HENRY CHARLES LEA

A HISTORY

OF

AURICULAR CONFESSION

AND

INDULGENCES

IN THE LATIN CHURCH

VOLUME I

CONFESSION AND ABSOLUTION

A HISTORY

OF

CONFESSION AND INDULGENCES.

A HISTORY

OF

AURICULAR CONFESSION

AND

INDULGENCES

IN THE LATIN CHURCH.

BY

HENRY CHARLES LEA, LL.D.

VOLUME I.

CONFESSION AND ABSOLUTION.

———————

LONDON:

SWAN SONNENSCHEIN & CO.,

PATERNOSTER SQUARE.

1896.

PREFACE.

PERHAPS in treating the subject of the present work I may be accused of threshing old straw. For nearly four centuries it has served as material for endless controversy, and its every aspect may be thought to have been exhausted. Yet I have sought to view it from a different standpoint and to write a history, not a polemical treatise. With this object I have abstained from consulting Protestant writers and have confined myself exclusively to the original sources and to Catholic authorities, confident that what might thus be lost in completeness would be compensated by accuracy and impartiality. In this I have not confined myself to standard theological treatises, but have largely referred to popular works of devotion in which is to be found the practical application of the theories enunciated by the masters of theology. I have purposely been sparing of comment, preferring to present facts and to leave the reader to draw his own conclusions.

I may perhaps be pardoned for the hope that, in spite of the arid details of which such an investigation as this must in part consist, the reader may share in the human interest which has vitalized the labor for me in tracing the gradual growth and development of a system that has, in a degree unparalleled elsewhere, subjected the intellect and conscience of successive generations to the domination of fellow mortals. The history of mankind may be vainly searched for another institution which has established a spiritual autocracy such as that of the Latin Church, or which has exercised so vast an influence on human destinies, and it has seemed to me a service to historical truth to examine somewhat minutely into the origin and

*

development of the sources of its power. This can only be done intelligently by the collocation of a vast aggregate of details, many of them apparently trivial, but all serving to show how, amid the clash of contending opinions, the structure gradually arose which subjugated Christendom beneath its vast and majestic omnipotence, profoundly affecting the course of European history and moulding in no small degree the conception of the duties which man owes to his fellows and to his God. Incidentally, moreover, the investigation affords a singularly instructive example of the method of growth of dogma, in which every detail once settled becomes the point of departure in new and perhaps wholly unexpected directions.

The importance of the questions thus passed in review is by no means limited to the past, for in the Latin Church spiritual interests cannot be dissociated from temporal. The publicist must be singularly blind who fails to recognize the growth of influence that has followed the release of the Holy See from the entanglements consequent upon its former position as a petty Italian sovereign, and the enormous opportunities opened to it by the substitution of the rule of the ballot-box for absolutism. Through the instrumentality of the confessional, the sodality and the indulgence, its matchless organization is thus enabled to concentrate in the Vatican a power greater than has ever before been wielded by human hands.

PHILADELPHIA, DECEMBER, 1895.

CONTENTS.

PART I.

CONFESSION AND ABSOLUTION.

CHAPTER VIII.—Confession.

CHAPTER IX.—Enforced Confession.

CHAPTER X.—JURISDICTION.

CHAPTER XI.—RESERVED CASES.

CHAPTER XIV.—ABSOLUTION.

PART I.

CONFESSION AND ABSOLUTION.

CONFESSION AND ABSOLUTION.

CHAPTER I.

PRIMITIVE CHRISTIANITY.

When Christ described his mission— "They that are whole need not a physician but they that are sick . . . for I am not come to call the righteous but sinners to repentance,"[1] he assumed as a postulate that in the dealings of God with man repentance suffices to procure pardon for sin.   In this he was merely giving expression to traditional Hebrew thought.   The Psalmist had said long before "A sacrifice to God is an afflicted spirit; a contrite and humbled heart O God thou wilt not despise;" and the Deutero-Isaiah "Let the wicked forsake his way and the unjust man his thoughts: and let him return to the Lord and He will have mercy upon him; and to our God for He is bountiful to forgive."[2]   Hebrew tradition however prescribed certain outward manifestations of the internal change of heart.   When the Ninevites desired to avert the vengeance of God they put on sackcloth and cast ashes on their heads, turned from their evil ways, fasted and prayed and were spared.[3]   The purer prophetical school, however, made light of these observances; Joel says to the sinner "rend your heart and not your garments, and turn to the Lord your God;"[4] and Christ, who sought to spiritualize the prevailing materialism of Judaism, assumed in all his acts that change of heart was the only thing needful.   The woman com-

---

[1] Matt. IX. 12–13. It is perhaps worthy of note that the Vulgate and the Douay version omit the words "to repentance."   The original has εἰς μετάνοιαν, and even so orthodox a scholar as Benito Arias Montano adds to the Vulgate "ad pœnitentiam."   A still higher authority is Pope John XIX. who in 1032 quotes the text in the same way (Johan. PP. XIX. Epist. 17).

[2] Ps. L. 19; Isaiah, LV. 7.   Cf. Ezek. XVIII. 23; XXXIII. 11.

[3] Jonah, III.   [4] Joel, II. 13.

monly identified with Mary Magdalen, of whom he said "Many sins are forgiven her because she hath loved much," the woman taken in adultery, the parable of the prodigal son, the salvation of the penitent thief, the forgiveness of Peter for denying his Master, the exhortation to become as little children, the parable of the king and his servants, his identification of himself with the poor, all show that in the teachings of Jesus externals were of no importance, that man dealt directly with God and that repentance, love, humility, pardon of offences or charity sufficed to win forgiveness.[1] It required all the ingenuity of theologians for thirteen centuries to build up from this simplicity the complex structure of dogma and observance on which were based sacramental absolution and the theory of indulgences.

Materials for this structure were contributed early. James and John both dwelt upon the redeeming character of mutual confession of sins "one to another," and the power of intercessory prayer, and James prescribed the cure of the sick by calling in the presbyters to anoint with oil and pray "And the prayer of faith shall save the sick man, and the Lord shall raise him up; and if he be in sins they shall be forgiven him."[2] Paul attributes the remission of sin to the blood of Christ,[3] and he gives countenance to the theory that it may be expiated by temporal suffering, in the well-known passage "To deliver such a one to Satan for the destruction of the flesh that the spirit may be saved in the day of our Lord Jesus Christ."[4] The early Christians however adhered to the teaching of the Master and to the traditional Hebrew view of the expiatory power of almsgiving.[5] Towards the close of the first century we

---

[1] Luke, VII. 47; XIII. 5; XV. XXIII. 40–43; John, VIII. 3–11; Matt. XVIII. 3–4, 35; XXV. 31–46; XXVI. 69–75.

[2] James, V. 14–16; I. John, I. 9; v. 16.   [3] Ephesians, I. 7.

[4] I. Cor. V. 5. This would seem to be the most probable explanation of the somewhat enigmatical text, especially as it was the current belief of the Jews of the period that sin is punished here rather than hereafter. This is seen in the question of the disciples, "Rabbi, who hath sinned, this man or his parents, that he should be born blind?" (John IX. 2), and though on this occasion Christ answered, "Neither hath this man sinned nor his parents," yet in the cure of the palsied (Matt. IX. 2–5) he accepted the belief by asking, "Whether it is easier to say, Thy sins are forgiven thee; or to say, Arise and walk."

[5] "Water quencheth a flaming fire and alms resisteth sins."—Ecclesiasticus, III. 33.—"Wherefore O king let my counsel be acceptable to thee, and redeem .

find St. Clement of Rome assuming that repentance and prayer to God for pardon suffice, without any formula for priestly intermediation, though he also recommends intercessory prayer for those who have fallen into sin.[1] About the same period the Didache and Barnabas both inculcate almsgiving as a means of redeeming sins,[2] and so soon afterwards does the second epistle which passes under the name of Clement.[3] St. Ignatius speaks only of repentance as requisite for reconciliation to God,[4] and about the middle of the second century the Shepherd of Hermas seems to know of no other means of remission.[5]

Yet as the Church grew and extended itself among the nations, absorbing converts of every race and every degree of intellectual development and moral fitness, its old simplicity of faith and organization disappeared. Philosophers and rhetoricians sought to explain the relations between God and man, leading to the evolution of doctrine which we shall consider hereafter. Converts, too, there were in multitudes whose weakness under temptation created the necessity of some rules of discipline by which the intercourse between the brethren should be regulated. Every Church, like all other human associations, must determine its own conditions of fellowship, and among Christians the test of this speedily came to be admission to the love-feast or Lord's Supper. He whose conduct was at variance with his Christian profession was liable to excommunication—suspension from communion until his repentance and amendment satisfied the rulers of his congregation. Thus gradually and insensibly grew up the enormous power derived from the control

thou thy sins with alms, and thy iniquities with works of mercy to the poor; perhaps he will forgive thy offences."—Daniel, IV. 24. "For alms delivereth from death and the same is that which purgeth away sins."—Tobias, XII. 9.— "Give alms and behold all things are clean unto you."—Luke, XI. 41.

[1] Clement. Epist. I. ad Corinth. VIII. 1; XXII. 1; XXIII. 1, 15.

[2] Didache, c. IV.—Barnabas Epist. XIV. 20. But already the evil of indiscriminate almsgiving was recognized—"Let thine alms sweat in thy hands till thou hast learned to whom to give" (Didache, c. I.).

[3] Pseudo-Clement. Epist. II. ad Corinth. 8, 13. "Fasting is better than prayer and almsgiving than both . . . . for almsgiving lifteth the burden of sin"—Ib. 16. So Pius IX. in proclaiming the jubilee of 1875, urges the bishops to exert themselves "ut peccata eleemosynis redimantur."—Pii P.P. IX. Encyc. *Gravibus* (Acta, T. VI. p. 358).

[4] Ignat. Epist. ad Philadelph. c. III. VIII.

[5] Hermæ Pastor. Lib. I. Vis. ii. Lib. II. Mandat. iv. Lib. III. Simil. ix.

of the Eucharist which formed so controlling a factor in establishing the domination of the Church over Christendom.   I have considered this subject in some detail elsewhere[1] and need only refer to it here in so far as it forms the leading feature in the system of discipline which insensibly arose to determine the relations between the sinner and his fellow Christians.   When his guilt was made manifest and proven he was suspended from communion; when restored he was said to be reconciled.   What were the rules in force in the infant Church it is impossible now to say.   Probably at first the power to suspend and restore lay with the spiritual teachers of the congregation, as indicated by the injunction of St. Paul—"Brethren and if a man be overtaken in any fault, you who are spiritual instruct such a one in the spirit of meekness;"[2] although when addressing the whole body of believers in Corinth he seems to regard the function as inherent in the congregation at large,[3] and when they refrained, in a peculiarly scandalous case, he had no hesitation in passing judgment on the offender himself,[4] subsequently ratifying the pardon granted by the local church on the repentance of the sinner.[5]   Towards the close of the first century, St. Ignatius, who magnified on all occasions the sacerdotal and episcopal office, assumes that the advice and consent of the bishop are requisite for restoration; no formulas or ceremonies are necessary, simple repentance suffices to win from God pardon of the sin, provided the sinner is readmitted to the unity of the Church.[6]   Half a century later Dionysius of Corinth, in his epistle to the Armastrians, orders them to receive back kindly all repentant sinners and even heretics.   No formalities are prescribed and no penance is indicated.[7]

---

[1] Studies in Church History, 2d edition, 1883.   [2] Galat. VI. 1.

[3] "But now I have written to you not to keep company, if any man that is named a brother, be a fornicator, or covetous, or a server of idols, or a railer, or a drunkard, or an extortioner: with such a one not so much as to eat."—I. Cor. V. 11.

[4] "I indeed, absent in body, but present in spirit, have already judged, as though I were present, him that hath so done"—Ibid. 3.

[5] "And to whom you have pardoned anything, I also."—II. Cor. II. 10.

[6] S. Ignat. Epist. ad Philadelph. c. VIII.   The shorter Latin version says "Omnibus igitur pœnitentibus dimittit Deus si pœniteant in unitatem Dei et concilium (συνέδριον) episcopi."   The longer version is "Omnibus igitur pœnitentibus dimittit Deus, si ad unitatem ecclesiæ concurrerint et ad consensum episcopi."   (Petermann's Ignatius, pp. 206-7.)

[7] Euseb. H. E. IV. 23.

In a body such as the primitive Church, composed of earnest souls striving to earn salvation amid obloquy and persecution, there was little chance that aggravated and permanent sin would find a lodgment; for the most part the law of love would suffice to preserve purity; those who lapsed would be eager to regain their standing and to make their peace with God and with their fellows, and the simplest rules would be ample to maintain discipline. Yet the weakness of human nature occasionally asserted itself, and there was sometimes friction. The epistle of Clement of Rome quoted above was called forth by a revolt against the priests of the Corinthian church, showing that even among the faithful of that early time those entrusted with control might exercise it arbitrarily, or that those who were subordinate might recalcitrate even against that rudimentary authority. Thus everywhere in the teachings and in the nascent organization of the Church lay the germs which, after countless struggles and vicissitudes, were to develop into a system so strangely at variance with the simplicity out of which it has grown.

Of these germs the first for us to consider is the jurisdiction over the sins and crimes of the faithful which gradually established itself in the hands of those who controlled the administration of the Eucharist. In dealing with this and with the numerous questions to which it gave rise we must bear in mind that during these early centuries there was no central authority and consequently no uniformity of practice. At first it may be said that every local church, and, after general organization had been introduced, each province, and almost each diocese, was a law unto itself in matters of discipline. As churches were organized numerous points had to be decided for which there was no precept in evangel or epistle. Doctrine and practice had to evolve themselves out of the confused struggle of warring opinions and interests, and it is frequently impossible at present, from the fragmentary remains of that period, to decide as to what was the prevailing consensus of opinion at any given time on a given subject. No one was empowered to speak for the Church at large and the most that we can do is to gather, from what we know of the customs of local churches and the expressions of leaders of thought, such facts and views as may serve to illustrate the gradual evolution and crystallization of Latin Christianity in relation to sin and its remission.

CHAPTER II.

DISCIPLINE.

THE code of morality taught in the gospels was wholly different from that prevailing in the society from which converts to Christianity were drawn. In the latter, license was all-prevailing and the standard erected by Christ and the apostles was one not easily enforced. Some effort consequently was made to test the sincerity of the postulant's conversion. The simplicity of the earliest time which required only a two days' fast preliminary to baptism[1] was soon found to be insufficient. The pardon symbolized by the baptismal rite was only to be earned by a cleansing of the heart, confession of sin to God and earnest repentance.[2] According to the Clementine Recognitions, which probably date towards the end of the second century, this period of probation was extended to three months, to be spent in self-examination and frequent fasts.[3] The catechumen wept and mourned over his past delinquencies, praying God for pardon, the congregation fasted and prayed with him ; he pledged himself to live righteously for the future and when the rite was accomplished he was assured that he was released not only from original sin but from all actual sin.[4] He was regenerate, he was born again without sin

---

[1] Didache, c. vii.

[2] "And he confesses to God, saying In ignorance I did these things ; and he cleanses his heart and his sins are forgiven him because he did them in ignorance in former time."—Apology of Aristides, c. xvii. (Rendel Harris's Translation, p. 51).

[3] Clement. Recogn. Lib. III. c. 67. The Catechism of the Council of Trent (Ed. Viennæ, 1838, p. 161) is careful to inform us that these preliminaries were not works of satisfaction but only to impress the convert with the venerable character of the sacrament.

[4] Justin. Mart. Apologiæ III.—Clement. Recogn. Lib. I. c. 69.—Tertull. de Baptismo c. xx.—S. Zenonis Lib. I. Tract. xxxix., xl., xli. (Migne's Patrolog. XI. 486–90).—Epist. Theodori *ap.* S. Hieron. (Migne, XXIII. 106).—S. Augustin. Lib. de Fide et Operibus.

According to the *Didascalia Petri* the sins of a convert were only remitted after twelve years of repentance.—Clement. Alex. Stromata Lib. VI. (Ed. Sylburg. p. 636).

and it was his duty to maintain this condition of purity. If he failed
in this it was the duty of the heads of the congregation to summon
him to repentance and amendment. In the simple Ebionitic society
of Palestine this was enforced by segregation from his fellows—" To
everyone who acts wrongly towards another let no one speak, nor let
him be listened to till he repents."[1] In the expanding and more
complex organizations of the Gentile churches, with their tendencies
to sacerdotal development, the means of enforcement lay in the control of the Eucharist. The offender was suspended and if persistently
impenitent he was ejected from the church, outside of which, as
Cyprian tells us, there was no more hope of salvation than in the
Deluge outside of the ark; no one could have God for father who
had not the Church for mother; he was slain with the sword of the
spirit.[2]

Thus alongside of the secular criminal courts there grew up at each
episcopal seat another criminal court of which the function was to
determine the relations between sinners and their congregations.
These were however in no sense spiritual courts or courts of conscience. Their jurisdiction was exclusively in the *forum externum;*
any influence which they might exert over the *forum internum,* over
the relations of the sinner with God, was merely indirect and incidental, and this is a point which it is important to keep in view for
it has been systematically overlooked or confused by apologists whose
duty it is to find precedent in the first three centuries for all the institutions and dogmas of the middle ages.[3] It is true that the Church

---

[1] Didache, c. xv.

[2] Cypriani de Unitate Ecclesiæ p. 109. Cf. Epist. ad Pomponium p. 9
(Ed. Oxon.).

[3] See Estius in Lib. iv. Sententt. Dist. xv. § 13. Modern theologians find
it difficult to reconcile the facts with their necessities. Francisco Suarez, S. J.,
frankly admits that the early penance was not sacramental, but wholly in the
forum externum, regulating the relations of the sinner with the Church but not
with God (Fr. Suarez in 3 P. Disp. xlix. § 2, *ap.* Amort de Indulgentiis, II.
172-3). Juenin (De Sacramentis, Diss. vii. Q. vii. cap. 4 art. 3) says that
Domingo Soto is alone among canonists and theologians in denying the sacramental character of ancient reconciliation.

The question is a troublesome one for apologists as the antiquity of indulgences depends wholly upon the sacramental character of ancient penance.
See Bouvier *Traité des Indulgences,* Ed. 1855, pp. 17 sqq. Gröne (Der Ablass, seine
Geschichte und Bedeutung, Regensburg, 1863, p. 27) endeavors to reconcile
the difficulty by assuming that the old penance was a censure, identical with

could destroy by expulsion, but it claimed as yet no correlative power to save. It could grant the penitent " peace " and reconciliation, but it did not pretend to absolve him, and by reconciliation he only gained the opportunity of being judged by God. St. Cyprian, who tells us this, had evidently never heard of the power of the keys, or that what the Church loosed on earth would be loosed in heaven; it cannot, he says, prejudge the judgment of God, for it is fallible and easily deceived.[1] This was not merely the opinion of the African Church, for the council of bishops assembled in Rome after the Decian persecution decided that homicides and those who had lapsed to idolatry, if truly repentant, could be admitted to reconciliation on the death-bed, but what this reconciliation was worth it declined to say, for the judgment lay in the hands of God.[2] When Cyprian allowed, in case of necessity, the ceremony of reconciliation by the imposition of hands to be performed by deacons, in order that the penitent might go to God with the peace of the church, it shows clearly that no sacramental exercise of the power of the keys was involved, for this has never been conferred on the diaconate, of which the functions are ministerial and not sacerdotal, and the proceedings of several Spanish councils

---

modern minor excommunication, and thus *in foro externo*, but having in connection with it sacramental satisfaction. Palmieri (Tract. de Pœnit. Romæ, 1879, p. 77) controverts the views of those who assert that the penitence of the early Church was only *in foro externo*, to reconcile the sinner to the Church, and condemns it as opposed to Catholic opinion. Subsequently, however, when he has to face the troublesome question of the old deprecatory form of absolution he boldly affirms (pp. 127–41) that public reconciliation was not sacramental, and he adopts (pp. 463–4) the theory of Dr. Amort, that when the sinner confessed his sin he received absolution, and that reconciliation was only another form of indulgence. All this of course is the baldest assumption, but these questions will come up for consideration hereafter.

Innocent I. (Ad Exsuperium cap. iv.) indicates how accusations were brought and how the accused was deprived of communion. The power of oppression thus lodged in the hands of an unscrupulous prelate is exhibited in the prosecution of the priest Isidor by Theophilus, the arbitrary archbishop of Alexandria.—Palladii Vit S. Jo. Chrysost. c. vi.

[1] Cypriani Epist. LV. ad Antonianum "Et quia apud inferos confessio non est nec exomologesis illic fieri potest, qui ex toto corde pœnituerint et rogaverint in ecclesia debent interim suscipi et in ipsa Domino reservari, qui ad ecclesiam venturus, de illis utique quos in ea intus invenerit, judicabit."

[2] Cleri Roman. Epist. ad Cyprian. (Cypriani Epist. xxx.) "Ipso Deo sciente quid de talibus faciat et qualiter judicii sui examinet pondera."

of the fourth century prove that diaconal reconciliation was not confined to the African Church.[1]

Reconciliation thus was merely a matter of discipline.   When Marcion the heretic returned to the faith and repented he was promised reconciliation under the condition that he would bring back to the fold those whom he had led astray—a condition which had no relation to the state of his own soul, for it depended wholly upon the free will of others, as was shown by his death before he was able to accomplish it.[2]   The account which Dionysius of Alexandria, about the middle of the third century, writes to Pope Fabianus of the miracle attending the death of Serapion, who had sacrificed to idols and had vainly sought reconciliation, shows that pardon by God was not dependent upon the ecclesiastical ceremony, though that was also needed to restore him to the Church, and so little doubt of it had Dionysius that he enquires whether Serapion ought not to be included in the glorious list of confessors.[3]   St. Augustin gives us clearly to understand that the so-called penitents of the early Church were simply excommunicates;[4] and when Bishop Therapius received the priest Victor to the peace of the Church before he had satisfied God

---

[1] Cypriani Epist. xviii.—C. Illiberitan. can. 32.—C. Toletan. I. ann. 400, c. 2. Cf. C. Carthag. IV. ann. 398, c. 4 " Diaconus cum ordinatur, solus episcopus que eum benedicit manum super caput illius ponat quia non ad sacerdotium sed ad ministerium consecratur."

These passages naturally give concern to modern apologists, who endeavor with more zeal than success to argue them away. See, for instance, Binterim, Denkwürdigkeiten der Christ-Katholischen Kirche, B. VI. Th. ii. pp. 201-7.

We shall see that even after the sacramental character of penance was accepted in the twelfth century there was difficulty in preventing deacons from administering it.

[2] Tertull. de Præscriptionibus c. xxx.

[3] Euseb H. E. vi. 44.

[4] S. Augustin. Epist. cclxv. n. 7. "Agunt homines pœnitentiam si post baptismum ita peccaverint ut excommunicari et postea reconciliari mereantur, sicut in omnibus ecclesiis illi qui proprie pœnitentes appellantur."

In referring to St. Augustin it is important to bear in mind the immense influence which he exercised in moulding the doctrine and discipline of the medieval and modern Church. This is illustrated in the *Decretum* of Gratian, where no less than 607 canons are taken from his works, genuine and suppostitious. Much as current Christianity owes to St. Paul, he furnishes only 408 canons. It was on Augustin rather than on Paul that the schoolmen built, as is obvious in the Sentences and the commentaries upon them which form the main body of scholastic theology.

by due penitence Cyprian allowed the reconciliation to stand, thus showing that reconciliation to God and to the Church were two different things.[1]

The episcopal tribunals which were established to administer this discipline, were not, like the modern confessional which has been affiliated upon them, simply designed to ease the conscience of despairing sinners who came forward to unburden their souls and seek salvation at sacerdotal hands. They were the prototypes of the Officiality, or episcopal court in the *forum externum*. Their sessions were public, they heard accusations, they examined witnesses, they convicted or acquitted the accused according to the evidence, and they apportioned the punishment or penance to be endured before he should be admitted to reconciliation. If he came forward voluntarily and confessed before the congregation, this evidence of repentance gained for him a mitigation of the penalty. The earliest account we have of these proceedings is in the Canonical Epistle of Gregory Thaumaturgus, written about the year 267, after the invasion of Pontus by the Goths, when many Christians had committed serious offences, aiding the invaders, plundering their neighbors, and even enslaving their fugitive brethren. The magnitude and novelty of the crimes and the number of the criminals were apparently so great that the bishop of the culprits seems to have been at a loss and applied to Gregory for instructions. His answer shows that the system was still crude and rudimentary. He sends a learned clerk, Euphrosynus to guide his colleague in the trials and to inform him who may be received as accusers. He specifies the length of penance to be inflicted for the several offences and the diminution to be granted for voluntary self-accusation. The whole business is evidently intended merely to settle the relations of the sinners with the Church, and there is no allusion to obtaining pardon from God. It is exclusively a matter of the *forum externum ;* the penalties inflicted are punishment in the guise of penance, deterrent as well as medicinal.[2]

The Apostolic Constitutions, which reflect the customs of nearly the same period, represent the bishop not only as a judge but as in some sort a prosecuting officer. Whenever he learns that a member of his flock has sinned it is his duty to investigate the case. There

---

[1] Cypriani Epist. lxiv.

[2] Greg. Thaumaturg. Epist. Canon. (Harduin. Concil. I. 191–4).

must be at least three witnesses of good reputation and not inimical to the accused. If the offence is proved the bishop orders the deacons to eject the offender from the church; on their return they are to intercede for him; he is sent for and interrogated and if he is found to be repentant a moderate penance of fasting is to be assigned to him, after the performance of which he is to be received back with fatherly kindness. The bishop is warned that he who refuses to welcome back one who seeks to return is a slayer of his brother, but if the sinner is obdurate to prayers, entreaties, exhortations, warnings and threats, then is he to be cut off.[1]

A hundred years later we find the same judicial system in force in the canons of St. Gregory of Nyssa, who lays down the rule that voluntary confession is a sign of amendment and that therefore a man who reveals what was not known and seeks a remedy should be visited with a shorter penance than he who is convicted through suspicion and accusation.[2] About the same period St. Basil the Great recognizes this principle; he gives alternative penances for confession and conviction and says that the bishop to whom is entrusted the power of binding and loosing will not be blameable if he diminishes the term of those who confess and show signs of amendment.[3]

All this demonstrates that in its penitential functions the Church was engaged in framing a system of criminal jurisprudence adapted to its needs and supplementing the civil jurisdiction. It did not trouble itself about the distinction between crime and sin.[4] It pun-

---

[1] Constitt. Apostol. Lib. II. c. xix , xxiv., xli., xlv.

[2] Greg. Nyssæn. Epist. Canon. c. iv.

[3] Basil. Epist. Canon. II. c. lxi., lxv., lxx., lxxi., lxxiv. About the same period St. Pacianus objurgates the sinner who will not confess and who baffles the investigation of his bishop (St. Paciani Paranæsis ad Pœnit. c. viii.). Synesius, Bishop of Ptolemais, tells us that in the case of the priest Lampridianus, although the accused anticipated conviction by confession he inflicted the full punishment and referred him to the see of Alexandria for mitigation (Synesii Epist. lxvii.). This indicates that even when the confession was not spontaneous, but was elicited by accusation and the dread of conviction, it still was considered as giving a claim to mercy.

[4] The distinction between crime and sin would seem to have been unknown to the early Fathers. St. Augustin uses the words *crimen* and *peccatum* as indicating only difference in degree. The saints are without *crimen* though no man is without *peccatum* (Enchirid. c. 64. Cf. Serm. CCCXCIII.). Towards the close of the fifth century the *Sacramentarium Leonianum* makes communion purge from *crimen* (Jejunii Sept. III., Octobris IV.—Muratorii Opp. T. XIII.

ished the crime; if the criminal was rebellious and refused to undergo the punishment designated it ejected him as the only means of enforcing discipline. If he was repentant and performed the penance enjoined on him it received him back to peace and reconciliation: he had paid the penalty of his crime and he settled for himself with God the question of his sin. He was invited to voluntary confession by a mitigation of the penalty incurred, but if he did not confess it made only the difference that he was tried and convicted and incurred the full rigor of the canons. We shall find these features of the penitential system of the Church continue with some gradual modifications until the middle ages were well advanced. Penance might be voluntarily assumed by a sinner seeking salvation, but, if it were not, and if his sin could be discovered, it was imposed on him and its performance enforced by the severest penalties within reach.[1] It was the duty of every member of the congregation to denounce any sin of which he might have cognizance, but St. Augustin tells us that this duty was neglected by some because they might need the sinner's favor in their own cases, and by others because they were unable to produce proof sufficient for conviction. He warns the bishop moreover that he must not condemn without positive evidence; and though suspension from communion was medicinal and not mortal, it was not to be inflicted without confession or conviction in some secular or ecclesiastical court.[2] Thus the jurisdiction of the Church was wholly in the *forum externum*; how little it imagined that it had any coercive power in the forum of conscience is seen in the com-

---

P. I. pp. 669, 729). Gregory I. follows St. Augustin in regarding the distinction between *crimen* and *peccatum* as one merely of degree and not as involving the difference between the external and internal forum. (Moral. Lib. XXI. c. xii.) In another passage he seems to use *peccatum* in the sense of crime and *delictum* in that of sin. "Hoc enim inter peccatum et delictum distat quod peccatum est mala facere, delictum vero est bona delinquere quæ summopere sunt tenenda. Vel certe peccatum in opere est, delictum in cogitatione" (Homil. in Ezek. Lib. II. Homil. ix. c. 3). Yet again, he uses *delictum* as synonymous with *peccatum* (Moral. XIII. v.). It all shows how completely vague as yet were the conceptions as to jurisdiction over conscience.

[1] Concil. Venetici ann. 465 c. 1.—Concil. Agathens. ann. 511 c. 37.

[2] S. August. Serm. CCCLI. n. 10. St. Augustin's assertion that excommunication was purely medicinal does not find support in the earlier penitential canons, such as those of St. Gregory of Nyssa, where the character of the penalties is almost purely vindictive.

plaint of Chrysostom when he dwells upon the difficulty of the task imposed upon the bishop who is charged with the consciences of his flock, for in this forum of conscience he has no power to coerce, and if he had he could not use it, for God pardons those only who come to him freely and willingly.[1] Apparently soon after this there was an effort to extend the jurisdiction to the forum of conscience and it was emphatically repressed. A canon of 419, subscribed to by St. Augustin himself, provides that if a bishop suspends from communion a sinner for a sin known to him only through private confession, and the sinner denies it and refuses to submit, the neighboring bishops shall refuse communion to their offending brother so long as he persists in the suspension, to teach him not to punish unless he can produce conclusive evidence.[2]

One notable feature of this system of discipline is that it was confined to certain sins of especial heinousness. In this however, as in so much else, the practice of the Church was by no means persistently uniform. We have seen that St. Paul enumerated quite a number of offences for which offenders were to be segregated. In this he was followed by the canons of Hippolytus, which date from about 230 and

---

[1] S. Joan. Chrysost. de Sacerdotio Lib. II. c. 2–4.

[2] Cod. Eccles. African. c. cxxxii–iii. (Concil. African. VI. ann. 419 c. 5). —Photii Nomocan. Tit. IX c. 20.

This canon is so absolutely destructive of the antiquity claimed for the power of the keys and the sacrament of penitence that efforts have naturally been made to pervert it. To accomplish this some of the ancient collectors of canons did not scruple to substitute for the final clause a wholly contradictory one—"secrete tamen [episcopus] interdicat ei communionem donec obtemperet" (Burchardi Decr. Lib. XIX. c. 127). It does not reflect much credit on modern Catholic criticism and candor to find Binterim (Denkwürdigkeiten der Christ-Katholischen Kirche, Bd. V. Th. ii. pp. 269 sqq.) seriously quoting it in this shape, without alluding to the forgery. The final clause "Quamdiu excommunicato non communicaverit suus episcopus eidem episcopo ab aliis non communicetur episcopis ut magis caveat episcopus ne dicat in quemquam quod aliis documentis convincire non potest" is in all editions accessible to me. See Surii Concil. Colon. Agripp. 1567 T. I. p. 587; Voelli et Justelli Bibl. Juris Canon. Vet. I. 398; Harduin. Concil. I. 938, 1250; Bruns, Canones Apost. et Concil. I. 196. This canon only expresses what was the current practice. A tract against the Novatians, which long passed current under the name of St. Augustin, tersely puts it "eum abjicere non liceat qui publice detectus non fuerit." Pseudo-Augustin. Questiones ex Vet. et Novo Testam. c. 102 (Migne, XXXV. 2310).

form the foundation of the later code known as the Apostolic Constitutions. Here we find numerous sins and evil customs specified for which the offender is to be expelled from the Church until he performs penance with weeping, fasting and works of charity, and the minuteness of the code is seen in including in the list the artist who uses his art for any purpose save supplying human wants.[1] These passages are omitted from the Apostolic Constitutions, and as a rule the only crimes of which the Church felt itself bound to take cognizance were three—unchastity, idolatry, and homicide—and for this it had ample Scriptural warrant, in spite of the conflicting instructions of St. Paul.[2] Even late in the fourth century St. Pacianus tells us that all other offences can be redeemed by good works and amendment,[3] and this opinion was still widely current in the time of St. Augustin.[4] How, towards the close of the fourth century, the Church gradually extended its cognizance over a wider range of less serious offences, is well set forth in the canons of St. Gregory of Nyssa. After providing definite punishments for the three crimes, unchastity, homicide and heresy (which by this time had virtually replaced idolatry) he proceeds " For avarice and the sins arising from it the Fathers have provided no remedy. The apostle has said that money is the root of

---

[1] Canones Hippolyti XI. 65; XIV. 74; XV. 79 (Achelis, Die Canones Hippolyti, Leipzig, 1891).

No periods of penance are specified in this, and the whole shows a very crude and archaic form of discipline, the origin of which I would be disposed to attribute an earlier period than the third century.

[2] "For it hath seemed good to the Holy Ghost and to us to lay no further burden upon you than these three necessary things: That you abstain from things sacrificed to idols, and from blood, and from things strangled, and from fornication: from which things keeping yourselves you shall do well."—Acts, XV. 28-9.

Pliny states of the Bithynian Christians, in 112, that when on trial they asserted that in their assemblies they took a mutual oath not to commit theft or robbery or adultery, not to break faith or deny the receipt of deposits, showing these to be the sins most deprecated at that time.—C. Plin. Secund. Lib. IX. Epist. xcvii.

[3] Reliqua peccata meliorum operum compensatione curantur; hæc vero tria crimina metuenda sunt.—S. Paciani Parænesis ad Pœnit. c. iv.

[4] Qui autem opinantur cætera eleemosynis facile compensari, tria tamen mortifera esse non dubitant et excommunicatione punienda donec pœnitentia humiliori sanentur, impudicitiam, idololatriam, homicidium.—S. August. de Fide et Operibus c. xix.

all evil, and yet this disease has been neglected and no cure provided for it. Thus it abounds in the Church and no one enquires whether he who is admitted to the priesthood is infected with it. Our authority however suffices for this. The robber is prepared to commit murder. His penance therefore should be that of voluntary homicide. For secret theft, if the thief repents and spontaneously confesses, his disease can be cured by contraries. Let him therefore give to the poor all he has; if he has nothing but his body, let him mortify his body. The violation of sepulchres is also divisible into pardonable and unpardonable. If it is merely carrying away of stones to use in other constructions, this is not laudable but custom sanctions it for works of utility; but violation of the grave in search of ornaments of value is to be punished like fornication. Sacrilege, or the theft of things dedicated to God, used to be punished with lapidation, according to Scripture, but I know not why this has been treated with greater leniency and the Fathers punish it with a shorter period than adultery."[1] Tentative as this is, the process of extending the jurisdiction of the Church proceeded even more slowly in the West. It is true, as we shall see hereafter, that elaborate codes were provided by local councils, such as that of Elvira, but the offences aimed at can mostly be referred, directly or indirectly, to one of the three crimes, and even in the beginning of the sixth century St. Cæsarius of Arles tells us that sins of the eye and heart, of speech and of thought can be cured by prayer and private compunction, but perjury and false witness, unchastity and homicide and abandonment to the devil through augurs and diviners require public penance.[2]

It is true, as the council of Elvira shows us, that all Christians were not satisfied with this laxity, and discontent with it led to the heresy of the Montanists. Tertullian, while yet orthodox, taught that God pardons all sins through repentance,[3] but when he became inflamed with Montanism he rejected the limitation of mortal sins to the three; he added to them fraud, blasphemy and some others, as

---

[1] S. Gregor. Nyssæn. Epist. Canon. c. vii. viii.

[2] S. Cæsar. Arelatens. Serm. CCLXII. c. 1, in Append. S. Augustin.

The Council of Elvira had included usurers, actors, informers, and false accusers of priests among capital offenders (C. Illiberit. c. 20, 62, 73, 75). We shall see hereafter the contrast between these simple delimitations of sins with the bewildering perplexities of modern classification.

[3] De Pœnitent. c. 4.

those for which Christ would not intercede and gave a long list of minor offences for which Christ would procure pardon.[1] It may perhaps be assumed from Tertullian's burst of indignation and arguments when Pope Zephyrinus admitted adulterers to penitence that during the first two centuries the Church, or at least a portion of it, resolutely refused reconciliation for the three crimes and refused to intercede for them with God.[2]

It is evident from all this that the Church in dealing with sinners considered them only as criminals and confined its action to defining its own relation with them.   The penance which it inflicted was punishment, medicinal, it was hoped, but also vindictive, and a passage in St. Augustin would seem to show that the secular courts sometimes would release convicted criminals at the intercession of bishops, on the understanding that they should be subjected to penance.[3]   The modern assumption that alongside of this jurisdiction in the *forum externum* there was a corresponding authority exercised over the *forum internum*, and that a system existed through which absolution was granted for secret sins, which the sinner shrank from confessing openly before the congregation, is wholly gratuitous and it is admitted that there is no evidence to prove it.[4]   That repentant sinners sought to placate an offended God by mortification and almsgiving, and occasionally by confession of their sins, is a matter of course; doubtless they often sought the advice of priest or bishop as experts in spiritual medicine, and they asked the prayers of the congregation to intercede for them with God.   That the Church, however, made no claim to exercise any control over them in this is rendered evident by the very absence of evidence.   When exhortations to repentance formed so large a part of the early patristic writings it is impossible that if the Church had prescribed any formulas, or had exercised the power to grant or withhold absolution, no allusions would have been made

---

[1] De Pudicit. c. 19.

[2] De Pudicit. c. 1, 5.   There has been an active controversy as to the custom of the Church on this point, in which the Doctors are about equally divided. See Morini de Administratione Sacram. Pœnitentiæ Lib. IX. c. 20, and Palmieri Tract. de Pœnit. pp. 85, 91.   The fact doubtless is that there was no universal rule, each local church having its own practice.

[3] S. Augustin. Epist. CLIII. c. 3.

[4] Binterim, Denkwürdigkeiten, Bd. V. Th. ii. pp. 269 sqq.

to them in the works of the Fathers, and that no instructions would have been given in the numerous bodies of canons which have reached us. The proof is as strong and incontrovertible as any negative proof can be. We have indirect evidence, moreover, that public confession and public penance were the only process recognized by the Church in a passage of Origen recommending the anxious sinner to lay bare his soul to some expert in whom he has confidence, and, if the latter advises confession in the face of the congregation, to follow the counsel.[1] The confessor, whether priest or layman, had evidently no power either to impose penance or to grant absolution ; he could only suggest whether the case was one in which the penitent could best deal directly with God, or humiliate himself before the Church and ask its prayers in public penance.

There have been various theories elaborated to explain the manner in which Christian morality supplanted that of the pagan philosophy, yet it should seem that the process is not far to seek. The philosophers had only moral suasion with which to enforce their ideals on their disciples. The secular legislator contented himself with laws to preserve the peace of society and the rights of property. On the other hand, Christianity, at the period of the conversion of Constantine, presented itself as an organized body, armed with penalties more or less severe to coerce the faithful who should transgress the moral code of which the propagation formed its real mission. In becoming the religion of the state it soon found means of reinforcing its ethical sanctions with penalties in which secular privations and disabilities were added to spiritual. It cannot be said that the moral status of the community was elevated to any great degree, but at least the ideal standard was accepted and the teachings of the philosophers rapidly disappeared before those of the gospels.

---

[1] Origenis Homil. II. in Psalm XXXVII. c. 6.

CHAPTER III.

PUBLIC PENANCE.

In the criminal code which was gradually developed under the conditions which I have described, the Church at first was necessarily restricted to so-called spiritual penalties. Bishops had not, in the early centuries, like their medieval successors, prisons at their command; they could pass no sentence of death or mutilation; the discipline had not yet been adapted as a feature of penance, and they were even forbidden to strike a sinner under pain of deposition:[1] Yet they could inflict on him the keenest pangs of humiliation and they could enjoin on him the severest macerations, nay more, they could destroy his career in life and condemn him to an existence of ignominy, poverty, and isolation. They were thus abundantly provided with resources for the rigorous punishment of offences, and they used their opportunities with a freedom which, however efficient in a punitive sense, must have rendered voluntary confession and assumption of penance comparatively rare. Jerome's well-known description of the penitence of the noble Roman matron Fabiola, who exhibited herself in the porch of the Lateran with hair unbound, face livid and swollen with weeping and neck and hands unwashed, shows that such spontaneous manifestations of repentance must have been uncommon indeed thus to excite his wondering admiration and his declaration that such tears and lamentations would cleanse the soul from any sin.[2] Pacianus, indeed, gives us to understand that many penitents were distinguishable only by greater luxury in vestments and banquets.[3]

---

[1] Canon. Apostol. xxvi. (Ed. Dion. Exig. xxviii.). One of the accusations against Chrysostom in the Synod ad *Quercum* was that he had in church struck Memnon with his fist and drawn blood, in spite of which he performed divine service. Other charges as to his cruelty would seem to show that chains and prisons were by that time among the recognized episcopal resources (Harduin. Concil. I. 1039, 1042).

[2] Hieron. Epist. LXXVII. § 4 ad Oceanum.

[3] Paciani Paraenesis ad Poenitentiam.

For at least the first four centuries the Church prescribed only public penance. It is the penance "secundum morem ecclesiæ" repeatedly alluded to by St. Augustin,[1] who tells us that it was only administered for grave sins, lighter ones being removed by daily prayer.[2] The first allusion to private penance occurs in the middle of the fifth century, and then it is a special privilege accorded by Leo I. to priests and deacons, who, as we shall presently see, were governed by different rules from those imposed on the laity as regards penance.[3] As late as the commencement of the seventh century the only form of penance which St. Isidor of Seville seems to know is that of sack-cloth and ashes, which is public penance.[4] There has been much discussion among orthodox theologians whether this applied to private sins revealed in confession as well as to those publicly confessed or proved; the weight of learning is on the affirmative side, and the only argument urged against it is that to concede it would be fatal to the divine origin of the seal of the confessional, which is *de fide*.[5] The fact is that there is no evidence against it. The only penance known was public, for it comprised suspension from communion. Every one was required to take the Eucharist whenever he attended divine service; if he abstained it was a sign that he was in penance and in most churches he was obliged to withdraw on a summons from the deacon, so that secret penance for secret sins was impossible.[6] St.

---

[1] S. Augustin. Enchirid. c. lxxxii; Serm. ccexcii. c. iii.

[2] In his sermon *De Symbolo* to the catechumens (cap. 7) he tells them "Illi enim quos videtis agere pœnitentiam scelera commiserunt, aut adulteria aut aliquæ facta immania; inde agunt pœnitentiam. Nam si levia peccata eorum essent ad hæc quotidiana oratio delenda sufficeret." We shall see hereafter, however, that St. Augustin was by no means consistent in his classification of sins.

[3] Leon. PP. I. Epist. clxvii. c. 2. At the same time there seems to be springing up a practice of less rigorous penance for minor offences. Leo says that for eating sacrificial meats in banquets with gentiles a man can be readmitted to the sacraments by fasting and the imposition of hands, but for the three sins of idolatry, fornication and homicide he must undergo public penance.—Epist. clxvii. Inquis. 19 (Bened. Levitæ Capitul. v. 133 and the collections of canons).

[4] S. Isidor. Hispalens. de Ecclesiæ Officiis Lib. ii. c. xvii. §§ 4, 5.—Cf. Epiphan. Panar. Hæres. lix.

[5] See Palmieri, Tract. de Pœnit. pp. 393–402.

[6] "Audis præconem stantem et dicentem *Quicunque estis in pœnitentia abite.* Omnes qui non participant sunt in pœnitentia. Si es ex iis qui sunt in pœni-

Ambrose prescribes public penance for secret sins,[1] and a sermon attributed to St. Augustin speaks of endeavoring to persuade sinners to undertake it—persuasion which only could be necessary to those whose crimes were unknown.[2] St. Augustin indeed had advanced to the point of considering secret repentance insufficient and that pardon was only to be obtained through the power of binding and loosing lodged in the Church as the mystical body of Christ, and he assumes that this can only be accomplished through public penance.[3] Even at the close of the fifth century, when, as we shall see, private penance was commencing to be employed, Gennadius still recommends public for all mortal sins; he does not deny that they can be redeemed by private, but only on condition that the penitent abandon secular garments and by life-long amendment and sorrow win the pardon of God[4]—a process in which the priest had no share.

This public penance was an observance of the severest kind, and we can readily understand from it why the early Church only took cognizance of the three crimes. Tertullian and Cyprian tell us in general terms of the rigors and austerities which alone were accepted as proof of the sincerity of repentance—the ashes sprinkled on the head, the garments of sack-cloth, the fasting, the days spent in grief and the nights in tearful vigils, the continuous prayer, the devotion to good works and almsgiving whereby forgiveness is obtained.[5] Nor were

---

tentia non debes participare, nam qui non participat est in pœnitentia."—S. Joh. Chrysost. in Epist. ad Ephesios Hom. III. n. 4.

It would seem that in time the rule requiring the withdrawal of those unable to take communion received but slack obedience, for Gregory I. felt obliged to warn them with a story of two nuns conditionally excommunicated by St. Benedict. They died and were buried in the church, but regularly at mass when the deacon ordered those not communicating to withdraw they were seen to rise from their tombs and go out until St. Benedict kindly removed the ban. —Dialog. Lib. II. c. 23.

[1] S. Ambros. de Pœnitent. Lib. I. c. 16.

[2] S. August. Append. Serm. 258 § 2.

[3] S. Augustin. Serm. 392, cap. 5.

[4] Gennadii de Eccles. Dogmat. c. 53.

[5] " Quod inlotos, quod sordulentos, quod extra lætitiam oportet deversari, in asperitudine sacci et horrore cineris et oris de jejunio vanitate." Tertull. de Pœnit. c. xi.

"Orare oportet impensius et rogare, diem luctu transigere, vigiliis noctes et fletibus ducere, tempus omne lachrymosis lamentationibus occupare, stratos solo adhærere, in cinere et cilicio et sordibus volutari, post indumentum

these manifestations of the profoundest contrition a merely transitory
matter, though it is impossible in the earlier periods to determine
definitely the terms imposed as they varied with time and place, and
show a constant tendency to augmentation. In the Apostolic Constitutions, fasts of two or three, or five, or seven weeks only are
alluded to.[1] The Apostolic Canons only once prescribe a term of
penance, which is three years for a layman mutilating himself.[2]
Originally the rule seems to have been that each case was considered
on its merits, and an appropriate length of penance prescribed to the
culprit.[3] This was the plan proposed by Cyprian after the Decian
persecution[4] and as late as the middle of the fifth century Leo I. lays
it down as the rule in spite of the multifarious legislation of councils
on the subject.[5] This manifestly however was productive of confusion and uncertainty and efforts were made to introduce definite terms
for each offence, though the independence of the episcopate rendered
them purely advisory and not obligatory. In 252 Cyprian tells us
that in Africa some bishops refused absolutely to assign penance to
adulterers while others admitted them;[6] and after the second council
of Carthage had prescribed rules for the reconciliation of the lapsed
in the Decian persecution, Cyprian admits that they were not binding
on the bishops,[7] though again he speaks of received rules and an
established order of discipline.[8] We obtain, however, some idea of
what was regarded as an appropriate term of penance for the supreme
crime of idolatry in the case of Ninus, Clementianus and Florus,
who had lapsed only after prolonged prison and torture, and who

---

Christi perditum nullum jam velle vestitum, post diaboli cibum malle jeju-
nium, justis operibus incumbere quibus peccata purgantur, eleemosynis frequenter insistere, quibus a morte animæ liberantur."—Cyprian. de Lapsis xxxv.
Cf. C. Agathens. ann. 506 c. xv.

[1] Constitt. Apostol. Lib. ii. c. xix.
[2] Canon. Apostol. c. xxiv
[3] Euseb. H. E. Lib vi. 28.
[4] Cyprian. Epist. lvii.
[5] Leon. PP. I Epist. clvii. c. 5, 6.
[6] Cypriani Epist. lv. Cf. S. August. Epist. xciii. § 42.
[7] Cyprian. Epist. lvii.
[8] "Agunt peccatores pœnitentiam justo tempore et secundum disciplinæ
ordinem ad exomologesin veniant."—Cyprian. Epist. xvi. xvii. For virgins
who had allowed themselves to be seduced he threatens " pœnitentiam plenam "
(Epist. iv.) but what this was it would be impossible now to say.

after three years spent in penance Cyprian thinks might be received to reconciliation.[1] Yet the matter was wholly discretionary, for when a second persecution became imminent the African Church resolved to admit at once all penitents, alleging as a reason that it was to strengthen them for the trial—they could not become martyrs unless they were members of the Church.[2] Somewhat similar was the action of Peter Archbishop of Alexandria in 306, three years after the Diocletian persecution. Those who had been in penance during that time, if they had lapsed only through torture were reconciled after an additional fast of forty days, while those who had yielded to prison without torture were to be kept on probation for another year.[3] We shall have occasion to see hereafter how confused a medley of legislation sprang up, first in the local councils and afterwards in the Penitentials.

Thus a sort of code gradually established itself in each region with more or less authority, prescribing the length of penance proportioned to each offence, and rules were framed dividing it into several stages. These in their perfected form were devised to symbolize the gradual readmission of the sinner to the Church which had expelled him and were modelled on those through which converts advanced to baptism.[4] The first was *fletus* or weeping, in which he stood outside the church, lamenting his sins and begging the prayers of the faithful as they entered : the second was *auditio* or hearing, when he was admitted to the porch among the catechumens and heard the sermon, but went out before the prayers : the third was *substratio*, lying down or kneeling during the prayers uttered for his benefit : the fourth was *consistentia* or *congregatio*, in which he remained with the faithful during the mysteries, but was not allowed to partake ; and after this stage had been duly performed he was finally admitted to the Eucharist after the ceremony of reconciliation by the episcopal imposition of

---

[1] Ejusd. Epist. lvi. When Bishop Therapius admitted to communion the priest Victor before he had performed full penance, a council of sixty-six bishops scolds Therapius and orders him not to do so again but concludes not to withdraw communion from Victor (Cyprian. Epist. lxiv.). This effectually disposes of the customary claim of antiquity for episcopal indulgences which all modern authorities seek to find in the reconciliation of the lapsed under Cyprian.

[2] Ejusd. Epist. lvii.

[3] Petri Alexandri Canones (Max. Bibl. Patrum, III. 370 sqq).

[4] Concil. Neocæsar. ann. 314 c. 5.

hands.[1] This elaborate system was of gradual development. Tertullian seems only to know the single stage of *fletus*.[2] Cyprian in his multifarious discussions on penance apparently is ignorant of any stages, and so is Peter of Alexandria in 306. The Apostolic Constitutions of about the same date speak only of one stage, in which the penitent left the church before the commencement of prayer.[3] The Council of Ancyra, held in 314, knows only the three stages of *auditio*, *substratio* and *consistentia* and for those who had lapsed under persecution it orders one year of the first, three of the second, and two of the third.[4] The great council of Nicæa, in 325, also speaks of only three stages and provides for the lapsed three years of the first, six of the second and two of the third.[5] In the East, the adoption of the four stages by St. Basil the Great rendered them traditional in the Greek Church,[6] but the West never adopted the system wholly or generally. It is not alluded to in any of the Latin Fathers, in spite of the authority of the Nicene Council. In 443 the council of Arles, while quoting that of Nicæa, reduces the stages to two, *auditio* and *consistentia*, and the whole term to seven years,[7] and we hear little more of it in the Latin Church, although, in 488, the synodical epistle of Felix III. prescribes, for the readmission of those rebaptized by heretics, three years of *auditio*, seven of *substratio* and two of *consistentia*,[8] a provision which was carried into the Capitularies of Benedict the Levite and through the various collections of canons into the Decretum of Gratian.[9] Yet even so recent a writer as Father de

---

[1] Gregor. Thaumaturg. Epist. Canon. c. xi. As the date of this epistle is about 267, and as these four stages were not known until considerably later, there would seem to be little doubt that this canon is a subsequent interpolation. See Morin. de Pœnitent. Lib. VI. c. 1. ？ 9 sqq.

[2] Tertull. de Pœnitent. c. 6.   [3] Constitt. Apostol. II. xliii.

[4] Concil. Ancyran. ann. 314 c. 4.

[5] Concil. Nicæn. I. ann. 325 c. 11.

[6] One Greek writer, posterior to the sixth century, counts five stages, reckoning admission to communion as the fifth, but this is merely a question of words. Joan. Abbat. Raythu Schol. in S. Joan. Climac. c. 12 (Bibl. Max. Patr. VI. II. 304). In 706 the Council of Constantinople provides for adulterous wives one year of *fletus*, two of *auditio*, three of *substratio* and one of *consistentia*, and at the end of the seventh year the culprit is admitted to communion.—Quinisext in Trullo ann. 706, cap. 87 (Harduin. III. 1671).

[7] Concil. Arelatens. ann. 443, c. x.

[8] Felicis PP. III. Epist. vii.

[9] Capitul. v. 134.—C. 118, P. III. Dist. iv.

Charmes describes the four stations as the regular *pœnitentia canonica*, although he says they have long been obsolete.[1]

Thus the duration of these several stages could be lengthened or shortened indefinitely, or one or more of them could be omitted, producing an infinite variety of penalties, and they were prolonged with little mercy. Towards the end of the fourth century St. Basil the Great drew up a code for the information of a neighboring bishop, which shows us how rugged was the path laid out for the sinner, especially when he did not confess but was convicted. Thus for involuntary homicide the penance lasted for ten years, divided into two of *fletus*, three of *auditio*, four of *substratio* and one of *consistentia;* for fornication the term was seven years, two each of the first three, and one of the last; for voluntary homicide the period was extended to twenty years, the stages being respectively four, five, seven and four years; for denying Christ the stage of *fletus*, the severest of all, lasted through life, communion being administered at death in reliance on divine clemency.[2]

This pitiless legislation, however, was wisely rendered to a greater or less extent dependent on the discretion of the bishop who administered it. The Apostolic Constitutions, indeed, assume that the whole matter is subject to his judgment; they exhort him to give careful consideration to the details of each case, and in warning him not to sell exemptions for filthy gain they indicate the abuses that were already creeping in.[3] When definite terms of penance came to be

---

[1] Th. ex Charmes Theol. universalis Diss. v. cap. v. Q. 2, Concl. 2.

[2] S. Basil. Epist. Canon. III. c. lvi., lvii., lix., lxxiii., lxxx. The uncertainty of these rules is illustrated by Basil's prescribing fifteen years for adultery, divided into terms of four, five, four, and two years, while in a subsequent clause he says that for dismissing a wife and taking another the penance is the same as for adultery, eight years in terms of two, two, three and one year. (Ibid. c. lviii., lxxvii.). It is evident that his epistle as it has reached us has suffered many changes and interpolations.

According to the council of Ancyra in 314 (can. xli., xlii.) the penance for voluntary homicide was life-long, for involuntary, five or seven years. Various other councils, notably those of Elvira and Nicæa, busied themselves with prescribing penances for crimes of various grades, but there is little to be gained by investigating their discordant legislation. Its chief importance consists in its having served as the groundwork of the Penitentials, which will be considered hereafter.

[3] Constitt. Apostol. Lib. II. c. ix., x., lii.

prescribed, the councils ordering them were frequently careful to instruct the bishops to temper or increase them as the behavior of the penitent before and during his penance might render advisable.[1] Basil the Great seems to limit the episcopal power to diminish penance to cases where the culprit has earned it by confession, and even this he admits rather grudgingly,[2] while Gregory of Nyssa asserts it unreservedly when there is real repentance and amendment.[3] The African Church went further and in 397 declared that the whole subject of penance was in the hands of the bishops, who were empowered to use their discretion in its imposition,[4] and even in the Eastern Church, despite the authority of the Basilian canons, Chrysostom assumes that the duration of penance is entirely within his control, and that in assigning it he is governed solely by the temper of the penitent.[5] In the West also this was declared to be the rule of the Church by both Innocent I. and Leo I., whose decisions were carried through all the collections of canons to the time of Gratian—the bishop was to watch the repentance of the penitent and release him when he had rendered due satisfaction for his offence.[6] Various councils in Gaul,

---

[1] Concil. Ancyran. ann. 313 c. xxiv.; Concil. Neocæsariens. ann. 314 c. iii.; Concil. Nicæn. I. c. xii. The Council of Elvira however has no such provision, for the Spanish Church of the period, under the guidance of Hosius of Cordova was excessively rigid, but in time it softened, at least in favor of priests guilty of lapses of the flesh, and authorized the bishops to increase or diminish their punishment (C. Ilerdens. ann. 523, c. v.). Soon afterwards Pope Vigilius in 538, writing to the Spanish Bishop Eutherius assumes to grant this discretion as a special grace to converts from Arianism (Vigilii PP. Epist. ad Eutherium c. iii.).

[2] S. Basil. Epist. Canon. III. c. lxxiv.

[3] S. Gregor. Nyssæni Epist. Canon. c. iv. v.

[4] "Ut pœnitentibus secundum peccatorum differentiam episcopi arbitrio pœnitentiæ tempora decernantur."—C. Carthag. III. ann. 397 c. xxxi.

[5] S. Joh. Chrysost. Homil. XIV. ad II. Corinth. ℥ 3.

[6] "Ceterum de pondere æstimando delictorum sacerdotis est judicare, ut attendat ad confessionem pœnitentis et ad fletus atque lacrymas corrigentis ac tunc jubere dimitti cum viderit congruam satisfactionem."—Innoc. PP. I. Epist. xxv. c. 7, ad Decentium.—Gratian. c. 17 P. III. Dist. iii.

"Tempora pœnitudinis habita moderatione constituenda sunt tuo judicio prout conversorum animas perpexeris esse devotas."—Leon. PP. I. Epist. clix. c. 6, ad Nicetam.—Gratian. c. 2 Caus. xxvi. Q. 7.

By the early Fathers the word *sacerdos* was commonly used as synonymous with *episcopus*.

from the fifth to the seventh century, take the same position[1] so that it may be a assumed to be the rule of the Latin Church, until the rise of the Penitentials reintroduced the system of determinate periods for each class of crimes, and even then, as we shall see, a certain amount of discretion was conceded to the confessor.

During the lengthened periods prescribed for penance, the head was kept shaven, or in the case of women it was veiled, the vestments were of sack-cloth sprinkled with ashes, baths were forbidden and abstinence from wine and meat were strictly enjoined—as St. Jerome tells us, the filthier a penitent is the more beautiful is he.[2] The time was to be passed in maceration, fasting, vigils, prayers and weeping—the penitent, as St. Ambrose tells us, must be as one dead, with no care for the things of this life.[3] In fact, he was

---

[1] Concil Andegavens. ann. 453 c. xii.; C. Aurelianens. IV. ann. 541 c. viii.; C. Cabilonens. ann. 649 c. 8.

This question of discretion in the prescription of penance has its importance as it is the main reliance of the Church in justifying the assertion of the Council of Trent that indulgences were known and granted from the earliest times (C. Trident. Sess. XXV. Decr. de Indulg.). Of course the two have no connection, belonging, as we shall see hereafter, to entirely different systems. The great development of indulgences, in fact, only took place at a time when the Penitentials were obsolete and the arbitrary discretion of the priest in assigning penance was fully conceded, so that the distinction between the two powers was taken for granted.

[2] "Quanto fœdior tanto pulchrior." S. Hieron. Epist liv. c. 7 ad Furiam.

The custom of shaving the heads of male penitents in public penance continued at least until the fourteenth century.—Bened. Levitæ Capitular. Lib v. c. 116.—Alex. de Ales Summæ P. IV. Q. xiv. Membr. 6 Art. 3.—T. Aquinat. Summæ Suppl. Q. XXVIII. Art. 3.—J. Friburgens. Summæ Confessorum Lib. III. Tit. xxxiii. Q. 8.—Astesani Summæ de Casibus Lib. v. Tit. xxxv. Q. 2.

At the same time there was also a custom of allowing the hair and beard to grow during the whole period of penance. See Greg. Turon. Hist. Franc. Lib. VIII. c. 20. In a forged indulgence of the eleventh or twelfth century among the privileges enumerated is that of shaving and haircutting, showing the contrary to be the sign of penance (D'Achery, Spicileg. III. 383). Early in the twelfth century Hildebert of Le Mans says (Sermo xxxiv.) that the hair and beard are not to be cut in penance; and Sicardo Bishop of Cremona, in speaking of the tonsure and shaven chins of ecclesiastics observes (Mitrale, Lib. II. c. 1) "sed in jejuniis capillos et barbam crescere permittimus ut habitum pœnitentium repræsentamus." Probably the contradiction may be explained by a difference in the penance of clerics and laymen, each following the custom that would render most conspicuous the fact of his penance.

[3] Tertull. de Pœnit. c. ix.—Cyprian. de Lapsis *ad calcem.*—S. Paciani Para-

forbidden to engage in secular pursuits; if he threw off his penitential garments and returned to the world, he was cut off from all association with the faithful and was segregated with such strictness that anyone eating with him was deprived of communion.[1] Whenever the faithful were gathered together in church, the penitents were grouped apart in their hideous squalor, and either left the church before the sacred mysteries, or, if they were allowed to remain, they were not admitted to the Eucharist, but were brought forward to be prayed for and received the imposition of hands—in short their humiliation was utilized to the utmost as a spectacle and a warning for the benefit of the congregation.[2] In view of the fragility of youth, it was recommended that penance should not be imposed on those of immature age; and, as complete separation between husband and wife was enforced, the consent of the innocent spouse was necessary before the sinful one could be admitted to penitence.[3] Trade, if not absolutely forbidden to the penitent, was at most grudgingly allowed; he was prohibited from litigation, but if the matter was of urgent necessity, he might seek justice in an ecclesiastical court. In some respects, indeed, the effects of penance were indelible; no one who had undergone it was allowed to resume the profession of arms or to partake of wine and meat if fish and vegetables were accessible; Pope Siricius forbade absolutely marriage to reconciled penitents, and the Council of Arles in 443, in cases of infraction of this rule, expelled from the Church not only the offender but the newly-wedded spouse. Leo I. however, in case the penitent was young and found continence perilous, was willing to admit that marriage was a venial

---

næsis ad Pœnit c. x. xi.—Concil Cabillon. ann. 813 c xxxv.—S Ambros. de Lapsu Virginis § 35; de Pœnitent. Lib. ii. c. x.

[1] Concil. Turonici ann. 460 c. viii.—C. Venetici ann. 465 c. iii.—C. Aurelianens. I. ann. 511, c. xi.—C. Aurel. III. ann. 538 c. xxv.—C. Barcinonens. I. ann. 540 c. vi. vii.

[2] Sozomen. H. E. vii. 16 The imposition of hands was not confined to the final act of reconciliation; it was performed on all occasions (Statuta Eccles. Antiq. c. lxxx.). The custom however varied somewhat according to time and place, and the learned are sadly at variance as to the rules which governed it; see Binterim, Denkwürdigkeiten, Bd. V. Th. ii. pp. 403–15. The importance of the matter lies in the fact that the repeated imposition of hands shows that it did not confer absolution and had no sacramental character.

[3] Concil. Agathens. ann. 506 c. xv.—C. Aurelianens. III. ann. 538 c. xxiv.—C. Arelatens. II. ann. 443 c. xxii.

sin, not to be forgiven as a rule, but to be tolerated as the least of two evils, for after performing penance life-long chastity was proper. It was not till the ninth century was well advanced that permission to marry was freely given by Nicholas I.[1] The life of the penitent truly was hard, and we can readily believe the assertion of a council of Toledo in 693 that despairing escape from it was sometimes sought in suicide.[2] Optatus, indeed, in scolding the Donatists for impiously condemning bishops to perform penance, asserts that it is worse than death.[3]

With these tremendous penalties in view, it is easy to imagine that voluntary penitents were few, and that those who persevered were still fewer, a fact which may be inferred from a remark of St. Pacianus.[4] St. Ambrose indeed tells us that it was easier to find a man who had preserved his innocence than one who had properly performed penance, and he denounces the frequent practice of postponing it till the approach of death in the same way that catechumens postponed the saving waters of baptism.[5] Yet where the episcopal police was vigilant the number was not small, and as they were obliged during their prolonged terms always to be present in church, the ceremony of imposition of hands upon them lengthened greatly the services.[6] These involuntary penitents did not always submit peaceably, especially in the earlier periods when, after the cessation of a persecution, there were great numbers of the lapsed whose public idolatry admitted of no concealment and who were necessarily condemned to penance in its full rigor. The troubles of Cyprian are well known with the

---

[1] Siricii PP. Epist. I. c. 5 ad Himerium.—S. Cæsar. Arelatens. Serm. CCLXI. c. 3, in Append. S. Augustin.—Concil. Arelatens. II. ann 443 c. xxi.—Leonis PP. I. Epist. CLXVII. c. x–xiii.—Ivon. Carnotens. Decr. P. xv. c. lxxii. lxxx.— Gratian. c. 16 Caus. XXXIII. Q. ii.

The decretals of Siricius and Leo were carried through all the collections of canons up to Gratian and were held to be the law of the Church.

[2] Concil. Toletan. XVI. ann. 693 c. iv.

[3] "O impietas inaudita quem jugulaveritis inter pœnitentiæ tormenta servare! in comparatione operis vestri latronum levior videtur immanitas. Vos vivum facitis homicidium; latro jugulatis dat de morte compendium."—Optati de Schism. Donatist. Lib. II. c. xxi. Cf. c. xxv.

[4] S. Paciani Paranæsis ad Pœnitent. c. x. xi.

[5] S. Ambros. de Pœnitent. Lib. II. c. x. xi.

[6] "Abundant hic pœnitentes: quando illis manus imponitur fit ordo longissimus."—S. August. Serm. CCXXXII. c. 7.

turbulent violence of the lapsed in the Decian persecution of 250, who clamored and insisted on speedy reconciliation, urging the recommendations to mercy which they had obtained from the martyrs and confessors, till even Cyprian's firmness gave way and the second council of Carthage, as we have seen, reconciled them by wholesale on the plea of strengthening them for an expected revival of the persecution. Even more determined was the resistance of the Roman lapsed after the persecution of Diocletian: finding it impossible to obtain from Pope Marcellus a relaxation of rigor they rose in open sedition, leading to bloodshed and culminating in his banishment, nor was his successor Eusebius more fortunate. He refused to yield to the demands of the malcontents and in a few months he was driven from the city and died exiled in Sicily.[1]

The Church thus held at a high price restoration to its communion but it made no promises that the reconciliation thus dearly purchased comprised absolution or pardon from God. Towards the close of the fourth century St. Epiphanius repeats what St. Cyprian had already admitted, the assertion of ignorance as to what was in store for the penitent sinner. This rested with God and he alone knew; we can only hope that in his infinite mercy he will pardon the repentant.[2] St.

---

[1] The epitaph on Marcellus, attributed to Pope Damasus, says—

> Veridicus rector lapsos quia crimina flere
> Prædixit miseris fuit omnibus hostis amarus :
> Hinc furor, hinc odium, sequitur discordia, lites,
> Seditio, cædes, solvuntur fœdera pacis.
> —Baron. Annal. ann. 309, n. 7.

There is a similar epitaph on Eusebius, which shows that a certain Heraclius was the leader of the malcontents :

> Heraclius vetuit lapsos peccata dolere
> Eusebius miseros docuit sua crimina flere.
> Scinditur in partes populus gliscente furore,
> Seditio, cædes, bellum, discordia, lites.
> Exemplo pariter pulsi feritate tyranni [Maxentii]
> Integra cum rector servaret fœdera pacis,
> Pertulit exilium omnino sub judice lætus
> Littore Trinacrio mundum vitamque reliquit.
> —Migne's Patrolog. T. VI. p. 28.

[2] "Suscipit enim Deus pœnitentiam etiam post baptisma si quis lapsus fuerit. Quomoda vero postea facit, ipse solus novit. . . . Neque igitur promittimus libertatem omnino his qui post baptisma lapsi sunt, neque desperamus de vita

Augustin tells us virtually the same thing. A sinner who undergoes penance and is reconciled and subsequently commits no sin may feel secure of salvation, but if one leaves repentance to the last and is reconciled on the death-bed, the matter is in the hand of God and the presumption is against him :[1] reconciliation thus was only an outward sign, it concerned only the relations between the sinner and the Church, and the real issue lay between him and his God. So little importance, in fact, did St. Augustin attribute to the jurisdiction and ministration of the Church, that in spite of Cyprian's opinion he admits that there may be salvation outside of it, and that its refusal to receive a sinner to penance and reconciliation does not signify that God will not pardon him, for he can still earn eternal life by amendment.[2] That penance was simply punitive and deterrent and not medicinal is seen by the way in which Pope Siricius speaks of the treatment of those who relapsed subsequently into sin.[3] This

---

ipsorum . . . Secundum vero novimus quod misericors est Deus si ex tota anima pœnitentiam egerimus a delictis. Habet enim in manu vitam et salutis benignitatem. Et quid quidem ipse facit ipsi soli notum est."—S. Epiphan. Panar. Hæres. LIX.

We shall have frequent occasion to see how little correspondence there is between the opinions of the Fathers and the modern doctrines of the Church —a fact candidly admitted by the Salamanca theologians when they remark that there is much apparent heresy in the ancient writings; in view of the sanctity of the writers this is explained away by theologians, but if uttered by men of less authority it would be condemned as heresy. "Inventæ sunt multoties in scripturis SS. Patrum propositiones ex vi terminorum hæresin dicentes, tamen, attenta sanctitate et doctrina prædictorum Sanctorum, præfatæ propositiones in aliquum verum sensum interpretatæ sunt Doctoribus, quæ in aliis hominibus inferioris notæ inventæ, ut hæreses sunt damnatæ."—Salmanticens. Cursus Theol. Moral Tract. XVII. c. ii. n. 106.

A more effective plan of preserving the faithful from the errors of the Fathers was that of expurgating their works. In 1570 we find the great Spanish scholar Arias Montano thus employed on St. Augustin, St. Jerome and other leading writers (Colleccion de Documentos inéditos, T. XLI. 175).

[1] S August. Serm. CCCXCIII. Yet by this time the theory was gaining ground that pardon might be had from God through the power of the keys lodged in the Church at large, and this was shared in some degree by St. Augustin (Serm. CCCXCII. § 5). His views on the subject will be considered hereafter.

[2] Ejusd. Epist. CLIII. c. iii. ad Macedonian.

[3] "Et ipsi in se sua errata castigent et aliis exemplum tribuant."—Siricii PP. Epist. I. c. 5.

evidently was the current opinion of the Church, for a hundred years earlier the council of Elvira gives a long list of offences for which culprits were to be denied reconciliation even on the death-bed, and we cannot imagine that even the rigid Spanish Church supposed that it was thus depriving them of all hope of salvation and condemning them to hell. The crimes, it is true, are mostly serious ones, but among them is included the accusation of a bishop, priest or deacon and failing to prove the charge.[1] It marks a radical change wrought by the growth of sacerdotalism when in 428 Cœlestin I. speaks with horror of the denial of the sacrament to the dying sinner as consigning his soul to perdition.[2] By this time belief in the power of the keys was growing and an advance is seen in Leo I.'s allusion to reconciliation as the gate through which the sinner, purged by penance, is admitted to communion and gains pardon through the supplications of the priests.[3]

What were the ceremonies connected with the imposition of penance in the early church it would be difficult now to determine. The only case of which we have accounts is that of Theodosius in 390 which would seem to be wholly irregular. The offence was the slaughter of Thessalonica, which, as voluntary homicide, involved a penance under the canons either life-long or of twenty years, yet the emperor was admitted to reconciliation after eight months' excommunication, and though during that period he laid aside the imperial insignia, he was not debarred from resuming them or from military command.[4] At a later period the imposition of penance had become one of the great annual solemnities of the Church. Even as baptism was an elaborate ceremony, to be performed on the Saturday of Easter, after preliminary observances the previous week,[5] so penance was imposed at the beginning of Lent, on Ash Wednesday, and reconciliation on Holy Thursday. On the former day, all those undergoing or about

---

[1] Concil. Illiberitan. c. 1, 2, 7, 8, 12, 13, 17, 18, 63, 64, 65, 66, 70, 71, 72, 73, 75.

[2] Cœlestin PP. II. Epist. II. cap. 2..

[3] Leonis PP. I. Epist. CVIII. ad Theodorum cap. 2.—This passage sufficiently shows that there was no absolution preceding reconciliation as has been imagined by some modern apologists.

[4] S Ambros. Orat. de Obitu Theodos. c. 34.—Paulini Vit. S. Ambros. c. 34.— Rufini H. E. Lib. II. c. 18.—Theodoriti H. E. Lib. v. c. 18.

[5] Sacramentarium Gelasianum, Lib. I. n. xxix. xlii. xliv.

to assume penance in the diocese, were ordered to present themselves to the bishop in front of the cathedral porch. Thither also came their priests and the archpriests of the several parishes, instructed to investigate diligently their conversation and to enjoin penance in accordance with their several deserts. They were then led into the church; the bishop and clergy prostrated themselves and with tears sang the seven penitential psalms. Then the bishop arose, laid his hands on the sinners, sprinkled them with holy water, cast ashes over them, covered their heads with sack-cloth, and with sighs and groans announced to them that, as Adam was expelled from Paradise, so they were to be ejected from the Church, and with this he ordered the clergy to drive them out, which was done, chanting " In the sweat of thy face shalt thou eat bread."[1] It was a spectacle dramatically arranged to be as impressive as possible, and its effect upon the assembled crowd could not fail to be edifying. In the later periods the penitents were sometimes confined in the sacristy, or in the *dia-conium* (a place of imprisonment for clerical criminals), where they were duly starved and made to watch and pray.[2] Every year this ceremony was repeated, as long as the penance lasted.[3]

A remarkable feature of this ancient penance was that, like baptism, it could be undergone but once in a lifetime. This rule was established at a very early period, in fact, almost as soon as allusions occur to penance of any kind. The Shepherd of Hermas tells us that but a single opportunity for repentance is open to the servants of

---

[1] This formula is detailed by Regino (De Eccles. Discipl. Lib. I. c. 291), Burchard (Decr. Lib. XIX. c. 6), Ivo (Decr. P. XV. c. 45) and Gratian (Decr. Dist. 50 c. 64) and is credited by all of them to the Council of Agde. That council has a brief canon on the subject (C. Agathens. ann. 506 c. 15) representing a much simpler ceremony. It probably received accretions at various times and developed into that described in the text, which is sufficiently in accord with the *Ordines ad dandam Pœnitentiam.* As late as the middle of the thirteenth century Alexander Hales describes it in substantially the same detail (Summæ P. IV. Q. xiv. Membr. 6 Art. 3).

In the Ambrosian Church however reconciliation took place on Good Friday (Morin de Pœnit. Lib. IX. cap. 29, § 3, 4) and this custom prevailed in Spain at least until the seventh century.—Concil. Toletan. IV. ann. 633, c. 7.

[2] Gregor. PP. II. Epist. xiii. The sixteenth council of Toledo (ann. 693, c. 4) speaks of penitents "sub pœnitentiæ satisfactione custodiæ mancipati."

[3] Innoc. PP. I. Epist. XXV. c. 7.—Abbonis Sangermanens. Serm. iii. (D'Achery, Spicileg. I. 339).—Gloss. super Dist. 50, c. 64.

God.[1] Tertullian argues that he who had once received pardon in baptism, had lapsed into sin and had again been pardoned, could ask and expect no further mercy; his reincidence into sin shows that he repents of his repentance and aims to satisfy Satan, not God.[2] St. Clement of Alexandria argues that to require repeated penitence is no penitence.[3] For mortal sins Origen tells us that there is but one chance of repentance.[4] St. Ambrose warns the penitent that he should not undertake it unless he knows that he can persevere to the end, for if he fails his only chance is lost as he cannot repeat it.[5] In the East it would seem still to have been an open question at the end of the fourth century, for we hear of a synod in which it was determined that penance should only be allowed once to a sinner. Chrysostom dissented from this, saying that if a man performed penance a thousand times, he should still be admitted to penance, but opinion was against him and even his friends took him to task severely.[6] In the West it had already become a recognized law of the Church. In 385 Siricius, in an authoritative decretal, says that those who after penance return to their worldly ways, not only by committing fresh sins, but by going to the theatres and games, marrying and having children, since they cannot be again admitted to penance, are to be allowed to remain in the churches during the mysteries, but are not to be allowed communion until the death-bed.[7]

This shows that the refusal of a second penance and reconciliation by no means debarred the sinner from salvation. Though not at peace with the Church he could be at peace with God. St. Augustin had no doubt as to this and is at pains to explain that although a second penance is denied to one who had relapsed into sin, this is by

---

[1] Pastor. Hermæ Lib. II. Mandat. iv. 1, 3. "Servis enim Dei una pœnitentia est."

[2] Tertull. de Pœnitent. c. v. vi. vii. ix. "Sed amplius nunquam quia proxime frustra. Non enim et hoc semel satis est? Habes quod non jam merebaris; amisisti enim quod acceperas."

[3] S. Clement. Alexand. Stromata, Lib. II (Ed. Sylburg. p. 386).

[4] Origenis Homil. in Leviticum xv. 2. "In gravioribus enim criminibus semel tantum pœnitentiæ conceditur locus."

[5] S. Ambros. de Pœnitent. Lib. II. c. xi. Cf. c. xcv.

[6] Socrat. H. E. VI. xxi. Chrysostom in fact says "Si quotidie peccas, quotidie pœnitentiam age."—De Pœnitent. Homil VIII. § 1.

[7] Siricii PP. Epist. I. c. 5. The Council of Nicæa (c. 13) had ordered that communion should never be refused at death.

no means to be understood as denying that God may pardon him and
that he may earn eternal life by amendment.[1]   Though he could be
reconciled to the Church but once, St. Jerome tells us that he could
have his sins pardoned by God seventy times seven by repentance.[2]
As far as the Church was concerned, however, he was cut off.   Among
the accusations brought against Chrysostom in the Synod *ad Quercum,*
in 403, was that he gave license to sinners by saying to them " If you
sin again, again perform penance, and as often as you sin come to me
and I will heal you,"[3] and whatever we may think of the motives of
those who persecuted the saint, the bringing of such a charge shows
that what is the universal daily practice of the modern confessor was
regarded in those times as heresy.   The same lesson is taught by the
third council of Toledo, in 589, which deplores the execrable presumption of some priests who grant reconciliation to penitents as often as
they ask it, an abuse which it strictly prohibits and requires the
ancient canons to be observed.[4]   It is true that, about the same period,
Victor Tunenensis asserted that the sinner can be cured as often as
he lapses,[5] but the Church held fast to the ancient ways and the rule
is theoretically still in force though it has long since ceased to be operative.   We shall see hereafter how this public penance gradually came
to be supplanted by private penance and sinners no longer allowed
their sins to accumulate through life to be erased by a spasmodic
paroxysm of repentance as it drew to a close.   Public penance
gradually grew rare and came to be known as solemn penance, imposed only for crimes that were notorious and scandalous, for by that

---

[1] S. August. Epist. CLIII. c. iii. ad Macedonian.

[2] S. Hieron. Epist. CXXII. c. 3, ad Rusticum.

[3] Synod. ad Quercum (Harduin, I. 1042).   The Pseudo-Justin Martyr was
apparently of the same opinion as Chrysostom.—Pseudo-Justin. Mart. Explicationes Q. 97.

[4] C. Toletan. III. ann. 589 c. xi —" Quoniam comperimus per quasdam His-
paniarum ecclesias, non secundum canonem sed fœdissime pro suis peccatis
homines agere pœnitentiam, ut quotiescunque peccare voluerint toties a presbyteris se reconciliari expostulent; ideo pro coercenda tam execrabili præ-
sumptione id a sacro concilio jubetur, ut secundum formam canonicam
antiquorum detur pœnitentia . . . . hi vero qui ad prævia vitia vel infra
pœnitentiæ tempus vel post reconciliationem relabuntur secundum priorum
canonum severitatem damnentur."

[5] Victoris Tunenens. de Pœnit. Lib. c. xii.—" Unde dudum curatus fueras
inde iterum curaberis."   And this is the rigorous penance—" Saccum indue,
cinerem asperge, in jejunio semper ora, in oratione jejuna " (Ibid. c. xviii.).

time the seal of the confessional had been invented and sins revealed in confession could not be betrayed by penance visible to the public. In this survival the rule was maintained that solemn penance could be imposed but once. During the transition period, and before the sacramental system was solidly established with auricular confession and secret penance, the conflict between the old practice and the new was somewhat puzzling to the schoolmen. Hugh of St. Victor, who did so much to bring about the change, about 1130, argues the question of a single penance at much length and in a way to show that there were still upholders of the old forms. Some, he says, explain it by saying that the sinner should repent and abstain from sin during life; others that it referred only to the public penance which could not be repeated on account of its rigor; personally he seems to incline to the former opinion, but he leaves the matter in doubt.[1] In the middle of the century Gratian shows the importance and difficulty of the question by the long array of authorities cited for its resolution, but he hopelessly confuses it by the standing difficulty of the ambiguity of the word *pœnitentia,* meaning both penance and repentance. His conclusion, however is that the refusal of repetition refers to solemn penance which in some churches is administered only once, and in this Peter Lombard agrees with him.[2] Toward the close of the century, when the new system was fairly established, Alain de Lille refers the rule exclusively to solemn penance and endeavors to explain it on the score of the solemnity of the ceremony and that its repetition would breed contempt.[3] After the Lateran canon of 1216 had rendered annual private confession to the priest obligatory, of course the distinction between it and public penance became absolute. St. Ramon de Peñafort differentiates them clearly; solemn penance is imposed by the bishop on Ash Wednesday, it cannot be repeated and the penitent incurs the old disability of marriage.[4] By this time it had lost whatever medicinal character it may have had of old and was wholly vindictive and deterrent. Alexander Hales explains the prohibition of repetition by its symbolizing the expulsion from Para-

---

[1] Hugon. de S. Victore de Sacramentis Lib. II., P. xiv. c. 4. Cf. Ejusd. Summæ Sentt. Tract. vi. c. 12.

[2] Grat. Decr. Caus. XXXIII. Q. iii. Dist. 4. *ad calcem.*—P. Lombard. Sententt. Lib. iv. Dist. xiv. § 3.

[3] Alani de Insulis Lib. Pœnitent. (Migne's Patrol. CCX. 296).

[4] S. Raymond. Summæ Lib. II. Tit. xxxiv. § 3.

dise which was once for all, and adds that it is not designed to grant immunity to persistent sinners, for they are to be punished for relapse in some other way with equal severity, but he says that it was the greatest error to hold that penance could not be repeated for it forced sinners to despair.[1] The matter continued to be a *crux* for the schoolmen, especially in consequence of the ambiguity between penance and repentance. Aquinas says penitence can be repeated except the *pœnitentia solemnis*.[2] Yet there seem to have still been some who owing to the confusion of terms held that repentance could not be repeated, for Astesanus de Asti in 1317 denounces this energetically as a most wicked and cruel error; at the same time he describes very fully the solemn penance, with its disabilities as to marriage and bearing arms, and says that it can be imposed but once, except in some churches which allow its repetition; he also asserts that it is sacramental.[3] Durand de Saint-Pourçain is equally mystified by the assertions of Ambrose and the other fathers and exerts himself to prove that a man can have penance as often as he lapses into sin.[4] When ecclesiastical archæology had come to be better understood, Juenin tells us that the custom of denying a second penance died out in the East early in the fifth century, but was continued in the West until the seventh, when the habit arose of imposing public penance only for public sins, while private sins were penanced as often as necessary—in which he is correct, except as to the dates.[5]

The applications of the penitential system to ecclesiastics offer one or two points worthy of brief consideration. The indelible character of penance in the early Church and the life-long disabilities which it entailed render it a matter of course that no one who had undergone it was eligible to holy orders. This seems at first to have been tacitly assumed as a necessary implication, and may be inferred from canons of the council of Nicæa.[6] Toward the close of the fourth century how-

---

[1] Alex. de Ales Summæ P. IV. Q. xiv. Membr. 5, Art. 2; Membr. 6, Art. 2. "Debet enim punire tanta pœna ut confusio solemnis pœnitentiæ in acerbitate et magnitudine recompensatur."

[2] S. Th. Aquinat. Summæ P. III. Q. lxxxiv. Art. 10.

[3] Astesani Summæ de Casibus Lib. V. Tit. vi. Q. 3; Lib. V. Tit. xxxv. Q 3, 4.

[4] Durandi di S. Portiano Comment. super Sententt. Lib. IV. Dist. xiv. Q. 6, § 6.

[5] Juenin de Sacramentis Diss. VI. Q. vii. Cap. 1, Art. 2, § 2.

[6] C. Nicæn. ann. 325 c. ix. x.

ever Pope Siricius orders it as though it were a new regulation, and mitigates it by providing that if a penitent has been ordained ignorantly he can retain his position and functions.[1] Soon afterwards the fourth council of Carthage is more severe; if he has been ordained in ignorance, he is to be deposed; if the bishop has done it knowingly, he is to be deprived of the power of ordination.[2] This more rigorous view prevailed. St. Augustin speaks of it as an established rule, that no penitent could enter or remain in or return to clerkship.[3] This however was not strictly observed and the prohibition had to be occasionally repeated. In 465 the council of Rome forbade penitents to aspire to holy orders.[4] In 506 the council of Agde repeated the injunction, adding that those who had been ordained through ignorance could retain their position with limited functions.[5] The council of Epaone in 517 again enunciated it, and that of Arles in 524 declared it to be the universal rule; if any bishop violated it by ordaining a penitent he was to be suspended for a year from celebrating mass.[6] Evidently the rule was one which it was not easy to enforce. Some of the Sacramentaria in the *Ordo de sacris ordinibus benedicendis* enunciate it, showing that it had to be kept perpetually before the eyes of bishops;[7] and about 700 the established formula of papal instructions to the suburbicarian bishops on their consecration contains a clause reminding them of it.[8] Gratian, in the twelfth century, gives the decretal of Siricius and the Carthagenian canon, but restricts

---

[1] Siricii PP. Epist. I. c. 14.—Innocent. PP. I. Epist. xxxix.—Yet a letter which is variously attributed to Siricius and to Innocent I. limits the prohibition to those who after performing penance have returned to a military career. —Siricii Epist. ad Episc. Afric.; Innoc. PP. I. Epist. ii. ad Victricium c. 2.

[2] Statuta Ecclesiæ antiqua c. lxviii. But about the same period the Council of Toledo allowed penitents to be admitted to the lower orders.—Can. Toletan. I. ann. 400 c. 2.

[3] St. Augustin. Epist. clxxxv. ad Bonifacium § 45. Carried through all the collections of canons to Gratian, Dist. 50 c. 25.—"Ut constitueretur in ecclesia ne quisquam post alicujus criminis pœnitentiam clericatum accipiat vel ad clericatum redeat, vel in clericatu maneat, non desperatione indulgentiæ sed rigore factum est disciplinæ."

[4] C. Roman. ann. 465, c. 3.

[5] Concil. Agathens. ann. 506, c. 43.

[6] Concil. Epaonens. ann. 517, c. 3.—C. Arelatens. IV. ann. 524 c. 3.

[7] Sacramentar. Gelasianum, Lib. i. n. xcv. (Muratori Opp. XIII. ii. 208).— Sacramentar. Gregorian. (Ibid. XIII. iii. 26).

[8] Lib. Diurn. Roman. Pontiff. Cap. iii. Tit. ix. n. 2.

the rule of course to those who have undergone solemn penance, and nullifies the sentence of deposition for bishops by adding the clause, "unless the necessity of the Church demands it or a contrary custom prevails;" he also gives the milder Toledan canon.[1] Nominally the rule was preserved by the canonists, but we may safely assume that in practice it became obsolete.[2]

The early Church honestly endeavored to keep the ranks of the clergy pure and to exercise a strict supervision over admission. How great an honor this was esteemed to be may be gathered from the emphasis with which Cyprian announces to his flock that he had conferred the inferior grade of lector on Celerinus who had earned the title of confessor by his constancy under persecution in Rome.[3] The council of Nicæa forbade admission to the newly baptized or to those who had been guilty of any crime; all postulants were to be strictly examined and any one who confessed to sin was to be rejected.[4] Siricius ordered that admission should be refused to any one who since baptism had been stained with unchastity, had administered justice or performed military service,[5] and Innocent I. added to the causes of exclusion the discharge of any public functions because this inferred that the candidate had been concerned in the public games of the circus.[6] Innocent deplored the inobservance of these rules in Spain, where lawyers, judges, soldiers, courtiers, and officials were received to orders though they must be burdened with sins; what has been done, he says, may be left to the judgment of God, but hereafter all such and those who ordain them must be degraded and deposed, and the Nicene canons must be obeyed.[7] Whether this produced a reform in Spain may be doubted, though two centuries later Isidor of Seville tells us that no one convicted of mortal sin is eligible to ordination.[8]

It was easy to adopt canons and issue decrees, but their enforcement

---

[1] Gratiani Decr. c. 55, 66, 68, Dist. 50.

[2] Astesani Summæ de Casibus Lib. v. Tit. xxxv. Q. 1.

[3] Cypriani Epist. xxxix.

[4] Concil. Nicæn. ann. 325 c. ii. ix.

[5] Siricii PP. Epist. x. c. 8, 13.

[6] Innocent. PP. I. Epist. ii. c. 12. For the frenzied passion of the Christians for the public games see Salvianus, *De Gubernatione Dei.*

[7] Innoc. PP. I. Epist. iii. c. 4, 6. Yet with singular inconsistency Innocent decided (Epist. vi. c. 3.) that administering torture or passing capital sentences was no bar to orders, thus reversing the mandate of Siricius.

[8] Isidor. Hispalens. de Eccles. Officiis Lib. ii. c. 5 § 14.

was a different matter, and the Church, which it had been difficult to keep pure during the periods of persecution, when Christianity became the state religion rapidly filled with ambitious, self-seeking and unprincipled men. Pope Siricus denounces the habit of some bishops in conferring the diaconate, priesthood and even the episcopate on vagrants styling themselves monks, rather than be at the expense of aiding them, and this without even knowing whether they were orthodox or baptized, while others ordained neophytes and laymen as deacons and priests.[1] St. Isidor of Pelusium tells us that Bishop Eusebius of that see sold ordination to a number of wretches stained with every vice and crime, and when Hermogenes succeeded Eusebius Isidor cautioned him about them, sadly adding that it would be of no use to eject them as experience showed that they would have no difficulty in obtaining positions elsewhere.[2] St. Jerome does not hesitate to apply to the clergy of his own period Jeremiah's denunciations of the wickedness of the priests of Judah.[3] If Optatus is to believed in his account of the Donatist schism the African Church was filled with criminals of the worst type, both bishops and priests,[4] and if Cyprian is to be believed this degradation of morals had existed since the middle of the third century.[5] Salvianus gives an even more deplorable account of the condition of clerical morals in Gaul in the fifth century and declares that Rome, the ecclesiastical city, is the most polluted of all.[6] When in 496 a certain Eucaristus endeavored to purchase consecration to the episcopate for sixty-three solidi, it is true that Gelasius I. condemned him in a synod, but the fact that he made the attempt shows that such transactions were familiar to men's minds.[7] Indeed, a provision in the Apostolic Canons punishing with

---

[1] Siricii. PP. Epist. vi. c. 2, 3.

[2] S. Isidori Pelusiot. Lib. ii. Epist. 121, 127; Lib. iii. Epist. 17, 103, 127, 224, 259.

[3] Hieron. Comment. in Jeremiam Lib. ii. c. viii. v. 10–11.

[4] Optati de Schismate Donatistar. Lib. i. c. 15–20. In the synod of Cirta, held about 307, Purpurius, Bishop of Limata, was accused of having slain his nephews while they were in prison, to which he fiercely replied that he had done so and that he did so to all who were opposed to him.

[5] Cyprian. de Lapsis. Yet when Cyprian, who attacked his fellow bishops so vigorously, was himself assailed, he assumed that to accuse bishops is to accuse God who sets them over his Church. The mere fact that they are bishops is sufficient proof of their innocence.—Epist. lxvi.

[6] Salviani de Gubern. Dei Lib. v. c. 10; Lib. vii. c. 17, 18, 22.

[7] Lowenfeld, Epistt. Pontiff. Roman. ined. n. 22.

deposition both the ordainer and the ordained guilty of this peculiarly objectionable simony indicates that it was a vice of old standing,[1] and two general councils felt it necessary to repeat the provision,[2] while Gregory the Great speaks of its occurrence as a matter within his own knowledge.[3] In fact, it subsequently became a received rule of the Church that its offices could be sold if the money was to be applied to a charitable purpose such as the redemption of captives.[4]

The Church thus in its members offered ample material for both repentance and penance, but unfortunately it came to adopt a rule that no cleric should be subjected to penance. This originally was not an expression of laxity, but rather of severity. Even as no criminal was to be admitted to orders, so none was to be allowed to retain them. The layman could be punished by penance of greater or less duration. For the cleric the only punishment was deposition, and it shows how purely all these penalties were disciplinary and not sacramental, how completely confined to the *forum externum*, that the culprit thus degraded was not suspended from communion but was allowed to receive the Eucharist as a layman. The loss of position was considered to be sufficient punishment, and scripture was cited forbidding two punishments for the same offence[5] If the sinner chose to placate the wrath of God by voluntary repentance and mortification of the flesh, there was nothing to prevent him, as Jerome advises the deacon Sabinian, who had been guilty of adultery, to do—to enter a

---

[1] Canon. Apostol. c. xxviii.

[2] Concil. Chalced. ann. 451, c. 2.—Concil. Quinisext. in Trullo ann. 701, c. 22. Cf. Concil. Namnetens. c. ann. 895, c. 7 (Harduin. VI. 458.).

[3] Gregor. PP. I. Homil. XVII. in Evangel. n. 13.

[4] S. Anselmi Lucens. Collect. Canon. Lib. v. c. 48. "Quod ministeria ecclesiæ pro captivorum redemptione vendenda sunt."

[5] Cyprian. Epist. lxviii. lxxii.—Canon. Apostol. xxiv. "Dicit enim Scriptura: bis de eodem delicto vindictum non exiges."—S. Basilii Epist. Canon. I. ii.—Concil. Carthag. v. ann. 401 (Cod. Eccles. Afric. c. xxvii.). So Basil the Great in laying down the rule adds "non enim vindicabis bis in idipsum." (Basil. Epist. Canon. II. c. xxxii. cf. III. li. lxx). Yet in the case of the priest Victor, who had lapsed in the Decian persecution, there was both deposition and penance (Cyprian. Epist. lxiv.), and Basil advises that the priest Bianor be admitted to penance for taking an oath (Epist Canon. II. c. xvii.). Synesius, also, in the case of the priest Lampronianus already alluded to above, seems to have inflicted penance for he deprived the offender of communion, reserving the right to admit him on the death-bed, when, if he recovered, he was to fall back into excommunication.—Synesii Epist. LXVII.

monastery and implore "divine mercy" with tears and sack-cloth and ashes.[1]

With the development of sacerdotalism this, which was a simple matter of proportioning punishment, came to be claimed as a privilege of immunity, releasing the clergy from all responsibility for their crimes. One of the most serious offences of the Donatists was that they subjected clerics to penance, reducing them thus to the condition of laymen, although, as Optatus claims, the consecrating oil releases them from human judgment and they are to be left to that of God.[2] When, however, Pope Siricius enunciated the rule that ecclesiastics were not to be penanced, he did not base it on that ground, and when Innocent I. pronounced that heretical ordination conferred no such exemption he ridiculed the claim put forward that the sacerdotal benediction removed all sin—the time had not yet come to recognize a power of absolution in the ceremonies of the Church.[3] With such material as we have seen existing in the higher grades of the Church, this practical immunity from all punishment short of the extreme penalty of degradation, which, for the avoidance of scandal, can rarely have been exercised except for purposes of persecution, could only work an increase of evil, while for the conscientious priest who had yielded to temptation it was a hardship that he could not relieve his conscience without suffering expulsion.[4] It was, we may assume, to meet these difficulties that, about the middle of the fifth century, Leo I. introduced an innovation destined in time to modify the whole theory and practice of the Church in relation to sinners. After reciting the fact that priests and deacons were not liable to public penance for any crime, he proposes that they should seek mercy from God in private, and promised that if they should thus render due satisfaction it should be sufficient.[5] At the time this seems to

---

[1] S. Hieron. Epist. CXLVII. § 8, ad Sabinian.

[2] Optati de Schism. Donatist. Lib. II. c. xxiv.–xxv.

[3] Siricii PP. Epist. I. c. 14.—Innoc. PP. I. Epist. XVII. c. 3, 4; Epist. XXIV. c. 3. He attributes to the necessities of the times the fact that the council of Nicæa (c. viii) admitted the validity of the ordinations of the Novatians and that those of the heretic bishop Bonosus held good in Macedonia (Epist. XVII. c. 5).

[4] We have a hint as to this in a canon of the first council of Orange in 441 relaxing the rule that clerics could not be admitted to penance—"Pœnitentiam desiderantibus clericis non denegandam"—C. Arausican. I. ann. 441 c. 4.

[5] Leon. PP. I. Epist. CLXVII. Inquis. ii. "Alienum est a consuetudine eccle-

have been speedily forgotten and produced no observable effect, but we shall see hereafter how this recognition of secret penance by the Church germinated and developed until it virtually replaced the time-honored public penance.

In the East the ancient rules continued to be obeyed. John the Faster, who was Patriarch of Constantinople from 586 to 596 asserts that bishops, priests and deacons are not to be heard in confession unless they furnish security in advance that if they have done aught which should prevent performance of their functions they will not minister in future, for no penance can be assigned to them. They may still however officiate as lector and need not abstain from communion.[1] In the West the confusion caused by the Barbarian invasions and the gradual development of the new order of things caused the rule to be virtually forgotten for a time. In 511 the council of Orleans says that a deacon or priest who had withdrawn himself from com-

siastica ut qui in presbyterali honore aut in diaconii gradu fuerint consecrati, ii pro crimine aliquo suo per manus impositionem remedium accipiant pœnitendi: quod sine dubio ab apostolica traditione descendit, secundum quod scriptum est: Sacerdos si peccaverit quis orabit pro illo. . . Unde hujusmodi lapsis ad promerendum misericordiam Dei privata est expetenda secessio, ubi illis satisfactio si fuerit digna sit etiam fructuosa."

Leo's invocation of apostolical authority for clerical immunity from penance is an instructive illustration of the exegesis which finds warrant for whatever is needed. The text cited has not much bearing on the subject, but doubtless it served as a demonstration when enunciated with such solemnity in a papal utterance. Yet it was a simple imposition on the presumptive ignorance of the people. The editors of Leo refer it to the Septuagint Leviticus V. but there is no such text there, and Leo can hardly have been unaware that the Levitical regulations are wholly opposed to his thesis. The Vulgate says—

"Si sacerdos qui unctus est peccaverit, delinquere faciens populum, offeret pro peccato suo vitulum immaculatum Domino."—Levit. IV. 3 (virtually the same in LXX.).

"Et expiabit sanctuarium et tabernaculum testimonii atque altare, sacerdotes quoque et universum populum."—Ibid. XVI. 33 (the same in LXX.).

When Pope Zachary (Epist. VIII. c. 14) quoted Leo, the text "Sacerdos si peccaverit," etc., is referred to I. Kings II.—but this is equally incorrect, the passage being "si autem in Dominum peccaverit vir quis orabit pro eo?"— which is destructive of all intercession for sins against God.

[1] Johann. Jejunator. Libellus Pœnitentialis (Morini Tract. de Pœnitent. Append. pp. 85–6). Cf. Ejusd. Sermon. (Ibid. p. 97). Yet the Justinian legislation empowered the bishop to diminish the penance and restore to his functions a cleric guilty of dicing or attending the public games, and this was embodied by Photius in the Nomocanon, Lib. IX. c. 39.

munion by profession of penance can still baptize.[1] In 523 the
council of Lerida shows priests and deacons subject to penance by
suspending from function and communion for two years those who
shed human blood, ordering them to pass the time in vigils, prayers
and almsgiving, and, though allowing them to resume their functions, pronouncing them incapable of promotion.[2] It is shortly after
this that we may date the rise of the system of Penitentials, or collections of canons prescribing the administration of penance, by
which until the twelfth century the Church governed the faithful.
In these public penance was assigned to cleric and laic alike, the
only distinction being that a longer period was assigned to the cleric,
and that this was increased in proportion to his rank. This begins
with the earliest collection, attributable to the sixth century, which
provides that for voluntary homicide, fornication or fraud the bishop
shall perform thirteen years of penance, the priest seven, the deacon
six, the monk not in orders four; adding that the saints of old had
prescribed twenty-three years for the bishop, twelve for the priest,
seven for the deacon, and four for monk, nun and lector, while the
nature of the observances prescribed and the suspension from communion rendered this a public and not a private penance.[3]

In the rudeness of those dreary ages, as we shall see more fully
hereafter, the distinction between secular and spiritual penalties was
well-nigh lost; they were combined together and penance became
more and more a temporal punishment, with little trace of its medicinal character. Thus a canon which is found in a whole class of
Penitentials provides that if a cleric commits homicide he shall be
exiled for ten years; on his return, if he can bring testimonials from
bishop or priest that during this period he has duly repented on
bread and water he can be received back, but he must satisfy the
parents of the slain and serve them as a son. If he will not do this
he shall be like Cain a wanderer on the face of the earth.[4] Another
penitential provides that if a man wounds another he shall pay him

[1] Concil. Aurelianens. I. ann. 511, c. 12.
[2] Concil. Ilerdens. ann. 523, c. 1. Cf. c. 5.
[3] Excerpta ex Libro Davidis §§ 7, 10 (Wasserschleben, Bussordnungen der abenländischen Kirche, pp. 1, 2).
[4] Pœnitent. Columban. B. c. 1 (Wasserschleben, p. 355).—P. Merseburgens. a. c. 1 (p. 391).—P. Bobiens. c. 1 (p. 407).—P. Parisiens. c. 1 (p. 412). The prescriptions of time in these codes are very uncertian. Cap. 13 of the P. Columban. repeats the above with the substitution of three for ten years.

the *wer-gild* or compensation and provide a physician to cure him; then, if a layman, he shall do penance for forty days, if a simple cleric twice forty days, if a deacon, seven months, if a priest a year.[1] This rigor of punishment had full papal assent. In 742 St. Boniface consulted Pope Zachary as to what measures he should adopt to check the universal licence of the clergy, such as deacons keeping four or five concubines, and while leading this scandalous life rising to the priesthood and episcopate. The same year St. Boniface held a synod in conjunction with Carloman and the prescriptions of that body may presumably be held to embody the papal counsel. All clerics and nuns guilty of unchastity were ordered to perform penance in prison on bread and water. If a priest, he was to be scourged and flayed and his imprisonment was to last for two years, with power to his bishop to increase it. If a simple clerk or monk he was to have three scourgings and a year's imprisonment, and the same for nuns, besides shaving the head.[2] In Spain shortly before the Saracenic invasion a council of Toledo had no hesitation in prescribing a year's penance for any priest, deacon or monk who sheltered a fugitive cleric from a sentence of his prelate.[3] Evidently Pope Leo's prescription had been forgotten. The Church made no distinction between public and private penance, and there was no hesitation in subjecting cleric and laic to either indiscriminately, though Rabanus Maurus argues that for public crimes a cleric should be deposed on account of the scandal, while for secret sins he can confess, and perform penance.[4]

The incompatibility of sin and clerical functions gradually also faded out. A council of Toledo in 633 decided that if a man in mortal sickness accepted penance but only made a general confession that he was a sinner, if he recovered he was eligible to ordination, but any one who had publicly confessed a mortal sin must still be excluded.[5] The question of the deposition of clerical penitents was settled in the Toledan council of 683, where Bishop Gaudentius of Valeria asked whether he should continue to perform his functions, seeing that he had accepted penance. To this the answer was long and argumentative, showing that the decision in his favor was known

---

[1] Pœnitent. Pseudo-Roman. c. vii. § 7 (Wasserschleben, p. 369.)

[2] S. Bonifacii Epist. XLIX.—Capit. Carolomanni I. c. 6 (Baluz. I. 105).

[3] Concil. Toletan. XIII. ann. 693, c. xi.

[4] Rabani Mauri Pœnitentium Liber, cap. 1.

[5] Concil. Toletan. IV. ann. 633, c. liv.

to be a reversal of the ancient rule. Penitents are to abstain from sin and from secular affairs, but not from what is holy; but if they have confessed mortal sin it is left for the metropolitan to decide.[1] Thus the incompatibility was practically set aside. It was in vain that Nicholas I., about 865, insisted that a priest after lapsing could not be restored to his functions,[2] in 1089 Urban II. decided like the Toledan council that it was a matter within the discretion of his bishop.[3] At the same time he retained a portion of the ancient rigor by ordering that a layman who had undergone penance and reconciliation should not be admitted to orders, or a cleric be promoted to a higher grade.[4] About the same period Anselm of Lucca assumes this as regards laymen, and explains that it is a matter of discipline and need not make them despair of pardon from God, while any deviation from the ancient rigor is a matter reserved for papal decision, and those who truly amend and render satisfaction may be restored.[5]

The men who were concerned in the manufacture of the False Decretals, during the first half of the ninth century had, while accepting the liability of the clergy to public penance, sought to remove all the disabilities which it inflicted on both clerks and laymen, in a passage which found its place in the collections of canons.[6] Yet Benedict the Levite, who belonged to the same school, endeavored to resuscitate the old rule; priests and deacons were not to be subjected to penance, but were to be degraded and never restored.[7] That in practice, however, they could be both degraded and penanced is shown by an edict of the Emperor Lothair, about 850, in which he orders that priests and deacons who have been deposed shall perform penance according to the canons in the places assigned to them and not wander around; if they do not obey they are to be scourged, and if this fails they are to be thrust into prison and undergo their penance there.[8]   Even

---

[1] Concil. Toletan. XIII. ann. 693, c. x.

[2] Nichol. PP. I. ad Arducium c. vi. (D'Achery, I. 597).

[3] Löwenfeld, Epistt. Pontiff. Roman. inedd. p. 63.

[4] Harduin. Concil. VI. II. 1653.

[5] Anselmi Lucens. Canon. Lib. VIII. c. 3, 30, 37.

[6] Pseudo-Calixti Epist. ad Galliæ Episcopos (Migne's Patrol. CXXX. 136.) Possibly this may have been framed to justify Louis le Debonnaire's resumption of the empire after the Penance of Attigny.

[7] Capitularia, Lib. V. c. 131.

[8] Capit. Lothar. Imp. Tit. IV. c. 3 (Baluz. II. 223). Lothair states that all the laws in Tit. IV. are excerpts from those of Charlemagne and Louis le Débonnaire.

slenderer respect for the tonsure and equal disregard for the distinction between secular and spiritual remedies are exhibited in an Hungarian canon of 1099 which orders that clerics accused of theft shall be tried by the bishop or archdeacon, when any one found guilty is to be deposed and his property confiscated, or if he has nothing to confiscate he shall he sold as a slave.[1]

With the gradual revival of learning the antagonism of these conflicting rules greatly puzzled the canonists who sought to bring into something like order the medley of legislation developed in the successive epochs of the Church. Ivo of Chartres is much worried by the prescription that no one who had performed penance is to be admitted to orders, or if in orders is to be degraded. It was the unquestioned ancient law of the Church, but in spite of Urban II. it was nowhere observed. Ivo can only explain it by showing that in many other things the observances of the Church had been modified, and comforts himself with the reflection that charity covereth a multitude of sins.[2] Gratian find the question equally insoluble; he gives thirteen canons on one side and twelve on the other and vainly endeavors to reconcile them.[3]

As in the matter of the repetition of penance, the trouble finally settled itself through the happy invention of private penance and its gradual superseding of public penance. When the latter became exceptional and was known as solemn penance, to be applied only in cases of notorious crimes which had scandalized the community, it was easy to enforce the ancient rule that it must not be applied to clerics, and at the same time tacitly to drop the alternative penalty of degradation. The schoolmen came to define three varieties of penance—private, public, and solemn. In this the later so-called public penance differed from private only in being inflicted in sight of the congregation, or in consisting of observances which could not be concealed, such as pilgrimages. The old expulsion from the church on Ash Wednesday and reconciliation on Holy Thursday became known as "solemn penance." Clerics were still held liable to the later public penance, and towards the end of the twelfth century Alain de Lille tells us that for them it consisted in exclusion from the choir during singing and from the table during meals, the knowledge of it thus being con-

---

[1] Synod. Strigonens. II. c. ann. 1099 (Batthyany, Legg. Eccles. Hung. II. 128.)
[2] Ivonis Decreti Prologus.   [3] Decreti Dist. 50.

fined to their fellows. If solemn penance was not to be imposed on them, it was not, as of old, on account of the purity required of them, but, it was a special favor, granted, as he says, on account of the dignity of the cloth, and chiefly because their sins are to be concealed, for if known to the laity they would be an evil example and a scandal, and the name of God would be blasphemed among the nations[1] —a candid admission of the reasons, not particularly creditable to the Church, which continued to be put forward in justification.[2] It thus became a received rule among the canonists and theologians that solemn penance was not to be imposed on clerics on account of scandal, unless the offender was previously degraded or reduced to the lower orders. Some say, however, that he was simply rendered ineligible to promotion without a papal dispensation, and others that the prohibition of solemn penance extended to nobles and men of rank.[3] The authorities are not altogether in harmony, but this is natural and is of little importance for practically the time-honored public penance of the Church had become obsolete.

---

[1] Alani de Insulis Lib. Pœnitentialis (Migne's Patrol. CCX. 295–6).

[2] About 1325, after scholastic theology had been fully constructed, the reasons alleged for the exemption of clerics from solemn penance show how widely the Church had strayed from the ancient landmarks. It was now regarded as a favor, the justification advanced for which was thoroughly discreditable " Hæc autem pœnitentia non est imponenda clericis, non propter favorem personæ sed ordinis, quia agens publicam pœnitentiam non debet ad ordines promoveri . . . primo propter dignitatem eorum. Secundum propter timorem recidivi. Tertio propter scandalum vitandum quod in populo posset oriri ex memoria præcedentium delictorum. Quarto quia non haberet frontem alios corrigendi cum peccatum ejus fuerit publicum."—Durand. de S. Portiano super Sententt. Lib. IV. Dist. xiv. Q. 4 §§ 6–7.

[3] Raymund. de Pennaf. Summæ Lib. II. Tit. xxxv. § 3.—Alex. de Ales Summæ P. IV. Q. xiv. Membr. 6, Art. 3.—Aquinat. Summæ P. III. Q. lxxxix. Art. 3.—Astesani Summæ de Casibus Lib. v. Tit. xxxiv. xxxv. Q. 1.—Angeli de Clavasio Summ. Angel. s. v. *Pœnitentia* §§ 4, 5.

CHAPTER IV.

RECONCILIATION.

RECONCILIATION, as we have seen, was merely a matter of discipline. The sinner's path to salvation was rendered easier by his redintegration to the Church, but it was not assured, nor did his exclusion infer that he was not pardoned by God. Still there are some points concerning it which merit consideration, especially as the old reconciliation gradually merged into the modern absolution, and it has been the aim of most of the apologists to prove their identity.

The essence of the ceremony of reconciliation was the imposition of hands, the exact original significance of which it would be at present impossible to define with accuracy. It could not have been considered as conferring the Holy Ghost, for according to Cyprian it was participated in by the bishop and all the clergy,[1] nor was it confined to the final act, but was also performed at the commencement when the sinner asked for penance and received the sack-cloth,[2] and was repeated whenever penitents were present in church during their term of penance,[3] while, as we have already seen (p. 10) in case of necessity the final imposition conferring the peace of the Church could be performed on the dying by a deacon. Yet in some quarters it was held to confer the Holy Ghost and that this was essential to the redintegration of the penitent in the Church. Thus the Apostolic Constitutions compare it to baptism, and represent the apostles as saying that by it they gave the Holy Ghost to believers.[4]

---

[1] Cypriani Epistt. XVI. XVII.

[2] C. Agathens. ann. 511, c. 15.—Leonis PP. I. Epist. CLXVII. Inquis. 2.—Bened. Levit. Capitularia, Lib. V. c. 116, 122, 123.

[3] C. Laodicens. ann. 324 c. 19.—S. August. Serm. CCXXXII. c. 7.—In the African Church it would seem that this was only done during Lent.—C. Carthag. IV. ann. 398, c. 80 (Gratian. Decr. c. 6, Caus. XXVI. Q. vii.).

[4] Constitt. Apostol. II. xlv. "Et erit ei in locum lavacri impositio manuum. Nam per impositionem manuum nostrarum credentibus Spiritus sanctus dabatur." Cf. Acts VI. 6; VIII. 17–19; I. Tim. V. 22.

Had this belief been accepted and current this last assertion would have

As yet the ceremony of reconciliation was much simpler than it became subsequently. It could be performed on any Sunday; the deacon uttered a prayer entreating God to pardon the sinners, and the bishop, in imposing hands, prayed God to accept the penance of the suppliants, to lead them back into the Church and to restore them to their previous honor and dignity.[1] There was no pretence of exercising any sacerdotal power of absolution, and the episcopal function was simply intercessory.

That the imposition of hands thus administered merely readmitted the sinner to the Church and had nothing to do with his relations to God is seen in the regulations with respect to dying penitents. It is easy to understand how men would postpone penance to the last and ask for it on the death-bed. The prevailing rule was that penance and communion were never to be denied to the dying[2] and if after their reception the sinner unexpectedly recovered he would be apt to claim that he was reconciled and in communion with the Church. To obviate this the plan was adopted that communion was to be administered to the dying, who was thus furnished with the viaticum which was sufficient for his consolation, but the imposition of hands which reconciled him to the Church was withheld, so that in case of recovery he could be required to perform penance and seek reconciliation in a legitimate way.[3] The Eucharist thus reconciled him to God but

---

been superfluous. It is perhaps significant that there is nothing of all this in the Canons of Hippolytus.

[1] Constitt. Apostol. VIII. xi. xii.—" Recipe nunc quoque supplicantium tibi pœnitentiam . . . et reduc eos in sanctam tuam ecclesiam, restitutis illis priori dignitate et honore per Christum Deum et Salvatorem nostrum."

Palmieri (Tract. de Pœnitent. p. 159) following Sirmond, endeavors to reconcile the ancient use of the imposition of hands with the modern dogmas by arguing that there were three varieties of it—one used at the imposition of penance, one during its performance and the third at reconciliation. This is of course purely supposititious.

[2] C. Nicæn. I. ann. 325 c. xiii.—Cœlest. PP. I. Epist. IV. c. 2 (Gratian. c. 13 Caus. XXVI. Q. vi.). A canon attributed to Julius I. which is found in all the collections says "Si presbyter pœnitentiam morientibus abnegaverit reus erit animarum" (Gratian. c. 12 Caus. XXVI. Q. vi.—P. Lombard. Sententt. Lib. IV. Dist. XX. § 5).

[3] " Qui recedunt de corpore, pœnitentia accepta, placuit sine reconciliatoria manus impositione iis communicari, quod morientis sufficit consolationi secundum definitiones patrum, qui hujusmodi communionem congruenter viaticum nominarunt. Quod si supervixerint, stent in ordine pœnitentium, et ostensis

not to the Church, the imposition of hands accomplished the latter and had nothing to do with the former.

As the Church gradually asserted the power of the keys and reconciliation began to assume the character of absolution, Benedict the Levite, who in the ninth century labored so earnestly in the development of sacerdotalism, asserts that only through imposition of hands, accompanied by the invocation of the Holy Ghost and the prayers of the bishop, or of the priest to whom he delegated the function, could sins be absolved, and for lack of other explanation he asserts it to be derived from the precept in the Old Law by which the priest in sacrifice laid his hand on the head of the victim.[1] When, however, in the thirteenth century the schoolmen had thoroughly elaborated the theory of the sacraments and the power to bind and to loose, and when, as we shall see, the formula of absolution became an absolute assertion of sacerdotal control over pardon, it became evident that this was incompatible with the necessity of invoking the Holy Ghost by the imposition of hands. Conservative theologians who objected to the change in the formula used as one of their main arguments the immemorial custom of imposition of hands, and they cited in support the great authority of William Bishop of Paris.[2] When Aquinas

---

necessariis pœnitentiæ fructibus legitimam communionem cum reconciliatoria manus impositione percipiant."—Concil. Arausican. I. ann. 441 c. 3.—Concil. Arelatens. ann. 443 c. 28. This was not a mere local regulation. It is virtually the same in Concil. Nicæn. I. c. 13 and C. Carthag. IV. ann. 398 c. 78. Cf. Gregor. Nyssæn. Epist. Canon. c. 5.

Yet another canon (c. 76) of the same council of Carthage provides that if the dying man is delirious or insensible the testimony of his friends that he has asked for penance suffices "et si continuo creditur moriturus, reconcilietur per manus impositionem et infundatur ori ejus Eucharistia" So also Leo I. (Epist. CVIII. c. 5 ad Theodorum.). "Testimonia eis fidelium circumstantium prodesse debebunt et pœnitentiæ et reconciliationis beneficium consequantur." This is only another instance of the contradictory character of the prescriptions of the early Church. In the Capitularies of Benedict the Levite an attempt is made to reconcile the incongruity by quoting cap. 76 of the Council of Carthage and only part of that of the Council of Agde (Capitular. Lib. v. c. 120, 121).

[1] Bened. Levit. Capitul. Lib. v. c. 127 (Isaaci Lingonens. Canon. Tit. I. c. 11.)

Again—" Nec se quisquam a peccatis absolutum sine reconciliatoria manus impositione credat, sed per manus impositionem precibus sacerdotum reconcilietur."—Ibid. c. 129 (Isaaci Lingon. Tit. I. c. 13). So in a Roman Ordo of the ninth century priests touch the heads of the penitents while the bishop officiates.—Morin. de Discipl. Sacr. Pœnit. App. p. 67.

[2] But William of Paris does not seem to regard the imposition of hands as

was summoned to defend the new formula, he brushed aside William of Paris as a canonist of insufficient weight to be conclusive on so great a matter; he argued that the words of absolution constitute the sacrament of which the penitent is the material, and that imposition of hands is unnecessary.[1] The tendency to sacerdotalism was irresistible. The innovators triumphed over the conservatives; the new formula gradually spread everywhere, and the imposition of hands became a mere unimportant adjunct in the ceremony. Still it held its place for awhile. In 1284 the synod of Nîmes, in its elaborate instructions to confessors, directs them to perform it when granting absolution,[2] but not long afterwards John of Freiburg accepts the dictum of Aquinas; making the sign of the cross over the penitent he says is more important than imposition of hands, but neither is essential.[3] About 1325 Durand de Saint-Pourçain argues that while imposition of hands is requisite in ordination because a *character* is conferred on the recipient, it is unnecessary in absolution for no change is made there in the status of the penitent[4] which shows that the schoolmen were still seeking for arguments to justify the abandonment of the old rite. About the middle of the next century St. Antonino of Florence shows that the change had been fully accepted: imposition of hands is unnecessary, and in the case of female penitents it is not decent; besides, the sign of the cross replaces it.[5] Early in the sixteenth century Prierias tells us that it is not performed, and that crossing is more effective though not essential.[6] Still the custom had been so inseparably connected with the remission of sins that it was not easily eradicated. In 1524 the council of Sens felt obliged to assert that it was not necessary and that the sign of the cross was more fitting.[7] About 1550 Domingo Soto admits that

---

conferring the Holy Ghost.—"Manus enim sacerdotis super caput pœnitentis manum divinam sive virtutem adesse significat ad sanctificandum vel significandum pœnitentem.—Guill. Paris. de Sacram. Pœnitentiæ c. 3 (Ed. Paris, 1674, T. I. p. 461).

[1] Th. Aquinat. Opusc. XXII. c. 4. Cf. Summæ P. III. Q. lxxxiv. Art. 3.

[2] Synod. Nemaus. ann. 1284 (Harduin. Concil. VIII. 911).

[3] Joh. Friburgens Summ. Confessor. Lib. III. Tit. xxxiv. Q. 90.

[4] Durand de S. Portiano Comment. sup. Sententt. Lib. IV. Dist. xxii. Q. 2 § 7.

[5] S. Antonini Confessionale (Ed. *sine nota*, fol. 69ᵃ); Summæ P. III. Tit. xvii. c. 21 § 1.

[6] Summa Sylvestrina s. v. *Absolutio* VI. § 2.

[7] Bochelli Decr. Eccles. Gallicanæ Lib. II. Tit. vii. c. 138.

it was still used by some confessors ;[1] towards the close of the century or beginning of the next Bellarmine uses the terms imposition of hands and absolution as synonymous ;[2] soon afterwards Zerola and Vittorelli regard it as desirable though not necessary ;[3] and the prevalence of its employment is seen in the advice of Willem van Est that the confessor should not omit it, especially if from any cause the penitent is dismissed without absolution and there are bystanders near, as its absence would betray the fact of the denial[4]—which further shows that by this time it was regarded as a mere formality, without real significance. At this period, however, the use of confessionals in churches was rapidly spreading and with their universal introduction the performance of imposition became an impossibility. Thus the rite which until the thirteenth century had been regarded as the one indispensable condition of reconciliation and absolution was discarded as useless and devoid of all significance.[5]

Strictly speaking, reconciliation was an episcopal function. As the executive head of his church, it was naturally part of the duties of the bishop to enforce its discipline and determine when and how the sinner who had been ejected should be readmitted, and we have seen above that to the bishop alone was entrusted the discretion of deciding whether the contrition of the sinner required a reduction or prolongation of the term of penance. If reconciliation had involved any supernatural power to bind and to loose, if it had concerned the *forum internum* as well as *externum*, the priest would have been equally

---

[1] Dom. Soto Comment in IV. Sententt. Dist. xiv. Q. iv. art. 3.

[2] Bellarmin. Concio viii. de Domin. 4 Adventus (Opp. Neapoli, 1861, T. VI. p. 50).

[3] Zerola, Praxis Sacr. Pœnitentiæ c. xxiv. Q. 4.—Victorelli Addit. ad. Aphoris. Confessarior. Emanuelis Sa. s. v. *Absolutio* n. 25.

[4] Estius in IV. Sententt. Dist. xv. § 5.

[5] Naturally this complete change in practice, which infers a corresponding change in dogma, is puzzling to Catholic writers. Palmieri, as we have seen, endeavors to show that there were several species of imposition of hands. Binterim (Denkwürdigkeiten, Bd. V. Theil II. p. 453) tells us that it is impossible to determine when the rite disappeared, but that all trace of it is lost after the sixth century, except in the solemn reception of public penitents on Ash Wednesday which is alluded to in c. 76 of the Council of Meaux in 845.

The Lutherans naturally retained the custom and considered that private absolution was conferred by it.—Steitz, Die Privatbeichte und Privatabsolution der Lutherischen Kirche, II. § 40 (Frankfurt a M. 1854, p. 143).

competent to perform it, for in the early ages of the Church there was no distinction between the spiritual functions of the two offices. The Canons of Hippolytus give the same formula of ordination for both, and distinctly assert that the only difference between them is in the name and in the fact that the bishop alone can ordain ;[1] and Jerome and Chrysostom both incidentally say that their functions are the same, except as to ordination.[2] Thus, as a matter of discipline, the infliction of penance and the admission to reconciliation naturally fell to the bishop, and it is always spoken of as performed by him or by

---

[1] "Etiam eadem oratio super eo oretur tota ut super episcopo cum sola exceptione nominis episcopatus. Episcopus in omnibus rebus æquiparetur presbytero excepto nomine cathedræ et ordinatione, quia potestas ordinandi ipsi non tribuitur."—Canon. Hippolyti c. IV. 31-2.

In this, as in so much else, however, it is impossible to assert that the rule was universal. One recension of the Egyptian Ordo, based on Hippolytus, says nothing about equality and gives a different formula of prayer (Achelis, Die Canones Hippolyti, p. 61), and this is followed in the Apostolic Constitutions, VIII. 25.

[2] "Quid enim facit, excepta ordinatione, episcopus quod presbyter non faciat?"—S. Hieron. Epist. CXLVI. ad Evangelum.

So Chrysostom in explaining why Paul alludes only to bishops and deacons and not to priests, says "Quia non multum spatii est inter presbyteros et episcopos . . . et quæ ille de episcopis dixit etiam presbyteris competunt. Sola namque ordinatione superiores sunt et hinc tantum videntur presbyteris præstare."—Chrysost. Homil. XI. §1 in I. Timoth.

In fact it is fair to infer from I. Peter IV. 10-11 that at the period when it was composed there were no definite officials set apart for special duties but that each member of the congregation performed such functions as his gifts enabled him to do, while from the Pastoral Epistles (I. Timoth. III.) it would appear that at that time there were only bishops and deacons, and that, as the churches grew, assistants under the name of elders or priests were furnished to the bishops and were also placed over congregations springing up in the smaller towns. These latter came to be known as chorepiscopi; all were on an equality with the bishop as to function, with the exception of ordination, which it was necessary to reserve to the bishop in order to preserve his authority as executive overseer or superintendent of the district or diocese. Yet Aquinas says it was an error of the Arians to assert that there was no difference between bishops and priests (S. Th. Aquinat. Opusc. V.) and when the Bishop of Chartres, in 1700, ventured to say that there was no distinction between bishops and priests under the apostles his chapter complained of him to the assembly of the Gallican Church which pronounced his assertion erroneous, rash, scandalous, etc. (D'Argentré Collect. Judic. de novis Erroribus III. II. 413). For the discussion on this subject see S. Alph. Liguori, Theol. Moral Lib. VI. n. 738.

his authority.[1]   How entirely devoid of all sacramental character was this is seen, about the year 310, when, after the Maxentian persecution, a number of African bishops who had been " traditores "—that is, had surrendered the sacred books to the Pagans—assembled together and mutually reconciled each other.[2]

There was no difficulty however, when the case required it, in the performance of the ceremony by priests and deacons. Although in 390 the second council of Carthage positively forbade priests from administering public reconciliation,[3] the third council in 397 relaxed the rule and permitted it when the bishop was consulted, and in cases of necessity in his absence,[4] and this must have been by no means infrequent with the dying. As regards deacons, we have seen the function confided to them, about 250, under Cyprian. Early in the fourth century the council of Elvira requires that bishops alone, to the exclusion of priests, shall grant penance, but in case of necessity in sickness priests can admit to communion and even deacons by command of priests.[5]   This long continued to be the rule of the Church. Up to the eleventh century the Carthaginian canon continued to be embodied in the collections, either textually or in spirit,[6] and in the absence of the bishop or priest, a deacon could officiate.[7]

---

[1] "In societatem nostram nonnisi per pœnitentiæ remedium et per impositionem episcopalis manus communionis recipiant unitatem."—Leon. PP. I. Epist. CLIX. c. 6.

[2] Optati de Schismate Donatistarum Lib. I. c. xix.

[3] Concil. Carthag. II. ann. 390, c. 3.

[4] "Ut presbyter inconsulto episcopo non reconciliet pœnitentem, nisi absente episcopo et necessitate cogente."—C. Carthag. III. ann. 397, c. 32. This canon also provides that when the crime has been notorious the penitent shall receive the imposition of hands in front of the apse, which would imply that there was also a private reconciliation. There may have been a local custom of this nature, but no other allusion is to be found to it anywhere.

[5] Concil. Eliberit. can. 32. It is probably in allusion to death-bed repentance that the apostolic canons class bishop and priest together as receiving the sinner back—"Si quis episcopus aut presbyter eum qui a peccato revertitur non recipit sed rejicit, deponitor, eo quod Christum offendat qui dixit ob unum peccatorum qui resipiscat gaudium oboriri in cœlo."—Can. Apost. 51.

[6] Bened. Levit. Capitul. v. 127, VII. 202.—Isaaci Lingonens. Canon. I. 35.—Regino de Discip. Eccles. I. 306.—Burchardi Decr. XIX. 40, 70.—Pœnitent. Pseudo-Theodori c. 5 (Wasserschleben, Bussordnungen, p. 571).

[7] Morini de Discipl. Sacram. Pœnitentiæ Lib. VIII. c. xxiii. n. 12.—Martene de antiq. Ecclesiæ Ritibus, Lib. I. c. vi. art. 7, Ord. 2, 10.—Hadriani PP. I. Epitome Canonum, Regulæ Ancyrani II. (Harduin. Concil. III. 2036).—

As reconciliation gradually developed into absolution the irregularity of this exercise of the power of the keys by those not in priest's orders became recognized and efforts were made to restrict the practice —efforts which only betrayed the consciousness of the incompatibility of the ancient system of the Church with the new theology, while yet making the fatal admission that extreme necessity would justify the administration of the sacraments by deacons. Thus the council of York in 1196 forbids deacons to baptize, to give the Eucharist or administer penance except under pressure of the gravest necessity:[1] and that of London in 1200 defines this necessity to be when the priest is unable or foolishly refuses and there is danger of death.[2] Eudes, Bishop of Paris, in 1198, utters the same injunction and shows the novelty of the principle involved by explaining that deacons do not possess the keys and cannot grant absolution.[3] Peter Cantor, about the same time, takes the same position, but adds that they can do so if they have a delegated power from the pope,[4] which manifests how confused were the ideas of the period as yet concerning the mode by which control of the sacraments could be acquired. It was long before deacons were finally excluded from the function of granting absolution in cases of necessity. Even in the authoritative Decretals of Gregory IX., issued about 1235, there is a curious canon to the effect that robbers slain in the act of robbery are not to be prayed for, but if they have confessed to a priest or a deacon they may have the Eucharist.[5] The canons of various councils to the end of the thirteenth century continue to admit that in case

---

Pseudo-Alcuini Lib. de Divinis Officiis c. 13.—Pœnitent. Floriacens. (Wasserschleben, p. 423).—Pœnitent. Merseburg. a. (Ibid. p. 389).—Reginon. de Discip. Eccles. Lib. I. c. 296.—Burchardi Decr. Lib. xix. c. 154.—Canons of Ælfric 16 (Thorpe's Ancient Laws, II. 349).—Pez Thesaur. Anecd. II. II. 611.—Ivon. Decr. P. XVI. c. 161, 162.—Stephani Augustodun. de Sacram. Altaris c. vii. (Migne, CLXII. 1279).

This assertion of Stephen of Autun called forth a special correction by Brisighelli in his expurgation of the Fathers. Index Expurg. Brasichillens. Romæ (Bergomi) 1608.

[1] Concil. Eboracens. ann. 1196, c. 4 (Harduin. VI. II. 1931).

[2] Concil. Londinens. ann. 1200, c. 3 (Ibid. 1958).

[3] Odonis Paris. Synod. Constit. c. 56 (Ibid. 1946).

[4] Morini de Discipl. Sacram. Pœnitent. Lib. VIII. c. xxiii. n. 14.

[5] C. 2 Extra Lib. v. Tit. xviii. Singularly enough this purports to be taken from the council of Tribur, in 895, which in c. 31 has a similar prescription, but it says nothing about deacons and only alludes to confessions to priests.

of necessity deacons can grant valid absolution, although sometimes the good fathers seek to hedge by adding the incompatible proposition that deacons have not the power of the keys.[1] Gradually, however, the practice became forbidden. In 1268 the council of Clermont prohibits deacons from hearing confessions and priests from committing that office to them as they have not the power to bind and to loose.[2] In 1280 Gautier, Bishop of Poitiers, speaks of it as a prevalent abuse, arising from ignorance, which must be eradicated, and he proceeds to argue against it in a manner to show that the scholastic theology had not yet penetrated to the rural parishes.[3] The prohibition triumphed finally everywhere, however, though stringent laws were still requisite to prevent the administration of the sacrament of penitence by deacons, which had become a most serious offence as it was deluding souls to perdition. In 1574 Gregory XIII., in 1601 Clement VIII. and in 1628 Urban VIII. issued bulls which pointed out that absolution granted by any one not in priest's orders was null and void. The offender was handed over to the Inquisition; if over the age of twenty he was to be degraded and relaxed to the secular arm to be put to death, and ignorance was declared to be no excuse.[4] This apparently remains the law of the

---

[1] Concil. Rotomagens. ann. 1231, c. 36 (Harduin. VII. 189).—Constitt. S. Edmundi Cantuarens. circa 1236, c. 12 (Harduin. VII. 269).—Constitt. Waltheri de Kirkham Episc. Dunelm. ann. 1255 (Ibid. p. 492).—Nich. Gelant. Episc. Andegav. Synod. XV. ann. 1273, c. 1 (D'Achery Spicileg. I. 731).—Statuta Eccles. Meldens. c. 77 (Martene Thesaur. I. 904).

This is so completely destructive of the accepted sacramental theory that efforts are naturally made to argue it away. Palmieri however can only assert (Tract. de Pœnit. p. 166) that all this refers to reconciliation and not to absolution, in which he is flatly contradicted by the words of the statutes themselves.

[2] C. Claromontens. ann. 1268, c. 7 (Harduin. VII. 596, 599).

[3] Constitt. Gaulteri Episc. Pictav. ann. 1280, c. 5 (Ibid. p. 851). Père Guillois endeavors to meet this difficulty of the administration of a sacrament by deacons by assuming that anciently there were two kinds of reconciliation, perfect and imperfect, of which the latter could be performed by deacons as it had been preceded by absolution granted by the priest (Guillois, History of Confession, translated by Louis de Goesbriand, Bishop of Burlington; New York, 1889, p. 133). Of course there are no facts on which to base such a theory.

[4] Gregor. PP. XIII. Const. 21, *Officii nostri*, 6 Aug. 1574 (Mag. Bullar. Roman. II. 415).—Clement. PP. VIII. Const. 81, *Etsi alias*, 1 Dec. 1601 (Bullar. III. 142).—Urbani PP. VIII. Constit. 79, *Apostolatus officium* 23 Mar. 1628 (Bullar. IV. 144).—Cf. Marc. Paul. Leonis Praxis ad Litt. Maior. Pœnitentiar.

Church, and is a striking illustration of the change wrought by the elaboration of the sacramental theory.

Although during the middle ages public penance became almost obsolete, as we have seen, yet it still retained its place in theory and served the theologians as a means of reconciling the old formulas with the new practice. The questions connected with the transition from reconciliation to absolution will be considered hereafter, and meanwhile it will suffice to observe that although public reconciliation had been freely delegated to priests and deacons not only at a time when it was the only process known but subsequently when private reconciliation was gradually supplanting it, yet when the process was fully accomplished there was a revival of the old rule that it appertained strictly to the episcopal office. About the middle of the twelfth century Peter Lombard repeats the Carthaginian canon which prohibited the priest from granting reconciliation, except in case of necessity, without consulting the bishop, and makes no attempt to harmonize this with the existing earnest effort to render confession universal and frequent and to bring every one under control of the parish priest, but Gratian in giving the same canon rather clumsily seeks to evade this difficulty by applying it to excommunicates who by this time were by no means necessarily the same as penitents.[1] When the sacramental system and annual confession had been established with the distinction between public or solemn and private penance it became the recognized rule that only bishops could impose solemn penance and reconcile for it, or priests to whom they delegated the faculty.[2] It was by this time administered only for reserved cases, and even in them it was scarce more than a theoretical prescription, recognized in the books but forgotten in practice.

The question as to the administration of death-bed reconciliation has already been incidentally alluded to and will require but brief consideration. The subject is obscure, the practice of the Church was not uniform, and the questions concerning it are complicated by the

---

Mediolani, 1665, p. 297.—Ferraris, Prompta Biblioth. s. v. *Absolvere* Art. 1. n. 58, 59.

[1] P. Lombard. Lib. IV. Dist. xx. § 6.—Gratiani Decr. can. xiv. Caus. XXVI. Q. 6.

[2] Durandi Spec. Juris Lib. I. Partic. 1, § 5, n. 22.—Astesani Summæ de Casibus Lib. v. Tit. xxxv. Q. 3.

difference which at times was recognized, as we have seen, between reconciliation and admission to communion. The epistle of the Roman clergy to Cyprian after the Decian persecution, quoted above, advises that the truly penitent be granted reconciliation at death, without prejudice to the judgment of God. Cyprian himself takes the ground that those who have not repented during life are not to be received to reconciliation and communion when in fear of impending death.[1] The council of Elvira, held probably in 313, under the influence of the rigid Hosius of Cordova, gives a long list of sins for which communion is to be denied on the death-bed, implying of course also the refusal of reconciliation. At Nicæa, in 325, in spite of the presence of Hosius, the laxer party triumphed and it was ordered that communion was never to be refused to the dying who asked for it. Yet at Sardica in 347, where Hosius again was the dominant spirit, it was ordered that any bishop translated from one see to another should be deprived of communion, and if he had intrigued for the change he was not to be readmitted even at death.[2] The matter remained in doubt, for it formed one of the questions put by Exsuperius, Bishop of Toulouse, to Innocent I. about 405. Innocent replied that there had been two customs in the Church; one, more rigid, during the period of persecution, granted penance, but denied communion to those who after a life of pleasure asked for penance and the reconciliation of communion; but after God gave peace to the Church a milder rule was introduced and communion was granted as a viaticum in view of the mercy of God and to avoid appearing to follow the harshness of the Novatians.[3] This practice prevailed. Cœlestin I. soon afterwards in a decretal, which passed into all the

---

[1] "Nec dignus est in morte recipere solatium qui se non cogitavit esse moriturum."—Cypriani Epist. 55.

[2] C. Sardicens. ann. 347, c. 1, 2. Hosius was a man of the highest repute. Before the council of Nicæa Constantine sent him to Alexandria to suppress the Arian heresy (Sozomen. H. E. I. 17). Eusebius says of him, in describing the council of Nicæa "Ab ipsa quoque Hispania vir ille multo omnium sermone celebratus, unacum reliquis aliis consedit" (Euseb. Vit. Constant. III. 7.—Socratis H. E. I. 8, 13).

[3] Innocent. PP. I. Epist. 6, c. 2. The expression "reconciliationem communionis" is noteworthy, as showing that the distinction between communion and reconciliation was not recognized in Rome, though it had been in the councils of Nicæa and Carthage, and continued to be in those of Orange and Arles.

collections of canons, speaks with horror of those who refused to receive to penance the dying seeking for it, as though they despaired of the mercy of God who carried to Paradise the penitent thief for a single word.[1] We have seen however that the viaticum did not always imply reconciliation and that precautions were taken to avoid conferring the latter with the former. On the other hand there arose a custom of posthumous reconciliation, whereby those undergoing penance and dying without the opportunity of communicating received Christian burial, their memories were included in the services and oblations made for them were accepted.[2] Finally Leo I., while warning sinners of the danger of delaying repentance and satisfaction to the last, laid down the positive rule that the dying who asked for it should receive both penance and reconciliation; if the moribund had become speechless when the priest arrived, the testimony of the bystanders as to his desire sufficed and the rites were to be administered —a decision which was carried through the collections of canons and has remained the law of the Church since the old reconciliation became the new absolution.[3] Yet in spite of the authority of St. Leo his precept did not receive universal obedience, for some of the rigid prescriptions of the council of Elvira still continued occasionally to show themselves in the collections of canons.[4]

The efficacy of these final rites was a matter about which the Church

---

[1] Cœlest. PP. I. Epist. IV. c. 2 (Gratian. c. 13 Caus. XXVI. Q. vi.).

[2] Concil. Vasens. I. ann. 442, c. 2.

[3] Leonis PP. I. Epist. 108, c. 5.—Gratian. c. 10, Caus. XXVI. Q. vi.—Rodulfi Bituricens. Capit. c. 44 (Migne CXIX. 724). During the middle ages in some places when there was a doubt as to death-bed repentance it was necessary for a friend to prove it by undergoing the cold-water ordeal before Christian burial was accorded to the corpse. Very moderate external evidence however sufficed. At a time when all participating in tournaments were subject to *ipso facto* excommunication a knight slain in one was refused sepulture. His friends appealed to the pope and proved that his right hand had been raised to his face as though to make the sign of the cross; this was admitted as showing his repentance and he was duly interred in consecrated ground. (Dollinger, Beiträge zur Sektengeschichte des Mittelalters, München, 1890, II. 622-3.) Leo I. was more rigid; if a penitent died before the completion of his penance and prevented by some obstacle from receiving the viaticum, he was refused the services of the Church; it was useless to discuss his acts and merits, for God had reserved him to his own judgment (Epist. 108 c. 2).

[4] Canon. Ingelramni lxii. (Hartzheim Concil. German. I. 256).—Pœnitent. Pseudo-Gregor. III. c. 4, 12, 14 (Wasserschleben, Bussordnungen, pp. 539, 541).

was long in coming to a decision. We have seen that St. Augustin considered death-bed repentance and reconciliation as a doubtful matter with the chances against the penitent.[1] A homily variously attributed to St. Ambrose, St. Augustin and St. Cæsarius of Arles takes the same ground—the wishes of the dying are to be gratified, but no promises are to be made, and there is no presumption in favor of the sinner.[2] The severer virtue of St. Salvianus regards as useless the repentance postponed till there is no time to redeem sin by prolonged penance, and of course priestly ministrations in such case, could effect nothing.[3] On the other hand the great advocate of sacerdotalism, Gregory I., illustrates the efficiency and necessity of priestly intervention by the story of the priest Severus who on being summoned to a dying man delayed in order to finish pruning his vines, and on reaching the spot found that he had been anticipated by death. His remorse at thus slaying a soul was so intense that the dead was brought to life, performed penance for seven days and passed away happily.[4] Then again the Penitential of Gregory III. in repeating the prescription that if the priest finds the patient delirious or speechless, he is to perform the rites and pour the Eucharist down his throat, adds that the result depends on the judgment of God.[5] Finally when the schoolmen had worked out the theory of contrition, of infused grace and of purgatory, Peter Lombard tells us that death-bed repentance may save from hell and the penance be replaced by purgatory, or that contrition may be so ardent that it will suffice in itself as full punishment for sin.[6]

---

[1] S. Augustin. Serm. ccxxciii.

[2] " Fateor vobis non illi negamus quod petit, sed nec præsumo quia bene hinc exit; non præsumo, non polliceor, non dico, non vos fallo, non vos decipio, non vobis promitto. . . . Pœnitentiam dare possum, securitatem dare non possum."—S. Cæsar. Arelatens. Homil. xix.

[3] Salviani adv. Avaritiam Lib. I. §. 10.

[4] Gregor. PP. I. Dialog. IV. 12

[5] Pœnitent. Pseudo-Gregor. c. 31 (Wasserschleben, p. 546).

[6] P. Lombard. Sententt. Lib. IV. Dist. xx. § 1. "Nisi forte tanta sit vehementia gemitus et contritionis quæ sufficiat ad delicti punitionem."

CHAPTER V.

THE HERESIES.

THUS far we have been considering the theories and practices which, however divergent and even contradictory, were yet held to come within the limits of orthodoxy. In the fluid condition of dogma much freedom of opinion was allowed, and indeed was inevitable, especially as there was as yet no central source of authority, short of the cumbrous device of a general council, to decide between different opinions, and when debates arose it was not easy to foretell which would be finally accepted as orthodox by a general consensus. If a hardy disputant differed from his bishop and refused submission, he would be excommunicated; if he had followers, and if the neighboring bishops or the patriarch concurred in the sentence, a sect arose which was freely anathematized and consigned to perdition. Or the heresiarch might himself refuse obedience, defiantly proclaim his independence, and gather what disciples he could. Thus through endless debates and more or less peaceful clash of opinions the structure of doctrine and practice gradually arose, and the simple teachings of the Master developed into a complicated mass of theology and ritual, absorbing many elements from speculative philosophy and pagan observance. The tenets which had satisfied the needs of the little Ebionitic band at Jerusalem were manifestly insufficient for the cravings of the Athenian schools and the cultured courts of Rome or Constantinople, and the effort to enlarge them so as to meet these growing demands necessarily led to many tentative developments which in failing to be generally received became naturally stigmatized as heretical. Struggles there were also between rival factions for power, and as these either grew out of some doubtful point of belief or practice, or created in their development antagonisms on such matters, each side held the other to be heretical and the ultimate decision as to orthodoxy depended upon which should finally triumph. In this confused medley of warring opinions our special subject did not figure largely; for the most part the differences which we have noted excited no particular animosities and were allowed to coexist. Few heresies arose from them, and the consideration of these need not detain us long.

The earliest of the heresies which is usually asserted to be concerned with the pardon of sins is that of the Montanists, otherwise known as Cathari or Pure, Cataphrygæ, Phrygastæ, Pepuzeni or Tascodrugitæ, who are said to have denied all pardon to sinners. Yet it would seem more than doubtful whether errors on this subject formed a portion of their beliefs. Montanus, we are told, flourished in Phrygia in the nineteenth year of Antoninus Pius (A. D. 156–7), where he proclaimed himself the Paraclete and the Holy Spirit, gifted with the spirit of prophecy. His followers reverenced him and his two leading female disciples, Priscilla and Maximilla, as prophets, ranking them even above Christ and their writings as superior to Scripture. In their ardent seeking for purity they prohibited as some say marriage and as others say second marriages, but none of the earlier authorities allude to any refusal by them to admit sinners to penance, an assertion which makes its first appearance towards the close of the fourth century in Jerome, though even then his contemporary Epiphanius, who made a special study of heresies, is silent as to this feature of their doctrines, while saying that they were still numerous in Phrygia, Cappadocia, Cilicia and Constantinople.[1] It is probable that the ascription of this implacability to them has arisen from the rigor of their most conspicuous convert, Tertullian, who after combating their heresy adopted it. He seems to have been alarmed at a tendency manifested to exalt the functions of the Church in the remission of sins and his protest took the shape of quoting I. John v. 16,[2] and dividing sins into remissible and irremissible—peni-

---

[1] Hippolyti Refut. Omn. Hæres. VIII. 19.—Tertull. de Præscriptionibus cap. lii.—Euseb. H. E. v. 16, 18, 19.—Philastrii Lib. de Hæres. n. LXXXIII.—Epiphan. Panar. Hæres. 48.—S. Basilii Epist. Canon. I. 1.

St. Jerome in 384 says of the Montanists "Illi ad omne pene delictum ecclesiæ obserant fores" (Epist. XLI. n. 3, ad Marcellam) and in 399 he classes Montanus with Novatus as refusing admission to penance (Epist. LXXVII. n. 5 ad Oceanum). Possibly this may be true of the Cathari who are spoken of by Basil the Great (*loc. cit.*) as a branch of the sect. St. Augustin makes no allusion to any special rigor as to penitence but tells a wild story as to their using the blood of an infant in place of the Eucharist.—S. August. de Hæresibus XXVI., XXXII.

[2] "He that knoweth his brother to sin a sin which is not to death, let him

tence and the intercession of the faithful secure pardon of the one; for the other, man can assume nothing save that penitence will not be in vain; though man may withhold pardon the reward will come from God.[1] It was in no sense a denial of the power of repentance to wash out mortal sin; it was merely an assertion that the wholesome discipline of the Church though binding on earth was not binding in Heaven. Tertullian soon wearied of his Montanist alliance, though his aggressive and independent spirit would not permit his return to the ranks of the orthodox. He founded a church of his own in Carthage, which was still in existence in the early years of the fifth century, but it had dwindled away and St. Augustin chronicles the reception of the survivors and of their property by the Catholics in his time.[2] There was in fact little or nothing to distinguish the views of Tertullian from those which were regarded as perfectly consistent with orthodoxy, for, as we have seen, St. Cyprian mentions that in his time there were African bishops who would not admit repentant adulterers to reconciliation.

The same may be said of Novatus and Novatianus, whose so-called heresy was in reality only a schism, to which vastly greater importance has been customarily ascribed than it is really entitled to. The epistles of Cyprian show how vague and uncertain, in the middle of the third century, were the doctrine and practice of the Church as to the readmission of sinners to peace and reconciliation. The African Church, after the Decian persecution, was in an uproar; the lapsed were clamoring for readmission; a strong faction urged that they should be gratified without undergoing due penance; Cyprian re-

---

ask and life shall be given to him who sinneth not to death. There is a sin unto death: for that I say not that any man ask."

[1] Secundum hanc differentiam delictorum pœnitentiæ quoque conditio discriminatur. Alia erit quæ veniam consequi possit, in delicto scilicet remissibili; alia quæ consequi nullo modo possit, in delicto scilicet irremissibili."—Tertull. de Pudicit. c. ii.

"Et si pacem hic non metit, apud Dominum seminat: nec amittit sed præparet fructum; non vacabit ab emolumento si non vacaverit ab officio. Ita nec pœnitentia hujusmodi vana, nec disciplina ejusmodi dura est. Deum ambæ honorant."—Ibid. c. iii.

But amendment is indispensable—"Sed etsi venia est potius pœnitentiæ fructus, hanc quoque consistere non licet sine cessatione delicti. Ita cessatio delicti radix est veniæ ut venia sit pœnitentiæ fructus."—Ibid. cap. x.

[2] S. Augustini de Hæresibus n. LXXXVI.

sisted until it nearly cost him his see and then he yielded under
pretext of arming the sinners for another impending persecution.
The Roman Church was involved in the same troubles. In January
250 Pope Fabianus was martyred and after an interregnum of about
a year his successor Cornelius was chosen to the perilous dignity.
A large portion of the Roman Christians, led by Trophimus, a priest
who had sacrificed to idols, refused to acknowledge him, doubtless
for the purpose of forcing him to admit them to reconciliation. He
yielded and admitted Trophimus to communion.[1] This was a serious
offence, especially in view of the turbulent conduct of the lapsed who
demanded reconciliation. It was just at this time that the Carthaginian clergy refused communion to a priest and deacon who
had communed with the lapsed, and Cyprian approved of it and
ordered it extended to any who might commune with the offenders.
Moreover, not long afterwards, among the misdeeds of Fortunatus
and Felicissimus, he enumerates the admission to peace of the lapsed
without enforcing due penance.[2] The laxity of Cornelius naturally
excited strong antagonism. The confessors who had survived refused
to acknowledge him and the Roman Church was in turmoil. At this
juncture Novatus, a Carthaginian priest whom Cyprian describes as
the leader of the opposition to him and consequently as stained with
every vice, hurried to Rome.[3] What share he had in the subsequent
disturbances we do not precisely know, but he seems to have organized the opponents of Cornelius, who elected as the first antipope
Novatianus, an aged priest of exemplary character and learning.
Cornelius says, in a letter to Fabian of Antioch, that Novatianus got
together three ignorant bishops of obscure Italian sees, made them
drunk and forced them to ordain him, but this may safely be set
down as part of the exaggerations customary in the ecclesiastical
squabbles of the period.[4] The rivals at once endeavored to secure
support, sending envoys and letters to all the churches. A synod
of sixty bishops held in Rome accepted Cornelius and condemned
Novatianus, and the Roman Christians generally submitted, but elsewhere there was dissension. Cyprian cautiously waited till he could
receive the report of two bishops whom he sent to Rome to investigate
the case; it was favorable to Cornelius and Cyprian acknowledged

---

[1] Cypriani Epist. LV.
[2] S. Cypriani Epist. XXXIV., LVIII.
[3] Ibid. Epist. LII.
[4] Eusebii H. E. VI. xliii.

him. So did Dionysius of Alexandria, but St. Firmilian of Cappadocia and Theoctistus of Palestine called a council at Antioch in support of Novatianus, and Marcianus of the great Gallic see of Arles was energetic in his favor. Each side endeavored to supplant the other by getting bishops favorable to them elected in all the sees of their opponents and a schism was fairly started.[1]

It naturally became the fashion of the orthodox controversialists to exaggerate the rigor of the Novatians, or *Mundi* or *Cathari* as they called themselves, and to ascribe to them the teaching that God was unforgiving, penitence useless, and the case of the sinner hopeless.[2] It is true that in their debates they occasionally used a text of the Epistle to the Hebrews, which would seem to justify this position,[3] but in reality their practice differed little if any from that of many churches which, by acknowledging the line of Roman bishops, were held to be thoroughly orthodox—that is, there were certain sins for which they refused communion and reconciliation to the last. One of the accusations brought against Novatianus by Cyprian was that he pardoned adulterers and refused to receive to penitence *libellatici*, or those who during persecution had purchased exemption by procuring *libelli* attesting their paganism from the officials, and he admits that Novatianus urged sinners to repentance, while refusing them readmission to the Church.[4] The epistle of the Roman clergy

---

[1] Cypriani Epist. XLIV., XLV., XLVI., XLVII., XLVIII., XLIX., L., LI., LV., LVIII.—Euseb. H. E. VI. xliv., VII. viii.

[2] Euseb. H. E. VI. 43.—Hilarii Pictaviens. Tract. in Ps. CXXXVIII. n. 8.—Paciani contra Novatianos Epist. iii.—Epiphan. Panar. Hæres. LIX.—Philastrii Lib. de Hæres. n. xxxiv.—Zacchæi Consultationum Lib. II. c. xvii. xviii. St. Augustin adds that they forbade second marriages.—S. August. de Hæresibus XXXVIII.

[3] "For it is impossible for those who were once illuminated, have tasted of the heavenly gift and were made partakers of the Holy Ghost,

"Have moreover tasted the good word of God and the powers of the world to come,

"And are fallen away: to be renewed again to penance, crucifying again to themselves the Son of God, and making him a mockery."—Hebrews, VI. 4–6. Cf. S. Ambros. de Pœnitent. Lib. II. c. ii.

They also quoted Matt. XII. 31–2 concerning the sin against the Holy Ghost, but were naturally unable to define it.

[4] Cypriani Epist. LV. Cyprian in the heat of controversy became subsequently more fervid in his descriptions of the errors of Novatianus—"ut servis Dei pœnitentibus et dolentibus . . . lenitatis paternæ solatia et

to Cyprian in 250, prior to the election of Cornelius, is ascribed to Novatianus : in it the position is taken that the ancient rules must be observed, in spite of the turbulence of the lapsed, clamoring for reconciliation ; those who die, showing marks of true contrition, may be helped and the result left in the hands of God.[1] It is quite possible that the laxity shown by Cornelius may have reacted on Novatianus and rendered him somewhat more rigid, for in the letters which he sent to the churches, after his schismatic election to the papacy, he urged them not to admit to communion those who had sacrificed to demons but to excite them to repentance and leave the question of reconciliation to God, with whom it lay to reconcile sinners.[2]

St. Ambrose thus was mistaken in saying that Novatianus taught that penance was not to be assigned to any one, but he is correct in describing the Novatians of his time as admitting the efficacy of repentance for minor sins and leaving the graver ones for God.[3] The habit of exaggerating the opinions of an opponent, so customary in secular as well as ecclesiastical polemics, could not, however, be restrained, and the Catholics continued to ascribe to them the pitiless condemnation of all sinners, in spite of their assertions that they only deprived of communion those guilty of mortal sin.[4] Probably they only followed the custom which was prevalent in many orthodox churches of denying death-bed communion and reconciliation for the graver sins of idolatry, fornication and homicide. The divergent tendency of the Church is strikingly exhibited in the contemporaneous councils of Elvira and Ancyra, both held about 314 to reorganize the faithful after the tenth persecution—the former denying death-bed communion for many offences which at the latter were subjected to various terms of penance. At Nicæa, as we have seen, the laxer party seems to have obtained control and the rule was adopted that death-bed communion should never be denied, while at Sardica this was disregarded in the case of bishops seeking trans-

---

subsidia claudantur . . . sed sine spe pacis et communicationis relicti ad luporum rapinam et prædam diaboli projiciantur."—Epist. LXVIII. Cf. Pseudo-Cyprian. Epist. ad Novatianum (Ed. Oxon. App. pp. 19-20).

[1] Novatiani Epist. §§ 2, 6, 7 (Migne's Patrol. III. 994, 997-1000).—Cypriani Epist. XXX.

[2] Socrat. H. E. IV. 28.   [3] Ambros. de Pœnit. Lib. I. c. 3.

[4] Socrat. H. E. IV. 28, VII. 25.—Hist. Tripart. Lib. XII. c. 2.—Sozomen. H. E. I. 22.

fer to other sees. The Novatians evidently only adhered to what had been regarded as a perfectly proper exercise of the judgment of the local churches.

That the Novatians were not considered as heretics, in spite of their protest against the growing sacerdotalism which was commencing to attribute a pardoning power to priestly ministrations, shows that that question had not as yet become a crucial one, but that it was open for all men to entertain their own opinions.[1] The council of Nicæa invited them to unity and promised that their priests and bishops should retain their positions where the whole Christian community belonged to their sect, and where there was already a Catholic bishop they should if they chose retain the title and be provided for.[2] Constantine invited to the council the Novatian Bishop Acesius, who professed his adhesion to the dogmas there adopted but refused to subscribe them and resisted the entreaties of the emperor to join in communion with them.[3] Under Constantius they were subjected with the Catholics to the fierce persecution of the Arians : deprived of their churches, both parties worshipped together and they came near agreeing to join in communion, but some unquiet spirits succeeded in keeping them apart, until the accession of Julian brought them peace in common.[4] When in 383 Theodosius the Great made an effort to unite all the warring sects, he consulted Nectarius Bishop of Constantinople as to the best means of effecting it. Nectarius applied for advice to the Novatian Bishop Agelius, who in turn called in his lector Sisinnius, and it was in accordance with the counsel of the latter that a general colloquy was held. On its failure, Theodosius issued a severe edict to repress heresy, but the Novatians were unaffected, as their faith was the same as that of the Catholics.[5] Thus they continued to exist, numerous and respected, with their bishops alongside of those of the Catholics, especially in the East. In the West, in 426, Cœlestin I. found it irksome to have a rival bishop of Rome, and so persecuted his competitor Rusticus that the

---

[1] The Council of Trent (Sess. XIV. de Pœnit. c. 1) evinces its customary disregard of historical accuracy in asserting that the Novatians were condemned by the Fathers in consequence of their heretical denial of the power of the Church to pardon sin.

[2] Concil. Nicæn. I. c. 8.
[3] Sozomen. H. E. I. 22.
[4] Socrat. H. E. II. 38.—Sozomen, IV. 20.
[5] Sozomen. H. E. VII. 12.

latter was obliged to celebrate in secret.[1] The growing power of Rome throughout the Western Empire caused the Novatians thereafter to be treated as heretics, and in 443 the council of Arles decreed that they should not be received to communion unless they would condemn their errors and perform due penance.[2] As late as the eighth century, in the profession of faith made by the popes on their installation, they were required duly to curse Montanus, Novatus and Donatus.[3] Thus schism grew to be heresy under the development of sacerdotalism and papal authority. Some modern writers have attributed to Novatianism an important change in the practice of the Church with regard to penance, but there is no evidence to that effect :[4] it was merely a protest, and an ineffectual one, against change. Innocent I. admitted this when he ascribed the relaxation in granting communion to penitents to a desire to avoid seeming to follow the harshness of the Novatians.[5]

The heresy of the Donatists was a much more serious one, which for nearly three centuries plunged the whole African Church into the most deplorable confusion. We have seen that although clerics could not be subjected to penance they were, theoretically at least, punished with degradation for the sins which entailed on laymen submission to penitence. When these sins were notorious the corollary seemed to follow that if man did not degrade them God would deprive them of the power of performing the mysteries. Thus in the African Church there sprung up the belief that sinful priests and bishops were incapable of administering the Eucharist or baptism or ordination, and consequently that these rites when so administered were invalid, that an ordination thus performed was null, and a baptism must be repeated. The repetition of a baptism administered by heretics had been a question somewhat hotly discussed. Cyprian and the council of Carthage in 256 had pronounced in its favor against the dictum of Pope Stephen. The East followed the same practice, while in Egypt Dionysius of Alexandria was inclined to be neutral ; he had

---

[1] Hist. Tripart. XI. 10.—Socrat. H. E. VII. 12.

[2] Concil. Arelatens. II. ann. 443, c. 9.

[3] Lib. Diurn. Roman. Pontif. Tit. viii.

[4] Juenin de Sacramentis Dist. VI. Q. vi. c. 8 Art. 1 § 2. For a different view see Binterim, Denkwürdigkeiten, Bd. V. Th. II. pp. 356–61.

[5] Innocent. PP. I. Epist. VI. c. 2.

learned, he said, from his preceptor Heraclas, to admit heretics without rebaptism, but he knew the other to be the custom of the most populous churches, confirmed by the councils of Iconium, Synnada and others, and he was loath to disturb his neighbor's landmarks.[1] Rome finally triumphed though not till after a prolonged struggle. The council of Nicæa required rebaptism of Paulicians received into the church.[2] In 360, after the council of Rimini, Pope Liberius sent an epistle through the provinces prohibiting rebaptism, but as late as 385 Himerius of Tarragona reports that in Spain opinions were divided on the subject, wherefore he asks Pope Siricius for instructions concerning Arians who were converted, and in 404 Innocent I. was called upon by Victricius of Rouen to decide the same question concerning the Novatians who sought admission into the Church, while Basil the Great treats it as an open question dependent on local custom.[3] Even St. Augustin was so carried away by the heat of the Donatist controversy as to assert his agreement with Cyprian that although the heretics could baptize their baptism conveyed no remission of sin,[4] of which the necessary corollary was that rebaptism was essential to salvation. It is quite possible that the antagonism created by the Donatists, with whom the rebaptism of Catholics was the most prominent dogma, may have contributed to the ultimate triumph of the rule that there can be but one baptism whether administered by Catholic or heretic.[5]

---

[1] S. Cypriani Epist. LXIX. LXX. LXXI. LXXII. LXXV.—Euseb. H. E. VII. 9. —S. Hieron. de Viris Illust. c. lxix.

[2] C. Nicæn. I. c. 19.

[3] Siricii PP. Epist. I. c. 1.—Innocent. PP. I. Epist. II. c. 8.—S. Basil. Epist. Canon I. 1. Curiously enough, the most authoritative of the Penitentials, that of Theodore, adopts fully the Donatist heresy that baptism by a priest whose sins are notorious is invalid and must be repeated—"Presbyter fornicans si postquam compertum fuerit baptizaverit, iterum baptizentur illi quos baptizavit."—Pœnit. Theodori Lib. II. c. ii. § 12. (Wasserschleben p. 203.)

[4] "Proinde consentimus Cypriano hæreticos remissionem dare non posse, baptismum autem dare posse, quod quidem illis et dantibus et accipientibus valeat ad perniciem, tanquam tanto munere Dei male utentibus."—St. August. de Baptismo contra Donatistas Lib. IV. c. 22.

[5] Theory and practice as to the administration of baptism have undergone many vicissitudes. Originally the rite was performed only by bishops. Towards the close of the fourth century we hear of priests and deacons allowed to act, but only in the name of the bishop, and the sign of the cross on the forehead, by which the Holy Spirit was granted, was reserved for the bishop.—(Siricii

The origin of the Donatist heresy lay in this ancestral scruple as to the validity of the ministrations of the guilty. In the Maxentian persecution many priests and bishops had committed the grave offence of surrendering to the pagans the sacred vessels and books, and were thus known as *traditores*, and this in the African Church incapacitated them from performing their functions. On the death, about 305, of Mensurius Bishop of Carthage, the African bishops assembled and elected as his successor Cæcilianus, who was ordained by Felix Bishop of Aptungis. Doubtless there were disappointed ambitions ready to kindle strife. Felix was accused of being a *traditor*, rendering void the ordination of Cæcilianus, and a large portion of the African Church refused to recognize him, electing in opposition to him Majorinus, and, after the death of the latter, Donatus, a priest justly respected for learning and probity. It was in vain that Constantine interposed his authority and held councils which decided in favor of Cæcilianus, the schism spread and organized itself till it covered all the African provinces. At a Donatist council held at Carthage, about 330, there were assembled 270 bishops; even after

---

Epist. x. c. 4.—Innocent. I. Epist. xxv. c. 3). As for laymen, according to the Apostolic Constitutions any laic daring to baptize is threatened with the fate of Ozias, for laying unhallowed hands upon the Ark of God (Constit. Apost. III. 10). It is true that the council of Elvira, about 314, permitted it in case of necessity on the death-bed, but if the neophyte survives he must be brought to the bishop for imposition of hands (C. Eliberitan. c. 38), and this custom was preserved in Spain (S. Isidor. de Eccles. Officiis Lib. II. c. 25, § 9). The rule of the Apostolic Constitutions prevailed elsewhere and in the Penitentials of the seventh and eighth centuries it was provided that if a layman performed the rite he was to be ejected from the Church and could never be received into orders. If a priest discovered that he had never been baptized, all those whom he had baptized were subjected to rebaptism (Canones Gregorii 32; Pœnitent. Theodori I. ix. § 11; II. ii. § 13.—Wasserschleben, pp. 164, 194, 203). In the ninth century however, Nicholas I. decided that a number of baptisms by a man of whom it was not known whether he was a Jew, a Pagan or a Christian, were valid (Gratian. Decr. de Consecr. IV. xxiv.), and at the close of the eleventh century an epistle of Urban II. shows that baptism by women in case of necessity was recognized as valid and proper (Ibid. c. 4, Caus. XXX. Q. iii.). In the thirteenth century we find priests instructed to impart to their parishioners the formula of baptism that they may perform it in case of necessity (Constitt. Coventriens. ann. 1237; Concil. Wigorn. ann. 1240, c. 5; Constitt. Waltheri de Kirkham ann. 1255.—Harduin. 278, 303, 332, 487). Alexander Hales draws the line at the devil who he says cannot baptize (Reschinger Reportor. Alex. de Hales s. v. *Baptisare*, Basileæ, 1502).

long decades of persecution when, in 411, Honorius ordered a conference held between the warring factions it was attended by 286
Catholic and 279 Donatist bishops. They even maintained a church
in Rome under a succession of so-called popes, though they were
obliged to meet in secret in the suburbs, whence they were variously
known as Montenses, Campitæ, Rupitæ, Cutzupitæ, etc. The fiery
African blood did not permit this strife to be peaceful. The orthodox accounts, which alone have been permitted to reach us, are full of
recitals of the oppression, rapine and slaughter committed by the
Donatists, but their admission of the thirst for martyrdom which
distinguished the sectaries shows that the extremity of violence was
not confined to the heretic side. After bitter persecution under
Constantine and Constans, Julian, in 362, restored to the Donatists
the churches of which they had been deprived and granted them
freedom of worship. In 373 Valentinian I., and in 377 Gratian,
endeavored to repress them. In 400 the rescript of Julian was formally withdrawn by Honorius; in 404 the Catholic council of Carthage petitioned him for still bitterer persecution, to which he
responded the next year by savage edicts, and these were followed
in 413 by still others from Theodosius II. The stubbornness of the
Donatists carried them through the sufferings in which they were
involved, together with the Catholics, under the domination of the
Arian Vandals; when Justinian reconquered Africa, his retention of
the old laws against rebaptism shows that he labored to suppress
them, but it was in vain. In 594 Gregory the Great complains of
their still performing rebaptism and ousting Catholics from their
churches and he orders the civil power to enforce the laws against
them. With such tenacity it is safe to assume that their existence
was prolonged until the land was overwhelmed in the Saracen con-
quest.[1]

A special complaint of the Catholics against the Donatists was
the unsparing severity with which they inflicted penance on all
without distinction. We have seen that in orthodox practice clerics
were not liable to penance and that penance disqualified from ordi-

---

[1] S. Optat. de Schism. Donatist. Lib. I. c. 20, 24; Lib. II. c. 4, 16, 17, 18.—
S. August. Epist. XCIII. n. 43; Contra Lib. Petilian. II. 97; Brevic. Collat.
Diei I. c. 14.—Cod. Eccles. African. c. 92–3.—Cod. Theodos. XVI. v. 37, 38; vi.
1. 2, 3, 4, 5, 6, 7.—Lib. I. Cod. Tit. vi.—Gregor. PP. I. Epist. Lib. IV. 34, 35.

nation and function. By disregarding the former and enforcing the latter the Donatists found in this an easy method not only of disabling those of their antagonists who fell under their jurisdiction, but of rendering even the laity incapable of ordination and of supplying the places thus vacated, which would seem to indicate that the Catholics felt themselves obliged to recognize the penance imposed by the Donatists and respect its indelible character.[1] According to their view Catholicism was heresy, and it was the universal rule that heretics were not to be received back without penance. Thus when, after being driven from their churches by persecution, a lull would occur and they were able to return, the whole population, which had submitted to Catholic ministrations, could only be reconciled by penance. This was perfectly logical according to the practice of the time, but the Catholic controversialists made it a special crime, and curiously enough raised the further objection that all were not subjected to a similar prolonged term, but were treated individually, some escaping with a day, others with a month, while others were subjected to a year, and this penance moreover was assigned to the people in masses.[2]

St. Optatus could scarce have anticipated the time when the Church would imitate these erroneous practices of heretics by rendering penitence virtually compulsory on all the faithful and administering, if not penance, absolution and indulgences to the people in crowds and masses. He animadverts moreover on several other errors of the Donatists, which, though not directly connected with our subject, are yet of interest as illustrating how far the Church has drifted from its old moorings and how the heresy of one age becomes the orthodoxy of another. Thus he accuses them of applying their theory of the vitiation of the sacraments in sinful hands only to Catholic prelates and of holding that when their own sinned his faculties continued to operate irrespective of his personality;[3] which is the well-known orthodox theory of effects wrought *ex opere operato*

---

[1] S. Optati Lib. II. c. 24.   [2] Ibid. II. c. 26.

The heresiologists class the Donatists with the Novatians as refusing forgiveness to all who lapsed after baptism, which is a curious blunder seeing that the Novatian error was the refusal of penance while that of the Donatists was its indiscriminate infliction. — Epiphan. Panar. Hæres. LIX.—Philastrii Lib. de Hæres. n. 35.

[3] S. Optati Lib. II. c. 9.

and not *ex opere operantis.* The Donatists also anticipated Latin Christianity in declaring the Church independent of the State, greatly to the disgust of St. Optatus, who little thought that the doctrine which he so emphatically taught of the supremacy of the State over the Church would be condemned as an error from the time of Hildebrand to the present day.[1] In another matter the Donatists were only in advance of their time. Regarding Catholics as heretics, they refused to them burial in their cemeteries, for which St. Optatus takes them severely to task, arguing that hatred should end with death and that this was simply an insult to the dead for the purpose of terrifying the living.[2] He would probably have been indignantly incredulous had he been told that the time would come when Catholicism would not only deny Christian burial to heretics but would dig up their bones and burn them, not merely to terrify but to edify the living.

---

[1] "Cum super imperatorem non sit nisi solus Deus, qui fecit imperatorem, dum se Donatus super imperatorem extollit, jam quasi hominum excesserat metas, ut prope se Deum non hominem æstimaret, non reverendo eum qui post Deum ab hominibus timebatur."—S. Optati. Lib. III. c. 3.

[2] Ibid. Lib. VI. c. 7.

CHAPTER VI.

THE PARDON OF SIN.

HITHERTO we have been dealing with the *forum externum*—with the relations between the sinner and the Church. It remains for us to consider what were the current beliefs as to his relations with God, and the means by which he could obtain pardon for sins committed after the cleansing waters of baptism had for the moment restored him to primal purity.

We have seen that in the simplicity of the earliest times repentance and charity were relied upon as the means of reconciling the soul with God; that the intercessory prayers of the faithful were regarded as efficient aids, and that the Divine wrath was sometimes placated by patient endurance of temporal sufferings sent as punishment. All this continued to be taught. It would be useless to seek any universally received theory when every writer framed his own and dwelt with especial stress upon what best suited his individual temperament, without caring what his predecessors or contemporaries thought—in fact, when an eloquent and emotional preacher like Chrysostom would let himself be carried away by the impulse of the moment and utter in one homily what, if rigidly interpreted, would contradict what he had said in another. It would be unprofitable and would carry us too far to enumerate all the teachings of the Fathers as to the means of procuring pardon for sin. It must suffice to allude to a few which illustrate the general tendencies of thought.

For the most part the Church as yet taught the sinner to rely upon himself, to address himself directly to God and to work out his own salvation. But there was one notable exception to this in the importance ascribed to intercessory prayer, which as we have seen had Apostolic warrant and was practised from the earliest times. This introduced an element out of which eventually grew the enormous development of sacerdotalism, interposing mediators of every kind, terrestrial and celestial, between man and his Creator. The extravagant power attributed to it, even in the second century, is shown by the remark of Aristides, which might seem borrowed from some Brahmanic revery, "And I have no doubt that the world stands by reason of the intercession of Christians."[1] There is a well-known story of St. John the Divine, which has been used by modern apologists, in lack of other evidence, to prove the antiquity of indulgences, reciting how he won back a youth who had gone astray and become a robber chief, by adjuring him to repent and offering his own soul as an expiatory sacrifice to satisfy the justice of God ; this softened the robber and they prayed and fasted together until the sinner was regenerated and restored to the Church.[2] Rufinus, at the close of the fourth century, relates of Apollonius, a Nitrian monk of his acquaintance, how that holy man sought to make peace between two villages about to engage in war, by promising to a robber, who was captain of one of the opposing forces, that he would pray to God to pardon his sins. Arms were thrown aside and the robber accompanied the monk to his monastery, where they prayed together till they were rewarded with a vision of heaven and a voice which said " The salvation of him for whom thou hast prayed is granted to thee."[3] The prayers of the congregation for those who were in penance are a further instance of this belief; while the Church was exercising its disciplinary power, and the sinner was awaiting reconciliation, the faithful prayed for him that he might also be redeemed from sin, and the tears and prayers of the people were held to be efficacious in thus purifying his heart and reconciling him with God as well as with the Church.[4] This is a subject to which we shall have to recur hereafter, and these instances will suffice to indicate the germ to which are traceable the productive theories of vicarious satisfaction and the Spiritual Treasury of the Church.

The expiatory power of misfortunes sent by God as a punishment for sin might seem also to be beyond the control and action of the sinner, but their efficacy in this respect depended upon the temper with which they were endured; if with humility and resignation, they took the place of future punishment. To so great a length was

---

[1] Apology of Aristides ch. xvi. (Rendel Harris's Translation).
[2] Euseb. H. E. III. 23. [3] Rufini Historia Monachorum cap. 7.
[4] Velut enim operibus quibusdam totius populi purgatur, et plebis lacrymis abluitur, qui orationibus et fletibus plebis redimitur a peccato, et in homine mundatur interiore.—S. Ambros. de Pœnitent. Lib. I. c. 15. Cf. Tertull. de Pœnitent. c. 10.

this belief carried that Origen argues that capital punishment expiates the crime for which it is inflicted; it absolves from the sin and leaves nothing of it which at the Judgment Day shall condemn the sinner to eternal torment,[1] and Jerome seems to be of the same opinion in his explanation of the prohibition to slay Cain.[2] Augustin is more moderate, but yet countenances the belief in the expiatory character of worldly troubles.[3] We shall see hereafter how an all-pervading sacerdotalism has assumed control of this and made it dependent on the priestly utterance in absolution.

Apart from these, the teaching of the Fathers is that the salvation of the sinner depends upon himself, although some lay special stress on one pious manifestation and others on another. To Tertullian, while yet orthodox, amendment is the main thing, without which repentance is vain and fruitless.[4] To Lactantius also repentance is merely the resolution to sin no more: this and almsgiving wash away sin, but not sin committed in expectation of its pardon through almsgiving.[5] In view of its scriptural warrant, almsgiving naturally is mainly relied upon by many authorities, with an insistance that explains the acquisitive use of it by the medieval Church. St. Am-

---

[1] Mors quæ pœnæ causa infertur pro peccato purgatio est peccati ipsius pro quo jubetur inferri. Absolvitur ergo peccatum per pœnam mortis nec superest aliquid quod pro hoc crimine judicii dies et pœna æternæ ignis inveniant.—Origenis in Levit. Homil. xiv. n. 4.

This doctrine was still held in the middle ages. Duns Scotus even says that natural death may redeem sin, but Astesanus de Asti denies this and only admits that violent death if patiently endured may diminish punishment and even replace it altogether.—Astesani Summæ de Casibus Conscientiæ, Lib. v. Tit. xxiii. Q. 3.

[2] S. Hieron. Epist. xxxvi. ad Damasum.

[3] S. August. Enchirid. c. 66.—The pseudo-Justin Martyr (Explicationes Quæstt. Q. 124) seems to know nothing of expiation and holds that the good and the evil have the same experiences in life. Bede teaches that although sickness and death are often sent in punishment of sin they are valueless for redemption unless there are sincere contrition and intention of amendment.—Bedæ Exposit. in c. 5 Epist. Jacobi.

[4] Ubi emendatio nulla pœnitentia necessario vana, quia caret fructu suo.—Tertull. de Pœnit. c. 1.

[5] Agere autem pœnitentiam nihil aliud est quam profiteri et affirmare se ulterius non peccaturum.—Firm. Lactant. Divin. Instit. Lib. vi. c. 13. In a subsequent passage (cap. 24) he develops these views more fully, but makes no reference to almsgiving. See also his Lib. de Ira Dei c. 21.

brose is careful to explain that its efficacy depends upon the disposition of the giver and that without the spirit of charity it is useless.[1] Chrysostom, carried away by the extravagance of his own rhetoric, would persuade us that almsgiving is the sole thing needful, and that salvation is secured by the gift of a farthing or of a cup of cool water.[2] The cooler Augustin follows Lactantius and warns his disciples that, while past sins may be redeemed by alms, amendment is indispensable and liberality will not bring impunity for the commission of future ones.[3] His contemporary, St. Gaudentius of Brescia is a little less reserved. Almsgiving, like baptism, will wash away all the accumulation of past sins, but the penitent ought not to add new ones as fast as he redeems the old.[4] In the sixth century St. Cæsarius of Arles is more emphatic—with the help of God every man can redeem his sins with alms.[5] From all this we may fairly conclude that the assiduous teaching of the expiatory power of alms-

---

[1] "Neque ego abnuo liberalitatibus in pauperes factis posse minui peccatum, sed si fides commendat expensas. Quid enim prodest collatio patrimonii sine gratia charitatis?"—S. Ambros. de Pœnit. Lib. II. c. 9.

The word "charity" has acquired in our language so completely the subsidiary sense of almsgiving that perhaps it is necessary to remind the reader of its theological significance, which is far wider and higher, embracing the love of God and all that this implies.

[2] Habes obolum? eme cœlum, non quod vili pretio venale sit cœlum, sed quod clemens sit Dominius. Non habes obolum? da calicem frigidæ aquæ. . . . Da panem et accipe paradisum : parva da et magna suscipe : da mortalia, immortalia recipe : da corruptibilia, incorruptibilia accipe. . . . Pretium redemptionis animæ eleemosyna est.—S. Jo. Chrysost. de Pœnitent. Homil. III. § 2. See also the doubtful Homil. VII. § 6.

[3] S. August. Enchirid. c. 70. This warning was not superfluous, for the assiduous and not wholly disinterested teaching by the Church of the power of almsgiving to remit sins naturally led to their commission in expectation of thus purchasing pardon. In 813 the council of Châlons warns those who do so that in such cases almsgiving is fruitless.—(C. Cabillonens. II. ann. 813 c. 36) and Ivo of Chartres considers it necessary to include the canon in his collection (Decr. P. XV. c. 70).

[4] Sicut aqua baptismi salutaris extinguit flammam gehenni per gratiam, ita eleemosynarum fluviæ omnis ille coacervatus post acceptam fidem peccatorum ignis extinguitur. . . . Is enim qui eleemosynis remedium peccatorum pœnitens quærit debet jam non agere pœnitenda, ne quod uno latere extinguitur alio succendatur.—S. Gaudentii Serm. XIII. Cf. Serm. XVIII.

[5] Nullus sine peccato esse potest, sed peccata sua omnis homo, Deo auxiliante, redimere potest.—S. Cæsar. Arelatens. Homil. XIV. (Migne, LXVI. 1076).

giving led not a few of the faithful to imagine that it conferred a licence to sin, and that, in the words of Chrysostom, heaven was purchasable.

The example of the pardon of St. Peter for denying Christ leads St. Ambrose to argue that tears alone suffice to wash away sin, and in this he is copied a century later by St. Maximus of Turin.[1] The irrepressible enthusiasm of Chrysostom, in urging the sinner to consult some expert physician of souls, causes him to assert that the mere act of confession abolishes the sin.[2] The belief that worldly tribulations were expiatory naturally suggested the idea that self-inflicted suffering was especially pleasing to God and therefore peculiarly effective. Bachiarius the Monk in arguing with a fellow cenobite, who was involved in a guilty passion with a married woman, exhorts him to return to his monastery and wipe out his sin with austerities and mortifications, thus by sufferings on earth redeeming himself from the torments of hell.[3] The development of this idea led to the extravagant self-tortures of the anchorites of Palestine and the Thebaïd, of which the aim seemed to be to reduce man as nearly as possible to a level with the brute, which fill so many records of the hagiology and which bear so singular a kinship to the Yoga system of the Brahmans. It is a relief to turn from these deplorable exhibitions of human wrongheadedness to the more Christian asceticism of John Cassianus, the founder of the Abbey of St. Victor of Marseilles, who, though fully trained in the cenobitic life of Egypt, had a truer conception of the religion of Jesus and of the mode of reconciliation with an offended but loving God. There are many aids, he says, to the expiation of sins, love and almsgiving, and weeping and confession, either to man or God, mortification of the heart and flesh, and greatest of all, amendment. Sometimes the intercession of the saints is useful; mercy and faith assist, and often the labor to convert others and the forgiveness of offences procure pardon for ourselves.[4] Nearly contemporary with Cassianus was St.

---

[1] Et tu si veniam vis mereri, dilue lacrymis culpam tuam : eodem momento, eodem tempore respicit te Christus.—S. Ambros. Exposit. Evang. sec. Lucam. Lib. v. n. 95, Lib. vi. n. 18, Lib. x. c. 88. Cf. S. Maximi Taurinens. Homil. liii.

[2] Confessio enim peccatorum abolitio etiam est delictorum.—S. Jo. Chrysost. in Genesi Homil. xx. n. 3.

[3] Bachiarii Monachi de Reparatione Lapsi c. 15.

[4] Jo. Cassiani Collat. xx. c. 8.

Eucherius, the saintly bishop of Lyons, whose series of homilies to monks is instinct with the highest and purest moral teaching. The way of salvation is hard and is only to be reached through earnest and prolonged repentance. Love, charity, humility, self-abnegation coupled with zealous striving for self-amendment, win the pardon of God—not the repetition of barren formulas or the intercession of priests on earth or saints in heaven, while even austerities are of little use. Secret contrition suffices, not outward confession, though as a lesson of humility the daily acknowledgment of faults to the assembled brethren is a wholesome exercise. No sacerdotal ministration is inculcated—the sinner wrestles with his own heart and deals directly with his God.[1] Very similar are the teachings of St. Fulgentius of Ruspe, who is classed with the Doctors of the Church. Confession and tears and repentance are useless without true conversion of the heart, and this conversion means living a good and virtuous life, free from evil, and loving and helpful to others.[2] Hesychius assumes that the mere act of confession with prayer causes sins to disappear, and also that repentance shown in fasting, prayer, tears and almsgiving procures full pardon.[3]

Thus there were many ways in which the sinner could obtain pardon for himself without the ministrations of the Church, and teachers sometimes briefly grouped them together, to the mystic number of seven. Origen seems to have been the first to attempt such a computation, and he enumerates them in order: I. Baptism, II. Martyrdom, III. Almsgiving, IV. Forgiveness of offences, V. Converting a sinner from the error of his ways, VI. Abundant loving charity, VII. and lastly, the hard and laborious way of repentance, when the sinner washes his couch with tears, when tears are his daily and nightly bread, and he does not blush to reveal his sin to the priest of God and ask for medicine.[4] Chrysostom also summarizes the

---

[1] "Non levi agendum est contritione ut debita illa redimantur quibus mors æterna debetur; nec transitoria opus est satisfactione pro malis illis propter quæ paratus est ignis æternus."—S. Eucherii Homil. v.—"Parum prodest carnis contritio si non habeatur cordis sollicitudo et mentis intentio. . . . Ac sic fratres de omnibus negligentiis nostris compungamus in cubilibus, id est in cordibus nostris; si ita egeritis nos quidem de profectu vestro lætabimur, sed vos de acquisita salute gaudebitis."—Ib. Homil. IX.

[2] S. Fulgentii Ruspensis de Remissione Peccatorum Lib. I. c. 6, 11, 12, 28.

[3] Hesychii in Levit. Lib. V. c. 17, 18; Lib. VII. c. 25, 26, 27.

[4] Origenis in Levit. Homil. II. c. 4.

methods of pardon.   The commencement of repentance is confession
—not to a priest, but to God.   Tears also are sufficient and so is humility, also almsgiving and also prayer, and fasting too is efficacious,
but pardon is the work of God, who is to be addressed directly.[1]
About the middle of the sixth century St. Cæsarius of Arles gives a
more elaborate enumeration of twelve methods—baptism, charity,
almsgiving, tears, confession, mortification of heart and flesh, amendment, the intercession of saints, mercifulness and faith, the conversion of others, the forgiveness of offences and martyrdom.[2] A century
later St. Eloi of Noyon reduces the number to eight, either of which
suffices to cleanse the soul from sin without priestly intervention.[3] To
this period may be assigned the commencement of the vogue of the
Penitentials, by which for three centuries or more the conscience of

---

[1] S. Jo. Chrysost. de Pœnitentia Homil. II. § 1–4; Homil. v. § 1.—" Profer
lachrymas et ipse [Deus] indulgentiam impertitur: profer pœnitentiam et ipse
tribuit remissionem peccatorum."

[2] Prima remissio est peccatorum qua baptizamur in aqua (Joan. III.).
Secunda remissio est charitatis affectus (Luc. VII.).
Tertia remissio est eleemosynarum fructus (Ecclus. III.).
Quarta remissio, profusio lacrymarum (III. Reg. XI.).
Quinta remissio est criminum confessio (Psal. XXXI.).
Sexta remissio est afflictio cordis et corporis (I. Cor. v.).
Septima remissio est emendatio morum (Joan. v.).
Octava remissio est intercessio sanctorum (Jac. v.).
Nona remissio est misericordia [et] fidei meritum (Matth. v.).
Decima remissio est salus aliorum (Jac. v.).
Undecima remissio est indulgentia et nostra remissio (Luc. VI.).
Duodecima remissio est passio martyrii (Luc. XXIII.).—S. Cæsar. Arelatens.
Homil. XIII.
How insignificant a factor in all this was sacerdotal ministration is seen in
Homil. XIX. The priest can promise nothing; everything is left to the judg-
ment of God.
In another Homily (Homil. XI.) he represents the forgiveness of offences as
in itself the surest means of pardon: "Qui enim omnibus in se peccantibus
clementer indulserit nullius peccati vestigium, nullius macula in ipsius anima
remanebit."

[3] Sed etiam fit absolutio peccatorum per charitatis affectum, per eleemosynarum fructum, per profusionem lacrymarum, per confessionem criminum, per
cordis et corporis afflictionem, præcipue per morum emendationem, interdum
etiam per sanctorum intercessionem, per indulgentiam quoque ac remissionem
nostram, qua peccantibus in nobis dimittimus, quibus omnibus modis aboleri
posse peccata.—S. Eligii Noviomens. Homil. IV.

Latin Christendom was regulated, and in these authoritative handbooks for the guidance of priest and sinner enumerations of these modes of remission frequently find a place. These vary of course with the idiosyncrasies of the compilers, but they are all closely fashioned after the elder authorities. Those in the Penitential of Cummeanus and the *Confessionale* of Egbert of York for instance, are an accurate transcript from that of St. Cæsarius of Arles; and, with a slight injection of sacerdotalism, this is repeated in the ninth century in the Penitential which also passes under the name of Egbert.[1] This is also the model of the list in the Merseburg Penitential, and that which passes under the name of Gregory III., save that they show a still higher degree of sacerdotalism by bringing in pardon by the priest as the twelfth remission.[2] The Origenian computation of seven however was more popular and lasting, and is found with little variation in the Pœnitentiale Bigotianum and Vallicellianum.[3] It is further given in the ninth century by the Bishops Theodulf of Orleans, Jonas of Orleans and Haymo of Halberstadt,[4] and it is also to be found in

---

[1] Pœnitent. Cummeani Prooem. (Wasserschleben, Bussordnungen, p. 461).—Confessionale Pseudo-Egberti c. 2 (Ib. 304.) — Pœnitentiale Pseudo-Egberti Lib. IV. c. 63 (Ib. 341.)

[2] Pœnitent. Merseburgens. *a.* Prolog. (Ib. 388).—Pœnitent. Pseudo-Gregor. III. c. 2.

[3] Pœnitent. Bigotianum Prolog. (Ib. p. 444).—Pœnitent. Vallicellianum II. Ordo Pœnitent. (Ib. 552).

[4] Theodulfii Aurelianens. Capitula ad Presbyteros XXXVI. — Jonæ Aurelianens. de Institutione Laicali Lib. I. c. 5.—Haymonis Halberstat. Homiliæ de Sanctis, Hom. 11.

Rabanus Maurus gives virtually the same modes of redeeming sins, but at greater length.—Rab. Mauri de Universo Lib. v. c. 11.

Throughout this period there is the same confusion as we have observed in the earlier centuries as to the requisites for pardon. Some authorities tell us that confession alone suffices (S. Donati Vesontiens. Regulæ c. 23.—Canones sub Edgaro, *ap.* Thorpe. II. 260). Others conjoin repentance with confession (Isidor. Hispalens. de Eccles. Officiis Lib. II. c. 17 § 6). Others hold penitence alone to be sufficient (Responsa Nicholai PP. I. ad Consulta Bulgaror. c. 16.—S. Theodori Studitæ Serm. LXXXII.). Sometimes almsgiving suffices (Ecclesiastical Institutes Prolog. *ap.* Thorpe, II. 395.—Sacramentarii Gelasiani Lib. III. n. 49), and sometimes it is linked with fasting (Sacram. Gelas. Lib. I. n. 82.—Sacram. Gregoranium *op.* Muratori Opp. T. XIII. P. II. p. 973), sometimes fasting alone answers (Missale Gothicum, *ap.* Muratori T. XIII. P. III. pp. 295, 364), and sometimes amendment is added (Sacram. Gregor. Ibid. p. 976), while forgiveness of injuries is declared to be indispensable (Missale Gallicanum,

an Anglo-Saxon collection, which probably represents the sacerdotal movement started by St. Dunstan under Edgar the Pacific, for
it orders annual confession at Easter.[1] The twelfth century naturally
wrought a change, with the development of the sacramental theory
and the idea of absolution. The Origenian list had become too
widely diffused to be abruptly cast aside, although priestly ministrations were becoming indispensable to salvation, and it accordingly
underwent successive modifications. In the hands of Honorius of
Autun the sacerdotal element is rendered more prominent.[2] By the
middle of the century the schoolmen were remodelling theology
after their own fashion, and Peter Lombard revised the formula by
introducing into it the scholastic idea of satisfaction for sin and an
older one of the Eucharist as an expiatory sacrifice.[3] This seems to
to have become, for a time at least, the accepted teaching, for it is
repeated without modification by Alain de Lille towards the close
of the century.[4]

Ibid. p. 534). In the Sacramentary which passes under the name of Leo I.
the Holy Ghost is declared to be in itself a remission of all sins—"quia ipse
[Sanctus Spiritus] est omnium remissio peccatorum" (Sacram. Leonian. *ap.*
Muratori T. XIII. P. i. p. 527).

[1] Ecclesiastical Institutes § xxxvi (Thorpe's Ancient Laws and Institutes
II. 435.—Spelman, Concil. Britann. I. 612).

[2] Primo per baptismum; secundo per martyrium, tertio per confessionem et
pœnitentiam; quarto per lacrymas; quinto per eleemosynam; sexto per indulgentiam in nos peccantibus; septimo per charitatis opera.—Honor. Augustodun. Elucidarium, Lib. II. c. 20.

[3] Septem sunt præcipui modi remissionis quibus peccata delentur, scilicet
baptismus, eleemosyna, martyrium, conversio fratris errantis, remittere in se
peccanti, fletus et satisfactio pro peccatis, communicatio corporis et sanguinis
Domini.—Pet. Lombardi Comment. in Psalmos, Ps. VI.

[4] Alani de Insulis Lib. Pœnitent. (Migne's Patrol. CCX. 298).

A more sacerdotal conception is found in Peter of Poitiers' enumeration of
the seven modes of justification, which are all stages of a single process and
inoperative without the final one of confession—"Cogitatio de Deo et viis
ejus, voluntas sive desiderium bene operandi, gratia Dei, motus surgens ex
gratia et libero arbitrio, contritio, peccatorum remissio, confessio."—Petri
Pictaviens. Sententt. Lib. III. c. 16.

Towards the close of the thirteenth century William Durand (Rationale
Divin. Offic. Lib. VI. c. xxiv. n. 8) recurs to the older form "per baptismum,
per martyrium, per eleemosynas, per indulgentiam, per prædicationem, per
charitatem, per pœnitentiam," but by this time the *pœnitentia* was assumably
the sacrament.

The idea that the Eucharist had a special virtue in remitting sin was perhaps not unnatural in view of the text "For this is my blood of the new testament which shall be shed for many unto remission of sins" (Matt. xxvi. 28), where the allusion to a general atonement whereby man was redeemed and reconciled to God was readily wrested to apply to the sacrifice of the altar for the benefit of the individual.[1] This belief, which contributed so largely to the development of sacerdotalism, assumed two shapes. One was that partaking of the Eucharist remitted sin. We have already seen this illustrated in the story of Serapion. St. Ambrose seems to restrict it somewhat in assuming that when the sin has been already condoned it is then remitted on the sinner partaking of the Eucharist;[2] but the holy Apollonius, whom Rufinus describes as a real prophet of God, asserted more broadly that remission of sins was granted to the faithful in communion.[3] This is accepted and asserted in the most positive manner by the third Council of Braga in 675, in a canon which was carried by Gratian into his compilation and credited to Pope Julius I.,[4] and it is assumed in the prayers of the Sacramentaries, especially in the *Missa pro peccatis.*[5] As the sacrament was under priestly control this served for awhile to satisfy the aspirations of sacerdotalism, but when penitence was erected into a sacrament and the confessor held the keys of heaven it became a serious impediment to the enforcement of the new discipline and it had to be gotten rid of. This was accomplished by rendering confession and

---

[1] This process is very clearly illustrated in the False Decretals, where the text is quoted with the interpolation "qui *pro vobis* fundatur," and the deduction is crudely drawn "Crimina enim atque peccata, oblatis his Domino sacrificiis, delentur . . . atque hæc Domino offerenda, talibus hostibus delectabitur et placabitur Dominus et peccata dimittet ingentia."—Pseudo-Alex. I. Decr. 1.

[2] Ita quotiescumque peccata donantur corporis ejus sacramentum sumimus, ut per sanguinem ejus fiat peccatorum remissio.—S. Ambros. de Pœnitent. Lib. II. c. 3. (Gratian. c. 52 § 4 Caus. XXXIII. Q. iii. Dist. 1.)

[3] Addebat autem his quod etiam remissio peccatorum per hæc [mysteria] credentibus detur.—Rufini Hist. Monachor. c. 7. Had this been at the time an accepted belief of the Church, Rufinus would not have taken the trouble to mention it.

[4] Cum omne crimen atque peccatum oblatis Deo sacrificiis deleatur —C. Bracarens. III. ann. 675 c. 1.—Gratian P. III. Dist. II. c. 7.

[5] Hanc igitur oblationem Domine quam tibi offerimus pro peccatis atque offensionibus nostris ut omnium delictorum nostrorum remissionem consequi mereamur, etc.—Sacram. Gregor. (Muratori Opp. T. XIII. P. II. p. 812).

absolution a condition precedent to worthily partaking of the Eucharist, under the precept of St. Paul (I. Cor. xi. 29) and declaring it a mortal sin to take communion when not in a state of grace.[1] The schoolmen exerted themselves to argue away the old belief that the Eucharist remits sin, for they clearly saw and acknowledged that if it was admitted it would render all the other sacraments superfluous. Their ingenuity was equal to the task, though they had a narrow and tortuous path to thread, and they did not at once agree on the result. Alexander Hales asserts that the Eucharist remits venial sins but not mortal ones absolutely, whether as to the *pœna* or the *culpa* into which scholastic ingenuity had divided sin.[2] Aquinas tells us that it remits venial sins, and also mortal ones when there is no consciousness of sin, but when such consciousness exists it only aggravates them; moreover it does not remit all the *pœna*, but only more or less according to the devotion with which it is taken.[3] As venial and forgotten sins by this time were remitted by various simple observances, including the general confession in the ritual,[4] this was virtually eliminating communion as a factor in penitence. The council of Trent thus limits its efficacy to the pardon of

---

[1] St. Augustin, in arguing the question whether a man conscious of sin ought to pretermit the daily communion customary at the period says: "Cæterum si peccata tanta non sunt ut excommunicandus quisque judicetur non se debet a quotidiana medicina Dominici corporis separare."—Epist. LIV. c. 3, ad Januarium.

In the twelfth century it began to be asserted that confession is an indispensable preliminary to communion in those conscious of sin (Rich. S. Victoris de Potestate Ligandi et Solvendi cap. xxi.); in the thirteenth it was a matter of counsel for those unabsolved to abstain (Constitt. Richardi Poore cap. xxx. *ap.* Harduin. VII. 97), and the rule was made *de fide* by the council of Trent, Sess. XIII. De Eucharist. cap. vii., xi.

[2] Alex. de Ales Summæ P. IV. Q. x. Membr. 8 Art. 1, §§ 1, 2.

[3] S. Th. Aquinat. Summæ P. III. Q. lxxix. Art. 3, 4, 5. He adds (Art. 6) that it strengthens the soul within and repels the attacks of demons from without, so that it preserves the recipient from future sin.

John of Freiburg follows Aquinas. Before taking communion a man must diligently search his conscience and confess any mortal sin. If one escapes his memory he does not sin in taking the sacrament "imo magis ex vi sacramenti peccati remissionem consequitur."—Jo. Friburg. Summ. Confessorum, Lib. III. Tit. xxiv. Q 69. See Juenin de Sacramentis Diss IV. Q. 7. cap. 1, art. 1, 2, for the effort to reconcile ancient theories with modern practice.

[4] Jo. Friburg, *Op. cit.* Lib. III. Tit. xxxiv. Q. 147, 156.

venials and preservation from mortals, while the Catechism of the council reconciles the old teaching and the new by attributing its agency to its conferring the grace of repentance.[1]

The other development of the pardoning power of the Eucharist lay in the efficacy attributed to the celebration of Mass, and proved of vastly greater utility to the Church. Originally the bread and wine of the sacrifice were contributed by the faithful on the spot and were known as oblations, the priest with his deacons moving through the congregation to collect them in a bag and pitcher and place them on the altar: if there was a superfluity the solid portion was cut into pieces of convenient size and distributed as *eulogiæ* or blessed bread among those unable to attend the services. In the earlier period, daily attendance was expected, which subsequently was diminished to weekly, so that these oblations constituted a substantial contribution to the expenses of worship.[2] They were only to be received from members in good standing; if conscious of sin they ought not to offer; if the sin were known the oblation was refused, and it thus became a sort of spiritual tribunal.[3] At first these contributions were voluntary,[4] but

---

[1] Concil. Trident. Sess. XIII. De Eucharistia c. 3.—Catechism. ex Decr. Con. Trident. De Eucharistiæ Sacramento c. xiii. "Hujus enim victimæ odore ita delectatur Dominus ut gratiæ et pœnitentiæ donum nobis impertiens peccata condonet."

[2] Canon. Hippolyti XXX. 214, XXXI. 216 (Achelis, p. 122).—Canon. Apostol. iv.—Concil. Carthag. III. ann. 397 c. 24.—Sacramentar. Gregor. (Muratori Opp. T. XIII. P. III. pp. 9, 12).—Missale Francor. (Ibid. p. 443)—Ordo Romanus (Ibid. 945, 947).—Amalarii Eclogæ de Off. Missæ (Migne's Patrol. CV. 1324).— Concil. Matiscon. II. ann. 585 c. 4.—Hincmari Capit. Synod. c. 7.—Concil. Nannetens. circa 890 c. 9, 10.—S. August. Epist. CCXXVIII. ad Honorat. n. 6.— Theodori Pœnitent. Lib. I. c. 12.

The obligation to make the oblation weekly continued after communion was required only thrice a year, and it thus became a source of revenue to the Church (Regino de Discip. Eccles. Lib. II. v. 56, 63, 89). Benedict the Levite however urges daily oblations and weekly communion (Capitul. VI. 170).

[3] Constitt. Apostol. V. 6, 7.—Concil. Carthag. IV. ann. 398 c. 93, 94.—Atton. Vercellens. Capitulare, c. 68.—Towards the close of the ninth century the council of Nantes orders the priest before celebrating mass to enquire whether any of those present are at enmity with each other. If so, they must be reconciled on the spot or be ejected from the church. "Non enim possumus munus vel oblationem ad altare offerre donec prius fratri reconciliemus (C. Nannetens. circa 890 c. 1).

[4] Justin. Mart. Apolog. Lib. II.—S. Cyprian. de Op. et Eleemos. c. 15.— S. Augustin. Serm. Append. CCLXV. c. 2 (Ed. Benedict.).

this soon changed, and St. Jerome complains bitterly of the harshness with which they were enforced, no one being allowed to plead poverty under a threat of excision from the Church.[1] In process of time the contributions in kind were converted into a money payment leading to a system which it would be interesting to trace in detail if it were not somewhat foreign from our purpose. It may possibly have been as a stimulus to liberality that the making of these oblations was held to procure remission of sins, and, that no encouragement might be lacking, a practice arose of the priest reciting the names of the contributors. St. Jerome objects to this because it converted into glorification what was meant to be a redemption of sin;[2] but Innocent I. ordered the oblations to be solicited and the names of the givers to be recited.[3] Thus the custom continued and many passages in the rituals show that God was expected to remit sins in return for the oblations, either directly or through the intercession of the saint on whose feast-day they were made: indeed, there is one prayer which indicates that they had a cleansing power over future sins as well as past.[4] This inevitably fostered the mercantile spirit which rendered all the functions of the Church a matter of profit, and occasionally a voice was raised in protest. In the ninth century

---

[1] S. Hieron. Epist. xiv. ad Heliodor. c. 8. This long continued a debatable question. About the year 900 Regino shows us that it was considered obligatory on the parishioner, but indecent for the priest to require it (De Discipl. Eccles. Lib. i. Inquis n. 72, 73). In 1078 Gregory VII. seems to have felt it necessary to enforce the rule that every one who attended at mass should make an oblation (C. Roman. V. ann. 1078 c. 12). This was the less excusable, as by this time the Church was richly endowed, but the observations in the Micrologus (cap. 10) show that the custom was regularly observed.

In the previous century it is recorded that Queen Matilda, mother of Otho the Great, went to church at least twice a day, and she never went empty-handed.—Vit. S. Mathildis c. 10 (Migne, CXXXV. 900.) In another passage it is said that daily at the mass she made the oblation of wine and bread "pro salute et utilitate totius sanctæ ecclesiæ."—Ib. c. 19.

[2] At nunc publice recitantur offerentium nomina et redemptio peccatorum mutatur in laudem.—S. Hieron. Comment. in Jeremiam Lib. ii. Cap. 11, vv. 15, 16.

[3] Innocent PP. I. Epist. xxv. c. 2.

[4] Et a præteritis nos delictis exuant et futuris.—Sacrament. Gregorian. (Muratori, T. XIII. P. ii. p. 769. Cf. pp. 617, 642, 645, 646, 651, 684, 697 etc.) —Missale Gothicum (Ib. T. XIII. P. iii. pp. 287, 293. Cf. pp. 297, 303, 336, 428) See also the Sacramentt. Leonianum et Gelasianum, *passim.*

Walafrid Strabo ridicules the prevailing notion that special oblations secured special graces directed at the will of the giver, and he rebuked the tendency which held that merit consisted in liberal offerings rather than in the spirit of devotion, so that frequently men would come and make their gift and then go out without waiting to hear the mass.[1] The spirit of the age was against him however, and the ministry of the altar became more and more an affair of trade.

If this was the effect of the trifling contribution made by the devotee, the sacrifice of the altar itself, the tremendous offering in the mass of the body and blood of Christ, would naturally be held to be of far greater efficacy. The belief sprang up and was sedulously inculcated that there was scarce any object of human desire that might not be obtained by Votive Masses—masses celebrated in the name of the worshipper for the fulfilment of his wishes. The mass was an unfailing resource, and in the ancient rituals there are formulas of masses for rain and for fair weather, for peace, for victory in war, for the cessation of cattle pests, for success in law-suits, against unjust judges, against slanderers, against tempests etc. etc. They were even celebrated in private houses to obtain for the inmates safety, peace and prosperity.[2] That they should also be used to obtain pardon for sin was inevitable, and thus there came to be rituals of masses "pro peccatis," "pro confitente," "pro pœnitente," in which the sacrifice is offered as an expiation to propitiate God and lead him to pardon the sinner, and this apparently was considered so efficacious that it was not thought worth while to assume that he was repentant or contrite.[3] What relations this bore to the established systems of

---

[1] Walafridi Strabi de Rebus Ecclesiæ c. 22.

[2] Sacrament. Gregor. (Ibid. P. II. pp. 813-26).—Sacrament. Gallican. (Ibid. P. III. pp. 833, 835, 842).—As recently as the sixteenth century, Grillandus (De Sortilegiis Q. 17) treats of the question of the punishment due to priests who use the Mass for improper purposes by mingling in it wicked and filthy prayers, and he emphasizes this by a recent case of a Spanish cleric in Rome, madly in love with four nuns, who bribed some mendicant priests to offer in their masses prayers to enable him to seduce them.

[3] Hanc igitur oblationem quam tibi offerimus pro famulo tuo [illo] ut omnium peccatorum suorum veniam consequi mereatur, quæsumus Domine placatus accipias et miserationis tuæ largitate concedas ut fiat ei ad veniam delictorum et actuum emendationem . . . et famulum tuum [illum] ab omni culpa liberum esse concede etc.—Sacramentar. Gregor. (Ibid. P. II. pp. 102, 1051, 812).—

penance it would be impossible now to determine with accuracy, but with the tendency of the Church in the Dark Ages to exploit all its powers it is perhaps not unjust to assume that it served as a precursor to indulgences, and that judicious liberality on the part of the so-called penitent might in this way diminish the terrors of the long years of mortification prescribed by the canons. In the twelfth century Abelard had no hesitation in ascribing to the avarice of the clergy their habit of thus selling masses to the dying, which he denounces as a trade of empty promises of salvation for money—a *denier* being the charge for a single mass, while a foundation of an annual mass cost forty.[1] The council of Trent seeks to palliate the custom by arguing that God, placated by the oblation, grants to the sinner the gift of repentance and thus remits the greatest crimes[2] and such masses are still authorized.[3] The most fruitful development of this

---

Alcuini Lib. Sacramentarium c. 2, 17.—Excerptt. ex Cod. Liturg. Fontanellan. (Migne, CLI. 902).

In a Sacramentarium Gallicanum (Muratori T. XIII. P. III. p. 847) there is a *Missa Dominicalis* which is more elevated in tone, asking pardon for the penitent sinner and praying that he may be granted strength to resist temptation and merit salvation.

In a Maronite *Ordo* the propitiatory and absolvatory power of the sacrifice is fully expressed. "Sacerdotes . . . qui sanctificarent in unitate et concordia corpus et sanguinem suum ad propitiationem debitorum et remissionem peccatorum."—Martene de Antiq. Ecclesiæ Ritibus Lib. I. c. viii. Art. 11 Ordo 20.

[1] Et quia plerunque non minor est avaritia sacerdotis quam populi . . . multos morientium seducit cupiditas sacerdotum vanam eis securitatem promittentium si quæ habent sacrificiis obtulerint et missas emant, quas nequaquam gratis haberent. In quo quidem mercimonio præfixum apud eos pretium constat esse, pro una scilicet missa unum denarium et pro uno annuali quadraginta. —P. Abælardi Ethica cap. 17.

[2] Huius quippe oblatione placatus Dominus gratiam et donum pœnitentiæ concedens, crimina et peccata etiam ingentia dimittit.—C. Trident. Sess. XXII. De Sacrific. Missæ c. 2.—Arguing from this Juenin (De Sacramentis Diss. v. Q. vi. Cap. 1) asserts that the sacrifice of the mass remits both the *culpa* and the *pœna* of sin.

[3] Ferraris, Prompta Bibliotheca s. v. *Missa*, Art. VII. n. 2.

The authority alleged in support of the custom is Hebrews, v. 3.—"And therefore he [the high priest] ought, as for the people so also for himself, to offer for sins."

The immense revenue accruing from the "stipends" or "alms" paid for masses led to a most careful and minute subdivision of the merits of the sacrifice. Following Scotus there is recognized a threefold partition—to the Church

practice was in the direction of mortuary masses which does not belong to our immediate subject and cannot be discussed here.[1]

There were various other religious ceremonies which were held to have a power of remitting sins. Thus the prayers in the mass of

---

at large, to the person for whom it is offered, and to the celebrant himself (Addis and Arnold, Catholic Dictionary, s. v. *Mass*), the intention of the celebrant determining how it shall be directed. All this has led to the most curious and intricate questions, which by their very nature are insoluble, though their correct solution to the believer is of such infinite importance. When there are two benefactors of the church equally entitled to the benefit of a mass, the priest is instructed to divide his intention equally between the two, which is admitted to be a difficult matter. When one of these is living and the other dead there are nice discussions as to which should be preferred to the other—the living who may be advanced in grace or the dead who will only have his purgatory shortened—and the priest under these circumstances is advised to utter a preliminary prayer to God to distribute the merits according to the need of the recipients (Nic. Weigel Claviculæ Indulgentialis c. 74). When a man pays a priest for a mass, some doctors hold that the celebrant is required only to apply the benefit *ex opere operato* and not that *ex opere operantis,* including the prayers uttered during the ceremony. To this the objection is urged that in this case the mass of a wicked priest is as efficacious as that of a good one, and people are thus discouraged from bestowing their custom on the virtuous (Summa Diana s. v. *Missam applicare* n. 8). It can readily be seen that the complexities of the subject are endless. For the scandalous quarrels to which the system gave rise, see the suits recorded in the *Formularium Advocatorum et Procuratorum Romanæ Curiæ,* Basiliæ, 1493, fol. 93-4, 132-5.

The purely mercantile character of these transactions is seen in the rule that, if a priest receives pay for a mass to be celebrated about an important matter and delays it for a few days, he is guilty of mortal sin and must refund the money, if during that time the matter is decided so that the mass is useless, as for example if a sick man dies or a law-suit is settled; but if no harm has arisen from the delay he commits no sin and can keep the money.—Benedicti XIV. Casus Conscientiæ, Apr. 1741, c. iii.

The industry of selling masses at a full price and having them performed elsewhere, where the tariff is lower, has been a flourishing one, but is forbidden by Pius IX. under excommunication reserved to the Holy See in the bull *Apostolicæ Sedis,* 12 Oct. 1869.

[1] How this, like all other sacerdotal functions, was exploited is seen in the complaints presented to the *Grands Jours* of Troyes in 1405, by the people against their parish priests. In the long catalogue of exactions is enumerated that when a death occurred the heirs were required daily for thirty days, and then weekly to the end of the year, to offer oblations of bread, wine, and other matters. The court ordered this to cease and that the priest should not

Exaltatio Crucis indicate that the sinner who adored the cross was liberated,[1] and the same is seen in the *Oratio ad capillaturam* on bestowing the tonsure.[2]   Entrance into religion was also regarded as a second baptism which washed away all the sins of the monk.[3] Extreme unction, however, was a more important and more durable means of obtaining pardon, which, as it has direct apostolic warrant[4] one is somewhat surprised not to find included in the various enumerations which are referred to above.   Doubtless, in the earlier time, this was practised generally with the sick, in the hope that the promise of cure of body as well as of soul might be realized ; as the result of the former could be tested, while that of the latter necessarily remained an assumption, it came to be reserved for desperate cases and for the moribund, and when the theory of the sacraments was definitely settled, the "chrism," which was one of the original three, was divided into two, confirmation and extreme unction.

The confection of the chrism on Holy Thursday was a ceremony performed with much solemnity.   In a Sacramentary, which is probably of the sixth century, the ritual for it comprises an exorcism in which it is assumed to have the power of remitting all sins.[5]   The formulas for the ministration of extreme unction show that it was held to be a cure for disease as well as a pardon for sin, which is further indicated by the application of the chrism to the head, eyes, ears, nostrils, mouth, neck, throat, back, breast, heart, hands, feet, joints,

---

demand more than five *sous tournois* for the office of the dead.—Preuves des Libertez de l'Eglise Gallicane, II. ii. 89, 92 (Paris, 1651).

[1] Sacramentarium Gregorianum (Muratori T. XIII. P. ii. p. 680).

[2] Ibid. p. 917.

[3] Theodori Capitula c. 2 (Wasserschleben p. 145).—Theodori Pœnitent Lib. II. c. iii. § 3 (Ibid. p. 204).   Thus in a life of St. Nilus, written by a contemporary, it is said concerning his desire to become a monk—"in uno momento rejuvenescere velut aquilæ juventus atque omnibus prioribus delictis liberari" (Martene Ampl. Coll. VI. 928).

[4] Is any man sick among you? let him bring in the priests of the church; and let them pray over him, anointing him with oil in the name of the Lord. And the prayer of faith shall save the sick man, and the Lord shall raise him up ; and if he be in sins they shall be forgiven him.—James, v. 14-15.

[5] Eisque ex eo ungere habent in remissionem omnium peccatorum.—Sacrament. Gelasianum Lib. I. n. 40 (Muratori T. XIII. P. ii. p. 105).   In the Sacram. Gregorianum (Ibid. pp. 578–80) the formula expresses the virtue of the chrism in more general terms.

and place of chief suffering.[1] Curiously enough Peter Lombard, in quoting the text of James, omits the words "and the prayer of faith shall save the sick man," thus attributing the whole virtue of the operation to the chrism : he holds that it is beneficial to both body and soul, but if it is not fitting that the sick man recover, at least he gains health for his soul, for there is an interior unction which operates remission of sin and amplification of virtue. There was a question among the theologians whether, like baptism, confirmation and orders, it could be performed but once, but Lombard proves that like the Eucharist, penitence and matrimony, it can be repeated.[2]

It would carry us too far beyond our scope to undertake a detailed investigation of the controversies over Pelagianism and justification by faith and grace, but we cannot escape some allusion to the part assigned by the doctors of the Church to God in the conversion and pardon of the sinner—a subject which has been perennially debated with all the more heat that all knowledge concerning it is unattainable.

As early as the Shepherd of Hermas we find the doctrine that the elect of God are saved through faith,[3] and in the middle of the fourth century this is amplified by St. Hilary of Poitiers who asserts that faith is the only means of justification ; no one can remit sins but God, therefore all remission is from him ; even the repentance which is a condition precedent to pardon is a gift from heaven : it is

---

[1] Thus a formula of the eleventh century has " Ungo te in nomine Patris et Filii et Spiritus sancti, oleo sancto atque sacrato, ut virtute Spiriti sancti tribuat tibi hæc sacra unctio sanitatem animæ et corporis in remissionem omnium peccatorum et vitam æternam." And the final instructions are " Deinde communicet eum sacerdos corpore et sanguine Domini, et sic septem continuos dies, si necessitas contigerit, tam de communione quam de alio officio, et suscitabit eum Dominius ad salutem, et si in peccatis fuerit dimittentur ei, ut apostolus ait.—Morini de Sacram. Pœnitent. Append. p. 27. Cf. pp. 49–50, 52.

The modern ceremony is somewhat less elaborate ; the unction is performed with blessed olive oil and is applied only to the organs which are the cause of sin—the eyes, ears, nostrils, mouth, hands, feet and reins—the latter being now omitted in the case of women —C. Florent. Decr. Unionis (Hard. IX. 440).—Addis and Arnold's Catholic Dict. s. v. *Extreme Unction.* Cf. Bonizonis Placentini Lib. de Sacramentis.

[2] P. Lombard. Sententt. Lib. IV. Dist. xxiii. §§ 1–3.

[3] Pastor Hermæ, Vis. III. 8.

not the reward of merit but a free and spontaneous pardon.[1] There was fair warrant for these deductions in the Fourth Gospel,[2] yet they struck at once a comprehensive and fatal blow at human free-will, at all incentive for moral improvement, and at all the claims of sacerdotalism. Yet if the priest was powerless to save he could at least condemn, for St. Hilary explained St. Paul's delivery of sinners to Satan (I. Cor. v. 5 ; I. Tim. i. 20) by expulsion from the Church, when they were at once abandoned bodily to the devil.[3] Not long afterwards Marius Victorinus softened this somewhat. While justification could only come from the grace of God and could not be asked for through merits, we may seek by repentance to placate God to grant it.[4] St. Jerome perhaps hardly realized how he denied all virtue to the ministrations of the Church when he insisted on the influence of the Holy Ghost as a prerequisite to the remission of sins ; even the waters of baptism could not wash a soul that had not been previously washed by the Spirit.[5] Rufinus, in attempting to answer the mocking pagans, who asked how the Christians by a formula could make a murderer to be not a murderer, explains that the acts are not changed but the soul is, and this is by the influence of God, and faith suffices for this.[6] St. Basil the Great, or the Rule which passes under his name, recognized how destructive this was to the doctrine of free-will and endeavored to reconcile them, but without success.[7]

The question broadened and deepened, and the assertions of the orthodox became more accentuated, in the controversy with Pelagian-

---

[1] Fides enim sola justificat . . . Verum enim nemo potest dimittere peccata nisi solus Deus : ergo qui remittit Deus est.—S. Hilar. Pictaviens. Comment. in Matt. c. viii. n. 3.

Peccata vetera flentibus et crimina quibus obsordescimus conscientia ærumnosis, hæc sedula in cœlo consolatio præparatur.—Ib. c. iv. n. 4.

Et peccatorum remissio non probitatis est meritum, sed spontaneæ indulgentiæ voluntas.—Ejusd. Tract. in Psalm. LXVI. n. 2.

[2] No man can come to me except the Father who has sent me draw him. . . . No man can come to me unless it be given him by the Father.—John, VI. 44, 66.

[3] S. Hilar. Pictav. Tract. in Ps. CXVIII. Lib. xvi. n. 5.

[4] Marii Victorini in Epist. ad Ephes. Lib. I. Vers. 7 ; de Physicis Libri cap. 15.

[5] Neque enim aqua lavat animam sed prius ipsa lavatur a Spiritu.—S. Hieron. Dial. contra Luciferanos ʒ 6.

[6] Rufini Comment. in Symbol. Apostol. c. 40.

[7] S. Basilii Regula, Interrog. CXXIII. (Migne, CIII. 532).

ism. Such teachings as the above could hardly go unchallenged, and Pelagius not only denied original sin in the sense of culpability leading to damnation unless remitted, but argued that man enjoys freewill and that his eternal destiny lies in his own hands, to make choice between good and evil. In combating this, St. Augustin was forced to define predestination and prevenient grace with a sharpness which led to considerable opposition. In Gaul, his *Liber de Correptione et Gratia* gave especial offence to men who stood so high as St. Hilary of Arles and John Cassianus. Their arguments were difficult to refute, and St. Prosper of Aquitaine, who was carrying on the unequal combat, wrote to St. Augustin for aid. He responded in one of the latest works of his fluent pen, the *Liber de Prædestinatione Sanctorum*, which a century later received the unqualified approbation of Pope Hormisdas, but the controversy continued and in 529 the second council of Orange was held to define the faith on this subject. Its definitions were confirmed by Felix IV. and as it is impossible from the premises to frame a rational and consistent theory, we need not wonder that the doctors have found in it matter for endless debate ever since.

In the system thus laboriously constructed justification comes only by faith and the free grace of God,[1] and the one insurmountable obstruction to salvation is despair—Judas would have been pardoned had he not despaired of pardon and hanged himself.[2] Yet faith is

---

[1] Fides igitur et inchoata et perfecta donum Dei est: et hoc donum quibusdam dari, quibusdam non dari omnino non dubitet qui non vult manifestissimis sacris litteris repugnare. . . . Unde constat magnam esse gratiam quod plurimi liberantur . . . Cur autem istum potius quam illum liberet inscrutabilia sunt judicia ejus et investigabiles viæ ejus.—S. August. de Prædestinatione Sanctorum cap. 8. Cf. c. 3, 10.

Quicunque dixerit gratiam Dei qua justificamur per Jesum Christum Dominum nostrum ad solam remissionem peccatorum valere quæ jam commissæ sunt, non etiam ad adjutorium ut non committantur, anathema sit.—Cœlest. PP. I. Epist. xxi. c. 10.

Si quis ut a peccato purgemur voluntatem nostram Deum expectare contendit, non autem ut etiam purgari velimus per sancti Spiritus infusionem et operationem in nos fieri confitetur, resistit ipsi Spiritui sancti.—Concil. Arausican. II. ann. 529 c. 4. Cf. c. 3, 5, 15, 19.—S. Prosperi Aquitan. Responsiones ad Capit. Vincentian. c. 15; Ejusd. contra Collatorem c. 11.—S. Eligii Noviomens. Homil. xi.—Rabani Mauri Homil. in Evang. et Epistt. Hom. cxi.

[2] Immo pœnitendo deterius peccant cum de peccatorum remissio desperant. —S. Fulgentii Ruspens. de Remiss. Peccatorum Lib. ii. c. 16.

only to be had through the prevenient grace of God and the will to believe is due to God.[1] Merits are rather a drawback—if there were merits there would not be grace and what is given would be the payment of a debt and not a free gift,[2] and repentance of course is superfluous.[3] Of course human free-will was incompatible with all this, and it was argued away in the most absolute fashion.[4] Man's will only serves him to displease God, when he serves God the will is God's, not his.[5] But the crowning doctrine in this deplorable theory was the assertion of predestination, of election and reprobation, for which ample warrant was found in the strange utterances of St. Paul.[6] These texts were used and carried to their ultimate consequences without regard to their practical nullification of the fundamental theory of the Atonement. When the Pelagians argued that God foreknew who would save themselves by the exercise of their free-will in good works, St. Augustin would have none of such temporizing and easily showed that the distribution of salvation was regulated and predestined by the divine will,[7] nor had he any greater trouble in disposing of the Gallican Semipelagian saints whose doc-

---

[1] S. August. Lib. de Prædestinat. c. 3, 6. "Cum aliis præparetur aliis non præparetur voluntas a Domino."

[2] Ibid. c. 3.—Prosperi Aquitan. (?) De Vocatione omnium Gentium Lib. I. c. 17.—C. Arausican II. ann. 529 c. 6.

[3] S. August. Lib. de Prædestinat. c. 16. For this there is the authority of St. Paul, Romans, XI. 29, which was duly quoted.

[4] S. August. Lib. de Prædestinat. c. 10.—Pseudo-Augustin. Hypognasticon Lib. III.

[5] C. Arausican. II. c. 23. "Suam voluntatem homines faciunt, non Dei, quando id agunt quod Deo displicet; quando autem id faciunt, quod volunt ut divinæ serviant voluntati, quamvis volentes agant quod agunt, illius tamen voluntas est a quo et præparatur et jubetur quod volunt."—Cf. c. 7, 8, 9.

Gregory the Great endeavored to remove one of the incongruities of the system by arguing that those predestined to salvation only obtain it by labors which merit what God had predestined for them (Gregor. PP. I. Dialog. I. 8) —but this postulates free-will for good and was not accepted. See Flori Diac. Lugdunens. Serm. de Prædest. (Migne CXIX. 97); Gratian. Decr. Caus. XXIII. Q. 4 post c. 19.

[6] Romans, VIII. 29, 30; XI. 5, 6.—Ephesians, I. 3–11.

[7] S. August. Lib. de Prædestinat. c. 17. "Non qui eliguntur quia credunt, sed qui eliguntur ut credant. . . . Sed jam electos in se ipso ante mundi constitutionem. Hæc est immobilis veritas prædestinationis et gratiæ."—Cf. Ejusd. de Correptione et Gratia c. 15; Epist. CII. ad Deogratias, n. 15.—S. Fulgentii Ruspens. de Remiss. Peccator. Lib. II. c. 2.

trines were nearly the same as those of the heretic.[1] For them there was a *crux* in the fate of infants dying before the age of responsibility, for they admitted original sin. To solve this they argued that such infants were saved or damned according to what their lives would have been had they lived, but Augustin easily exposed the fallacy of this, for it conceded fate and foreknowledge; his own view is that when infants die they either are saved by God's grace or damned by his judgment.[2] The council of Orange did not proclaim the doctrine of predestination and election in all its repulsive crudeness, but it adopted a canon in which foreknowledge and consequently predestination is assumed.[3] How completely this was accepted by the Church is seen by the clear definition of St. Isidor of Seville, in his assertion that one man tries to be good and is unable while another wishes to be wicked and is not permitted, and in his admission that the whole is inexplicable by human intelligence.[4]

The Pelagians argued, but in vain, that this system removes all pressure on men to be righteous. In fact it neutralizes all the influence of the promise of future rewards and punishments and relegates man to the position of a blind puppet of a supreme and

---

[1] S. August. Lib. de Prædest. c. 19. One argument which St. Augustin seems to regard as conclusive (Ibid. c. 15) is a happy illustration of the theological habit of regarding illustrations as reasons. Christ was a man. His sinless career was predestined. He was conceived of the Holy Ghost and Christians are regenerate in baptism. As the cases are parallel the careers of all Christians are predestined, for they are all members of Christ. This is also the only argument that Peter Lombard can adduce.—P. Lombard. in Epist. ad Romanos, n. 11.

[2] S. Augustin. Lib. de Prædestinat. c. 12.—Monastic asceticism found a reason for the damnation of innocent infants. St. Odo of Cluny asks "Quare justus judex Deus infantem legitimo matrimonio et absoluto tempore conceptum, etiam si priusquam peccare possit moritur, cur æternaliter condemnet? Sed dum proprio reatu minime punitur, manifestum est illud fieri propter illud peccatum quod fit hora conceptionis. Si ergo tanta est culpa in conjugali concubitu ut infans pro illa sola puniri debeat etc."—Odonis Cluniac. Collationum Lib. II. c. 24.

[3] Tales nos amat Deus quales futuri sumus ipsius dono, non quales sumus nostro merito.—C. Arausican. II. ann. 529 c. 12.

[4] Gemina est prædestinatio, sive electorum ad requiem, sive reproborum ad mortem. . . . Vult quis esse bonus et non valet; vult alter esse malus et non permittitur interire. . . . Et in hac tanta obscuritate non valet homo divinam perscrutari dispositionem, et occultem prædestinationis perpendere ordinem.—S. Isidori Hispalen. Sententt. Lib. II. c. 6.

mysterious power, working for its own inscrutable ends, regardless
of human virtue and happiness, here and hereafter. Moreover it
struck at the root of the growing sacerdotalism, for logically it
eliminated the ministrations of the priest; if man had no free-will,
if repentance and good works were indifferent, if he were predestined
to bliss or to perdition, the power to bind and to loose was a figment,
and the sacraments were the merest simulacra. It is a most striking
illustration of the human faculty of self-deception that these dogmas
continued to be taught while sacerdotalism in all its forms was spreading, while men were earnestly urged to win God's favor by good
works and repentance and amendment and to earn salvation through
the sacraments, as though the freedom of the will had never been
questioned and predestination had never been heard of. The whole
practice of the Church assumed the truth of the Pelagian heresy
that every man holds in his own hands the destiny of his soul for
good or for evil, while yet the Church anathematized Pelagius and
condemned the astrologers for denying free-will.[1] When in the
ninth century the monk Gotteschalck taught the unvarnished doctrines of S. Augustin, it was easy to condemn and punish him in the
councils of Mainz and Quierzy, but he could not be condemned without also condemning what the Church had held for more than four
centuries as unquestioned verity, and a theological storm arose which
ended only with the exhaustion or death of the participants, leaving
the riddle as far from solution as ever.[2]

Yet the ingenuity of churchmen sufficed to reconcile predestination

---

[1] A sermon attributed to St. Cæsarius of Arles says " Per mathematicos sic
loquitur: Numquid homo peccat? Stellæ sic sunt positæ, necesse est ut faciat
homo peccatum . . . quia stella facit ut homo peccet; nam ipse non peccat."
—S. Augustin. Append. Serm. CCLIII. n. 2 (Ed. Benedict). This continued to
the last to be the ground for condemning astrology. Cecco d'Ascoli was burnt
because his predictions of future events by the stars inferred denial of free-will.

[2] Gotteschalci Fragmenta (Migne, CXXI. 347) —Concil. Mogunt. II. ann. 848
(Harduin. V. 15).—C. Carisiac. I. ann. 849 (Ibid. p. 18). —C. Carisiac. II. ann.
853 (Ib. p. 58).—C. Valentin. III. ann. 855 (Ib. p. 87).—Ratramnus Corbeiens.
de Prædestinat. Dei.—Amulonis Lugdunens. Sententt. de Prædestinat. —S.
Remigii Lugdunens. de Tribus Epistolis Liber.—Hincmarus Remens. de Prædestinatione.—Joan. Scoti Erigenæ Lib. de Prædestinat.—Flori Diac. Lugdunens adv. Jo. Scot. Erigenam.—Lupus Ferrariens. de Tribus Quæstionibus;
Ejusd. Collectaneum de Tribus Quæstionibus.—S. Prudentius Trecens. de
Prædestinat. contra Jo. Scotum.

with the necessity of priestly ministrations, if not logically yet coer-
cively. When Gerard of Cambrai, at his synod of 1025, undertook
to convert the heretic Cathari, he told them that justification is a
matter of grace, reserved for the predestined,[1] but when he came to
treat of the sacerdotal power he argued that the sentence of the priest
absolved those whom God had visited with the grace of compunction,[2]
and as the priestly sentence of excommunication or absolution had a
very effective value in worldly affairs, there would have been small
use in arguing that God had already granted his grace to the offender.
In the next century Abelard is thoroughly orthodox on the subject,
teaching prevenient grace and predestination.[3] Towards the middle
of the century Cardinal Robert Pullus in one breath lays down the
most rigid definitions of predestination, election and reprobation, and
in another assures us that faith and charity suffice to obtain pardon[4]
—the naked Augustinian doctrine was too orthodox to be denied and
too repulsive not to be rejected at whatever cost of inconsistency. Yet
his contemporary Gratian accepts it in all its crudity : reproof and
punishment, he says, are either superfluous or useless—superfluous
to those predestined to salvation, useless to those predestined to
damnation.[5] It would be difficult to strike a more damaging blow
at the whole system of the Church, whether in exhortation or the
imposition of penance, whether as a teacher or as a judge. All her
functions in the *forum internum* were idle. The same conclusion can
be drawn from Peter Lombard ; it is impossible for those predestined
to be saved to be damned, for those predestined to be damned to be
saved : but God, he argues, is not responsible for the latter, he
simply acts by withholding his grace, and leaves them to their evil
ways.[6] Thus we return to the old postulate that man has free-will
only for evil and the Church is powerless to save or to condemn, yet

---

[1] Synod Atrebatens. ann. 1025 c. 16 (D'Achery, Spicileg. I. 623).

[2] Ut quos omnipotens Deus per compunctionis gratiam visitat, illos pastoris
sententia absolvat.—Gerardi Camerac. Epist. (Gousset, Actes de la Prov. Eccles.
de Reims, II. 51).

[3] P. Abælardi Ethica, c. 20.

[4] Card. Roberti Pulli Sententt. Lib. I. c. 12 ; Lib. V. c. 11.

[5] Prædestinati enim ad vitam sine correptione mutantur sicut Petrus. . . .
Præsciti ad mortem inter flagella deteriores fiunt, sicut Pharao. Bonis ergo
superflua, damnandis hæc inveniuntur esse inutilia.—Gratian. Decr. Caus.
XXIII. Q. 4, post c. 19.

[6] P. Lombard. Sententt. Lib. I. Dist. 40.

this does not prevent Lombard from subsequently dwelling upon repentance and the sacraments and the power of the keys, as though he had never heard of predestination, election and reprobation.

It would be mere weariness to follow the intricacies of the subject through the endless dialectics of the schoolmen. It had never exercised the slightest influence on the policy or the practice of the Church, and even as a scholastic question its interest diminished with the rise of the sacramental system and the establishment of the power of the keys. When the function of absolution came to be conceded to the priest it made little difference to him or to his penitent whether the latter was one of the elect or of the reproved. Predestination remained necessarily an accepted dogma, to be used hereafter with tremendous effect by the heretics, but it was not allowed to hinder the growth of the confessional or the development of indulgences, however incongruous and contradictory it was to them. The only effort made to reconcile the conflicting principles, in constructing a working theory of penitence, was the assumption that as contrition is a condition precedent of absolution, so there can be no true contrition save through infused or prevenient grace. It was all the work of God who in this way saved the elect. There is no heart so hardened, says Richard of St. Victor, but that God can soften it, and there can be no repentance without his initiative for he has reserved this function to himself.[1] Thus the definition of contrition came to be that infused grace is its necessary commencement and that God alone can fit the sinner for the absolution of the priest.[2] The benumbing effect of this was recognized by the practical moralists, and the Dominican Peter of Palermo complains of the fools who say that they will satisfy for their sins when God shall give them the grace of repentance.[3] It is true that there was a reaction in favor of free-will; William of Paris asserts that there are three modes of justifi-

---

[1] Rich. a S. Victore de Potestate Ligandi et Solvendi c. 3, 7.

[2] Pet. Cantor. Verb. Abbrev. c. 141.—S. Raymundi Summæ Lib. III. Tit. xxxiv. § 5.—Alex. de Ales Summæ P. IV. Q. xiii. Membr. 1 Art. 3; Q. xvii. Membr. 2, Art. 1 § 3.

Yet toward the end of the twelfth century Master Bandinus omits infused grace in his enumeration of the essentials of penitence. The three things are "cordis compunctio, oris confessio, operis satisfactio."—Bandini Sententt. Lib. IV. Dist. 16.

[3] Petri Hieremiæ Sermones; De Pœnitentia Serm. IV. (Brixiæ, 1502).

cation, the first by the gratuitous grace of God, without coöperation by the sinner, the second by the suffrages of the saints, the third by the coöperation of the penitent;[1] Alexander Hales specifies that it must precede the infusion of grace and that justification requires four things—the movement of the free will, infusion of grace, contrition and remission of sin,[2] and Aquinas argued that grace is infused by repentance, thus rendering it an effect rather than a cause,[3] which led to a scholastic discussion as to whether the sinner by repentance opened his soul to grace, or whether the preparation for grace is the operation of God[4]—a highly important difference, but one not easily decided, involving on the one side a limitation of the omnipotence of God and on the other of human free-will. The position of Aquinas would seem to have been abandoned, for Domingo Soto tells us that a legitimate act of penitence cannot be had by nature but only by the grace of God whose special help is essential,[5] and when Cardinal Lugo denied that God could pardon sin unless there is at least virtual repentance, Palmieri answers him that God can infuse sanctifying grace without an act either precedent or consequent.[6]

The whole question however sank for a while into the condition of a theological abstraction, of interest only as a subject of dialectics. The schoolmen might expatiate on the saving grace of God and its influence on the soul in producing perfect contrition and change of heart, but experience showed that if this were a condition precedent of absolution few penitents would escape perdition. For practical purposes in the confessional some new expedient must be invented, and the difficulty was solved by the discovery that imperfect contrition or "attrition," which does not require grace and charity, becomes

---

[1] Guillel. Parisiens. de Sacr. Pœnitentiæ c. 9 (Ed. 1674, p. 472).

[2] Alex. de Ales Summæ P. IV. Q. xvii. Membr. 4 Art. 6 § 4.

[3] S. Th. Aquinat. Summæ P. III. Q. lxxxix. Art. 1.

Yet Aquinas in his *Summa contra Gentiles* had assumed that charity and grace were necessary to conversion "Nam mens nostra debite ad Deum converti non potest sine charitate; charitas autem sine gratia haberi non potest." (Lib. IV. c. 72). The initiative and the responsibility rested with God—"Quod Deus aliquos a peccato liberat et aliquos in peccato relinquit." (Lib. III. c. 162). Human free-will is powerless to win grace, but it is efficient to impede it (Lib. III. c. 160).

[4] Astesani Summæ de Casibus Lib. V. Tit. xxii. Q. 2.

[5] Dom. Soto Comment. in IV. Sententt. Dist. XVII. Q. ii. Art. 5.

[6] Palmieri Tract. de Pœnitent. p. 38.

contrition in the confessional through the operation of the sacrament. This consolatory fact has been hidden from the earlier schoolmen. The first germ of it, I think, is to be found in Alexander Hales, about 1245, though he does not attribute it to the sacrament but to the act of confession which sometimes he says intensifies attrition into contrition.[1] His contemporary William of Paris suggests that sometimes the power of the keys in the sacrament may supply defects in those who come to confession with a vehement desire to regain the grace of God, and he even ascribes infusion of grace to the sacrament.[2] Cardinal Henry of Susa seems to know nothing of it.[3] Aquinas denied that attrition could become contrition, but he argued that the penitent could acquire grace in confession and absolution if he imposed no impediment, and thus became fitted for the exercise of the power of the keys.[4] St. Bonaventura however asserts positively that the sacrament of penitence converts attrition into contrition;[5] this view was generally held by the Franciscan school,[6] and finally the Dominicans adopted it. St. Antonino of Florence asserts it as an accepted fact[7] and Chancellor Gerson, who detested equally both Thomists and Scotists, alludes to it as a matter of course.[8] Prierias not only assumes it but quotes Aquinas in its support,[9] while the Council of Trent in carefully balanced phraseology[10] approached it sufficiently to

---

[1] Alex. de Ales Summæ P. IV. Q. XVIII. Membr. ii. Art. 1.

[2] Guillel. Paris. de Sacram. Pœnitent. c. 4, 21.

[3] Hostiensis Aureæ Summæ Lib. V. De Pœn. et Remiss. § 5.

[4] S. Th. Aquinat. Summæ Supplem. Q. 1, Art. 3; Q. 18, Art. 1.

[5] S. Bonavent. in Lib. IV. Sententt. Dist. XVIII. P. i. Art. 2, Q. 1.

[6] Jo. Scotus super IV. Sententt. (Ed. Venet. c. 1470 fol. 285a).—Astesani Summæ de Casibus Lib. V. Tit. 18.—Guillermus Vorrillong super IV. Sentt. Dist. 14, 17, 18, 20.

William of Ware is now a forgotten theologian of the early fourteenth century, but in his day he was known as the *Doctor Fundatus*. The wide extent of his reputation is seen in the various disguises which his name underwent. He is cited as Anglicus, Guill. Anglicus, Guaro, Guaronis, de Oona, Varillio, Varrilionis, Varro, Verus, de Waria, Warrillo, Warro, Vorlyon, and, as the early Venice edition has it, Vorrillong.

[7] S. Antonini Summæ P. III. Tit. xiv. c. 19 § 3. Yet in another passage (P. I. Tit. x. c. 3 § 5) he speaks of it as only occasional—"cum per confessionem efficiatur quis aliquando de attrito contritus."

[8] Fit etiam ut attritio minus sufficiens fiat in confessione contritio.—Joh. Gersoni Regulæ Morales (Opp. Ed. 1488, XXV. G.).

[9] Summa Sylvestrina s. vv. *Claves* § 4, *Confessio Sacrament.* I. § 1.

[10] C. Trident. Sess. XIV. De Pœnit. c. 4. Yet in an earlier session the Council

justify subsequent theologians in laying it down as a rule of practice.[1] Thus the grace of God was brought within the reach of lukewarm penitents.

While thus the tremendous doctrines of predestination, election and reprobation, of justification by faith and grace, were made the sport of the schools and were nullified in practice; while they were admitted speculatively as articles of faith and were contradicted by the efficiency ascribed to priestly ministrations, it is no wonder if the heretics who arose from time to time eagerly seized them as the most effective weapons against the Church. Wickliffe and his disciple Huss thus made ample use of them, and Thomas of Walden, while quoting St. Augustin largely, is virtually obliged to abandon predestination and reprobation in order to refute the heretic arguments.[2] Luther's teaching of justification by faith, which we have seen was as old as St. Hilary of Poitiers, was the most direct attack that he could make on all the paraphernalia of sacerdotalism. Calvin carried out the dogma of predestination with a pitiless logic that shrank from no conclusions however repulsive. When the council of Trent assembled to repel these heretic assaults and to frame a definition of faith that should separate at once and forever the true Church from the false teachers, it was forced to throw to the winds the dogmas of St. Augustin and the council of Orange. It could not in words repudiate them, nor could it abandon the sacerdotal system that had been built up in their despite. It had a narrow path to tread and it picked its way with tolerable skill, regardless of consistency, for the heretics had taken possession of its old position and it was obliged to occupy a new one. Justification by faith was admitted but argued away in favor of justification by works; human free-will was recognized as a

---

had asserted the contradictory proposition that prevenient grace is a necessary condition of justification; that man can do nothing of himself and that his will is powerless without the grace of God.—Sess. VI. De Justificat. cap. 5; can. 3.

[1] Attritio, id est imperfectus de peccato dolor, sufficit cum sacramento pœnitentiæ ad gratiam impetrandum.—Eman. Sa Aphorismi Confessariorum s. v. *Contritio* § 4.—Reiffenstuel, Theologia Moralis Tract. XIV. Dist. vi. n. 37, 38.

The theologians hold with Aquinas that attrition cannot become contrition, but that when the love of God is added to it, contrition is the result (Pereyra, Elucidarium Theol. Moral. n. 1610). The distinction is too refined to be recognizable in practice).

[2] Thomæ Waldens. de Sacrament. cap. CLX. CLXI. CLXII.

factor in good works and their merits; predestination was kept out of sight as much as possible—it could not be denied but it was only recognized by limiting it.   The faithful were warned that no one without a special revelation could know that he was among the elect, thus inferring that all need the aid of the Church, and this was followed by a declaration which virtually destroyed predestination by denying its universality : those not elect may be justified by grace and it does not follow that they are predestined to evil.[1]   Thus at Trent Pelagius triumphed over St. Augustin, and this was emphasized by the fact that in the Tridentine Catechism there is no allusion to predestination, election and reprobation.   Even the parish priests were not to be trusted with a hint of so dangerous a doctrine.   When the Jansenists endeavored to reconcile the doctrines of St. Augustin with those of Trent they were promptly denounced as heretics of the worst description.[2]

It would carry us too far from our subject to enter into the disputes which agitated the Church for two centuries and which can scarce even yet be said to be settled, between Molinism and Jansenism, between the doctrines of sufficing grace and efficient grace.   They will occasionally emerge into view and need only here be alluded to as one of the most notable instances of human effort to define the undefinable.

---

[1] C. Trident. Sess. VI. De Justificatione cap. 5, 8, 12; can. 4, 9, 17.—Free-will was weakened but not destroyed by the sin of Adam—Ibid. cap. 1.—Yet Bellarmine teaches that there is no remission of sin save by infused grace "Sol justitiæ et Pater hominum non remittit peccata nisi per gratiam sive justitiam quam infundit."—R. Bellarmini Exposit. Psalmi XXXI.

[2] Scavini Theol. Moral. Univ. Tract. I. Disp. 1, Cap. 2, Art. 2.

CHAPTER VII.

THE POWER OF THE KEYS.

THUS far we have examined the various theories which Christians framed as to the methods of God in dealing with the sins of man. We have seen that the sinner appealed directly to his Creator and was taught, except under the baleful shadow of predestination, to earn his own salvation without assistance, save what he might gain by the intercessory prayers of the faithful. No special power was attached to the prayers of the priest; those of the laity were equally efficient; presumptively the entreaties of the righteous were more acceptable than those of the impious, but no distinction is anywhere indicated that ordination conferred any particular control over the grace and mercy of God. Martyrs, confessors and saints however were regarded as enjoying peculiar favor as mediators. Tertullian shows that the tendency to this began early when, after he had embraced Montanism, he argues that it is sufficient for a martyr to have purged his own sins, and asks who except Christ had saved another by his own death;[1] and a passage in Cyprian shows us the belief fully current.[2] When martyrdom went out of fashion with persecution the intercessory office was transferred to the saints. Early in the fifth century, a passage in the life of St. Honoré by his successor St. Hilary of Arles, shows that the saints were regarded as the patrons of the living, to intercede for them with God.[3] So crude, indeed, were the notions of the age that Bachiarius argues that a sinner, whose crime was so gross that it was an insult to the saints to beg their suffrages, might so weary them with his importunities that they would intercede, when their intercession would be the more effective because they

---

[1] Tertull. de Pudicit. c. 22.—"Sufficiat martyri propria delicta purgasse. Quis alienam mortem sua solvit nisi solus Dei filius?"

[2] Cypriani Epist. XIX.—"Qui libellum a martyribus acceperunt et auxilio eorum adjuvari apud Dominum in delictis suis possunt si . . . cum pace a martyribus suis promissa ad Dominum remittantur."

[3] S. Hilarii Arelatens. Vit. S. Honorati c. 7.

themselves were injured parties.[1] Yet direct prayers to the saints do not seem as yet to be officially recognized. In the earliest of the Sacramentaries, attributed to Leo I., prayers are offered only to God, and the extraordinary expedient is adopted of praying him to make the saints and martyrs pray for the suppliants and obtain from him pardon for them.[2] When the mediator could only be addressed

---

[1] Bachiarii Monachi de Reparatione Lapsi c. 14.

[2] "Fac eos et majestatem tuam jugiter exorare et salutaria impetrare pro nobis." "Cunctos martyres tuos fac orare pro nobis quos digne possis audire." —Sacram. Leonian. (Muratori Opp. T. XIII. P. i. pp. 483, 487). Even on the saints' days it is God who is thus addressed and not the saint whose feast is celebrated.—Ibid. pp. 485, 491, 507, 511, 559, 624, 646, 655, 663, 737.

Considering the supreme intercessory power ascribed to the Virgin in medieval and modern Catholicism it is instructive to see how subordinate was her position at this period. In the Calendars of the fourth and fifth centuries printed by Muratori, there is no feast for her (loc. cit. pp. 63–8). In a Gallican Sacramentary of the eighth century, there is only one, the Assumption, and this occurs in January (Ib T. XIII. P. iii. p. 676) and not as at present in August. It is true that in the fourth century St. Gregory of Nyssa speaks of the feast of Purification, but this was probably only a local custom, for its introduction is commonly ascribed to Justinian about 542 to avert a pestilence (Martene de antiq. Ecclesiæ Ritibus, Lib. iv. c. 15). In a calendar presumably of the seventh century there are four feasts, Purification. Annunciation, Assumption and Nativity (Sacrament. Gelasian. *ap.* Muratori T. XIII. P. ii. pp. 238, 243, 276, 285). In the Leonine Sacramentary she is only alluded to three or four times as the mother of Christ, and never as an intercessor and her suffrage is never asked for. Evidently her cult had not yet commenced, and in the early allusions to pilgrimages to the tombs and relics of saints there is no reference to shrines of the Virgin.

It is quite possible that her cult may be attributable to the zeal of the Barbarians who may have regarded her as a subordinate deity. In a Gothic Missal of the sixth or seventh century the mass on Assumption day is in a strain of laudation and adoration much beyond the contemporary Roman ones (Muratori T. XIII. P. iii. pp. 254-6). Yet the progress was slow. In the Sacramentarium Gelasianum the prayers on her feast days represent her as no more an advocate or intercessor than any other saint (Lib. ii. c. 8, 14, 47, 54). In the Sacramentarium Gregorianum there is some advance. The Virgin is named before the other saints as if deserving of peculiar honor and she is invoked on other feast days than her own (Muratori T. XIII. P. ii. pp. 494, 527). Yet in the middle of the seventh century, St. Eloi in speaking of the prayers and merits of the saints as a means of reconciliation with God makes no mention of the Virgin (S. Eligii Noviomens. Homil. 8). Even in the ninth century, when a holy priest had a vision in which he saw the saints interceding for sinners, there is no allusion to her (S. Prudentii Annal. ann. 835). A Sacramentary

through God it evidently was difficult to shake off the primitive idea that God, as the sole source of pardon, was to be approached directly. He evidently had not entrusted to any one, in heaven or on earth, the dispensation of his mercy.

Yet alongside of this there had for some time been quietly growing a claim that God had entrusted to the Church a mysterious and undefined power over the forgiveness of sins. This was founded on the celebrated texts in the gospels of Matthew and John—

"And I will give to thee [Peter] the keys of the kingdom of heaven. And whatsoever thou shalt bind on earth, it shall be bound also in heaven: and whatsoever thou shalt loose on earth it shall be loosed also in heaven" (Matt. XVI. 19).

"Amen I say to you, whatsoever you shall bind upon earth shall be bound also in heaven; and whatsoever you shall loose upon earth shall be loosed also in heaven" (Matt. XVIII. 18).

"Receive ye the Holy Ghost. Whose sins you shall forgive, they are forgiven them; and whose sins you shall retain, they are retained" (John XX. 22-23).[1]

of the eleventh century however regards her as the chief intercessor "Beata Maria semper virgine intercedente cum omnibus sanctis" (Sacramentarium Vetus, *ap.* Migne, CLI. 872). After this the progress was rapid, yet it was long before she attained the position assigned to her in modern belief. When in 1179 the Waldenses applied to the third Lateran Council for authority to preach, Walter Mapes relates (De Nugis Curialium Dist. I. cap. 31) that he was deputed to ascertain their acquaintance with theology, and he demonstrated their ignorance by asking them successively whether they believed in God, in Christ, in the Holy Ghost and in the Virgin Mary, when their answer in the affirmative to all the questions showed that they did not understand the difference between the belief required as to the Trinity and as to the Virgin. In contrast to this is the case of Juan Hidalgo who was penanced in 1590 by the Inquisition of Toledo because he asserted that we must say we believe in God and believe the Virgin (MSS. Königl. Bibl. Halle, Yc, 20, Tom. I.).

Modern devotion, in fact, assigns to the Virgin more than an intercessory power and makes her share the attributes of God. Père Huguet tells us (Vertu miraculeuse du Rosaire et du Chapelet, Paris, 1870, p. 4) "Nous reconnaissons, selon la foi Catholique, à la très-sainte Vierge dans le ciel, deux sortes de pouvoirs . . . un pouvoir d'*intercession* pour nous auprès de Dieu, et un pouvoir de coopération avec Dieu auprès de nous. Nous invoquons en Marie le premier de ces pouvoirs . . . en lui disant PRIEZ POUR NOUS! et le second . . . en lui criant SAUVEZ NOUS!"

[1] The orthodox explanation of the reiteration of the grant of power by Christ, after his resurrection, is that in Matthew he merely made a promise, the fulfilment of which is recorded in John.

Even admitting that the texts have the sense ascribed to them by the Church,

Whatever sense may be attributed to this grant of power, the primitive Church evidently regarded it as personal to the holy men whom Christ had selected as his immediate representatives. At the time the gospels were composed the apostles were not expected to have any successors, for Christ had foretold the coming of the Day of Judgment before that generation should pass away,[1] and the presence of this in all the synoptic gospels shows how universal among Christians was the expectation of its fulfilment.   In fact, how slowly the idea was developed that even the apostles had this power is seen in Philip's referring Simon Magus to God for forgiveness after repentance[2] and in the legend related above from Eusebius of St. John and the robber.   Had the belief existed the apostle would not have been represented as offering his own soul in exchange and as interceding long and earnestly with God: as soon as assured of the sinner's repentance he would have been recorded as absolving him. The early Christians would have stood aghast at the suggestion that God would confer such awful authority on every vicious or ignorant man who through favor or purchase might succeed in obtaining ordination.   That such a pretension should be accepted by Europe, even in the Dark Ages, would be incredible if it had not proved a fact. The transmission of the power from the apostles to those who were

---

there is a serious deficiency in the grant, for they do not say that no sins shall be remitted save those pardoned by the Apostles; the power must be exercised to be effective, and a sinner may make his peace with God otherwise.   The point is of no importance save as affording an illustration of the boundless assumptions by which Catholic teachers maintain the power of the keys. Thus Palmieri (Tract. de Pœnitent. p. 102) asserts that the Apostles bind whomsoever they do not loose—"Apostoli autem tamdiu retinent quamdiu non absolvunt," and he even has the audacity to represent Christ as saying "independenter a ministerio Apostolico nolo remitti quodlibet peccatum."

Equally audacious was the attempt made in 1625 by the Jesuit Santarel to prove that the text in Matthew was not confined to the forum of conscience but that it gave the Church and the pope supreme temporal power over all rulers (D'Argentré, Collect. judic. de novis Erroribus II. II. 213). Bellarmine reaches the same result, but by a different process (De Controversiis Christianæ Fidei, Cont. III. Lib. v. c. 6) and it was the received Jesuit doctrine. See *La Theologie Morale des Jésuites* (Ant. Arnauld), Cologne, 1667, pp. 121 sqq.

[1] Matt. XXIV. 34; Mark, XIII. 30; Luke XXI. 32.

[2] Acts, VIII. 22. This did not escape Wickliffe in his controversies over the power of the keys. See Thomas of Walden's *De Sacramentis* c. CXLV. n. 2.

assumed to be their successors is the most audacious *non sequitur* in history, and the success of the attempt can scarce be overestimated as a factor in the development of religion and civilization.[1]

That the primitive Church knew nothing of this is plainly inferable from the silence of the early Fathers. It is proverbially difficult to prove a negative, and in this case the only evidence is negative. They could not discuss or oppose a non-existent doctrine and practice and their only eloquence on the subject must perforce be silence, but as they treated earnestly on the methods of obtaining pardon for sins, their omission of all allusion to any power of remission lodged in priest or Church is perfectly incompatible with the existence of contemporaneous belief in it. We have seen already (Chapter I.) that St. Clement of Rome, the Didache, Barnabas, St. Ignatius and the Shepherd of Hermas, while counselling sinners as to reconciliation with God, know nothing of any authority under God. St. Ignatius, who magnified the episcopal office, speaks indeed of the council of the bishop (p. 6) as an element, but ascribes to him no individual power. Irenæus asks how sins can be remitted unless God against whom we have sinned remits them to us[2] and evidently is ignorant of any intermediary function. St. Dionysius of Corinth orders all returning sinners to be received back kindly and says nothing about absolving them.[3] The Epistle of St. Polycarp to the Philippians is a summary exhortation as to conduct and practice in which, if confession and absolution were customary or recognized, he could not avoid referring to them, but he says nothing about

---

[1] When Luther, who followed his master St. Augustin in holding that the power of the keys was lodged in the Church at large, argued that otherwise there would be no reply to the heretics who asserted that the gift was personal to Peter and died with him, the only answer which his antagonist Faber deigned to make was that there are no heretics so foolish as to make an assertion so futile and shadowy, and with this he declares that the whole of Luther's position is swept away.—Joh. Fabri Opus adversus nova Dogmata Lutheri, Roma, 1522, H. ij.

Faber was a Dominican Humanist, allied with Erasmus, Zwingli and other early reformers until alarmed at the progress of the Reformation he became one of its most active and efficient opponents. His book won him much applause in Rome; he became bishop of Vienna, where he manifested his zeal by earnest labors to reform his clergy and also by procuring the burning of Balthasar Hubmeier, March 10, 1528.

[2] Irenæi contra Hæreses Lib. v. c. xvii. §§ 1, 2.

[3] Euseb. H. E. iv. 23.

them. Nor in the paragraph as to the duties of priests is there any allusion to such functions or to mediation between God and man. As for the priest Valens and his wife, who had misbehaved he only says, "May God grant them true repentance!" The whole epistle pictures a church of the utmost simplicity, in which man deals directly with his Creator.[1] In fact the custom which prevailed, as we have seen, of not admitting clerics to penance shows that the whole penitential system had nothing to do with the relations between the sinner and his God.

The first allusion to any power of pardoning sin occurs early in the third century, when Tertullian protested vigorously on hearing that it was proposed at Rome to remit the sin of fornication and adultery to those who had duly performed penance.[2] Whether this purpose was carried out or not we have no means of knowing positively, but there is every appearance that the project was allowed to drop as there is no trace in any subsequent document that adultery was treated with greater mildness than homicide or idolatry—indeed, we have seen that in some African churches those guilty of it were not even received to penitence. Yet that the subject was beginning to attract attention and provoke discussion is shown by Tertullian's argument that the grant to Peter was personal; the apostles had the power of forgiving sins, and this has been transmitted to the Church; if the bishop of Rome claims it, let him show his right by performing miracles like the apostles.[3]

The idea gradually made its way in some churches, though under varying conditions. Not long after Tertullian the canons of Hippolytus, in the ritual of episcopal ordination, show that God was prayed to bestow on the bishop the power of remitting sins,[4] and the

---

[1] S. Polycarp. Epist. ad Philippenses.

[2] Audio etiam edictum esse propositum et quidem peremptorium Pontifex scilicet maximus quod et episcopus episcoporum edicit 'Ego et mœchiæ et fornicationis delicta pœnitentia functis dimitto.'—Tertull. de Pudicit. c. 1.

[3] Ibid. c. 21.

[4] Tribue etiam illi O Domine episcopatum et spiritum clementem et potestatem ad remittenda peccata.—Canon. Hippolyti III. 17.
This was not the only supernatural gift which the superstition of the age ascribed to the episcopal office. As the shadow of Peter cured the sick, Acts v. 15 was made the basis of a claim, as well as Matt. xvi. 19, that the bishop was held to be able to relieve disease. The prayer of ordination adds "et tribue ei facultatem ad dissolvenda omnia vincula iniquitatis dæmonum et ad

Apostolical Constitutions, based on these canons, have nearly the same formula at the close of the third century.[1] How completely dependent on local usage however was this claim is seen in the ordination of priests. In the Canons of Hippolytus the same prayer was used for them as for bishops; in an Egyptian Ordo based on the canons, the prayer for the priest has no allusion to the remission of sins, and the same is observable in the Apostolic Constitutions.[2]

Thus in some churches the bishops were claiming the power of the keys, but in others their pretensions were ridiculed. Origen tells us that they cited the text in Matthew as though they held the power to bind and to loose; this is well, if they can perform the works for which Christ made the grant to Peter, but it is absurd in him who is bound in the chains of his own sins to pretend to loosen others, simply because he is called a bishop.[3] Evidently to Origen ordination conferred no such power; to him the priest was a mediator who propitiated God at the altar.[4] We have already seen that Cyprian disclaimed all power to absolve; the Church could condemn by refusing reconciliation, but those whom it admitted to peace were only referred to the judgment of God to confirm or annul the decision. In another passage he is even more emphatic. Let no one, he says,

---

sanandos omnes morbos et contere Satanam sub pedibus ejus." This was accomplished by a visit and a prayer of the bishop—"Magna enim res est infirmo a principe sacerdotum visitari; quia umbra Petri sanavit infirmum" (Ibid. XXIV. 199). See also Irenæi contra Hæreses, II. 32-4 and Tertull. ad Scapulam c. 4. It was a common belief that sickness was caused by demons and that driving them away ensured recovery (Tatiani contra Græcos Oratio). The canons of Hippolytus do not cite Mark XVI. 17-18, which is more to the purpose, probably because the conclusion of that gospel as we have it was unknown at the time.

[1] Da ei Domine omnipotens per Christum tuum participationem sancti Spiritus ut habeat potestatem dimittendi peccata secundum mandatum tuum (κατὰ τὴν ἐντολήν σου)."—Constitt. Apostol. Lib. VIII. c. 3.

It is worth while to remark the deprecatory character of these rituals in contrast with the indicative form of the later "Accipe Spiritum sanctum."

[2] Achelis, Die Canones Hippolyti, pp. 61-2.—Constitt. Apost. VIII. 24.

[3] Alioquin ridiculum est ut dicamus eum qui vinculis peccatorum suorum ligatus est, trahit peccata sua sicut funem longum et tanquam juge lorum vituli iniquitates suas, propter hoc solum quoniam episcopus dicitur, habere hujusmodi potestatem ut soluti ab eo sint soluti in cœlo aut ligati in terris sint ligati in cœlo."—Origenis Comment. in Matt. Tom. XII. § 14.

[4] Origenis in Levit. Hom. VII. n. 2.

deceive himself, for none but Christ can pardon ; man is not greater
than God, nor can the servant condone an offence committed against
his master. The most that he will admit is that the intercession of
priest and martyr may incline God to mercy and change the sentence.
It is the height of arrogance for man to assume that he can do what
God did not concede even to the apostles—to separate the grain from
the chaff and the wheat from the tares.[1] A phrase of Cyprian's
contemporary, St. Firmilian of Cappadocia, has been quoted as asserting the power of the keys, but it occurs in his furious letter to Pope
Stephen on the rebaptism of heretics and refers only to the remission
of sin in baptism ; [2] that Firmilian made no claim for such power is
shown by his assembling a council in support of Novatianus.[3] Com-
modianus, in his instructions to penitents, says nothing of any priestly
ministrations ; as he had himself endured a course of penance he
had every opportunity of knowing that the sinner dealt directly
with God ; nor in his remarks to priests and bishops does he make
any allusion to their possession of such authority.[4] St. Peter of
Alexandria, in 305, in his instructions for the reconciliation of those
who had lapsed in the persecution of Diocletian knows nothing of
any power to remit sin ; the Church can only pray that Christ may
intercede for sinners with the Father.[5]

---

[1] Nemo se fallat, nemo se decipiat. Solus Dominus misereri potest. Veniam
peccatis quæ in ipso commissa sunt solus potest ille largiri qui peccata nostra
portavit, qui pro nobis doluit, quem Deus tradidit pro peccatis nostris. Homo
Deo esse non potest major; nec remittere aut donare indulgentia sua servus
potest quod in dominum delicto graviore commissum est.—S. Cyprian. de
Lapsis n. 17. Cf. n. 18, 29 ; Epist. 4, 55, 56 ; De Unitate Ecclesiæ.
   Potest ille [Deus] indulgentiam dare, sententiam suam potest ille deflec-
tere . . . potest in acceptum referre quidquid pro talibus et petierint martyres
et fecerint sacerdotes.—De Lapsis n. 36.
   Tum deinde quantus arrogantiæ tumor est, quanta humilitatis et lenitatis
oblivio, arrogantiæ suæ quanta jactatio ut quis aut audeat aut facere se posse
credat, quod nec apostolis concessit Dominus, ut zizania a frumento putet se
posse decernere, aut quasi ipsi palam ferre et aream purgare concessum sit,
paleas conetur a tritico separare.—Epist. 55.
   [2] Cypriani Epist. 75 (Ed. Oxon). It is somewhat remarkable to find this
abusive epistle quoted by a Catholic, as Binterim does (Denkwürdigkeiten
Bd. V. Th. ii. p. 183) and to see it moreover coolly attributed to Cyprian
himself.
   [3] Euseb. H. E. vi. 44.   [4] Commodiani Instructiones, n. 49, 69.
   [5] S. Petri Alexandr. Can. xi.

Yet when a claim such as that inferred in the ordination ritual of the Canons of Hippolytus had once been made, it was sure, in the plastic condition of doctrine and practice, to develop with the increasing power and pretensions of the Church as it emerged from persecution to domination. Appetite grows by what it feeds on and it would have required abnegation not often predicable of human nature for bishops not to grasp at such authority after it had been advanced and exercised by a few. There is a hint of this in the remark of the Novatian Bishop Acesius who attended the council of Nicæa and subscribed to its canons but refused to join in communion with his fellow members, and when asked by Constantine the reason replied that he considered those unworthy of communion who would admit to the sacraments a man who had sinned since baptism, for such remission of sin depended on the power of God and not on the will of a priest, whereupon the emperor said to him "Acesius, get a ladder and go up to heaven by yourself."[1] Still the development of the power of the keys was wonderfully slow. As Lactantius was not a priest but a philosopher, his testimony on such a subject does not count for much, but he knows nothing of the priest as an intermediary ; the sinner deals directly with God.[2] St. Hilary of Poitiers is a more significant witness, and in his Commentary on Matthew he seems ignorant of the claim that the power of binding and loosing was conferred on the apostles to be transmitted to their successors. He treats it wholly as a personal grant to them and makes no allusion to any other view of the matter.[3] Various other writers of the second half of the fourth century ascribe no pardoning power to the Church ; the fate of the sinner depends exclusively on God.[4] St.

---

[1] Sozomen. H. E. I. 22. There is something of the same to be gathered from the conference between Atticus Bishop of Constantinople and Asclepiades, the Novatian Bishop of Nicæa.—Socrat. H. E. VII. 25.

[2] Lactant. Divin. Institt. Lib. IV. c. 17 ; Lib. VI. c. 13, 24.

[3] S. Hilarii Pictav. Comment. in Matt. c. xvi. n. 7 ; c. xviii. n. 8. Possibly his assertion that the Pharisees claimed to hold the keys of heaven (c. xii. n. 3) may have been intended as a covert rebuke to the high sacerdotalists.

Juenin (De Sacram. Diss. VI. Q. v. Cap. 1 Art. 2 § 2) admits that Hilary does not claim the power as transmitted to the successors of the apostles, but Palmieri (Tract. de Pœnit. p. 114) boldly quotes what he says as to the apostolic power, as though he conceded the transmission.

[4] Philastrii Lib. de Hæres. n. 34.—Marii Victorini in Epist. ad Ephes. Lib. I. n. 7.—S. Epiphanii Panar. Hæres. 59.

Pacianus, when controverting the Novatians, asserts that the power of the keys was transmitted to the successors of the apostles, to be exercised with the utmost caution and only in accordance with the Divine will, but this was a mere speculative argument, for in his exhortation to sinners he only ascribes to the Church a power to assist, and it is Christ who obtains pardon for us.[1] The Manichæans seem to have been the first to discover the power of the keys. Their elect could not handle money and when in want of food would undertake to remit sins for bread. Ephraim Syrus denounces them bitterly for this; there is but One who can remit sins, except in the rite of baptism.[2] Possibly this example may have begun to infect the Church, for his contemporary, St. Basil the Great, claims that authority to bind and to loose is lodged with the bishops.[3]

It is highly probable in fact that the Novatian schism stimulated greatly the progress of sacerdotalism against which it was a protest. The schismatics doubtless did not forego the advantage offered them by the hazy and dubious character of the *pax ecclesiæ* which the priests conferred and contemptuously asked what was after all the advantage of the reconciliation purchased at so heavy a cost, and the orthodox in answering them would naturally be led to exalt the efficacy of its redeeming power and to assert that it was equivalent to divine pardon. This process is well illustrated by the contradictory utterances of St. Ambrose. Stimulated by conflict with the Novatians, in some passages he asserts the power of the keys in the hands of bishops in an unqualified manner; Christ, he says, could remove sin

---

[1] S. Paciani contra Novatianos Epist. I.—Paranæsis ad Pœnitentiam.—"Qui fratribus peccata sua non tacet, ecclesiæ lacrymis adjutus, Christi precibus absolvitur."

[2] Wegnern Manichæorum Indulgentiæ pp. 187–88 (Lipsiæ, 1827).—"Canes morbidi sunt qui, cum panis buccellas non inveniant, peccata et debita remittunt. Qua in re admodum rabiosi sunt et digni qui contundantur; quum unus tantum qui peccantibus peccata remittere posset."

It is generally assumed that St. Maximus of Turin (Homil. CIV.) in the latter half of the fifth century is describing the Manichæans when he speaks of the invasion of the land by heretics whose priests sell pardon of sin for money, and say "Pro crimine da tantum mihi et indulgetur tibi. Vanus plane et insipiens presbyter, qui cum ille prædam accipiat putat quod peccatum Christus indulgeat." St. Maximus could hardly have anticipated the time when, as we shall see hereafter, the teaching which he thus denounced was practiced by pardoners in all the lands of the Roman obedience.

[3] S. Basil. Epist. Canon. III. c. 74.

by a word, but he has ordered that it should be done through men.[1]
Thus he pushes this to an extent so insane that he represents God
as wishing to be asked to pardon and as virtually unable to do
so without the action of the priest.[2] In cooler moments he assumes
that this power is lodged in the Church at large, and limits it to
intercessory prayer denying that the priest can exercise any power ;[3]
and when it came to the practical exertion of the power he denies
that he possesses it and attributes it solely to God,[4] while his biographer Paulinus tells us that he regarded himself merely as an intercessor.[5] The same inconsistency is found in Chrysostom. We have
seen how he assumes that pardon is to be had by almsgiving and
other good works. Elsewhere he emphatically declares that no
intercessor is needed ; God freely forgives those who seek him with
heartfelt tears ; the prayer of the wicked is much more efficacious
with God than any intercessory prayers can be.[6] In other passages
he exalts the power of the priesthood beyond the most extravagant
claims put forward since his time. Whatever they do is confirmed
by God, who ratifies the sentences of his servants ; their empire is
as complete as though they were already in heaven ; it is not only in
baptism that they regenerate us, but they can pardon subsequent

---

[1] S. Ambros. in Ps. cxviii. Serm. x. n. 17.—In Ps. xxxviii. Enarrat.
n. 37, 38.—Exposit. Evangel. sec. Lucam Lib. v. Serm. 10 n. 13.—De Cain
et Abel Lib. ii. c. iv. n. 15.—De Pœnitent. Lib. i. c. 7, 8.

[2] Quis enim tu es qui Domino contradicas, ne cui velit culpam relaxet, cum
tu cui volueris ignoscas? Vult rogari, vult obsecrari. Si omnium justitia,
ubi Dei gratiæ? Quis es tu qui invidias Domino?—Exposit. Evangel. sec.
Lucam Lib. vii. n. 235-6.

[3] De Pœnitent. Lib. i. c. 2.—Exposit. Evangel. sec. Lucam Lib. v. Serm.
x. n. 11, 92; Lib. vii. n. 225.—In Ps. xxxviii. Enarrat. n. 10.—De Spiritu
Sancto Lib. iii. c. xviii. n. 137.

[4] In his well-known letter to Theodosius St. Ambrose says, "Peccatum non
tollitur nisi lacrymis et pœnitentia. Nec Angelus potest nec archangelus:
Dominus ipse qui solus potest dicere *Ego vobiscum sum*, si peccaverimus nisi
pœnitentiam deferentibus non relaxat."—S. Ambros. Epist. li. c. 11.

[5] Paulini Vit. S. Ambros. c. 39.

[6] Nam ipse solus cordi medelam afferre potest . . . sine intercessore
exorabilis est, sine pecuniis sine sumptibus petitioni annuit: sufficit solo corde
clamare et lacrymas offerre et statim ingressus eum attraxeris. —S. Joh.
Chrysost. de Pœnit. Homil. iv. § 4. Cf. Homil. viii. § 2.—In Epist. ad
Hebræos Homil. ix. § 4.—Homill. xi. non hactenus editæ Hom. vi.—Homil.
in Philippens. i. 18.

sins.[1] St. Jerome is less inconsequent. It is true that in one passage he speaks of the bishops as succeeding to the Apostles and, as holders of the keys of heaven, judging after a fashion before the Day of Judgment, but he qualifies this by adding that all bishops are not bishops; there was Peter but also there was Judas; it is not easy to hold the place of Peter and Paul, and the salt that has lost its savor is useless save to be cast out.[2] Ordination evidently conferred no power on those unworthy of it. In commenting, moreover, upon the text of Matthew he is much more condemnatory of the claim, for he declares that bishops and priests have misinterpreted the words of Christ and have assumed the arrogance of the Pharisees, so they think that they can condemn the innocent and release the guilty, when in truth God only considers the life of the sinner and not the sentence of the priests. The only power he will allow is that of the priest in the old law, who did not render the leper clean or unclean, but distinguished between those who were clean and those who were unclean.[3] Luther himself could scarce have said more.

This shows that the priesthood were beginning freely to claim and exercise the power of the keys, with the inevitable abuses thence arising, of which we have further evidence in the complaints of St. Isidor of Pelusium. Priests he says can deprecate but not judge, they are mediators, not kings. The power of the keys comes from the Holy Ghost and is not possessed by those who are in sin, otherwise the promise would be tyrannical and only for the benefit of priests.[4] Evidently the claim was gaining ground and the power naturally was grasped most eagerly by those least fitted for its exercise.

It was impossible that so voluminous a writer as St. Augustin, moved by varying impulses during a long series of years, should be

---

[1] S. Joh. Chrysost. de Sacerdotio Lib. III. c. 5, 6.—"Neque enim tantum cum nos regenerant [aqua baptismi] sed etiam post regenerationem admissa peccata condonare possunt."

[2] S. Hieron. Epist. XIV. ad Heliodor. c. 8, 9.

[3] Istum locum [Matt. XVI. 19] episcopi et presbyteri non intelligentes aliquid sibi de Pharisæorum assumunt supercilio, ut vel damnent innocentes vel solvere se noxios arbitrentur: cum apud Deum non sententia sacerdotum sed reorum vita quæratur.—S. Hieron. Comment. in Evangel. Matthæi Lib. III. c. xvi. v. 19. We shall see hereafter what a stumbling-block was this passage to the theologians until they concluded to ignore it.

[4] S. Isidori Pelusiot. Lib. III. Epist. 260.—"Ministri enim sunt, non participes, deprecatores non judices, mediatores non reges."

wholly consistent in his treatment of a subject which was as yet so debatable. In one of his latest productions, reproaching the bishops and priests for the abandonment of their posts on the approach of the Vandals, he argues that it is the destruction of those who for lack of their ministrations die either unbaptized or not released from their sins.[1] This however is probably rather a rhetorical amplification than an expression of conviction, for elsewhere his position is uniform. The power granted to St. Peter was transmitted to the Church at large, which consists of the whole body of the faithful; amendment combined with faith in its power to save is all that is needed to obtain forgiveness.[2] In combating the Donatists, who assumed that the power was personal in the priest, he argues that this is fatuous and heretical. Christ had said "Thy faith hath made thee whole" and now man presumes to do what Christ as a man had refrained from doing, and arrogates the power to himself.[3] The passage in John (xx. 22-3) he explains as meaning that the charity of the Church diffused in our hearts by the Holy Ghost dismisses the sins of those

---

[1] Ubi si ministri desint quantum exitium sequitur eos qui de isto seculo vel non regenerati exeunt aut ligati.—S. Augustin. Epist. CCXXVIII. n. 8 ad Honoratum.

[2] After quoting Matt. XVI. 19, he says the power of the keys was conferred on the Church "scilicet ut quisquis in Ecclesia ejus dimitti sibi peccata non crederet non ei dimitterentur; quisquis autem crederet, seque ab his correctus averteret, in ejusdem Ecclesiæ gremio constitutus, eadem fide atque correctione sanaretur."—S. August. de Doctrina Christiana Lib. I. c. 18.

"Ergo Petrus figuram gestabat Ecclesiæ; Ecclesia corpus est Christi. Recipiat igitur jam mundatas gentes quibus peccata donata sunt."—Ejusd Serm. CXLIX. c. 6. Cf. Enarratio in Ps. CI. Serm. II. § 3.—Serm. CCXCV. c. 2.—Serm. CCCLI. c. 5.—De Agone Christiano c. 31.—Enchirid. c. 65.—Serm. CCCXII. c. 3.

It will be seen how nearly Luther followed in the footsteps of his master.

[3] Medicus bonus [Christus] ægros non solum præsentes sanabat sed et futuros etiam prævidebat. Futuri erant homines qui dicerent: Ego peccata dimitto, ego justifico, ego sanctifico, ego sano quemcunque baptizo . . . Audet sibi homo hoc usurpare? Quid contra hæreticus? Ego dimitto, ego mundo, ego sanctifico. Respondeat illi non ego sed Christus: "O homo quando ego a Judæis putatus sum homo, dimissionem peccatorum fidei dedi." Non ego, respondet tibi Christus: "O hæretice tu cum sis homo dicis: Veni mulier, ego te sanam facio. Ego cum putarer homo dixi: Vade mulier, fides tua salvam te fecit."—S. August. Serm. XCIX. c. 8.

We shall see hereafter that the heresy of the Donatists became the orthodoxy of Trent.

sharing it, and retains them in those who do not share it.[1] Yet
with all his learning and acuteness St. Augustin had the vaguest possible conception of what was the nature of this mysterious power to
bind and to loose. In one place he explains it by the judgments
rendered by the martyrs who are to sit on thrones during the Mil-
lennium (Rev. xx. 4).[2] Again, in praying for the conversion of the
Manicheans, he assumes that conversion and repentance will win
remission of their sins and blasphemies, and, if he refers casually to
the power of the keys lodged in the Church, it is apparently only to
indicate that by baptism in the Church they will be in a position to
obtain pardon.[3] And yet again he argues that through the keys the
Church has the power of inflicting punishment worse than death by
the sword, by fire or by the beasts,[4] though the individual priest has
no power; God pardons or condemns wholly irrespective of what the
priest may say or do.[5]

For the next few centuries the question remained in the same state
of fluctuation and uncertainty. On the one hand Cœlestin I. in 431
assumes the necessity of priestly ministrations by denouncing as mur-
derers of souls those who refused penance to the dying.[6] Leo I., who
was so strenuous a sacerdotalist, only ascribes to the priest as we
have seen (p. 33) a deprecatory and mediatory power, but the
exercise of this is essential to the reconciliation of the sinner. Zac-
cheus, in controverting the Novatians, claims the transmission of the
grant from Peter, but limits it to sins that have been duly expiated,
for the sentence of the bishop requires the assent of heaven.[7] St.
Cæsarius of Arles in a remarkable passage admits that the office of
the priest is merely to fit the sinner for the judgment of God; he can
promise nothing, but he can advise that which will enable the truly

---

[1] S. Augustin. in Joannis Evang. Tract. cxxi. n. 4.

[2] De Civitate Dei Lib. xx. c. ix. ¿ 2.

[3] De Natura Boni c. 48.

[4] Contra Adversarium Legis ¿ 36.

[5] Quid volunt ut ego promittam quod ille non promittit? Ecce dat tibi
securitatem procurator; quid tibi prodest si paterfamilias non acceptet? . . .
Securitatem tibi procurator dedit: nihil valet securitas procuratoris. . . .
Domini enim securitas valet etiamsi nolim; mea vero nihil valet si ille nolue-
rit.—S. August. Serm. xl. cap. 5.

[6] Cœlestin. PP. I. Epist. iv. c. 2.

[7] Zacchæi Consultationum Lib. ii. c. 17–18.

repentant to win for himself access to heaven.[1] On the other hand, toward the close of the sixth century, John the Faster of Constantinople asserts that the power of the keys has been handed down from St. Peter,[2] but nearly all the writers of this period assert the capacity of the sinner to make his peace with God directly. There is no denial of the power of the keys, but it is quietly ignored, or regarded as confided to the Church at large, and at most the functions of the priest are treated as subordinate and indifferent. It is not worth while to detail these views at length, and a few references will suffice for the enquiring student.[3] In the Sacramentaries of the period moreover the allusions to the grant to St. Peter are singularly few.[4] Gregory the Great, though he alludes to the elect obtaining expiation at the hands of bishops, yet reminds his prelates that their power to bind and to loose depends upon the use they make of it; if they

---

[1] Sed unde scis inquis, si forte Deus mihi misereatur et dimittet mihi peccata mea? Verum dicis, frater, verum dicis. Unde scio, et ideo tibi do pœnitentiam quia nescio. At ille inquit: Ergo dimitte causam meam Deo: quid tu me verbis affligis et judici me Deo dimittis? Illius judicio te committo cujus judicio me commendo. Nam si scirem nihil tibi prodesse, non te admonerem, non te terrerem. Duæ res sunt, aut ignoscetur tibi aut non tibi ignoscetur. Quid horum tibi sit nescio: sed do consilium, dimitte incertum et tene certum. Et cum vivis age pœnitentiam veram ut cum veneris in judicium Dei non ab eo confundaris, sed ab eo in regnum ipsius inducaris.—S. Cæsar. Arelat. Homil. XIX.

[2] Joh. Jejunatoris Libellus Pœnitentialis (Morin. de Discipl. Pœnitent. App. p. 90). A work of this kind is especially liable to interpolation as it passes from generation to generation and probably this passage is an addition to the original text. As late as the ninth century St. Theodore Studita (Serm. LXXXII.) in urging his brethren to seek pardon from God by contrition knows nothing of absolution or priestly ministration.

[3] Bachiarii Monachi Professio Fidei, c. 7; Ejusd. de Reparatione Lapsi c. 22, 23.—Joh. Cassiani Collat. XX. c. 5.—S. Prosperi Aquitan. contra Collatorem c. 11.—Gennadii Massiliens. de Ecclesiæ Dogmatibus c. 53.—Pseudo-Augustin. Serm. de Symbolo c. 16 (Migne, XL. 1199).—S. Cæsarii Arelatens. Homil. 18. Ejusd. Serm. in Append. S. Augustin. CCLXI. c. 2 (Migne, XXXIX. 2228).—S. Fulgentii Ruspens. de Remiss. Peccator. Lib. I. c. 15, 19, 22, 24; Lib. II. c. 20. —Juliani Pomerii de Vita Contemplativa Lib. II. c. 7.—Victor Tunenens. de Pœnitentia c. 24.—Hesychii in Leviticum Lib. VII. c. 27.

[4] In the Leonine Sacramentary, although there are twenty-eight masses for the feast of Peter and Paul there is only one incidental reference to the power of the keys (Muratori Opp. T. XIII. P. I. p. 545). In the *Missale Gothicum*, of a later date, there are only one or two allusions of merely a passing nature, and no conclusions are drawn from it (Ibid. P. III. p. 365).

abuse it they forfeit it, and it is only effective when the grace of God and the internal judge have pronounced sentence—or in other words it merely makes manifest the judgment of God.[1] At the same time, when he warns the laity that if unjustly bound they must submit, for resistance will bring sin where there was none before, he shows that at least in Rome the power of the keys was beginning to be vigorously exercised.[2] Yet he infers that all priestly ministrations were superfluous in his story of a monk praying on a mountain, and followed by his curious abbot, who as he watched saw the monk suddenly suffused with a divine light, and subsequently learned from him that at that moment a heavenly voice had said " Thy sin is forgiven."[3] In the East at this period the symbolical commentary on Leviticus by Hesychius of Jerusalem indicates the advancing claims of sacerdotalism in attributing to the priests of the New Law the functions of the Levites of the Old, enlarged so as to render them the dispensers and not merely the instruments of divine mercy.[4] Yet at the same time S. Anastasius of Sinai describes the priest as merely a mediator who propitiates God, and no supernatural functions are ascribed to him.[5] About the middle of the seventh century the good bishop St. Eloi, in his Holy Thursday homilies, naturally dwells on the importance of the imposition of hands in the ceremony of reconciliation, while with simple earnestness he warns his penitents that God will not absolve them unless they are truly contrite.[6] In the next century a homily, attributed to the Venerable Bede, says that only heresy or pagan superstition, or Jewish infidelity or schism requires the intervention of the priest; all other sins God himself cures in the conscience and intellect of the sinner.[7]

By this time the use of the Penitentials—collections of canons

---

[1] Gregor. PP. I. Homil. in Evangel. Lib. I. Homil. xvii. § 18; Lib. II. Homil. xxvi. §§ 5, 6. "Unde fit ut ipse hac ligandi et solvendi potestate se privet qui hanc pro suis voluntatibus et non pro subjectorum moribus exercet . . . ut quos omnipotens Deus, per compunctionis gratiam visitat illos pastoris sententiam absolvat. Tunc enim vera est absolutio præsidentis cum interni arbitrium sequitur judicis."

[2] Ibid. Lib. II. Hom. xxvi.   [3] Ibid. Lib. II. Hom. xxxiv. § 18.

[4] Hesychii in Levit. Lib. I. c. 4; Lib. IV. c. 13; Lib. VI. c. 22.

[5] Nam cum sacerdos mediator inter Deum et homines existat, ac pro peccato multitudinis Deum propitiet.—S. Anastas. Sinaitæ Orat. de S. Synaxi (Canisius et Basnage, I. 471).

[6] S. Eligii Homil. vii. xi.   [7] Bedæ Homil. Lib. III. Hom. xiii.

prescribing the penance to be assigned to each sin—was becoming general among the priests scattered through the lands occupied by the recently converted Barbarians. The size of the dioceses, the insecurity of the roads, and the troubles of those centuries of transition rendered it impossible for the bishops to listen to penitents and for penitents to be confined to episcopal reconciliation. Much of this work necessarily fell into the hands of the parish priests, in many cases ignorant leaders of ignorant flocks, and a change in practice was inevitable, leading eventually to a change in doctrine. The bishop still performed the functions of public reconciliation on Holy Thursday, but public reconciliation was daily becoming a smaller part of the dealing of the Church with sinners; it was gradually growing obsolete and its place was being taken by the private dealings of the priests with their penitents, thus creating a new want which was filled by the compilation for daily use of the manuals which we know as Penitentials. We shall have to consider them further hereafter and meanwhile it suffices to point out the radical change which this introduced in the administration of penance, resulting in time in a complete modification of the theory of the power of the keys.

The power of binding or loosing attributed to the sacerdotal office is founded on the bestowal of the Holy Ghost in ordination.[1] We have seen (p. 55) that in the Canons of Hippolytus this was prayed for equally in the case of bishops and priests, while in the later Apostolical Constitutions there was a distinction drawn, the prayer for the Holy Ghost being retained in episcopal ordination, while it was omitted in that of priests. Thus whatever function of binding and loosing was admitted to exist was confined to the episcopal office, to which likewise was entrusted the exclusive control over reconciliation. It is quite possible that this may not have been the case everywhere, for each local Church was autonomous, and the complaints of Jerome and Isidore of Pelusium indicate that at least

---

[1] Durand. de S. Portiano Comment. super Sententias Lib. IV. Dist. xix. Q. 1 § 6.—Astesani Summæ de Casibus Lib. v. Tit. xxxvi. Q. 2.

For reasons that will presently be apparent Aquinas passes over this in his Opusc. v. *de Fide et Sacramentis*, which is followed in the Council of Florence (Decr. Unionis, Harduin. IX. 440), but he plainly infers it in his Summa, Suppl. Q. xxxvii. Art. 5 ad 2. See also his *Summa contra Gentiles*, Lib. IV. c. 21.

in some places priests were found claiming and exercising the privilege, but this may safely be assumed to have been the rule in the West, so far as the Holy See could exercise control, and in the petty dioceses into which Italy and Africa were divided it could create but little practical inconvenience, especially so long as penance was mostly a judicial and not a voluntary act. In all the early Sacramentaries and rituals, a portion of the formula of episcopal ordination is a prayer to God to grant to him the keys of heaven, so that what he may bind on earth shall be bound in heaven, and what he looses on earth shall be loosed in heaven, that whose sins he retains shall be retained and whose sins he forgives shall be forgiven,[1] while in the formula for the ordination of priests there is no such power asked for, but only that of offering the sacrifice and celebrating mass for the living and the dead. Evidently thus far the bishop, as the successor of the apostles, was the sole inheritor of the power of the keys, as St. Eloi in the seventh century represents him.[2] The forgers of the false decretals in the ninth century evidently desired to confine the power to episcopal hands. In a decretal attributed to Pope Anaclet, after quoting the text of Matthew and stating that bishops succeeded to the apostles, he is made to say rather pointedly that priests represent the seventy-two disciples.[3] This distinction continued in spite of the fact that under the Penitentials the priests gradually invaded the episcopal territory and administered a kind of quasi absolution. Dom Martene's exhaustive researches into ancient rituals show that these formulas remained in use until the close of the thirteenth century, although the immense development of sacerdotalism in the twelfth century had been followed in many places by the introduction of the modern formula, in which the power of binding and loosing is conferred on the priest, and this no longer in the deprecatory form, but in an absolute and

---

[1] Da ei Domine claves regni cœlorum ut utatur, non glorietur, potestate quam tribuis in ædificationem non in destructionem. Quodcunque ligaverit super terram sit ligatum et in cœlis, et quodcunque solverit super terram erit solutum et in cœlis. Quorum detinuerit peccata detenta sint, et quod dimiserit tu dimittas.—Sacramentar. Gregorian. (Muratori Opp. T. XIII. P. III. p. 84). Cf. Sacrament Gelasian. Lib. I. n. 99 (Ib. P. II. p. 218).—Missale Francor. (Ibid. p. 458).

[2] S. Eligii Noviomens. Homil. 4.

[3] Pseudo-Anacleti Epist. 2. Cf. Ivonis Carnot. Decr. P. v. c. 58.—The same distinction is drawn in Pseudo-Clement. Epist. 1.

imperative one—"Receive the Holy Ghost. Whose sins you shall forgive, they are forgiven them: and whose sins you shall retain they are retained."[1] The earliest instance of the use of this formula which the industry of Dom Martene has discovered, occurs in the life of St. Liébert, who was ordained a priest after his election to the see of Cambrai in 1151, when the emotion ascribed to him on hearing it indicates that it was a novelty,[2] and the earliest formulary in which it occurs dates from about the year 1200. For a century longer the two forms of priestly ordination coexisted, but the one containing the grant of power gradually triumphed and became universal. Then for awhile it was dropped as superfluous for bishops, who had already obtained it on acquiring priesthood, but subsequently it was resumed for them, and is still retained.[3] The fact that there is no clause conferring the keys in nearly all the Oriental rituals—the Orthodox *Euchologium*, the Maronite, the Jacobite and the Coptic—

---

[1] Accipe Spiritum sanctum; quorum remiseris peccata, remittuntur eis, et quorum retinueris retenta sunt (John xx. 21-23).—Ferraris, Prompta Biblio-theca, s. v. *Ordo* art. 1. n. 49.

[2] Vit. S. Lietberti Camerac. c. 17 (D'Achery, Spicilegium, II. 142).

[3] Ferraris s. v. *Ordo* art. 1 n. 52.—Martene de antiquis Ritibus Ecclesiæ Lib I. c. viii. art. 9, 10, 11.

The question as to whether the power of the keys is conferred by this clause in the ritual of ordination is necessarily a burning one. The antiquarian ignorance of the schoolmen led them naturally to assume as a matter of course that it is (Mag. Bandini Sentt. Lib IV. Dist. 18.—Pet. de Aquila in Sentt. Lib. IV. Dist. xviii. Q. 1) and it was not questioned until researches unveiled the forgotten customs. Dom Martene holds this view to be a gross error, because the absence of the clause from the old Sacramentaries would otherwise show that priests prior to its introduction had no power of absolution (loc. cit. art. 9 n. 12). But this gross error is shared by such authorities as Melchor Cano, Bellarmine, Estius, Layman, Escobar, Vazquez, Diana etc., and it is only the more modern theologians, Juenin, Concina, Tournely, Menard and others, who in the light of these revelations have recognized the error. All that Liguori will say, after balancing the contradictory opinions, is that the latter is the more probable (S. Alph. de Ligorio, Theol. Moral. Lib. VI. n. 749).

In fact the change of practice places the Church on the horns of a dilemma, either of which is sufficiently damaging to its infallibility as the custodian of the sacraments. Benedict XIV. felt this, for, after discussing the matter at length and stating the different arguments, he leaves it undecided, instructing bishops moreover not to allow such subjects to arise in their synods, for they will find themselves involved in intricacies from which extrication is impossible (De Synodo Diœcesana Lib. VIII. c. 10).

would seem to show that these have been handed down unchanged from a period before the ascription to the sacerdotal order of the power to bind and to loose.[1]

Even while, under the Penitentials, the priests were everywhere receiving such penitents as presented themselves, and, except in cases of aggravated public scandal, were administering a sort of quasi absolution, they were exercising a power not inherent in their office but only delegated to them by their superiors. We have already seen how jealously the bishops endeavored to retain control over reconciliation, and they did not recognize that ordination to the priesthood conferred the power to admit to penance. At the council of Pavia, in 850, they strictly prohibited priests from reconciling penitents, except on the death-bed, or by special instruction, for the reason that it is exclusively an episcopal function, like making the chrism and consecrating nuns, since the bishops are the sole representatives of the apostles to whom was said "Receive ye the Holy Ghost," etc.[2] The schoolmen had not yet invented the theory of "jurisdiction" whereby the cure of a parish invested the incumbent with authority to bind and loose his "subjects." Even at the close of the eleventh century we have evidence that the special assent or license of bishop or pope was requisite to enable the priest to perform the functions of a confessor. In 1065 we find two priests, Rodolf and Theobald, applying to Alexander II. for authority to assign penance to penitents confessing to them, which the pope grants, providing their bishop does not object.[3] In 1084 Berthold of Constance relates that the Cardinal Legate of Ostia promoted him to the priesthood and at the same time gave him papal authority to receive penitents—authority which evidently he would otherwise not have had;[4] and in 1095 the great

---

[1] Martene, *loc. cit.* Ord. XIX. XX. XXII. XXIII.—In the Nestorian *Ordo* there is no thing about the keys in the ordination to the priesthood, but in that of bishops there is the clause "Tibi commendo ego claves thesauri spiritualis ut liges et solvas quidquid est in terra et in cœlo."—Ibid. Ord. XXI.

[2] Synod. Regiaticinæ c. 7 (Harduin. V. 26–7).

[3] Pœnitentiam confitentibus vobis causa religionis injungere, quandoquidem vos igne divini amoris fervere non dubitamus, nisi episcopi in quorum parœchiis estis prohibuerint, licentiam damus.—Löwenfeld, Epistt. Rom. Pontiff. inedd., p. 54.

[4] Eique potestatem ad suscipiendos pœnitentes ex apostolica authoritate concessit.—Berthold. Constant. App. ad Herman. Contractum (Urstisii Germ. Histor. p. 355).

council of Piacenza, presided over by Urban II., repressed the aspirations of priests by formally prohibiting them from administering penance unless their bishops had confided this duty to them, a command which was confirmed by the council of Clermont in the same year.[1] The synod of Gran, about 1099, took the same position, asserting that neither in ordination nor under the authority of the Fathers has the priest power to receive penitents, but only by concession of the bishops.[2] A somewhat different plan of obtaining the same result was adopted by a council of Normandy about this period : no priest or monk, it says, is to receive a public sinner to penitence without command of the bishop ; secret sinners may be received to confession, but the case is to be referred to the bishop to determine the penance without reporting the name of the penitent.[3] It is quite possible that this determined assertion of episcopal control may be connected with the fact that at this period the use of the power of the keys was, as we shall see hereafter, increasing enormously the wealth of the Church. Evidently the priests were endeavoring to obtain a right to claim a share in this profitable faculty and the bishops were struggling to retain control over it. Even after the change in the formula of ordination towards the close of the twelfth century, Peter of Poitiers asserts that priests have only potential power of the keys and cannot exercise it without delegation from the bishop.[4]

All this vagueness and uncertainty explains to us why, when the priests were everywhere handling the Penitentials, listening to such penitents as might come to them, prescribing penance, and restoring sinners to communion, there was no clearer admission than before of the power of the keys. Alcuin is as inconsistent as the earlier Fathers. In one passage he tells us that the recital of the seven penitential psalms will win the mercy of God ; in another he assumes that repentance is the sole requisite for pardon, in yet another he

---

[1] Concil. Placentin. ann. 1095.—Concil. Claromont. ann. 1098 c. 5. (Harduin. VI. 1713, 1736).

Even as late as the latter part of the twelfth century Peter of Blois objects to monks confessing to bishops " vel illis quos pro se delegant episcopi" (P. Blesens. de Pœnitent.) showing that the power was still only a delegation from that of the bishops.

[2] Synod. Strigonens. II. c. ann. 1099, c. 21 (Batthyani, II. 157).

[3] Post Concil. Rotomagens. ann. 1074 c. 8 (Harduin. VI. I. 1520).

[4] Petri Pictaviens. Sententt. Lib. VI. c. 16.—"Sed illam potestatem habet tantem in habitu et non in actu, nisi concedatur ei ab episcopo."

asserts that the prayers of the priest will render confession acceptable to God and obtain pardon from him, and in another he asserts the power of the keys as a matter of belief.[1] In a similar spirit many rituals of the period give a prayer of the priest in which he only describes himself as an humble mediator constituted by God to intercede for penitent sinners.[2] Smaragdus indicates the uncertain conceptions of the time in saying that mortal sins are to be submitted to the priest who will regulate the penance for them, but, after all, the sufficiency of the satisfaction is weighed by divine and not by human judgment,[3] thus reducing the power of the keys to the merest formality.

With the commencement of the Carlovingian decadence came the effort to establish the supremacy of the Church, of which the most conspicuous embodiment is to be found in the False Decretals. With the crumbling of the secular power the way lay open for the Church, which had been enormously strengthened by Charlemagne in his policy of using it as an instrument for the civilization of his empire. In the disintegration of existing institutions and the foundation of the medieval commonwealths which then occurred, the Church had ample opportunity for the development of its ambitious schemes. For the nonce these lay in the direction of temporal supremacy rather than of spiritual, and the full evolution of the latter was postponed until the twelfth century, after the former had been completely established by Gregory VII. and his successors. Still the opportunity was not wholly neglected to bring into prominence and to practically exercise the power of the keys, which thus far had been rather a theoretical claim of the high sacerdotalists than an actually conceded authority. In 829 the bishops assembled at the great council of Paris complain that many Christians hold that those who persevere in their wickedness until death are punished only

---

[1] Alcuini de Psalmorum Usu Præfat.; Ib. n. 12.—Ejusd. de Virtut. et Viciis c. 13.—Ejusd. Epistt. 12, 112.

[2] Me exiguum humilemque mediatorem constituisti ad advocandum et intercedendum Dominum nostrum Jesum Christum pro peccantibus et ad pœnitentiam revertentibus. — Pez, Thesaur. Anecdot. II. ii. 613.—Martene de antiquis Ritibus Ecclesiæ. Lib. i. Cap. vi. Art. 7, Ord. 3, 4, 9.

[3] Smaragdi Diadema Monachor. c. 15, 16.—"Quia pœnitentiæ satisfactio divino pensatur judicio, non humano."

temporarily in purgatory and not eternally in hell, showing how slowly the populations were accepting the idea that sacerdotal ministrations were required to escape damnation. Further remarks coupled with extracts from Bede indicate that absolution for sin was procured by prayer direct to God without human mediation.[1] Evidently some means were necessary to support the claims of the Church as controlling the gates of heaven and hell. Thus in an endeavor to revive the decaying practice of public penance, an Isidorian decretal assumes that it reconciles not only to the Church but to God.[2] Another forgery, attributed to Clement I., is a recital of his ordination as bishop of Rome by St. Peter, in which the apostle formally transmitted to him the power of the keys granted by Christ, showing that the question of transmission was felt to be doubtful and required this authentic corroboration.[3] In the same decretal St. Peter is made to say that bishops are the keys of the Church; they have power to open and close the gates of heaven for they are the keys of heaven.[4] In all this, the attribution of the power to bishops alone and the silence respecting priests are significant. It was Benedict the Levite however, in his collection of Capitularies, who labored most strenuously in this direction. Perhaps the earliest claim to the absolute remission of sins and the absolution of the sinner is his assertion that Christ gave to his disciples and their successors the power of binding and loosing, so that they were able to remit the sins of those who performed due penance, and that he knew this to be a novelty is seen in his explanation that no one should wonder at it, seeing that masters can confer upon their slaves

---

[1] Con. Parisiens. ann. 829 Lib. II. Cap. x. xii. xiii. (Harduin. IV. 1344, 1347–8).

[2] Ipsam quoque infamiam qua sunt aspersi delere non possumus, sed animas eorum per pœnitentiam publicam et ecclesiæ satisfactionem sanare cupimus, quia manifesta peccata non sunt occulta correctione purganda. Pseudo-Calixti Epist. ad Galliæ Episcopos.

[3] Propter quod ipsi trado a Domino mihi traditam potestatem ligandi et solvendi, ut de omnibus quibuscunque decreverit in terris hoc decretum sit et in cœlis. Ligabit enim quod oportet ligari et solvet quod expedit solvi.—Pseudo-Clement. Epist. I. Carried into Ivonis Decret. P. XIV. c. 1.

[4] Ecclesiam . . . cujus claves episcopos esse dicebat. Ipsi enim habent potestatem claudere cœlum et aperiri portas ejus, quia claves cœli facti sunt.—Pseudo-Clement. Epist. I. Carried into Burchard. Decr. Lib. I. c. 125 and Ivon. Carnotens. Decr. P. v. c. 225.

authority over their fellow slaves.[1] This he follows up by assuming
in his instructions for the process of reconciliation that in it the
sinner is absolved and his sins remitted by the invocation of the
Holy Ghost in the prayers of the priest.[2] As up to this time, and
for three centuries to come, the only formulas in use were prayers to
God to pardon the penitent, Benedict had no hesitation in forging
interpolations in papal decretals to show that these prayers had an
absolving power. An epistle of Leo I. is thus falsified by injecting
in it the phrase "by the absolution of the priestly prayers,"[3] and
the Synodical Epistle of Felix III. has a similar forgery inserted in
it.[4] Having thus manufactured papal authority for the absolutory
function of the priestly prayers over the penitent he had no hesitation in employing the same phrase in his instructions for the conduct
of public reconciliation.[5] It is probably to these efforts that we may
attribute the efficacy subsequently ascribed to the deprecatory formulas of absolution until they were replaced by the indicative one
which is still in use, for these Capitularies were not issued simply
on the authority of Benedict or of the church of Mainz, where he
professed to have discovered them, but were presented and received

---

[1] Et ideo Dominus et magister noster discipulis suis et successoribus eorum
ligandi ac solvendi dedit potestatem ut peccatores ligandi habeant potestatem,
et pœnitentiam condigne agentes absolvi ac peccata cum divina invocatione
dimitti queant. Nec mirum etc.—Capitular. Lib. v. c. 116.

[2] Ibid. c. 129, 137.

[3] Ibid. c. 133. He quotes from Leo's Epist. CLIX. c. 6 "oportet ei per sacer-
dotalem sollicitudinem communionis gratia subvenire," injecting after "sollicitudinem" the words "id est per manus impositionem, absolutione precum
sacerdotalium."

[4] Ibid. c. 134. The Epistle VII. of Felix III. in ordering the viaticum for
dying penitents says "aut similiter a presbytero viaticum abeunti a sæculo non
negetur." Benedict inserts after "presbytero" "jussu aut permissu tamen
proprii episcopi, per manus impositionem, absolutione precum sacerdotalium "

Both these canons are carried in this shape into Isaac of Langres' collection,
Tit. I. c 16, 29.

[5] Ibid. c. 136 (Isaaci Lingonens. Tit. I. c. 17).

Much stress is laid by modern apologists on a letter of Pope John VIII. in
879 to the Frankish bishops respecting those who had recently fallen in battle
against the pagan Northmen, as proving the exercise of the power of the keys
at this period. There was from an early time a certain, or rather uncertain,
amount of influence claimed for the prayers of the Church over the fate of the
disembodied soul after death which will be more conveniently treated hereafter
when we come to consider the subject of purgatory.

as laws promulgated by Pepin, Charlemagne and Louis le Debonnaire, and thus as entitled to unquestioned respect and obedience. The Capitularies of Benedict were not the least audacious and successful of the great cycle of Isidorian forgeries. It is to the same influences that we may attribute the incorporation of remission by the priest in the twelve methods of obtaining pardon, by the Penitentials of Merseburg and of Gregory III., as mentioned in the previous chapter (p. 83).

In spite of the forgeries the theory of the power of the keys made slow advance. It is true that Jonas of Orleans, who, as we have seen, retained the Origenian list of seven modes of remission, in another passage speaks of priests reconciling men to God,[1] and the Penitential which passes under the name of Egbert of York speaks of bishops granting remission of sins in reconciliation[2] On the other hand Rabanus Maurus, Archbishop of Mainz and perhaps the most authoritative writer of the age, quotes approvingly the damaging passage of St. Jerome; he is inclined to ascribe the power to all the elect in the church, and the special grant to Peter he construes as a warning that outside of the Petrine Church there is no salvation, yet priests and bishops can relieve the penitent from the dread of eternal death and threaten the hardened sinner with endless torment.[3] Similarly the learned Haymo Bishop of Halberstadt, while freely conceding that the power of the keys was transmitted to bishops and priests who represent the Apostles, proceeds to illustrate it by the Levitical law of leprosy, which was to be shown to the priest, not that he could cleanse the leper or make him clean, but that he should distinguish between leprosy and leprosy—that is, between the greater and lesser sins.[4] That he attached no importance to the keys

---

[1] Moris est Ecclesiæ de gravioribus peccatis sacerdotibus, per quos homines Deo reconciliantur, confessionem facere.—Jonæ Aurelianens. de Instit. Laicali Lib. I. c. 16.

[2] Pœnitent. Pseudo-Ecberti Lib. I. c. 12.—"Et episcopus super eos cantat et remissionem dat. . . . et ita ei juxta illud remissionem dat."

[3] Rabani Mauri Comment. in Matt. Lib. v. c. xvi.

[4] After quoting Matt. XVI. and XVIII. Haymo says "eandem potestatem tribuit [Christus] episcopis et presbyteris, qui officio Apostolorum funguntur." Then, after referring to the Levitical law, he adds "non quod ipse leprosum mundare aut mundatum leprosum facere posset, sed quia ad ministerium ipsius sacerdotis pertinet ut discernat inter lepram et lepram, id est inter peccatum majus et minus."—Haymon. Halberstat. Homil. de Sanctis, Hom. III.

is seen when in treating elsewhere somewhat fully on confession, repentance and the forgiveness of sins he makes no allusion to sacerdotal ministrations.[1] Almost identical with Haymo's conception is that of an Anglo-Saxon tract, probably of the tenth century, in which annual confession at the beginning of Lent is prescribed, where the priest assigns penance to be performed before Easter, and the penitent obtains pardon without further ceremonies—"because penance is like a second baptism, and in baptism the sins before committed are forgiven, so also through penance the sins are purified which were committed after baptism."[2] About the year 900 Abbo of St. Germain tells the penitents whose penance was not completed that they must go on with it cheerfully, for no bishop can grant absolution until it is fully performed, which would seem to recognize the function of absolving, but this was mere reconciliation with the Church for he had previously told them that if the penance assigned be insufficient they must add to it voluntarily to satisfy God.[3] As the distinction between *culpa* and *pœna* had not yet been evolved by the schoolmen this was a practical denial of the power of the keys and of the authority of the Church to act for God.

Regino, whose collection of canons, so much more complete than those of his predecessors, virtually superseded the Penitentials during the tenth century, has no hesitation in asserting that the keys of heaven are granted to bishops and priests to exercise judgment on penitents, though he admits that in case of necessity a deacon can admit a penitent to communion,[4] showing that the recognition of the power to bind and to loose was gradually making its way, though the conception as to its exercise was still very vague. The Council of Trosley, also, in 909, specified as an article of faith that repentance with sacerdotal ministration obtains pardon for sins.[5] The darkness of the tenth century, however, was too dense, both intellectually and spiritually, for progress of any kind, and it has left us scarce any expression of its conceptions on this subject by which to estimate the direction of its currents of thought. One of the few scholars of the age, Atto, Bishop of Vercelli, in vindicating episcopal

---

[1] Haymon. de Varietate Librorum Lib. II. c. 61–67.
[2] Ecclesiastical Institutes c. 36 (Thorpe, II. 435).
[3] Abbonis Sangermanens. Serm. II. III.
[4] Reginon. de Discipl. Eccles. Lib. I. c. 295, 296.
[5] Concil. Trosleian. ann. 909 c. 15 (Harduin. VI. I. 544).

immunity from secular jurisdiction, declares that they are not to be rashly judged of men who have received from God the power of judging even the angels, which was carrying the function of the keys to its highest denomination, but how little reference this had to any practical exercise of it is seen in his elaborate instructions to his priests, in which there is no reference to anything but reconciliation to the Church by the bishop.[1] St. Ulric of Augsburg, in his synodal constitutions, which are very minute, tells his priests to invite their parishioners to confession on Ash Wednesday, and to impose due penance on them, but he says nothing about absolution and seems ignorant of anything save the reconciliation of the dying.[2] St. Odo of Cluny claims for prelates the power to bind and to loose but, like Atto of Vercelli, it is as a weapon of defence against the lawless oppressors of the Church, and he relies to terrify them wholly on the worldly punishments with which God afflicts the wicked.[3] Save at the approach of death, the age was too cruel and carnal to care much for spiritual terrors, and the less the Church deserved and enjoyed the respect of the laity the greater became the claims which it put forward to serve as a shield. Ratherius, Bishop of Verona, who was thrice driven from his see by the secular power, at the instance of his clergy unable to endure the rigidity of his virtue, naturally seeks to exalt in the most extravagant manner the authority of his office. Bishops, he says, are Gods, they are Christs, they are angels, kings, and princes ; they are physicians of souls, the janitors of paradise, bearing the keys of heaven, which they can close or open at will.[4] Yet of these divine beings he admits that there is scarce one fitted for the position or fit even to lay hands on another when elected, while the priests are only to be distinguished from the laity by shaving, the tonsure, some slight difference in garments and the negligent performance of the offices, to satisfy the world rather than God.[5] It would be curious to enquire what was his conception

---

[1] Atton.Vercell. de Pressuris Ecclesiasticis Pars. I —Ejusd. Capitulare, cap. 90.

[2] S. Udalrici Augustani Sermo Synodalis.

[3] S. Odonis Cluniacens. Collationum Lib. I. c. 19.   Cf. Lib. II. c. 16.

[4] Talibus igitur, O rex, subdi ne dedigneris, quia velis nolis ipsos deos, ipsos angelos, ipsos principes, ipsos judices habebis . . .   Medici animarum sunt, janitores paradisi sunt, claves cœli portantes, reserare et claudere cœlum valent. —Ratherii Veronens. Præloquiorum Lib. II. n. 11, 12.

[5] Ejusd. de Contemptu Canonum P. II. §§ 1, 2.

of the God who would entrust such powers to such hands, or what was the intellectual condition of the populations that could be brought to admit such claims.

The eleventh century does not afford us much material for the illustration of the subject, but what it does indicates that little advance was made in the theory of the power of the keys. Thietmar, Bishop of Merseburg, was one of the most cultured men of his day, and yet his idea of the authority of his office was of the vaguest and crudest description. When, about 1015, Bishop Bernar built a church and invited Thietmar to consecrate it, he handed his guest a long written confession of his sins and reading it with groans begged for pardon. Thietmar thereupon granted him absolution (apparently without penance) by divine power, and then, fearing that in his impotence this was of no service to the sinner, after consecrating the church, he placed the confession on a reliquary so that the saints whose relics it contained might by earnest intercession obtain the desired remission of sin for the postulant.[1] Thietmar tells us that he had never heard of this being done, but the spirit which prompted it was not confined to him. A ritual of the period instructs the priest, when his penitent is a cleric, to lead him before the altar and say, " I am not worthy to receive thy penitence. May the omnipotent God receive thee and liberate thee from all thy sins, past, present and future."[2] Burchard of Worms, in his collection of canons, gives the extract from the forged decretal of Clement I. already cited, in which bishops are declared to have the power of opening or closing heaven, because they are the keys of heaven,[3] but St. Fulbert of Chartres seems to know nothing of all this. In an exhortation to sinners he tells them to perform the penance enjoined on them, but this is useless without amendment; many, he says, have escaped eternal death by penitence and many by prayer, but the saving power of the Church does not appear to be a factor in his scheme of

---

[1] Hoc nunquam vidi aliquem fecisse vel audivi; sed quia infirmitatem meam huic nil prodesse timui, ad sanctos intercessores confugi.—Dithmari Chron. Lib. VII. c. 7.

[2] Non sum dignus ego tuam suscipere pœnitentiam. Suscipiat te omnipotens Deus et liberat te de omnibus peccatis tuis, præteritis, præsentis et futuris.—Garofali, Ordo ad dandam Pœnitentiam, Roma, 1791, p. 21.

[3] Burchardi Decret. Lib. I. c. 125. This forgery evidently was the basis of the assertion of Ratherius of Verona just quoted.

salvation.[1] Towards the close of the century the blessed Lanfranc of Canterbury evidently holds that the power of the keys is lodged in the Church at large, to be exercised in case of necessity by any of its members, whether in orders or not. He tells the penitent that if his sin be public it should be confessed to a priest, through whom the Church binds and looses what it publicly knows : if the sin be private it can be confessed to any cleric, but if none is to be found then to a righteous layman, for the righteous can purify the unright-eous without respect to orders. If this likewise fails, there is no cause for despair, for the Fathers agree that confession is then to be made to God.[2] How vague as yet were all conceptions on the sub-ject is seen in Gregory VII. assuming to absolve correspondents at a distance from their sins, by authority of Peter and Paul, and this without requiring confession or knowing what were the sins thus pardoned by writing,[3] and we shall see hereafter, when we come to treat of indulgences, that various popes about this period, in return for services rendered or expected, made indefinite promises of the pardon of sin without reference to the internal disposition of the sinner. All this was wholly irregular and had no influence on the general theories of the Church. St. Anselm of Lucca apparently pays no attention to the matter in his compilation, and about the year 1100 St. Ivo of Chartres, the highest authority of his day, virtually denies the power of the keys by citing in his *Decretum* the story of an abbot who expelled a negligent brother and received by an angel a message from God telling him never to condemn any one before the Lord should have judged him.[4] It is true that St. Ivo inserts the exaggerated description of bishops as keys of heaven from the Pseudo-Clement, but he likewise gives the emphatic con-

---

[1] Fulbert. Carnot. Serm. II. Cf. Ejusd. de Peccatis capitalibus.

[2] De occultis omni ecclesiastico ordini confiteri debemus ; de apertis vero solis convenit sacerdotibus, per quos Ecclesia, quæ publice novit et solvit et ligat. Sin nec in ordinibus ecclesiasticis cui confitearis invenis, vir mundus ubicumque sit requiratur. . . . Sed diligenter intuendum quid est quod sine determinatione cujusquam ordinis homo mundus lustrare immundum dicitur: et quosdam sanctorum Patrum legimus qui animas rexerunt, et tamen eorum ordinum nescimus. Quod si nemo cui confitearis invenitur, ne desperes quia in hoc Patrum conveniunt sententiæ ut Domino confitearis.—B Lan-franci Lib. de Celanda Confessione.

[3] Gregor. PP. VII. Regest. Lib. I. Ep. 34 ; Lib. II. Ep. 61 , Lib. VI. Ep. 2.

[4] S. Ivon. Carnot. Decr. P. II. c. 109.

demnation of the keys by St. Jerome,[1] and in a sermon he describes priests and bishops as mediators; they absolve and reconcile, but it is through eminent sanctity, and there is no allusion to any power derived from the apostles.[2] As a bishop himself, however, in performing his functions he could not abnegate the power of the keys, and in an Ash Wednesday sermon to penitents he speaks of the Church to which God through its pastors had given license to bind and to loose.[3] St. Bernard seems to know little of the power of the keys. In his book of counsel to his sister he says nothing as to her confessing to the priest and accepting penance and absolution: it is God alone who absolves from sin, and repentance is to be manifested by amendment and mortifications.[4] Elsewhere he dwells earnestly and repeatedly on the virtues of confession, which of itself suffices to wash away sins, and he only refers to priestly absolution in the most cursory manner.[5] He adopts without credit the passage of Smaragdus quoted above, while he also exalts the power of the priest over that of cherubim and seraphim, thrones, dominations and virtues, but this is because of the function of transubstantiating the Eucharist, no reference being made to the power of the keys.[6] Yet by this time the schoolmen were at work, commencing to lay the foundations for the structure of sacerdotalism. Hugh of St.

---

[1] Ibid. P. v. c. 225; P. xiv. c. 7; Ejusd. Panorm. Lib. v. c. 86.

[2] Ejusd. Serm. ii. [3] Ejusd. Serm. xiii.

[4] S. Bernardi Lib. de Modo bene vivendi c. 27.—"Deus misereatur tui et dimittat tibi omnia peccata tua; Deus retribuat tibi indulgentiam tuorum delictorum; Deus indulgeat tibi quidquid peccasti; Deus te lavet ab omni peccato."

[5] S. Bernardi Serm. de Diversis, Serm. xl.; Lib. ad Milites Templi c. 12; Epist. cxiii. § 4; Vit. S. Malachiæ c. 25; Serm. in Nat. Domini, Serm. ii. § 1; Serm. in Temp. Resurrect. § 10; Serm. iii. in Assumpt. B. Virginis; Serm. ii. in Festo Omn. Sanctt. § 13; Serm. de Diversis, Serm. xci. § 1.—"Omnia siquidem in confessione lavantur."

[6] S. Bernardi Lib. de modo bene vivendi cap. xxvii; Instructio Sacerdotis cap. xxiii.

The belief in transubstantiation effected by the priest of course vastly stimulated the growth of sacerdotalism and led directly to the assumption of the power of absolution. At an earlier period the fact that the character of the priest did not affect the efficacy of the mass was explained by saying that an invisible angel stood by who. at the words of consecration, changed the bread and wine into the body and blood.—Pœnitent. Vallicellian. II. cap. 49 (Wasserschleben, p. 565).

Victor, who did so much to create the theory of the sacraments, argues strenuously that the priest remits sin; he will not listen to those who hold the old theory that the sacerdotal function is merely to make manifest the pardon of God, and he explains the text, Matt. XVI. 18, to mean that priestly absolution precedes that of heaven—a step in which St. Bernard follows him in spite of the indifferent tone of the passages just cited.[1]

Still more illustrative of the vague and uncertain character of thought at this period is the position of Gratian in his authoritative compilation. He does not treat the question directly, though in his section on excommunication he inserts a portion of the passage of St. Jerome and other texts from St. Augustin and St. Gregory the Great which virtually deny the power of the keys, without giving any opposing opinions.[2] When he comes to treat of confession and satisfaction, however, which are recognized as conditions precedent of the exercise of the power to bind and to loose, he gives a long array of authorities to the effect that they are unnecessary for pardon, and then another array arguing their necessity. Between these two he confesses his inability to decide and leaves the question for the reader, merely remarking that each side is supported by wise and pious men. Thus up to this period the Church had arrived at no conclusion: it could not as yet decide whether the sinner should deal directly with God, or whether priestly interposition was necessary: it could not say that absolution was essential and it had not framed a working theory of the mysterious power of the keys.[3] Nay more. This non-committal position offended no one at the time. The Decretum was at once received in the most favorable manner by the great University of

---

[1] Hugon. de S. Victore de Sacramentis Lib. II. P. xiv. c. 8.—Bernardi Serm. I. in Festo SS. Pet. et Paul. n. 2.

[2] Gratian. c. 44, 45, 60, 62 Caus. XI. Q. iii.

[3] Gratian. Decr. post can. 89 Caus. XXXIII. Q. iii. Dist. 1. Gratian's only allusion to the keys is incidental (P. I. Dist. xx. *initio*) and there he evidently regards them as belonging to the *forum externum*—the power of receiving in or ejecting from the Church.

It is a curious fact that a century later, after the power of the keys had been generally accepted in the schools, the authoritative Gloss on the Decretum (Caus. XXXIII. Q. iii. Dist. 1, *in princip.*) gives various opinions as to the remission of sins, without alluding to priestly absolution, and sums up "Si tamen subtiliter intueamur gratiæ Dei non contritioni est attribuenda remissio peccatorum."

Bologna. Though not official its use spread everywhere and it was adopted universally as the foundation of the canon law. From time to time it was added to as papal legislation increased, but no one ever ventured to alter it. We shall see hereafter that Gratian's conservatism respecting the theory of the sacraments was as pronounced as in regard to confession and the power of the keys, and the fact shows in the clearest light how completely modern Catholic theology is the creation of the University of Paris. Gratian labored in Rome, where the chief concern was to develop a working body of canon law, and where little heed was taken of the speculations which were agitating the University. His compilation shows no trace of their influence and they evidently as yet were regarded by the curia as matters of mere theory, devoid of all interest for the practical churchman.[1]

Yet little as the practical churchman might imagine it, his labors were of small account in comparison with those of the schoolmen who, in the University of Paris, were destined to modify so greatly the whole structure of Catholic belief—to impose, we may almost say, a new religion on the foundations of the old faith. The two great development periods of ecclesiastical power were in the ninth and the twelfth centuries. In the former, the dissolution of the empire of Charlemagne gave rise to an era of social reconstruction during which feudalism and ecclesiasticism clutched at the fragments of shattered sovereignty. It was then that the Church emancipated itself from the State, and, by skilful use of the doctrines promulgated in the False Decretals, formulated the principles which eventually enabled Gregory VII. and his successors to triumph over monarchs.

. [1] Dante gives to Gratian full meed of praise for his labors—

> Quell' altro fiammeggiare esce del riso
> Di Gratian, che l'uno e l'altro foro
> Ajuto sì che piace in Paradiso.—Paradiso, X.

But when the schoolmen had succeeded in revolutionizing theology, canon law underwent a corresponding change, and the compilation of Gratian, as representing an earlier order of things, ceased to have the authority of law. It had done its work and was superseded. The admissions and conclusions which represented the ideas and practice of the twelfth century are unsuited to modern times, and though it retains its place in the Corpus Juris and the papal compilations which follow are merely addenda to it, it is not to be quoted as authority, save in its extracts from the Fathers.—Alph. de Leone, de Offic. et Potestate Confessarii, Recoll. II. n. 55.

No less important was the silent revolution of the twelfth century which gave to the Church unquestioned domination over the souls and consciences of men. As the human mind began to awaken after the dreary slumber of the Dark Ages, and thinkers once more commenced to debate the eternal questions of man's relations with God, and the Divine government of the universe, all culture and intelligence were at the service of the Church, and the answers to these questions could not fail to be given in favor of sacerdotalism. The race of schoolmen arose, whose insatiable curiosity penetrated into every corner of the known and of the unknowable, framing a system of dialectics through which their crudest and wildest speculations assumed the form of incontrovertible logical demonstration. With keen subtilty and untiring industry, through successive generations, they advanced from one postulate to another, building up the vast and complex fabric of Catholic theology. Fashioned by their hands the Christian faith emerged from the schools a very different thing from what it had been on entering, and the modifications which it underwent were all directed to the exaltation of ecclesiasticism. The whole was moulded into symmetry by the master hand of St. Thomas Aquinas, the most perfect product of scholasticism, who grasped all the labors of his predecessors and reduced them to a system which, despite the opposition of the Scotists, has held its place to the present day. Scarce more than thirty years after his death Dante already introduced him as the spokesman and greatest of the schoolmen.[1] His *Summa* might well be laid upon the altar at the council of Trent, along with the Scriptures and the Papal Decretals, for, of the three, it was the most important bulwark of the principles and policy which the Reformation sought to destroy. Leo XIII. is not mistaken in ceaselessly urging its study in all institutions of learning as a cure for the evils which threaten the Church, for the *Summa* is vastly better suited than the Pauline Epistles to the needs and desires of the papacy, and he was not wasting his revenues when he appropriated 300,000 lire to defray the expenses of a new edition of the writings of the Angelic Doctor, in which he tells us that all philosophy and all doctrine are to be found.[2]

---

[1] Paradiso x. xi.

[2] Ut longe lateque fluat Angelici Doctoris excellens sapientia, qua opprimendis opinionibus perversis nostrorum temporum fere nihil est aptius, conservandæ veritati nihil efficacius.—Leonis PP. XIII. Motu Proprio *Placere*

If Gratian was non-committal as to the power of the priest to remit sins it was not because the question had escaped discussion in

---

Nobis, 18 Jan. 1880. Cf. Epist. Encyc. *Æterni Patris*, 4 Aug. 1879; Litteræ *Jampridem*, 15 Oct. 1879; Epistola *Quanto Noster*, 12 Dec. 1884; Epistola *Qui te*, 19 Junii 1886.

In the Litt. Apostol. *Cum hoc sit*, 4 Aug. 1880, Aquinas is made the patron saint of all Catholic schools, academies and universities, which are ordered to pay him the appropriate cult. It would not be easy to overestimate the effect upon the minds of the younger generation of ecclesiastics of this persistent and determined effort to bind them in the chains of the thirteenth century and to hold them rigorously to medievalism. When the Church is thus training its ministers it can afford to shake hands with Democracy and to affect an external liberalism.

An instructive illustration of the system of exegesis which enabled the schoolmen to reach whatever conclusion was desired from a given text is to be found in the use made of the Raising of Lazarus (John, XI.) as a staple argument for the power of the keys. In fact a history of the development of that power can be traced in following the various explanations of the text. It will be remembered that, on that occasion, Christ was accompanied by Mary and Martha "and the Jews that were with her," and that in his preliminary prayer he asks for the miracle "because of the people that stand about have I said it that they may believe that thou hast sent me." Then he ordered Lazarus to come forth "and presently he that had been dead came forth bound feet and hands with winding bands; and his face was bound about with a napkin. Jesus said to them [αὐτοῖς]: Loose him and let him go." To any but a theological mind it would seem impossible to connect this simple and straightforward story with the power of the keys and absolution, but it was seriously adduced as scriptural proof and adapted to every successive change of doctrine.

St. Ambrose (De Pœnit. Lib. II. c. 7) employs it to illustrate the redemption and revivification of the sinner, but the lesson he draws from it shows how different was the belief of his day from that of subsequent ages. Christ performs the whole work, save in ordering the stone to be removed from the mouth of the tomb, showing that it is for us to remove the impediments and for him to resuscitate and to lead out from the tomb those released from their bonds. St. Augustin goes a step further; in his exegesis the unbelieving Jews who stood around become the disciples; Christ resuscitates the sinner and orders the disciples to remove the bands, which, as he argues, means that the Church loosens them (S. August. Serm. LXVII. c. 1, 2. Cf. Serm. XCVIII. c. 6; Serm. CCXCV. c. 3; Enarratio in Ps. CI. Serm. II. § 3; De Diversis Quæstionibus n. 65). With Gregory the Great there is a still further advance. Confession was now becoming a process inculcated by the Church, so Lazarus coming out of the tomb signifies the sinner's confession of his sin, after which the bishops can relieve him of the punishment incurred (S. Gregor. PP. I. Homil. in Evangel. XXVI. § 6). St. Eloi sees in the story a proof of justification by grace, for the priest can only loosen those whom God has revived

the schools. Hugh of St. Victor, who preceded him by some twenty years, is the first to treat the subject at length, and he tells us there

---

by sanctifying grace (S. Eligii Noviomens. Hom. XI.), thus showing that by his time it was assumed as a matter of course that the unbinding of Lazarus meant the release of the sinner by the priest. In some rituals of the eighth century there are allusions to Lazarus as typifying the soul buried in the tomb of its sins and revived by the call of God, but the comparison is carried no further (Missale Gothicum; Sacrament. Gallican. *ap.* Muratori Opp. T. XIII. P. III. pp. 300, 712). About 800 Alcuin uses Lazarus to prove the necessity of the intervention of the priest (Alcuini Epist. CXII.) and soon afterwards Benedict the Levite shows by him that the priest in the imposition of hands loosens the bonds of the sinner (Capitular. Lib. V. c. 127). Druthmar of Corbie, about the same time, uses the story as a lesson to priests to be cautious, because if the disciples had loosened Lazarus before Christ revived him they would have only produced a stench (Christiani Druthmari Exposit. in Matthæum XVI.). A tract of uncertain date, ascribed to St. Augustin, asserts that, in delivering Lazarus to the disciples to be unbound, Christ showed the power of loosing granted to priests (Pseud. August. de vera et falsa Pœnitentia c. X. n. 25). Then the schoolmen took hold of the story and made the most of it. Hugh of St. Victor sees in it that Christ only excites the heart to repentance by his grace, while the priest does the rest (Hugon. a S. Victore de Sacramentis Lib. II. P. xiv. c. 8), but a further refinement was soon discovered. We shall see how, to reconcile the competing functions of God and priest in the sacrament of penitence, the theologians shrewdly divided the effects of sin into *culpa* and *pœna*, and Peter Lombard utilizes Lazarus to prove that God pardons the *culpa* and leaves the *pœna* to the hands of the priest (Sententt. Lib. IV. Dist. xviii. § 4). Cardinal Pullus, in his vague effort to explain absolution, which neither he nor any of his contemporaries understood, takes refuge in Lazarus, who, when recalled to life by Christ, was bound and torpid until released by the disciples (Card. Rob. Pulli Sententt. Lib. VI. c. 60). Now purgatory was beginning to assert itself as the *pœna* left after the pardon of the *culpa*, and Richard of St. Victor has no difficulty in proving this also by Lazarus (Rich. a S. Victore de Potestate Ligandi etc. c. 10. Cf. c. 16, 17). Adam of Perseigne, on the other hand, tells us that the bonds of Lazarus, from which the priest releases the sinner, are three—dishonor of public crime, fear of hell and denial of the sacraments (Adami de Persennia Epist. XXVI.). Alexander Hales goes further than his predecessors in holding that Lazarus shows that the priest releases from damnation (Alex. de Ales Summæ P. IV. Q. xx. Membr. 6 Art. 3. Cf. Q. xxi. Membr. 1; Membr. 3 Art. 1), for he considers that the power of the keys extends to the *culpa* as well as the *pœna*. St. Thomas Aquinas uses Lazarus to prove that confession can be made only to priests (Summæ Supplem. Q. VIII. Art. 1), while Cardinal Henry of Susa finds in the story evidence to prove that pardon does not come from Christ alone but from the Trinity (Hostiens. Aureæ Summæ Lib. V. de Pœn. et. Remiss. n. 6). Astesanus contents himself with asserting that Christ instituted absolution in the mystery of the raising

were those who argued that God alone remits sins, that man has no share in it, and that to attribute such power to the priest is to make of him a God.[1] Hugh himself was an earnest sacerdotalist, who contributed greatly to the framing of the theory of the sacraments, but while he asserted the power of the keys, his uncertainty about it and the limitations with which he surrounded it show how hesitatingly the idea was received, even by its advocates. God, he says, has really and truly granted to priests the power of absolution ; they receive it in consecration from bishops, but some who are not consecrated have it, and some priests have it not; still as a rule it may be said that all priests and only priests have it, but if they use it unjustly he who is bound or loosed by them is not bound or loosed by God. In fact, priests do bind and loose many who are not bound or loosed by God, and their power is conditioned on its being exercised in conformity with the will of God[2]—all of which showed common sense vainly struggling with dogmatism and reaching the conclusion that God, in order to carry out the scheme of the Atonement, had invented a plan of salvation so vicious that it resulted in the blind leading the blind. In another passage he is rather more decided : God, it is

---

of Lazarus (Astesani Summæ de Casibus Lib. v. Tit. ii. Art. 4). On the other hand, John Gerson, who was inclined to miminize sacerdotal power, finds in Lazarus proof that Christ absolves and that the priest only makes the fact manifest to the people (Joh. Gersoni de Reform. Eccles. c. 28). Nicholas Weigel rallies to the support of sacerdotalism by discovering that Christ handed over Lazarus to St. Peter himself to unbind (N. Weigel Claviculæ Indulgentialis c. 9). The Council of Trent had the good sense to omit all reference to this much abused text, but subsequent theologians have not always imitated its discretion. Willem van Est gravely tells us that Christ gave Lazarus to the apostles to unbind and that this prefigures the sinner vivified by Jesus and absolved by the priest (Estius in IV. Sentent. Dist. XVII. ? 3) and he thinks so much of the argument that he recurs to it repeatedly (Dist. XVIII. ?? 1, 4); Bellarmine contends vigorously for its significance against Calvin (De Pœnitent. Lib. III. c. 3); while Binterim, in his efforts to prove that the old reconciliation was modern absolution, brings in the inevitable Lazarus as confidently as though he had anything to do with the question (Denkwürdigkeiten, Bd. V. Th. III. p. 222).

The story of the leper (Matt. VIII.) and that of the ten lepers (Luke XVII.) were also largely used as evidence of the power of absolution. See Rich. a S. Victore de Potestati Ligandi etc. c. xii. xiii. xiv. xv.; Thomæ Waldensis de Sacramentis Cap. cxlii.

[1] Hugon. de S. Victore de Sacramentis Lib. II. P. xiv. c. 8.
[2] *Loc. cit.*—Ejusd. Summæ Sententt. Tract. VI. c. 14.

true, pardons for contrition, but the Church has yet to be satisfied; if the sinner has no opportunity to confess, the pardon is good; if he has opportunity and does not confess he is not absolved for the ministry of the priest is necessary in such case.[1] Abelard, who was the *enfant terrible* of the schools, was not likely to allow the rising claims of the power of the keys to pass without question. He argues that God had not bestowed on their successors the wisdom and sanctity which he had granted to the apostles, and he quotes Origen, Jerome, Augustin and Gregory to prove that the sentence of a bishop is void if it is not in accord with divine justice.[2]

Difficulties evidently arose as soon as the powers claimed for the Church were made the subject of investigation and definition. The basis on which they rested was so narrow and the claims to which they gave rise were becoming so broad that the acquiescence which they enjoyed when they were little more than a theoretical point of dogma required some more positive exposition. The schoolmen moreover were subjecting everything to analysis and were called upon in debate to furnish dialectic demonstration and some kind of proof of all assertions, so that questions arose on all sides and centuries of discussion were still required before arguments could be agreed upon to substantiate all the pretensions of the Church—in fact the authoritative declarations of the Council of Trent were necessary to establish a formula intended to be final. Richard of St. Victor tells us that some asserted that the successors of the Apostles could release from damnation; others asked whether a priest can loose a sinner and bind a righteous man; if he can remit the sins of an impenitent man and retain those of a penitent.[3] These were all

---

[1] Hugon. de S. Victore Summæ Sententt. Tract. VI. c. 11.

[2] P. Abælardi Ethica, c. 26.—St. Bernard includes these views among the errors of Abelard which he pointed out to the college of Cardinals (S. Bernardi Epist. CLXXXVIII.). In another letter (Epist. CXCII.) he says of him "Nihil vidit per speculum et in ænigmate, sed facie ad faciem omnia intuetur." Similarly the prelates of the council of Sens, in 1140, writing to Innocent II. about the appeal which Abelard had made against their sentence of condemnation, characterize him in the same way—"Ascendit usque ad cœlos et descendit usque ad abyssos; nihil est quod lateat eum, sive in profundum inferni sive in excelsum supra" (Gousset, Actes de la Province ecclés. de Reims, II. 224).

These expressions describe accurately enough the besetting weakness of all the schoolmen, but they usually escaped condemnation because they worked in unison with sacerdotalism.

[3] Rich. a S. Victore de Potestate Ligandi et Solvendi cap. 1.

pertinent questions, for if the texts in Matthew and John mean what the Church claims for them they mean this, and the theologians, as we shall see, have never been able to frame a satisfactory solution of this problem.

It was not easy to reconcile the theory of the keys with the supremacy of an all-wise God, and the earlier schoolmen, like Hugh of St. Victor, while manfully asserting the power as a general theorem, could not avoid surrounding it with conditions which practically reduced it almost to a nullity, by denying to it all certainty in application. When the vague declamations of emotional preachers like Chrysostom, or the confident assertions of the Forged Decretals were submitted to the scrutiny of minds trained in all the subtilties of dialectics, difficulties presented themselves which seemed incapable of settlement. To consider them all and the conflicting opinions of the leading doctors concerning them would carry us too far, but the chief of them may be grouped under three heads—the share to be allotted respectively to God and to the priest in the pardon of sin, the nature and certainty of priestly absolution, and the guidance which priests, who as a class were notoriously ignorant, might expect in the exercise of the awful authority conferred upon them.

As regards the function of the power of the keys in the remission of sin, or how much was contributed by it and how much directly by God, Peter Lombard reviews despairingly the contradictory utterances of the doctors, and concludes that we may believe that God alone releases or retains sins, and yet he has granted to the Church the power to bind and to loose, but he and the Church bind and loose in different ways. He only dismisses the sin, purifying the soul from its stains and releasing it from the debt of eternal death, and this power he did not concede to the priest, but only that of showing that men are bound or loosed, for though a man may be loosed before God, he cannot be so considered in the face of the Church save by the judgment of the priest.[1] This reduced the

---

[1] P. Lombardi Sententt. Lib. IV. Dist. 18, §§ 5, 6. In order to give the priest some substantive power of binding and loosing he adds (§ 7) that the priest binds when he imposes penance and looses when he remits part of it or admits to communion those who are purged by its performance.

The place of Peter Lombard—the "magister" *par excellence*—is unique in the history of theology, for he was the first who brought into order the newly growing science of scholastic theology. The schoolmen were everywhere pushing their

priestly function to the wholly subordinate one of guessing and announcing the judgments of God; it gave rise, as we shall see, to vigorous discussion and was finally cast aside. Although it seems to have satisfied Peter himself, he also timidly brings forward, as an opinion held by some, a division of the pardon of sin into the remission of guilt and the remission of punishment—into *culpa* and *pœna* —in which God removes the sin by cleansing the soul, and allows the priest to remit the punishment of eternal damnation.[1] Cardinal Pullus, a contemporary, seems to have had a vague conception of this distinction between *culpa* and *pœna*, which was destined to become of such supreme importance, for in answering the question why, if contrition and faith secure pardon, confession and satisfaction should still be required, he urges the commands of the Church,

---

subtile and daring enquiries into all the secrets of life and all the mysteries of the invisible world. Not content with the simple faith inculcated by Scripture, they sought to support it, and sometimes to supplant it, with reason, and to complete with their dialectics the work which St. Augustin had commenced. If, as has been argued, Peter Lombard sought to set bounds to their dangerous labors, to define the limits beyond which they should not stray, and to decide all questions finally, he signally failed. His labors became simply the starting-point for future generations of schoolmen; his Sentences were the recognized basis of all teaching in the schools, and almost the highest ambition of all succeeding scholars was to write a commentary upon them—a hundred and sixty of these are said to have been composed by English theologians alone and even as late as the commencement of the seventeenth century the learned Willem van Est wrote one in four folios which continued to be reprinted for more than a hundred years longer. But in the eager wrangling of the schools it was not to be expected that their skilled dialectitians would be content with what Peter imagined that he had established, and the process of adding dogma to dogma continued with greater zeal than ever, for in place of reaching a finality he had simply furnished them with a foundation on which to construct more and more subtile theories as to the details of the mysterious unknown.

[1] Quidam arbitrati sunt. . . . Solus enim Christus, non sacerdos, animam resuscitat, ac pulsis tenebris interioribus et maculis eam illuminat et mundat, qui animæ faciem lavat; debitum vero æternæ pœnæ solvere concessit sacerdotibus—Sententt. Lib. IV. Dist. 18 § 4.

Hugh Archbishop of Rouen is apparently one of those alluded to by Lombard as dissociating the pardon of sin from the remissions of its punishment (Hugon. Rotomag. Dialogor. Lib. V. Interrog. iii.). Efforts have been made to trace it back to St. Augustin (De Peccatorum Meritis et Remissione Lib. II. c. 34) but the passage relied upon is only an endeavor to explain why, when death was the punishment decreed for the primal sin, men who are relieved from all sin, both original and actual, should still be obliged to die.

and adds that the penance delivers the sinner from purgatory.[1] This was an important contribution to the theory, in the substitution of purgatory for hell, for the opinion recorded by Peter was monstrous, that a sinner might be pardoned by God and yet be condemned to eternal perdition for lack of priestly ministrations.

These two points, first as to whether the priest absolved or merely made manifest the absolution by God, and second, the distinction between *culpa* and *poena* and the power of the priest over one or over both, were only settled after long and varying discussion, and it will be more convenient briefly to follow them out separately. In these as in other investigations into changes of belief, it is to be borne in mind that these were not mere academic debates but the expressions of faith actually held and taught. In the plastic condition of medieval theology there were a vast number of unsettled questions which might eventually be decided in one way or in another. General councils rarely troubled themselves with such matters, while the Holy See looked placidly on without uttering final definitions, save the brief and imperfect statement in the Decree of Union with the Armenians drawn up by Eugenius IV. at the council of Florence in 1439, and until the council of Trent was obliged by the heretics to formulate an authoritative exposition of the faith we have no surer source of information as to the details of medieval belief than the writings of the leading scholars which convey to us the doctrines taught in the principal schools. Occasionally a university might condemn a proposition or a series of propositions, or the opinions of a heretic such as Wickliffe or Huss or Pedro of Osma might be anathematized, but outside of these scanty materials it is to the books of such men as St. Ramon de Peñafort, Alexander Hales, Bonaventura, Aquinas and others down to St. Antonino, Prierias and Caietano that we must turn to know what our forefathers really believed.

The theory that the priest does not absolve but merely makes manifest the absolution by God had its warrant in the passage of St. Jerome cited above, and it is clearly indicated in the middle of the

---

[1] Card. Rob. Pulli Sententt. Lib. VI. c. 59. How perfectly tentative was all this is seen in Pullus's next remark (Ib. c. 60) that he who confesses and is absolved is held to punishment until his penance is performed, but what that punishment is God only knows.

ninth century by Druthmar of Corbie.[1] It is true that the high
sacerdotal Hugh of St. Victor rejects it,[2] but when Peter Lombard
adopted it he only expressed the prevailing opinion of his time.[3]
Cardinal Pullus, who was papal chamberlain and an undoubted authority at the period, not only thus explains the function of the priest
but adds that the only use of absolution is to quiet the anxieties of
the penitent.[4] Not long afterwards Richard of St. Victor attacks
this opinion as so frivolous and so absurd that it is to be laughed at
rather than confuted, but, in the insuperable difficulty of assigning
their respective shares to God and the priest, he reduces the functions
of the latter to that of an automaton : according to his theory what
the priest really does is not what he may wish to do or what he may
think that he does ; it is decided not by his wishes and acts but by
the immutable laws of God, and these laws moreover provide only
for the remission of sins committed through infirmity or ignorance ;
for those committed through malice there is no pardon, they are
remitted through penitence, but yet not remitted, and the final punishment will be exacted of them, for they are sins against the Holy
Ghost.[5] Toward the close of the twelfth century Peter of Poitiers,

---

[1] S. Hieron. Comment. in Evangel. Matthæi Lib. III. c. xvi. v. 19.—Christiani Druthmari Exposit in Matt. xvi.

[2] Hugon. S. Victor. Summæ Sententt. Tract. VI. c. 11.

[3] It is evidently in this sense that we must understand the well-known *post-
mortem* absolution of Abelard by Peter the Venerable of Cluny. Abelard had
died in the Cluniac house of Châlons, in 1142, confessing his sins and receiving
the viaticum, and though there is nothing said as to absolution, Peter assumes
that the viaticum was to him the pledge of eternal life. The body was taken
to the Paraclete and buried there, when Heloise asked for a sealed patent of
absolution to be hung over the tomb. Peter sent it duly sealed in this form
"Ego Petrus Cluniacensis qui Petrum Abailardum in monachum Cluniacensem
suscepi, et corpus ejus furtim delatum Heloisæ abbatissæ et monialibus Para-
cleti concessi, auctoritate omnipotentis Dei et omnium sanctorum absolvo eum
pro officio ab omnibus peccatis suis."—Pet. Venerab. Epist. Lib. IV. Ep. 21 ;
Lib. VI. Epp. 21, 22, cum not. Andreæ Chesnii (Migne, CLXXXIX. 428).

[4] A peccatis ergo presbyter solvit, non utique quod peccata dimittat sed quod
dimissa sacramento pandat. Et quid est opus pandi nisi ut consolatio fiat pœni-
tenti ?—Card. Rob. Pulli Sententt. Lib. VI. c. 61.

[5] Rich. a S. Victore de Potestate Ligandi etc. c. 11, 12.—Ejusd. de Statu Inte-
rioris Hominis Tract. II. cap. iii.
Dante classes Richard of S. Victor among the most eminent of theologians—
Vedi oltre fiammeggiar l'ardente spiro
D'Isidoro, di Beda, e di Riccardo,
Che a considerar fù più che viro.—Paradiso, X.

Adam of Perseigne and Master Bandinus all adopt the views of Peter Lombard that the priest only manifests who are bound and who loosed,[1] while Peter Cantor, when he declares that repentance can end only with life if we are to hope for pardon, denies inferentially that the priest can even make manifest a pardon by God.[2] The manifestation theory maintained its place in the schools for a considerable period. It was taught by St. Ramon de Peñafort, the most distinguished authority of the first half of the thirteenth century.[3] Alexander Hales is not willing formally to admit it, but he approaches to it very closely,[4] and so does St. Bonaventura, who endeavors to reconcile the contending opinions by arguing that as to *culpa* the priest manifests the pardon and as to *pœna* he grants it.[5] Aquinas, while he accepts it, endeavors to explain it away ; the priest by the power of the keys has control to some extent over both *culpa* and

---

[1] Petri Pictaviens. Sententt. Lib. III. c. 16.—Adami de Persennia Epist. XX. —Magist. Bandini Sentt. Lib. IV. Dist. 18.

Peter of Poitiers was the most eminent disciple of Peter Lombard. He was chancellor of the University of Paris and one of the leading theologians of the day.

[2] P. Cantoris Verb. abbreviat. cap. 145.

[3] Judicium sacerdotis qui auctoritate clavium ligat et solvit in terris, id est, ostendit esse ligatum vel solutum a Deo.—S. Raymundi de Pennaforte Summæ Lib. III. Tit. XXXV. § 5.

[4] Alex. de Ales Summæ P. IV. Q. XXI. Membr. 1.

[5] S. Bonavent. in Lib. IV. Sentt. Dist. XVIII. P. 1. init. ; Ibid. Art. 2 Q. 1.

Willem van Est admits that Lombard's opinion was followed by a host of authoritative doctors but adds that it is false and erroneous leading directly to the Wickliffite heresy—"Si homo debite fuerit contritus omnis confessio exterior est ei superflua et inutilis"—condemned by the council of Constance (Artic. Joann. Wicliff n. 7, Harduin. VIII. 299), and that it was finally set aside at Trent.—(Estius in IV. Sentt. Dist. XVII. § 1). It was also condemned as a heresy by the council of Alcalá, in 1479, when taught at Salamanca by Pedro de Osma (Alfonsi de Castro adv. Hæreses Lib. IV. s. v. *Confessio*).

The Tridentine Catechism reconciles the discrepancy by describing the degree of contrition requisite for the remission of sin as so intense and ardent that few mortals can attain it, wherefore God in his mercy has supplied the sacrament of penitence which enables a lower degree of repentance to suffice. —Catech. ex Decr. Con. Trident. De Pœnit. Sacram. c. 7.

Azpilcueta, on the other hand, asserts that this sufficing contrition is frequent, and cites in support a host of authorities, including the Council of Trent itself, Sess. XIV. De Pœnit. c. 4.—Azpilcuetæ Manuale Confessarior. c. 1 n. 24.

pœna, though he can exercise this power only on those properly prepared.[1] This however only introduced a new difficulty which Aquinas strove to meet by asserting that the use of the keys was only efficient when in accordance with the will of God, and that when the priest disregarded the divine impulse his action was invalid,[2] which was even more damaging than the old theory, for it denied him even the power of manifesting that the penitent was absolved. Duns Scotus endeavors to escape the manifestation theory by adducing the power of the sacrament which he administers, through which he becomes the arbiter between the sinner and God.[3] In 1317 Astesanus admits that a penitent may win absolution from God, in which case the priest would only have to make it manifest, but as the priest cannot know this he is obliged to give absolution and impose penance, which is not amiss as it tends to increase the accumulation of merits in the Church.[4] Shortly afterwards Durand de St. Pourçain rejects wholly as incompatible with the dignity of the sacrament the idea that the priest only manifests the absolution.[5] At the council of Constance Chancellor Gerson renewed the assertion[6] but before the council was ended, in 1418,

---

[1] S. Th. Aquin. Summæ Suppl. Q. XVIII. Art. 2, 3.—Opusc. XXII. c. 2.

It is strange that so acute a reasoner as Aquinas should not see that, as the texts of Matthew and John, on which the power of the keys is based, impose no limitation on its exercise, any limitation however reasonable is fatal to the significance of the texts. Either *tantum valent quantum sonant* or else they are worthless. They must be accepted as they stand or it must be admitted that they have no such meaning as that attributed to them.

[2] Summæ Suppl. Q. XVIII. Art. 1, 4.

[3] Jo. Scotus in Lib. IV. Sententt. Dist. XIX. Q. 1.

[4] Astesani Summæ de Casibus Lib. V. Tit. 23.

Astesanus summarizes four theories of the *modus operandi* of the keys, current at the period—I. That of Peter Lombard, that the priest only makes manifest the pardon. II. That of Bonaventura and Duns Scotus that they have no power of their own but operate by the divine virtue in coöperation. III. Another of Bonaventura that they operate through deprecation and impetration. IV. That of Aquinas and Peter of Tarentaise that they work instrumentally in predisposing to grace and justification and immediately effecting this grace and justification (Cf. Aquin. in IV. Sentt. Dist. xviii. Q. 1, Art. 2). Of these four Astesanus prefers the second.—Ibid. Lib. V. Tit. xxxvii. Q. 1.

William of Ware also rejects Lombard's theory and inclines rather to Duns Scotus. The sacrament produces its effect *opere operato*, through which God works upon the sinner.—Vorrillong super IV. Sentt. Dist. xiv.

[5] Durandi de S. Portiano Comment. super Sententt. Lib. IV. Dist. xviii, Q. 3 § 6.

[6] Jo. Gersoni de Reform. Ecclesiæ c. xxviii. (Von der Hardt, I. v. 136).

Martin V. condemned it by implication when he included among the errors of Wickcliffe and Huss the denial of priestly power of absolution,[1] and Thomas of Walden, in controverting the Wickliffite errors, assumes as a matter of course that the absolution by the priest precedes the absolution by God.[2] St. Antonino tells us that contrition deletes the sin *quoad Deum*, and the penance imposed in confession manifests that it is deleted *quoad ecclesiam*.[3] In 1439 the Council of Florence formally declared that the sacrament effects absolution.[4] Subsequently Prierias describes the manifestation of the absolution of the penitent as the first operation of the functions of the keys.[5] About the same period Cardinal Caietano shows how impossible it was for the keenest minds to construct a consistent theory out of the incongruous mixture of divine and human elements, for in one passage he virtually admits that the priest manifests the pardon by God, while in another he denies it.[6] The Dominican Giovanni Cagnazzo (or de Tabia) in 1518 not only asserts it but adds that the keys may err and the absolution not be ratified in heaven.[7] Domingo Soto on the other hand denounces the theory of manifestation as blasphemous towards the Church and impious as regards Scripture.[8] In fact, it too nearly approached the views of the heretics to be permitted, and the Council of Trent in 1551 solemnly blasted it with the anathema, thus branding as heresy what had been received as orthodoxy by nearly the whole Church through the greater part of the twelfth and thirteenth centuries.[9] Yet the authorities in its favor were so numerous and unimpeachable that van Est feels it necessary to disprove it by an exhaustive argument.[10]

[1] C. Constant. Sess. ult. (Harduin. VIII. 915).

[2] Thomæ Waldens. de Sacramentis cap. CXLIV. This work may be regarded as authoritative. It was written by command of Martin V. who formally approved it after examination by theologians delegated for the purpose.

[3] S. Antonini Summæ P. I. Tit. xx. (Ed. Venet. 1582, T. I. fol. 299 col. 1).

[4] C. Florent. Decr. Unionis (Harduin. IX. 440).

[5] Summa Sylvestrina s. v. *Claves* § 4.

[6] Caietani Tract. IV. De Attritione Q. 4; Tract. XVIII. De Confessione Q. 5.

[7] Summa Tabiena s. v. *Sacerdos* § 4, 5.

[8] Dom. Soto Comment. in IV. Sententt. Dist. XIV. Q. 1, Art. 3.

[9] Si quis dixerit absolutionem sacramentalem sacerdotis non esse actum judicialem, sed nudum ministerium pronuntiandi et declarandi remissa esse peccata confitenti, modo tantum credat se esse absolutum . . . . anathema sit.—C. Trident. Sess. XIV. De Pœnitent. can. 9.—Cf. Ferraris Prompta Bibliotheca s. v. *Absolvere* Art. III. n. 12.

[10] Estius in IV. Sententt. Dist. XVIII. § 1.

An even more important revolution in the doctrine of the Church is to be found in its teachings on the subject of *culpa* and *pœna*—the remission of guilt and the remission of punishment, into which the pardon of sin became divided. As this had an important bearing upon the theory of indulgences it will repay a somewhat minute examination into the varying opinions to which it gave rise. Originally there was no conception of any differentiation between pardon of sin and remission of punishment; the one included the other.[1] A foreshadowing of the distinction is to be found in Hugh of St. Victor, who tells us that the sinner is bound both by sin and the penalty of sin.[2] Abelard seems to have some conception of it when he says that penance is useful as an expiation for the temporal punishment which remains after contrition has secured pardon for the sin, but his hazy explanation shows that the theory had not yet been worked out.[3] St. Bernard apparently knows nothing of it in his numerous exhortations to confession and good works as remitting sin. We have seen it take a somewhat more definite shape in the works of Peter Lombard and Cardinal Pullus, but to Richard of St. Victor belongs the honor of fashioning it into the form in which it left a profound and indelible impression on Latin Christianity, though as we shall see it underwent important modifications with the advance of sacerdotalism. He argues that although God alone can dissolve the obligation of sin he sometimes seeks the co-operation of his ministers. As soon as the sinner experiences true repentance, the eternal punishment due to his sin is changed to a temporal one, the vindictive fires of hell give place to the cleansing fires of purgatory, but release from purgatory is conditioned on confession to the priest and the performance of the penance which he may enjoin. This is the function which God commits to his ministers, and this is the part which they play in the sacrament of penitence, though they are not always necessary, for God sometimes performs this also, and sometimes commits it to those who are not priests. This grace of co-operation with God some enjoy at one time and some at another, but priests have it always through the power to bind and to loose.

---

[1] Sacramentarium Gregorianum (Muratori Opp. T. XIII. P. ii. p. 1043).

[2] Hugon. de S. Victore Summæ Sententt. Tract. vi. c. 11. Cf. Ejusd. de Sacramentis Lib. ii. P. xiv. c. 2.

[3] P. Abælardi Expos. Theolog. Christianæ cap. 37.

Moreover God releases the debt of damnation only under condition of seeking absolution from the priest, if it is possible, and of performing the penance that he may enjoin, for if this is neglected the sinner is consigned to eternal punishment.[1] This theory of *culpa* and *pœna* was comprehensive enough to reconcile the old practice of the Church with the new ideas which were fermenting in the schools. It is true that it met with opposition from those who could not understand how a sin could be said to be remitted when the penitent was still subjected to prolonged punishment,[2] while on the other hand there were already zealous sacerdotalists who claimed that although God remitted the sin it was the priest who granted release from hell.[3] The time however had not yet come for conceding such powers to the ministers of the Church, and the theory of Richard of St. Victor obtained general currency. Although Master Bandinus does not recognize it Alain de Lille virtually does.[4] Early in the thirteenth century the idea had become generally diffused, so that the good monk Cæsarius of Heisterbach teaches it, though he evidently had no very clear conception of its working.[5] Ramon de Peñafort adopts it, although he eliminates purgatory, when he says that for every mortal sin there is a double punishment, the eternal which is remitted by contrition, and the temporal which is inflicted by the Church.[6] William of Paris admits the division between *culpa* and

---

[1] Rich. a S. Victore de Potestate Ligandi c. 2, 3, 4, 6, 7, 8. Of course it was not easy for these early explorers in the unknown to be at all times consistent and it need not surprise us to find in another passage (c. 23) that sacerdotal absolution liberates from both hell and purgatory.

[2] Sunt adhuc qui mirantur et quærunt quomodo dicitur Deus et Dei ministri peccata remittere cum profecto inveniatur uterque pœnitentium peccata et puniendo expiare et expiando punire. Quæ est, inquiunt, ista remissio ubi exigitur diuturna sæpe et satis molesta expiatio?—Rich. a S. Victore de Potest. Ligand. c. 23.

[3] Petri Pictaviens. Sententt. Lib. III. c. 16.—Peter readily disposes of this claim by showing that when God remits the sin the sinner necessarily is in charity and as such becomes worthy of eternal life and not of eternal punishment.

[4] Alani de Insulis Lib. de Pœnitentia (Migne CCX. 299).

[5] Cæsar. Heisterb. Dial. Dist. III. c. 1, 40.

[6] Nota ergo quod pro quolibet peccato mortali duplex pœna debetur, temporalis videlicet et æterna: æterna remittitur per cordis contritionem; remanet postea temporalis ab ecclesia infligenda.—S. Raymundi Summæ Lib. III. Tit. XXXV. § 5.

pœna, but his confused and labored explanation only shows how vague were as yet the conceptions of the schools, and in a subsequent passage, where he ascribes to the sacrament infusion of grace and liberation from both hell and purgatory, he virtually eliminates contrition as an element of complete pardon.[1] Alexander Hales defines it clearly in a completed shape : contrition justifies from the *culpa* of mortal sin and changes the eternal punishment to the temporal one of purgatory, which God remits if the penitent performs the penance enjoined on him by the priest, but not otherwise ; thus Christ releases from hell and the priest from purgatory.[2] In this way a division was established between the functions of God and the priest which seemed to promise finality, for its acceptance by such authorities as Cardinal Henry of Susa and St. Bonaventura show that it became firmly established in the schools and was taught as the rule of practice.[3] Having gained this much, however, sacerdotalism asked for more. It was not satisfied with the limitation on its powers inferred from the premises that true contrition was requisite in order to free the sinner from the *culpa*, without which the priest could not remit the *pœna;*[4] this left the value of absolution perfectly uncertain, and granted too much efficacy to the unassisted striving of man to reach God. To meet this we have seen (p. 102) how the Franciscan school taught the agency of the sacrament in converting attrition into contrition. Before this was accepted by the Dominicans the latter solved the difficulty in another way by attributing to absolution a power over the *culpa* as well as over the *pœna*. Alexander Hales will only admit that the priest by prayer can exercise some influence over God in the remission of the *culpa*, as any righteous man can, without personally granting it, and he even has to resort to the treasure of salvation to explain the power of dimin-

---

[1] Guillel. Paris. de Sacram. Pœnitent. c. 5, 21 (Ed. 1674, T. I. pp. 464, 510).

[2] Alex. de Ales Summæ P. IV. Q. xvii. Membr. 4 art. 3 ; Membr. 6 art. 3.— "Dicendum quod aliud et aliud in peccato remittit Christus et sacerdos ; quia Christus culpam et pœnam æternam et sacerdos pœnam purgatoriam et aliquid de pœna præsenti taxata in canone si discretioni ejus videtur."

[3] Hostiens. Aureæ Summæ Lib. v. De Pœnit. et Remiss. § 46.—S. Bonavent. in Lib. IV. Sententt. Dist. XVIII. P. I. art. 2, Q. 1, 2.—Durand. de S. Portian. Comment. super Sentt. Lib. IV. Dist. xiv. Q. 2, § 9.

[4] Si autem aliquis non vere contritus est, sacerdotes eum non possunt absolvere, quia cum culpa remissa non est, pœna demi non potest.—Johan. de Deo Pœnitentialis Lib. I. c. 1.

ishing the *pœna;*[1] Aquinas ventures further, though his confused
and contradictory utterances prove that he had no clear opinions on
the subject: whatever virtue repentance has in the remission of the
culpa is due to the power of the keys; to this the efforts of the
penitent are secondary, and thus the sacrament removes both *culpa*
and *pœna*, yet God alone removes the *culpa* and the priest contrib-
utes in some undefined way, not as an efficient but as a predisposing
cause.[2] Yet in an earlier work he had followed Alexander Hales
in an explanation which threatened a complete revolution in the
doctrine of the keys, by attributing their power to the merits of
Christ and the saints, forming the treasure of the Church. This he
utilized to explain that the keys derive their efficacy from the treasure, of which they apply an equivalent to satisfy God for the sins
of the penitent.[3]

---

[1] Alex. de Ales Summæ P. IV. Q. xxi. Membr. i.; Membr. ii. art. 1.

[2] S. Th. Aquinat. Summæ P. iii. Q. lxii. art. 1; Q. lxiv. art. 1; Q. lxxxiv.
art. 3; Q. lxxxvi. art. 4, 6; Supplem. Q. x. art. 3; Q. xvii. art. 3; Summæ
contra Gentiles Lib. iv. cap. 72.

In another passage Aquinas represents God as the efficient cause and the
keys as only an instrument, yet indispensable, like water in baptism.—Opusc.
xxii. cap. 2.

[3] Dicendum est quod meritum ecclesiæ est sub dispensationem clavium, et
idcirco tam ex merito Christi quam aliorum qui sunt de ecclesia, ecclesiæ
claves efficaciam habent.—S. Th. Aquin. in IV. Sentt. Dist. xviii. Q. ii.
art. 5.

This is a simple explanation of the virtue of sacramental absolution which
has long maintained itself (Caietani Tract. iv. De attritione Q. iv.; Dom. Soto
in IV. Sentt. Dist. xxi. Q. ii. art. 3; Palmieri Tract. de Pœnit. p. 422). As
the treasure, however, was assumed to be the basis of indulgences and as these
became the exclusive prerogative of the pope, who was asserted to be the sole
dispenser of the treasure, it was seen that there was danger in admitting the
priest to such control over it, and some theologians restricted his function in
this respect to applying it in diminishing the penance, and thus explaining
the nominal satisfaction which, as we shall see hereafter, gradually replaced
the severity of the canons (Astesani Summæ de Casibus Lib. v. Tit. xxxvii.
Q. 2). Thus when Luther pointed out that if the sinner is released by the
application of the merits of Christ there is no exercise of the power of the
keys, Ambrogio Caterino retorted that it is impious to question the power of
the keys and that the application of the treasure is made only to those already
absolved by the keys (Ambr. Catherini adv. impia ac valde pestifera Martini
Lutheri Dogmata Lib. v.—Florentiæ, 1520, fol. 89). The council of Trent
discreetly avoided all allusion to the treasure in its definitions as to the sacrament of penitence and only referred to it as removing original sin in baptism

These exaggerations of the priestly function by no means met with prompt acceptance. The Franciscans held to the old landmarks and Duns Scotus even casts doubts upon the division of *culpa* from *pœna*.[1] In 1317 Astesanus holds that contrition liberates from *culpa*, leaving only the *pœna* to be remitted by the priest, though he of course follows what was by that time the accepted rule that true contrition includes a vow of sacramental confession, and his vagueness as to the character of the *pœna* shows how hazy as yet was the scholastic mind on the subject.[2] William of Ware substantially agrees with him.[3] Pietro d'Aquila is even more reactionary : God does not limit his power to the sacraments but only confers his grace on those who have sufficient *dispositio congrua ;* contrition (including the vow to confess) will remit all sins and even serve also as satisfaction ; it is only imperfect contrition that has to be supplemented by penance ; the function of the priest and the power of the keys are confined exclusively to the temporal *pœna* of which they can remit only a portion.[4]

As a rule the Dominicans followed Aquinas and developed his views. Durand de S. Pourçain argues that if the contrition is insufficient the power of the keys extends over the *culpa* and by the application of grace supplies what is lacking.[5] Peter of Palermo

---

and as employed in indulgences (C. Trident. Sess. v. De Pecc. Orig. § 3 ; Sess. XXI. De Reform. cap. xi.).

The questions involved are intricate and abstruse, as the schoolmen in framing the theory of the sacraments were unanimous in ascribing their virtue to the Passion of Christ.—P. Lombard. Sentt. Lib. IV. Dist. ii. n. 2.—Alex. de Ales Summæ P. IV. Q. v. art. 4, Membr. iii. § 7.—S. Th. Aquinat. Summæ P. III. Q. xlix. art. 2 ad 2 ; Q. lii. art. 8, ad 2 ; Q. lxi. art. 1 ad 3 ; Q. lxii. art. 5 ; Q lxix. art. 1 ad 3.

[1] Bart. Mastrius in IV. Sentt. Disp. VI. Q. ix. Art. 6 (Amort de Indulgentiis II. 182-3).

[2] Astesani Summæ de Casibus Lib. v. Tit. xix. Q. 2 ; Tit. xxxvi. Q. 2.

[3] Vorrilong super IV. Sentt. Dist. XVIII.

[4] P. de Aquila in IV. Sentt. Dist. XIV. Q. 3 ; Dist. XV. Q. 1 ; Dist. XVII. Q. 1 ; Dist. XVIII. Q. 1, 2.

Pietro d'Aquila was highly esteemed by Clement VI., who, in 1347, made him bishop of Sant-Angeli de' Lombardi and transferred him the next year to the see of Trivento. He was one of the most eminent of the Scotists and was honored with the appellation of *Scotellus.* His commentary on the Sentences was printed at Speyer in 1480 and in Venice in 1501 and 1600.

[5] Dur. de S. Portiano in IV. Sentt. Dist. XVII. Q. ii. ; Q. iii. §§ 4, 5 ; Dist. XVIII. Q. ii. §§ 3, 7.

admits that Gregory the Great taught that the priest only makes manifest the pardon of the sinner, but he says that this is false except in case of sufficing contrition; where there is only attrition the sacrament converts it into contrition and thus the priest absolves from both *culpa* and *pœna*.[1] St. Antonino of Florence, though a Dominican, however, recurs to the older theory that repentance remits the *culpa* and if perfect the *pœna*, wholly or partially, but he adds the saving clause that the penitent thus freed from sin must subsequently submit himself to the keys by confession and penance under pain of mortal sin.[2] Gabriel Biel adopts the opinion of William of Ockham, that the sacrament of penitence is only the certain sign of the remission of the *culpa* through previous contrition.[3] Aquinas however finally carried the day. The rigorous virtue of Caietano was disposed to exalt as much as possible the efficiency of contrition, but he admits that, after long debate, the question had been decided in favor of the power of the keys, and for this he cites the council of Florence, where the effect of the sacrament was described as the absolution of sin.[4] The Dominican Prierias has no question about it, and leaves nothing for God to do; the priest by the power of the keys remits the *culpa*, changes the eternal punishment to temporal, and diminishes the latter or sometimes removes it altogether.[5] Sacerdotalism could ask no more; by successive steps it had succeeded in eliminating God from the pardon of sin and had replaced him with the priest. It was the practical use made of these doctrines that provoked the Reformation, and when the council of Trent was assembled to select from the speculations of the schoolmen the faith to be thenceforth professed by Catholics, it had before it a somewhat difficult task in defining the power of the keys. In its first convocation, in 1547, it considered the subject of justification; it could not deny justification by grace, and all it could do was to assert that the *culpa* was not so remitted by grace but that a *pœna* remained to be

---

[1] Petri Hieremiæ Quadragesimale, Serm. xx.

[2] S. Antonini Summæ P. iii. Tit. xiv. cap. 17, § 3; cap. 18.

[3] Gab. Biel in IV. Sentt. Dist. xiv. Q. ii. Art. 2, Concl. 3, 4, 5.

[4] Caietani Tract. iv. De Attritione Q. 4; Tract. xviii. Q. 5.

[5] Summa Sylvestrina s. v. *Claves* § 4.—"Tertio, solvit absolvendo a culpa. Quarto, remittendo pœnam æternam et commutando eam in temporalem purgatoriam. Quinto minuendo pœnam temporalem vel aliquando totaliter abolendo."

satisfied either on earth or in purgatory.[1]   When therefore, in 1551, it treated of the sacrament of penitence its hands were somewhat tied, but it did the best it could, without formally declaring that the power of the keys extended over the *culpa*.   It asserted that the sacrament conduces to obtaining grace for imperfect contrition or attrition, that the perfect contrition which sometimes reconciles the sinner to God necessarily involves the vow to confess, that to obtain full pardon not only contrition but confession and satisfaction are requisite, and that satisfaction consists either in afflictions sent by God or in penance imposed by the priest, while it forbade anyone, however contrite, to take the Eucharist without previous confession.[2]

For a while these cautious utterances imposed a similar caution on theologians, and there was a tendency to return to the older formulas, but when Michael Bay taught that God justifies and that the priest only removes the penalty his opinions were emphatically condemned by St. Pius V. in 1567, by Gregory XIII. in 1579 and by Urban VIII. in 1641.[3]   Bishop Zerola came perilously near to this, but escaped condemnation, in asserting the old doctrine that contrition removes the *culpa* and part or all of the *pœna*, according to its intensity, only adding that if it does not contain the vow to confess the *culpa* is not remitted.[4]   Escobar only defines the power of the keys as a faculty which enables the ecclesiastical judge to admit the worthy to heaven and to exclude the unworthy[5]—which would seem to render the whole function a trifle superfluous.   But it is not deemed necessary to enlighten the people on these niceties or to diminish their simple faith in the all-embracing efficacy of priestly ministrations.   Cardinal Bellarmine, in a popular catechism, informs the reader that, by the words of the priest in absolution, God internally releases the soul from the bonds of sin, restores his grace and liberates it from

---

[1] C. Trident. Sess. VI. De Justificatione can. 30.

[2] C. Trident. Sess. XIII. De Eucharistia c. 7, can. 11; Sess. XIV. De Pœnitentia cap. 4; can. 4, 12, 13.—Father Sayre (Clavis Regiæ Sacerd. Lib. I. cap. 6, n. 6) uses this as an example of change of doctrine.   All the older theologians, he says, taught the sufficiency of contrition, but since the utterances of the council of Trent they necessarily teach the opposite.

[3] Urbani PP. VIII. bull *In eminenti* Prop. 43, 58 (Bullar. Ed Luxemb. V. 369).

[4] Zerola, Praxis Sacr. Pœnitent. cap. vii. Q. 29.

[5] Escobar Theol. Moral. Tract. VII. Examen iv. cap. 5, n. 29.

the fate of being cast into hell;[1] or, as he expresses it elsewhere, it is the absolution granted by the priest that drives away sin,[2]—thus extending the power of the keys over both *culpa* and *pœna*. Benedict XIII. in a series of instructions for children at their first confession, requires them to be told that the priest stands to them in the place of God and that it is his absolution that remits their sins and saves them from hell.[3] The Tridentine utterances have come to be thus interpreted by theologians of all schools. Juenin expressly says that the sinner cannot obtain justification or remission of sin without sacerdotal absolution.[4] Palmieri is as confident and as uncompromising as Prierias: the power of the keys is the absolute power of admitting to or of excluding from heaven; it remits the *culpa* and with that remission the eternal punishment due to it is remitted; the old schoolmen limited the power incorrectly when they asserted that sacramental absolution can be granted only to those whose contrition had won justification from God, for they were insufficiently versed in the sacraments.[5] Who can deny that Catholic theology is a progressive science, and who can predict what may be its ultimate development? Yet the satisfaction with which modern teachers

---

[1] Bellarmino, Dottrina Cristiana, Della Penitenza (Opp. Neapoli, 1862, T. VI. p. 193)—" Ed il sacerdote esteriormente pronunzia l'assoluzione: così Iddio interiormente per mezzo di quelle parole del sacerdote scioglia quell' anima dal nodo de' peccati col quale era legata; se le rende la grazia sua, e la libera del obbligo che aveva d'esser precipitata nell' Inferno."

[2] Bellarmin. de Pœnit. Lib. III. cap. 2 (Ibid. III. 679)—" Ut enim flatus extinguit ignem et dissipat nebulas, sic enim absolutio sacerdotis peccata dispergit et evanescere facit."

[3] Instruzione per gli figliuoli, in Concil. Roman. ann. 1725; Tit. xxxii. cap. 3 (Romæ, 1725, pp. 138, 432).

[4] Juenin de Sacramentis Diss. VI. Q. vii. cap. 5, Art. 1.

[5] Palmieri Tract. de Pœnit. p. 72, cf. p. 118.—There are some other knotty and disputed points involved. Palmieri asserts absolutely (pp. 102–3) that sin cannot be remitted without submission to the keys, at least by a vow. Yet he had previously pointed out the difference between actual and virtual penitence, the latter of which exists when an act of charity is performed without remembering the sin, and though the sufficiency of this for justification is denied by some theologians he affirms it (pp. 40–1). The two assertions seem irreconcilable, but he gets rid of the contradiction by asserting (p. 106) that in the act of charity there must be an implied admission of the power of the keys, tantamount to a vow. How this can be when in virtual penitence, *ex vi termini*, there is no recollection of sin it might not be easy to explain.

may well regard their conquests over the infinite must be tempered with regret that for the greater part of its existence the Church misled the faithful as to the extent of the gifts bestowed upon it by God.

When we come to consider the nature and certainty of the absolution thus wrought by the power of the keys we find ourselves at once confronted with limitations suggestive of human impotence in its attempt to act for the Omnipotent. The hopeless incongruity between the weakness, ignorance, or vices of the man and the tremendous powers of the keys conferred upon him was self-evident in almost every parish ; this could not escape the attention of the schoolmen and their efforts to bridge the chasm, while striving to confirm the efficacy of the sacrament, contribute an instructive chapter to the history of human error. Peter Lombard, while defining the power to bind and to loose as merely the manifestation of those bound or loosed by God, admits that sometimes the priest exhibits as bound or loosed those who are not bound or loosed with God ; the sentence of the Church only harms or helps according as it is merited and is approved by the judgment of God. Still, the priest has the power, though he may not use it righteously and worthily : only God and the saints in whom dwell the Holy Ghost can worthily and correctly remit or retain sins, yet it is done by those who are not saints, but it is not done worthily and correctly.[1] Evidently the dialectics of the period could not enable him to frame a coherent theory. Cardinal Pullus is equally emphatic in asserting that God pronounces his judgments irrespective of the action of the priest, and he seeks to save the power of the keys by the ingenious suggestion that he who uses it improperly loses it[2]—an eminently scholastic device but not conducive to the peace of mind of those who paid in money or mortifications for salvation. Richard of St. Victor can see no way out of the difficulty save by admitting that an unjust sentence of pardon or condemnation by the priest is void, for he can use the power not arbitrarily but only in accordance with the merits of the case and the will of God. At the same time Richard endeavors to retain something for the keys by the extraordinary assumption that, when God pardons, the pardon is only conditional and does not become absolute

---

[1] P. Lombard. Sentt. Lib. IV. Dist. xviii. § 7 ; Dist. xix. §§ 3, 5.
[2] Rob. Pulli Sentt. Lib. VI. cap. 52, 61.

without the priestly absolution.[1] Master Bandinus, while asserting that the sentence of the priest is to be dreaded, admits that it must be in accordance with justice to be valid.[2] With the progress of sacerdotal development there were enthusiastic theologians who were not satisfied with these moderate claims. William Bishop of Paris about 1240 asserts for the priestly order the control of the fate of the soul; absolution releases it from the sentence of damnation and the terrors of the Day of Judgment; God commits irrevocably to the priest the consideration of the sinner's case—and yet with inevitable inconsistency he admits that to the majority of penitents absolution is illusory through their lack of due contrition, thus avowing that it is merely a snare by lulling them in false security.[3] S. Ramon de Peñafort, about the same period, is more cautious. He puts the question, What is it that the priest remits in penitence? and essays to answer it, but fails. He states various opinions then current, which show how unsettled as yet was the matter in the schools, and concludes by conceding that the binding and loosing are absolute only when just.[4] Cardinal Henry of Susa solves the question in a manner highly derogatory to the keys: sin creates a double responsibility, to God and to the Church; contrition obtains pardon from God, but the offence to the Church remains and must be expiated by confession and satisfaction; if the contrite sinner neglects this the sin does not return, but new mortal sin is committed which again consigns him to perdition.[5] Thus the only function of the priest is to assign or remit penance. Aquinas admits that the priest cannot use the power of the keys at his pleasure, but only as God prescribes, and he relies on divine inspiration to guide the confessor aright, but the futility of this was apparent when an objector asked him how, without a revelation from God, the priest can know that the penitent is absolved, and Aquinas could only reply that any judge may acquit a guilty man on the evidence of witnesses and to the confessor the penitent is the only witness, for and against himself.[6] Giovanni Balbi follows

---

[1] Rich. a S. Victore de Potestate Ligandi c. 8, 9, 11, 12.

[2] Mag. Bandini Sentt. Lib. IV. Dist. 18.

[3] Guillel. Parisiens. Opera de Fide; Ejusd. de Sacramento Pœnitentiæ c. 6, 21.

[4] S. Raymundi Summæ Lib. III. Tit. xxxiv. § 5.

[5] Hostiens. Aureæ Summæ Lib. V. De Pœn. et Remiss. § 6; De Remissionibus § 1.

[6] S. Th. Aquinat. Summæ Supplem. Q. XVIII. Art. 4; Ejusd. Opusc. XXII. cap. 3.

Aquinas as to the necessity of the priestly discretion being divinely guided and adds that the priest, in using the power of the keys, acts only as the instrument and minister of God and no instrument acts efficiently save as it is moved by its principal.[1] Astesanus admits that the priestly judgment is not final but requires ratification in heaven; indeed, he quotes approvingly from Peter of Tarantaise (Innocent V.) that the forum of God and the forum of the Church are distinct and that a man may be absolved in one and not in the other.[2] William of Ware disputes this, for such uncertainly would drive the penitent to despair, as the confessor cannot know the judgment of God; there is a certain latitude in the punishment and God increases or diminishes it in accordance with the sentence of the priest.[3] Marsiglio of Padua, in his bold revolt against sacerdotalism, recurs to Peter Lombard and Richard of S. Victor and develops their theories to their ultimate results. He proves from them that the priest only makes manifest to the Church the binding or loosing by God; he may err through prejudice, favor, ignorance, or corrupt motives, so that his sentence has no influence on the judgment of God, and the pope has no greater power than any other priest.[4] Marsiglio however exercised no influence on the current of thought; it was running too strongly towards sacerdotal development and it continued to flow. Thus Durand de S. Pourçain boldly claims that the priest is an arbiter between God and man, first selected by God and then by the penitent; but he confesses the idleness of this and the vice of the whole system when he says that in the forum of the Church the penitent must perform the penance enjoined, whether suitable or not, while in the forum of God if it is too little it does not suffice, if too much it is superfluous.[5] Thomas of Walden and Dr. Weigel revert to the older theory : the power of the keys to be effective must be exercised justly; the sentence of the priest only binds or looses when it conforms to the sentence of God.[6] Gabriel Biel minimizes the power of the keys; God alone removes sin and

---

[1] Joannis de Janua Summa quæ vocatur Catholicon s. v. *Pœnitentia.*

[2] Astesani Summæ Lib. v. Tit. xxxi. Q. 2.

[3] Vorrillong super IV. Sentt. Dist. XVIII.

[4] Marsilii Defensoris Pacis P. II. cap. 6.

[5] Durand. de S. Port. in IV. Sentt. Dist. XIX. Q. ii. § 7; Dist. XX. Q. 1, §§ 5, 6, 8.

[6] Thomæ Waldensis de Sacramentis cap. CXLIV. n. 4.—Weigel Claviculæ Indulgentialis cap. 7.—Thomas of Walden moreover (cap. CLVIII. n. 3) makes

opens the gate of heaven; the priest merely sentences; if his sentence is in accordance with the law of God it is confirmed, if not it is revoked.[1] Prierias naturally returns to the opinion of Aquinas; the priest is to act according to Divine inspiration, when he is the instrument of God's will; if he arbitrarily varies from this he sins and his decision is void.[2] To this Bartolommeo Fumo assents, except as to the invalidation of the sentence,[3] while Domingo Soto asserts positively that the sentence of the priest is powerless if it is erroneous.[4] Since the council of Trent discussion on this subject seems to have been avoided. The council strictly withheld any intimation that the priestly sentence is subject to doubt, except as to the intention of the ministrant; that it may be rejected by God is not hinted.[5] Modern theologians accordingly have no hesitation in asserting that the effect of absolution is certain and infallible;[6] there

the admission that it is impossible to define the degree of innocence conferred by absolution, as this is known only to the Searcher of hearts.

It is worthy of note that practically there is no difference between Thomas of Walden's opinion and that of the heresiarch whom he is controverting. Wickliffe says—"But oure bileve techis us that no synne is forgiven but if God hymself forgif furste of alle. Ande if his trewe vicare acorde to Gods wille, he may assoyle of synne as vicary of his God. But if he discorde from juggement of his God he assoyles not, boste he never so muche." Jo. Wickliffe's Septem Hæreses, Hæresis V. (Arnold's Select English Works, III. 444).

[1] Gab. Biel in IV. Sentt. Dist. xviii. Q. 1, Art. 1, not. 2; Dist. xx. Art. 3, Dub. 1.

[2] Summa Sylvestrina s. v. *Claves* § 6.

[3] Bart. Fumi Armilla Aurea s. v. *Clavis* n. 6. This work was an acknowledged authority in the second half of the sixteenth century. My edition is of Medina del Campo, 1552; there was one of Paris, 1561, and I have met with Venitian editions of 1554, 1558, 1563, 1565, 1578, 1584 and 1588.

[4] Dom. Soto in IV. Sentt. Dist. xviii. Q. ii. Art. 5 ad 5.

[5] C. Trident. Sess. xiv. De Pœnitentia cap. 6.

[6] Caramuelis Theol. Fundament. n. 1120.—Palmieri Tract. de Pœnit. p. 120. —The summary of Father de Charmes (Theol. Universalis Diss. v. cap. vii.) is that the sacrament of penitence confers infusion of sacramental and habitual grace, the remission of *culpa*, and release from eternal torment, but not always total remission of temporal punishment, though it diminishes this in accordance with the greater or less disposition of the penitent.

There is another question which need not detain us here as it is one on which the wisest doctors differ—whether sins deleted in confession will be made manifest at the Day of Judgment. It is agreed however that if they are they will not cause humiliation, because the glorified penitent will have performed penance for them during life.—Clericati de Virt. et Sacr. Pœnit. Decis. xlix. n.

is of course theoretically the condition precedent that the penitent is properly disposed, but this is a matter for the priest to determine at the time. This question of the disposition, however, has been the subject of interminable and intricate debates in the schools and will be considered hereafter.

The evil lives and the ignorance, both invincible and crass, of those to whom this tremendous power was committed were the subject of denunciation too general throughout the middle ages for the schoolmen not to seek some explanation or palliation of the incongruity. Hardly had the existence of the power of the keys been defined in the schools when its abuse led Alain de Lille—perhaps the most learned doctor of his time—practically to deny their efficacy; they should rather, he says, be termed keys of hell than of heaven, for they betray souls to eternal death, and the text in Matthew ought to read, "Whatsoever you shall bind upon earth shall be loosed in heaven, and whatsoever you shall loose upon earth shall be bound in heaven," while priests are rather vicars of Simon Magus than of Simon Peter.[1]

The fact that the plural word "keys" is used suggested a method of partially eluding these objections, at least in theory. Already in the ninth century Rabanus Maurus had said that Christ designated as keys of heaven the power and the knowledge of discerning between those fit and unfit for heaven.[2] Hugh of St. Victor, to whom the keys were a more concrete conception, calls them respectively

---

14.—I shall frequently have occasion to quote this work which appeared in 1702 and was dedicated to Clement XI. For more than forty years the author had been examiner of applicants for license to hear confessions in the diocese of Padua and thus had ample opportunity to test his learning by the exigencies of practice. His voluminous writings are now well-nigh forgotten.

[1] Alani de Insulis Sententt. cap. 27.—"Sed jam istæ claves mutatæ sunt in adulterinas, quia non jam Dei intuitu et rationis ductu ligant aut solvunt sed amore pecuniæ non ligandos ligant, ut de eis posset dici: Quodcumque ligaveris super terram erit solutum in cœlis et quodcumque solveris super terram erit ligatum in cœlis. Et isti clavigeri sunt non a clave sed a clava: claves mutant in clavas, quia non eis viam aperiunt sed potius seducendo ad mortem æternam percutiunt. Isti potius videntur habere claves infernorum quam regni cœlorum. Isti miseri non sunt vicarii Simonis Petri sed Simonis Magi."

[2] Rabani Mauri Comment. in Matt. Lib. v. cap. xvi.

discrimination and power.[1] Gratian, in his incidental reference to
the keys, alludes to one as giving the power to eject from or retain
in the Church, and to the other as conveying the knowledge to decide
between leprosy and leprosy.[2] This evidently had become a current
idea and Peter Lombard adopted it, but in a manner highly derogatory to the claims of sacerdotalism and of apostolical transmission.
Deploring the unfitness, both as to learning and morals, of so many
of those who obtained orders, he says that on them the key of knowledge is not bestowed; only those who are properly trained receive it.
There are some authorities, he adds, who hold that only worthy successors of St. Peter receive the keys, but he is obliged to assume that
all priests receive the key of power, however ignorantly and unworthily they may use it.[3] The belief that only the fit representatives of St. Peter receive the keys was not ephemeral, for towards
the close of the twelfth century we find it still enunciated by Master
Bandinus.[4] Peter of Poitiers tells us that the ignorance of a majority
of priests precludes them from receiving the key of knowledge, but
the question as to their use of it, he confesses, is too intricate for
him to decide.[5]

This theory of the key of knowledge continued to be generally
taught, but it was not as a rule pretended that knowledge is divinely
conferred in ordination. If an ignorant man took orders he remained ignorant, and the general admission was that as he used the
key of power ignorantly his judgments were of no weight for they
were as likely to be unjust as just,[6] nor did the learned doctors, who
made this concession to the evidence of their everyday experience,

---

[1] Hugon. de S. Victore Summæ Sentt. Tract. VI. cap. 14.

[2] Gratian. P. I. Dist. XX. *initio.*

[3] P. Lombard. Sentt. Lib. IV. Dist. XIX. §§ 1, 2, 3.

[4] Bandini Sentt. Lib. IV. Dist. XIX.

[5] Pet. Pictav. Sentt. Lib. III. cap. 16.

[6] Rich. a S. Victore de Potestate Ligandi cap. 13.—Adami de Persennia
Epist. XXI.—Alani de Insulis Sententt. cap. 27.—Bonaventuræ in IV. Sentt.
Dist. XVIII. P. 1, art. 3, Q. 1.—Astesani Summæ Lib. V. Tit. XXXI. Q. 2.
The utterances of a few of the schoolmen on the subject will show how
diverse were the conclusions respecting it.
Alexander Hales (Summæ P. IV. Q. XX. Membr. iii. art. 1; Membr. vi. art.
3) says—"Et intelligendum quod multi habent clavem qui non habent beati-
tudinem clavis, et ita multi habent claves qui possunt errare."
Cardinal Henry of Susa (Aureæ Summæ Lib. V. De Remissionibus § 1)—

pause to think what an extraordinary scheme of salvation they were attributing to God in their efforts to reconcile the claims of the Church to common-sense. This definition of the two keys continued to be received, though after the Reformation theologians were more reticent in their admissions and taught that the ignorant receive the key of knowledge though they remain ignorant.[1] Yet all agree that the keys may err, in which case they are powerless—a fatal admission for a system based upon a supernatural power specially granted by God for the salvation of mankind.[2] The phrases *clave*

"Sed sive dicas unam clavem vel duas hæc est rei veritas quod quicquid ligatum est in terris a sacerdotibus ligatum est et in cœlis, subaude tu, clave non errante."

William of Ware (Super IV. Sentt. Dist. xviii.). " Unde potest esse auctoritas cognoscendi sine scientia."

Pietro d'Aquila (In IV. Sentt. Dist. xviii. Q. 1) denies that there is a key of knowledge; the two keys are one of discerning and the other of deciding, " ita potestas cognoscendi non est scientia, imo est sine scientia, sicut de facto in multis hodie est sacerdotibus."

St. Antonino of Florence is more cautious (Summæ P. iii. Tit. xvii. cap. 16)— "Scientia autem acquisita non est clavis sed juvat bene uti clavi."

Gabriel Biel carries out the definition of Pietro d'Aquila and dispenses with knowledge (In IV. Sentt. Dist. xx. Q. 1, art ii. concl. 3)—"Clavis scientiæ non est habitus scientiæ neque scientia actualis, sed autoritas discernendi inter dignum et indignum in foro pœnitentiæ quæ esse potest in idiota, et ea carere potest eruditissimus."

Dante adopts the theory of the two keys and has no hesitation in saying that when they err they fail in their effect:

> "L'un era de oro e l'altra era de argento . . .
> Quandunque l'una d'este chiavi falla,
> Che non si volga dritta per la toppa,
> Diss' egli a noi, non s'apre questa calla.
> Più cara è l'una, ma l'altra vuol troppa
> D'arte e d'ingegno, avanti che disserri,
> Perch' egli è quella che 'l nodo disgroppa."—Purgatorio, xx.

[1] Joh. Eckii Enchirid. Locor. commun. cap. viii. De Confessione.—Dom. Soto in IV. Sentt. Dist. xviii. Q. 1, art. 1.—Estii in IV. Sent. Dist. xviii. § 1. " Est igitur utraque clavis tam scientiæ quam potestatis penes sacerdotes, non tantum doctos et bonos, verumetiam penes indoctos et malos " (Ibid. Dist. xix. § 1).

[2] Alex. de Ales Summæ P. IV. Q. xx. Membr. vii. art. 1.—Hostiens. Aureæ Summæ Lib. v. De Remiss. § 1.—Joh. Gersonis de Reform. Eccles. cap. 28.— Weigel Clavic. Indulgentialis cap. 7.—Dom. Soto in IV. Sentt. Dist. xviii. Q. ii. art. 5.—Estii in IV. Sentt. Dist. xix. § 1.

errante and *clave non errante* are a confession that the whole fabric of the power of the keys rests upon a delusion.

Some of the schoolmen were shrewd enough to see the destructive character of admissions such as these and that the supernatural gift of the keys must be supplemented with a supernatural gift of wisdom. Thus William of Paris piously asserts that, in the case of ignorant and inexperienced confessors, God inspires them with most wholesome counsel as to the penance which they are to impose.[1] We have seen that Aquinas assents to this theory of inspiration, though when he treats of the key of knowledge he loses himself in contradictory speculations which he reports without affirming.[2] Durand de S. Pourçain cuts the knot resolutely ; the priest ought to have knowledge, but its absence does not invalidate his power.[3] Thomas of Walden can only meet the scoffing Lollards by exhorting the priest not to be disturbed and the penitent not to doubt the validity of the sacrament but to have faith and trust in Christ who will supply all defects and not allow the keys to err.[4] This is virtually a return to the theory of inspiration, in which Cardinal Caietano concurs when he asserts that the confessor is without doubt moved by the Holy Ghost in binding or loosing.[5] However necessary such an assumption must be to complete the theory of the power of the keys, in practice it is recognized as illusory. According to Escobar it is the general opinion that inability to distinguish between mortal and venial sins renders the priest incapable of conferring absolution,[6] and the distinction between these classes of sins is so tenuous that, as we shall see, the wisest doctors are frequently

---

[1] Guillel. Paris. de Sacr. Pœnitent. cap. 20.

[2] S. Th. Aquin. Summæ Supplement. Q. XVII. art. 3.

[3] Durand. de S. Port. in IV. Sentt. Dist. XVIII. Q. 1.

[4] Th. Waldens. De Sacramentis cap. CL. n. 1.

[5] Caietani Tract. XVIII. De Confessione Q. 5.

[6] Escobar Theol. Moral. Tract. VII. Exam. iv. cap. 7, n. 36. Authorities are, however, as usual divided on this point. Chiericato (De Pœnitent. Decis. XXXI. n. 16, 17) says the truer opinion is that the *bona fides* of the penitent supplies all such defects if the confessor knows enough to repeat the formula of absolution, which reduces the priestly function to that of a conjuror. When he cannot even do this the sacrament of course is void. Marchant (Trib. Animar. Tom. I. Tract. II. Tit. 5, Q. 3, Dub. 8) holds that the absolution of an ignorant confessor is valid, but it does not release from obligations which he may have neglected to prescribe.

at odds over it. This throws an unpleasant shade of doubt over almost all absolutions, for the penitents are few who are fitted to gauge the learning of their confessors and consequently the remedy prescribed by St. Alphonso Liguori against such invalid absolution is for the most part inapplicable—that is to seek a more competent spiritual judge.[1] As a remedy, confessors are sometimes recommended, before hearing a confession, to utter a fervent prayer, in view of the great danger which exists of their making mistakes in granting absolution where it ought to be refused and refusing it where it ought to be granted.[2]

There are other causes besides ignorance which throw a doubt over the validity of the sentence pronounced in the confessional. The priest may not understand the confession through ignorance of the language of the penitent, or through deafness or drowsiness or inattention, and yet he may grant absolution. Whether this is valid or not is a question on which the doctors have differed. Some hold the negative, but St. Antonino, followed by Busenbaum and most of the moderns, considers it more probable that if the penitent is not aware of the confessor's condition the absolution is good before God, and the confession need not be repeated; if, however, he finds that some of his sins have not been understood he must repeat them,[3] though, oddly enough, we are told that this need not be done if it causes sufficient inconvenience to render confession odious.[4] Another view is that if the priest hears nothing the absolution is invalid, but if he happens to catch a single venial sin it is good and covers all that have been confessed[5]—all of which shows how little

---

[1] S. Alph. de Ligorio Theol. Moral. Lib. VI. n. 568. "Si autem ignorantia esset tanta ut confessio illi facta foret invalida aut illicita neque esset alius privilegiatus aut habens jurisdictionem, licere alteri confiteri docent Nav. Vasq. etc."

[2] Synod. Sutchuens. ann. 1803 cap. vi. §7 (Collect. Concil. Lacens. Tom. VI. p. 608).

[3] S. Antonini Summæ P. III. Tit. xvii. cap. 15; cap. 21, §3.—Summa Diana s. v. *Confessarius* n. 26.—Escobar Theol. Moral. Tract. VII. Exam. iv. cap. 7, n. 36.—Layman Theol. Moral. Lib. V. Tract. vi. cap. 9, n. 5.—Gobat Alphab. Confessar. n. 489-92.—Busenbaum Medullæ Theol. Moral. Lib. VI. Tract. iv. cap. 1, Dub. 3, art. 4.—Mig. Sanchez, Prontuario de la Teología Moral. Trat. VI. Punto 5 §8.—S. Alph. de Ligorio Theol. Moral. Lib. VI. n. 499.

[4] La Croix Theol. Moral. Lib. VI. P. ii. n. 1210.

[5] Piselli Theol. Moral. Summæ P. II. Tract. 5 cap. 4 (Romæ, 1748).

importance is really attached to the function of the confessor as a judge. There is also a source of error when a priest exceeds his jurisdiction and grants absolution in cases reserved to the bishop, or wrongfully absolves the subject of another priest—complex questions which will be considered more fully hereafter.[1]

It shows how slender is the value really attributed to the power of the keys by modern theologians that when an absolution is invalid through mistakes committed by the priest he is told, on the unimpeachable authority of St. Alphonso Liguori, that he must seek to induce the penitent to confess again, but if he cannot do this without scandal or loss of reputation or other injury to himself, he can let it pass.[2] A similar conclusion is deducible from the advice of the moralists in the case, by no means very infrequent, when the priest through forgetfulness omits to utter the formula of absolution. There has been considerable speculation as to how the error should be repaired. Absolution has to be granted in the presence of the penitent, though the exact distance at which it is effective has never been positively determined. If the priest, after remembering the omission, meets the penitent he can absolve him, provided the latter has not meanwhile committed a mortal sin: to require him to confess this and render himself capable of absolution would be apt to lead to scandal, and if there is danger of this the pious advice of the doctors is to leave the matter in the hands of God.[3]

Thus through successive steps and under varying conditions the power of the keys gradually established itself and the Church acquired the awful and mysterious power of regulating the salvation

---

[1] Clericati De Pœnitent. Decis. xix. n. 34. His definition of sources of error and his claims of infallibility are characteristic—"Utrum autem hi effectus clavium sint infallibiles? Respondetur affirmative dummodo clavis scientiæ non erret circa species aut circumstantias mutantes illas; vel clavis potentiæ pariter non erret in absolvendo a peccatis reservatis super quibus sacerdos non habeat jurisdictionem. In his duobus casibus cessarent prædicti effectus quia judicium esset invalidum et sacramentum nullum. At ubi validitas sacramenti et absolutionis est salva prædicti effectus sunt infallibiles, etsi sacerdos in aliquo peccaret circa clavem scientiæ vel potentiæ, imponendo scilicet vel majorem vel minorem pœnitentiam, vel non interrogando exacte omnes circumstantias."

[2] S. Alph. de Ligorio Theol. Moral. Lib. vi. n. 618.

[3] Gobat Alphabetum Confessariorum n. 283-90.

or perdition of her children. Theologians may among themselves admit that the keys can err and that the judgments passed on earth may not be ratified in heaven, but the plain people are taught that the priest holds their eternal destiny in his hands and that to them he is virtually God, for he has the power to convert guilt into innocence.[1]

---

[1] "So great is the power of the priest that the judgments of heaven itself are subject to his decision. . . . 'This man,' says God, speaking to the priest, 'this man is a sinner; he has offended me grievously; I could judge him myself but I leave this judgment to your decision. I shall forgive him as soon as you grant him forgiveness. He is my enemy, but I shall admit him to my friendship as soon as you declare him worthy. I shall open the gates of heaven to him as soon as you free him from the chains of sin and hell.' 'Yea, Lord,' the priest can answer, 'when I forgive him my arm is strong like thine, for I break the chains of sin. My voice thunders like thine for it bursts the fetters of hell; my voice changes thine enemy into thy friend; it transforms the slave of hell into an heir of heaven.' The power of forgiving sins surpasses that of any created being either in heaven or on earth. An earthly judge has great power, yet he can only declare one innocent who has been falsely accused; but the Catholic priest has power to restore to innocence even those who are guilty."—Müller's Catholic Priesthood, I. 48, 50 (New York, 1885.)

As this work bears the *imprimatur* of Cardinal McCloskey and of the Redemptorist General Mauron, I presume that it correctly represents the current teaching of the Church.

In this Father Müller only amplifies the assertion of Peter of Palermo in the fourteenth century who says that in conferring absolution the ordinary priest is superior to the angels and even to the Virgin Mary, for they cannot do what he does.—Pet. Hieremiæ Quadragesimale, Serm. xx.

CHAPTER VIII.

CONFESSION.

DURING the middle ages it was a point debated between theologians whether sacramental confession is a divine law or merely a precept of the Church. To the earlier schoolmen, indeed, like Hugh of St. Victor and Peter Lombard, the idea of its being a divine law seems to have been unknown, and they only advance human reasons in its favor.[1] S. Ramon de Peñafort apparently desires to imply a divine origin when he says that confession, like contrition and satisfaction, are all comprised in the command of Christ "Do penance" (Matt. IV. 17).[2] Alexander Hales explains the absence of divine command by God's desiring confession to be voluntary and not extorted, and he expounds a passage of St. Ambrose by the fact that confession had not been as yet instituted by Christ.[3] Bonaventura follows him in saying that Christ only suggested it and left it to be instituted by the apostles.[4] The Gloss on the Decretum concludes that it is not to be found in the Old or the New Law, but is a tradition of the Church, binding on the Latins but not on the Greeks, for at this time there was a current belief that confession was not practised in the Eastern Church.[5] Apparently Aquinas was the first who boldly declared confession to be of divine law; as he has no gospel text to quote he argues that it cannot be of human law because it is a matter of faith; faith and the sacraments are beyond human reason and therefore they must be of divine law,[6] which is

---

[1] Hugon. de S. Victore de Sacramentis Lib. II. P. xiv. cap. 1.—P. Lombard. Sentt. Lib. IV. Dist. xvii. ⸹ 6.

[2] S. Raymundi Summæ Lib. III. Tit. xxxiv. ⸹ 4 De Confess. ii.

[3] Alex. de Ales Summæ P. IV. Q. XVIII. Membr. iii. Art. 2; Membr. ii. Art. 1.

[4] S. Bonavent. in IV. Sentt. Dist XVII. P. ii. Art. 1, Q. 3.

[5] Gloss. sup. Decr. Caus. XXXIII. Q. iii. Dist. 5.—As this gloss was in universal use, Durand de S. Pourçain (In IV. Sentt. Dist. XVII. Q. viii. ⸹ 9) is much scandalized by the perilous errors contained in this passage—"et mirum est quod in tam solenni libro ecclesia sustinuit et adhuc sustinet tam perniciosam glosam."

[6] S. Th. Aquin. Summæ Supplem. Q. VI. Art. 2. Cf. Art. 6.

virtually to assume that, as we cannot understand it, it must be of divine command though no such divine command is recorded. The authority, if not the reasoning, of Aquinas gave a standing in the schools to this view and we find it accepted by many succeeding writers.[1] The Scotists reached the same conclusion by a somewhat different line of argument: the Church, they said, would not have imposed so heavy a burden on her children except by divine command and that as there is no trace of any canon prescribing it, prior to the Lateran council of 1216, it could not have been a mere human precept.[2] Chancellor Gerson makes no pretence that it is of divine origin save that the Decalogue commands us to honor our parents and as Mother Church has commanded it we must honor her by obedience.[3] Thomas of Walden can answer Wickliffe only by saying that everything which Christ said and did is not recorded in Scripture.[4] Cherubino da Spoleto speaks of it as not absolutely of divine or natural law although it was impliedly commanded by Christ.[5] There was thus ample latitude of opinion, and on the eve of the Reformation Baptista de Saulis and Prierias both inform us

---

[1] Joh. Friburgens. Summæ Confessor. Lib. III. Tit. xxxiv. Q. 31.—Astesani Summæ Lib. V. Tit. x. Art. 2, Q. 1.—Guill. Vorillong super IV. Sentt. Dist. XVII.—Durand. de S. Port. in IV. Sentt. Dist. XVII. Q. viii. §§ 9, 11, 12.

Astesanus (loc. cit. Q. 2) points out that the divine origin of confession renders it obligatory on all mankind, the infidel and the unbaptized as well as the faithful, which would not be the case if it were merely a precept of the Church. Cf. Summa Angelica s. v. *Confessio* II. § 2. This point seems to have originated with Richard Middleton (Rob. Episc. Aquinat. Opus Quadragesimale Serm. XXVII. cap. 3).

[2] Joh. Scoti in IV. Sentt. Dist. XVII. Q. unic.—Pet. de Aquila in IV. Sentt. Dist. XVII. Q. ii.—Summa Angelica s. v. *Confessio* II. § 1.—Gab. Biel in IV. Sentt. Dist. XVII. Q. 1, Art. 1.—Domingo Soto repeats this argument and claims it as novel (In IV. Sentt. Dist. XVIII. Q. 1, Art. 1).

I shall have frequent occasion to quote the *Summa Angelica*, of which the enduring authority throughout the sixteenth century is shown by editions of Chivasso in 1486; Speyer, 1488; Nürnberg, 1488 and 1492; Strassburg, 1495, 1498, and 1513; Lyons, 1534; Venice, 1487, 1489, 1492, 1495, 1499, 1504, 1511, 1569, 1577, 1578 and 1593, and probably numerous others. The author, Angiolo da Chivasso was Cismontane Vicar-general of the Observantines, who died in 1485 with the highest reputation for piety and learning (Rodulphii Hist. Seraph. Relig. p. 307).

[3] Joh. Gersonis Compend. Theologiæ (Ed. 1488, XXVII. F.).

[4] Thomæ Waldens. de Sacramentis cap. CXLVIII.

[5] Cherubini de Spoleto Sermones Quadragesimales Serm. LXII.

that the canonists hold that confession is of human precept, while the theologians declare it to be of divine law;[1] but when Pedro de Osma taught the former doctrine at Salamanca it was condemned as an error by the council of Alcalá in 1479 and Sixtus IV. confirmed the decree.[2] In the Lutheran controversy, Caietano speaks of it only as a precept, while Dr. Eck argues that it is of divine origin because the practice of the Church is the best interpreter of Scripture. Caterino reverts to the view of St. Ramon de Peñafort, escaping the necessity of proof by treating confession as inseparable from repentance which was commanded by Christ, while Fisher of Rochester argues that much was handed down orally by Christ and the Apostles and not committed to writing.[3] From all this it is evident that Erasmus was not especially culpable in assuming that confession is a human institution, and his doing so did not detract from his reputation until after the appearance of Luther, when the altered position of the Church is seen by the inclusion of this in the list of his heresies drawn up for the Spanish Inquisition by Dr. Edward Lee, subsequently Archbishop of York.[4] Domingo Soto is much scandalized that such doctors as Hales, Bonaventura and Duns Scotus should admit that confession was not prescribed by Christ, for if this is granted the orthodox would have nothing wherewith to confute the heretics.[5] The continued assaults of the latter compelled the Church to take the most advanced position, and it was perhaps necessary for the council of Trent to declare that sacramental confession is of divine law and to anathematize all who should deny the assertion.[6] As this belief is thus *de fide,* discussion on the subject has of course ceased within the Church, for the Tridentine canon has removed all

---

[1] Summa Rosella s. v. *Confessio* II.—Summa Sylvestrina s. v. *Confessio Sacram.* II. § 4. Baptista de Saulis, the author of the *Summa Rosella,* is also known as "de Salis" and "Tornamala."

[2] Alfonsi de Castro adv. Hæreses Lib. IV. s. v. *Confessio.*

[3] Caietani Tract. XVIII. De Confessione Q. 1.—Jo. Eckii Enchirid. cap. VIII. De Confessione.—Ambr. Catherini Apologia pro veritate Lib. I. (Florent. 1520, fol. 78).—Jo. Roffensis Assertionis Lutheranæ Confutatio, Art. 5.

[4] Erasmi Colloq. Confabulatio Pia. — Menendez y Pelayo, Heterodoxos Españoles, II. 90.

[5] Dom. Soto in IV. Sentt. Dist. XVIII. Q. 1, Art. 1.

[6] C. Trident. Sess. XIV. De Pœnit. can. 6.—"Si quis negaverit confessionem sacramentalem vel institutam vel ad salutem necessariam esse jure divino . . . anathema sit."

cause for doubt, being the infallible assertion of an œcumenical council confirmed by the Holy See.[1] Yet still there were the unbelieving heretics to answer and this has forced on modern theologians the somewhat onerous task of proving from history that the council of Trent is right and that so many of the brightest lights of the medieval Church taught heresy.

To accomplish this every shred of patristic literature has been searched with the result of finding a few scattered and irrelevant passages which at best are but indirect allusions or exhortations. This is in itself sufficient evidence of the fruitlessness of the effort. So infinitely important a priestly function, in a population so corrupt as that of the Empire, would necessarily have formed the subject of detailed treatises for both penitents and confessors. The Apostolic Constitutions embody the customs of the Church towards the end of the third century, but they are silent as to this. A hundred years later St. Augustin, with untiring industry, covered the whole ground of Christian ethics and duties, but he gives no counsel to confessors how to perform their most delicate and responsible functions. The councils, in a fragmentary manner, prescribe penances for the grosser sins, but they lay down no commands as to confession. A few more or less imperfect codes of penance were drawn up by individuals, like the Gregories and Basil, but they contain nothing about confession save a bribe for it in a diminution of penalties. No formulas have reached us as to the treatment of penitents by confessors. It is not till about the seventh century that the Penitentials begin to afford indications of the kind and these are of a nature to show how rare as yet was confession. It would be idle to argue that such a literature existed and has utterly perished. The proof by tradition is as vague as that by Scripture—wholly an inference to justify a foregone conclusion.

To estimate the full force of this negative evidence it is only necessary to compare the silence of the early centuries with the clamor which arose as soon as confession was made habitual by the Lateran council in 1216. Scarce a local synod was held for a century which did not allude in some manner to the new functions thus thrust upon

---

[1] Qui quidem canon tollit omnem dubitandi ansam, quia reddit hanc veritatem infallibilem, cum emanaverit in concilio œcumenico confirmato a Summo Pontifice, ut bene docent Fagnanus etc."—Clericati de Pœnitent. Decis. XVII. n. 1.

the parish priests. Everywhere we see the Church organizing the new system, enforcing it, devising methods to render it effective and to curb the abuses that followed in its wake. Bishop after bishop issued instructions to guide their priests in their unaccustomed duties —instructions which presuppose the densest pre-existing ignorance. Systematic writers speedily took up the subject and compiled huge volumes of the complicated details which it involved, and from that time to this there has been devoted to it an increasing mass of literature which has swollen to vast proportions. It cannot be imagined that men like the Christian Fathers could have been blind to what has been so clearly seen since the thirteenth century, that the duties of the conscientious confessor are the most arduous and exacting, the most intricate and complex, that can be imposed on the fallibility of human nature, and that, seeing this, should not have left on record some expression of their own experiences for the benefit of their less gifted brethren. Nor would there have been left open the numberless questions which, as we shall see hereafter, required for their settlement the discussion of the acutest intellects of medieval and modern times during six centuries—questions the very existence of which demonstrate that the whole theory and practice of the confessional required to be worked out after it had been rendered obligatory in 1216. Yet the custom had an origin, and it is our business to trace its development from its inconspicuous beginnings to the growth which has overshadowed the whole of Latin Christianity.

There is scriptural warrant for the confession of our sins in various texts duly cited by the theologians.[1] There is also the direct com-

---

[1] The texts generally relied upon are—

" When a man or woman shall have committed any of the sins that men are wont to commit . . . they shall confess their sin and restore the principal itself and the fifth part over and above."—Numbers, v. 6, 7. See also Eccles. IV. 31: Proverbs, XXVIII. 13.

" And were baptized of him in the Jordan, confessing their sins." Matt. III. 6.

" And many of them that believed came confessing and declaring their deeds." Acts, XIX. 18.

" If we confess our sins he is faithful and just to forgive us our sins and to cleanse us from all iniquity." I. John, I. 9.

Less to the point is " Go, shew thyself to the priest " (Luke, v. 14; XVII. 14) of which the exegesis is very like that of the Raising of Lazarus.

For an abstract of the various futile and contradictory efforts of the theolo-

mand of St. James in his Catholic epistle, of which the theologians are somewhat chary.[1] Evidently among the primitive Christians the practice of acknowledging sins was regarded as a wholesome exercise, contributory to their pardon and leading to self-restraint. The term

---

gians to find scriptural warrant for auricular confession see Tournely, *De Sacramento Pœnitent.* Q. VI. Art. ii. Guillois (History of Confession, translated by Bishop Goesbriand, p. 12) furnishes an accessible compilation of all that can be gathered to support the orthodox view, commencing with the answers of Adam and Eve to the questions of God.

[1] " Confess therefore your sins one to another and pray one for another."— James, v. 16.

The difficulty about this text is its precept for mutual confession—*alterutrum* in the Vulgate and ἀλλήλοις in the original. It was freely cited before confession became sacramental and confined to the priesthood, but subsequently it was handled discreetly. Hugh of St. Victor (Summæ Sentt. Tract. II. cap. xi.) relies wholly upon it, and Peter Lombard (Sentt. Lib. IV. Dist. xvii. ⸶ 4) argues that *alterutrum* means to the priest. The Gloss on the Decretum (Caus. XXXIII. Q. iii. Dist. 5. Cf. c. 3 Dist. XXV.) says that some attribute confession to it, but it is preferable to rely on tradition. As usual, the Franciscans and Dominicans divided on the question. It is true that Bonaventura accepts it (In IV. Sentt. Dist. XVII. P. ii. Art. 1, Q. 3) but Duns Scotus shows clearly that James had not sacramental confession in view and is forced to rely on Matt. XVI. and John XX. (In IV. Sentt. Dist. ii. Q. 1) in which he is virtually followed by François de Mairone (In IV. Sentt. Dist. XIV. Q. 1), by Astesanus (Summæ Lib. V. Tit. viii. Art. 2, Q. 1) and William of Ware (In IV. Sentt. Dist. XVII.). On the other hand Aquinas and his followers hold with Peter Lombard that *alterutrum* means to the priest (S. Th. Aquin. in IV. Sentt. Dist. XVII. Art. 2; Summæ Suppl. Q. VI. Art. 6; Q. VIII. Art. 1.—Jacopo Passavanti, Lo Specchio della vera Penitenza Dist. v. cap. 2.—S. Antonini Summæ P. III. Tit. xiv. cap. 19). A tract of uncertain date, long attributed to St. Bernard relies exclusively upon it (Ps. Bernardi Meditatio de Humano Conditione, cap. 9). Some of the theologians, as Angiolo da Chivasso and Domingo Soto prudently avoid reference to it. Palmieri (Tract. de Pœnit. p. 167) in one passage doubts whether the confession thus commanded was sacramental; he suggests that certain persons were selected to hear confessions and that these must have been priests; besides, the tradition from other sources forbids the interpretation of mutual confession. Subsequently, however (p. 389) he takes heart of grace and argues that ἀλλήλοις means to priests.

Luther did not fail to quote the text in support of his system of lay confession (Steitz, Die Privatbeichte etc. der Lutherischen Kirche, p. 62), while the ardent Catholic controversialist Martin van der Beek (De Sacramentis, Tract. III. P. ii. cap. 38, Q. 1. n. 5) is obliged to argue that if the confession alluded to is sacramental, then *alterutrum* means to priests; if it is not sacramental then it may be to any one.

exomologesis, by which confession is designated in the New Testament, came to signify in time the whole act of confession to God, with prostration and humiliation, whereby repentance was excited through which his wrath might be appeased.[1]

In the primitive Church this confession to God was the only form enjoined. According to St. Clement of Rome the Lord requires nothing of any man save confession to Him.[2] The Didache shows us that this confession was public, in church, and that each believer was expected to confess his transgressions on Sunday, before breaking bread in the Eucharistic feast, for no one was to come to prayer with an evil conscience[3]—a precept which is repeated in Barnabas, evidently copied from the Didache.[4] This practice of public confession is also shown in the instances given by Irenæus of the disciples of Marcus who returned to the Church.[5] That the custom was not universal is presumable from the fact that in the detailed instructions given by Polycarp in his epistle to the Philippians there is no allusion to confession, nor does Dionysius of Corinth enjoin it in his advice to the Amastrians concerning the reception of sinners.[6] Where it was in use, however, nothing else was regarded as necessary. The Shepherd of Hermas seems to know only of confession to God, which, with repentance, prayer and faith, procures pardon.[7] Tertullian shows us that in the African Church the precepts of the Didache were still observed; that this confession to God was performed publicly, the penitent casting himself at the feet of the priests and of the people and begging them to aid him with their prayers. Tertullian bids

---

[1] Tertull. de Pœnit. cap. 9.—" Is actus qui magis Græco vocabulo exprimitur et frequentatur, exomologesis est, qua delictum Domino nostro confitemur; non quidem ut ignaro, sed quatenus satisfactio confessione disponitur, confessione pœnitentia nascitur, pœnitentia Deus mitigatur . . . Itaque exomologesis prosternendi et humilificandi hominis disciplina est."

Finally exomologesis was understood as including penance; that originally the confession and petition were addressed to God is seen by its becoming in time synonymous with *litaniæ* or litanies.—Con. Magunt. ann. 813 cap. 32 (Hartzheim Concil. German. I. 411).—Rabani Mauri de Universo Lib. v. cap. 15.

[2] S. Clement. Epist. I. ad Corinth. 52.—Οὐδὲν οὐδενὸς χρῄζει εἰ μὴ τὸ ἐξομολογεῖσθαι αὐτῷ.

[3] Didache, IV. XIV.—See also Hesychius in Levit. VI. 22.

[4] Barnaba Epist. XIV. 24.   [5] Irenæi contra Hœreses I. xiii. 5, 7.

[6] S. Polycarpi Epist. ad Philippens.—Eusebii H. E. IV. 23.

[7] Pastor Hermæ Vis. III. Mand. ix.

him feel no shame in this, for the Church and Christ are in each of the brethren, and he is humbling himself not before them but before Christ.[1] That up to the early portion of the third century, hearing the confessions of penitents formed no recognized part of sacerdotal functions is clearly shown by the Canons of Hippolytus, in which the duties of all orders of the clergy are minutely detailed and the only allusion to confession is to that made by the catechumen to the bishop before baptism.[2]

It is not until we reach the middle of the third century that we find any evidence of an occasional custom of sinners unburthening their souls to priests. That anxious repentance should seek counsel at the hands of the holy men versed in Scripture and the ways of God, is perfectly natural, and doubtless it was practised more or less from the beginning, but it was in no sense enjoined nor did it form part of the discipline of the Church. The first allusion to it occurs in Origen, who, in the seven modes of pardon (p. 81) includes the remission of sins by repentance, when the sinner washes his bed with tears and does not feel shame in revealing his sin to a priest and in seeking medicine from him, and the terms in which this is described as hard and painful show that it was by no means a usual expedient.[3] We have already seen that Origen ridiculed the idea that the power of the keys had been transmitted from St. Peter, and we have further evidence that this private consultation with a physician of the soul had in it nothing capable of remitting sin or of obtaining absolution, but that it was merely a wholesome practice recommended by preachers and that the only confession as yet recognized by the Church was in public before the congregation, for in another passage he exhorts the sinner to select carefully some competent adviser (apparently either layman or cleric) and, if he counsels public confession, to follow the advice, whereby the spiritual disease may be cured and the faithful be edified.[4] Evidently public confession, with its conse-

---

[1] Tertull. loc. cit. As this was written while Tertullian was yet orthodox, it has given much concern to modern theologians, who vainly endeavor to explain it away. See Bellarmine, De Pœnitentia Lib. III. cap. 6, and Juenin, De Sacramentis, Diss. VI. Q. 5, cap. 1, Art. 1, § 1.

[2] Canon. Hippolyti XIX. 103.

[3] Origenis Homil. II. in Levit. cap. 4—"Est adhuc et septima, licet dura et laboriosa etc."

[4] Origenis Homil. II. cap. 6, in Ps. XXXVII.—"Probas prium medicum cui

quences of public penance, was not a matter to be lightly undertaken, and we have already seen how unusual it was becoming as a
voluntary act. A passage in Cyprian is often quoted in which he
urges the lapsed in the Decian persecution to confess and undergo
penance before they die, but such confession was necessarily public
and without it they could not apply for penance.[1] In another place
he says that pardon is to be had, through the mediation of Christ,
by repentance and confession, or by promising amendment, but he
does not specify whether this confession is to be in secret to God or
in public.[2] Early in the fourth century Peter of Alexandria, like
Origen, recommends confession to a priest as part of the means of
securing pardon, though it is the penitent then who, with amendment and almsgiving, cures himself and not the priest that cures
him, so that it was merely a wholesome exercise.[3] A story told soon
after this by Eusebius shows that public and notorious sinners were
required to confess publicly and undergo penance before being admitted to the sacred mysteries. It relates that the Emperor Philip
(244–249) was a Christian and that on entering a church at Easter
he was stopped by the bishop (supposed to be St. Babylas of Anti-

---

debeas causam languoris exponere . . . ut ita demum si quid ille dixerit,
qui se prius et eruditum medicum ostenderit et misericordem, si quid consilii
dederit, facias et sequaris, si intellexerit et præviderit talem esse languorem
tuum qui in conventu totius ecclesiæ exponi debeat et curari, ex quo fortassis
et cæteri ædificari poterunt, et tu ipse facile sanari, multa hoc deliberatione et
satis perito medici illius consilio procurandum est."

Another passage (Homil. xvii. in Lucam) has evidently in view this public
confession before the Church—"Si enim hoc fecerimus et revelaverimus peccata nostra non solum Deo sed et his qui possunt mederi vulneribus nostris
atque peccatis, delebuntur peccata nostra ab eo qui ait Ecce delebo ut nubem
iniquitates tuas etc."

All these are stock quotations, relied upon to prove the antiquity of sacramental confession.

[1] Cyprian. de Lapsis n. 29. "Confiteantur singuli quæso vos fratres dilec-
tissimi delictum suum dum adhuc qui deliquet in sæculo est, dum .admitti
confessio ejus potest, dum satisfactio et remissio facta per sacerdotes apud
Dominum grata est."

[2] Cyprian. Epist. xi.

[3] Deinde per confessionem peccatum suum sacerdoti manifestans, nitens in
contrarium, eleemosynas scilicet faciens, curabit infirmitatem." I give this on
the authority of Palmieri (Tract. de Pœnit. p. 366) who quotes Mai Spicilegii
Tom. VII. to which I have not access.

och) and made to confess, after which he took his place among the penitents.[1] Apologists cite a passage in Lactantius, in which he distinguishes the true Church from the Novatians, as that which cures the wounds of the soul through confession and repentance, but another passage shows that Lactantius relied on confession to God.[2] St. Hilary of Poitiers is also customarily adduced in support of sacramental confession, on the strength of a passage evidently corrupt,[3] the truth being that he knows nothing of any confession save to God, the sufficiency and necessity of which for the pardon of sin he is never tired of reiterating, though his definition of this confession includes amendment.[4] St. Pacianus, in his exhortation to repentance, speaks of confession as an integral part of it; he does not specify that this confession is to God, and his allusions to the shame connected with it would seem to indicate that it was public, in the congregation.[5] In fact the stress laid by the Fathers on the humiliation of confession as part of the expiation of sin shows that it must have been public, and they have a somewhat grotesque effect when applied by modern writers to the wholly different practice of auricular confession.[6] A passage or two in the so-called Rule of St. Basil the Great have been quoted to show the existence in the fourth century of sacerdotal confession, but the recensions in which these occur are evidently of a date considerably

----

[1] Euseb. H. E. VI. 34. An immense amount of discussion has been provoked by the statement that Philip was the first Christian emperor. It will be found exhaustively summed up by Le Nain de Tillemont, *Hist. des Empereurs*, III. 494–499.

[2] Lactant. Divin. Institt. Lib. IV. cap. 7, 30.

[3] In describing the power of the keys granted to the apostles he says "ut quos ligaverint, id est peccatorum nodis innexos relinquerint, et quos solverint confessione [concessione] videlicet veniæ receperint in salutem, hi apostolica conditione sententiæ in cœlis quoque absoluti sint aut ligati."—S. Hilar. Pictav. Comment. in Matt. cap. XVIII. n. 8. Cf. cap. XVI. n. 7.

The emendation of *concessione* for *confessione* would seem to be self-evident. It was suggested two centuries ago by the Protestant Daillé, but is rejected by Catholic scholars, who are loath to abandon even so trivial a piece of evidence.

[4] "Iniquitati enim alia nulla medicina est nisi confessio ad Deum."—S. Hilarii Tract. in Ps. XXXI. n. 5. Cf. Tract. in Ps. CXVIII. Litt. iii. n. 19; Litt. iv. n. 4; Lit. xviii. n. 13.—Tract. in Ps. CXIX. n. 4.—Tract. in Ps. CXXXV. n. 3.

[5] S. Paciani Parænesis ad Pœnit. cap. 6, 8, 9.

[6] The current phrase is "Erubescentia quæ est maxima pars satisfactionis."—S. Antonini Summæ P. III. Tit. xiv. cap. 19, § 9.

posterior and consequently prove nothing.[1] Moreover, his contemporary, St. Gregory of Nyssa, lays down the rule that voluntary confession is a sign of amendment, and that therefore it should be rewarded by a shorter penance than when the offender is convicted of his sin, thus showing that he regarded such confession as a matter of the *forum externum.*[2]

About this period we meet with three forms of voluntary confession in more or less frequent use—confession to God, to the congregation gathered in the church, and to a priest or some other holy man. St. Ambrose supplies us with evidence of them all. In some passages he speaks of confession to God as though that were the ordinary and recognized practice.[3] In another he seeks to remove the shame of confession in the church and soliciting the prayers of the brethren, showing that this public confession was voluntary and for secret sins; this he says procures admission to the sacrament which removes the sin, showing further that it was the Eucharist that secured pardon.[4] Concurrently with this we learn from his biographer that he was very sympathetic with those who sought him privately to confess their sins to him, but he assumed to do nothing more than to intercede for them with God and to prescribe abstention from sin and humiliation before God.[5] This passage is the main reliance of modern apologists, but there is in it evidently nothing of sacramental confession and absolution; it was a practice

---

[1] S. Basilii Regulæ Interrog. XXI. CXCIX. CC. (Migne CIII. 508, 551-2).—S. Basil. Regulæ Breviores Q. 288. In S. Basil. *Liber Regularum fusius disputatarum,* Q. 46, 51, 52, evidently embodying an earlier form and purporting to be the utterance of the saint himself, sin is treated as a matter of the *forum externum,* as in the monastic Rules of the West.

[2] S. Gregor. Nyssen. Epist. Canon. cap. 4.

[3] "Et nos ergo non erubescamus fateri Domino peccata nostra?"—S. Ambros. de Pœnit. Lib. II. cap. 1. Again, "Novit omnia Dominus sed expectat vocem tuam non ut puniat sed ut ignoscat.—Ibid. cap. 7. This is an essential preliminary to pardon—De Paradiso cap. xiv. n. 71.

[4] S. Ambr. de Pœnit. Lib. II. cap. 3, 10.—"Hoc ergo in ecclesia facere fastidis ut Deo supplices, ut patrocinium tibi ad obsecrandum sanctæ plebis requiras, ubi nihil est quod pudori esse debeat nisi non fateri, cum omnes simus peccatores." Alexander Hales (Summæ P. IV. Q. XVIII. Membr. iv. Art. 5, § 8) admits with the early Fathers that the humiliation of public confession is the chief source of pardon and remission, but he argues that the shame is too great and that the consequences may be serious.

[5] Paulini Vit. S. Ambros. cap. 39.

permitted but not recognized by the Church; it might aid the sinner in winning for himself reconciliation to God, but the Church took no cognizance of the matter as its formulas were framed only for public confession. St. Ambrose himself knows only of public penance for grave sins; the venials of daily occurrence were removed by repentance, and there is no class intermediate between them.[1] The confessor had no power to do anything but to pray and advise, as indicated by Origen. If reconciliation with the Church were wanted the sin secretly confessed had to be published to the congregation in order that public penance might be imposed, but this rule was relaxed in the case of adulteresses, lest it should lead to their death, though they were suspended from communion for the period assigned by the canons.[2]

With the development of sacerdotalism the custom of private confession naturally spread, for it was a vast relief to the sinner thus to quiet his conscience without public humiliation and the hardships of public penance. St. Jerome refers to it several times and a canon of the first council of Toledo in 398 shows that in Spain it was becoming a recognized function of the priest, at least for virgins under vows.[3] In the East, also, the custom seems to have been established of deputing an experienced priest in each cathedral church as *pœnitentiarius* to listen to all who desired to make confession. Socrates and Sozomen relate that Nectarius, the predecessor of Chrysostom in the see of Constantinople, did away with the practice in consequence of a fair penitent being seduced by a deacon and that his example was imitated by other bishops.[4] The accuracy of this story has been

---

[1] S. Ambros. de Pœnit. Lib. II. cap. 95.

[2] S. Basil. Epist. Canon II. 34. This necessity of public confession as a preliminary to admission to penance is naturally an obstacle in proving the antiquity of auricular confession. To evade it the ingenious assumption is made that private confession always preceded public and that the latter was merely part of the penance imposed.—Guillois, History of Confession, pp. 121 sqq.

[3] S. Hieron. Epist. XLI. n. 3; Comment. in Ecclesiastæ cap. 10.—Con. Toletan. I. ann. 398 cap. 6.

[4] Socrat. H. E. v. 19.—Sozomen. H. E. VII. 16. Both writers say the custom originated in Rome. Socrates attributes it to the troubles arising in the middle of the third century from the Novatian controversy. Sozomen ascribes it to the growing distaste for public confession, for which it was a substitute, and proceeds to describe the existing practice of the Roman Church, which exhibits the form of public penance, the penitents being grouped together in church;.

questioned, owing to certain discrepancies and improbabilities in the
narratives, but there would seem little doubt that by this time in the
East private confession, as an escape from public, was gaining ground.
That this was regarded by the Church with disfavor as an irregularity is shown by the accusation against Chrysostom in the synod
ad Quercum referred to in a former chapter (p. 36). Chrysostom
himself, as might be expected, is by no means consistent in his treatment of the subject. In some passages he speaks of confession to
God as all sufficient to procure pardon.[1] In another he suggests
that the anxious sinner will find relief in unburdening his conscience
to an expert who can show him how to mend his ways, and again he
speaks of confession as though it were open and public.[2] Of these
three, however, confession to God is the one essential; it is that
which secures pardon, the others may be performed or not.[3] Evidently as yet in the East there was no formal and recognized practice
of private confession.

In the African Church St. Augustin seems to set little store on
confession when he omits it entirely from his enumeration of what
is requisite to obtain pardon for sin.[4] Yet in his exposition of the
Raising of Lazarus he assumes that by confession the sinner is revived, after which his bonds are loosed by the Church.[5] One passage
has been quoted to show that he was opposed to public confession,

---

after mass, in which they are not allowed to take communion, they prostrate
themselves; the bishop comes and prostrates himself with them, and they perform in private the penance assigned to them. We shall see that in the Roman
Church private confession was not recognized till the middle of the fifth
century.

[1] S. Jo. Chrysost. de Pœnitent. Homil. II. n. 1; Homil. III. n. 1.

[2] S. Jo. Chrysost. in Genesim Homil. XX. n. 3; in Johannem Homil. XXXIV.
n. 3. Cf. De Davide et Saule Homil. III. n. 2; in Epist. ad Hebræos Homil.
IX. n. 4.

[3] In Epist. ad Hebræos Homil. XXXI. n. 3.—"Non tibi dico ut ea tanquam
pompam in publicum proferas, neque ut apud alios te accuses, sed ut pareas
prophetæ dicenti; *Revela Domino viam tuam.* Apud Deum ea confitere, apud
judicem confitere peccata tua, orans, si non lingua saltem memoria, et ita roga
ut tui misereatur."

[4] S. Augustin. Serm. CCCLI. cap. 5.

[5] Ejusd. Serm. LXVII. cap. 1, 2; Enarrat. in Ps. CI. Serm. ii. cap. 3. It is
true that in the *Enarrat. in Ps.* LXVI. n. 6, he says "damnaberis tacitus qui
posses liberari confessus," but the context shows that this alludes to confession
to God, who thus becomes both advocate and judge.

but it is only an argument against the bishop's public reproof of sins of which he has obtained cognizance, as this may lead, in case of crime, to prosecution before the secular authorities.[1] It is in the same line of thought as the canon referred to above (p. 15) subscribed to by him in the African council of 419, directing all' bishops to withdraw from communion with any bishop who should deprive of communion any one on account of a sin revealed to him in confession, if the sinner chose to deny it. That in fact he considered public penance to be essential for any action by the Church is seen by his urging that without it the Church could not make use of the power of the keys,[2] and the canon just cited shows that public penance inferred public confession. No one, he says elsewhere, has true repentance who is deterred from penance by fear of the humiliation.[3] Evidently confession to priest or bishop had no recognized place in the discipline of the African Church, nor was the necessity for it apparent, in the middle of the sixth century, to Victor of Tunnone, who seems to regard confession to God as the one thing needful, for the very act of confession to him cures the soul.[4] Man still dealt directly with his God and required no intermediary.

In the Latin Church of the early part of the fifth century John Cassianus seems to know only public confession and confession to God, when he counsels the sinner who is ashamed to reveal his lapses before men to have recourse to the Lord from whom nothing is hidden.[5] Confession to the priest as an alternative seems to be unknown to him. In his monastic institutes, indeed, Cassianus orders the young monk to reveal to some older one all the evil thoughts that arise in his mind and take counsel with him how to avoid the snares of the enemy,[6] but this has nothing to do with sacramental confession and is akin to the monastic custom of daily confession of faults in the chapter or assembly of the convent.[7]

Meanwhile the claims of the Church as the source of pardon through the power of the keys were constantly advancing, and sacerdotalism was gradually interposing itself more and more between

---

[1] Ejusd. Serm. LXXXII. cap. 8.

[2] Ejusd. Serm. CCCXCII. cap. 3.   Cf. Serm. CCCLI. n. 9.

[3] Ejusd. Enarrat. in Ps. XXXIII. Serm. ii. n. 11.

[4] Victor. Tunenens. de Pœnitent. Lib. I. cap. 3.

[5] Jo. Cassian. Collat. XX. cap. 8.   [6] Ejusd. Institutt. Lib. IV. cap. 9.

[7] S. Eucherii Lugdun. Homil. VIII.

the sinner and his God. We have seen how St. Jerome and St. Isidor of Pelusium rebuked the priests and bishops who assumed to remit sins and such remission was manifestly impossible without a preliminary declaration of the offences to be forgiven. Voluntary public confession had long been irksome; it required a vehemence of contrition not predicable of the average Christian, especially after the faith had become dominant and had spread over mixed and motley populations, and the warning of St. Augustin shows that incautious revelations of crime in this way were liable to lead to public prosecution. That private confession should be hailed as a relief was inevitable, but the Church resisted it long and endeavored to stave it off by expedients. The biographer of St. Hilary of Arles describes for us a system bearing some analogy to that ascribed to the Western Church about this time by Sozomen. He would announce that on Sunday he would administer penance; crowds would flock to hear him and he would excite their fears to the utmost by powerful descriptions of the torments of hell and the terrors of the Day of Judgment; with tears and sobs and groans they would beg for pardon, when he would bestow on them the imposition of hands and pray earnestly that their repentance might bear the proper fruit.[1] Evidently in such a scene as this there could be no confession except the general one of being in sin, and St. Hilary relied upon the impression produced on the souls of the penitents to win pardon from God. Another method by which the humiliation of public confession was evaded was by writing out the confession of the penitent, which was then read in the congregation, thus sparing him the personal mortification of uttering it himself. It is probable that St. Basil refers to this when he orders that the sin of adulteresses shall not be published lest they incur risk of death.

It would seem that the pressure for relief from this severity increased, while the tendency of bishops to arrogate to themselves the right of dealing with sinners in secret developed until the Church gave way. In 452 we find St. Leo I. defining a wholesome confession as a condition precedent to reconciliation, without specifying the character of the confession.[2] When in 459 he forbade, in an epistle to the bishops of Campania, the custom of reading confessions in

---

[1] Vit. S. Hilarii Arelatens. cap. 13.
[2] Leonis PP. I. Epist. cviii. cap. 2, ad Theodorum.

public he could scarce have conceived the ultimate importance of his act, for centuries were still to elapse before its full significance was developed. The terms in which he proposed this momentous change show that he regarded it merely as a matter of expediency. The faith is laudable which leads men to disregard the mortification of having their transgressions made known, but it prevents many sinners from seeking pardon, either through shame or through fear of letting their enemies learn their crimes and of becoming subject to the laws. Having thus shown that public confession, either personally or by writing, was the only form as yet recognized, he proceeds to define that it suffices to confess to God and then to the priest (or bishop) who should pray for the sinner. In this way, he adds, more sinners can be allured to repentance when they know that their sins will not be published to the people.[1] Yet sinners do not seem to have availed themselves of the opportunity as eagerly as was hoped, and, about 470, another inducement was offered when the pope, St. Simplicius, set apart a week in each of the three churches, St. Peter's, St. Paul's and St. Lawrence's, in which priests should remain there to receive penitents and administer baptism[2]—the first authentic evidence we have of confessors stationed in churches—and this slender provision for the imperial and papal city indicates how rare as yet was confession.

The practice of private confession, in fact, developed but slowly. If we would look for it anywhere it might be expected to occur in the monastic rules which were framed in order that earnest seekers after salvation should be led to the performance of all things salutary

---

[1] Ejusd. Epist. CLXVIII. cap. 2.—C. 61, Caus. XXXIII. Q. iii. Dist. 1. Yet the custom of *libelli* of confession long continued. In 892 Pope Formosus required them when he received to reconciliation the clerics who had been ordained by Photius.—Formosi PP. Epist. II. (Migne, CXXIX. 840).

It required a notable ignorance of church history for the Baltimore council of 1866 to declare that God could have required of sinners the humiliation of public confession but that "tantum a nobis postulavit ut sacerdoti secreto et sine testibus conscientiæ arcana panderemus" (Con. Plen. Baltim. II. ann. 1866, Tit. v. c. 5, n. 276). Thomas of Walden, in controverting Wickliffe, knew better than this when he admitted (De Hæresibus Antiquor. Cap. LXXI. n. 1) that in the early Church confession was public, though he endeavors to recover himself by asserting that the apostles instituted secret confession, which was wrongfully supplanted by public and was restored by Leo.

[2] Anastas. Biblioth. in Simplicio PP.

to their souls and acceptable to God. Yet the Rule which St. Pacho-
mius is said to have received from an angel has in it no precept of
confession; trifling infractions are punished with two or three days'
penance, and serious offences with scourging; it is wholly an affair of
the *forum externum.*[1] The same may be said of the Rule of St. Orse-
sius and the *Regula Orientalis* compiled by the deacon Vigilius from
the Eastern Rules, and also of those which passed under the names
of St. Antony, the Abbot Isaiah, St. Serapion, the Holy Fathers,
and St. Macarius.[2] In that of St. Cæsarius of Arles there is only the
provision that those who have done what they know not to be right
shall ask pardon of each other, and the conception of earning remission of sins is the assiduous daily practice of good works.[3] In the
Rule of Benedict, private confession is not a matter of prescription
but is recommended as a sign of humility, and a monk who is conscious that there is lurking in his soul a cause of sin is told to reveal
it to the abbot or to one of the elders who know how to cure wounds
and not betray them.[4] As the abbots of the period were rarely priests
there was nothing sacramental about these regulations. The Rule of
St. Fructuosus of Braga has a somewhat similar provision as a method
of moral discipline and not as a means of obtaining pardon from God.[5]
Even in the ninth century we are told that daily confession one to
another was a monastic custom,[6] and St. Chrodegang prescribed that
every day after prime each member of the house should confess his
faults and accept punishment according to his station.[7] Grimlaic, in his
rules for monks, about the year 900, orders them to meet in the evening and examine their consciences for all sins committed during the

---

[1] Regul. S. Pachomii cap. 119, 121, 128.

[2] S. Benedicti Ananiens. Codex Regularum (Migne, CIII.).

[3] Regul. S. Tetradii cap. 12, 20. But in a homily attributed to St. Cæsarius
(Homil. XIX.) death-bed confession to God and to the priest is regarded as
essential.

[4] Regul. S. Benedicti cap. 7, 45, 46.

[5] S. Fructuosi Bracarens. Reg. Monachor. cap. 13. See also the Regula S.
Aurelii Arelatens. cap. 41 (Migne LXVIII. 392).—Reg. SS. Pauli et Stephani
cap. 34 (Ib. LXVI. 957).—Reg. S. Ferreoli Uzetensis (Ib. LXVI. 959-76).—
Reg. S. Isidor. Hispalens. (Ib. CIII. 568-9).—Reg. Magistri cap. 13, 14, 15 (Ib.
LXXXVIII. 967-9, 981).—S. Benedicti Ananiens. Concord. Regularum cap. 30,
31, 33 (Ib. CIII. 973-1006).

[6] Jonæ Aurelian. de Instit. Laicali Lib. I. cap. 16.

[7] Reg. S. Chrodegangi cap. 18.

day ; confession leads to repentance and repentance to pardon, but nothing is said as to penance or absolution. It was a wholesome exercise and nothing more.[1] In 829 an expression of the council of Paris shows that the confession of nuns to priests was a wholly voluntary matter, not governed by any precept.[2] The monks thus had adopted the custom of daily chapters or assemblies in which sinners were expected to confess their faults and accept punishment, and where accusations could be brought against those who did not voluntarily accuse themselves, even as in the congregations the faithful were more or less accustomed to do the same. This answered all purposes of discipline and private confession would have been a manifest surplusage.

Among the laity, Julian Pomerius, about the year 500, assumes that the penitent can either confess his sins or keep them to himself and assume penance for them, through which he will secure salvation.[3] St. Fulgentius of Ruspe teaches that confession is useless unless the sinner by good works overcomes the demerits of his past transgressions,[4] thus denying all value to the intermediation of the priest, while Gennadius of Marseilles speaks of public lamentation over sin as the mode of securing pardon ; he stigmatizes as Novatians those who deny this and evidently knows nothing of private confession to the priest as a remedy.[5]

Gregory the Great, who did so much for the advancement of sacerdotalism, assumes as a matter of course that confession is necessary for the remission of sin and that the process is in sacerdotal hands,[6] although in one passage he speaks of the public confession of secret sins as a salutary exercise and as a practice still followed.[7] In the East, his contemporary, John the Faster of Constantinople, seems to recognize no other form than private confession to the priest ;[8]

---

[1] Grimlaici Reg. Solitarium cap. 25, 29 (Migne CIII. 606, 618).

[2] Con. Paris. ann. 829, cap. 46 (Harduin. IV. 1323).

[3] Juliani Pomerii de Vita contemplativa Lib. II. cap. 7.

[4] S. Fulgent. Ruspens. de Remiss. Peccator. Lib. II. cap. 16.

[5] Gennadii Massiliens. de Eccl. Dogmata cap. 80.

[6] Gregor. PP. I. Homil. in Evangel. Lib. II. Homil. 26.—Moral. Lib. VIII. cap. 21.—Exposit. in I. Regum Lib. VI. cap. ii. n. 4, 33.

[7] Ejusd. Moral. Lib. XXV. cap. 13.

[8] Johann. Jejunatoris Libellus Pœnitentialis (Morin. de Discipl. Pœnit. App. p. 79.) I have already alluded to the likelihood of modifications in a code such as this handed down through the centuries.

and St. Anastasius of Sinai gives formal directions for it, though he admits that many great sinners are justified without it.[1]

It was at this period that Gregory, by sending forth St. Austin of Canterbury to convert the Anglo-Saxons, gave impulse to the missionary enterprises which were destined to work such benefit to the Church and to civilization, subduing to Christianity the wild tribes which were to be the ancestors of so many European common-wealths. In this the Barbarian and his teacher exercised a mutual interaction, each influenced the other, and the result was the medieval Church. To the new and ignorant converts the priest was the direct representative of God, regarded with a veneration very different from that which he excited in the polished citizens of Nîmes or Rome or Constantinople, and any claim which he might put forward of super-natural power was not likely to be gainsaid.[2] I have already alluded to the influence of this movement on the substitution of priest for bishop in the office of reconciling penitents; it could have no less in establishing the claim of the priest to hear confessions. As early as the seventh century the fact that Pepin of Landen condescended to confess to Bishop Wito was cited as a conspicuous proof of his well-known piety,[3] and though this would show that confession was as yet exceptional, yet the simple fact that Penitentials were beginning to be found necessary, that in time they multiplied so enormously and were in such universal use, indicates how, under these favoring influences, the practice of confession spread and how firmly it became lodged in priestly hands. Yet among the more southern communi-

---

[1] S. Anastas. Sinaitæ Orat. de S. Synaxi (Canisii et Basnage Thesaur. I. 470, 477)—"Confitere Christo per sacerdotem peccata tua. . . . Nam multi crebro reperiuntur qui cum palam peccassent magnam in occulto pœnitentiam egerunt . . . ac a nobis quidem judicantur velut peccatores, apud Deum autem justificati sunt."

[2] A notable instance of this occurs during the Carlovingian reconstruction, after the social disorganization in France under the Mayors of the Palace. One of the most troublesome opponents of St. Boniface in this work was a certain Bishop Adelbert, who pretended to be inspired and who was regarded as a saint by his numerous followers. When the people would assemble before him and desire to confess their sins he would say "I know all your sins, for nothing is hidden from me. It is not necessary for you to confess for all your sins are remitted to you, so you can go home in the peace of the Church and safe in your absolution."—S. Bonifacii Epist. LVII.

[3] Baron. Annal. ann. 631 n. 8.

ties and races of older civilization the progress was slower. In Spain, St. Isidor of Seville, early in the seventh century, while treating in detail of the duties of bishop and priest, makes no mention of their hearing confessions; he knows only of the public penance of sackcloth and ashes and is evidently altogether unfamiliar with auricular confession and private penance.[1] In the East, at the same period, St. Dorotheus the Abbot, in his instructions as to securing salvation, speaks of repentance and amendment and prayer and doing good, but nothing of confession and priestly ministrations.[2] Even in the ninth century, St. Theodore Studites holds that repentance suffices for pardon; confession is only a wholesome exercise, for through it evil thoughts are dissipated in place of infecting the soul.[3]

Throughout the greater part of Europe, however, the custom was establishing itself permanently. It was declared to be indispensable to the awarding of penance and to the reconciliation of the sinner, and formed a necessary portion of the formalities connected with these ceremonies.[4] The ardent missionaries who were spreading the faith among the barbarian tribes, eager to lead and keep their converts in the right path, could imagine no more effective method than to inculcate regular and habitual confession, and it was easy for them to prescribe it as a rule among their neophytes who knew nothing to the contrary. The earliest attempt at inducing periodical confession would seem to be by Egbert of York, in the latter half of the eighth century, who says that Theodore of Canterbury introduced the custom that, within twelve days of Christmas, all, both clerics and laymen, should seek their confessors as a preparation for the communion of the Nativity.[5] Early in the ninth century, again, there was a

---

[1] S. Isidori Hispalens. de Eccl. Officiis Lib. II. cap. xviii. n. 4–7.

[2] S. Dorothei Archimandr. Doctrina XII. De Timore et Pœnis Inferni.

[3] S. Theodori Studitæ Serm. LXXXII., CXXXIII.

[4] Con. Cabillonens. ann. 649, cap. 8.—S. Eligii Noviomens. Homil. IV. XI. XV.—Jonæ Aurelianens. de Instit. Laicali I. 15.

The *Ordines ad dandam Pœnitentiam* contained in so many of the Penitentials show that confession to the priest was expected of all penitents.

[5] Ecberti Dialog. Interrog. xvi. (Haddan and Stubbs, III. 413).

Nearly contemporary with this was the Rule framed by St. Chrodegang for the order of canons regular which he instituted. This has been commonly quoted in proof of the institution of periodical confession, but it is of no authority. In the recension printed by D'Achery there is a precept that the

decided effort to introduce annual confession on Ash Wednesday. A ritual of the period orders the priest to call upon all accustomed to confess to him to renew their confessions on that day, and another ritual even orders three confessions a year.[1] In 821 Theodulf of Orleans prescribes it annually on Ash Wednesday,[2] and in 822 the statutes of Corbie order a holiday on that day, so that the laboring folk may have time to confess.[3] The Penitential which passes under the name of Egbert speaks of it as a custom existing beyond seas and urges its adoption,[4] and a forged decretal attributed to Pope Eutychianus orders the priest to invite his flock to confess on that day.[5] Nor

---

people shall confess thrice yearly to their priests, and monks every Saturday to the bishop or to their prior (Reg. S. Chrodegangi cap. 32, *ap.* Migne LXXXIX. 1072). In another recension, which is evidently older, there is nothing concerning the laity, and the canons are only required to confess twice a year to the bishop—once early in Lent and again between Aug. 15 and Nov. 1 (Reg. S. Chrodeg. cap. 14, *ap.* Harduin. IV. 1196). Even this however is a later regulation, for the Rule evidently was revised from time to time to adapt it to the evolution of the Church. In 816, the council of Aachen drew up a minute and extended series of regulations for the canons, in which there is no trace of secret confession, while there is ample provision for the punishment of offences. A man might, if he chose, confess a crime in the chapter and accept the penalty provided for it, and if he did not do so he was carried before the bishop who inflicted public penance on him.—Con. Aquisgranens. ann. 816 Lib. I. cap. 134 (Hartzheim I. 509). See also the *Regula Canonicorum ab Amalrico collecta* Lib. I. cap. 134 (Migne, CV. 927). In the later recension the clause concerning confession by the laity is evidently an interpolation by some zealous sacerdotalist, for it has no relation to the rest of the Rule.

Hartzheim (Concil. German. I. 32) prints a canon of a council of Liége in 710 prescribing yearly confession to the parish priest, but it is evidently either a forgery or an erroneous date. If genuine it cannot be earlier than the Lateran canon of 1216.

[1] Martene de antiq. Eccles. Ritibus Lib. I. cap. vi. Art. 7, Ord. 4, 10. Cf. Ord. 3.

[2] Theodulfi Aurel. Capit. ad Presbyt. XXXVI.

[3] Statuta antiqua Abbatiæ Corbiens. Lib. I. cap. 2 (D'Achery, I. 587).

[4] Pœnit. Ps. Ecberti Lib. I. cap. 12 ; Lib. IV. cap. 65.

[5] Ps. Eutychiani Exhortatio ad Presbyteros (Migne, V. 65). Another forgery, ascribed to Eutychianus, which passed into all the collections of canons (Theodulf. Aurelian. cap. 26; Burchardi Lib. XII. cap. 14; Anselmi Lucens. Lib. XI. cap. 71; Ivon. Carnot. Decr. P. XII. cap. 71; Gratian cap. 17 Caus. XXII. Q. 1) threatens segregation for refusal to confess, but it is concerned only with public and notorious crime, so that confession is used to signify application for penance and reconciliation.

was this all: the reluctant people were stimulated by assuring them that confession was all-important, that it was the source of all hope and that of itself it secured justification and the pardon of sin.[1] It was even asserted to be the means of securing earthly good fortune. When a young friend was setting out on a campaign against the Saxons, Alcuin advises him to secure himself by confession against the dangers of the expedition; with this and the protection of priestly prayers, to be obtained by liberal payments, he will be able to return in safety.[2] Charlemagne gave practical realization to this belief when, in his efforts to Christianize his Saxon conquests, he enacted that those secretly guilty of capital crimes, who would confess them to the priest and accept penance, should escape other punishment on the testimony of the confessor.[3] Yet with all this so little conception was there, in the Church of the period, of any sacramental character attaching to auricular confession that Theodulf of Orleans, whom we have just seen prescribing it annually, orders daily confession to God and regards that to the priest only as an assistance whereby to obtain wholesome counsel as to penance and mutual prayer,[4] and Benedict the Levite speaks of it as placating God and merely seeking counsel of the priest,[5] while Rabanus Maurus defines confession as confessing to God and seems to know nothing of priestly mediation.[6]

In spite of all endeavor the custom of auricular confession made provokingly slow progress, though it is evident that some people adopted it, for Ghaerbald Bishop of Liége urges diligence on his priests in listening to all who come to confess and in assigning them

---

[1] Ordo ad dandam Pœnitentiam (Pez, Thesaur. Anecd. II. II. 622).—"Confessio sanat, confessio justificat, confessio peccati veniam donat; omnis spes in confessione consistit, in confessione locus misericordiæ est."—Cf. Alcuin. de Virtut. et Vitiis cap. 12.

[2] Alcuini Epist. XLIV.

[3] Capit. Carol. Mag. de Partibus Saxoniæ ann. 789, cap. 14.

[4] Theodulf. Aurel. Capit. ad Presbyteros cap. XXX.

[5] Bened. Levit. Capitular. Lib. VII. cap. 385.   Addit. III. cap. 19.

[6] Rabani Mauri de Clericorum Instit. Lib. II. cap. 14.

A synodal sermon to be preached at all synods is ascribed to Leo IV. about 850, giving minute directions as to the duties of priests, among which is summoning all their parishioners to confession on Ash Wednesday, and imposing on them due penance according to the Penitentials, but its date and authority are equally uncertain (Harduin. VI. I. 786).

due penance.[1] Yet over-curious folk asked what warrant there was for it in the New Testament, to which Jonas of Orleans replies by quoting certain texts, wholly irrelevant so far as the priestly function is concerned.[2] In 747 the council of Clovesho, in its elaborate instructions to priests as to their duties, says nothing about hearing confessions or imposing penance, though it assumes that their people will come to them to consult about their spiritual welfare.[3] Even the Venerable Bede considers that only heresy, infidelity, judaism and schism are to be brought to the Church; other sins God cures by himself in the mind and conscience,[4] and Smaragdus echoes him in advising that grievous sins alone be revealed to the priest, and urging confession to God who diminishes sin.[5] In fact, the old belief that confession to God suffices had been too deeply implanted to be readily eradicated. It is still indicated in the formulas of the Gregorian Sacramentary and of a Gallic Sacramentary of the seventh or eighth century.[6] It is to be found in many of the Penitentials— the place of all others where we should least expect to meet it—in case of the absence of a priest.[7] Alcuin, with the indecision customary at the period, wavers between confession to God and to the priest.[8] A still more emphatic testimony to the complete uncertainty which as yet reigned on the subject, and to the resistance of inertia offered to the introduction of auricular confession, is found in the proceedings of the council of Châlons in 813. Charlemagne had summoned the prelates of his vast empire to meet in five great synods, at Arles, Châlons, Tours, Reims and Mainz, to consult as to the welfare of the Church and to offer him suggestions to be embodied in legislation. The synods of Arles and Mainz paid no attention to confession and

---

[1] Ghaerbaldi Instruct. Pastoral. (Martene Ampliss. Collect. VII. 27).

[2] Jonæ Aurelian. de Instit. Laicali I. 15.

[3] Con. Cloveshoviens. ann. 747 cap. 8–12 (Haddan and Stubbs, III. 365–66).

[4] Bedæ in Lucæ Evang. Exposit. Lib. V. cap. 17.

[5] Smaragdi Diadema Monachorum cap. 16.

[6] Sacrament. Gregorian. (Muratori Opp. T. XIII. P. II. pp. 886–93).—Sacrament. Gallican. (Ibid. P. III. p. 873).

[7] Capitula Dacheriana cap. 58, 150.—Canones Gregorii cap. 38.—Theodori Pœnitent. Lib. I. cap. xii. § 7.—Cummeani Pœnitent. XIV. 13.—Pœnit. Ps. Gregorii III. cap. 30 (Wasserschleben, Bussordnungen, pp, 150, 158, 164, 196, 493, 545.)

[8] Alcuini de Psalmorum Usu P. II. cap. 3, 8, 9; Ejusd. Officia per Ferias, Feria 2, 4, 5; Ejusd. de Confessione Peccatorum cap. 2, 7.

penance. Those of Reims and Tours complain of the carelessness and ignorance of priests in hearing confessions and assigning penance.[1] That of Châlons, however, endeavored to define the questions which evidently were occasioning debate in the Church. Some persons, it says, hold that confession is to be made only to God, others think that it should be made to the priest; both customs are followed in the Church with great profit. David tells us to confess to God, the apostles to confess to each other; confession to God purges sin; confession to the priest shows how sins are to be purged; God often confers salvation by his invisible power, and often by the ministration of the spiritual physician.[2] Evidently the good fathers of the council were endeavoring to still discussion by a definition which should satisfy both parties.

The effort to extend and popularize the practice of auricular confession evidently was meeting with scant success. Alcuin, in writing

---

[1] C. Remens. II. ann. 813, cap. 12, 16.—C. Turon. III. ann. 813, cap. 22.

[2] C. Cabillonens. II. ann. 813, cap. 33 (Harduin IV. 1037).—" Quidam Deo solummodo confiteri debere dicunt peccata, quidam vero sacerdotibus confitenda esse percensent: quod utrumque non sine magno fructu intra sanctam fit ecclesiam. Ita dumtaxat ut et Deo, qui remissor est peccatorum, confiteamur peccata nostra, et cum David dicamus *Dixi; confitebor adversus me injustitias meas, et tu remisisti impietatem peccati mei* (Ps. XXXII. 5). Et secundum institutionem Apostoli, confiteamur alterutrum peccata nostra et oremus pro invicem ut salvemur. Confessio itaque quæ Deo fit purgat peccata; ea vero quæ sacerdoti fit docet qualiter ipsa purgentur peccata, Deus namque salutis et sanitatis auctor et largitor plerumque hanc præbet suæ potentiæ invisibili administratione, plerumque medicorum operatione."

In this shape the canon was included in the collections of Benedict the Levite (Capitul. Add. III. cap. 57). As auricular confession, however, became more and more a policy to be enforced, this recognition of its subsidiary character could not be permitted and zealous churchmen resorted to the customary device of interpolation. Burchard prints it (Decreti Lib. XIX. cap. 145), crediting it to the Penitential of Theodore, in which it does not exist, and inserting after the first "peccata" the words *ut Græci* and after "percensent" *ut tota sancta ecclesia*, thus giving it a totally different significance. In this shape it was carried into Ivo (Decr. P. XV. cap. 155) and Gratian (cap. 90 Caus. XXXIII. Q. iii. Dist. 1). To this falsification is attributable the notion which prevailed during the middle ages that confession was unknown in the Eastern Church, as we have seen in the Gloss on the Decretum.

For futile attempts to explain away the plain meaning of the canon see Estius in IV. Sentt. Dist. XVII. § 7 and Palmieri Tract. de Pœnit. p. 388.

to the brethren in Aquitaine and Languedoc, praises highly their piety and reverence, but reproves them because he is told that no layman is willing to confess to a priest.[1] In spite of the exhortations and commands to confess annually it is apparent from the formulas in the Penitentials and the books of ritual that voluntary confession was an extraordinary incident in the life of a sinner and an unusual one in that of a priest. The long recital provided for, of sins from childhood to maturity, shows that penitents were expected to come forward only when in fear of approaching death or of some unusual danger, and that the misdeeds of a lifetime were accumulated to be rehearsed in a single effort to quiet the conscience. The long protracted ceremonies, moreover, rendered it impossible for a priest to expedite more than a very few penitents, and could only have been framed at a time when a confession was an infrequent occurrence. When a penitent applies, the priest is instructed to retire to his *cubiculum*, or prayer-cell, and pray to God as a preliminary, after which he returns to the sinner, preaches a sermon to him, or perhaps even says mass over him and at the least sings several psalms, listens to the long catalogue of crime, consults with the penitent as to the amount of penance that he can endure, enjoins it, and the performance concludes with a number of prayers. Still more convincing as to the rarity of the occasion is the fact that, in many of the *Ordines*, the priest is directed to encourage the penitent by sharing with him a portion of the penance and fasting with him for two or three weeks —an amount of self-sacrifice only to be expected when penitents were as few as black swans, and scarce adapted to lead the priest to encourage confession among his flock unless some notable pecuniary advantage was anticipated as a result.[2] Many of these *Ordines* comprise

---

[1] Alcuini Epist. CXII.—"Dicitur vero neminem ex laicis suam velle confessionem sacerdotibus dare."

[2] For the inordinately long and complicated ceremonial of confession see Pœnitentiale Sangermanense, Pseudo-Romanum, Merseburgense, Sangallense and Vallicellianum II. (Wasserschleben, pp. 349, 361, 389, 437, 551).—Garofali, Ordo ad dandam Pœnitentiam, Romæ, 1791, p. 11.—Ordo ad dandem Pœnit. (Pez Thesauri Anecd. II. II. 611).—Martene de antiq. Eccles. Ritibus Lib. I. cap. vi. Art. 7, Ord. 2, 6, 12.—Morini de Sacr. Pœnit. App. p. 25.

For instructions to the priest to share the penance see Pœnitentiale Pseudo-Bedæ, Sangermanense, Pseudo-Romanum, Merseburgense, and the Corrector Burchardi (Wasserschleben, pp. 250, 349, 361, 389, 676).—Garofali loc. cit.— Muratori Antiq. Ital. Diss. 68 (T. XIV. pp. 27, 37)—Martene, *loc. cit.* Ord. 2,

formulas of confession evidently drawn up to guard against lapses of memory in penitents confessing the crimes of a whole life. They are hideous catalogues of vice and sin, containing all that the dismal experience of the confessional could mass together and apparently were repeated by the penitent whether or not he was guilty of all the wickedness thus detailed.[1] How different, moreover, was all this from sacramental confession is seen in the rule that the penitent must also reveal whatever he knows of the sins of other persons, with a view to their amendment, and failure to do this is denounced as a fresh sin.[2]

The popular resistance of inertia was evidently hard to overcome either by allurements or commands, but the Church persevered with its ordinary persistence. Every diocese, however, was a law unto itself. In 889 Riculfus of Soissons, in his very minute instructions to his priests, makes no allusions to private confession and penance; they are instructed to look after the public penitents and in due time to bring them in for reconciliation, but nothing more.[3] Yet within a few years, about 900, Regino of Pruhm shows us that, in some places, annual confession was assumed to be the rule, for in episcopal visitations one of the points to be inquired into is whether any one does not come to confession at least once a year on Ash Wednesday,[4]

10.—Pseudo-Alcuin. Lib. de Divinis Officiis cap. 13.—Ivonis Decr. P. xv. cap. 51.

That death-bed confession had become customary is inferable from cap. 29 of the council of Paris in 829.

[1] A good example of these will be found in Martene, *loc. cit.* Ord. 3. This custom probably explains the curious confession of Ratherius of Verona, in which he represents himself as the most abandoned wretch on earth—he who was the sternest moralist of the age.—Ratherii Veronens. Dial. Confessional. (Migne, CXXXVI. 397).

How deeply ingrained and almost ineradicable was the custom of deferring confession till the death-bed is shown by the repeated exhortations against it in many of the sermons which pass under the names of St. Augustin and St. Cæsarius of Arles. See S. Augustini Serm. Append. Serm. 255, 256, 257, 258, 259.

[2] Bened. Levit. Capitul. Lib. vii. cap. 386.—Ivon. Decr. P. xvi. cap. 360.

[3] Riculfi Suession. Constitt. cap. ix. (Harduin. VI. i. 416).

[4] Reginon. de Eccles. Discipl. Lib. ii. 5, n. 65. Lib. i. cap. 288 (copied into Burchard, xix. 2) orders priests to invite all conscious of mortal sin to come to confession on Ash Wednesday.

Binterim (Denkwürdigkeiten, V. iii. 267) rather recklessly quotes Regino

and some other canons of nearly the same period indicate the same.[1] On the other hand the council of Trosley, in 909, in its elaborate exhortations to sinners, speaks only of confession to God, to be followed by mortification and almsgiving.[2] Under the powerful influence of St. Dunstan, King Edgar the Pacific was led about 967 to recommend that all polluted with mortal sin should confess to their bishops on Ash Wednesday, which he says is a custom observed beyond the seas,[3] and in a body of English ecclesiastical observance, probably of nearly the same period, daily confession to God and yearly to the priest is enjoined; indeed, when any evil thoughts arise they should at once be confessed to the ghostly leech.[4] In 1009 the council of Enham orders frequent confession without specifying any definite intervals.[5] The little that was accomplished by all this is visible in the pious King Cnut's exhortations to confession which are in general terms, make no allusion to periodicity, and are hortatory, not mandatory,[6] while Ælfric's Pastoral Epistle, minute and detailed as it is, seems to know of no confession save on the death-bed, as a preparation for extreme unction.[7]

On the Continent, about the middle of the tenth century, St. Ulric of Augsburg ordered his priests to invite their parishioners to confess yearly on Ash Wednesday,[8] and doubtless there was much more legislation of the kind the records of which have been forgotten, but it was useless. Few prelates of that age were more earnest than Atto of Vercelli in enforcing the rights and powers of the priesthood,

---

Lib. I. cap. 195 to prove that at this period confession and communion were required thrice a year. This is virtually Conc. Turon. III. ann. 813 cap. 50, carried by Ansegise into Capitul. II. 45; it orders communion thrice annually, but not confession, for confession, as we have seen, was not at that time a condition precedent of communion. See also Reginon. Lib. II. 5, n. 56, where the meaning is unmistakable.

[1] Statutu Synodalia Remens. cap. 8 (Harduin. III. 575).—Reginon. Lib. I. cap. 272.—Burchard. Lib. II. cap. 62.

[2] Con. Trosleian. *ad calcem* (Harduin. VI. I. 764).

[3] Canons under King Edgar (Thorpe, Ancient Laws of England, II. 267).

[4] Ecclesiastical Institutes §§ 21, 30, 36 (Thorpe, II. 417, 427, 435).

[5] Con. Ænhamens. ann. 1009, cap. 20.

[6] Cnuti Leges Eccles. Tit. 18. This passage is lacking in the recension printed by Kolderup-Rosenvinge, Havniæ, 1826, p. 28.

[7] Ælfric's Pastoral Epistle n. 47 (Thorpe, II. 385.) Cf. Ælfric's *Quando dividis Chrisma* (lb. p. 393).

[8] S. Udalric. Augustan. Sermo Synodalis (Migne CXXXV. 1072–4).

yet in the elaborate instructions which he framed for his priests there is no allusion to any duty incumbent on them to hear confessions or to impose private penance. The only form he recognizes is public penance for public sins; if a priest hears of a sin committed he is to summon the offender and to impose penance according to the canons, but is not to reconcile him without permission of the bishop; if the sinner refuses, the bishop is to be notified, who will then take the requisite action. So, in the admonitions which the priest is to give to his flock, there is no word of exhortation to auricular confession, but they are daily to confess their sins to God with sighs and tears.[1] All the efforts of the Church to introduce private confession are ignored and we find ourselves transported back to the fourth century. When, in the year 1000, the council of Poitiers allowed bishops to accept, but not to exact, payment for receiving to penance and conferring confirmation it infers that both were strictly episcopal functions in which priests could not participate.[2] A Norman council of about 1025 classes confession merely as an alternative when it declares that any mortal sin since baptism closes the portals of heaven, unless it is washed away either by confession or contrition or by other good works.[3] Thietmar of Merseburg is evidently of the same opinion, when he relates how Archbishop Walterdus of Magdeburg and another notoriously licentious man redeemed their lapses of the flesh by contrition and liberal almsgiving, without any allusion to confession and absolution. Sometimes an intercessor aided in this, like the holy recluse virgin Sisu, to whom sinners used to flock with gifts, by distributing which among the poor she redeemed the sins of the donors. The manner in which Thietmar chronicles occasionally the confessions of individuals, especially on the death-bed, shows that it was regarded as rather a noteworthy occurrence, and an experience of his own is highly suggestive. He tells us that he violated a sepulchre to bury his brother's wife and adds that he confessed the sin the next time that he was sick.[4] On the other hand, it is related of the pious Emperor Henry III. that

---

[1] Attonis Vercellens. Capitulare cap. 90, 96.

[2] Con. Pictaviens. ann. 1000 cap. 2 (Harduin. VI. I. 764).

[3] Con. Normanniæ incerto anno cap. 14 (Bessin, Concil. Rotomagensia, p. 37).

[4] Dithmari Merseburgens. Chron. Lib. IV. cap. 14, 43; Lib. VI. cap. 30, 31, 46; Lib. VII. cap. 52; Lib. VIII. cap. 6.

he never put on the regal insignia without having first confessed and undergone the discipline in satisfaction of his sins,[1] and about 1099 the synod of Gran enjoins three confessions a year—at Easter, Pentecost, and Christmas.[2]

On the whole the Church during this period was rather losing ground, and it may be assumed as a rule that confession was rarely made save on the death-bed or when some threatening danger warned the sinner to set his house in order and prepare to meet his God. That penitents were few is inferable from a regulation already alluded to of a council of Rouen, about this time, requiring the confessor to report all confessions to his bishop who will then determine the penance.[3] This was not encouraging to penitents and still less so was a persistent effort made by successive popes to enforce the rigor of the ancient penance, including the abandonment of all occupations in court, camp or trade that could not be followed without sin, together with the forgiveness of all injuries and atonement to those injured.[4] The men of that day might well desire to postpone until life was spent the reconciliation which could only be purchased by surrendering all that rendered life attractive to them. Accordingly delayed confessions seem to be the rule. St. Peter Damiani describes the dowager Empress Agnes, widow of Henry III., on her visit to Rome about 1060, confessing to him all her sins since she was five years old.[5] About 1095 St. Anselm writes to his

---

[1] Reginandi Vit. S. Annonis n. 6 (Migne, CXLIII. 1521).

[2] Synod Strigonens. II. (Batthyani Legg. Eccl. Hung. II. 120). The same synod prohibits abbots from administering penance, showing how strong was the jealousy between the secular clergy and the regular.

[3] Post. Concil. Rotomagens. ann. 1074 cap. 8 (Harduin. VI. II. 1520).

[4] Synod. Urbani II. ad Melfiam ann. 1089 cap. 16; Concil. Claromont. ann. 1095 cap. 5; Concil Lateran. II. ann. 1139 cap. 22 (Harduin. VI. II. 1687, 1736, 2212).—C. 8 Caus. XXXIII. Q. iii. Dist. 5.

[5] S. Petri Damiani Opusc. LVI. cap. 5. Yet the empress grew more anxious as to her soul as she drew near her end. Her latter years were passed in the strictest ascetic observances, confessing daily not only her acts but her thoughts and even her dreams and performing religiously whatever penance was assigned to her.—Berthold. Constant. Annal. ann. 1077.

A similar assertion is made of Archbishop Gerhard, about 1105, whose body was for years refused Christian sepulture in consequence of strife with St. Anselm. It is said of him that whatever soil he contracted from the world he washed off by daily confession and tears.—Quadripartitus P. II. (Ed. Liebermann, Halle, 1892, p. 163).

brother Burgundius, who was about to depart on a pilgrimage to the Holy Land, neither to take his sins with him nor to leave them behind him, but to make confession of them all since infancy—and Burgundius was at that time a man of middle age with a son in holy orders.[1] Similarly when, in 1125, Archbishop Gelmirez of Compostella published an indulgence for a foray against the Moors, he offered absolution for all sins committed since baptism, showing that he presumed his recruits would never have confessed.[2] In fact, as yet auricular confession does not seem to be recognized as part of the regular functions of the priest. In the rituals of ordination at this period, not only is there no allusion to any power of absolution, but, in the enumeration of duties, hearing confessions and imposing penance are not mentioned.[3] Up to this time, as we have seen (p. 124) when priests administered penance it was only as a power delegated by the bishop.

Perhaps the most convincing evidence of the slender importance attached to auricular confession at this period is its neglect by the monastic orders, and their adherence to the customs described above (p. 183). From the earliest organization of monachism, they adapted to themselves the existing custom of public confession in the congregation, which was represented by daily or weekly chapters in which the brethren assembled and were expected to confess their faults or to be accused, when immediate punishment, usually scourging, would be inflicted,[4] consisting, in the eleventh century, according to St. Peter Damiani, usually of from twenty to forty stripes for each fault confessed.[5] There was nothing in the slightest degree sacramental about this, but it sufficed. After penitence, as we shall

---

[1] S. Anselmi Epist. Lib. III. Epist. 66. Yet St. Anselm, when treating of the forgiveness of sins (Cur Deus Homo cap. 11–15. 19, 20, 25), seems to know nothing of the efficacy of confession. The soul deals directly with God; for every sin there must be punishment or satisfaction, and the ordinary means of satisfaction are repentance, a contrite and humble heart, mortification of the flesh, almsgiving, forgiveness of sins and obedience, but all these are useless without faith.

[2] Hist. Compostell. Lib. II. cap. 78 (Florez, Hispaña Sagrada, XX. 429).

[3] Martene de Antiq. Eccles. Ritibus Lib. I. cap. viii. Art. 11, Ord. 7, 13.— "Qui ordinandi estis presbyteri offerre vos oportet et benedicere, præesse et prædicare, baptizare et bonis operibus et Deo placitis undique redundare."

[4] S. Eucherii Lugdunens. Homil. VIII.—S. Benedicti Regulæ cap. 45, 46.

[5] S. Petri Damiani Lib. VI. Epist. 27.

see, was erected into a sacrament, there naturally arose the question as to the sacramental character of these capitular proceedings—that is, whether they were only in the *forum externum* or whether they conferred absolution in the *forum internum*, which by that time was considered to be the exclusive function of the sacrament. In the early thirteenth century, Cæsarius of Heisterbach, who, though not a theologian, represents the views current among the convents of the time, has no hesitation in assuming that they are sacramental and sufficient in both forums.[1] Soon after this, William of Paris shows the commencement of applying to them the new theories by arguing that they are wholly judicial and complaining that they are generally regarded as sacramental, so that those who had undergone punishment in them considered themselves absolved and that no further confession or penance was required.[2] Aquinas on the other hand admits that, although a chapter may be held by one who is not a priest, yet the absolution granted is good in the forum of penitence, and he seems disposed to attribute to them a quasi-sacramental character, in which he is followed by Astesanus,[3] but later theologians had no difficulty in deciding that they were not sacramental.[4] At the period under consideration these questions had not yet arisen, and the public confession or conviction in the chapter, with its resultant punishment and pardon by the abbot or other presiding officer, was held to be sufficient, so that no provision was considered necessary for auricular confession—the conservatism of monachism handed down the traditions and customs of the early Church undisturbed by the developments and changes of the outside world.

In the old Benedictine Order, Alcuin, in 793, writing to the monks of Tynemouth, urges them to adopt private confession, and towards the close of the eleventh century the Blessed Lanfranc recommends it as a wholesome custom.[5] A century later, when confession had become a sacrament and was insisted upon as essential to salvation, Peter of Blois complains of monks being compelled to confess to bishops instead

---

[1] Cæsar. Heisterbac. Dial. Dist. III. cap. 49.

[2] Guillel. Parisiens. de Sacram. Pœnitentiæ cap. 20.

[3] S. Th. Aquin. in IV. Sentt. Dist. XX. Q. iv. ad 2; Summæ Suppl. Q. XXVIII. Art. 2 ad 2.—Astesani Summæ Lib. V. Tit. 11.

[4] Summa Rosella s. v. *Indulgentia* § 7.—Summa Sylvestrina s. v. *Indulgentia* § 21.—Caietani Opusc. Tract. XVI. cap. 2.

[5] Alcuini Epist. XIV.—B. Lanfranci Sermo (D'Achery Spicileg. I. 443).

of to their own abbots ;[1] but in 1196 Matthew Paris's account of the dying confession of a pious monk of Evesham shows that no regular system had yet been instituted.[2] The abbey of St. Victor of Paris was the focus of sacerdotalism and doubtless one of the first to set an example, and here, at the close of the twelfth century, while the custom of public confession and accusation in the daily chapters was still maintained, we find the abbot appointing a monk as confessor, to whom his brethren could confess and be absolved when they felt so inclined,[3] but the vague conceptions still prevailing are seen in the custom of some monasteries, as described by Peter Cantor, in which the monks confessed to each other and were absolved by the abbot, thus dividing the sacrament.[4] The adoption of regular and stated confession was of later introduction. It was not until 1312 that the council of Vienne required the Benedictines to confess once a month, and this was changed to once a week in 1337 by the *Constitutio Benedictina* of Benedict XII. ; but we are told at the end of the fifteenth century that the observance of this was irregular.[5]

The Cluniac Order was a rigid reform of the Benedictine. We possess a very complete account of the discipline of the mother-house of Cluny, about the year 1080, including details as to the semi-annual bathing of the monks, their stated times of blood-letting, and how the novices were drilled to bend their necks without curving their backs. We are told all the signs that were used to replace the voice, so that the holy silence of the monastery might not be broken even to express the wants of human nature.[6] The daily chapters for confession and accusation were duly held, but so little confidence was felt in the candor of the brethren that discipline and morals were maintained by officials known as *circatores*—spies or detectives, who had entrance everywhere and who were always moving around

---

[1] Petri Blesens. de Pœnitentia Liber.

[2] Matt. Paris Hist. Angl. ann. 1196.

[3] Antiquæ Consuett. S. Victoris Parisiens. c. 37, 39 (Martene de antiq. Eccles. Ritibus T. III. Append.).

[4] Morin. de Sacram. Pœnit. Lib. VIII. cap. ix. n. 23.—Martene de antiq. Eccles. Ritibus Lib. I. cap. vi. Art. 6, n. 5.

[5] Cap. 1 § 2 Clement. Lib. III. Tit. x.—Chron. Cassinens. Append. p. 862 (Ed. Du Brueil, 1603).—Bart. de Chaimis Interrogatorium sive Confessionale fol. 101*a* (Venetiis, 1480).

[6] Udalrici Consuetudd. Cluniacenses, Lib. II. cap. 2, 4, 21 ; Lib. III. cap. 17 (Migne, CXLIX.).

to observe and report offences. Yet the only prescription of auricular confession was that the novice when received confessed all the sins committed in secular life, and the monk when dying confessed again as a preparation for extreme unction.[1] Some half a century later, in the new statutes which Peter the Venerable introduced in the Cluniac Rule there is still no allusion to confession.[2]

We have already seen (p. 188) that in the early Rule of the Canons Regular there was no precept of auricular confession. About 1115 Peter de Honestis drew up an elaborate account of their discipline, including baths and blood-letting, but the only provision for private confession is on the death-bed, where the dying brother unburdens his soul to the prior, or to priests deputed for the purpose, after which he receives absolution from the whole body of the brethren.[3] The rules of S. Jacques de Montfort, probably about the close of the twelfth century, have no provision for auricular confession, but the public confession and accusation in the daily chapters is in full force, when the prior grants absolution and adjudges the penance or punishment.[4]

When, in 1084, St. Bruno founded the ascetic Carthusian Order he framed no formal Rule or statutes. The earliest written one is by Abbott Guigo about 1128. It is very full, ordering the monks to shave six times a year and let blood five times, but its only allusion to confession is on the death-bed, when the dying monk is expected to confess to a priest and receive absolution.[5] In the Order of Fontevraud, the founder, Robert d'Arbrissel, shows by his rule that confession was purely voluntary and could be postponed to the death-bed;[6] for the nuns of the Order there is no precept as to con-

---

[1] Ibid. Lib. II. cap. 26; Lib. III. cap. 7, 27, 28.

[2] Statuta Congr. Cluniacens. (Migne, CLXXXIX. 1025). The Cluniac death-bed confession is illustrated by Peter the Venerable, who relates that in returning from England he passed a night in a priory of the Order of which the prior was mortally sick. Peter at once urged him to make confession of his sins, which he did, but as he wilfully concealed a portion he had a warning vision that night which induced him to perfect the confession the next day.— Petri Venerab. de Miraculis Lib. II. cap. 32.

[3] Petri de Honestis Regulæ Clericor. Lib. II. cap. 22 (Migne, CLXIII.).

[4] Antiquæ Consuetudd. Canon. Regular. cap. 4–7 (Martene Thesaur. IV. 1218–20).

[5] Guigonis I. Consuetudines cap. 12, § 2 (Migne, CLIII.).

[6] R. de Arbrisello Præcepta recte vivendi n. 22 (Migne, CLXII.).

fession, save that if when sick they desire to confess they must be carried to the chapel, and on no account must the priest be admitted to the bed-side.[1]

St. Robert of Molesme, the founder of the severe Cistercian Order, left no written rules, as it was only a concourse of hermits who placed themselves under his direction. The third abbot, St. Stephen Harding, between 1110 and 1120, when the Order began to spread, issued the *Charta Charitatis*, or rules concerning the intercourse between the mother-house of Citeaux and its daughters. After his death, in 1134, the regulations devised by him were collected and are known as the *Usus Antiquiores*, though in the shape in which they have reached us there are interpolations as late as 1202. They are very prolix and minute, prescribing every detail of monastic life, even for the sudden nose-bleeding of a priest while celebrating mass. Like the other Rules they provide for accusation and self-accusation in the chapters, followed by punishment and absolution, but there is no injunction of private confession, though the abbot, prior and sub-prior are empowered to listen to those who desire to confess such things as illusions in sleep. Even on the death-bed no formal or detailed confession is prescribed. The dying man merely said "Confiteor" or "Mea culpa, I pray you to pray for me for all my sins" and the absolution was equally informal.[2] The schoolmen were now at work, however; the sacramental character of penitence was taking shape and passages in sermons of St. Bernard not long after this justify the assumption that confession and communion at Easter were becoming customary.[3] Early in the thirteenth century a story told by Cæsarius of Heisterbach shows that by that time the monks made sacramental confession to the abbot in addition to the capitular confessions.[4]

The ascetic Order of Grammont was founded by St. Stephen of Thiern who died in 1124. The Rule in the earliest shape in which it has reached us was confirmed by Adrian IV. in 1156 and by suc-

---

[1] Regula Sanctimonialium Fontis Ebraldi. — Vetusta Statuta cap. 16 (Ibidem).

[2] Usus antiquiores Ordinis Cisterciensis, cap. 70, 75, 94 (Migne, CLXVI.).

[3] S. Bernardi Serm. in Die Paschæ n. 15 ; Serm. IX. in Cantica n. 3.

[4] Cæsar. Heisterb. Dial. Dist. III. cap. 23. Other stories (Ibid. cap. 25, 53) indicate that only the abbot, or sometimes the prior, could administer sacramental absolution.

cessive popes till Innocent III., who made some changes in it in 1202, so that it represents a period during which the sacramental character of penitence was acknowledged and confession was becoming increasingly important. Yet in it the discipline of the daily chapters is strictly enforced and the only allusion to confession is a prohibition to confess to any one outside of the Order; the brethren might, if they so chose, confess to each other, and as many of them were laymen there was no recognition of the sacramental nature of such practice. Crimes of violence and theft, lapses of the flesh and possession of private property could only be confessed to the Prior of Grammont himself so that in the affiliated houses sinners desirous of doing so were sent from one priory to another till they reached the mother-house.[1]

The ancient Rule which passes under the name of St. Augustin contains no allusion whatever to confession.[2] Of the Orders based upon it, the Premonstratensian canons were founded by St. Norbert about 1120, and the earliest description that we have of their Rule is by Adam the Scot, about 1180. In this, the system of accusation and self-accusation in the chapters is fully developed; the punishment there inflicted is held to secure absolution for sins and there is no precept of sacramental or auricular confession. *Circatores*, or official spies, are freely employed and there is an elaborate criminal code, classifying offenses as *leves*, *mediæ*, *graves*, *graviores* and *gravissimæ*, for which the penalties range from a penitential psalm through scourging to excommunication and expulsion—a typical illustration of the lack of distinction between the *forum externum* and *internum* pervading all these monastic institutes. In a somewhat later statement of the Rule there is a provision that any one desiring to do so may confess to a priest.[3] The Rule of the Augustinian Canons Regular was virtually the same as this, as we learn from a collection of usages drawn up about the year 1200. We have some documents concern-

---

[1] Regulæ S. Stephani Grandimont. cap. 50 (Migne, CCIV. 1155).—Ordinis Grandimont. Statuta Antiqua, cap. 41, 42, 43, 52, 62 (Martene Thesaur. IV.). —P. Cantor. Verb. abbreviat. cap. 79.

[2] Migne, XXXII. 1447, 1449.

[3] Adami Scoti de Ordine et Habitu Canon. Præmonstrat. Serm. x. cap. 8, 9; Serm. xiv. cap. 18 (Migne, CXCVIII.)—Primaria Institt. Canon. Præmonstrat. Dist. I. cap. 3, 4; Dist. II. cap. 4; Dist. III. cap. 1–9 (Martene de antiq. Eccles. Ritibus, T. III. Append.).

ing the house at Oignies, founded in 1192, which show the practical development of the system and we learn further that when, in 1250, Peter Cardinal of Albano reformed the house, which had fallen into a shocking state of indiscipline (among the abuses which he prohibits are keeping a tavern within the walls for the sale of wine and beer, the employment of women as nurses in the infirmary etc.) he said nothing as to introducing auricular confession. It was not until John of Bavaria, Bishop-elect of Liége, again reformed the house in 1404, that he ordered the canons and even the novices to confess monthly.[1]

I have dwelt thus in detail upon the monastic regulations concerning confession during the critical and revolutionary period of the twelfth century because they seem to me to throw an important light upon the transition from the ancient custom of public confession in the congregation to the innovation of auricular confession. They furnish us a nearly perfect and unbroken chain of tradition preserving that ancient custom down to the times of the schoolmen and the development of penitence as a sacrament. In this survival the only significant change is the introduction, in the later period, of absolution in a manner which shows that the distinction between the *forum internum* and *externum* was as yet practically unrecognized. To the monk his daily or weekly chapter represented the congregation of the early Church, and in this he was bound to make public confession of his sins; if he failed to do so he could be accused by any one cognizant of his offence, and in the later period the office of the *circatores* was devised to aid in enforcing the discipline of the Rule. In the Rule of Benedict, and presumably in the rest, there is a provision, like that which we have seen of old, that voluntary confession entitles the sinner to a mitigation of the penalty.[2] Anxious as was the Church to introduce auricular confession everywhere it saw nothing to object to in all this. On the eve of the Lateran council, which was to render confession obligatory on every one, the papal legate, Cardinal Robert de Curzon, in 1212, held a great coun-

---

[1] Consuetudd. Canon. Reg. S. Augustini, cap. 20, 73, 74, 83; Antiquæ Consuetudd. Oigniacens. Monast. cap. 19–29; Statuta ann. 1250 pro Monast. Oigniacens; Statuta Reformatoria Oigniacens. Monast. ann. 1405, cap. 3 (Martene de antiq. Eccles Ritibus, T. III. Append.).

[2] S. Benedicti Regula, cap. 46.—Adami Scoti de Ord. et Hab. Canon. Præmonstratens. Serm. x. cap. 8.

cil in Paris for the reform of the clergy. It ordered the seculars to confess to their superiors, but in the twenty-seven canons devoted especially to the regulars it said not a word about confession, while a command to the abbots to deal mercifully with penitents shows that the existing system of chapters was deemed sufficient.[1] It was not long after this that, in rendering confession obligatory, the Lateran council ordered bishops to appoint penitentiaries in all conventual churches, showing that the regulars were no longer to be allowed to consider their chapters as sufficient,[2] and in time, as we have seen in the case of the Benedictines and Augustinian canons, they were required to confess oftener than once a year. The Cardinal legate Ottoboni, at the council of London in 1268, promulgated a rule inferring that monks should be obliged to confess monthly,[3] but Aquinas pronounces this improper, for monks are only bound to do what is required of other men, except in performance of their vows, which do not include confession.[4]

Under the influence of the new system the capitular proceedings gradually became merely formal. I have traced this elsewhere somewhat in detail in the case of the Templars[5] and need not dwell upon it here except to point out that the change was probably hastened by the desire of the monks to substitute the secret confessional, with its rapidly diminishing penances, for the humiliation of self-denunciation and scourging at the discretion of the presiding prelate. Among the Templars this was replaced by three annual confessions to the chaplain and was one of the causes of the demoralization of the Order. During the Templar trials, one of the brethren, Robert le

---

[1] Conc. Parisiens. ann. 1212 P. III. cap. 16 (Harduin. VI. II. 2013). In the nunneries confession was already established, doubtless because the abbess or prioress presiding over the chapters could not, as a woman, grant the absolution which by this time was accepted as sacramental. The council prohibits nuns from confessing, except to their regular chaplains, and orders the bishops to provide them with virtuous and discreet confessors (Ibid. P. III. cap. 7, p. 2012).

[2] Conc. Lateran. IV. ann. 1216, cap. 10.

[3] Conc. Londiniens. ann. 1268, cap. 54 (Harduin. VII. 644).

[4] S. Th. Aquin. Summæ Suppl. Q. VI. Art. 5. This continued an open question (Astesani Summæ Lib. V. Tit. 11) and as late as the sixteenth century Prierias still adheres to the opinion of Aquinas (Summa Sylvestrina s. v. *Confessio Sacram.* I. § 3.

[5] Papers of the American Church History Society, Vol. V.

Brioys, related how Giraud de Villiers, Visitor of France, about 1300, reproached the priest Jean de Calmota, for the facility with which he and the other Templar chaplains absolved the guilty members of the Order. If the custom of confession and penance in the chapters had been preserved, he said, the brethren would be more cautious in stealing the property of the Order, and in other wickedness, but now the chaplains absolved them for money and shared with them the stolen goods of the Temple.[1]

While the monastic Orders thus in the twelfth century preserved the early traditions of public confession, which had become obsolete among the laity, the Church persisted in its efforts to popularize the auricular confession which was the only practicable substitute. We have seen how unavailing had been these efforts to overcome the resistance of inertia, nor, as the twelfth century wore on, did there seem much prospect of improvement. Had the usage of regular confession become general, with the elaborate formula in use, this function alone would have required the services of a large body of priests, and when we note how imperfectly the Church was manned, at a time when religious fervor was almost exclusively directed to the extension of monachism, we can estimate how infrequent was the resort to the confessional. Early in the twelfth century we are told that Antwerp already was a populous city, and yet it had but one priest, who was involved in an incestuous amour and paid no attention to his duties.[2] In 1213, just before confession was rendered obligatory on all Christians, the city of Montpellier had but one church in which the sacrament of penitence could be administered,[3] and as late as 1247, when Ypres boasted of two hundred thousand inhabitants, it had but four parish churches.[4] When this was the case with large and opulent towns it is reasonable to assume that the spiritual needs of the rural population and peasantry were even more scantly provided for.

Yet in spite of these deficiencies there was no relaxation in the urgency with which auricular confession was enjoined to fill the gap

[1] Michelet, Procès des Templiers, I. 448.
[2] Vit. S. Norberti cap. 79 (Migne, CLXX. 1311).
[3] Innoc. PP. III. Regest. xv. 240.
[4] Berger, Registres d'Innocent IV., n. 2712.

left by the disuse of public confession. A curious passage in Honorius of Autun, about 1130, throws light on the manner in which the one was gradually supplanting the other and the confusion still existing between the old and the new. The memory of the former was preserved in the ritual wherein the congregation and priest made a general confession of sins. As yet this was not couched in vague and unmeaning phrase, but was a specific admission on the part of all joining in it of having polluted themselves with each and every mortal sin recited in it, and on its conclusion the priest administered absolution in the only form as yet known to the Church by praying for it.[1] Although this survival of the original practice had become a mere formality, doubtless the faithful largely regarded it as a sufficient expiation for their sins, and to remove this the priest is directed to follow it with an admonition that it is valueless except for sins which had already been confessed to the priest and for which penance had been performed, or for those committed in ignorance.[2] Thus as yet both public and private confession were requisite and neither was effective without the other and without satisfaction. Yet so vague as yet were the current notions that in another passage Honorius describes confession as equal to baptism in remitting sins, without conditioning it on contrition and satisfaction.[3]

Hugh of St. Victor, who laid the foundation of the sacramental theory, shows us that at this period there were two opposite errors to be combated respecting auricular confession. There were those who boldly denied its necessity, asserting that confession to God suffices and demanding in vain to be shown scriptural proof that priestly intervention is requisite. On the other hand, the assiduous teaching

---

[1] Honorii Augustod. Speculum Ecclesiæ; De Nativitate Domini. The formula of absolution is "Indulgentiam et absolutionem de omnibus peccatis vestris per intercessionem omnium Sanctorum suorum tribuat vobis Pater et Filius et Spiritus Sanctus, et custodiat vos amodo et a peccatis et ab omnibus malis, et post hanc vitam perducat vos in consortium omnium sanctorum suorum. Amen."

[2] Ibidem.—"Fratres ista confessio tantum valet de his peccatis quæ sacerdotibus confessi estis, vel quæ ignorantes gessistis. Cæterum qui gravia crimina commiserint et pœnitentiam inde non egerunt, quæ sunt homicidia et adulteria, pro quibus instituta est carina, nichil valet ista confessio."

[3] Honorii Augustod. Elucidarii Lib. II. cap. 20.—"D. Quid valet confessio? M. Quantum baptismus, sicut etiam in baptismo originalia, ita in confessione remittuntur peccata actualia."

of the necessity of confession and the exaggeration of its effectiveness had naturally led many to regard it as a matter of mere routine and that forgiveness of sins resulted from it without repentance and without fear or love of God.[1] The subject was evidently one which was engaging the attention of the schools; opinions were as yet unsettled, but the practice was gaining ground and was becoming a matter of habit with a portion of the community.

Abelard probably reflects the average views of the schoolmen of this time when the sacramental quality had not yet been assigned to confession. Its object is the inculcation of humility in revealing sins to and accepting penance from a fellow man : auricular confession is not essential to salvation, but if avoided through neglect or contempt perdition ensues, for no one can have true contrition who despises the institutes of the Church. There are many reasons, however, which justify its omission ; penitents incur great risks through ignorant and indiscreet priests, and there are many who omit it altogether without sin because they believe it rather injures than benefits them. There are many prelates neither pious nor discreet; these are to be avoided and there is no offence against God when no contempt is felt towards him.[2]

On the other hand, Abelard's great antagonist, St. Bernard, who exercised more influence than any other man on the current of thought of his generation, is never weary of extolling the virtues of confession. Yet it is not sacramental confession that he urges, for this had not yet been formulated ; we hear from him nothing of absolution and little of penance. Confession itself is the great thing, but it is often doubtful whether he means confession to God or to the priest, and the prayers, mortifications and almsgiving which render it effective are self-imposed and not enjoined by a confessor. Yet his conception of confession shows how vague and indefinite were as yet the ideas concerning it : in one passage he says it consists first in knowledge of oneself, second in repentance, third in grief, fourth in oral confession, fifth in mortification of the flesh, sixth in amendment and seventh in

---

[1] Hugon. de S. Victore de Sacramentis Lib. II. P. xiv. cap. 1.—"Isti nonnunquam, sine aliquo compunctionis motu, sine aliquo timoris vel amoris Dei attractu, pro sola consuetudine explenda, ad dicenda peccata sua se ingerunt, existimantes se propter solam verborum prolationem a debito peccatorum suorum absolvi."

[2] P. Abælardi Epit. Theol. Christianæ cap. 36; Ethica, cap. 19, 24, 25.

perseverance, while in another he tells us that true confession and true repentance are when a man so repents that he does not repeat the sin.[1] He did not hesitate, moreover, to attribute a magic power to confession in a miracle which he relates of St. Malachi. A woman of ungovernable temper was brought by her two sons to the saint, who asked her whether she had ever confessed ; on her answering in the negative he ordered her to do so, after which he enjoined penance and prayed over her, with the result that she thereafter was the most amiable of women. Apparently confession had previously not been practised in Ireland for St. Bernard includes it among the unknown rites introduced by Malachi when he Romanized the Irish Church.[2]

As we have seen in the case of the power of the keys, the battle for auricular confession was fought by the French schoolmen. Rome apparently at this period took little interest in it. Allusion has already been made (p. 135) to the non-committal position of Gratian on the subject. After stating that opinions are divided, he gives a long series of authorities to show that oral confession is not a necessity, for the sin has already been pardoned through contrition, and he sums them up emphatically in that sense ;[3] then he gives a series on the other side, and draws the opposite conclusion,[4] finally leaving the question to be decided by the judgment of the reader, as both sides have the support of wise and pious men.[5] Even more significant of the indifference with which these questions were regarded by the Roman canonists, absorbed in the effort to

---

[1] S. Bernardi Serm. de Diversis Serm. XL. n. 2, 3, 9.—Tract. de interiore Domo n. 61.—Cf. Lib. ad Milites Templi cap. 12 ; Epist. CXIII. n. 4 ; Serm. in Nat. Dom. Serm. II. n. 1 ; Serm. in Tempore Resurrect. n. 10 ; Serm. in Assumpt. B. M. Virg. n. 4 ; Serm. II. in Festo Omn. Sanctt. n. 13 ; Serm. de Diversis Serm. XCI. n. 1, 2 ; Serm. CVII.

The eloquent formula of private confession attributed to St. Bernard is addressed to God.—S. Bernardi Confessionis Privatæ Formula.

[2] S. Bernardi Vit. S. Malachiæ cap. 3, 25.

[3] Post cap. 30 Caus. XXXIII. Q. iii. Dist. 1.—"Luce clarius constat cordis contritione non oris confessione peccata dimitti."

"Non ergo in confessione peccatum remittitur, quod jam remissum esse probatur. Fit itaque confessio ad ostensionem peccati, non ad impetrationem veniæ."—Post cap. 37, loc. cit.

[4] Post cap. 60, loc. cit.—"Ex his itaque appareat quod sine confessione oris et satisfactione operis peccatum non remittitur."

[5] Post cap. 89 loc. cit.

extend ecclesiastical jurisdiction in the *forum externum,* is the careless manner in which Master Roland (afterwards Alexander III.) dismisses the subject in his summary of the Decretum; he passes it over, he says, on account of its prolixity and practical inutility, but promises to treat it elsewhere.[1] Evidently at Rome no one as yet dreamed of the divine origin of confession or of its being an indispensable part of a sacrament. Paris, however, took a truer view of its importance to the new theology which was evolving itself in the schools, and Peter Lombard boldly reconciled the conflicting views which Gratian abandoned in despair; the sinner must confess first to God and then to the priest, without which he cannot hope for paradise.[2]

In proving this the most conclusive authority on which he relied was a spurious tract, bearing the revered name of St. Augustin, which mysteriously came into circulation about this time, when such aid was so much needed by the sacerdotal school. Gratian had drawn from it the strongest evidence which he was able to produce in favor of confession, but admitted that it could not overcome the array on the other side. The Paris schoolmen felt no such misgivings; they found in it exactly what they required in teaching authoritatively the power of the keys and the indispensable functions of the priest in their ministration. It is through the priest that God must be approached; the penitent must submit himself to him in blind obedience and must be prepared to follow his commands in order to obtain salvation, as though he were seeking to escape from bodily death.[3] The extent of the citations from the tract in

---

[1] Summa Rolandi caus. XXXIII. Q. 3 (Innsbruck, 1874, p. 193).

[2] P. Lombard Sententt. Lib. IV. Dist. xvii. §§ 3, 4.

[3] Ps. Augustin. Lib. de Vera et Falsa Pœnitentia cap. XV. n. 30.—"Ponat se omnino in potestate judicis, in judicio sacerdotis, nihil sibi reservans sui ut omnia eo jubente paratus sit facere pro recipienda vita animæ quæ faceret pro vitanda corporis morte."

The date and sources of this forgery have naturally been the subject of some discussion. To me it seems unquestionably to be the work of two writers at widely different periods. The earlier portion, up to the end of chap. IX. bears the mark of the teaching of the fifth century; through true repentance the penitent reconciles himself to God and washes away his sins with his tears. With the exception of chapters XIII., XVI. and XVII. the latter half of the tract is in direct opposition to this and is undoubtedly a work of the middle of the twelfth century. Some schoolman of the period probably met

the works of the schoolmen shows the inestimable service which it rendered in furnishing ancient authority for the new theories, and

---

with an anonymous and forgotten exhortation to repentance and after interpolating and adding to it the new theories in their most absolute expression launched it on the schools as a book of St. Augustin's, to whom it was the fashion to attribute a vast variety of spurious writings.

As early as the close of the sixteenth century the authenticity of the tract was questioned by Abbot Trithemius, who recognized that the style is not St. Augustin's and that the saint himself is quoted in chapter XVII. The truth of this was soon generally conceded, but the work was not on that account abandoned. In 1525 Latomus quotes it as St. Augustin's and argues that its genuineness is of no importance for it represents the period and having been inserted in the canons it has the full force of law (Jac. Latomus de Confessione secreta, Antverpiæ, 1525). The Catechism of the council of Trent (De Pœnit. cap. 6, 12, etc.) cites it without an intimation of its unauthenticity. Azpilcueta (Comment. de Pœnit. Dist. I. pp. 1–2, Romæ, 1581) says that in his first and second editions of 1542 and 1569 he did not wholly dissent from its spuriousness, but now he does, for the reference to St. Augustin may have been a gloss inserted by a copyist and the style is no criterion; moreover, tradition should not be set aside and the book is a most useful one. Even after its genuineness ceased to be defended it continued to be quoted as St. Augustin's at least until the close of the seventeenth century (Clericati de Pœnit. Decis. XVIII. n. 2.— P. Segneri Instructio Confessariorum, Dilingæ, 1699, p. 31), and subsequently with more or less admission of the fraud (Amort de Indulgentiis, II. 183).

Another spurious tract circulated under the name of St. Augustin (De Visitatione Infirmorum Lib. II. cap. 4, 5) continued to be quoted until the middle of the seventeenth century in proof of the antiquity of confession. See Marchant, Tribunal Animarum Tom. I. Tract. I. Tit. 1, Q. 14, concl. 1 (Gandavi, 1642).

A grosser forgery, with the object of popularizing confession, was perpetrated in the thirteenth century by the manufacture of the *Sermones ad Fratres in Eremo* under the name of St. Augustin. There was safe presumption on the ignorance of the age when he was represented as relating his disputes with Arius and Fortunatus and his adventures in Ethiopia (Serm. XXXVI. XXXVII.). The people are told not to hesitate to confess their sins for they are at once obliterated from the memory of the confessor, and the supreme virtues of the act are set forth with eloquent exaggeration—"Hæc est enim salus animarum, dissipatrix vitiorum, restauratrix virtutum, oppugnatrix dæmonum, pavor inferni, lumen et spes omnium fidelium. O sancta et admirabilis confessio! tu obstruis os inferni et aperis paradisi portus!" (Sermo XXX.). No fraud was too clumsy if it contributed to advance sacerdotalism. So uncritical was the age that these sermons were accepted and quoted as St. Augustin's (Astesani Summæ Lib. V. Tit. xxii. Q. 4), and despite the exposure of the imposture by Erasmus, they continued to be so till the seventeenth century (Alonso Perez de Lara, Compendio de las Tres Gracias, p. 18).

the eagerness with which they availed themselves of the unexpected reinforcement. Few forgeries in the history of the Church, which owes so much to such means, have been so successful or have left a deeper impress on its dogmas. It was virtually the foundation on which the new superstructure was reared.

The great obstacle to the development of the power of the keys and the necessity of confession lay in the belief, to which the Church was fully committed, that the sinner could be justified by contrition and faith. So long as man could deal directly with God the interposition of the priest was not essential; if sacerdotal ministration was necessary, confession followed as a matter of course, for the priest must know the sins before he could absolve the sinner and assign to him the performance of due satisfaction. To render confession obligatory it was thus only requisite to prove that the penitent must approach God through his minister, and to accomplish this some means must be found of evading the established doctrine of justification by contrition and faith. To this Hugh of St. Victor pointed the way when he asserted that the sinner who had a contrite heart must want to confess.[1] The hint however was not immediately taken, for Cardinal Pullus endeavors to answer the question why, if contrition and faith secure pardon, confession and satisfaction should be required in surplusage, and he admits his inability to answer it when he can only urge the statutes of the Church as a reason and boldly affirms that without confession repentance is valueless.[2] Stephen of Tournay dismisses the question of the necessity of confession after contrition as one on which opinions are divided,[3] and the theologians long continued to admit, as a matter of theory, that contrition may be so perfect as to render priestly intervention unnecessary and even to obtain exemption from purgatory.[4] Yet Peter

---

[1] Hugon. de S. Victore Summæ Sentt. Tract. VI. cap. 11.

[2] R. Pulli Sentt. Lib. V. cap. 51, 59. He recurs to it, Lib. VI. cap. 51 and endeavors to argue away as exceptional the cases of St. Peter and Mary Magdalen, the penitent thief and the woman taken in adultery.

[3] Steph. Tornacensis Summa Decr. Gratiani Caus. xxxiii. Q. 3 (Ed. Schulte, Giessen, 1891, p. 246).

The contemptuous indifference with which Stephen treats the whole subject shows that, like the Roman canonists, he regarded it as a profitless scholastic dispute and that he failed completely to recognize the importance of its consequences.

[4] P. Lombard Sentt. Lib. IV. Dist. xx. §§ 1, 2.—R. a S. Victore de Potestate

Lombard hit upon a method to reconcile this with the necessity of confession, when, with the assistance of the Pseudo-Augustin, he suggested that contrition to be sufficing must contain a vow to confess to a priest if there is opportunity to do so.[1] It is true that he puts forward this definition rather hesitatingly and inferentially than directly, but it was too ready a solution of the vexed problem to be allowed to remain doubtful. Richard of St. Victor seized upon it and asserted it positively—true repentance is the detestation of sin with a vow of amendment, of confession and of satisfaction; it needs therefore the intervention of the priest when one can be had.[2] He has no authorities to cite for this, he starts with it as a postulate based on authentic doctrine and does not trouble himself to prove it, though he condescends to meet the argument that no one who is in charity can be damned by pointing out that the patriarchs and

---

Ligandi cap. 25.—S. Raymundi Summæ Lib. III. Tit. xxxiv. ¿ 4.—Alex. de Ales Summæ P. IV. Q. XXI. Membr. ii. Art. 1.—Hostiens. Aureæ Summæ Lib. v. De Pœn. et Remiss. ¿¿ 51, 61.—S. Th. Aquin. Summæ P. III. Q. lxxxiv. Art. 1; Q. lxxxvi. Art. 1; Suppl. Q. iv. Art. 1; Summæ contra Gentiles Lib. IV. cap. 73.

The effort to reconcile the conflicting theories is seen in various stories current during the succeeding centuries. Thus Guido de Monteroquer tells us (Manipulus Curatorum P. II. Tract. iv. cap. 5) that once when Clement IV. (Gui Foucoix, the most eminent lawyer of his day) was riding through the streets of Rome he was approached by a woman with a baby in her arms, crying for penance and saying that she had borne the child to her son. The pope prescribed for her Friday fasting during a year. Reflecting on the inadequacy of this for her grievous sin she sought him the next day and repeated her confession, when he reduced the penance to three Paternosters. Still more perplexed she came a third time and he cut the penance down to a single Pater, and when his courtiers asked him the reason of this leniency he replied that the woman's contrition and the humiliation of her public confession were more effective than life-long fasting on bread and water. Somewhat similar is a story told of St. Vincent Ferrer, when, after imposing a sharp penance for three years the sinner told him it was not enough, whereupon the saint promptly reduced it to three days; the penitent expostulated at this and asked for more, when St. Vincent diminished it to three Paters and Aves and his judgment was confirmed, for at the sinner's death his soul was seen to soar to heaven without stopping in purgatory.—S. Leonardo da Porto Maurizio, Discorso Mistico e Morale, ¿ xxix.

[1] P. Lombardi Sentt. Lib. IV. Dist. xvii. ¿¿ 1, 2; xviii. ¿¿ 1, 4.

[2] R. a S. Victore de Potestate Ligandi cap. 5—"Vera pœnitentia est abominatio peccati cum voto cavendi, confitendi et satisfaciendi . . . Eget ergo sacerdotis absolutione quandiu datur hoc posse."

prophets were in charity, yet were they damned in hell and would have remained there through eternity, had not Christ liberated them.[1] Thus the priest was permanently interposed between God and man and confession, unless prevented by insuperable obstacles, was proved to be indispensable for the pardon of sin.

Of course so arbitrary a solution, based simply upon a definition, did not meet with immediate and universal acceptance, and the question continued for some time to be debated. Peter of Blois earnestly exhorts sinners to confess, but he makes no allusion to the intervention of priestly absolution.[2] Peter of Poitiers takes the position that, although contrition remits sins, the penitent who does not confess commits a mortal sin through which the previous ones return.[3] Adam of Perseigne can assign no reason for the obligation to confess save the precept of the Church and says it is presumptuous to ask more.[4] Master Bandinus makes no allusion to the definition of Richard of St. Victor and strives to solve the difficulty by some unintelligible talk about the sacrament and the unity of Christ with the Church.[5] Yet Richard's view gradually prevailed. St. Ramon de Peñafort adopts it, but describes other opinions as still maintained.[6] William of Paris does not include the vow to confess in his definition of the requisites for the remission of sin; contrition in itself is sometimes sufficient satisfaction and God asks nothing more, and he only argues that the Church would be deceiving the faithful if confession and absolution did not augment grace.[7] Alexander Hales adopts unconditionally the definition of Richard of St. Victor,[8] but Cardinal Henry of Susa admits that the confession and satisfaction may be internal: he reaches the same result however by adding that oral confession and open satisfaction are due to the Church which has been offended, and this he says is the prevailing

---

[1] Ibidem cap. 19.

[2] Petri Blesensis Lib. de Confessione Sacramentali (Migne CCVII. 1077–92). It is highly probable that the word "sacramentali" in the title of this is a later interpolation.

[3] Petri Pictaviens. Sententt. Lib. III. cap. 12.

[4] Adami de Persennia Epist. xx. (Martene Thesaur. I. 751).

[5] M. Bandini Sententt. Lib. IV. Dist. 19.

[6] S. Raymundi Summæ Lib. III. Tit. xxxiv. § 4.

[7] Guillel. Parisiens. de Sacram. Pœnitent. c. 4, 19.

[8] Alex. de Ales Summæ P. IV. Q. XVII. Membr. 1, Art. 3 ; Q. XVIII. Membr. 2, Art. 1; Q. XXI. Membr. 2, Art. 2.

opinion and is to be held. He further quotes Cardinal Hugo of S. Claro to the effect that if the vow to confess and satisfy is not fulfilled when occasion offers the old sins do not return but a new mortal sin is committed—a view which has been generally adopted.[1] Aquinas is not entirely consistent in his treatment of the question. He adopts Richard's definition, but he admits that contrition alone can efface both *culpa* and *pœna*, and argues that confession and satisfaction are required to obtain certainty and to obey the precepts of the Church ; moreover, he uses the vow to confess in order to prove that the keys remove *culpa* as well as *pœna*.[2] It would be superfluous to continue further the examination of the progress of the definition of sufficing contrition as including the vow to confess and satisfy, which became accepted as a commonplace of the schools. It was inferred by Martin V. in 1418, at the council of Constance, when he assumed that contrition does not suffice and that confession is necessary if a fitting priest can be found.[3] Thomas of Walden yielded the position when, in answering the Wickliffites, he admitted that repentance and amendment secure pardon and added that confession and satisfaction can do no harm and must do good,[4] and on the eve of the Reformation Geiler von Keysersberg bases the claim of confession only on the necessity of reconciliation to the Church as well as to God before taking the Eucharist from the hand of an ecclesiastic, otherwise contrition would suffice.[5] Finally the council of Trent put the question at rest by adopting Richard of St. Victor's definition of contrition[6] and since then it has been *de fide* that a

---

[1] Hostiens. Aureæ Summæ Lib. v. De Pœn. et Remiss. § 6.—Petri Hieremiæ Quadragesimale Serm. XXI.— Zerola, Praxis Sacr. Pœnit. cap. VII. Q. XXX. XXXI.

[2] S. Th. Aquin. Summæ Suppl. Q. I. Art. 1; Q. IX. Art. 1; Q. XVIII. Art. 1.—Opusc. XXII. cap. 2.

[3] Martini PP. V. Bull. *Inter cunctas*, 22 Feb. 1418 (Harduin. VIII. 915). Yet Astesanus (Summæ Lib. v. Tit. x. Art. 2, Q. 1) admits an exception. A man can be saved without confession if his contrition is so intense as to cause him to forget the precept, but if the omission is caused by contempt or by absorption in worldly affairs the contrition does not suffice.

[4] Thomas de Walden de Sacramentis cap. CL. n. 1.

[5] Jo. Keysersperg. Navicula Pœnitentiæ (Aug. Vindel. 1511, fol. xxiii. col. 1).

[6] C. Trident. Sess. XIV. De Pœnitentia cap. 4; can. 4, 7. Cf. Sess. VI. De Justificatione cap. 14.

According to Melchor Cano the vow to confess must be explicit and not im-

mortal sinner cannot be pardoned without auricular confession if a priest is accessible.

When Peter Lombard and Richard of St. Victor had thus proved the necessity of confession to secure pardon for sin the use of the confessional naturally became more common. It was encouraged in every way, and the path of the sinner was made wide and easy. Theologians might amuse themselves with defining the prevenient grace and the detestation of sin, the change of heart and the firm resolution of amendment which were requisite along with the vow of confession, but in practice these were disregarded in reliance on the power of the keys. When the Bishop of Beauvais enquired of Alexander III. what should be done with penitents who came to confess and declared that they could not abstain from crime the pope who, as Master Roland, had recorded his contemptuous indifference to the subject, benignantly replied that, although this was not true penitence, yet they should be received to confession and penance be duly imposed with wholesome exhortations.[1] Although this was placing a very low estimate on the newly discovered sacrament of penitence, it was not a mere temporary expression of papal opinion, but was included in the Decretals of Gregory IX. and thus became part of the permanent law of the Church. The natural consequence of the tendency thus displayed was the popularization of the confessional by converting it into an avenue to sin, giving rise to active protests from the stricter members of the clergy. John of Salisbury complains bitterly of the horde of monks who promptly commenced to wield the keys and make market of the mercy of God, teaching that despair was the only unpardonable offence, encouraging sin by promising pardon in advance for money and absolving with special ease the rich and powerful.[2] We can readily understand how the resistance of inertia, which had so long arrested the

---

plicit (Relectio de Pœnitentia P. v.). Cf. Clericati De Pœnit. Decis. ii. n. 4, 5; Palmieri Tract. de Pœnit. pp. 103, 108.

The doctors continued to amuse themselves with debates as to the degree and intensity of the contrition which justifies without the sacrament, but it is a purely speculative question of no practical importance. The curious in such matters will find the various opinions set forth by La Croix, Theol. Moral. Lib. VI. P. ii. n. 761 sqq.

[1] C. 5 Extra Lib. v. Tit. xxxviii.   [2] Jo. Salisburiens. Polycrat. VII. 21.

extension of auricular confession, melted away under the combined influence of the increased value of absolution derived from the establishment of the power of the keys and of the increased facility for obtaining it. We have already seen how Alain de Lille re-echoed these complaints soon afterwards, and in his instructions to confessors we can realize how different were the conditions now imposed on the penitent from those prescribed in the older canons and in the Penitentials : he was allured to confession and no longer rejected if he refused in advance to declare that he forgave all his enemies.[1] Yet even at this time periodical confession was as yet infrequent, for Alain admonishes the penitent when going to the confessional to scrutinize all the recesses of his conscience and recall all his offences against God since childhood.[2]

The popularization and extension of auricular confession, which thus was at length secured, is proved by the council of Paris, about 1198, in which we find the earliest synodical code of instructions for confessors. That such a code was needed shows that confession was spreading, and the character of the instructions infers that priests were as yet wholly unversed in its duties. From one clause we see that the shocking laxity of Alexander III. was not yet accepted, for after confession the priest is told to ask the penitent whether he will abstain for the future and if he will not promise he is to be refused penance and absolution lest he rely upon them. Another clause infers that periodical confession was yet infrequent, for all priests are ordered earnestly to enjoin confession on their flocks, especially at the beginning of Lent.[3] Briefer and less elaborate instructions, issued by the council of London in 1200, indicate that across the Channel the attention of prelates was attracted by the increasing prevalence of the custom and the necessity of regulating it.[4] In Italy it does not seem to have spread as fast as it was doing within the sphere of influence of the University of Paris, for Sicardo of Cremona, in

---

[1] Alani de Insulis Lib. Pœnitentialis (Migne CCX. 286).

[2] Ibidem (p. 299). This is followed by a precept that every one at Easter should go to confession whether conscious of sin or not, in obedience to the mandate of the church. This is evidently an interpolation as it conflicts with the preceding and as no such mandate had yet been issued.

[3] Odonis Episc. Paris. Synod. Constitt. cap. vi. §§ 8, 13 (Harduin. VI. ii. 1940–1).

[4] Concil. Londiniens. ann. 1200, cap. 4 (Harduin. VI. ii. 1958).

enumerating the functions of priests, says nothing about the duty of hearing confessions, though he alludes to binding and loosing penitents.[1]

Thus after an apparently hopeless struggle for centuries, auricular confession finally won its way to recognition as an incident in the revolution of thought in the twelfth century, whereby the schoolmen established the power of the keys and the sacrament of penitence, with the contingent result of facilitating in every way the pardon of sin. That it should prove an instrument of such incalculable power can hardly have occurred to any one concerned in the movement, for it was reserved for Innocent III., at the great Lateran council of 1215-16, to effect the momentous change in its character from voluntary to obligatory. That change of supreme importance opens a new epoch in its history, involving many complicated considerations, the discussion of which must be treated individually. Before doing so, however, it is necessary to trace the gradual absorption by the priesthood of the exclusive function of hearing confessions—a point not without importance in its bearing on the development of sacerdotalism.

We have seen that the only apostolic command of confession—that by St. James—simply prescribes it as mutual and does not recognize the priestly class as specially fitted for it. We have also seen that during the early centuries the only confession recognized by the Church was in conformity with this precept and was made by the sinner in the congregation of the faithful, unless, indeed, he might be on trial before his bishop and then it was public in the episcopal court—customs which were faithfully handed down in the monastic chapters, long after they had been abandoned elsewhere. Also, that when the sinner had recourse to confession to a priest or other holy man, the latter determined whether the case required public confession, and that the penitent's susceptibilities might be spared by committing the confession to writing and reading it in public. As private or auricular confession gradually supplanted public, it naturally fell into the hands of the priestly class, who were regarded as experts in the matter of repentance and penance and who, in the Penitentials, had standards by which to apportion the penalty to the sin. They had however no prescriptive or exclusive right to this. It is true

---

[1] Sicardi Cremonens. Mitrale, II. 2 (Migne CCXIII. 66).

that the Penitential of Theodore claims it for them, but the claim shows that the people were accustomed to apply even to women for penance, and that an exclusive sacerdotal privilege was a matter which required to be asserted.[1] A passage from the Venerable Bede has been largely quoted in support of this claim, in which he says that the lighter and daily sins can be confessed to one another and be redeemed by prayers, while the graver ones should be revealed to the priest, but we have already seen that by these graver sins he means only heresy, Judaism, infidelity and schism, leaving a large field for mutual confession between laymen.[2] Even confession to women was by no means unknown. In the seventh century, St. Donatus of Besançon drew up a Rule for the nuns of Joussan in which he prescribed confession to the abbess several times daily,[3] but after the establishment of the sacrament of penitence this was considered irregular, and when Innocent III. learned that in Spain Cistercian abbesses were in the habit of hearing confessions of the sisters he promptly forbade it.[4] Still later than this, however, Cardinal Henry of Susa still quotes St. Augustin to the effect that in case of necessity confession may be made to laymen and even to women,[5] and Count Louis of Liége, when on his death-bed, sent for a holy virgin named Christiana, to whom he confessed all his sins, not to obtain absolution, which by that time was a priestly function, but in order that her prayers might intercede for him. She undertook to bear half of his purgatorial pains, and thenceforth for some hours a day she suffered alternations of burning agony and chilling rigors, till he appeared to her and announced his release from purgatory.[6] Even as late as the fourteenth century the synod of Cahors approves of death-bed confession to laymen and women, not that they can absolve, but that the reverence thus shown for the sacrament enables the priest to absolve

---

[1] Theodori Pœnit. II. vii. § 2; Canones Gregorii cap. 41 (Wasserschleben, pp. 165, 209).

[2] Bedæ Exposit. super Epist. Jacobi cap. 5; in Lucæ Evang. Exposit. Lib. v. cap. 17.—In fact, a large portion of the sins subsequently classed as mortal were at this period reckoned as venial. See S. August. Serm. Append. Serm. CCLVII. n. 4 (Migne, XXIX. 2220).

[3] S. Donati Vesont. Regulæ cap. 23 (Migne, LXXXVII. 282).

[4] Cap. 10 Extra Lib. v. Tit. xxxviii.

[5] Hostiens. Aureæ Summæ Lib. v. De Pœn. et Remiss. § 14.

[6] Thomæ Cantimpratens. Bonum Universale, Lib. II. cap. 52.

the sinner after his death[1]—a highly irregular way of reconciling to existing tenets what was evidently a prevailing custom. Even after this Bishop Alvaro Pelayo complains that women fulminate excommunications and hear confessions.[2]

In the absence of a priest, death-bed confession to a layman was long held to be sufficient. In 1015 Thietmar of Merseburg relates as an example for all men to follow the case of Ernest Duke of Suabia who was killed while hunting : summoning his followers around him he confessed aloud to one of his knights so that all might hear, and Thietmar seems to thinks that remission of sins cannot fail to be thus secured.[3] In 1085 Richer de l'Aigle, when mortally wounded, confessed his sins to his comrades.[4] Cases of this kind were not apt to find their way into the chronicles except when conspicuous personages were concerned, but Dom Martene has collected quite a number of them,[5] and there can be no doubt that it was a common practice. A well-known example is that of the Sire de Joinville in 1250, when, after St. Louis and his army had been captured, Joinville and those with him were in momentary expectation of death. Joinville admits that he could not recall any of his sins, but Messire Gui d'Ibelin, Constable of Cyprus, knelt down beside him and made confession, when "je luy donnay telle absolucion comme Dieu m'en donnoit le povoir."[6]

But confession to laymen was not restricted to such cases of extremity. Lanfranc, as we have seen, says that for secret sins it can

---

[1] Epist. Synod. Guillel. Episc. Cadurcens. circa 1325, cap. 8 (Martene Thesaur. IV. 688).

[2] Alv. Pelag. de Planctu Ecclesiæ Lib. v. Art. xiv. n. 61, 72.

The extreme jealousy of the modern Church as regards confessions to women is seen in a decision of the Sacred Congregation of Bishops and Regulars, March 10, 1860, respecting the constitution of the Sisters of Christian Charity which requires the members at stated intervals to open their consciences to the Mother Superior. The Congregation strictly forbids this, so far as sins are concerned, which are to be reserved for the confessor, while only defects in the observance of the Rule and progress in virtue can be communicated to the Superior. This is prescribed for all female communities, where the Superior is never to be consulted as to matters of conscience.—Müller, Catholic Priesthood, III. 223, 226.

[3] Dithmari Merseburg. Chron. Lib. vii. cap. 10.

[4] Orderic. Vital. Hist. Eccles. P. iii. Lib. vii. cap. 8.

[5] Martene de antiq. Eccles. Ritibus Lib. i. cap. vi. Art. 6, n. 8.

[6] Mémoires du Sire de Joinville, Ed. 1785, Tom. II. p. 20.

be made to any cleric, from priest to ostiarius, and in their default to any righteous man.[1] We have also seen that in the monastic orders confession was made in the chapters and reconciliation or absolution was granted by the presiding officer, who was by no means necessarily a priest—indeed, in the Military Orders he never was until the Hospitallers adopted a rule that their priors should be in priest's orders, and this absolution by laymen was one of the accusations brought against the Templars at their downfall.[2] Hugh of St. Victor will only admit that venial sins can be confessed to laymen,[3] but the Pseudo-Augustin, in extolling the value of confession, asserts that its power is so great that if a priest is absent it suffices to confess to one's neighbor, and this statement was long quoted as authoritative by the schoolmen.[4] Peter Lombard, in commenting on it, says that opinions are divided; for himself he holds that both venial and mortal sins should be confessed first to God and then to a priest, and the penitent should endeavor to find an experienced one who can select an appropriate remedy, but if a priest is lacking then confession should be made to a neighbor or comrade.[5] A story attributed to St. Augustin was freely quoted by canonists in the first half of the twelfth century, relating how in a ship threatened with wreck the only Christian was a penitent; a pagan asked him for baptism, which he gave and then obtained reconciliation from the neophyte.[6] Cardinal Pullus asserts that it suffices to confess minor sins to a comrade, but the graver ones should be confessed to a priest, except in extreme necessity, and this is the view taken by Alain de Lille and Master Bandinus towards the close of the century—the desire for a priest renders the penitent worthy of pardon, in default of the power of the keys.[7]

---

[1] Lanfranci Lib. de Celanda Confessione.

[2] See Papers of the American Church History Society, Vol. V.

[3] Hugon. de S. Victore de Sacram. Lib. II. P. xiv. cap. 1.

[4] Tanta vis itaque confessionis est ut si deest sacerdos confiteatur proximo. —Ps. August. de vera et falsa Pœnit. cap. x. n. 25. Gratian even inserts it twice, cap. 89 § 2, Caus. XXXIII. Q. iii. Dist. 1, and cap. 1, Caus. XXXIII. Q. iii. Dist. 6.

[5] P. Lombardi Sententt. Lib. IV. Dist. xvii. §§ 1, 5, 6.

[6] Ivon. Carnot. Decr. P. I. cap. 191; Panorm. Lib. I. cap. 26.—Gratian, Decr. De Consecratione Dist. IV. cap. 21, 36.

[7] Rob. Pulli Sententt. Lib. VI. cap. 51.—Alani de Insulis Lib. de Pœnit; Contra Hæreticos Lib. II. cap. 10.—Mag. Bandini Sententt. Lib. IV. Dist. 18.

Though the theologians thus endeavored to restrict the old customs in accordance with the new dogmas, the belief continued that the virtue of confession lay in the act itself, irrespective of the person to whom it was made. Cæsarius, the Cistercian of Heisterbach, was fairly versed in the doctrines of his day, yet, in some of the stories which he tells, he shows that laymen could hear confessions and grant absolution as effectively as priests, even when there was no excuse such as that of the death-bed. One of the current superstitions was that a demoniac—or rather the possessing demon—was familiar with the sins of those present and took a malicious pleasure in exposing them, but as soon as sins were confessed and remitted they vanished from his memory. In illustration of this Cæsarius tells us that a certain priest was guilty of adultery with the wife of a knight, who suspecting it induced him, as though casually, to visit with him a demoniac whose demon reproached all comers with their sins. As they neared the place the priest suspected the object of his companion and made a pretext to go to a stable, where he found the knight's servant, forced him to hear his confession and demanded penance, when the man enjoined on him whatever he would enjoin on another priest guilty of the same sin. With full confidence he allowed himself to be confronted with the demon, who could only say "I know nothing about him; he was justified in the stable." In another similar case the adulterer justifies himself by confessing to a peasant in a wood while on his way to a demoniac.[1] Even later in the thirteenth century we hear of a miller, a lay-brother of the Abbey of Viller in Brabant, whose reputation for holiness was such that sinners flocked to him to lay bare their consciences, and though we are only told that he gave them wholesome advice, it is evident that those who thus preferred him to their parish priests must have believed that they were obtaining absolution.[2]

Meanwhile the theologians continued to admit the efficacy of confession to laymen in the absence of a priest. St. Ramon de Peñafort does not limit it to the approach of death but mentions embarking in a just war as a sufficient reason, and he even discusses the question whether confession can be made to a heretic, without positively

---

[1] Cæsar. Heisterbacens. Dial. Dist. III. cap. 2. Even so enlightened a man as Peter Cantor tells similar stories as to the efficacy of confession in preventing revelations by demoniacs.—Verb. Abbrev. cap. 144.

[2] Hist. Monast. Villariens. Lib. III. cap. 4 (Martene Thesaur. IV. 1364).

deciding it, except to advise against it, for such a confession may lead a penitent into error or despair.[1] William of Paris, it is true, will only admit that some hold that in case of necessity a layman can absolve for venial sins,[2] but Alexander Hales, without specifying the condition of necessity, says that confession to laymen may sometimes be highly meritorious and expedient; it is not sacramental, but if the layman is holy his intercession procures absolution.[3] Albertus Magnus takes nearly the same view — confession to laymen is valid, if it is not motived by contempt of religion, and in case of necessity laymen and even women have authority from God to grant absolution.[4] The Gloss on the *Decretum* considers confession to laymen sufficient for venial sins, but for mortal ones it suffices only in the absence of a priest.[5] Aquinas treats the question more thoroughly. He does not limit necessity to cases of shipwreck or sudden death; if a man or woman knows the parish priest to be a solicitor to evil or a revealer of confessions, and cannot get his licence to confess to another priest, he can confess to a layman; such confession is only quasi-sacramental, but God supplies the place of a priest; still, absolution thus obtained, while it reconciles to God, does not reconcile to the Church, and the penitent cannot be admitted to the sacraments until he has confessed to a priest, and if he dies without doing so he incurs greater purgatorial punishment than if he had had the benefit of the keys[6]—all of which shows how impossible even Aquinas found it to frame a working hypothesis for so purely artificial a system; no sooner had the priest become indispensable to pardon than it was necessary to find reasons for dispensing with him. Bonaventura takes a different view; he will not admit that there is any benefit from confession to laymen, even in the extremest necessity, except as a sign of contrition and as a proof

---

[1] S. Raymundi Summæ Lib. III. Tit. xxxiv. § 4. Cf. Hostiens. Aureæ Summæ Lib. v. De Pœn. et Remiss. § 7.

[2] Guillel. Parisiens. de Sacr. Pœnit. cap. 19.

[3] Alex. de Ales Summæ P. IV. Q. XIX. Membr. 1, Art. 1.

[4] Alberti Magni in IV. Sentt. Dist. XVII. Art. lviii. (Juenin de Sacramentis Diss. VI. Q. 5, cap. 4, Art. 2).

[5] Gloss in cap. 3 Dist. XXV.

[6] S. Th. Aquin. Summæ Suppl. Q. VIII. Art. 2; Art. 6 ad 3; Q. IX. Art. 4; In IV. Sentt. Dist. XVII. Q. iii. Art. 4 ad 3.—Cf. Joannis de Janua Summa quæ vocatur Catholicon s. v. *Confessio.*

that, if a priest could be had, confession would be made to him.[1] The question thus became a debatable one and, at the end of the thirteenth century, John of Freiburg reflects the uncertainty of the period by vaguely reporting the contradictory opinions of the different authorities.[2] Bonaventura's position seems to have become traditional in the Franciscan school. Duns Scotus will only admit that confession to a layman, which he says is habitual among condemned prisoners, can be made without committing sin and is excusable through the simplicity of those who do so; it is useless save as an expression of humility.[3] In 1317 Astesanus discusses the question with a minuteness that suggests that fresh attention had been called to it by the case of the Templars; he rejects the views of Aquinas, condemns those who say that laymen can absolve and adheres to Bonaventura and Duns Scotus.[4] William of Ware takes the same view and finds a new argument in the indicative formula of absolution which, as we shall see hereafter, had by this time become universal.[5] A more cogent reason may be sought in the demoralization of the time, when benefices with cure of souls were frequently given to those not in holy orders. The Franciscan opinion gained ground, and even the Dominican Durand de S. Pourçain denies that confession to a layman can be sacramental or obtain absolution; at the most, in cases of necessity, it is a praiseworthy humiliation.[6] Yet the old custom died hard; in the fourteenth and fifteenth centuries no two works had wider circulation as practical manuals than Guido de Monteroquer's *Manipulus Curatorum*, written in 1333 and Bartolommeo de S. Concordio's *Summa Pisanella*, written in 1338; of these the former tells us that death-bed confession to a layman, in the absence of a priest, though not sacramental, secures absolution, while the latter follows Aquinas in holding it to be quasi-sacramental.[7] So when, in 1418, at the council of Constance,

---

[1] S. Bonaventuræ Tract. *Quia Fratres Minores Prœdicent.*

[2] Jo. Friburgens. Summæ Confessor. Lib. III. Tit. xxxv. Q. 39, 43, 76.

[3] Jo. Scoti in IV. Sentt. Dist. xiv. Q. 4; Dist. xvii. Q. unica.—Franc. de Mayronis in IV. Sentt. Dist. xiv. Q. 1.

[4] Astesani Summæ Lib. v. Tit. xiii. Q. 2.

[5] Guill. Vorrilong in IV. Sentt. Dist. xiv., xviii.

[6] Durand. de S. Port. in IV. Sentt. Dist. xvii. Q. xi.

[7] Manipulus Curatorum, P. II. Tract. iii. cap. 4.—Summa Pisanella s. v. *Confessio* III. in princip. et n. 8.

Martin V. issued instructions for the detection and punishment of Wickliffites and Hussites, he was careful to infer that confessing to laymen was only a heresy when a proper priest was accessible.[1] Still, the Franciscan view continued to prevail in the schools and Dominicans like John Nider and St. Antonino of Florence abandoned the teachings of their master Aquinas.[2] Angiolo da Chivasso asserts that the opinion of Duns Scotus is followed by theologians in general, in opposition to Peter Lombard and Aquinas,[3] while Gabriel Biel argues that a layman can no more grant absolution than he can consecrate a host, but he finds it difficult to set aside the Pseudo-Augustin and Peter Lombard, and admits that it is beneficial as a counsel but not a precept.[4] While in the schools the Franciscan view was thus prevailing it seemed impossible to eradicate the old belief that a layman could absolve in case of necessity. This is positively asserted in a little anonymous manual for confessors at this period, which probably reflects more truly the popular practice

---

[1] Harduin. Concil. VIII. 915.—Nauclerus (Chron. Ed. Colon. 1544, fol. 930ᵇ) asserts, on the authority of Æneas Sylvius (which I have failed to identify), that, on the eve of the desperate battle of Agincourt, Henry V. ordered his soldiers to confess mutually and to administer to each other a pinch of earth as a symbol of the Eucharist. The story retained its currency through the moralists—Gobat Alphab. Confessor. s. v. *Confessarius quid* cas. 1; Clericati De Pœnit. Decis. XVIII.—but John Capgrave is much more likely to be accurate in saying (Lib. de Illustribus Henricis, ann. 1415) that Henry commanded his men to confess and that, owing to the scarcity of priests, the process was slow.

[2] Jo. Nider Præceptorium Divinæ Legis, Præcept. III. cap. 9.—S. Antonini Confessionale fol. 70; Summæ P. III. Tit. xvii. cap. 1, 4, 22 § 2. Yet he admits (P. I. Tit. x. cap. 3 § 5) that a man who holds a plenary death-bed indulgence can gain it *in articulo mortis* by confessing to a layman if no priest is accessible.

St. Antonino was the leading theologian of the fifteenth century, and his works are still quoted as authority by modern writers. His *Confessionale* and *Instructio de Audientia Confessionum* had an enduring circulation. My edition is without date or place, but the work was printed in Cologne, 1469–70; Erlangen, about 1474; Memmingen, 1483; Strassburg, 1492 and 1499; Lyons, 1564; Florence, about 1480; Ancona, 1533 and Venice, 1473, 1474, 1480, 1483, 1495, 1511, 1536, 1539, 1566, 1584, and 1592—and doubtless there were numerous other editions.

[3] Summa Angelica s. v. *Confessio* III. § 1. Cf. Bart. de Chaimis Interrogatorium sive Confessionale, Venet. 1480, fol. 1ᵇ, 12ᵇ.

[4] Gab. Biel in IV. Sentt. Dist. XIV. Q. ii. Art. 1, not. 1; Dist. XVII. Q. ii. Dub. 7.

than the more formidable treatises of the theologians.[1] Soon after this we find Sylvester Prierias returning to the full doctrine of Aquinas; confession can be made to a layman in the absence of one's own parish priest: the act is more important than the person to whom it is made; though the layman cannot absolve, the defect is supplied by God, and the lay confessor does not, as some assert, become "irregular," as though he celebrated mass.[2] On the other hand, in 1528, Frias declares that as the layman cannot absolve confession to him is worse than useless.[3] In 1551 the council of Trent, while condemning the heresy of asserting that the power of the keys was bestowed on all Christians and not on bishops and priests exclusively, is careful to avoid a definition as to lay confession, and the question was thus left open.[4] About this time Domingo Soto speaks of it as a custom formerly prevailing in the Church, but he denounces it as useless,[5] while Azpilcueta discusses it at a length which shows that it was still a matter of living interest. He says that many believe that death-bed confession to and absolution from a layman are valid, and he considers that in such act there is no sin, or at most a venial one.[6] Bartolommeo Fumo's remarks show that at this period it was still customary in Italy.[7] In 1584 Bishop Angles speaks of it as laudable but unnecessary.[8] The savage bulls of Paul IV., Sixtus V., Clement VIII. and Benedict XIV., under which all who, without being in priests' orders, administered the

---

[1] Casus papales Confessorum, *sine nota* (Hain, 4675). "Decimo, laicus potest absolvere pœnitentem in articulo mortis, cum non possit haberi sacerdos."

[2] Summa Sylvestrina s. vv. *Confessio Sacram.* I. § 16; *Confessor* I. §§ 1, 2.

Luther practically did not go much beyond this when, in 1518, he asserted that, in the absence of a priest, confession to a layman and absolution by him were as effective as to a priest. In theory however he had already advanced further, for he argued that the keys had been granted to all Christians and could be used by any one, irrespective of ordination.—Steitz, Die Privatbeichte etc. der Lutheranischen Kirche, I. § 11.

[3] Martini de Frias de Arte et Modo audiendi Confessiones, fol. 64 (Burgos, 1528). The approbation of this work bears the distinguished signatures of Francisco de Vitoria and Domingo Soto. The author was professor of theology at Salamanca.

[4] C. Trident. Sess. XIV. De Pœnit. cap. 6, can. 10.

[5] Dom. Soto in IV. Sentt. Dist. XVIII. Q. iv. Art. 1, 5.

[6] Azpilcueta Comment. in VII. Distt. de Pœnit. Dist. VI. cap. 1, n. 81, 83.

[7] Fumi Aurea Armilla, s. v. *Confessor* n. 8.

[8] Angles, Flores Theol. Quæstionum P. I. fol. 145 (Venet. 1584).

sacraments of penitence and the Eucharist were subjected to the Inquisition and were to be "relaxed" to the secular arm for burning[1] are evidently intended primarily for impostors and not for laymen who might honestly in extremity perform the function which de Joinville did for Guy d'Ibelin, yet they may have exercised some restraint on the custom and we hear little of it after the sixteenth century, though the question whether a layman administering absolution was thereby rendered "irregular" long continued to be disputed among the canonists.[2] Diana merely speaks of it as a useless and abusive practice which sailors adopt in danger of shipwreck[3] and Valerè Renaud only quotes and follows Azpilcueta.[4] Liguori emphatically declares that in no case, and with no matter what dispensation, can the sacrament be administered except by a priest,[5] and Palmieri alludes to it as a pious custom of the middle ages which fell into disuse in the fourteenth century and was finally abolished.[6] The Church appears never to have taken any formal action on the question, either of approbation or condemnation, other than the papal decrees just mentioned : as a mute protest against the exclusive sacerdotal control of the keys the custom died a natural death consequent upon the full recognition of that control, yet its persistence until the seventeenth century shows how strong a hold the ancient tradition held on the popular mind, and it is not without interest to observe that, in spite of the denial of the sacramental character of lay confession, a quasi-sacramental character has still been accorded to it in the rule that the seal of the confessional extends over all such confessions made to laymen.[7]

---

[1] Bullar. Roman. Ed. Luxemb. III. 142.—Bullar. Bened. PP. XIV. Tom. I. p. 152.

[2] Thesauri de Pœnis Ecclesiasticis P. II. s. v. *Absolutio* cap. 1.

[3] Summa Diana s. vv. *Confessarius* n. 2 ; *Confessionis necessitas* n. 13, 14.

[4] Reginaldi Praxis Fori Pœnitent. Lib. I. n. 8, 9.

[5] S. Alph. de Ligorio Theol. Moral. Lib. VI. n. 540.

[6] Palmieri Tract. de Pœnitent. p. 168.

[7] S. Antonini Summæ P. III. Tit. xvii. cap. 22 § 2.—Summa Sylvestrina s. v. *Confessio* III. § 4.—Aurea Armilla s. v. *Confessor* n. 8.—Clericati de Pœnit. Decis. XVIII. n. 15.

Diana however says (Summa, s. v. *Sigillum Sacram.* n. 3) that this is a disputed point among theologians.

CHAPTER IX.

ENFORCED CONFESSION.

Thus far auricular confession had been the spontaneous act of the sinner, anxious for reconciliation with God. The Church, with indifferent success, had long sought to popularize it, until the labors of the schoolmen constructed a theory under which the power of the keys, in the sacrament of penitence, promised absolution, and no contrition was held to be sufficing that did not comprise the vow to confess and to perform the penance to be imposed by the confessor. As that theory became accepted, the necessity of confession was apparent to all pious souls and to all who dreaded the judgment of God, and the practice increased in frequency. Yet how vague and crude were still the conceptions of the sacrament is seen in Peter Cantor's advice that the more priests the sinner confesses to the sooner will he obtain absolution for his sins.[1]

The logical development of the scholastic movement was to render confession obligatory on all Christians. Bishops, as we have seen, had occasionally, with scant success, attempted to reduce this to practice in their own dioceses, and it seems to have been felt that so profound a change in the functions and discipline of the Church could only be wrought through the authority of an Œcumenic Council—a parliament of all nations, empowered to make laws for Christendom. The council of Avignon, held in 1209, by the papal legates Hugo of Reggio and Master Theodisius, and that of Montpellier, held in 1215 by the legate Cardinal Stephen, were both silent on the subject;[2] that of Paris, in 1212, held by the legate Robert de Courzon, while it shows a desire to promote confession, only ventures to address itself to ecclesiastics. These are told to confess only to their superiors, while bishops and archbishops are ordered to attend personally to the duties of the confessional and to confess frequently to discreet confessors.[3] The opportunity for gen-

---

[1] P. Cantor. Verb. abbrev. cap. 143.   [2] Harduin. VI. II. 1985, 2045.

[3] C. Parisiens. ann. 1212, P. I. cap. 5; P. IV. cap. 6 (Harduin. VI. II. 2002, 2016).

eral legislation came with the great Lateran council of 1215–16. Probably Guido de Monteroquer may be correct in stating that one of the objects of the measure was the detection of heresy, with which the Church of the period was engaged in doubtful and internecine conflict.[1] It certainly was utilized for that purpose, but we can scarce believe that Innocent III., who has the credit of the initiative in devising and carrying it through, was blind to its far-reaching effects in other and more important directions. It was a move worthy of his far-seeing statesmanship and unbending purpose to establish ecclesiastical supremacy, yet even he can scarce have conceived what a mighty instrument he was fashioning for giving to the Church control over the conscience of every man and establishing its authority on an impregnable basis. Through this the scholastic theories of the power of the keys and the virtue of the sacraments were no longer the barren speculations of the closet, but became efficient levers in the hands of every parish priest to mould not only the internal but the external life of each member of his flock, and on this, transmitted through a skilfully organized hierarchy to the head of the Church, was founded a spiritual domination without example in the history of mankind. The dreams of the forgers of the False Decretals were realized at last. Aquinas recognized the full import of the Lateran canon in his argument to prove that it is heresy to deny the necessity to salvation of confession. With Gratian's admission of its being an open question staring him in the face, he acknowledges that this was not formerly the case, but since the decision of the Church under Innocent III., as recorded in the canon *Omnis utriusque sexus,* it is now to be considered as heresy. It thus became a new article of faith, and the assertion of Aquinas was duly accepted in the schools.[2]

---

[1] Manipulus Curatorum, P. II. Tract. ii. cap. 2.

[2] S. Th. Aquin. in IV. Sentt. Dist. XVII. Q. iii. Art. 5 ad 4.—S. Antonini Summæ P. III. Tit. xiv. cap. 19 § 1.—Summa Sylvestrina s. v. *Confessio Sacram.* II. § 2.

Duns Scotus admits that prior to the Lateran canon there was no obligation to confess except at any time prior to death (Guillel. Vorrillong in IV. Sentt. Dist. XVII.). Thomas of Walden, in refuting the Lollards, is more reckless, and boldly cites the dictum of Innocent I. (Epist. XXV. cap. 7) that in the Roman Church it was the custom to receive back on Holy Thursday the penitents who had performed their penance (Th. Waldens. de Sacramentis cap. CXLVIII. n. 6). Latomus, in his controversy with Œcolampadius, in endeavor-

This momentous canon is drawn in a fashion which shows that it was imposing not only new obligations on the laity but new duties on the priesthood, who required instructions for their discharge. It orders all the faithful of both sexes, after reaching years of discretion, to confess privately all their sins at least once a year to their own priests, and to endeavor, as far as their strength shall permit, to perform the penance imposed; also reverently to take communion, at least at Easter, unless for reasonable cause the priest advises postponement: otherwise ingress to the church is to be refused to the living and Christian sepulture to the dead. This salutary statute, it proceeds, is to be published frequently in the churches, so that no one shall be able to plead ignorance of it. If any one has just cause to desire to confess to another priest, he must obtain licence from his own, as otherwise no one else has power to bind or to loose. The priest must be discreet and prudent, so that like a skilful leech he may bathe with wine and oil the wounds of the wounded, diligently enquiring into the circumstances of the sinner and of the sin, whereby he may understand what counsel to give and what remedy to exhibit, using various experiments to cure the sick. But he must be specially careful not by word or sign in any way to betray the sinner, and if he is in need of wiser counsel he shall cautiously seek it without mentioning the sinner, for we decree that he who shall venture to reveal a sin known to him in the penitential judgment shall not only be deposed from the priestly office but shall be thrust into a rigid monastery to perform perpetual penance.[1]

---

ing to prove the antiquity of enforced confession is obliged to rely exclusively on the Forged Decretals and Pseudo-Augustin.—Jo. Latomus de Confessione Secreta, Antverpiæ, 1525.

[1] Omnis utriusque sexus fidelis, postquam ad annos discretionis pervenerit, omnia sua solus peccata saltem semel in anno fideliter confiteatur proprio sacerdoti; et injuctam sibi pœnitentiam pro viribus studeat adimplere, suscipiens reverenter ad minus in Pascha Eucharistiæ sacramentum; nisi forte de proprii sacerdotis consilio ob aliquam rationabilem causam, ad tempus ab hujusmodi perceptione duxerit abstinendum; alioquin et vivus ab ingressu ecclesiæ arceatur et moriens Christiana careat sepultura. Unde hoc salutare statutum frequenter in ecclesiis publicetur, ne quisquam ignorantiæ cæcitate velamen excusationis assumat. Si quis autem alieno sacerdoti voluerit justa de causa sua confiteri peccata licentiam prius postulet et obtineat a proprio sacerdote, cum aliter ipse illum non possit absolvere vel ligare. Sacerdos autem sit discretus et cautus ut more periti medici superinfundat vinum et oleum vulneribus sauciati, diligenter inquirens et peccatoris circumstantias et

This is the substance of what is perhaps the most important legislative act in the history of the Church. How little prepared was its organization for the stupendous duties thus assumed is seen in another canon of the council which orders all bishops to appoint penitentiaries in their cathedral cities and in all conventual churches.[1] It was evidently necessary that there should be provided everywhere skilled experts to whom penitents could be sent or whom the new confessors could consult in doubtful cases. Some bishops responded promptly to the requirements of the council. In 1217, a constitution of Richard Poore of Salisbury alludes to such officials as already existing.[2] In 1219, Everard Bishop of Amiens appointed a penitentiary in his church with a stipend of twenty-five livres per annum; he was to hear confessions from every part of the see, except those of priests, magnates and barons, which the bishop reserved to himself, and he was clothed with discretionary appellate power in all cases of doubt arising in the confessional.[3] Other prelates were more dilatory, and the custom established itself but slowly,[4] till at

---

peccati, quibus prudenter intelligat quale debeat ei præbere consilium et cujusmodi remedium adhibere diversis experimentis utendo ad salvandum ægrotum. Caveat autem omnino ne verbo aut signo aut alio quovis modo aliquatenus prodat peccatorem, sed si prudentiori consilio indiguerit illud absque ulla expressione personæ caute requirat; quoniam qui peccatum in pœnitentiali judicio sibi detectum præsumpserit revelare non solum a sacerdotali officio deponendum decernimus, verumetiam ad agendum perpetuam pœnitentiam in arctum monasterium detrudendum.—C. Lateran. IV. ann. 1216, cap. 21.—Cap. 12 Extra, v. xxxviii.

The ponderous jocularity of the schoolmen explained that the phrase *omnis utriusque sexus* was not intended to mean hermaphrodites exclusively and was to be construed distributively, not conjunctively.—Guillel. Vorrillong in IV. Sentt. Dist. XVII.

[1] C. Lateran. IV. cap. 10.

[2] Constitt. R. Poore Episc. Sarum cap. 30 (Harduin. VII. 98).

[3] D'Achery, Spicileg. III. 589.

[4] In 1233 one of the questions in an inquisition of the see of Lincoln is whether there are sufficient episcopal penitentiaries in each archidiaconate (Inquis. Lincoln. ann. 1233 cap. 44.—Harduin. VII. 235). In 1237 the council of London, held by the legate Otto, orders the bishops to appoint in each deanery prudent men to whom clerics can confess; also general confessors in all cathedrals (C. Londiniens. ann. 1237 cap. 5.—Ibid. VII. 294). In 1261 the council of Mainz commands all bishops to appoint penitentiaries in their cathedrals and to have another always with them (C. Mogunt. ann. 1261 cap. 33.—Hartzheim III. 604).

last the council of Trent was obliged to repeat the injunction, which met with only partial obedience.[1]

Evidently the enforcement of the Lateran canon was to be a work of time. The first prelate to make the attempt seems to have been the zealous Bishop of Salisbury who, in 1217, showed his earnestness by ordering three confessions and three communions a year, at Easter, Pentecost and Christmas, and by threatening exclusion from the church and deprivation of Christian burial for all who shall not at least confess and commune yearly.[2] In 1223 the council of Rouen ordered the Lateran canon to be diligently executed.[3] About the same time the constitutions of the Bishop of Paris indicate that the progress making in its enforcement was not encouraging and that its rigor had to be modified, for parish priests were ordered frequently to notify their flocks that all, or at least the fathers and mothers of families, should come to confession before Palm Sunday, under penalty of keeping their Lenten fast until after the octave of Easter, when they should have another chance of being heard. Lists of all penitents moreover were ordered to be kept and brought to the annual synod. Another regulation shows the progress of the rule that confession must precede all sacraments, for priests were told to enjoin on their people to confess before contracting marriage.[4] In 1227 the council of Narbonne ordered the Lateran canon enforced on all over fourteen years of age, and lists of those who obeyed were to be kept as evidence in their favor.[5] This has a decided appearance of using the confessional as a means of discovering the heretics of which Languedoc was full, and the object comes forward still more clearly in the council of Toulouse held, in 1229, to organize a system of persecution after the Peace

---

[1] C. Trident. Sess. XXIV. De Reform. cap. 8. This was not without effect. About 1700, Chiericato (De Pœnit. Decis. XLVIII. n. 18) speaks of episcopal penitentiaries as existing in all dioceses, but in 1725 Benedict XIII. issued a constitution ordering the rule to be observed wherever it had not been, and he caused a decree to the same purport to be adopted by the council of Rome of the same year.—C. Roman. ann. 1725, Tit. xxxiii. cap. 4 (Romæ, 1725, p. 139; Append. p. 175).

[2] Constitt. R. Poore Episc. Sarum. ann. 1217 cap. 25 (Harduin. VII. 96).

[3] C. Rotomagens. ann. 1223 cap. 9 (Ibid. VII. 128).

[4] Additiones Willelmi Paris. ad Constitt. Gallonis cap. 7, 8, 16 (Ibid. VII. II. 1798-9). This William may be either Guillaume de Seignelai (1220-3) or Guillaume d'Auvergne (1228-49) but presumably is the former.

[5] C. Narbonnens. ann. 1227, cap. 7 (Ibid. VII. 146).

of Paris, for three confessions and communions were ordered yearly and priests were instructed to watch keenly for absentees who were to be held suspect of heresy.[1] In 1236 Edmund of Canterbury adopted the regulations of Richard Poore,[2] and in 1240 they were repeated by the council of Worcester, though without the penalty.[3] In 1237 the Bishop of Coventry urged three confessions and communions a year, but if this could not be had the people were to be warned to confess and fast in Advent.[4] It was not till 1250 that Berenguer, Bishop of Gerona, instructed his priests to tell their people that they must confess once a year and that if they died without repentance they would be denied Christian burial.[5] Soon after this Cardinal Henry of Susa recommends that the precept be frequently published in the churches so that no one could plead ignorance,[6] and in 1268 we find the council of Clermont ordering all priests to teach the rule to their flocks.[7] It is scarce worth while to enumerate further the efforts to introduce the Lateran canon which continued until the end of the century and beyond. How slow was its acceptance is seen in the council of Ravenna, in 1311, which ordered all priests to publish it in the services of the mass during Advent and Lent and to explain it to the people in the vernacular, so that no one might be able to plead ignorance.[8] So little, indeed, as yet was the whole scholastic theory of the sacrament and the keys understood that in 1280 the synod of Poitiers was obliged to prohibit, under pain of excommunication, the hearing of confessions and granting of absolutions by deacons, an error, it said, of old standing, arising from ignorance, which must be eradicated.[9] How slowly, too, the priests

---

[1] C. Tolosan. ann. 1229, cap. 13 (Ibid. VII. 178).

[2] Constitt. S. Edmundi Cantuar. ann. 1236, cap. 18 (Ibid. VII. 270).

[3] C. Wigorn. ann. 1240, cap. 16 (Ibid. VII. 336). In spite of these repeated regulations the idea of confessors appears still to be a novelty, for not long afterwards Matthew Paris (Hist. Angl. ann. 1196) seems to feel it necessary to explain "quos religiosi confessores vocant."

[4] Constitt. Coventriens. ann. 1237 (Harduin. VII. 277).

[5] Florez, España Sagrada, XLIV. 20.

[6] Hostiens. Aureæ Summæ Lib. v. De Pœn. et Remiss. § 45.

[7] C. Claromont. ann. 1268, cap. 7 (Harduin. VII. 594).

[8] C. Ravennat. ann. 1311 Rubr. xv. (Ibid. VII. 1367). Somewhat similar are C. Senonens. ann. 1269 cap. 4 (Ibid. VII. 650) and C. Treverens. ann. 1310, cap. 90 (Martene Thesaur. IV. 260).

[9] Synod. Pictaviens. ann. 1280, cap. 5 (Harduin. VII. 851).

learned their unfamiliar duties is visible in the instructions issued by synod after synod for more than a century—instructions of greater or less detail which presuppose complete ignorance of the subject on the part of the priesthood.[1] As the duties of the confessional came to be more thoroughly understood, and it was recognized that they could be made to control nearly every act of external as well as of internal life and all the relations of man to his fellows, manuals of all kinds were prepared for the guidance of priests in their perplexing functions, from the humble fly-sheet to the stately folio, thus creating a literature which has in time swollen to vast proportions.[2]

That the people did not take kindly to the burden thus imposed upon them is evident from the devices which at once became necessary to coerce them, though it was admitted that confession must be voluntary and that if induced by the fear of expulsion from church it is worthless for the remission of sins.[3] Lists were ordered to be made out, sometimes of those who confessed and sometimes of those who neglected or refused. In the latter case the list is generally ordered to be sent to the bishop in order that the backsliders may be punished.[4] This shows that the exclusion from church and denial of funeral rites was speedily taken out of the hands of the priests, for the canonists decided that the punishment was not *ipso facto* but could only be inflicted after due conviction,[5] which doubtless greatly

---

[1] Constitt. Richardi Poore, cap. 22 (Harduin. VII. 96).—Constitt. Coventriens. ann. 1237 (Ibid. VII. 279-86).—C. Mogunt. ann. 1261, cap. 8; ann. 1281, cap. 8 (Hartzheim III. 664-6).—C. Coloniens. ann. 1280, cap. 8 (Harduin. VII. 826-9).—C. Nemausens. ann. 1284 (Harduin. VII. 907-11).—Statuta Synodal. Leodiens. ann. 1287, cap. 14 (Hartzheim III. 686-9).—Statuta Synod. Camerac. ann. 1300-10 (Hartzheim IV. 68-9).—Statuta Synod. Remensia circa 1330, Secundus locus, Præcept. 4 (Gousset, Actes de la Prov. ecclés. de Reims, II. 540).—C. Suessionens. ann. 1403, cap. 35-45 (Ibid. II. 630-1).

[2] Probably the earliest compilation for the special benefit of confessors was the *Summa de Casibus Conscientiæ* of Burchard or Brocardus of Strassburg, who flourished about 1230. Casimir Oudin describes it as existing in several MSS. but I believe it has never been printed (Canisii et Basnage, Thesaur. IV. 7).

[3] Summa Tabiena s. v. *Confessio sacram.* § 29.

[4] C. Arelatens. ann. 1275, cap. 19 (Harduin. VII. 731) —C. Coloniens. ann. 1280, cap. 8 (Ibid. VII. 829).—C. Nemausens. ann. 1284 (Ibid. VII. 912).—Statuta Synod. Leodiens. ann. 1287, cap. 4 (Hartzheim III. 689).—Statuta Synod. Camerac. ann. 1300-1310 (Ibid. IV. 70).—C. Ambianens. ann. 1454, cap. 5 § 3 (Gousset, op. cit. II. 709).—C. Tornacens. ann. 1484, cap. 4 (Ibid. II. 753).

[5] Tournely de Sacr. Pœnitent. Q. VI. Art. iii. In Spain however it was

diminished its efficacy. Yet the process described, about 1300, by John of Freiburg is that if a parishioner is known to be a sinner and refuses to confess and repent the priest should excommunicate him or report him to the superior; he is to be forced to perform penance and if he continues disobedient he is to be ejected from the church not to be readily readmitted.[1]

The people, thus coerced, resorted to any available means to elude the precept. The council of Arles, in 1265, relates how, when episcopal penitentiaries were sent through the parishes during Lent in order to enable the poor to obtain absolution for reserved cases, the people fraudulently pretended that they confessed fully to them, refused to confess to their priests and rejoiced in the deceit, wherefore the penitentiaries are instructed in future to hear no general confessions. Ten years later a subsequent council complains that the same trick was played by pretending that confession was made to the Mendicant friars, and, to check this, lists are ordered to be kept by both priests and friars which are to be compared in order that none may escape.[2] Yet in spite of the difficulty of enforcing annual confession there were earnest churchmen who considered it insufficient, in view of the difficulty of remembering sins during so long an interval. Thus, in 1429, the council of Paris orders all priests to induce if possible their parishioners to confess on the five other great solemnities of the year—Pentecost, Assumption, All-Saints, Christmas and Ash Wednesday.[3]

To overcome this general popular repugnance no effort was spared to exalt the virtues and benefits of confession in the estimation of the people. Cæsarius of Hiesterbach declares emphatically that it is so potent that the mere desire to perform it, if the act is prevented by necessity, suffices to remit all sins. He pours forth a wealth of marvellous stories to prove the advantages, both spiritual and ma-

---

rendered *ipso facto.* In 1528 Martin de Frias (De Arte et Modo Audiendi Confess. fol. viiᵃ) includes among the preliminary inquiries to be made of the penitent the question whether he had confessed the previous year. If answered in the negative and if there is a diocesan decree excommunicating all who neglect the annual precept he is at once to be sent to the Ordinary for absolution.

[1] Jo. Friburgens. Summæ Confessor. Lib. III. Tit. xxxiv. Q. 84.

[2] C. Arelatens. ann. 1260 (1265) cap. 16; ann. 1275, cap. 19 (Harduin. VII. 516, 731).

[3] C. Parisiens. ann. 1429, cap. 28 (Ibid. VIII. 1048).

terial, flowing from it, showing how industriously these pious frauds were invented and circulated from mouth to mouth. A demon in the shape of a youth watches the stream of penitents coming to confession; he sees them enter as sinners and depart justified with the assurance of eternal glory, and is so impressed that he presents himself as a penitent and pours forth a long catalogue of iniquities till the astonished confessor inquires who he is; on being told the priest assures him of redemption if he will thrice a day prostrate himself before God and sue for pardon, but demonic pride rejects the penance as too hard. The impression sought to be produced is especially manifest in the frequent miracles through which those who repent and confess escape the secular punishment due to their crimes. A more immoral lesson it would be difficult to conceive, and Cæsarius admits this when in answer to his interlocutor's question, why all criminals do not thus escape, he replies that this would lead many to commit sin.[1]

The same effort led to the forgery, about this time, of the absurd sermons attributed to St. Augustin to which reference has already been made (p. 210). The preacher complains that men are wont to say that God knows everything and therefore does not need our confession, whereupon he proceeds to extol in the most extravagant language the importance and advantages of auricular confession. He warns his hearers not to come to it laughing and gossiping and assures them that they need not fear to reveal their sins "for what I know through confession I know less than what I do not know."[2] William of Paris declares that confession is most sweet to the ears of

---

[1] Cæsar. Hiesterb. Dial. Dist. II. III. One noteworthy peculiarity is the slender attention paid to absolution and satisfaction. The former is alluded to but once (Dist. III. cap. 53). As yet contrition and confession were the main things; the sacrament seems scarce to be thought of.

The stories related by Cæsarius formed part of the stock in trade of the medieval preachers. See Fra Jacopo Passavanti, *Lo Specchio della vera Penitenza*, Dist. V. cap. iii.

[2] Ps. August. Serm. ad Fratres in Eremo, Serm. XXX. Wherever this expression may have originated, it seems to have become proverbial. It is used by St. Leonardo da Porto Maurizio, *Discorso Mistico e Morale*, § 30. Even in the middle of the nineteenth century the whole passage in which it occurs is quoted, with a few verbal changes as St. Augustin's by Bishop Zenner, Vicar General of Vienna, in his *Instructio Practica Confessarii* § 73 ad 4. There are some phrases in it which the forger borrowed from St. Augustin's Enarrat. in Ps. LXVI. n. 6, 7.

God and of the heavenly hosts, while it is most horrible and terrifying to the demons and drives them in dismay from those who truly and piously confess.[1] Aquinas argues that the shame experienced in the act of confession diminishes the punishment left after the remission of the *culpa*, and the oftener the same sins are confessed the more the *pœna* is reduced.[2] That such stories as we find in Cæsarius produced a profound impression on the popular mind is seen in the fact that persons in sickness and trouble sometimes confessed in hope of obtaining material relief, and St. Antonino feels obliged to explain that when the act is performed with this object it does no good; confession must be made to placate God, though as a secondary effect there is no objection to the penitent hoping for worldly benefit.[3] A more legitimate means of removing popular distaste for it was the injunction of the council of Nîmes, in 1284, to the parish priests to treat their people kindly so as to render them more willing to come to the confessional.[4] But whatever may have been the temper of the masses, by the end of the thirteenth century there was no question that confession was indispensable to salvation. In Dante's metaphorical theology the three steps by which admission is secured to purgatory are confession, contrition and satisfaction, among which confession occupies the first place.[5]

The enforcement of confession as a part of church discipline worked a change so profound, not only in practice but in the theory of the sacrament, that necessarily a cloud of questions arose which were discussed with the untiring acumen characteristic of this period of theological construction. Many of these will necessarily be dis-

---

[1] Guillel. Paris. Opera de Fide etc. (Nuremburgi, 1496, fol. 180, col. 3).

[2] St. Th. Aquin. Summæ Suppl. Q. x. Art. 2.

[3] S. Antonini Summa Confessionum fol. 13*a*; Summæ P. III. Tit. xiv. cap. 19 § 8.

[4] Synod. Nemausens. ann. 1284 (Harduin. VII. 939).

[5]   . . e lo scaglion primajo
    Bianco marmo era, si pulito e terso
    Ch'i'mi specchiava in esso, quale i'pajo.
  Era'l secondo tinto più che perso,
    D'una petrina ruvida e arsiccia,
    Crepato per lo longo e per traverso.
Lo terzo che di sopra s'ammassiccia
    Porfido mi parea si fiammegiante,
    Come sangue che fuor di vena spiccia.—Purgatorio, IX.

cussed hereafter, and I need here allude only to a few of a more general character. Bishop William of Paris still considers it incumbent on him to argue at great length against the belief that confession to God suffices, which he stigmatizes as a Jewish error; his instructions to penitents seem to take for granted that the sins of a lifetime are to be confessed, as though the annual prescription was still an innovation, but he stoutly declares that if the precept to confess at Easter is not obeyed the negligent sinner must be coerced. He debates various questions, which he says caused much perturbation among the faithful, and does not always resolve them in the manner finally accepted by the Church; he asserts that confession can be made to one person and absolution be obtained from another, and that after each relapse into sin it is advisable to confess in full, *de novo*, from the beginning.[1]

Alexander Hales treats the subject with greater thoroughness, and in a manner to show that the new rule had not as yet by any means been accepted and digested. Men still asked why, if contrition brought justification, a justified penitent had to confess, wherefore they held that the sole obligation to confess arose from the duty of obedience, to which Hales can only reply that the object of confession is not remission of *culpa* and *pœna*, but obedience to the Church, and that neglect or contempt of the sacrament is a new mortal sin which destroys the justification—apparently not recognizing that thus the sacrament becomes an impediment and not an aid to salvation. The phrase *omnia peccata sua* in the Lateran canon had led to the belief that every year the sinner had to make a general confession of all his sins and Hales is obliged to explain that the opinion of the masters is that only those committed since the last confession are to be included, unless indeed satisfaction had been neglected, in which case the enumeration of the former ones must be repeated. It is true that confession to be satisfactory must be performed in charity, but that which is made only in obedience to the precept need not be so, and it is not a mortal sin to confess in mortal sin. Obligatory confession, in fact, was so totally different from voluntary that what applied to one had no bearing on the other, and already the doctors were disputing with the subtlest dialectics over the question, which was not settled till the seventeenth century by

---

[1] Guillel. Paris. de Sacr. Pœnitentiæ, cap. 2, 12, 19.

Alexander VII., whether the impenitent, who were resolved not to abandon their sins, were required to make a pretended confession that was only in derision of God and of the sacrament, and the theologians sought to evade it by drawing the nicest distinctions between those on whom it was and those on whom it was not incumbent. Almost equally puzzling was the question as to the obligation resting on those who had no mortal sins to confess, to which Hales replies that, if a man has no mortals, he must confess venials; if he has no venials he must in general terms confess himself a sinner; even the perfect are not exempt from the rule any more than from Lenten fasting. It requires, indeed, an elaborate argument to prove that original sin need not be included in the confession.[1]

St. Bonaventura admits that there can be justification without confession, but the contrition requisite for this includes the vow of confession, and this is held to be the same as confession—but then, even after justification, confession is necessary to avert falling from righteousness. So little even yet was understood as to the practice of the confessional that he wrote his *Confessionale* for the purpose of instructing priests, the ignorance of many of whom he says is horrible, and is equalled by that which is almost universal among penitents, at least among country folk.[2]

Aquinas holds of course that the Lateran canon is obligatory on all, though as venial sins are not required to be confessed, it suffices, if a man has no mortals, to present himself to the priest and say so, when this is reputed as confession; if he is doubtful whether a sin is mortal or venial he should confess it. Some authorities, he says, argue that one should confess as soon as he feels contrition, and if this were the precept of the Church he would sin mortally in not doing so, but as the precept is annual he is bound to nothing more, unless, indeed, he is obliged to take communion. As confession is of divine law, even the pope cannot dispense for it any more than he can dispense for baptism in an unbaptized person who desires to be saved, but he can dispense for the annual precept, which is merely

---

[1] Alex. de Ales Summæ P. IV. Q. xviii. Membr. iv. Art. 1; Art. 2 § 1; Art. 5 §§ 1, 3, 4, 7.

[2] S. Bonaventura in IV. Sentt. Dist. xvii. P. 1, Art. 1, Q. 2; Art. 2, Q. 4.— Confessionale, Cap. 1 Partic. 1; Cap. 2 Partic. 1.

a regulation of the Church.[1] All the schoolmen, however, did not accept the Lateran canon with this saintly zeal. Those who assumed to be philosophers and not theologians looked down with contempt on confession, and, while they might, for the sake of comfort, comply with the precept, had no scruple in asserting that it need only be performed in appearance—an error which was duly condemned in 1276 by Stephen Tempier, Bishop of Paris.[2]

Although, as we shall see, the council of Trent made the Lateran canon *de fide* it did not define its exact meaning. It did not even settle the question discussed by Alexander Hales whether the precept is satisfied by a confession without repentance or intention to sin no more —whether it requires spiritual or only formal obedience. Curiously enough, the Lateran canon prescribed confession and the performance of penance but said nothing about the sacrament or obtaining absolution. The schoolmen were prompt to see this and two schools arose, one of which held that the canon must be construed to cover the whole sacrament of penitence, the other that a mere formal confession suffices—a confession theologically fictitious through the absence of all desire to placate God, to obtain valid absolution and to abstain from sin. Great names are ranged on either side and the most that Laymann can say is that the former opinion is the more common.[3] The latter reduced the precept to a mere barren formality, rendering the sacrament an object rather of contempt than of reverence, and divesting the confessional of all spiritual significance and moral efficiency, yet it was not until 1665 that it was condemned by Alexander VII.[4] The exact construction and application of the expression "at least once a year" have been the subject of a good deal of debate which

---

[1] S. Th. Aquin. Summæ Suppl. Q. VI. Art. 3, 4, 5, 6.

Domingo Soto says (In IV. Sentt. Dist. XVIII. Q. 1, Art. 5) that only the pope or a council can dispense for annual confession, as for instance to a hermit to confess once in two or three years. Billuart (Comment. in Aquin. *loc. cit.*) informs us that a papal dispensation ought not to extend beyond eight or ten years.

[2] D'Argentré, Collect. Judic. de novis Error. I. I. 182, 199.

[3] Dom. Soto in IV. Sentt. Dist. XVIII. Q. iii. Art. 3.—Henriquez Summa Theol. Moral. Lib. v. cap. 15, n. 1.—Layman Theol. Moral. Lib. v. Tract. vi. cap. 5, n. 10, 11.

[4] Alexand. PP. VII. Const. 7 Sept. 1665, Prop. XIV. For the controversy over the question see Trotta a Veteri Expos. et Impugn. Propp. Damnatar. Neapoli, 1707, p. 15. Also, Viva, Trutina Theologica in Prop. XIV. Alex. VII.

need not detain us here, except to mention an ingenious device, commonly accepted by theologians, by which the burden is sensibly diminished. This is to confess and take communion twice during the fortnight between Palm Sunday and Low Sunday, when one may count for the past and the other for the coming year, thus virtually enabling the sinner to escape with a biennial ceremony.[1]

Another question which has excited considerable discussion is whether the precept is binding on a man who has committed no mortal sin since his last confession. The canon makes no exceptions: it commands that every one shall confess all his sins once a year, but the doctors discovered that venial sins are not necessary matter for the sacrament and need not be confessed. This question will be considered more in detail hereafter and it suffices to say here that it is not yet fully settled whether this vacates the precept of annual confession in the absence of mortal sin. The suggestion of Aquinas (p. 238), that in such case a man should present himself to his priest and declare the fact, is generally recommended, but the corollary from this, that he can take his Paschal communion without previous confession, though admitted by some theologians is regarded by others as hazardous.[2] The pope, also, is not bound by the precept, though we are told that he ought to observe it for the avoidance of scandal. If he is in mortal sin he is subject, like other men, to the divine law of confession, especially if he desires to receive or administer the sacraments.[3]

It need cause no surprise if the enforcement of the Lateran canon encountered obstacles and if it met with tardy obedience. The Church in adopting it had somewhat recklessly ventured on a tre-

---

[1] Caramuelis Theol. Fundament. n. 751. There is an unsettled question whether the year runs from January to December or from Easter to Easter, or from the date of the last confession; also whether, if omitted one year there must be two confessions in the next.—Clericati de Pœnit. Decis. L. n. 9.—Gousset, Théol. Morale, II. n. 409.

[2] Clericati de Pœnit. Decis. L. n. 3.—Casus Conscientiæ Bened. PP. XIV. Apr. 1740, cas. 1.—Gousset, Théol. Morale, II. 407–8.

Chiericato informs us (*loc. cit.*) that as the Virgin never committed sin, either mortal or venial, she never confessed and never received the sacrament of penitence, though she did that of baptism, which in view of the Immaculate Conception would appear to have been a work of supererogation.

[3] Clericati *loc. cit.* n. 8.

mendous experiment, for which its organization was wholly unfitted and unprepared. We have seen (p. 205) how imperfectly the increase in parish churches and priests had responded to the growth of population and the ever enlarging development of the sacred functions; the larger the parish the greater the revenues of the incumbent, who naturally resisted any division of its boundaries, however inadequate he might be to the proper discharge of his accumulating duties, and consequently, while the nations were burdened with a constantly multiplying crowd of ecclesiastics the number entitled to administer the sacraments was insufficient to meet the new demand upon it. To some extent, as we shall see, this deficiency was supplied by the rise of the Mendicant Orders and their invasion of the province of the beneficed priests, but while this remedied partially the lack of numbers it did not remove a more serious source of trouble, for the character of the majority of those in holy orders rendered them in every way unfit to win the confidence of their flocks or to discharge adequately the supremely delicate responsibilities of the confessional. Allusion has been made above to the descriptions by Peter Lombard and Alain de Lille of the clergy of the twelfth century, who guided penitents to hell rather than to heaven, and Henry Archbishop of Salzburg shows us that Germany was infected equally with France.[1] As years passed on the unvarying reiteration of these complaints, by those best able to judge, unfortunately leaves no room for doubting that the ministers of God, to whom was now entrusted the awful power of the keys, were as a class too ignorant and too corrupt to employ it for the welfare of their subjects or to reconcile the people to the new and onerous burden.

Innocent III., at the very time when he was imposing on the priests of Christendom this most difficult duty, had no illusions as to their unfitness and unworthiness for, in a sermon at the Lateran council, he declared that they were the chief source of corruption to the people whom he was thus subjecting to them.[2] As he could

---

[1] Henrici Salzburg. de Calamitatibus Ecclesiæ cap. 9 (Migne, CXCVI. 1551). "Clericus etenim . . . a fornicationibus et adulteriis laicum publico pœnitentia compescit. Clericus nulla timore frenatur. Quia etsi turpissimæ vitæ fuerit, decanum contemnit atque archidiaconum nisi accusatus fuerit, nullusque accusator sit, omnibus idipsum facientibus et crimina propria in aliis faventibus."

[2] Innoc. PP. III. Sermo VI. in Concil. Lateran.—"Nam omnis in populo corruptela principaliter procedit a clero."

thus expect only increased corruption from the new rule it is not uncharitable to assume that its object was ecclesiastical aggrandizement and increased facilities for the detection of heresy. Innocent's assertion is confirmed, in 1219, by his successor Honorius III.[1] and by Bishop Grosseteste in his memorial presented to Innocent IV. in 1250. The priests, he says, are slayers of the souls committed to their charge; they not only flay their sheep, but strip the flesh from the bones and grind the bones; they are universally given over to fornication and adultery and incest and gluttony, and are an abomination to God. Besides, the churches are for the most part abandoned to mercenaries on stipends barely enabling them to live, generally too ignorant to punish sins and not daring to do so when they know their duty. In a sermon addressed to his clergy, he tells them that many of them do not know a single article of faith nor are able to explain a single law of the decalogue.[2] The key of science evidently was not conferred in ordination, nor did the council of Worcester, in 1240, define it rigidly when it told the priests that they must at least know what are the seven deadly sins and the seven sacraments so that they may be able to teach their flocks and exhort them to confession.[3] Alexander Hales describes in vigorous terms the prevalence of sin among the people, while as for the clergy, who should convert them, the world is full of priests, but it is rare to find a laborer in the harvest of the Lord; we are all ready to assume the sacerdotal office but not to perform its duties, and the universal negligence is best passed over in silence.[4] William of Paris com-

---

[1] Honorii PP. III. Epist. ad Archiep. Bituricens. (Martene Ampl. Collect. I. 1149).

[2] R. Grosseteste Sermo (Fascic. Rer. Expetendarum, Ed. 1690, II. 251-3); Sermo ad Clerum (Ibid. p. 265).

It is perhaps to this conviction of the unfitness of the clergy that is attributable the slender importance that Grosseteste seems to attach to confession, in his tireless efforts to elevate the morals of his great diocese. In his numerous sermons to his clergy, while reproving their vices and urging them to their duties, he only once alludes to confession, and then it is rather as a means by which a pastor learns to know his sheep (Ibid. pp. 262-306). In a letter to his archdeacons, requiring them to see that the priests do their duty, there is no allusion to the confessional (Ib. p. 315). In scolding H. de Pateshul (afterwards Bishop of Coventry) for his neglect of pastoral duties, there is no word about confession (Ib. p. 324).

[3] C. Wigorn. ann. 1240, cap. 18 (Harduin. VII. 337).

[4] Alex. de Ales Summæ P. IV. Q. XXXII. Membr. iv. Art. 3.

plains of the thousands of souls lost through the wickedness and neglect of a single prelate and the impossibility of obtaining the removal of such unfaithful pastors.[1] When, in 1247, Johannes de Deo framed his *Liber Pœnitentialis* for the guidance of confessors, the list which he gives of fifty-one sins committed by bishops in the exercise of their functions is a terrible arraignment of the prelates of the period, while as for the clergy, especially the priests, he declares that their wickedness is so great as almost to baffle computation.[2] Cardinal Henry of Susa tells us that the common vice of the clergy is that for which Sodom and Gomorrha and Segor were destroyed, but he adds that they ought not to boast publicly of their sins for in that case they incur suspension on account of the scandal and infamy.[3] Alexander IV. was therefore probably correct when, in 1259, he ascribed the increasing corruption of the people to the infection proceeding from the clergy.[4] Aquinas contents himself with denouncing their ignorance, which renders them most dangerous in the confessional ; many of them do not even know Latin and very few have ever looked into the Scriptures; besides, the size of the parishes is often such that if the priest devoted his whole life to it he could scarce shrive all the penitents.[5] Bonaventura is quite as emphatic in his description of the prevailing ignorance of the priests, rendering them utterly unfit to guide the souls committed to their charge ; besides, the incumbents, in nearly all the parishes, took no thought of their cures but abandoned them to vicars hired at the lowest possible price, and these were mostly not only ignorant but so vicious that decent people fear to confess to them and an honest woman would risk her reputation if one of them whispered to her ; they are vagabonds, wandering from cure to cure in search of a living and when employed always liable to be turned out by an underbidder. If the Mendicants, he says, arraign the secular priests in their sermons, it is because the crimes of the latter are so open and notorious that, if passed over in silence, the laity would argue that

---

[1] Guillel. Paris. de Sacr. Pœnitent. cap. 20.

[2] Jo. de Deo Pœnitentialis cap. 2-6, 20.

[3] Hostiens. Aureæ Summæ Lib. v. de Excess. Prælat. § 2. The ecclesiastical definition of scandal is that which gives occasion to sin in others.—S. Th. Aquin. Summæ II. ii. Q. xliii. Art. 1.—La Croix Theol. Moral. Lib. i. n. 189.

[4] Chron. Augustens. ann. 1260 (Freher et Struv. I. 546).

[5] S. Th. Aquin. contra Impugnantes Religiosos P. ii. cap. iv. § 10.

such enormous offences are not hateful to God and women would believe what some priests tell them that sin with a cleric is no sin.[1] Of
course St. Bonaventura excepts the Mendicant friars from his censure, but, in his little work directing them how to confess their sins
and repent, the large space devoted to sensual offences shows what
was their besetting weakness, how little the vows and habit influenced the carnal nature and how prohibition only concentrated the
thoughts on the forbidden fruit.[2] It is no wonder that he should
halt deplorably in his endeavor to prove the necessity that wicked
priests should enjoy the power of the keys.[3]

The vicars or chaplains whom St. Bonaventura criticizes so sharply
were a recognized and standing evil;[4] as a rule no supervision was
exercised over them; their installation by the parish priest was sufficient and they required no episcopal licence or approbation. Occasionally, it is true, some diocesan synod would endeavor to curb the
abuse by insisting that no one should hear confessions unless he were
either beneficed or licensed, but these efforts were local and temporary, and, in the fifteenth century, Chancellor Gerson tells us that
although some rigid doctors held that no assistant of a parish priest
could hear confessions unless he had been accepted by the bishop
others insisted that ordination and employment in the parish sufficed,
and this was the rule in practice for that everywhere parsons employed deputies who held no licence.[5]   It is easy to imagine how

---

[1] S. Bonaventuræ Libellus Apologeticus; Quare Fratres Minores prædicent
et Confessiones audiant; In Lib. IV. Sentt. Dist. XVII. P. ii. Art. 1, Q. 2.

It is true that Bonaventura excepts the clergy of France and England from
these denunciations, but we have seen from Bishop Grosseteste how little the
latter deserved the exception, and Guillaume Le Maire, Bishop of Angers, in
1293, shows that the French clergy was no less corrupt; nor, if he is to be
believed, were the regulars better fitted for the confessional than the secular
priests.—Guill. Majoris Episc. Andegav. Synod IV. cap. 1 (D'Achery, I. 735).

The "Formulary of the Papal Penitentiary" compiled by Cardinal Thomasius
(Philadelphia, 1892), which is for the most part devoted to dispensations rein-
stating sinful clerics, explains to some extent the all-pervading vices of the
clergy who were not amenable to secular justice and who, by application to the
curia, could obtain immunity from the operation of the spiritual law.

[2] S. Bonaventura de Puritate Conscientiæ.

[3] S. Bonaventuræ in IV. Sentt. Dist. XIX. P. 1, Art. 1.

[4] Hiring vicars at small stipends was an old abuse, complained of more than
a century earlier by Geroch of Reichersperg, Exposit in Ps. lxiv. n. 156.

[5] Van Espen Jur. Eccles. P. II. Tit. vi. cap. 6, n. 11.—C. Wigorn. ann. 1240,

useless was the complaint of Humbert de Romanis at the general council of Lyons, in 1274, that one of the evils most urgently requiring correction was the granting of the keys to those too ignorant to know how to bind or to loose.[1] At the next general council, that of Vienne, in 1312, the memorial for the reformation of the Church presented by Guillaume le Maire, Bishop of Angers, is almost wholly occupied with deploring the ignorance and the execrable lives of the clergy of all ranks.[2]

It would be surplusage to accumulate further this consensus of opinion as to the moral and intellectual character of the medieval clergy on whom was thus thrust the responsibility of the salvation of souls through enforced confession. The evidence continues throughout the fourteenth century—indeed the description of the all-pervading wickedness of ecclesiastics, by such unexceptionable witnesses as Bishop Pelayo, St. Catherine of Siena and St. Birgitta of Sweden, grows stronger and more outspoken.[3] That a progressive deterioration, indeed, should occur would seem inevitable when the Holy See,

---

cap. 39 (Harduin. VII. 343).—Statut. Eccles. Æduens. ann. 1299, cap. 13 (Martene Thesaur. IV. 487).—Statut. Eccles. Avenionens. ann. 1449, cap. 6; ann. 1509, cap. 31 (Ibid. pp. 392, 591).—Statut. Eccles. Biterrens. ann. 1368, cap. 4 (Ibid. p. 627).—Jo. Gersonis Compend. Theologiæ (Ed. 1488, xxvii. G.).

[1] H. de Romanis de Tractandis in Concilio P. III. cap. 9 (Martene Ampl. Collect. VII. 197).

[2] "Innumerose persone contemptibiles et abjecte, vita, scientia et moribus omnino indigne, ad sacras ordines et maxime ad sacerdotium promoventur. Ex quo fit quod totus ordo ecclesiasticus dehonestatur, ministerium ecclesiasticum vituperatur, Ecclesia scandalizatur, dum effrenata multitudo sacerdotum maxime indignorum in Ecclesia a laicis populis consideratur; ex quorum execrabili vita et perniciosa ignorantia infinita scandala oriuntur, sacramenta ecclesiastica a laicis contempnuntur; unde in plerisque partibus apud laicos sacerdotes Judeis viliores et contemptibiliores habentur." Much of the blame for this he ascribes to the Holy See—"Quia multi vita et moribus detestabiles, de diversis mundi partibus ad sedem apostolicam concurrentes, tam in forma pauperum quam alias beneficia cum cura vel sine cura cotidie impetrare noscuntur, maxime in locis quibus de vita eorum et moribus noticia non habetur, et a prelatis tanquam filiis obediencie, mandato sedis apostolice obtemperantibus, reverenter instituti vel admissi, ita detestabilem et deformem vitam ducunt quod ob hoc ecclesie destruuntur, populi scandalizantur, Dei ecclesia blasphematur, prelati hodie non possunt bonis personis de beneficiis nec beneficiis de bonis personis, obstante numerosa multitudine talium impetrancium, providere."—Mélanges Historiques, II. pp. 478, 481.

[3] Alvar. Pelagii de Planctu Ecclesiæ Lib. ii. Art. 7.—S. Caterina da Siena

in the fourteenth century, grasped almost the whole disposable patronage of the Church throughout Europe and openly offered it for sale. In this market for spiritualities it is significant to observe that benefices with cure of souls were held at a higher price than those without cure, as though there was a speculative value in the altar and the confessional: thus in Italy the price *cum cura* was sixty florins and *sine cura* forty, in Germany and England twenty-five and eighteen marks respectively.[1] In addition to this source of demoralization there was the shameless issue of dispensations to hold pluralities which had long been the cause of untold injury to the Church and which ever grew more reckless, and there was moreover the showering of numberless benefices on the creatures of the curia, the cardinals and their dependents, with dispensations for non-residence. After forcing confession upon the people, the Holy See busied itself in selling the office of confessor to the first comer who could pay its price, irrespective of his fitness for the responsibilities of the position, and it even turned into a source of profit the infringement of the very slender rules to guard against unfitness, for it openly sold dispensations as to age: a clerk at twenty-two could buy for sixteen

---

Epistole, Lett. 9, 13, 14, 15, 17, 18, 21, 35, 38 etc.—S. Brigittæ Revelationes Lib. IV. cap. 33, 37, 142.

The frate Jacopo Passavanti tells us (Lo Specchio della vera Penitenza, Dist. v. cap. 5) that great numbers of penitents sought out purposely ignorant and stupid confessors, the result of which was that both priest and sinner were damned. Doctor Peter of Palermo complains (Quadragesimale, Serm. xx.) that while the vilest mechanical art is considered to require training, the art of directing souls is carried on without it.

[1] That a fixed tariff was set on benefices first appears in the Rules of the Chancery of Benedict XII., issued about 1335, but no figures are mentioned— only the *summa consueta* is alluded to, showing that regular prices had been adopted under his predecessor, John XXII. (Regulæ Cancellariæ Benedicti PP. XII. n. 2, 3, *ap*. Ottenthal, Regulæ Cancellariæ Apostolicæ, p. 19). Under subsequent popes figures are given (Regulæ Urbani PP. V. n. 4, p. 14.—Regulæ Gregor. PP. XI. n. 14, p. 27.—Regulæ Johann. PP. XXIII. n. 14, p. 175). During the Great Schism the antipopes, Clement VII. and Benedict XIII., made exceptions in favor of masters of theology and doctors of civil and canon law, who were not to be taxed (Regulæ Clement. VII. n. 24, p. 95.—Regulæ Bened. XIII. n. 70, p. 135), probably in order to win the support of the learned class and the universities.

These "taxes" were in addition to the fees for the letters, which were not light. See Tangl, Mittheilungen des Instituts für österreichische Geschichtsforschung, XIII. 1.

gros a letter enabling him to receive priest's orders, while additional years of deficiency were taxed at two *gros* each, and similar letters could be had enabling him to hold benefices with cure of souls.[1] Under these adverse influences it is easy to see why the spiritual needs of the faithful throughout Europe were more and more neglected, and how they were abandoned to the guidance of pastors steadily depreciating in character. The reformatory efforts of the councils of Constance and Bâle came to naught, and the complaints of the ignorance and corruption of the clergy in general and of confessors in particular continue to the Reformation.[2] Even among the Mendicants the standard for the confessional was not high. The Dominican Prierias instructs the superiors of the Orders with regard to the selection of friars for presentation to bishops as fit to receive licenses to hear confessions, and says that if a candidate knows enough grammar to understand Latin when read and has read the *Defecerunt* or other similar book and is not so stolid but that he can doubt when doubt is required and is not rash or presumptuous he can be presented with entire safety.[3] In 1538 the commission of cardinals, appointed by Paul III. to consider the reforms necessary to check the progress of heresy, reported as the first thing to be reme-

---

[1] Tangl, *ubi sup.*—At a later period, towards the close of the fifteenth century, the tariff of the Papal Penitentiary for favors to minors was—

Absolutio pro eo qui minor XXV. annis existens se fecit ad omnes
    sacros ordines promoveri et non est in etate legitima   .   .   gros. vii.
Absolutio pro eo qui nondum venit ad etatem legitimam et petit
    secum dispensari ut possit ministrare   .   .   .   .   gros. xviii.
Dispensatio pro eo qui dum XX sue etatis annum attigerit petit
    quod ad omnes sacros ordines promoveri possit   .   .   gros. xxxiii.
Absolutio pro presbytero quia minorennis parrochialem ecclesiam
    obtinuit et se fecit promoveri   .   .   .   .   .   gros. viii.
Libellus Taxarum super quibusdam in Cancellaria Apostolica impetrandis (White Historical Library, Cornell University, A. 6124).

[2] Martene Thesaur. I. 1612-16.—Jo. Gersonis Sermo in Concil. Remens. ann. 1608 (Gousset, Actes de la Province de Reims, II. 656-8).—Nic. de Clemangis de Ruina Ecclesiæ cap. 19-36.—Jo. de Ragusio Init. et Prosec. Concil. Basil. (Acta et Monumenta Concil. Sæc. XV., I. 32).—Weigel Clavicula Indulgentialis cap. 45, 76.—Jo. Nideri Formicar. Lib. I. cap. 7.—S. Antonini de Audientia Confessionum, fol. 3*a*.—Œneæ Sylvii Opp. inedd. (Atti della Accad. dei Lincei, 1883, pp. 558-9).—Cherubini de Spoleto Quadragesimale, Serm. LXIV.—God. Rosemondi Confessionale, Antverpiæ, 1519, fol. 113*b*.

[3] Summa Sylvestrina s. v. *Confessor* III. § 3.

died the deplorable character of the priesthood which had brought
the Church and its functions into universal contempt.[1] Even after
the counter-Reformation was fairly under way there seems to have
been little improvement. About 1575 a memorial of matters requiring reform, presented to a cardinal, includes the ignorance prevailing
among those who preach and confess, adding that prelates and princes
usually desire to have such confessors.[2] Bartolomé de Medina complains bitterly that confession is abandoned to the more ignorant
priests, who, destitute of knowledge of scripture, undertake the cure
of souls, while learned theologians and canonists despise the function
and think it a disgrace to listen to penitents ; this he characterizes as
an intolerable perversity and terrible disease of these miserable times,
leading to the perdition of the people of God.[3] Cardinal Bellarmine
is unsparing in his denunciation of the vices of the clergy ; he deplores the perversity of the times when priests, who of old were not
even subject to public penance, are now condemned in numbers to the
galleys ; the secular clergy corrupt by their example the people whom
they should edify, while the regulars scandalize not only the faithful
but even the heretics and the Turks.[4]

Some of the stories related by Cæsarius of Heisterbach show how
these pastors fulfilled the duties thus thrust upon them. He tells us
of one priest saying to those coming in Lent for confession and absolution that he prescribed for them the same penance as his predecessor
had done, or the same penance as he had imposed on them the previous year. There was another who, when his parishioners flocked to him
at Easter, would call them up to the altar in groups of six or eight,
wind his stole around them as though for exorcism, and then repeat
to them in the vernacular a general confession, in the recital of which
they followed him, after which he would prescribe a general penance
for them all and dismiss them. When he died, his successor was

---

[1] Quod passim, quicunque sint, imperitissimi sint, vilissimo genere orti, sint
malis moribus ornati, sint adolescentes, admittantur ad ordines sacros, maxime
ad presbyteratum . . .   Hinc innumera scandala, hinc contemptus ordinis
ecclesiastici, hinc divini cultus veneratio non tantum diminuta sed etiam prope
jam extincta.—Le Plat, Monum. Conc. Trident. II. 598.

[2] Bibl. Ambros. MS. G. 22 (Döllinger, Beiträge zur politischen, kirchlichen
und Cultur-Geschichte, III. 241.)

[3] Bart. a Medina Instruct. Confessor. Prologus (Coloniæ, 1601).

[4] Rob. Bellarmini de Gemitu Columbæ Lib. II. cap. 5 ; Lib. III. cap. 5, 6.

called to the death-bed of an old parishioner who could not be persuaded to confess otherwise than in the accustomed routine—" I
confess to have sinned in adultery, theft, rapine, homicide, perjury
etc.," though he emphatically denied having committed any of these
sins.[1]

The Church of course could not admit that the validity of the
sacrament was impaired by the ignorance or wickedness of the ministrant, but the people, whose salvation was at stake, were not firm
in this conviction, though to doubt it was to revive the old Donatist
heresy. The schoolmen labored to remove this error, and Aquinas
triumphantly points out that no one can know whether another is in
a state of grace and therefore that no one could feel sure of his absolution if it depended on the fitness of the ministrant. He admits
that evil priests make evil use of the keys, but he casts the responsibility on God to evoke good out of this evil, forgetful that he is thus
practically denying the priestly power.[2] He further admits that
many penitents are so weak that they would rather die unhouselled
than confess to such priests, wherefore those who refuse to their
parishioners license to confess to others consign many souls to hell,
and in such case confession to a layman is the best course.[3] Guido
de Monteroquer advises confession to God if, under such circumstances, the licence is refused.[4] John Gerson says that parishioners
not infrequently, and with good reason, suppress some of their sins
when confessing to their priests, which is highly significant,[5] and

---

[1] Cæsar. Heisterb. Dial. Dist. III. cap. 44, 45. This routine confession of all
possible sins was long continued. There is a xylographic *Beichtspiegel nach
den zehn Geboten* which has been reproduced in fac-simile, consisting of a formula in which the penitent confesses himself guilty of every possible offence
arranged according to the Decalogue. Being in German, and having no formulas for absolution or penance, it was evidently intended for popular use,
showing how the indolence of priest and sinner was consulted in its recital,
covering everything of which the penitent could possibly be guilty.—Haltrop,
Confessionale, La Haye, 1861.

[2] S. Raymundi Summæ Lib. III. Tit. xxxiv. § 5.—Hostiensis Aureæ Summæ
Lib. v. De Remiss. § 3.—S. Th. Aquin. Summæ Suppl. Q. XIX. Art. 5 ad 2.

[3] S. Th. Aquin. in IV. Sentt. Dist. XVII. Q. iii. ad 5. The confirmation of
this dictum of Aquinas by subsequent writers shows that the trouble continued.
See Astesani Summæ Lib. v. Tit. xiv. Q. 3 ; Summa Pisanella s. v. *Confessio*
III. n. 4; Summa Angelica s. v. *Confessio* III. § 31.

[4] Manip. Curator. P. II. Tract. ii. cap. 4.

[5] Jo. Gersonis Orat. in C. Remens. ann. 1408 (Gousset, Actes, II. 659).

hardly less so is the advice of Roberto da Lecci to penitents to shut their eyes to the sins of their confessors; it should suffice if their lives are not conspicuously evil.[1] The penitent, in fact, seems to have had only a choice of evils, for Angiolo da Chivasso, himself an Observantine Franciscan, advises penitents to adhere to their own priests, in view of the ignorance and deceit which abound among others who are licensed to hear confessions.[2]

It is not strange, therefore, that wayward human nature continued to require to be coerced to avail itself of the easy means of salvation provided by God and offered by the Church. Among the regular questions to be put to a priest who is confessing is whether he has made all his subjects confess and has compelled the unwilling, or has denounced them to the bishop as he is bound to do under pain of mortal sin.[3] Yet with all these means of coercion at hand the success of compelling annual confession was very partial. After two centuries and a half of effort, Roberto da Lecci complains that we see multitudes who have not confessed for twenty or thirty years and who constitute a venomous synagogue of hell. He tells us, indeed, that there was growing up an opinion that confession is useless and superfluous, and he devotes a whole sermon to its confutation.[4] Even in orthodox Spain, the council of Seville, in 1512, was forced to adopt measures of a radical character to overcome popular indifference. Seeing that so many neglect the precept and care nothing for the consequent excommunication, it directs that each priest shall divide his parish into districts and assign to each district a day on which the inhabitants shall come to confession. Those who fail to do so are to be denounced from the pulpit as excommunicates, while not only is the ordinary list to be sent to the provisors, but a second list of the persistently contumacious is to be furnished by the octave of Corpus Christi, and against these the provisors are commanded to proceed by censures and punishment, invoking if necessary the aid of the secular arm.

---

[1] Roberti Episc. Aquinat. Opus Quadragesimale, Sermo XXVIII. cap. 2.

[2] Summa Angelica s. v. *Confessio* III. § 33. It is safe to assume from this that the rule was a dead letter which he elsewhere records (s. v. *Clericus* VIII. n. 1, 2), that it is not lawful to receive any sacrament save baptism from a notorious sinner.

[3] Bart. de Chaimis Interrogatorium, fol. 92b.—Somma Pacifica, composta dal P. Pacifico da Novara, cap. xxii.

[4] Rob. Aquinat. Episc. Opus Quadragesimale Serm. XXVII.

Those who remain for a year under excommunication, if clerics, are to be imprisoned until they repent and submit; if laymen they incur a fine of a hundred maravedises a month, and after another year confiscation of half their property.[1] It is evident that those who would not voluntarily go to heaven were to be driven there, nor apparently did the Church pause to weigh the worth of confession and absolution under such stress of punishment. Charles V. was not quite so emphatic when, in his Reformation Formula of 1548, he described confession as necessary for the preservation of public morals and contented himself with ejecting from the Church those who did not obey the precept to perform it annually.[2]

The Lutheran revolt only rendered the Church more eager to define its position with greater precision, and the council of Trent actually elevated the Lateran canon into an article of faith.[3] The Tridentine Catechism therefore naturally lays especial stress on the obligation incumbent on all pastors to inculcate on their flocks the duty of obedience to the canon, explaining its institution by Christ and its necessity for the salvation of sinners, for whatever of sanctity, piety and religion has been conserved to the Church is in great measure due to the practice of confession.[4] Still the faithful seem not to have been duly impressed and various devices were employed to stimulate them. The old plan of keeping lists and issuing certificates was revived. At Rouen, in 1584, the bishops, in their annual visitations, were directed to enquire particularly as to those who did not annually confess and take communion; at Breslau, in 1592, all parish priests were ordered before Easter to make a house to house inspection, taking the names of all who ought to come to confession and subsequently checking off those who complied. In 1604 the council of Brixen imposed a fine of a florin on all priests who did not, after Easter, furnish the bishop with a list of all recusants, but in all this there does not seem to have been any thought of inflicting penalties other than those prescribed by the Lateran

---

[1] C. Hispalens. ann. 1512, cap. 7, 8 (Aguirre, V. 365).

[2] Formulæ Reformationis cap. 13 (Le Plat, Monument. C. Trident. IV. 88).

[3] C. Trident. Sess. XIV. De Pœnit. can. 8.—"Si quis dixerit . . . ad eam [sc. confessionem] non teneri omnes et singulos utriusque sexus Christifideles, juxta magni concilii Lateranensis constitutionem semel in anno . . . anathema sit."

[4] Cat. Trident. De Pœnitentia, cap. 7, 8.

canon.[1] Even these seem to have fallen into desuetude, for, in 1587, the Congregation of the Council of Trent felt called upon to decide that a bishop can excommunicate those who neglect the precept of Easter confession and can then remove the excommunication in return for "almsgiving."[2]

In the Spanish colonies, however, the new converts were treated with less indulgence, and the flagging zeal of the Indians was encouraged by St. Toribio, Archbishop of Lima, with the gentle stimulus of thirty stripes for the omission of Easter confession—a provision, it is true, from which the women and caciques were exempted, who were to be coerced in some other manner not specified. It is perhaps not surprising that there was little fervor among the converts, for the Indies were a sort of ecclesiastical penal colony to which were sent troublesome clerics who could not be endured at home, and, in a council shortly before, St. Toribio had deplored the degradation to which the sacrament of penitence had been allowed to sink. Many, through fear or shame or hatred of their parish priests, concealed their gravest sins, wherefore he proposed to appoint extraordinary confessors to whom the Indians might confess without apprehension; he also rebuked the numerous priests who through ignorance of the language, or negligence, or impatience of the tedium of listening, perfunctorily granted absolution after hearing one or two sins, and he ordered the bishops to exercise greater care and discrimination in the examining and licensing of confessors, even of members of religious orders.[3]

---

[1] C. Aquens. ann. 1585, De Pœnit. (Harduin. X. 1531).—S. Caroli Borromei Instructiones (Brixiæ, 1676, p. 71).—C. Rotomagens. ann. 1584, De Episc. Offic. n. 29 (Harduin. X. 1232).—C. Tolosan. ann. 1590, P. ii. cap. 4, n. 5 (Ibid. p. 1800).—C. Wratislaviens. ann. 1592, cap. 8 (Hartzheim VIII. 392).—C. Tornacens. ann. 1600, Tit. viii. cap. 4 (Hartzheim VIII. 483).—C. Brixiens. ann. 1603, De Confessione cap. 4 (Hartzheim VIII. 545).

In Brixen the custom seems to have been kept up. In the program prepared for the visitation of his diocese by the Bishop Giovanni Molino, about 1758, one article requires the priest of each town to give him a written list of all *inconfessi* with the dates of their last confessions. In Padua the same instructions were given; the Bishop Minotto Otthoboni threatens recusants repeatedly with punishment while living and deprivation of sepulture when dead (From a collection of Italian episcopal letters in my possession).

[2] Pittoni Constitutiones Pontificiæ T. VIII. n. 390.

[3] Concil. Provin. Liman. ann. 1583, Act. ii. cap. 14, 15, 16.—Synod. Diœces. Liman. III. cap. 87 (Haroldus, Lima Limata, Romæ, 1672, pp. 10, 250).

In the zeal of the counter-Reformation for the confessional there was one noteworthy exception. Prostitutes enjoyed the favor of exemption from excommunication for omitting confession—an exemption necessary if they were allowed, as they were, to ply their trade without ecclesiastical interference.[1] Viva, it is true, looks a little askance at this; he argues that they are not released from the annual precept, but he regards as probable the opinion of those doctors who hold that they do not incur the penalties decreed against transgressors of the canon, for they never are denounced, no matter how many years they pass without confession.[2] Aquinas, in fact, had shown, on the authority of St. Augustin, that prostitutes are to be tolerated for the avoidance of greater evils,[3] and this was the accepted doctrine of the Church.[4] Rulers, therefore, are justified in allowing them to practise their industry, and there is no sin in renting houses for the purpose, provided they are in the proper quarter and the owner secretly detests the sin. The harlot is entitled to her pay and can sue for it and give alms with it; if she abandons her calling she can confess and be absolved, when the confessor can interrogate her closely, for which most suggestive instructions are given.[5]

With the diminution of penance, which, as we shall see hereafter, has become in modern times scarce more than nominal, the confessional must naturally have lost much of its old-time terror, yet the Church has apparently never been able to secure satisfactory obedience

---

[1] Em. Sa Aphorismi Confessariorum s. v. *Confessio* n. 42.—"Meretrices non comprehenduntur statutis synodalibus excommunicantibus non confitentes in Pascha, itaque tales nunquam denunciantur."

This little book of Manuel Sa's is of peculiar authority, as it underwent a minute censorship in Rome. Printed in 1595, it had a wide circulation and was one of the works revised in the *Index Brasichellensis* in 1607, the only expurgatory Index that has been issued by the Holy See. Many passages of the *Aphorismi* were stricken out or altered to suit the views current in Rome, so that subsequent editions may be regarded as authoritative. I quote from that of Venice, 1617, which has the corrections of Brisighelli.

[2] Viva Cursus Theol. Moral. De Pœnit. P. II. Q. iv. Art. 3, n. 7.

[3] S. Th. Aquin. Summæ Sec. Sec. Q. x. Art. 11.

[4] Liguori (Theol. Moral. Lib. III. n. 434) thinks the doctrine of Aquinas probable, but the contrary more probable, which, under the rules of probabilism, allows either opinion to be followed.

[5] Ferraris Prompta Biblioth. s. v. *Meretrix* n. 4, 5, 9, 10, 13, 14.

to the precept of annual confession, although its omission is a mortal sin. The penalties provided in the Lateran canon are still legally in force, but prudence counsels their tacit suppression in view of the multitude of offenders.[1] Van Espen, about the year 1700, says that in several of the Belgian Dioceses the precept was wholly neglected and that it could not be revived without vigorous episcopal action.[2] In Italy, about the same time, Chiericato speaks of the numbers who allow not one but many lustres to pass without visiting the confessional.[3] In our own day the injunctions of almost all the local councils on the parish priests to exhort their flocks to yearly confession is evidence that neglect is common and that constant stimulus is needed to secure observance, while occasionally there is an admission that a large portion of the faithful abstain from confession during nearly their whole lives.[4] We may readily believe this if there is truth in the current statement of the journals of the day that of the thirty-eight millions of so-called Catholics in France, not more than eight millions obey the precept of Paschal communion. All this, of course, does not apply to the fervently religious, who require no coercion, and with whom the sacrament of penitence is voluntary, not enforced. Those of the laity, who are accustomed to daily communion, usually, I am told, make a practice of weekly confession. It is to a standard like this that the parish priest is told that he ought to strive to bring his flock. To confess once, twice, or thrice a year may be allowable for rustics living in a sparsely settled region, but for those in thickly populated districts, with easy access to confessors, it is virtually certain that almost all such confessions are imperfect and sacrilegious.[5] Daily confession, we are informed, was

---

[1] Casus Conscientiæ Bened. PP. XIV. Apr. 1737, cas. 2; Sept. 1738, cas. 3.
—Gousset, Théol. Morale, II. n. 413-14.—In Naples, recusants fall under an interdict removable only by the archbishop (Manzo, Epit. Theol. Moral. P. I. De Pœnit. Append. n. 14) and there may be similar diocesan regulations elsewhere.

[2] Van Espen, Jur. Eccles. P. II. Tit. vi. cap. 5, n. 24.

[3] Clericati de Pœnit. Decis. XVIII. n. 13.

[4] C. Avenionens. ann. 1849, Tit. IV. cap. 5 § 1 (Collect. Lacens. T. IV. p. 339)—"Plurimos Christianorum esse qui a salutari Pœnitentiæ lavacro per totum fere vitæ curriculum abstineant nemini ignotum est."—Cf. C. Albiens. ann. 1850, Tit. V. Decr. 1 (Ibid. p. 428-9); C. Senonens. ann. 1850, Tit. III. cap. 5 (Ib. p. 891); C. Quebecensis ann. 1854, Decr. IX. § iv. n. 2 (Ibid. III. 638).

[5] Salvatori, Istruzione per i confessori novelli, P. I. § 3.

the practice of St. Catharine of Siena, St. Birgitta of Sweden, St. Carlo Borromeo and St. Ignatius de Loyola, while St. Francisco de Borja is said to have been in the habit of making two confessions a day.[1] This, however, is not considered a practice to be encouraged. Frassinnetti says "those persons—invariably women—who would wish to go to confession every day are generally ninnies, and the more frequently they confess the more silly do they become"[2]—an incautious utterance, for it reveals how little real confidence is felt in the sanctifying grace of the sacrament. Benedict XIV. would seem to regard monthly confession as the maximum, for he says that a parish priest fulfils his duty if he is ready to hear confessions on the first Sunday of every month ;[3] and Cardinal Gousset appears to be quite satisfied if the precept of annual confession can be enforced.[4]

If it is difficult to enforce the Lateran canon at the present day, the character of the average modern confessor offers less excuse for repugnance than did that of the middle ages. The rivalry of Protestantism and the necessities of the counter-Reformation have rendered it incumbent on the Church to shake off its old-time indolence and self-indulgence. The council of Trent rendered no greater service to the cause than when, in 1563, it ordered seminaries to be founded in every diocese, where aspirants for the priesthood were to be trained from early youth in its duties, and the special importance of those of the confessional was recognized in requiring the studies to be particularly directed to fitting them for it.[5] To the competent development of this plan the successful labors of the Jesuits as educators powerfully contributed, and with its general introduction the complaints of the ignorance of confessors diminish. Another method aided efficiently. In 1594, the council of Avignon deplores the ignorance of confessors and orders the bishops to institute lectures on cases of conscience to be attended by confessors, or to have con-

---

[1] Müller's Catholic Priesthood, IV. 218.

[2] Frassinnetti, The New Parish Priest's Practical Manual, p. 386 (London, 1893).

[3] Bened. PP. XIV. Casus Conscientiæ, Dec. 1724 cas. 2.—In the fourteenth century Astesanus says (Summæ Lib. v. Tit. xiv. Q. 8) that the parish priest is only under obligation to hear yearly confessions, though he ought to listen to his parishioners whenever they wish to confess.

[4] Gousset, Théol. Morale, II. n. 409-10, 413.

[5] C. Trident. Sess. XXIII. De Reform. cap. 18.

ferences of confessors to be held twice a week, presided over by some
learned man.[1]   Clement VIII. took the hint and, in 1599, ordered
all members of religious orders to assemble twice a week for the purpose of reading the Scriptures or discussing cases of conscience, a
command which was repeated by Urban VIII. in 1624.[2]   These
conferences and discussions on cases of conscience were widely introduced and could not fail to familiarize confessors with the intricacies
of their duties and the boundless resources of casuistry.[3]   Father
Gobat, however, sets little store by such training, for he says that
any priest of sound mind has knowledge sufficient, and though it is
a mortal sin intentionally to seek an ignorant confessor, his absolution is valid if obtained in good faith.[4]   Liguori does not assent to
this and considers it necessary to quote the older doctors as to ignorance rendering confessions invalid and justifying the penitent in
seeking another confessor,[5] which shows that the race of ignorant

---

[1] C. Avenionens. ann. 1594, cap. 18 (Harduin. X. 1846).

[2] Bullar. Ed. Luxemb. IV. 65.

[3] In 1703 Chiericato tells us (De Pœnit. Decis. XXXVIII. n. 28-9) that it was
customary for all the confessors of a city or district to assemble twice a month
and discuss cases of conscience, the parish priest of the place when the meeting was held-acting as host and furnishing a collation.   In Padua this led to
excesses in eating and drinking, which induced Cardinal Barbadico, when
bishop, to prohibit the banquet, whereupon the attendance notably decreased.
The custom, however, was long kept up in Padua.   In December, lists of cases
for discussion during the ensuing year were sent to all confessors that they
might prepare themselves.   Minotto Otthoboni, who was bishop from 1730 to
1743, was especially assiduous in the matter; he ordered all the *vicari foranei*
to be present to see that the collation was modest and to report the results to
the Visitor General.   His successor, Cardinal Rezzonico, in 1746, expresses the
strongest dissatisfaction at the neglect into which the custom was falling and
orders the vicars to revive it energetically.   Prospero Lambertini, when archbishop of Bologna, was sedulous in his personal attention to these monthly discussions and continued it after his elevation to the papacy as Benedict XIV.,
resulting in a well-known collection of cases of conscience to which I frequently
have occasion to refer.   This training is still kept up.   The Baltimore plenary
council of 1884 orders an assembly of the confessors of every diocese to be held
twice or four times a year and among the prescribed exercises is the discussion of cases of conscience (Concil. Plenar. Baltim. III. ann. 1884, Tit. v. cap.
5, n. 191-2).

[4] Gobat Alphab. Confessar. n. 188-93.   Cf. Clericati De Pœnit. Decis.
XXXVI. n. 4 and Marchant. Trib. Animarum Tom. I. Tract. II. Tit. 5, Q. 3.

[5] S. Alph. de Ligorio Theol. Moral. Lib. VI. n. 568.

confessors is by no means extinct; indeed, in 1736, Cardinal Veronese, then vicar-general of Padua, declares that the greater part of the evils of the people are the result of the ignorance of the clergy.[1] From these facts we may gauge the extent of the hallucination which leads Father Gury to repeat the assertion of Aquinas that the confessor is specially illuminated by God in the direction of consciences.[2]

The council of Trent took another important step for the improvement of the confessional by abolishing all privileges and ordaining that no one should be entitled to hear confessions unless he either held a parochial benefice or obtained an approbation from the bishop, who was empowered to require the applicant to submit to an examination before granting the licence.[3] While this, as we shall see, was more especially directed against the regular clergy, it put a check on the old abuse of the parochial chaplains, who were thus obliged to procure an episcopal approbation before they could be employed, although the council was powerless to reform the abuse of patronage, whereby unfit persons were presented to benefices with cure of souls, and any priest who, at the age of twenty-four, could obtain such preferment was empowered to hear the confessions of both men and women. It was even disputed whether the salutary Tridentine decree could prevent incumbents from employing priests who did not possess the episcopal approbation, and when the crowd of penitents was greatest about the Easter tide they were apt to be hired without scanning their credentials, throwing grave doubt upon the validity of their absolutions.[4] The efficiency of the Tridentine reform depended on the bishops; under careless prelates there was no improvement, but many were scrupulous and required careful examination into the fitness of all applicants for licenses. These licenses customarily were limited to a twelvemonth, at the expiration of which they had to be renewed, thus exerting a wholesome restrain-

---

[1] Padova, nella Stamperia del Seminario, 1736, p. 1.

[2] Gury, Casus Conscientiæ I. 53.

[3] C. Trident. Sess. xxiii. De Reform. cap. 15.

[4] Escobar Theol. Moral. Tract. vii. Exam. iv. cap. 7, n. 38.—Summa Diana s. v. *Parochus*, n. 13, 14. In 1581 the council of Rouen declared that the vicars of parish priests only deceive the people when they hear confessions without an episcopal licence (C. Rotomag. ann. 1581, De Curatorum Officiis cap. 1—*ap.* Harduin. X. 1235).

ing influence on the holder.[1] It is true that when, in 1650, the assembly of the French clergy adopted this limitation, as a general rule the Mendicant Orders recalcitrated and claimed that it was not in accordance with the Tridentine prescription; the issue was raised with the Bishop of Angers and carried to Alexander VII. who decided against the Mendicants.[2] These approbations always except the confession of nuns, and in some dioceses, such as that of Antwerp, even of Beguines.[3]

---

[1] Clericati de Pœnit. Decis. XXXVII. n. 9-12, 14-16, 25.

[2] Van Espen Jur. Eccles. P. II. Tit. vi. cap. 5, n. 17.—S. Alph. de Ligorio Theol. Moral. Lib. VI. n. 552.

[3] Van Espen loc. cit. n. 23.—Th. ex Charmes Theol. Univ. Dissert. v. De Pœnit. cap. vii. Q. 3.

The spiritual direction of nunneries was rightly regarded by the council of Trent as deserving of special attention. It required nuns to confess monthly and bishops were instructed to appoint extraordinary confessors who should in addition hear the confessions of all the nuns twice or thrice a year (Sess. XXV. De Reg. et Mon. cap. 10). In 1615, the Congregation of Bishops and Regulars decided that neither parish priests and their chaplains nor regulars could be so deputed (Clericati de Pœnit. Decis. XLI. n. 2-10. Cf. Bizzari Collect. Sacr. Cong. Episc. et Reg. pp. 346, 357, 368, 378, 437). In 1622, Gregory XV. subjected the confessors of all nunneries and all regular confessors to episcopal approbation (Gregor. PP. XV. Const. Inscrutabili §§ 4, 5, ap. Bullar. III. 452), and, in 1670, Clement X. decreed that each nunnery must have its own special confessor, who must have the approval of the bishop and can serve no other house; he can serve only three years (Bizzari, op. cit. pp. 13, 14), but is again eligible after three years' interval, while the extraordinary confessor requires a fresh episcopal faculty every time he makes a visitation (Clement. PP. X. Bull. Superna § 4, ap. Bullar. VI. 306). Confessors of nunneries must be at least forty years old (Bizzari op. cit. p. 383). In spite of all these careful provisions to guard the purity of the spouses of ·Christ, the investigation made by the Grand-duke Leopold into the morality of the Tuscan nunneries and their confessors, about 1785, revealed a most shocking state of affairs (De Potter, Mémoires de Scipion de' Ricci, I. 284 sqq.).

In the perpetual friction between the secular clergy and the Mendicants on the subject of confessions, the papal decisions were construed very differently by the rivals. The Mendicants claimed that their confessors had a right to shrive all nuns and Tertiaries subject to their respective Orders, even in all reserved cases, including those of the Cœna Domini. They held it to be unquestionable that these privileges could not, as pretended by the other side, be withdrawn by the revocatory bulls In tanta of Gregory XIII., Quœcumque of Clement VIII., In speculo militantis of Urban VIII. and Superna of Clement X. (Bernardi a Bononia Manuale Confessar. Capuccin. cap. III. § 2). Possibly it

Another and perhaps still more efficacious influence on the improvement of the priesthood has been the secularization of ecclesiastical property which the Church has resisted so bitterly. Deprived of the enormous revenues which it once enjoyed, it offers less attraction for the indolent and sensual, and patronage no longer places the cure of souls in the hands of the most unfit. What it has lost on the temporal side it has more than gained on the spiritual, and its influence on the souls of men was perhaps never stronger than it is to-day.

Although these movements within and without the Church have thus elevated the average character of the confessor, the function is one requiring so rare a combination of qualities that complaints of unfitness naturally continue. About 1700, Corella ascribes the general incapacity of the confessors of his time to the fact that those really suited to the duty refuse to undertake it and it is confided to those wholly unfit; the cure of souls is committed to men who would not be trusted with the care of bodies; churches are bestowed on those incapable of the government of a house.[1] The testimony of Père Habert may perhaps be questioned on account of his rigorism, when he describes the prevailing carelessness and negligence of the confessors of his time who say that it is impossible to observe in the confessional the prescriptions of the canons, and who, therefore, abandon them wholly,[2] but it is authoritatively re-echoed by St. Alphonso Liguori[3] and by the council of Suchuen in 1803, which

---

was this and similar pretensions that led to Fra Bernardo's book being placed on the Index.

In so artificial and complex a system, presenting so many debatable points, the validity of absolutions granted must often be questionable.

[1] Corella, Praxis Confessionalis P. II. Perorat. n. 7, 8.

[2] Habert, Praxis Sacr. Pœnit. Præfatio (Venetiis, 1744).

This work was prepared by order of Hippolyte de Béthune, Bishop of Verdun, for the use of his clergy. It was known as *La Pratique de Verdun* and was stigmatized by the Anti-Jansenists as *La Pratique impraticable*. That it is not Jansenist, however, is sufficiently shown by its condemnation of those who insist on the ancient rule of deferring absolution until after the performance of penance (Tract. v. p. 345). It is full of admirable moral teachings and, if its prescriptions could be carried out by men fitted for the office, the confessional might become an instrument of good.

[3] S. Alphons. de Ligorio Praxis Confessar. cap. 1 § 2, n. 6. Many confessors, he says, "si pœnitentem dispositum vident statim eum absolvunt; sin minus, quin unum verbum impendant illico dimittunt, oculo retorto dicentes: Discede a me quia te absolvere non possum."

describes how the teachings of the seminary are speedily forgotten and how confessors seek only to despatch their penitents as speedily as possible, casting some into despair by uncalled-for severity and leading others to license by injudicious laxity.[1] The council of Bordeaux, in 1859, reiterates these complaints and deplores the reaction against excessive rigor which leads confessors through mental imbecility to a blind and excessive laxity by which the gravest sins are treated as trivial and are dismissed without appropriate remedies.[2]

Far more serious is the indictment brought against the confessors of the present day by the good Redemptorist, Father Michael Müller. Unlike the council of Bordeaux, he especially condemns the rigorists who cast the sinner into despair and brutally abuse the awful power which the confessional gives them over sensitive souls—"Confessors who are cold, stiff and heartless, who instead of encouraging the poor sinner only repel and embitter him, are a terrible scourge to the Church."[3] But this is perhaps the least of his accusations. The motive which frequently impels men to embrace the clerical profession is tersely described by modifying the lament of the Prodigal Son—"Fodere non valeo, mendicare erubesco, ergo sacerdos ero." The terrible temptations of the sacerdotal career, moreover, lead many astray who as students were good and pious, and we are led to infer that drinking, gambling, licentiousness and the accumulation of ill-gotten gains are by no means uncommon, while "the majority

---

[1] C. Sutchuens. ann. 1803 cap. VI. §§ 3, 8, 9 (Coll. Lacens. VI. 607-9).

[2] C. Burdigalens. ann. 1859, Tit. III. cap. 5, § 2 (Coll. Lacens. IV. 760).

[3] Müller, The Catholic Priesthood, III. 135. This is emphasized with an account of a dying girl who refused to confess and on being pressed for the reason burst into tears and exclaimed "God knows I was a virtuous girl. I never missed my communion. Three years ago I went to confession to a certain priest. I tried honestly to make a good confession, but the priest spoke roughly and called me an infamous name. That morning I did not go to communion. . . . I have never confessed since and now that I stand on the brink of eternity I do not intend to confess. May God have mercy on my soul!"

If such scenes are frequent in the confessional Father Müller is justified in exclaiming "Oh! how many souls have been ruined by harsh and imprudent confessors." Whether they are frequent or not is not likely to be known as the penitent is virtually, though not positively, subject to the "seal" except in cases of solicitation to evil.

of priests lead a life more or less lukewarm."[1] This is encouraged by the dread of "scandal," which grants virtual immunity to those who do not by some public and notorious offence render action indispensable; as long as their vices can be prudently concealed they are sure of toleration,[2] so that we may believe Father Müller when he says "You will find indeed many an unworthy priest who will assure you that he gives no scandal," and further that "If God did not so often cast a veil over the sins of so many unworthy priests, what horrible scandals we would witness, how many souls would be ruined!"[3] This may be so, but it is not easy for the non-clerical intellect to grasp the reasoning which concludes that souls would be ruined by unmasking these wolves in sheep's clothing rather than by allowing them to ravage their flocks undisturbed. There may be exaggeration in Father Müller's statements, and I do not venture to sit in judgment on the Catholic priesthood of to-day, but at least it is apparent that, in constructing the system of compulsory confession and absolution, the Church has undertaken a task beyond the capacity of human strength and virtue. Laxity and rigor, as we have seen, are the Scylla and Charybdis between which only Divine wisdom could hope to escape shipwreck.

---

[1] Ibid. pp. 78–127, 140, 222, 258.—Lochon (Traité du Secret de la Confession, p. 277, Brusselle, 1708) shows us that these complaints of the deteriorating influence of the priesthood are by no means of modern origin, for he tells us that many young confessors are better than the old ones "que l'habitude et l'usage du confessionel a amolis et relachez extraordinairement."

[2] "The good bishop, perhaps, knew his crimes, at least in part. . . . What was the good bishop to do? Tear the mask from the brow of the hypocrite? Expel him from the altar he had profaned, from the parish he had scandalized? His crimes were known to but a few. Was the bishop to publish them to the whole world? What a scandal to the weak! What a triumph for the heretic and the scoffing infidel! The good bishop prayed and waited and hoped."—Müller, *loc. cit.* p. 139.

Good bishops in this only follow the decision rendered in September, 1707, by the Sorbonne and the Faculty of Douay on a case where a parish priest in good repute was accused of seducing his female penitents—"La Sainte Écriture, les Conciles, les Loix et grand nombre d'habiles et de sages Théologiens sont d'avis qu'il est plus àpropos dans ces circonstances de tolérer le mal que de scandaliser et perdre cet Ecclesiastique ou Religieux dans l'esprit des Fidelles, et ne point exposer à la risée des libertins un Ministre du Seigneur qui est en reputation d'honnête homme."—Lochon, *ubi sup.*

[3] Müller, *op. cit.* pp. 68, 71.

In one respect the Church, in its zeal for the salvation of souls, overstepped the boundaries of humanity. Confession on the deathbed is regarded as highly important, but not indispensable, for, as we shall see hereafter, absolution and the viaticum can be administered without it if the moribund has asked for a confessor and is speechless when the priest arrives. Yet, in its anxiety to render confession universal, and possibly with an eye to legacies for pious uses, the Lateran council ordered that all physicians when called in should commence by inducing the patient to confess and after the cure of the soul had been secured that of the body might claim attention. Two reasons were assigned for this—that sickness is often the punishment of sin and will disappear when the sin is removed, and that the warning to seek the consolations of religion, if postponed till the patient is seriously ill, is likely to plunge him in despair. The rule was enforced by denying admission to church to the physician disobeying it, and the whole precept was duly embodied in the canon law.[1] In 1244 a council of Barcelona enforced the rule by absolutely prohibiting physicians from taking charge of a case until after the patient had confessed and had been duly absolved[2]—sinners might neglect the duty of confession while in health, but sickness gave the Church a hold on them which it was resolved to utilize. All this was so repugnant to the instincts of humanity that its general enforcement was impossible, and already, in 1317, Astesanus informs us that the Lateran precept was a dead letter.[3] Yet where the Church had control, as in hospitals, it was observed, for Gerson, in 1408, tells us that in those of Paris all patients admitted were obliged to confess and receive absolution before they were allowed to enter,[4] and the general neglect of the rule was deplored, in 1429, by the council of Paris, which commanded physicians to obey it strictly in future.[5]

Notwithstanding the neglect into which the Lateran precept had fallen, the physician who did not obey it was held guilty of mortal sin, and among the interrogatories to be put to all medical men in the confessional was a question as to whether they had obeyed it, although in trivial cases it was held to be only good counsel, and in emergen-

---

[1] C. Lateran. IV. ann. 1216, cap. 22.—Cap. 13 Extra v. xxxviii.

[2] Villanueva, Viage Literario, T. XVII. p. 343.

[3] Astesani Summæ Lib. v. Tit. xvi.

[4] Jo. Gersonis Orat. in C. Remens. ann. 1408 (Gousset, Actes, II. 651).

[5] C. Parisiens. ann. 1429, cap. 29 (Harduin. VIII. 1048).

cies, when delay was dangerous, it might be pretermitted, nor was the patient obliged to follow the advice.[1] Early in the sixteenth century Cardinal Caietano feels obliged to concur in the established view that inobservance of the precept is mortal sin, but he evidently is expressing his own feelings when he adds that it is abrogated through non-user; it has never, he says, been accurately observed, nor has it been accepted by those concerned, for they have constantly opposed it as contrary to their duties, which they hold to be to inspire their patients with hope; where there is danger, observance of the precept increases it; where there is none, it exposes the sacrament to contempt.[2]

Thus by common consent the Lateran precept, almost from the date of its passage, had been treated as non-existent till it was admitted to have become obsolete, and, with the progress of enlightenment, it might have been expected to be allowed to rest in oblivion, if not formally revoked. The revival of zeal, however, caused by the counter-Reformation resuscitated it in a peculiarly objectionable form, and to Spain apparently belongs the credit. In 1565, the council of Valencia directs the physician, when first called in, to warn the patient to send for a confessor; if on his second visit he finds that this has not been done he is to cease his attendance and withdraw from the case.[3] This found a prompt response from St. Pius V., who was so implacably remoulding the Church according to his own standard. In 1566, he issued a decree reviving and confirming the Lateran precept which had become obsolete through proscription, and to insure its observance he added that if, by the third day, the patient had not confessed and did not furnish a written certificate to that effect, the physician must abandon him; all physicians neglecting this were to be deprived of the doctorate, declared infamous and fined at the discretion of the Ordinary, and all, moreover, at graduation, must take an oath before a notary to observe the rule.[4]

To what extent this inhuman law was enforced at the time it would be impossible now to determine, but at least some zealous prelates

---

[1] Summa Pisanella s. v. *Medicus* n. 1.—Somma Pacifica, cap. xv.—Summa Tabiena s. v. *Medicus* n. 10, 11.

[2] Caietani Summula s. v. *Medicus.*

[3] C. Valent. ann. 1565 Sess. II. cap. 8 (Aguirre V. 415). Cf. C. Tarraconens. ann. 1591 Lib. VI. Tit. xvi. cap. 6 (Ibid. VI. 324).

[4] Pii PP. V. Const. *Supra gregem,* 1566 (cap. 1 in Septimo Lib. III. Tit. vi.).

attempted it. S. Carlo Borromeo, at his first Milanese provincial council, caused the requisite statutes to be passed, and he furnished his priests with printed blanks on which to give the necessary certificates to physicians, but he evidently found an unsatisfactory response, for he ordered priests frequently to ask from the altar whether there were any sick in the parish, and to appoint two or four *infermieri*, from the membership of some confraternity, whose duty it should be to report all cases of sickness, when the priest was to visit them and urge the patient to confess.[1]   In 1583, St. Toribio of Lima ordered the penalties prescribed by St. Pius V. to be rigidly inflicted on all physicians and surgeons disregarding the precept,[2] and in 1616 Marcus Sittacus, Archbishop of Salzburg, did the same, in the instructions drawn up for the visitation of his province.[3]   Yet the ingenuity of the casuists found no difficulty in explaining away the papal decree and in proving that the physician was not obliged to abandon a patient who, after due warning, neglected to send for a confessor.[4] This was not acceptable to Rome, and in 1682 the Congregation of Bishops and Regulars complained that in some dioceses the rule was not observed, wherefore a circular letter was issued ordering the constitution of Pius V. to be publicly read on every second Sunday in Lent.[5]   This official utterance seems to have met with little more success than its predecessors.   Physicians cared more to cure their patients or to prolong their attendance than to obey, and it is probable that the penalties were not enforced.   The light, indeed, in which a conscientious physician would be apt to regard priestly interference with his patients may be guessed from a case related with great self-gratulation by Chiericato as an example to all his brethren.   He was called in the evening to a young man aged 22, whom he found in a high fever; when the paroxysm had passed the patient agreed to confess, which he had not done for two years, and Chiericato searched

---

[1] S. Caroli Borromei Instructiones (Brixiæ, 1676, pp. 51, 76).

[2] C. Provin. Liman. I. ann. 1583, Act. III. cap. 39 (Harold. Lima Limata, p. 32).

[3] Dalham Concilia Salzburgens. p. 603.

[4] Summa Diana s. v. *Confessionis necessitas* n. 15.   Yet Graffio (Practica Casuum Reservator. Lib. II. cap. xxvi.) is inclined to construe strictly the decree of Pius V. and Caramuel (Theol. Fundam. n. 1565) asserts absolutely the duty of the physician to abandon the obstinate patient.

[5] Lettera del S. C. de' Vescovi e Regolari, 30 Sett. 1682.

his conscience thoroughly—an exercise which occupied a couple of hours—and absolved him. Summoned again at midnight he found the youth delirious, in which condition he died next morning.[1] The shrift may have saved the soul, but it certainly hastened its separation from the body.

It was probably the desire to prevent final backsliding, on the part of forcibly converted Huguenots, which led to a strenuous effort in France, supported by the secular power, to enforce the papal decrees. Cardinal de Noailles, Archbishop of Paris, in 1707, issued an ordonnance to this effect, which received so little obedience that it was published again, in 1712, accompanied by a royal declaration to the effect that all physicians in cases of fever or other disease that may prove mortal must, on the second day, notify the patient or his family to send for a confessor; if indisposition to do this is manifested, the physician must summon the parish priest himself and take a certificate of having done so; no visit is to be paid on the third day unless evidence is produced of a confessor having been sent for, but after this the visits may be resumed. All this is enforced under penalties of 300 livres for a first offence, three months' suspension of practice for a second, and absolute exclusion from practice during life for a third. These rules seem to have remained unrepealed until the Revolution.[2]

Elsewhere, about this period, Viva shows us how in practice the papal precept was shorn of its most abhorent features. He treats it as in force and says that, in the diocese of Naples, the violation of the physician's oath is a reserved case, without excommunication. At the same time the physician is not bound to warn the patient personally but can do so through his friends, and this only when the case is grave or there is danger of its becoming grave, nor is he bound either to warn or to desert his patient if there is no hope of inducing him to confess and probable danger of death if abandoned. A written certificate of confession is unnecessary, but credible testimony suffices. Moreover, it is understood that the oath is taken with these reservations.[3]

---

[1] Clericati de Pœnit. Decis. XXI. n. 10

[2] Isambert, Anciennes Loix Françaises, XXI. 574.—Héricourt, Loix ecclésiastiques de France, II. 15.

[3] Viva Cursus Theol. Moral. De Pœnit. P. II. Q. iv. Art. 2, n. 4.—Laymann (Theol. Moral. Lib. V. Tract. vi. cap. 5, n. 5) simply quotes the Lateran canon

The wishes of the Holy See evidently received slender attention, and the curious contest between it and the theologians was resolutely fought out. In 1725 the council of Rome ordered the strict enforcement of the rule that the physician should abandon the patient after the third visit if a confessor had not been summoned.[1] The resultant confusion of thought is reflected in the cases of conscience of Benedict XIV. He treats the precept as in force, and says that all physicians at graduation are obliged to swear to its observance; the physician who merely warns the relatives and does not see to their acting commits a mortal sin; he does wrong when he only gives the warning in mortal cases and neglects it in light ones, and yet he does well in not abandoning the patient who is obstinate, for if he cures the hardened sinner there is a future opportunity of his repentance and conversion.[2] Liguori coolly copies the Salamanca theologians in holding that pontifical decrees only obligate in so far as they are currently observed; these are disregarded in Spain and Naples, and consequently are abrogated there. Elsewhere the common opinion of the moralists, followed in practice, is that the rule only applies in cases of serious disease, when, if the patient obstinately refuses and if it would imperil his life to abandon him, the physician is under no obligation to do so.[3] One might imagine that, in view of these successive rebuffs, the hopeless effort to overcome the common instincts of humanity would be abandoned, yet in 1855 the council of Ravenna ordered the punishment provided by the canons, together with an arbitrary penalty at the discretion of the bishop, for any physician disobeying the precept of St. Pius V.— yet with the saving clause that, if an obstinate patient utterly refuses and life be endangered by abandonment, an exception may be made.[4]

---

and adds that it applies only to grave cases where there is peril of death; the decree of St. Pius V. is not even alluded to. Cf. Mattheucci, Cautela Confessarii Lib. I. cap. x. n. 6.

[1] C. Roman. ann. 1725, Tit. xxxii. cap. 1.

[2] Bened. PP. XIV. Casus Conscientiæ, Jun., 1738, cas. 3; Jan., 1740, cas. 2; Apr., 1743, cas. 1.

[3] Salmanticens. Cursus Theol. Moral. Tract. XVII. cap. ii. n. 89-92.—S. Alph. de Ligorio Theol. Moral. Lib. III. n. 181-2; Lib. VI. n. 664.—Pittoni Constitt. Pontificiæ, T. VII. n. 239.

Tournely, however, as a Frenchman (De Sacr. Pœnitentiæ Q. VI. Art. ii.) quotes the pontifical decrees as being literally in force.

[4] C. Ravennat. ann. 1855, cap. 5 § 12 (Coll. Lacens. VI. 161).

In Naples, a modern theologian informs us that the papal decrees are still in force and that by disobedience a physician incurs a papal reserved case, though in practice he is not obliged to expose a patient to the risk of death by abandoning him.[1] In 1869 the journals reported the issue by Pius IX. of a confirmation of the older decrees requiring the abandonment of all patients who should not, within three days after warning, confess their sins and express their willingness to receive extreme unction. I have not been able to verify this, but the Roman Ritual still continues to instruct the priest that he must warn his sick parishioner and family that the physician must cease attendance after the third visit if confession is not made, and the most recent theologian asserts that the Lateran canon and the decree of St. Pius V. are still in force where they have been received and have not lapsed by disuse; he adds, however, from Liguori, that the physician is not bound to desert a patient if there are graver reasons for remaining and there is no hope of benefitting his soul.[2]

The application of enforced confession to ecclesiastics introduced some special factors which require consideration. We have seen (p. 48) how the old rule prohibiting a cleric from performing penance gradually disappeared and was revived as a privilege exempting him from public penance. Yet as regards auricular confession, when that came into vogue, he was precisely in the same position as the layman; the old rule that a priest guilty of mortal sin must abandon his sacerdotal functions had faded out, and the new rule prescribing confession and absolution prior to administering the sacraments had not as yet been evolved. His confession, like the layman's, before the Lateran canon, was wholly voluntary. An Ordo, probably of the eleventh century (see p. 132), prescribes that when a cleric comes for confession the priest shall take him to the altar, declare himself unworthy to receive his repentance and ask whether he wishes to confess his sins "to the Lord God omnipotent and all his saints and to me an unworthy priest,"[3] which would seem to

---

[1] Manzo Epit. Theol. Moral. P. III. Append. 1, n. 98–101 (Neapoli, 1836).

[2] Ritualis Roman. Tit. v. cap. 4 (Aug. Taurin. 1891).—Marc Institt. Moral. Alphonsianæ, n. 2332 (Romæ, 1893).—Cf. Varceno Comp. Theol. Moral. Tract. v. cap. vi. Art. 10.

[3] Garofali Ordo ad dandam Pœnitentiam, Romæ, 1791, p. 18.

indicate that as yet priestly confession was by no means a usual performance. About the middle of the twelfth century, Cardinal Pullus alludes incidentally to priests confessing their venial sins daily to the bystanders, whether lay or clerical, and says nothing to show that they were bound by any special rules of auricular confession.[1] As for monks, their capitular confession at this period has been sufficiently described in the preceding chapter.

Yet the utterance of St. Paul—" For he that eateth and drinketh unworthily eateth and drinketh judgment to himself, not discerning the body of the Lord " (I. Cor. xi. 29)—could not but be held especially applicable to the priesthood engaged in the sacred functions of the altar, however necessary it might be to assume that the validity of their ministrations was not affected by their being in mortal sin. It is, therefore, not surprising that the importance of their purifying themselves from sin before performing the sacrifice of the Eucharist was emphasized by the customary device of miraculous stories. As early as the eleventh century we hear of an unchaste priest who, on swallowing the wafer, was terrified at seeing it slip out unaltered at his navel, disdaining further lodgment in his polluted body, and of another who found the wine changed to a black and bitter draught.[2] Peter Cantor, towards the close of the twelfth century, insists that no layman can take communion until not only he has confessed but has performed the penance enjoined on him, and no priest can celebrate mass save under the same conditions, unless, indeed, there is unavoidable necessity for his so doing and he has no substitute to take his place.[3] The celebration of mass, moreover, is not the only question involved, for it is a mortal sin for a priest to administer any sacrament except in a state of grace, though some authorities hold that he is excusable if suddenly summoned to perform baptism or shrive the dying.[4]

It will be seen that the Church found itself in a dilemma with priests who, for the most part, were continuously in mortal sin and at the same time were under obligations not to allow interruption in

---

[1] R. Pulli Sentt. Lib. v. cap. 51.

[2] Rod. Glabri Histor. Lib. v. cap. 1.—Rogeri de Wendover Chron. ann. 1051.

[3] P. Cantor de Sacram. (Morin. de Pœnitent. Lib. x. cap. 24).

[4] S. Alph. de Ligorio Theol. Moral. Lib. vi. n. 32, 33.—S. Carlo Borromeo (Instruct. Confessor. Ed. 1676, pp. 49–50) strictly forbids priests to hear confessions while in mortal sin.

the daily services or to refuse their ministrations to the penitent. The incompatible conditions were sought to be reconciled in a series of halting compromises which in reality satisfied neither requisite. The question, moreover, was complicated by the indisposition of the priests themselves to submit to enforced confession, and when it was attempted to subject them to the Lateran canon a difficulty arose as to the persons to whom they should confess. Bishop Poore of Salisbury, in 1221, tried the expedient of appointing two special deputies in each chapter to whom priests and clerks should confess, but he recognized his inability to enforce this by providing that recalcitrants should go to the episcopal penitentiaries, or, if they refused to do this, to the bishop himself.[1] About the same time William, Bishop of Paris, ordered priests to confess twice yearly, in Advent and Lent, to persons duly appointed in each deanery.[2] The experiment was tried in England of making them confess to the deans, but this aroused opposition, as, notwithstanding the seal of the confessional, they feared to reveal their lapses to their immediate superiors, and, in 1237, the Legate Otto, at the council of London, ordered the bishops to appoint suitable persons in each deanery to receive the confessions of priests and clerics.[3] So far was this from satisfying them that their resistance to it caused its abandonment, until, in 1281, the council of Lambeth ordered it to be revived and observed inviolably in future.[4] Cardinal Henry of Susa lays down the general rule that priests are to confess to their superiors and never to each other, except by special licence, which should be sparingly granted, as they are apt to favor each other, to the great relaxation of discipline.[5] Yet such licenses in time came to be generally employed, for Guido de Monteroquer advises all priests on ordination to procure one from the bishop empowering them to select their own confessors, and he adds that, though in strictness this did not allow them to choose a priest not licensed to hear confessions, yet it may be considered as tacitly permitted if the bishop does not object.[6]

Thus far there does not appear to have been much effort to compel

---

[1] Constitt. R. Poore Episc. Sarum ann. 1221 cap. 30 (Harduin. VII. 98).
[2] Additiones Wilhelmi Paris. cap. 6 (Ibid. VI. II. 1978).
[3] C. Londiniens. ann. 1237, cap. 5 (Ibid. VII. 294).
[4] C. Lambethens. ann. 1281, cap. 9 (Ibid. VII. 865).
[5] Hostiens. Aureæ Summæ Lib. v. De Pœn. et Remiss. § 34.
[6] Manip. Curator. P. II. Tract. iii. cap. 4.

more frequent confession from ecclesiastics than the annual one prescribed by the Lateran canon. If this could be enforced the authorities were satisfied. In 1284, the council of Nîmes orders all clerics to confess yearly to the priest of the parish in which they reside, and, in 1287, that of Liége requires priests to do the same to their deans, who are to report the names of recusants to the bishop for punishment.[1] In 1454 the council of Amiens ordered confession and communion twice a year for priests, with reports of those who refused compliance,[2] but the example does not seem to have been followed. In 1574, S. Carlo Borromeo ordered that all ecclesiastics should confess to confessors selected by himself, on which Van Espen remarks that if all bishops would do the same the clergy would be vastly improved.[3] This is quite likely, for the manuals for confessors contain long chapters on the priestly duties and failings to be inquired into—that they do not perform their sacred function in a state of mortal sin, that they celebrate mass decently with clean vessels and napery, that they do not take two "alms" for one mass, or create scandal by excessive fees for sepulture, or publish fraudulent indulgences, or cause scandal by their conduct in the confessional, or commit simony with respect to their benefices, or frequent suspected company, or make improper use of their revenues, or pay anything for justice from the Holy See, etc.[4] Gradually more frequent confession came to be required. In 1600, the council of Tournay earnestly exhorted all priests to confess weekly, and, in 1604, that of Cambrai ordered them to do so.[5] Not long afterwards the Bishop of Freisingen required monthly confession of all clerics, who were obliged to furnish him with written certificates from their confessors.[6] In modern times weekly confession by priests is deemed desirable, but it is not a matter of general precept. To encourage it, Clement XIII., by a constitution of December 9, 1763, granted to

---

[1] Synod. Nemausens. ann. 1284 (Harduin. VII. 907).—Statuta Synod. Leodiens. ann. 1287, cap. 4 (Hartzheim III. 689).

[2] C. Ambianens. ann. 1454, cap. 5 § 3 (Gousset, Actes, II. 709).

[3] Synod. Diœcesan. Mediolan. IV. ann. 1574, Decr. 24.—Van Espen Jur. Eccles. P. II. Tit. vi. cap. 5, n. 24.

[4] Mart. Fornarii Institut. Confessar. Tract. II. cap. 8.—Bart. a Medina Instruct. Confessar. Lib. I. cap. xvi. § 2.

[5] C. Tornacens. ann. 1600, Tit. VIII. cap. 1; C. Cameracens. ann. 1604, Tit. VIII. cap. 13 (Hartzheim VIII. 483, 595).

[6] Layman Theol. Moral. Lib. V. Tract. vi. cap. 5, n. 13.

those who would practise it all indulgences, except the Jubilee, which are conditioned on confession—a goodly number—and that this inducement is still required is evident from the decree being quoted as still in force by an assembly of bishops at Loreto in 1850.[1] In the practice of to-day a priest who believes himself to be in a state of grace may go without confession for any length of time, and this, in scattered communities or in mission-work, may be necessary, but the general custom is to confess weekly.

With regard to the religious Orders, each one has its own rules, a detailed examination of which would teach us little. We have seen in the previous chapter (p. 204) that Aquinas held that monks are not bound to more frequent confession than laymen, but this has been changed, and the rules for the most part now prescribe frequent confession. In the seventeenth century, Juan Sanchez remarks that two or three confessions weekly are the utmost required.[2] In the more rigid Orders, like the Oratory of St. Philip Neri, three confessions a week are prescribed, but this is not binding under mortal sin. Nuns, as stated above (p. 258), were ordered by the council of Trent to confess monthly, with two or three special confessions annually in addition, but in practice they generally confess once a week.

In the case of priests engaged in their sacred functions the case is complicated by the principle that a state of grace is necessary for the worthy administration of the sacraments, and the anxiety to avoid "scandal" by letting it be known that the ministrant is not in fit condition. Aquinas tells us that a priest in mortal sin about to celebrate should confess, if another priest is accessible ; if not he can evade the difficulty by making a vow to confess[3]—which was an easy, if discreditable, solution of the dilemma. This was not accepted at Cambrai, where it seems to be assumed that priests are always in mortal sin, for in order to prevent interruption of the mass they were ordered to confess daily to the episcopal penitentiaries, or, if these were not accessible, to some other priest, in which case they were required to repeat the confession to the penitentiary ;[4] showing the suspicion felt as to mutual priestly confession and that what was good enough for the altar was insufficient as a sacrament. This was extreme rigorism,

---

[1] Conventus Lauretanus ann. 1850, Sect. IV. n. 25 (Coll. Lacens. VI. 785).

[2] Jo. Sanchez Selecta de Sacramentis Disp. XXXI. n. 4.

[3] S. Th. Aquin. Summæ Suppl. Q. VI. Art. 5.

[4] Statuta Synod. Cameracens. ann. 1300–1310 (Hartzheim IV. 68).

unsuited to the prevailing laxity, and John of Freiburg, about the same time, tells us that although a priest in mortal sin ought to confess before celebrating, still he can celebrate without it if necessary to avert scandal, and there is no sin in so doing if he has an intention to confess.[1] Astesanus indicates that priests were not held to be bound to more than annual confession and that, if in mortal sin with no confessor at hand, an "act of contrition" with an intention to confess sufficed to enable them to celebrate. He agrees however with Cardinal Henry of Susa in condemning the device through which they sought to evade the necessity of confession by adding the words *de pollutione* to the general confession in the ritual and by holding that this exempted them from the requirement of confession for lapses of the flesh.[2] The council of Lambeth, in 1330, takes note of this device; it denounces the error of those who believe that this general confession suffices for the remission of sins and orders all sinful priests to confess before celebrating.[3] Guido de Monteroquer makes no allusion to any methods of evasion; he simply quotes Aquinas that priests in sin should confess before celebrating.[4]

Various reasons were found for relieving priests from the necessity of confession before celebration. "Scandal" was always especially deprecated, and if the celebrant during the office should suddenly recall a forgotten sin his cessation of functions would be a scandal of the most pronounced character. The doctors, therefore, necessarily agreed that he should proceed, repenting internally and determining to confess at the first opportunity. It was easy to extend this to sins remembered in advance of celebration, which was accordingly done. In addition there was the secrecy involving everything connected with confession, and it was argued that anything that might lead to a suspicion of the pastor's sin would be an infraction of this. Then also there was the question of "jurisdiction," a subject to be considered in the next chapter, under which one parish priest had no power to confess and absolve another, and this in many cases threw an impediment in the way of prompt confession by a priest.[5] Reserved cases, as we shall see hereafter, introduced a

---

[1] Jo. Friburgens. Summæ Confessor. Lib. III. Tit. xxiv. Q. 70; Tit. xxxiv. Q. 69.

[2] Astesani Summæ Lib. v. Tit. xi.; Tit. xii. Q. 4.

[3] C. Lambethens. ann. 1330 cap. 3 (Harduin. VII. 1552).

[4] Manip. Curator. P. II. Tract. iii. cap. 3.

[5] Summa Pisanella s. vv. *Missa* n. 7; *Confessio* III. n. 7.—Summa Tabiena s. v. *Communicare* n. 30.

further complication. Thus, although confession by a sinful priest before celebrating was assumed as a wholesome rule, it was not absolutely insisted on, and St. Antonino says that he can find no clear assertion of it.[1] The council of Trent only requires confession if a confessor is accessible; if not, confession as soon as possible thereafter, and it says nothing as to eliciting an act of contrition.[2]

Thus in practice it may be assumed that for the most part sinners about to celebrate content themselves with a more or less genuine act of contrition and intention to confess, unless there is a fellow priest on the spot through whom a form of confession can be made. It would at least seem to be so in the case of concubinary priests whom the council of Trent ordered to be suspended from their functions.[3] This led to the question whether those who attended the masses of notorious concubinarians could do so without mortal sin, to which Henriquez replies in the affirmative, as custom seems to have abrogated the prohibition, and Laymann agrees with him.[4] Corella describes for us the manner in which such a priest prepares himself for his sacred functions by a hasty confession in the sacristy, a thing which he says is of no little frequency, nor does he appear to be scandalized by such a prostitution of the sacraments of the altar and confessional.[5]

---

[1] Bart. de Chaimis Interrogatorium fol. 20b, 86b.—S. Antonini Summæ P. III. Tit. xiv. cap. 19 § 3.

A Spanish Confessional of the early sixteenth century infers that for a priest to celebrate in mortal sin is only a sin if the offence was public.—Confessionario breve y muy provechoso, cap. xxiii.

On the other hand de Chaimis holds (fol. 98b) that even preaching in mortal sin is a mortal sin.

[2] C. Trident. Sess. XIII. De Eucharistia cap. 7.

[3] C. Trident. Sess. XXV. De Reform. cap. 14.

[4] Henriquez Summæ Theol. Moral. Lib. IX. cap. XXV. n. 13.—Layman Theol. Moral. Lib. IV. Tract. vi. cap. 4, n. 4.

[5] Corella Praxis Confessionalis P. II. Tract. xii. cap. 1, n. 11.

Gottschalk Rosemund (Confessionale cap. v. P. ii. § De Concubinariis) gives us a formula for the confession of such sinners—"Item in hac vita fornicaria subditos et populum scandalizavi et toto illo tempore irreverenter pollutis labiis et manibus et corde contaminato ad sancta sanctorum accessi et absolutionis sacramentum indigne suscepi."

How little was thought of such lapses of the flesh in priests is seen in the regulations forbidding bishops to make them reserved cases unless they are complicated with adultery.—Clericati de Pœnit. Decis. XLII. n. 13.

CHAPTER X.

JURISDICTION.

If the power of the keys is divinely conferred in ordination on every priest, it would seem futile for man to endeavor to limit it by human ordinances and to define conditions under which its exercise is invalid. Yet when human weakness seeks to control the infinite it can frame no system of universal application. Thus, as the theory of the sacrament of penitence established itself, there grew up the principle that, while the power to confer it is obtained in ordination, this is only a faculty *in posse,* and that to administer it validly requires the addition of what is known as "jurisdiction," and this again was found to be incompatible with certain necessities and had to be in turn limited and subjected to exceptions. The whole subject thus bristles with doubtful questions on which the authorities have been by no means in accord, until it forms one of the most intricate and involved branches of canon law. In its simplest expression it means that no one but the parish priest can administer validly the sacrament of penitence to his parishioners.

We have seen how, up to the twelfth century, the power of reconciliation was claimed exclusively by the bishops and that whatever function of the kind was permitted to the priests was merely as a delegation; also, that, as the power of the keys came to be more definitely asserted, the priests succeeded in establishing a claim to it, until finally in the twelfth century it was formally conferred upon them in ordination. During this prolonged and obscure struggle there is no trace of the existence of jurisdiction as a recognized principle. When, about the year 900, Regino assumes that every priest should possess a copy of a Penitential it would indicate that all could hear confessions and prescribe penance ;[1] yet we have seen (p. 124) that at the close of the eleventh century no priest could do so without possessing a special licence from his bishop or from the

---

[1] Reginon. de Discip. Eccl. Lib. I. Inquis. 95.

pope. This latter fact would indicate that as yet the possession of a parish did not confer spiritual jurisdiction, though we may assume as probable that, when the episcopal licence had been granted, parishioners would, for the most part, on the occasions when they desired to confess, apply to their pastor as the natural and most convenient person accessible. Yet the penitent still had full liberty in the selection of a confessor. In the ninth century we find Jonas of Orleans reproving those who seek laxer confessors and avoid the more rigid, and deploring the course of priests who know better and who yet attract penitents by imposing inadequate penance.[1] Early in the twelfth century we are told that St. Gerald, founder of the abbey of Grandselve, drew crowds of sinners by his sanctity and the mildness of his injunctions.[2] The holy virgin Sisu, chronicled by Thietmar of Merseburg (p. 195), shows that penitents sought relief in any quarter at their choice.

Yet, from an early period, there had been a sort of property claimed by the pastor in his flock. His support was to some extent derived from them, and he was naturally jealous of any interference with the oblations and other sources of revenue on which he depended to make up deficiencies in his tithes. There had long been standing quarrels over burial fees between the churches and the monasteries, when the faithful elected sepulture in the latter—quarrels which Leo I. in the fifth century and Leo III. in the ninth vainly sought to pacify by assigning to the parish church a half or a third of whatever pious legacies might be left by a decedent who chose to be buried in a convent [3] The forgers of the False Decretals had proclaimed the property of the priest in all the rights and emoluments of his parish,[4] and the confessional, like all other ministrations, was a source of profit as well as power to be battled for.[5] The council of Nantes,

---

[1] Jonæ Aurelianens. de Instit. Laicali Lib. i. cap. 10.

[2] Vit. S. Geraldi Silvæ Majoris cap. 24 (Migne CXLVII. 1040).

[3] Cap. 1, 2, Extra, III. xxviii.   [4] Gratian, cap. 1 Caus. XIII. Q. 1.

[5] At the close of the twelfth century, when the question had virtually been determined in favor of the parish priest, a canonist enumerating his rights says "Sacerdos habet in populo suo pœnitentias vivorum et morientium, visitationes infirmorum, primitias, oblationes, benedictiones sponsarum, missas surgentium a partu et multa alia quæ ei tum canonica constitutio tum consuetudo confirmavit; solemnes tamen pœnitentiæ sive publicæ cathedrali ecclesiæ reservantur."—Bernardi Papiensis Summæ Decretalium Lib. III. Tit. xxv. § 2 (Ed. Laspeyres, Ratisbonæ, 1861, p. 104).

towards the end of the ninth century, had recognized the closeness of the tie binding the parishioner to his church by a canon, carried through the collections of Burchard and Ivo, which directed the priest on Sundays and feasts to ask from the altar whether there were any present belonging to another parish, and if such were found they were to be expelled.[1] Towards the close of the eleventh century, the question as to penitents came to the surface owing to the intrusion of the monks on the parochial functions, which was sharply resented. Gregory VII., in a Roman council held about 1075, sought not only to repress this but to define the rights of the parish priest by forbidding anyone to receive to baptism or absolution the parishioners of another, except in cases of necessity, when all fees paid to him were to be at the disposal of the regular incumbent.[2] Yet that this was not held to bind the parishioner absolutely to his priest is shown by a decree of Urban II. at the council of Nîmes, in 1096, prohibiting interference with the bestowal of absolution by monks, and by another utterance of the same pope, which found its way into the canon law, inferring the free choice of a confessor, after which he is not to be interfered with unless his ignorance renders him unfit for his duties.[3] The profits connected with sacerdotal ministrations, however, rendered it inevitable that, with the development of the sacramental theory, the parish priest should claim the exclusive right to exercise such functions over his "subjects," as they came to be technically known.

Abelard alludes to the effort in a manner which shows that as yet the right was but partially recognized. Those, he says, who have

---

[1] C. Nannetens. circa ann. 890, cap. 1 (Harduin. VI. I. 457).

[2] C. Roman. circa 1075, cap. 7 (Pflugk-Harttung, Acta Pontiff. Roman. ined. II n. 161).—"Nullus presbyter parochianum alterius recipiat, nisi per necessitatem, in baptismo et in absolutione, et si quid caritative sibi oblatum fuerit ex consensu illius cujus parochianus fuerat, habeat vel reddat."

[3] C. Nemausens. ann. 1096, cap. 2, 3 (Harduin. VI. II. 1750).—Cap. 3, Caus. xxxiii. Q. iii. Dist. 6.

There is a canon attributed to a council of Reims in the seventh century which says "nemo tempore Quadragesimæ pœnitentium confessiones audiat præter pastorem" (Harduin. III. 575), but it evidently belongs to a period considerably later. The same may be said of a canon quoted by the learned Noël Alexandre (Summæ Alexandrinæ P. I. n 548), as occurring in a council of Langres in 1084, which is not in the collections and which evidently reflects the practice of the thirteenth century.

reason to distrust their priest are not to be blamed but to be praised for leaving him. It is well to consult him first and see if he can give good counsel and to ask his permission, but if he refuses through pride or because he imagines himself to be master he should be abandoned.[1] Yet the Pseudo-Augustin, copied by both Gratian and Peter Lombard, recognizes no such obligation and directs the sinner to seek out a priest who knows how to bind and to loose, for such must he be who sits in judgment on the sins of others.[2] They both vainly endeavor to reconcile this with the decree of Urban II. which they interpret as establishing the jurisdiction of the parish priest, and Lombard vaguely speaks of the canons prohibiting anyone to judge the parishioner of another, but he cites none, which he would assuredly have done had such existed.[3] It all reveals the effort making at the time to establish jurisdiction. Cardinal Pullus indicates the unsettled state of the question when he blames those who leave their own priests for others who will treat them more leniently, but he adds that it is praiseworthy, when one's own priest is of slender discretion, to seek a wiser one, either getting permission or accepting penance and then subjecting it to revision by another.[4]

By this time the power of the keys was formally bestowed on the priest in ordination, but the rule still existed that confessions could only be heard by those who held a licence from the bishop. There was an incongruity in this, for if the power to bind and to loose came from God, it was granted with the priestly character; if a delegation from the bishop, he certainly bestowed it in the ordination rite. Peter of Poitiers seems to be the first who endeavored to explain it by asserting that all priests possess the power, but those only can exercise it to whom the bishop concedes the faculty[5]—a sort of compromise between the old exclusive episcopal prerogative and the newly enlarged functions of the priests, clumsy enough, but still the only one available to systematize the conflicting claims arising from the development of the sacramental theory. Thus the distinction was drawn between the potential and the actual power of the keys, and the way

---

[1] P. Abælardi Ethica, cap. xxv.

[2] Ps. Augustin. de vera et falsa Pœnit. cap. 10.—Cap. 1 Caus. xxxiii. Q. iii. Dist. 6. Cf. c. 88 Dist. 1.—P. Lombard. Sentt. Lib. iv. Dist. xvii. n. 5.

[3] Gratian. post cap. 2, *loc. cit.*—P. Lombard. *loc. cit.* n. 7.

[4] R. Pulli Sentt. Lib. vi. cap. 52.

[5] P. Pictaviens. Sentt. Lib. iii. cap. 16.

was open to discover that its exercise was, or could be, limited. In the confessional, it was argued, the priest sat as judge, but a judge can only act where he has jurisdiction. Alexander III., who was familiar with the principles of the civil law and who did so much to engraft them on the canon law, had no hesitation in applying this limitation to the power of the keys.[1] Thus the only question could be as to the extent of jurisdiction and the person to exercise it, and the answer was inevitable—the priest in his parish, the bishop in his diocese and the pope throughout Christendom—and this had the ulterior advantage of establishing the supremacy of the papal jurisdiction everywhere, so that when the Treasure of the Church came to be discovered, with the pope as its dispenser, it was easy to assume that the power of the keys was a delegation from the Holy See. In practice, however, as yet there was still hesitation in construing strictly the exclusive prerogative of the parish priest. Alain de Lille, in one passage, says that if a parishioner goes to confession to another than his own priest he is not to be listened to unless he has already confessed to the latter; but elsewhere he contradicts this by observing that if a priest rightfully accuses a parishioner of a sin it is better for the latter to confess it to some one else, and again he speaks of obtaining a licence from an unfit parish priest as a preliminary to seeking another confessor.[2]

With the progressive development of sacerdotalism the lines were constantly drawn closer. The Cardinal-legate, Robert de Curzon, at the council of Paris in 1212, threatened suspension for any priest who, without a mandate from the bishop or parish priest, should receive the confession of a parishioner except in cases of immediate necessity.[3] Finally the Lateran canon, in 1216, which introduced compulsory annual confession, required it to be performed "proprio sacerdoti"— to the priest of the penitent. This could only be construed as designating the parish priest, and it further defined that he alone had power to bind and to loose; if the penitent desired to confess to another he could do so only by obtaining permission from his own priest.[4] Thus to the parish priest was given exclusive control over

---

[1] Post Concil. Lateran. P. xxxv. cap. 4 (cap. 4 Extra v. 38).—"Cum a non suo judice nullus ligari valeat nec absolvi."

[2] Alani de Insulis Lib. de Pœnit. (Migne CCX. 299, 304).

[3] C. Paris. ann. 1212, P. I. cap. 12 (Harduin. VI. II. 2003).

[4] C. Lateran. IV. cap. 21.

the salvation of his subjects, and it was assumed that God would disregard the remission of sins by any one else. As we have seen this was only the formulation of a principle which had been gradually taking shape in the schools, but it was regarded throughout the middle ages as the source and origin of the jurisdiction of the parish priest.[1] Of course the councils, which during the following years enforced the obligation of the Lateran canon, were careful to specify that the annual confession must be made to the priest of the penitent, and deacons were prohibited from administering the sacrament in future.[2]

Apparently the only resistance to this came from the nunneries. Monks had their own priests to whom they confessed when capitular confession gradually died out, but nuns had not this resource and, in the notorious unfitness of the secular clergy, they not unnaturally objected to being subjected to them in the confessional. A large portion of the religious houses had obtained exemptions which released them from the jurisdiction of the bishops and subjected them immediately to the Holy See; they claimed therefore that they should have confessors specially appointed for them by papal authority, and the papacy, nothing loath to extend its influence in local affairs, encouraged these claims by granting such requests. Even the non-exempt sought privileges of the same kind. Thus a nun of Limoges applies to the pope to have a proper confessor selected for her, whereupon the Penitentiary writes to the Dean of Limoges (the see being vacant) ordering him to select a fitting priest for her until the future bishop can provide better.[3]

Yet, even as the precept of annual confession was accepted but slowly, so that of applying only to the parish priest was not easily enforced. Alexander Hales disregards it when he argues that a man who is seeking a fit confessor can lawfully delay confession till he finds one, and St. Bonaventura informs us that the precept was vio-

---

[1] Thus St. Antonino relies on the Lateran canon and admits (Summæ P. III. Tit. xvii. cap. 2) that "a principio quilibet poterat quemlibet volentem se sibi subjicere absolvere," and Prierias does the same (Summa Sylvestrina s. v. *Confessor* I. § 3).

[2] Constitt. R. Poore ann. 1217 cap. 25.—C. Rotomagens. ann. 1223, cap. 10; ann. 1231, cap. 36.—Constitt. S. Edmundi Cantuar. ann. 1236, cap. 12 (Harduin. VII. 96, 128, 189, 269).

[3] Formulary of the Papal Penitentiary, Philadelphia, 1892, pp. 160–161.

lated every day, which he regards as a heinous sin.[1] In fact the long arguments, which the theologians found necessary to justify the rule against the ancient practice of free choice, show that there was some difficulty even for these keen intellects in finding reasons to justify it, though it afforded the advantage of easily proving that heretic, schismatic, excommunicated and degraded priests lost the power of absolution by losing jurisdiction while retaining the character impressed in ordination and the power of the keys in essence.[2] Nor could the theory be settled at once. St. Ramon de Peñafort sought to explain it by asserting that the power to bind or to loose conferred in ordination is so limited that it cannot be exercised without special authority from the diocesan or pope, and his *Postillator* sees nothing to object to in this.[3] Here we can recognize a remnant of the old theory which confined the power of reconciliation to bishops, but it soon disappeared and the current theory was adopted that as soon as a priest receives a cure of souls he acquires *ipso facto* the jurisdiction requisite for the exercise of the power without further authorization.[4] Aquinas put the theory into definite shape by arguing that all power requires appropriate material for its exercise and the penitent becomes appropriate material for the power of the keys through jurisdiction, without which it cannot be exercised on him ; or, as he puts it in another shape, to absolve requires a duplicate power, that of orders and of jurisdiction ; those who have general jurisdiction can apply the keys to all men ; those who have limited jurisdiction, only on their subjects.[5] St. Antonino, therefore, was only logical when to the two keys of St. Peter he added

---

[1] Alex. de Ales Summæ P. IV. Q. XVIII. Memb. 4, Art. 5, § 1.—S. Bonavent. Confessionale cap. IV. Partic. 1.

Yet Hales subsequently (*loc. cit.* Q. XIX. Membr. 1, Art. 2) argues laboriously to show that confession must be made to the parish priest, except by women when the priest is notoriously a solicitor to evil.

[2] Hostiens. Aureæ Summæ Lib. V. De Pœn. et Remiss. § 14.—S. Th. Aquinat. Summæ Suppl. Q. VIII. Art. 4 ; Q. XIX. Art. 6.—S. Bonaventuræ in IV. Sentt. Dist. XIX. Art. ii. Q. 2.—Jo. Friburgens. Summæ Confessor. Lib. III. Tit. xxxiv. Q. 176.—P. de Aquila in IV. Sentt. Dist. XVIII. Q. 1.

[3] S. Raymundi Summæ Lib. III. Tit. xxxiv. § 4.

[4] Hostiens. *loc. cit.*—Astesani Summæ Lib. V. Tit. xiv. Q. 1.

[5] S. Th. Aquinat. in IV. Sentt. Dist. XIX. Q. 1, Art. 3 ; Summæ Suppl. Q. XX. Art. 1.—Cf. P. de Palude in IV. Sentt. Dist. XVII. Q. iii. Art. 1.

a third one—the key of jurisdiction,[1] although this was an admission that there was no warrant for it in the apostolic deposit.

In practice the new regulation did not work without some friction. In 1272, the synod of Angers deplores that many of the faithful die without the sacraments, though anxious to confess, through the absence of their own priests and the refusal of others to come. Already it was apparent that a breach had to be made in the precept and in the elaborate theories as to jurisdiction, and the council, to prevent such unfortunate occurrences, felt obliged to threaten with deprivation all priests who should decline to respond to a call of this kind.[2] There was also trouble on the part of penitents who objected to being tied to their parish priests, and in 1298 Boniface VIII. was obliged to decree that no custom should confer on any one the right to select a confessor without special licence to that effect from the superior prelate.[3]

Thus the theory of jurisdiction as requisite to the exercise of the power of the keys was definitely accepted by the Church. In 1439, the council of Florence, in its definition of the sacrament of penitence, was careful to explain that its minister must have power, either ordinary or delegated, in order to be able to absolve,[4] whence Caietano draws the somewhat extreme conclusion that mere ordination does not render the priest a minister of the sacrament of penitence.[5] As time wore on and jurisdiction ceased to be a novelty it came, like all other innovations, to be regarded as having existed from the beginning. The earlier schoolmen, as we have seen, had no scruple in admitting that freedom of choice had existed prior to the Lateran council, but Domingo Soto rejects this view indignantly, and the inference that jurisdiction is a human precept; it is, he says, a divine law and has always been in force.[6] The same development is visible with regard to its strict construction. Many theologians held

---

[1] S. Antonini Summæ P. III. Tit. xvii. cap. 21. For the endless refinements which the schoolmen brought into the question and the disputes over the exact sense of *proprius sacerdos* see Gabriel Biel in IV. Sentt. Dist. xvii. Q. ii.

[2] Nich. Gelant Episc. Andegav. Synod. XII. ann. 1272, cap. 5 (D'Achery, I. 731).

[3] Cap. 2 in Sexto Lib. v. Tit. ix.

[4] C. Florent. ann. 1439 Decr. Unionis (Harduin. IX. 440).

[5] Caietani Opusc. Tract. VII.

[6] Dom. Soto in IV. Sentt. Dist. XVIII. Q. iv. Art. 2.

that a priest without jurisdiction—a heretic or excommunicate or one degraded—though he could not lawfully absolve yet his absolution when granted was valid.[1] The council of Trent settled this definitely in the negative, by declaring that absolution is worthless when granted to one over whom the priest has not ordinary or delegated jurisdiction.[2] No allusion was vouchsafed to the original contrary custom as shown in the compilation of Gratian, no consideration was shown for the unlucky souls which, prior to the Lateran canon, may have sought more holy confessors than their own priests; the council assumed to know the ways of God and defined what he would accept and what reject as a valid remission of sin, and this Palmieri admits to be the first authoritative declaration of the doctrine.[3] Ordination thus does nothing more than confer the capacity of obtaining jurisdiction,[4] and the Holy Ghost bestowed in it is powerless to act without an episcopal licence or a benefice with cure of souls.

As this was not merely a regulation of discipline, but a definition of a point of faith in the efficacy of the sacrament, there could be no further discussion as to the power bestowed in ordination being merely potential and inchoate, and when the synod of Pistoia, in 1786, spoke of its being "convenient" that, under the division of dioceses and parishes, each priest should confess his own parishioners, Pius VI. condemned this expression as false, audacious, pernicious, insulting and antagonistic to the council of Trent and erroneous.[5] Thus so completely does the power of the keys depend upon jurisdiction that a priest who resigns his benefice loses its exercise.[6] Of course no parish priest can grant valid absolution to the subjects of another, but this point of faith rests on conditions so tenuous that he can do so with the licence of the bishop, expressed or implied, and this

---

[1] Durand. de S. Porciano in IV. Sentt. Dist. XIX. Q. 2.

[2] C. Trident. Sess. XIV. De Pœnit. cap. 7.—"Nullius momenti absolutionem eam esse debere quam sacerdos in eum profert in quem ordinariam aut subdelegatam non habet jurisdictionem." For the discussion over this see *Summa Diana* s. v. *Sacerdos* n. 10.

[3] Palmeri Tract. de Pœnit. p. 173.   [4] Ibid. p. 175.

[5] Pius PP. VI. Bull. *Auctorem Fidei* n. 37. Guarceno (Comp. Theol. Moral. Tract. XVIII. cap. vi., art. 2) speaks of the Tridentine definition as *proxima fidei.*

[6] S. Alph. de Ligorio Theol. Moral. Lib. VI. n. 542.

is presumed when a custom to do so exists of which the bishop is cognizant and does not prohibit.[1]

Thus human ordinances, however much they may be assumed to reflect the divine will, require to be modified or suspended to meet the infinitely varying exigencies of human imperfection. Scarcely, in fact, had the Lateran canon been promulgated than the truth was recognized that it could not be invariably obeyed, and a cloud of perplexing questions arose which have continued to exercise the ingenuity of the casuists down to the present day. Exceptions to the rule at once began to be discovered. Of these the most immediately apparent was its conflict with the humane prescription of the Church that absolution is never to be refused to the dying sinner who seeks it. We have seen the solution which the council of Angers gave to this in 1272, and it became generally accepted that if in such cases the parish priest is not accessible another can act. This was confirmed by the council of Trent, which, in the decree just cited, admits that *in articulo mortis* any priest can confess and absolve any penitent.[2] Even this however gives rise to a disputed question as to whether in such cases excommunicated or degraded or suspended priests can act.[3]

This exception comes under the broader one of cases of necessity, in which the doctors agree that the limitation arising from jurisdiction is suspended, for, as Aquinas reminds us in this connection, necessity knows no law.[4] This throws us back on the definition of necessity, on the rightful interpretation of which, in any given case,

---

[1] Th. ex Charmes Theol. Univers. Diss. v. De Pœnit. cap. vi. Q. 2.

[2] C. Trident. *loc. cit.* The phrase *in articulo mortis* is not construed only as applicable to mortal disease, but extends to everything that may threaten death, as embarking on a long voyage, being in a beleaguered town or in an army on the eve of battle or, to pregnancy, or, what illustrates Italian civilization in the seventeenth and eighteenth centuries, "castrandis."—Clericati De Pœnit. Decis. XLV. n. 1.

[3] The *Somma Pacifica,* cap. 1, asserts that no excommunicate, degraded or suspended priest can absolve *in articulo,* and much less a schismatic or heretic, and Chiericato (*loc. cit.* n. 9) states that the Congregation of the Council of Trent has so decided. Subsequently, however, the authorities seem to take the opposite view. See Bern. da Bologna Man. Confessor. Ord. Capuccin. cap. 1, ? 4; Ferraris Prompta Biblioth. s. v. *Absolutio* I. n. 48–50; Varceno Comp. Theol. Moral. Tract. XVIII. cap. vi., art. 2, ? 1.

[4] S. Th. Aquinat. Summæ Suppl. Q. VIII. art. 6.

the salvation of a soul may depend, but necessity is not always easily recognizable, and the vague attempts to define it afford ample material for debate. Another knotty question is whether the parochial jurisdiction is territorial or personal—whether a man who commits sin in another parish is justiciable in his own parish or in that where the act was performed. The latter is an infraction of the rule that a priest has jurisdiction only over his own subjects, but it is upheld by St. Ramon de Peñafort, Aquinas, Bonaventura and others, while Angiolo da Chivasso decides against it on the ground that the offence is against God and that the parish priest stands in the place of God to his subjects, while Prierias adds the unanswerable argument that it entails divided confession and partial absolution which are not recognized.[1] This question again branches out into innumerable intricate problems arising from change of domicile, as with travellers, pilgrims, tramps, soldiers, students in universities, merchants, peasants who labor in summer in one place and in winter in another, nobles who hold possessions in different parishes and inhabit them alternately, etc. All these present difficulties of a somewhat intricate character which are discussed by the theologians at great length and with abundant subtilty, showing the inherent impossibility of reducing the dogma of jurisdiction to any practical general principle.[2] So troublesome is it that some authorities have thought it necessary that any one about to undertake a journey must provide himself with a licence from his bishop.[3]

In addition to these exceptions arising from the penitent there

---

[1] S. Raymundi Summæ Lib. III. Tit. xxxiv. § 4.—S. Th. Aquinat. in IV. Sentt. Dist. XXI. Q. iii. art. 3 *ad calcem.*—S. Bonavent. in IV. Sentt. Dist. XIX. art. iii. Q. 1.—Epist. Synod. Guillel. Episc. Cadurcens. cap. xiv. (Martene Thesaur. IV. 693–4).—Jo. de Janua Summa quæ vocatur Catholicon s. v. *Confessio.*—Summa Angelica s. v. *Confessio* V. § 11.—Summa Sylvestrina s. v. *Confessor* I. § 11.

[2] S. Raymundi Summæ Lib. III. Tit. xxxiv. § 4.—Hostiens. Aureæ Summæ Lib. V. De Pœn. et Remiss. § 44.—Synod. Nemausens. ann. 1284 (Harduin. VII. 907).—Jo. Friburgens. Summæ Confessor. Lib. III. Tit. xxxiv. Q. 38–42, 45–49, 59.—Epist. Synod. Guillel. Cadurcens. (Martene Thesaur. IV. 693–4). —S. Antonini de Audientia Confess. fol. 5*a*; Ejusd. Summæ P. III. Tit. xvii. cap. 4.—Summa Angelica s. v. *Confessio* IV. §§ 9–14.—Summa Sylvestrina s. v. *Confessor* I. § 10.

[3] Bart. de Chaimis Interrog. fol. 12*a*—"Imo non licet clericis vel laycis profiscisci sine licentia episcopi."

were others originating in the priest. We have seen what was the general character of the medieval clergy; how for the most part benefices were held or administered by men utterly unfit for the delicate and responsible duties of the confessional and that even to day the priesthood is not wholly impeccable. It, therefore, need not surprise us that theologians, with virtual unanimity, admit that incompetent priests forfeit their jurisdiction and justify their subjects in seeking shrift at other hands. The usual causes assigned for thus leaving the parish priest are three—his ignorance, his disregard of the seal of the confessional, and his being a solicitor to evil. Ignorance in the confessor is generally, though not universally, held to render a confession invalid, but its exact amount is not readily defined; inability to distinguish between mortal and venial sins is usually suggested as the test, but the difference between these classes of sin is often so nebulous that the wisest doctors are at issue, so that really no one can know whether his confessor is sufficiently learned to administer valid absolution and whether he ought to be abandoned for another who may be no better. Revealers of confession forfeit their jurisdiction; no one is bound to confess to them, and the constant reference to this in the manuals of practice show that it is a recognized source of trouble. Solicitation, or the seduction of penitents in the confessional, is likewise a danger to which all, and especially women, are exposed, though less so at present than formerly, and those who have reason to dread it are justified in seeking some safer confessor. Any risk, in fact, of exciting the evil passions of the confessor, whether lustful or vengeful, relieves the subject from his jurisdiction. It is easy to lay down general rules of this kind, but the difficulty lies in their application, and the long and intricate discussions over them show the impossibility of framing them to suit all cases or of furnishing the penitent with any sure guide of conduct.[1]

---

[1] S. Raymundi Summæ Lib. III. Tit. xxxiv. § 4.—Alex. de Ales Summæ P. IV. Q. XIX. Membr. 1, Art. 2.—S. Th. Aquinat. Summæ Supplem. Q. VIII. Art. 4. —Astesani Summæ Lib. V. Tit. xiii. Q. 2.—Manip. Curatorum P. II. Tit. iii. cap. 4.—S. Antonini Summæ P. III. Tit. xvii. cap. 4.—Gab. Biel in IV. Sentt. Dist. XVII. Q. ii. Art. 3, Dub. 4.—Bart. de Chaimis Interrog. fol. 10*b*.— Summa Sylvestrina s. v. *Confessor* I. §§ 10-11.—Summa Tabiena s. v. *Confessio Sacram.* n. 22.—Escobar Theol. Moral. Tract. VII. Ex. iv. cap. 5, n. 30.—S Alph. de Ligorio Theol. Moral. Lib. VI. n. 568.

Besides these three leading causes for avoiding the parish priest some authori-

When the penitent has thus just cause to regard his parish priest as unfit, his duty is to ask him for a licence to confess elsewhere. If this is refused, the doctors differ. Some hold that the penitent should apply to the superior for a licence; others that he is then released from jurisdiction and can select another confessor; others that he is in the position of one unable to get a confessor, which means that confession to God suffices; others again that he is still bound and that any other absolution which he may obtain is invalid. The question is evidently a difficult one, on which the authorities are at issue.[1] Priests, as a rule, are urged to grant such licences readily: Aquinas indeed says that it is a sin for them to refuse: S. Carlo Borromeo instructs them to make the offer spontaneously when they have a quarrel or a lawsuit with a parishioner, and adds that if difficulty is made the *vicario foraneo* has authority to issue them, but they are not to be in blank and must specify the confessor to be substituted.[2] It is easy to prescribe liberality in such matters to priests, but it is impossible not to recognize that a timid parishioner, or a woman dreading solicitation, might hesitate long before risking the ill-will of the priest by making a request which in itself is a direct and severe imputation on his fitness for his office.

Nor are these the only questions to which the introduction of jurisdiction has given rise. As without it there is no power to administer validly the sacrament of penitence, if it is improperly assumed, or is

---

ties specify others. Thus John Myrc's "Instructions to Parish Priests" (v. 829–54)—

> Or gef hym selfe had done a synne
> By the prestes sybbe kynne,
> Moder or suster or his lemmon
> Or by his doghter gef he had on . . .
> Or gef his preste, as doctorus sayn
> By any of his paresch have layn . . .
> And of mon that schal go fyghte
> In a bateyl for hys ryghte,
> Hys schryfte also thou myghte here
> Thogh he thy pareschen neuer were.

[1] S. Th. Aquinat. Summæ Suppl. Q. VIII. Art. 4.—Astesani Summæ Lib. v. Tit. xii. Q. 2; Tit. xiv. Q. 3, 4.—Manip. Curatorum P. II. Tit. iii. cap. 4.— S. Antonini de Audientia Confessionum fol. 5a.—Summa Sylvestrina s. v. *Confessor* I. § 13.—Em. Sa Aphorismi Confessar. s. v. *Confessio* n. 35.—Gobat Alphab. Confessar. n. 76–8.—S. Alph. de Ligorio Theol. Moral. Lib. VI. n. 568.

[2] S. Carol. Borrom. Instruct. (Ed. Brixiæ, 1676, pp. 73–5).

vitiated by simony, or is doubtful or erroneous, or only probably legal, all absolutions granted by the priest may be invalid or at best doubtful. The priest may be an intruder, he may be under excommunication, he may have obtained his position by simony, he may hold no benefice or licence, he may perhaps never have been validly baptized. The practical problems thus raised are numerous and have exercised the theologians for centuries without giving assurance to the penitent unknowingly exposed to these risks, other than by the pious hope that God or the Church may supply deficiencies and take the *bona fides* of the sinner as a substitute for the sacrament[1] How nice are the distinctions, and how perilous to the unsuspecting penitent, may be estimated from some of the rules reported by Father Gobat. Custom, he says, confers jurisdiction when bishop or priest tacitly consents, but if a parish priest internally dissents when his subjects confess to another, yet forbears to interfere because he dreads quarrels or wrongly imagines the other to have authority, then the absolutions so granted are invalid. If the parish priest is ignorant of the invasion of his jurisdiction, and, on being informed of it, says that he is content, it is almost certain that the absolutions are invalid, for the sacrament cannot be dependent on a subsequent contingency. Tacit consent requires external manifestation ; if a custom springs up of subjects of one parish confessing to a priest of another, and if it is brought to the attention of the pastor of the former and he assents, this validates subsequent but not prior absolutions ; but if the custom is notorious and no objection is made, this silence is the requisite external manifestation. Common popular error confers jurisdiction even where none exists, but this does not extend to the ministrations of a deacon who is thought to be a priest. All theologians, however, were not as liberal as Father Gobat, who mentions a case in which a parish priest absented himself and the magistrates of the town elected another, who officiated for two years. The questions which arose were referred to the learned Doctor Sanchez,

---

[1] S. Antonini Summæ P. III. Tit. xiv. cap. 19 § 18.—Summa Angelica s. v. *Confessio* IV. § 12.—Summa Sylvestrina s v. *Confessor* I. § 15.—Marchant Tribunal Animarum Tom. I. Tract. II. Tit. iii.—S. Alph. de Ligorio Theol. Moral. Lib. VI. n. 571-3.—Varceno Comp. Theol. Moral. Tract. XVIII. cap. 6, Art. 2. §§ 2, 4.

For unsettled questions concerning jurisdiction see *Casus Conscientiæ Benedicti* XIV. Dec., 1743 c. 3; Maii, 1744 c. 2, etc.

who decided that all the sacraments of penitence and marriage administered by the intruder were void. Gobat says that in view of the troubles caused by such a judgment he would have decided the other way.[1] One cannot help wondering whether either of these distinguished theologians imagined that his opinion affected the eternal destiny of the penitents who had departed with the valid or invalid absolutions. Some authorities indeed hold that, when it is the probable opinion of the doctors that a priest has jurisdiction, then his absolutions are valid, but unfortunately there are others of equal standing who deny it.[2]

Another puzzling question arises respecting the chaplains of armies on the march—must they obtain approbations from the bishops of every diocese through which they pass? La Croix ventures to express no opinion himself as to this, but says that he consulted two doctors who held that the regiment is the parish of the chaplain and that he carries his jurisdiction with him ; also that he can shrive the members of any other regiment who may apply to him, for they are all wanderers. But when troops are permanently quartered anywhere, a decision of the Congregation of the Council of Trent, in 1645, and again in 1694, requires the chaplain to procure an episcopal approbation.[3]

A natural result of the establishment of jurisdiction was the necessity of determining who were the authorized confessors of the higher classes, whose rank seemed to remove them from the position of subjects of a parish priest. In the earlier period they had exercised the power of selection as a matter of course, and were in the habit of having their own private confessors. St. Agobard complains that all who pretended to temporal rank had their own domestic chaplains, from whom they exacted not only spiritual but secular services ; these were often men of neither character nor train-

---

[1] Gobat Alphab. Confessar. n. 81, 82, 85, 86, 95, 96, 106, 110, 111. Yet Sanchez was right ; see Pet. de Aragon *de Justitia et Jure* Q. LX. Art. vi. and C. A. Thesauri de Pœnis Eccles. s. v. *Absolutio* cap. 2. Still there are doctors who hold that to prevent the peril of souls the Church supplies the defect of jurisdiction.

[2] Gobat Alphab. Confessar. n. 112, 114.

[3] La Croix Theol. Moral. Lib. VI. P. ii. n. 1518.—Summæ Alexandrinæ P. I. n. 529.—Pittoni Constitutiones Pontificiæ T. VII. n. 870.

ing—frequently serfs or retainers whose ordination was procured for the purpose.[1] This was an abuse against which Nicholas I. angrily protested, and the synod of Pavia, in 850, endeavored to limit it by requiring all such priests to be examined by the bishops and to be furnished with commendatitious letters[2]—a rule repeated by Urban II., in 1089, who forbade the residence of priests in courts, where they were kept in subjection to laymen and women; nobles desiring such chaplains must apply to bishops, who can grant temporary licences for the purpose.[3] Royal personages seem to have had private confessors as a matter of course. A certain Humbert, afterwards Bishop of Litchfield, is spoken of as the confessor of Offa II. of Mercia; Louis le Débonnaire selected the pious Aldric as his confessor, and then in four months gave him the bishopric of Le Mans; in 909 a charter of Ordoño II. of Leon is subscribed by Diego Hernando as *confessarius regis;* before the battle of Lechfeld, in 955, Otho the Great received the sacrament from his confessor Othelric; when, in 1017, the Cathari were burnt at Orleans, Queen Constance, standing at the church-door as they were led out to the stake, struck out with a stick the eye of the heretic Stephen who had been her confessor. The pious emperor Henry III. would seem to have had no regular confessor, for it is related of him that he never assumed the regalia without confessing to some priest, accepting penance and asking permission.[4] With the establishment of jurisdiction, this freedom of choice and the privilege of private chaplains was necessarily regarded as an interference with ecclesiastical organization. Accordingly, in the compilations for the guidance of confessors, we find elaborate enumerations of all the grades of society, with designations as to whom they are to seek for their shrift, and long lists of their habitual sins which are to be enquired for.[5] Thus we are told that dukes con-

---

[1] S. Agobardi de Privilegiis et Jure Sacerdotum cap. 11.

[2] Hugon. Floriacens. Chron. Lib. I. circa ann. 855.—Synod. Ticinens. ann. 850 cap. 18 (Harduin. V. 30).

[3] C. Melphitan. ann. 1089, cap. 9 (Harduin. VI. II. 1686).

[4] Vita Offæ II. (Matt. Paris Hist. Angl. Ed. 1644, App. p. 14).—Gesta Domini Aldrici (Baluz. et Mansi Miscell. I. 80).—Du Cange s. v. *Confessarius Regis.*—Dithmari Merseburg. Chron. Lib. II. ann. 955 —D'Achery Spicileg. T. I. p. 606.—Reginandi Vit. S. Annonis n. 6 (Migne, CXLIII. 1521).—See also Mabillon, Præfat. I. n. 86 in Sæc. III. Ord. S. Benedicti.

[5] Hostiens. Aureæ Summæ Lib. V. De Pœn. et Remiss. §§ 15–43.—Jo. Friburgens. Summæ Confessor. Lib. III. Tit. xxxiv. Q. 57–8.—Astesani Summæ

fess to the bishops of their capitals; there are various directions as to marquises and counts, whose rank and possessions were by no means uniform; a baron confesses to the parish priest of his chief town, while knights, merchants, peasants and children confess to the priests of their parishes. All this is simple enough, but crowned heads presented a more troublesome problem. As to the emperor, Cardinal Henry of Susa, who is copied by succeeding authorities, tells us that there were various opinions; some held that the pope was his confessor, others the Bishop of Liége in whose diocese is situated Aachen where he is crowned, others again that he can select his own confessor as he is subject to no law, but the truth is that by immemorial custom the emperor and empress have master chaplains and under them daily chaplains, to whom they confess at will, and this is approved by the pope, who could prohibit it if he chose. As for kings, Cardinal Henry says that some consider that they must confess to the pope, others to whom they please, but the truth is that they are subjects of the bishops of their capitals, unless by custom or by ancient licence they can exercise free choice. Astesanus declares that no custom can authorize kings to select their confessors, for this would be detrimental to church discipline. St. Antonino and Gabriel Biel say that the confessor of a king is the bishop or archbishop of the city in which he is crowned.[1] The probability is that, as a rule, they obtained from the popes permission to choose their confessors. Thus, in 1272, Philippe le Hardi procured such a privilege from Gregory X., and, in 1278, from Nicholas III. In 1281, Martin IV. granted one to Magnus of Sweden, and, in 1301, Boniface VIII. to Edward I. of England. Finally, in 1351, Clement. VI. granted in perpetuity to King John and his queen and their successors on the throne of France the right to select their confessors with the added privilege of absolution for papal reserved cases.[2] The struggles of the Reformation and the religious wars which followed emancipated

---

Lib. v. Tit. xv. Q. 15-16.—S. Antonini Summæ P. III. Tit. xvii. cap. 2, 3.—Gab. Biel in IV. Sentt. Dist. XVII. Q. ii. Art. 3, Dub. 2.

[1] Hostiens. Aureæ Summæ Lib. v. De Pœn. et Remiss. §§ 35 sqq.—Astesani Summæ Lib. v. Tit. xv. Q. 15, 16.—P. de Palude in IV. Sentt. Dist. XVII. Q. iii. Art. 2.—S. Antonini Summæ P. III. Tit. xvii. cap. 2, 3.—Gab. Biel in IV Sentt. Dist. XVII. Q. ii. Art. 3, Dub. 2.

[2] Raynald. Annal. ann. 1272, n. 59; ann. 1278, n. 37; ann. 1281, n. 23; ann. 1301, n. 23.—D'Achery Spicileg. III. 724.

royalty, and the principle became established that all great princes have the privilege of selecting their own confessors from among authorized priests.[1]

As regards ecclesiastics, the first question naturally is with regard to the pope, who, as Cardinal Henry says, not only can sin but sins more grievously than others on account of his exalted rank. It seems that at first there was doubt, and some affirmed, like the Greeks, that it sufficed for him to confess to God; others suggested that it should be to the Cardinal of Ostia or to some other cardinal bishop or to a monk, but the correct decision is that he can select whom he pleases.[2] As for the cardinals, according to Cardinal Henry and Bishop Pelayo, in the thirteenth and fourteenth centuries, some held that they must confess to the pope; others that the cardinal deacons confess to the priest-bishops, the bishops to the first bishop (Ostia) and he to the pope, but the real practice is that the cardinal bishops are privileged to select their own confessors, the rest confess their private sins to the papal Penitentiary and their public ones to the pope, but it is safer for each one to get a papal licence to choose a confessor.[3] In modern times all cardinals can make their own selection.[4] Archbishops, as Cardinal Henry tells us, if in Italy and subject immediately to the Holy See, must confess to the pope once a year, as they are required to come annually to the curia; outside of Italy, if the sin be public and enormous, it must be confessed to the pope, in all else they have freedom of election. Bishops, if exempt, have the same privileges as archbishops; if not exempt, they must confess to their archbishops at least once a year. Privi-

---

[1] Escobar Theol. Moral. Tract. VII. Ex. iv. cap. 5, n. 30.—Gobat Alphab. Confessar. n. 98.—S. Alph. de Ligorio Theol. Moral. Lib. VI. n. 565.—Varceno Comp. Theol. Moral. Tract. XVIII. cap. vi. art. 2, § 1.

[2] Hostiensis *loc. cit.* Johannes de Deo reaches the same conclusion, after saying (Pœnitentialis Lib. v. cap. 1) "Et forsan videtur quibusdam quod non peccaret papa . . . unde videtur se licere quidquid facere vellet. Ego autem Johannes de Deo cum aliis doctoribus contrarium teneo et dico quod si papa peccat magis offendit quam alius homo."—Cf. Alvari Pelagii de Planctu Ecclesiæ Lib. II. Art. xix.

In modern times the Apostolic Sacristan seems frequently selected as the papal confessor.—Grégoire, Histoire des Confesseurs des Empereurs etc. p. 188 (Paris, 1824).

[3] Hostiens. *loc. cit.*—Alv. Pelag. *loc. cit.*

[4] S. Alph. de Ligorio Theol. Moral. Lib. VI. n. 565.

leges, however, to choose a confessor were readily obtained, and in time bishops, both active and titular, gained the power to do so as a prerogative of their station. Elaborate rules at one time prevailed with regard to all other grades of the clergy, both regular and secular, but it is scarce worth while to enter into these details, especially as the tendency has been constant to relax the strictness of the old regulations, and already, in the seventeenth century, Escobar tells us that custom allows all priests to select their own confessors, and Martin van der Beek enumerates seven classes so privileged—popes, bishops and prelates, secular priests, emperors and kings, scholars, vagabonds and pilgrims.[1]

It is evident from all this that everywhere there was a desire to shake off the subjection to the parish priest and to exercise free choice in the selection of the person who should occupy the supremely delicate position of confessor. The motive might be laudable, to escape from the control of a licentious, ignorant or tyrannical pastor, or it might be evil, to seek some complaisant priest who, for a consideration, would confer absolution without due penance or requiring restitution of ill-gotten gains or abandonment of sin. Whatever the object, it was a privilege generally and eagerly sought. As the "superior" assumed to have power to grant it, the issuing of licences to choose a confessor became a recognized custom, nor, when the manners of the middle ages are considered, need it surprise us that they should be granted for a price. Hardly had the decree of Boniface VIII. been promulgated, forbidding the choice of a confessor without a licence, than we find the synod of Autun, in 1299, quoting it and requiring every one who desired the privilege to procure an episcopal licence, and, in 1335, a synodical epistle of William of Cahors reminds the possessors of such documents that they do not include power to absolve for reserved cases.[2] While this shows that episcopal licences were customary, the papal chancery seems to have been the most active agency in issuing them. We have seen that sovereigns sought them, and private individuals were no less welcome. As early as 1252, we find one granted to Siger, sieur

---

[1] Escobar, Liguori, Varceno, *ubi sup.*—Becani de Sacramentis Tract. II. P. III. cap. 38, Q. 8, n. 1.

[2] Stat. Synod. Eccles. Œduens. ann. 1299, cap. 14; Epist. Synod. Guillel. Episc. Cadurcens. circa 1335, cap. 8 (Martene, Thesaur. IV. 487, 688).

d'Aingen, in the diocese of Cambrai, empowering him to confess to any discreet priest, who shall have power to absolve even for papal reserved cases[1]—a clause which perhaps explains the preference felt for papal rather than for episcopal licenses. Doubtless the decree of Boniface VIII., in 1298, was intended to emphasize the necessity of procuring such letters, for their issue was becoming one of the recognized functions of the papal chancery.[2] In the tax list of John XXII. the price of a confessional letter for an individual was fixed at ten *gros tournois;* if it contained the additional clause of absolution *in articulo mortis* the charge was fourteen ; if for a husband and wife, sixteen ; other persons could be included at two *gros* apiece, if they were not individually named, but a letter for a college or other body in mass was taxed at fifty.[3] These were nominally the scrivener's fees, but the varying prices, without corresponding difference in the length of the document, show that there was a profit to the curia beyond the mere cost of production, and as there were further charges for engrossing, sealing, registering, etc., the total cost to the recipient was

---

[1] Berger, Registres d'Innocent IV. n. 6012. Possibly this may be the doctor of philosophy, Siger of Brabant, immortalized by Dante—

> Essa è la luce eterna di Sigieri
> Che leggendo nel vico degli strami
> Sillogizzò invidiosi veri.—Paradiso, X.

[2] For various letters of this nature issued by Boniface VIII., see Digard, Registres de Boniface VIII. n. 2687, 2692, 2730, 2943, 2968, 3103 etc.

[3] Tangl, Das Taxwesen der päbstlichen Kanzlei, pp. 91-2 (Mittheilungen des Instituts für österreichische Geschichtsforschung, Bd. XII.). Herr Tangl enumerates various documents of the kind which he has met ; one costing fourteen *gros*, as above ; another of 1353 cost twenty-two ; others to married couples, sixteen and fourteen ; one to seventy-two named conventuals of S. Maria della Scala of Siena, in 1318, is taxed at 127 *gros*. Other cases show great irregularity in price ; sometimes to convents they are issued gratuitously or partly so, as under Gregory XII., in 1407, two to S. Maria della Scala are taxed at four hundred and five hundred *gros* respectively, but are marked to be registered without charge (Ibid. p. 34). There seems to have been no additional fee for magnates, for only ten *gros* are charged to Leopold III., Duke of Austria, for one issued by Gregory XI. in 1373 (p. 40).

In a printed copy of the Taxes of the Chancery, of about 1500, the price of a licence to choose a confessor who can absolve once for papal cases and as often as wanted for others, including censures, is twenty *gros;* for simply choosing a confessor it is ten.—White Hist. Library, Cornell University, A. 6124.

The *gros tournois* was in value one-tenth of a florin.

four- or five-fold the amount in the tax table.[1]   When, about 1536, Paul III., in the threatening aspect of the Lutheran revolt and the demands for a general council to reform the Church in its head and its members, was considering plans for the reformation of the curia, a consultation submitted to him alludes to these confessional letters and argues that no one should be scandalized by them, for they were sold at the simple scrivener's fee; if the recipients abused them by committing enormous crimes in expectation of easy absolution, the Holy See was not responsible and the sinners only deceived themselves.[2]

All this made a serious inroad on the exclusive pretensions of jurisdiction, which were still further invaded by the development of the system of indulgences.   Many of these carried with them the right to choose the confessor who should administer the sacrament on which the indulgence was conditioned, and although this was for once only, the purchase of an indulgence a year liberated the penitent wholly from his parish priest.   These indulgences were of various kinds—jubilees, crusade indulgences, those for St. Peter's, and individual letters issued to applicants for a trifling sum.   The most conspicuous is the Cruzada, granted to the Spanish dominions, where the habit of taking it annually was so universal that Escobar gravely remarks that the only laymen who can choose their confessors are kings, princes and Spaniards and Sicilians under the Cruzada.[3] Whether the freedom of choice under licences and indulgences enables the penitent to select any simple priest, or whether he is restricted to those having cures or episcopal approbations, is a disputed point.   Domingo Soto asserts that any priest, not excommunicated or suspended, can be chosen, that the papal rescript confers

---

[1] By a regulation of Martin V., the papal secretaries had the emoluments of certain *minuta* (the rough drafts for which the charge was separate from the engrossed copies), viz., those of "tabellionatus officii, altarium portatilium, celebrandi in locis interdictis et ante diem, *confessionalis perpetui* et indulgentiarum in mortis articulo et in vita."   When, in 1487, Innocent VIII. raised the number of his secretaries from six to twenty-four and made them all purchase the office at 2600 florins apiece, to redeem his mitre and jewels which he had pawned, he confirmed this regulation and added other sources of profit.—Innoc. PP. VIII. Bull. *Non debet,* ₴ 15 (Bullar. I. 442).

[2] Döllinger, Beiträge zur politischen kirchlichen und Cultur-Geschichte, III. 232.

[3] Escobar Theol. Moral. Tract. VII. Ex. iv. cap. 5, n. 30.

the jurisdiction, and that such is the practice under the Cruzada.[1]
Similar construction was placed on grants made by Sixtus IV. and
Innocent VIII. empowering superiors of the Religious Orders to
authorize their members to select confessors, which Chiericato, about
the year 1700, considers a grave abuse.[2] More modern authorities,
however, assume that the selection is restricted to approved confessors.[3]

The jurisdiction of the parish priest over his subjects was thus so
largely encroached upon that respect for it was considerably shaken,
and Charles V., in the Formula of Reformation adopted by the Reichs-
tag of Augsburg, in 1548, proposed, for the purpose of encouraging
confession, that penitents should have free choice among fit confessors,
who should moreover have power to absolve for reserved cases at the
discretion of the bishop.[4] Two years after this the council of Trent
uttered the decree declaring invalid all absolutions granted without
jurisdiction, thus reaffirming its necessity in the most authoritative
manner. This seems to have received slack obedience, for, in 1583,
the council of Reims felt obliged to announce that no one must
imagine that he is at liberty to confess to whom he pleases, and in the
same year the council of Bordeaux asserted that absolution without
jurisdiction is worthless;[5] moreover, as we shall see hereafter, the
custom was growing of appealing to another confessor when a penance deemed unreasonable was imposed, and all confessors were
recognized as authorized to commute or mitigate a penance imposed
by another—a practice encroaching most seriously on the prerogative of jurisdiction. With the constantly increasing relaxation of

---

[1] Dom. Soto in IV. Sentt. Dist. XVIII. Q. iv. Art. 3.

[2] Clericati De Pœnit. Decis. XXXIX. n. 5–14.

[3] S. Alph. de Ligorio Theol. Moral. Lib. VI. n. 545.—Varceno Comp. Theol.
Moral. Tract. XVIII. cap. vi., art. 2, § 1.

[4] Formula Reformationis, cap. 13 (Le Plat, Monum. Concil. Trident. IV. 88).
In 1562 a similar project was adopted in Bavaria, but meanwhile the
council of Trent had spoken, and this clause was limited by requiring the
consent of the parish priests: heresy, homicide and excommunication were
also excepted from among the reserved cases.—Formul. Reform. Salzburgens.
cap. 11 (Knopfler, Die Kelchbewegung in Bayern, Actenstücke, p. 50).

[5] C. Remens. ann. 1583, De Pœnit. cap. 5 ; C. Burdegalens. ann. 1583, cap.
12 (Harduin. X. 1282, 1347). Although the council of Trent has never been
officially published in France the churches were at liberty to accept its discipline for their governance.

modern times the control of parish priests over the confessions of their subjects would seem to be disappearing and the right of free choice of confessors to be admitted. In 1736 we find Benedict XIV. assuming as a matter of course that a penitent who finds his confessor too rigid can go to another for absolution.[1] In 1768 the Bishop of Gerona alludes to the efforts of the Jesuits in endeavoring to induce their penitents to confess only to them, and he threatens that if any one shall seek to do this by persuasion or compulsion he shall, if a parish priest, be suspended, and all others shall have their licences withdrawn.[2] From 1835 to 1850 a number of diocesan and provincial councils in France declared that all penitents should enjoy the utmost liberty in the selection of their confessors, even for the annual confession of precept, the only restriction being that the confessor must possess the episcopal approbation or licence : all parish priests were instructed to give notice to this effect during Lent, and their opposition to the measure was assumed in the prohibition of their interfering directly or indirectly with this privilege.[3] This is evidently regarded as a matter of local discipline, to be settled in each province or diocese for itself, and it would probably not be easy to determine exactly how far this liberality extends, though expressions employed by recent Spanish, German and American writers would seem to indicate that in these countries it prevails generally.[4] This

---

[1] Benedicti PP. XIV. Casus Conscientiæ, Jan., 1736, cas. 1.

[2] Čarta de Edicto de Don Manuel Palmero y Rallo, Obispo de Gerona, 8 Feb., 1768, p. xxxiii.

[3] " Maximam libertatem habeant fideles in confessariis eligendis, etiam pro confessione sacramentali annua facienda de præcepto, cui satisfieri pro nostra provincia declaramus per confessionem factam cuilibet sacerdoti de approbatis ab Ordinario. Universi parochi moneant parochianos præsertim in quadragesima de ejusmodi facultate ipsis concessa, et nullus erga quascumque personas hanc libertatem directe vel indirecte lædere præsumat."—C. Turonens. ann. 1849, Decr. XVII. § 4 (Collect. Lacensis IV. 176).—C. Avenionens. ann. 1849, cap. v. § 8 (Ibid. p. 340).—C. Albiens. ann. 1850, Decr. VI. (p. 433).—C. Rothomagens. ann. 1850, Decr. XVII. § 4 (p. 530).—C. Burdegalens. ann. 1850, cap. v. § 2 (p. 571).

These were provincial councils. Similar regulations had been adopted in the diocese of La Rochelle in 1835, in that of Meaux in 1838, of Paris in 1839, of Aix in 1840, of Verdun in 1844.—Gousset, Théologie Morale, II. 412.

[4] Mig. Sanchez, Prontuario de la Teología Moral, Trat. VI. Punto ii. § 4; Punto v. § 8.—Gröne, Der Ablass, p. 144.—Müller's Catholic Priesthood, III. 172.

would seem to be in direct conflict with the Tridentine definition that absolution without jurisdiction is worthless, but the difficulty is presumably met by an elastic construction of the term jurisdiction, which may be held to be indirectly conferred on the confessor whom a penitent may select[1]—a typical illustration of the ease with which the most solemn definitions of the Church can be modified to suit the exigencies of changing customs, in the confident expectation that God will follow and conform his decisions to those of his ministers. There is a further discussion as to whether a bishop can forbid his subjects from going to confession outside of his diocese : the doctors assert that he cannot do so if the confession is made to a Regular, because the Regulars hold privileges to shrive sinners from every quarter, but if to a secular priest opinions are divided, with the weight preponderating in the affirmative, and this, we are told, is to be followed in practice.[2]

The most serious interference with the jurisdiction established by the Lateran council in favor of the parish priests was that which arose shortly afterwards from the privileges accorded to the Mendicant Orders. Hardly, indeed, had the canon been promulgated and efforts had commenced for its enforcement, when it was to a great extent neutralized by the unexpected and enormous development of the Dominicans and Franciscans, followed by the Carmelites and Augustinians, in whom the Holy See recognized its most useful instruments and whose influence it stimulated by delegating to them power everywhere to preach, to hear confessions and to administer the sacraments. There can be little doubt that the relief thus afforded to the oppressive character of the new parochial jurisdiction greatly weakened the opposition to the enforcement of confession. In view of the deplorable character, intellectual and moral, of the medieval clergy it may perhaps be questioned whether enforced confession could have been permanently established but for the intervention of these new volunteers. The secular clergy naturally resented the intrusion; the struggle was long and bitter and intricate; it cost the lives of two popes, Innocent IV. and Honorius IV., and

---

[1] This question does not seem to be treated by recent theologians, but the conclusion in the text is inferable from Marc, *Instit. Moral. Alphonsianæ,* n. 1751.

[2] Varceno Comp. Theol. Moral. Tract. xviii. cap. vi., art. 2.

possibly also that of John XXI.; it continued for centuries, and the jealousies which it aroused can scarce be said even yet to have faded away.

This was only an intensified renewal of an old contest, for hardly had the power of the keys begun to take shape when a contest arose between the secular and the monastic clergy over its exercise. At first the Holy See sided with the secular clergy, for a council held by Gregory VII. at Rome, about 1075, forbade monks from usurping the functions of parish priests except in case of necessity, and, in 1094, the council of Autun, held by the legate, Hugh of Lyons, repeated the prohibition.[1] Urban II. suddenly changed his policy, for, as we have seen above (p. 276), in 1096, at the council of Nîmes he sharply reproved those who sought to deny to monks the faculty of confession. This produced little effect, for, in 1100, the council of Poitiers and, in 1102, that of London took decided action against their pretensions.[2] At the Lateran council of 1123 the seculars won a still more substantial victory in a canon forbidding abbots and monks to impose public penance, to visit the sick and to administer extreme unction—the latter doubtless to prevent their securing the bequests which were the customary penances of the death-bed.[3] As voluntary confession during health was as yet unusual, this, if enforced, reduced their activity in the confessional to a minimum, but they were irrepressible and, towards the end of the century, John of Salisbury complains bitterly of their surreptitiously exercising the power of the keys, swinging their sickles in the harvests of others and rewarding the liberality of the rich and powerful by exaggerating the mercy of God.[4] As the idea of jurisdiction gained ground, this interference was admitted to be irregular. Alain de Lille, who was himself a Cistercian, lays down the rule that monks are not to . hear the confessions of parishioners unless invited by the priest or deputed by the superior prelate, and about the same time the Cistercian chapter forbade the abbot of Aigue-belle from in future preaching

---

[1] Pflugk-Harttung, Acta Pontiff. Roman. inedd. II. n. 161.—Bernold Constant. Chron. ann. 1094.

[2] C. Pictaviens. ann. 1100, cap. 10, 11; C. Londiniens. ann. 1102, cap. 18 (Harduin. VI. I. 1860, 1865).

[3] C. Lateran. I. ann. 1123, cap. 17 (Ibid. VI. II. 1113).—Cap. 10 Caus. XVI. Q. 1.

[4] Jo. Salisburiens. Polycrat. VII. xxi.

in secular churches or enjoining penance on laymen without the order of his bishop.[1]

Thus when the Lateran canon established jurisdiction as an acknowledged feature of ecclesiastical organization, the parish priests might congratulate themselves that their rights were too conclusively recognized to be trespassed upon in future. Scarce more than ten years elapsed, however, before they saw the swarms of the new mendicant friars pushing themselves everywhere, trained to the duties of the pulpit and confessional, eager for the salvation of souls and winning the confidence of the people by their self-denying zeal. On his accession, in 1227, Gregory IX. granted to the Dominicans, and not long afterwards to the Franciscans, the right to preach, hear confessions, and grant absolutions everywhere, and this without requiring consent from the diocesans,[2] and the long contest began. It would be interesting to follow its vicissitudes, which shook the Church from centre to circumference—even in the remotest corner of distant Spain the *Hermandad* of the bishops and abbots of Leon and Galicia, formed in 1283, specifies as one of the objects of the association resistance to the usurpations of the Mendicants[3]—but this would lead us too far from our theme, and I can find space only for one or two points bearing directly upon our subject.

At first there seems to have been naturally some question as to the papal power to confer these faculties on the mendicant friars, as it presupposed that the Holy See was the sole source of the remission of sins, and that the episcopal prerogative was a mere delegation from it—a proposition which had not yet been accepted. Alexander Hales, though himself a Franciscan, argues the matter in favor of the Mendicants doubtfully and hesitatingly. He thinks the pope has power to grant such privileges, whereby the " proprius sacerdos " of the Lateran canon may be anyone who has delegated power to hear confessions, especially in view of the ignorance and negligence and other defects of the parish priests.[4] Whatever doubts existed,

---

[1] Alani de Insulis Lib. Pœnit. (Migne CCX. 299).—Statuta Antiqua Ord. Cistercens. ann. 1191, cap. 8 (Martene Thesaur. IV. 1270).

[2] Ripoll. Bullar. Ord. Prædic. I. 18, 19.—Sbaralea Bullar. Franciscan. I. 215.

[3] Memorial Histórico Español, T. II. p. 96.

[4] Alex. de Ales Summæ P. IV. Q. XIX. Membr. 1, Art. 1.

however, were speedily dispelled, and subsequent schoolmen had no trouble in demonstrating that either bishop or pope had full authority to deputize priests for the purpose within the circumscriptions of their respective jurisdictions.[1] Whatever may have been the questions agitated in the schools, the people at large were vexed with no such scruples; they eagerly sought the mendicant confessionals, and St. Bonaventura tells us that the only difficulty lay in supplying the demand for confessors.[2]

Yet the episcopal jurisdiction was of so old a standing that it furnished a strong line of defence in the contest which raged between the regulars and seculars, and the assumption was made that not only was a general permission from the diocesan requisite to enable the Mendicants to administer the sacrament of penitence, but that each friar must be able to show a special and personal episcopal licence. Thus, in 1279, the council of Avignon required this and instructed all who had none to apply for them to the bishop.[3] It is easy to see how great an obstruction could thus be presented to the activity of the intruders, for a bishop, who would not venture to refuse a general permission to function in his diocese, could greatly limit it by declining to license individual friars. The struggle thus became hot around this key of the position. About the year 1300, Boniface VIII. endeavored to effect a settlement by requiring the prelates of the Mendicant Orders to select proper candidates and present them to the bishops for licensing; that the bishops were expected to abuse the power thus admitted to exist is seen by a further clause providing that, if they indiscriminately refuse to license any, then all can act under delegation from the pope. The Mendicants chafed under this; quarrels became fiercer than ever, and a few years later the Dominican Pope Benedict XI. virtually released them from all episcopal supervision. This aroused a still more threatening clamor, and Clement V., at the council of Vienne in 1312, restored the regulation of Boniface.[4] This continued to be the rule, but the

---

[1] S. Th. Aquinat. Summæ Suppl. Q. VIII. Art. 5 ; In IV. Sentt. Dist. XVII. Q. iii. Art. 3.—Durand. de S. Porciano in IV. Sentt. Dist. XVII. Q. xii. n. 8.

[2] S. Bonavent. Libell. Apologet. (Opuscula, Ed. Venet. 1684, II. 428).

[3] C. Avenion. ann. 1279, De Religiosis (Harduin. VII. 780).

[4] Bonif. PP. VIII. Bull. *Super cathedram* (cap. 2 Extrav. Commun. Lib. III. Tit. vi.).—Benedict. PP. XI. Bull. *Inter cunctas* (Cap. 1 Extrav. Commun. Lib. v. Tit. vii.) —Clement. PP. V. Bull. *Dudum* (cap. 2 Clement. Lib. III. Tit. vii.).

Mendicants were dissatisfied and had no difficulty in procuring from the papal chancery special letters, in which they were authorized, against the will of the parish priests, to preach and hear confessions in the parish churches. In 1402, Boniface IX. speaks of these letters as being extorted from the Holy See; they had been shockingly abused and had given rise to many scandals, wherefore he revoked them all.[1]

Under the bulls of Boniface VIII. and Clement V. the practice was for the local superiors of the Mendicants to select such friars as they deemed competent and present them to the bishop, who could reject those whom he considered unfit, but if he rejected all they could all act under papal authority; the presentation under the bull *Dudum* was required to be personal, but in time this was omitted and the application was made by letter, which rendered it merely a formal acknowledgment of the episcopal authority.[2] Clement V. had further ordered that the number presented should be restricted and proportioned to the population, but this received little respect, and, in 1455, the council of Reims complains that their multitude is so great as virtually to give to all penitents freedom of choice of confessors, rendering the people reckless as to the commission of grievous sins, wherefore the bishops are counselled to restrict the number of licences.[3] In 1481, the council of Tournay went further, and with the view of preventing the fraudulent use of licences, which was a subject of complaint, it required them to be limited to a year and to be renewed annually.[4] Still more emphatic was the utterance of the great national council of Seville in 1478. It complained bitterly of the papal

---

[1] Regulæ Cancellariæ Bonif. PP. IX. n. 73 (Ottenthal. *op. cit.* p. 76).

The immense success of the Dominicans and Franciscans naturally led to a host of imitators, whose unauthorized beggary became an intolerable nuisance. At the council of Lyons, in 1274, these surreptitious orders were forbidden to receive more members, in hopes that they would soon die out, and meanwhile were prohibited to preach, hear confessions, or perform burial service. There was a special declaration that the decree did not apply to the Dominicans and Franciscans, while the unauthorized Carmelites and Augustinians were allowed to exist on sufferance "donec de ipsis fuerit aliter ordinatum."—C. Lugdun. ann. 1274, cap. 23 (Harduin. VII. 716).

[2] Summa Pisanella s. v. *Confessio* III. n. 11.—S. Antonini de Audientia Confessionum fol. 6*a*.—Summa Angelica s. v. *Confessio* III. § 16.

[3] C. Remens. ann. 1455 (Gousset, Actes etc. II. 736).

[4] C. Tornacens. ann. 1481, cap. 4 (Ibid. II. 754).

privileges granted to the Mendicants as a disservice to God and a damage to the local churches, a derogation of the rights of the prelates and the cause of continual scandals, wherefore it prayed Ferdinand and Isabella to intervene with the pope and have these privileges reduced to the common law.[1] What representations the Catholic Kings made to Sixtus IV. we do not know; possibly they were forestalled, for, about the same time, the Archbishops of Mainz and Trier with other German prelates, the Duke of Bavaria and the Count Palatine of the Rhine had addressed to him an earnest petition to frame some accord that should put an end to the strife. He referred the matter to a commission of five cardinals who, after hearing both sides, presented a report which was accepted but which was little more than an exhortation to peace and charity with some concessions to the secular priests.[2] The fifth Lateran council, in 1515, wrestled with the problem, and under severe papal pressure made important concessions to the Regulars,[3] and a manual compiled in 1518 shows how liberally the latter construed the Clementine bull *Dudum* in their own favor, reducing the episcopal function to the merest ministerial act, denying the right of the bishop to limit the licences either in number or duration and that of the parish priest to have his consent asked.[4]

The foundation and rapid development of the Company of Jesus, and the extensive privileges in the confessional promptly granted to its members by the Holy See, were not calculated to soothe the permanent exasperation of the secular ecclesiastics; in 1549 Paul III. authorized all Jesuits to hear confessions of all Christians, without

---

[1] Concilio nacional de Sevilla, año 1478 (Fidel Fita, Boletín de la Real Acad. de la Historia, 1893, T. XIII. p. 229).

[2] Sixti PP. IV. Bull. *Vices illius* (cap. 2, Extrav. Commun. I. ix.).

[3] C. Lateran. V. Sess. XI. (Harduin. IX. 1832).—Paridis de Grassis Diarium, Romæ, 1874, pp. 21, 22, 34–5, 38.

[4] Summa Tabiena s. v. *Absolutio* I. §§ 24–34.—The curia made its profit out of the eagerness of the Mendicants to hear confessions, for in the Taxes of the Chancery a letter authorizing a friar to do so, with the consent of the parish priest, is priced at twenty *gros.*—White Hist. Library, A. 6124.

The perpetual strife over death-bed alms and legacies finds expression in the opinions of some doctors that a friar administering the viaticum to a dying man incurs excommunication removable only by the pope.—Bart de Chaimis Interrog. fol. 106*b.*

specifying the necessity of obtaining episcopal licences.[1] It was time for the episcopate to assert itself, and, at the council of Trent, the bishops vindicated their claims by a decree to the effect that no regular priest should hear confessions of the laity, unless he held a parochial benefice or obtained the approbation of the bishop, who was authorized to examine him if he saw fit, and all privileges, even immemorial, to the contrary, were declared inoperative.[2] This became, therefore, the law of the Church, and, in 1565, Pius IV. confirmed it by a bull in which all privileges and faculties not in accordance with the Tridentine decree were revoked. St. Pius V. was induced to grant letters in derogation of this, but he recalled them by a formal decree in 1571, in which he confirmed absolutely the Tridentine action, but the Regulars were untiring in their efforts to evade it, and the declaration had to be repeated, in 1628, by Urban VIII.[3] S. Carlo Borromeo had promptly availed himself of the Tridentine decree and required all Regulars applying for approbations to be strictly examined as to fitness, while, as their moral characters could not thus be ascertained, he instructed their superiors to send him none without a written certificate of virtue, for he would otherwise refuse the licence.[4] Chafing under these restraints, the Regulars endeavored to argue away or ignore the Tridentine decree, and, in 1666, Alexander VII. was obliged formally to condemn the proposition that they could exercise the privileges expressly revoked by the council.[5]

The Jesuits were naturally the foremost in the struggle. They had devoted themselves especially to the confessional and the school as offering the greatest means of usefulness and the surest avenues to the world-wide influence which was the object of their ambition ; they

---

[1] Pauli PP. III. Bull. *Licet debitum* (Litt. Apostol. Soc. Jesu, Antverpiæ, 1635, p. 48).

[2] C. Trident. Sess. XXIII. De Reform. cap. 15. For the discussion over this subject see Pallavicini Hist. Concil. Trident. Lib. VII. cap. 4.

[3] Pii PP. IV. Bull. *In principis Apostolorum* (Th. ex Charmes Theol. Univ. Diss. v. cap. vi. Q. 3).—S. Pii PP. V. Bull. *Romani Pontificis* (Benzi Praxis Trib. Conscient. p. 278).—Urbani PP. VIII. Bull. *Cum sicut accepimus* (Bullar. V. 173).

[4] S. Caroli Borrom. Instructiones (Ed. Brixiæ, 1676, p. 50).

[5] Em. Sa Aphorismi Confessar. s. v. *Confessor* n. 4.—Escobar Theol. Moral. Tract. VII. Ex. iv. cap. 5, n. 30.—Alex. PP. VII. Decr. 1666, Prop. 36.

felt secure in papal favor, and were in some degree intoxicated with their extraordinary success. It is true that in their instructions each member is ordered, when sent to a new diocese, to apply immediately to the bishop, personally or by letter, for a faculty to officiate,[1] yet, when they deemed it safe, they arrogantly asserted complete independence of episcopal supervision. This was abundantly manifested in their quarrel with Juan de Palafox, Bishop of Puebla de los Angeles in Mexico. He offered to licence any fathers whom they might present to him, but they refused to go through the formality, alleging that they had privileges releasing them from the obligation. Supported by the inquisitors they raised such a storm that Palafox was obliged to fly and lie hid among the mountains, until orders came from Spain in his favor; even then they did not obey, and the question was carried to Rome, where, after prolonged wrangling, they were defeated.[2] Even more significant of their independent spirit was the action of the Jesuits of Silesia and Russia after the suppression of the Society by Clement XIV. in 1773. Assured of the protection of Frederic the Great and of Catherine II., they refused obedience and continued the functions of which they had been de-

---

[1] Compend. Privilegior. s. v. *Confessarius*, § 2 (Antverpiæ, 1635, pp. 49–50). At the same time they are given clearly to understand (Ibid. § 1) that they are not obliged to ask the consent of the parish priests.

The Jesuits, rightly regarding as supremely important their reputation as confessors, were commendably careful in the selection of those to whom that function was confided. As in the other Orders, no one was allowed to act unless deputed by his superior, and the utmost discrimination was ordered to be exercised in selecting them. They were required to regard the confessional as a duty of the highest moment, to be discharged with the greatest zeal and alacrity. Curiously enough, no one was allowed to become the spiritual director of any penitent or to require obedience from him.—S. J. Regulæ Sacerdotum, n. 8–19 (Antverpiæ, 1635, pp. 192–4). In the earlier period St. Francis Xavier (Avvisi ai Confessori) is particularly emphatic in instructing the confessor to manifest submission to the prelate and to cultivate good relations with the clergy.

[2] Obras de Juan de Palafox, Tom. XII. To hide their discomfiture the Jesuits caused interpolated bulls of Innocent X. to be inserted in a Bullarium then printing in Lyons, with the remarkable result that the volume containing them was placed in the Index, *donec corrigatur*, by decrees of August 3, 1656, July 27, 1657, and June 10, 1658.—Index Alex. PP. VII. Romæ, 1664, pp. 372, 375.

prived by the Holy See, although the sacraments which they admin-istered were held in Rome to be invalid.[1]

As the Tridentine decree could not be got rid of, the Regulars naturally sought to reduce it to a nullity, as had been successfully done with previous antagonistic precepts. They argued that, as the council had not specifically revoked the Clementine canon *Dudum*, it was still in force and that bishops had no power to revoke licences or to restrict their duration. In France especially, they held that, as the council had never been formally published there, its decrees were not in force, although the crown, in steadily refusing to receive the council, had permitted the Church to accept its decrees in so far as they related to internal discipline, and this had been done by assem-blies of the clergy in 1625, 1635 and 1645. It was in vain that the Sacred Congregation of Bishops and Regulars, by decisions in 1615, 1619, 1625, 1629 and 1630 confirmed the right of the bishops to grant approbations revocable at will and to revoke unlimited ap-probations when the confessor should give any reasonable cause.[2] In spite of all this the Archbishop of Sens, in 1650, was involved in a long quarrel with the Jesuits who disputed his authority, and, in 1653, he published a decree excommunicating all who should confess to them.[3] The Jesuits of Anjou, as we have already seen, supported by the other Orders, raised a similar issue with the Bishop of Angers, but were emphatically defeated by the decision of Alexander VII. in 1659, who denounced the proposition that bishops cannot limit and restrict the licences granted to Regulars as false, audacious, scandal-ous, leading to heresy and schism, and insulting to the council of Trent and the Holy See, which was followed up by the assembly of the Gallican Church pronouncing it hypocritical and mendacious.[4] Defeated in this, the next attempt was to revive and extend the bull *Dudum* by asserting that, if a bishop unjustly refused a licence, the rejected applicant could still hear confessions and that those made to him satisfy the precept of the Church—a proposition which was duly condemned by Alexander VII. in 1665.[5]

---

[1] Theiner, Histoire du Pontificat de Clément XIV. T. II. p. 501.

[2] Barbosa, Summa Apostol. Decisionum s. v. *Approbatio*, n. 7, 16–18.

[3] Ant. Arnauld, Théologie Morale des Jésuites, Cologne, 1667, pp. 237–71.

[4] Juenin de Sacramentis Diss. VI. Q. vii. cap. 3, art. 3, § 1.—S. Alph. de Ligorio Theol. Moral. Lib. VI. n. 552.

[5] Alexand. PP. VII. Const. 1665, Prop. 13.

There was another question involved of considerable importance, for the Regulars argued that their delegation of power was from the pope, not the bishop, and thus, when a licence had been given, it was good in any diocese to which the recipient might be sent, which enabled them to secure multitudinous approbations from some favoring bishop and then send their men everywhere.[1] In 1607, the Congregation of the Council of Trent formally decided against this pretension, but to no purpose.[2] Clement X., in 1670, sought to settle this and all other questions by a comprehensive decree in which, after deploring the constant disturbances and quarrels, he emphatically required the episcopal approbation for all regular confessors, he confirmed the episcopal right of examination and defined that the licence was good only for the diocese of the grantor.[3] If he imagined that this would put an end to the bickerings and mutual jealousy of the seculars and regulars he undervalued the persistency of human passions, for the seculars accused their rivals of purchasing favor by relaxing penance, as we shall see hereafter, and Alexander VIII. felt obliged to condemn their assertions in 1690.[4] It was in vain

---

[1] For a long list of distinguished doctors teaching this opinion see Juan Sanchez, *Selecta de Sacramentis*, Disp. XLIV. n. 1. Manuel Sa was one of these (Aphorismi Confessar. s. v. *Confessor*, n. 4, 5), but when his book passed under the Roman censorship these passages were stricken out and others substituted affirming positively the opposite—"sed opus est approbatione episcopi ejus diœcesis in qua deget" (Index Brasichellens. I. 350). In 1643 Marchant (Trib. Animar. Tom. I. Tract. II. Tit. vi. Q. 4, Dub. 2) discusses the question at length in a manner to show that it was still hotly disputed.

[2] Barbosa, Summa Apostol. Decis. s. v. *Approbatio*, n. 12.

[3] Clement. PP. X. Const. *Superna* §§ 1, 4 (Bullar. VI. 305).

It appears to have been the custom of each new bishop to subject to examination all holding licences from his predecessor. In a collection of episcopal letters of Padua I find Cardinal Rezzonico doing this when appointed bishop in 1743. His successor Santi Veronese (afterwards Cardinal), in 1758, ordered all confessors, who were not parish priests, to present themselves with their licences at the episcopal palace on certain days and undergo a personal examination by him as to their fitness, and he warned them that those would not be easily confirmed who absented themselves from the monthly discussions of cases of conscience over which he presided.

[4] Alexand. PP. VIII. Constit. 1690, Prop. 21, 22. A century earlier S. Carlo Borromeo seems to justify this accusation by exhorting the Regulars not to absolve those whom the priests refuse on account of living in sin, or of not paying pious legacies, or of not satisfying public penance and the like.—S. Caroli Borrom. Instructt. pp. 53–4.

that successive popes thus endeavored to keep the peace; each side construed the papal utterances after its own fashion, and the debates have continued endlessly.[1]

Yet the bitterest source of quarrel between the rival parties was one which went to the very root of the jurisdiction created by the Lateran canon. If the penitent was obliged to obey it by annual confession to his parish priest, the latter need not care much for the voluntary intercalary confessions made to the intruding friars. His control over his subjects was maintained and he was relieved from an onerous task in listening to the scruples of conscience of the timorous. At first this was all that the Mendicants claimed. Alexander Hales thinks that those who confess to the friars are also bound to confess to their parish priests at least once a year if required; at the same time he adds that if the superior power decides otherwise the obligation will cease.[2] St. Bonaventura, who was so energetic a defender of the privileges of the Mendicants, was careful to respect the rights of the parochial clergy, and repeatedly insists on the necessity of annual confession to them, but he manifests some uncertainty, for in one passage he alludes to repeating confession and in another he says that sins which have been remitted by the friars need not be repeated.[3] The Church, in fact, was in a somewhat awkward position between the Lateran precept and the powers granted to the Mendicants, for the annual confession to the pastor could not be insisted on without denying the validity of the absolution conferred by the friar. Aquinas takes full advantage of this; he argues that no one is bound to confess sins that he has not got, therefore it is unnecessary to repeat *proprio sacerdoti* what he has confessed to another duly authorized to remit them, but he adds that the oftener a sin is confessed the less is the *pœna*, so a second confession is not lost; it is well for the friar to induce a penitent to confess again to

---

[1] Clericati De Pœnit. Decis. XXXVIII. n. 10–31.—La Croix Theol. Moral. Lib. VI. P. ii. n. 1505, 1545.—Bern. a Bononia Man. Confessar. Ord. Capuccin. cap. 1, § 3.

For the numerous nice questions involved and the manner in which they are resolved see Guarceno, Comp. Theol. Moral. Tract. XVIII. cap. vi. art. 2, §§ 1–3.

[2] Alex. de Ales Summæ P. IV. Q. XIX. Membr. 1, Art. 3.

[3] S. Bonavent. in IV. Sentt. Dist. XVII. P. ii. Art. 1, Q. 2; Confessionale cap. iv. Partic. 1.

his own priest, but if he refuses he is none the less to be absolved. Moreover, in penitence a man is to be believed both for and against himself; therefore, if he asserts that he has already confessed, the parish priest must accept his assertion.[1] Aquinas had the logic of the situation, but in spite of this Martin IV., in 1282, decreed absolutely that under the Lateran canon annual confession must be made to the parish priest no matter what other confession might have been made to the friars.[2] This would seem to settle the question, but in 1304 the Dominican pope, Benedict XI., in his zeal for his Order, reversed the decision in his bull *Inter cunctas*, when he adopted the views of Aquinas and declared that sins confessed to the friars need not be repeated to the parson, in spite of the Lateran canon. This bull, as we have seen, was revoked by Clement V. in the council of Vienne and the bull *Super cathedram* of Boniface VIII. was revived.[3] The latter had made no allusion to this question, so the decree of Martin IV. was again in force, but the matter seems to have been considered *sub judice* and was variously argued in the schools. The Franciscan Astesanus and the Dominican Pierre de la Palu seek at much length to prove that confession to the friars suffices and need not be repeated to the parson, while the Dominican Durand de S. Pourçain is rigid in upholding the rights of the parochial clergy ; the penitent must again confess and again be absolved by his priest, for the Church has reasonably ordered that pastors should have jurisdiction over their subjects ; by going to another the penitent has committed the sin of disobedience and while thus in mortal sin his confession is invalid.[4]

Matters might perhaps have remained in this uncertain condition but for the indiscretion of Jean de Poilly, a doctor of the University of Paris, where hatred of the Mendicants was traditional. Not content with teaching that sins confessed to the friars must be re-

---

[1] S. Th. Aquinat. in IV. Sentt. Dist. XVIII. Q. iii. Art. 2.

[2] Martini PP. IV. Bull. *Ad fructus uberes*, 1282 (Martene Thesaur. I. 1172).—Sbaralea Bullar. Francisc. III. 480).

The council of Mainz, in 1281, had ordered the yearly confession to the parish priest of those who had confessed to the friars (Hartzheim III. 666) showing that there was an endeavor to escape it.

[3] Cap. 1 Extrav. Commun. Lib. v. Tit. vii.—Cap. 2 Clement. Lib. III. Tit. vii.

[4] Astesani Summæ Lib. v. Tit. xiv. Q. 9.—P. de Palude in IV. Sentt. Dist. XVII. Q. iv. Art. 3.—Durand. de S. Porciano in IV. Sentt. Dist. XIX. Q. ii. §11.

peated to the pastor, he added that, so long as the Lateran canon stood, neither God nor the pope had power to decree otherwise. John XXII., who was then pope, was not especially tender in his dealings with the Mendicant Orders, and he would doubtless not have troubled himself to espouse their cause, but the Paris doctor had incautiously involved the papal prerogative in the matter, and this was a point on which Pope John was inflexible, for, at the time, he was burning Franciscan Spirituals by the score for holding that the pope could not dispense for vows of chastity and poverty. There could not have been lacking Mendicants connected with his court to call his attention to the insubordination threatened in Jean de Poilly's teaching, and, in 1321, the overzealous theologian was summoned to Avignon ; his theses were discussed in full consistory and pronounced erroneous ; he was forced to recantation, and a bull was issued declaring that it suffices to confess to the friars, and that sins so confessed need not be repeated to the parish priest.[1]

The question was settled in so far as the most authoritative utterance of the Holy See could accomplish it, but the secular clergy and the University of Paris were not prepared to submit. It is true that, in Spain, Guido de Monteroquer, who was himself parish priest of Teruel, accepted it as final, and even argued that it was inferable from the bull *Super cathedram* of Boniface VIII.,[2] but elsewhere bishop and priest were not so complying. When, in 1373, the Sicilian Franciscans applied to Gregory XI. for an official copy of the bull *Vas electionis*, it is apparent that the errors of Jean de Poilly were still taught in the island.[3] It was in France, however, that the most serious resistance was experienced. In 1409 the friars complained to Alexander V. that the errors of Jean de Poilly were openly taught and reduced to practice, and when he responded with the bull *Regnans in cœlis*, threatening punishment as heretics on all who upheld them, the University of Paris refused to receive the bull

---

[1] Johann. PP. XXII. Bull. *Vas electionis* (Cap. 2 Extrav. Commun. Lib. v. Tit. iii.).

[2] Manip. Curatorum P. II. Tit. iii. cap. 4.

[3] Cosentino, Archivio Storico Siciliano, 1886, p. 336.

In Italy doubtless the decision of John XXII. and his successors was respected. St. Antonino tells us (Summæ P. III. Tit. xvii. cap. 9) that a parish priest cannot refuse communion to a subject who says that he has confessed to the friars, unless he is excommunicate or a notorious sinner.

and expelled all the friars who would not agree to renounce it. The struggle continued throughout the fifteenth century; Eugenius IV. and Nicholas V. directed the Ordinaries to prosecute for heresy all who should maintain the doctrines of Jean de Poilly, and the University responded by denouncing the bulls as surreptitious and not to be respected.[1] When, in 1474, Sixtus IV. took a more advanced step and empowered the Inquisition to suppress by persecution these new heretics his action was equally fruitless, and he was finally obliged to yield the point. In the compromise arranged by him, about 1478, the friars were forbidden to teach that confession to them superseded the annual confession to the priest, for such confession was required by law.[2] It shows how little the papal authority was respected at this period that Gabriel Biel argues at great length to prove that confession to the friars need not be repeated, but does so without any allusion to papal decisions, and that, in 1493, the Archbishop of Mainz prohibited absolutely the Mendicants from exercising the function of confession.[3]

The papal acceptance of the whilom heresy as orthodoxy settled the dispute for but a short space, for, in 1515, the fifth Lateran council decreed that confession to a friar satisfies the precept of annual confession to the parish priest.[4] The question became still more pressing with the appearance of the Jesuits. When, in 1549, Paul III. granted to them the right to hear confessions without the permission of the parish priests, he expressly stated that sins remitted by them need not be again confessed to the pastor.[5] Yet S. Carlo Borromeo was emphatic in requiring annual confession to the parish priest, and, in 1592, a quarrel on the subject at Douai required for its pacification a brief from Clement VIII. and pastoral letters from the Bishop of

---

[1] D'Argentré, Collect. Judic. de novis Erroribus I. II. 184, 242, 251, 340, 347, 352, 354, 356.—Religieux de S. Denis, Hist. de Charles VI. Liv. xxix. chap. 10.

[2] Sixti PP. IV. Bull *Regimini* § 15 (Bullar. I. 394); Ejusd. Bull. *Vices illius* (Cap. 2 Extrav. Commun. Lib. I. Tit. ix.).

[3] Gab. Biel in IV. Sentt. Dist. XVII. Q. ii. Art. 1, not. 5; Art. 2.—Gudeni Cod. Diplom. III. 603.

[4] C. Lateran. V. Sess. XI. (Harduin. IX. 1832). Father Tournely tells us (De Sacr. Pœnit. Q. VI. Art. 3) that the fifth Lateran council is not received in France as œcumenic.

[5] Pauli PP. IV. Bull. *Licet debitum*, 1549 (Litt. Apostol. S. J., Antverpiæ, 1635, p. 48).

Arras and the Archbishop of Cambrai. Willem Van Est asserts positively that the Lateran canon requires annual confession to the pastor irrespective of what other confessions may have been made, and, about 1700, Van Espen dwells upon it with an insistance, and cites canons prescribing it from French and Netherlandish councils with a profusion, which show how active still was the controversy and how stubbornly, at least in the Gallican Church, the secular clergy maintained what they claimed to be their rights. It made little difference to them that, in 1645, Innocent X. settled adversely to them a quarrel between the Archbishop of Bordeaux and the Regulars, and that, in 1670, Clement X. finally decided the matter in favor of the latter by defining that confession to an approved friar superseded that to a parish priest and need not be repeated. In France the bull was denounced as surreptitious, its publication was prohibited and those who ventured to explain its purport to the people were prosecuted.[1] This position was consistently maintained by the Gallican Church, but elsewhere the papal policy prevailed at last, aided by the constantly increasing tendency to afford free choice of confessors to the penitent, and St. Alphonso Liguori declares without reserve that a parishioner showing to his priest a certificate of confession from any approved confessor is free from the annual precept, and further, that any episcopal decree in derogation of this is void.[2] This leaves the friars with one manifest advantage over the secular priests, that, whereas the jurisdiction of the pastor is confined to the boundaries of his own parish, the regular who holds an episcopal approbation can hear penitents from all parts of the diocese, even if he knows that their object in coming to him is to avoid their own priest.[3]

---

[1] Estius in IV. Sentt. Dist. XVII. § 13.—Van Espen Jur. Eccles. P. II. Tit. vi. cap. 5, n. 20.—Juenin de Sacramentis Dissert. VI. Q. 5, cap. 4, art. 3, § 2. —Tournely de Sacr. Pœnit. Q. VI. art. 3.—Clement. PP. X. Bull. *Superna*, § 5 (Bullar. VI. 306).

[2] Héricourt, Loix ecclésiastiques de France, Tom. II. p. 13 (Neufchâtel, 1774). —S. Alph. de Ligorio Theol. Moral. Lib. VI. n. 564.

[3] Cabrini Elucidarium Casuum Reservator. P. I. Resol. xxvi.

CHAPTER XI.

RESERVED CASES.

THE power of the keys in the hands of the parish priest was still further limited by what are known as reserved cases. These are sins for which he is unable to grant absolution, and are either episcopal cases, as reserved to the bishop, or papal, as reserved to the Holy See. They form an intricate and perplexing portion of the canon law, giving rise to a multitude of questions on which the authorities are by no means in accord and merit a more detailed enquiry than space will here permit.

We have seen (pp. 121 sq.) how the priest, in acquiring the power of the keys, gradually divested the bishop of his sole control over penance and reconciliation. In yielding, after a prolonged struggle, however, the bishop did not relinquish his claim of dominant authority and retained jurisdiction over such cases as he might, in his discretion, designate, and these became known as reserved. The process was confused and irregular, depending largely on the temper and policy of the individual prelates, and the practice in the different dioceses varied accordingly. In the Penitentials, we see no distinctions drawn between the lesser sins and those which subsequently came in general to be classed as reserved. A careless bishop might leave all penitents in the hands of the local priests; an active one might require them all to be brought before him, though the size of the northern dioceses, the insecurity of travel, and regard for the susceptibilities of newly converted barbarians naturally tended to localize jurisdiction. The earliest allusion to any distinction is of interest only as showing how vague as yet were the delimitations between spiritual and secular authority, between penance and punishment. It provides that the homicide of a monk or cleric shall be judged by the bishop, and assigns to it seven years' penance or abandoning the use of arms, while, if the victim be a priest or bishop, the slayer shall be judged by the king.[1] One of the later compilations, it is true,

---

[1] Theodori Canones Gregorii cap. 108; Theodori Pœnit. Lib. I. cap. iv. § 5; Ps. Ecberti Confessionale, cap. 23; Pœnit. XXXV. Capitular. cap. 1, § 2; Pœnit·

seems to indicate a tendency to differentiate between episcopal and priestly functions by directing that grave cases shall be sent to the bishop, but at the same time it recognizes that the bishop is the fountain of jurisdiction in the assignment of penance.[1] The earliest definite prescription reserving a case to the bishop, that I have met, occurs in the council of London, in 1102, where it is decreed that none but he shall absolve for unnatural crime.[2] The work of the schoolmen was now commencing, which was eventually to reduce to a system the indefinite claims and uncertain practice of the Church and to specify, with some approach to accuracy, the functions of the various ranks of the hierarchy. Public or solemn penance was rapidly being superseded by private—a process which will be considered hereafter—and, as a general rule, the latter was abandoned to the priests while the former was retained by the bishops ; crimes of peculiar atrocity were still held to be subject to public penance, and in this way the doctors came to explain why the priests, who had the power to bind and to loose, could only exercise it on the less important offences ; besides, as they said, the prelates were more experienced, so the greater sins were naturally reserved for them.[3] It was soon after this that, in 1195, the council of York ordered perjurers to be sent to the archbishop or bishop for penance, and Adam de Perseigne says that cases of homicide and arson are reserved for the diocesan.[4] The growth of the custom of thus reserving sins is seen, about the same period, in the instructions of Eudes of Paris that the greater sins, such as homicide, sacrilege, unnatural crime, incest, seduction of virgins, violence to clerics, broken vows and the like are to be sent to the prelates.[5] The matter was wholly at the discretion of the bishop, and an entirely different list is given in an undated document of the Paris church, probably not much later than this ; it enumerates abortion, perjury in the episcopal court, volun-

---

Ps. Gregorii cap. 3 ; Pœnit. Vallicellian. II. cap. 7 (Wasserschleben, pp. 172, 188, 310, 506, 538, 557).

[1] Ps. Ecberti Pœnit. Lib. I. cap. 11, 12 (Ibid. pp. 321-22).

[2] C. Londiniens. ann. 1102, cap. 28 (Harduin. VI. I. 1866).

[3] Alani de Insulis Lib. Pœnitent. Migne, CCX. 295).

[4] C. Eboracens. ann. 1195, cap. 11 (Harduin. VI. II. 1932).—Adami Persenniæ Abbatis Epist. XXVI. (Migne, CCXI.).

[5] Constitt. Synodal. Odonis Episc. Paris. circa 1198, cap. vi. § 5 (Harduin. VI. II. 1940).

tary homicide, counterfeiting the episcopal seal, redemption and commutation of vows, restitutions of more than twenty sous, sorcery committed with the Host or chrism, carrying arms and errors condemned by pope or bishop.[1] How completely the bishops retained control over the sacrament and assumed that the priests exercised only delegated power is manifest in the regulations of Everard of Amiens (p. 230), in 1219, after the Lateran council had conferred exclusive jurisdiction on the parish priests with no exceptions in favor of the bishops.

It thus was recognized that, in spite of the Lateran canon, the bishop in each diocese, acting individually or in his synod, should designate the sins which he reserved to his own jurisdiction, and that the priest should have cognizance only of the remainder. In view of the power to bind and to loose conferred in ordination, this was an arbitrary limitation of the power of the keys, but the incompatibility between the old episcopal function of reconciliation and the new sacramental theories had to be reconciled in some way, and as usual the doctrine of jurisdiction was invoked to accomplish this. Aquinas thus explains that the power of the keys conferred on priests extends to all sins, but for its exercise jurisdiction is required, and the bishop, in granting jurisdiction, can subject it to such limitations as he sees fit. Aquinas proceeds to enumerate five cases which must be referred to the superior prelate, an enumeration showing how confused was as yet the distinction between the *forum internum* and *externum.* These are, I. when solemn penance is to be imposed; II. excommunication pronounced by a superior; III. irregularity requiring dispensation by a superior; IV. arson; V. when in any diocese it is the custom to refer enormous crimes to the bishop.[2] Thus every see was a law unto itself, and the variations were infinite. The council of Mainz, in 1261, reserves no episcopal cases and leaves everything to the priest save what was assigned to the pope, while

---

[1] Cartularium Ecclesiæ Parisiensis, Tom. I. p. 3. The expression "Istos casus reservat sibi episcopus in confessionibus" shows that the reservation concerns the *forum internum.*

[2] S. Th. Aquinat. in IV. Sentt. Dist. XIX. Q. 1, Art. 3; Summæ Suppl. Q. XX. Art. 2.

St. Bonaventura (Confessionale, Cap. iv. Partic. 2) only specifies arson as a reserved episcopal case, but adds that each diocese has its own customs. Cf. Hostiens. Aureæ Summæ Lib. v. De Pœn. et Remiss. § 14.

those of Arles, in 1275, of Cologne, in 1280, and of Nîmes, in 1284, give long lists of reserved cases.[1] The tendency evidently was to their multiplication, which Benedict XI., in 1304, apparently endeavored to check, in his bull *Inter cunctas*, by declaring that the episcopal cases were arson, voluntary homicide, forgery, violation of ecclesiastical liberties and immunities, and sorcery, but this bull was revoked in the Council of Vienne, in 1312, and received little respect, though it served, as we shall presently see, as a basis for claims by the Mendicant friars to disregard the episcopal prerogative.[2] In 1324, the council of Toledo complains of the indiscretion of priests who absolve indiscriminately for perjury, leading to great injustice to individuals and loss of the rights of churches, wherefore this is declared to be a reserved case.[3] In fact, with the strongly marked tendency to laxity in the confessional, this seemed to be the only method by which rigorist bishops could exercise a control over the sacrament, and they were disposed to make the most of it, as did Bishop William of Cahors about this period, leaving little for his parish priests to absolve.[4]

---

[1] C. Mogunt. ann. 1261, cap. 8 (Hartzheim III. 548).—C. Arelatens. ann. 1275, cap. 12, 13 (Harduin. VII. 729-30).—C. Colon. ann. 1280 cap. 8 (Ibid. p. 829).—C. Nemausens. ann. 1284 (Ibid. pp. 913-14).

[2] Cap. 1 Extrav. Commun. Lib. v. Tit. vii.—Cap. 2 Clement. Lib. iii. Tit. vii.

[3] C. Toletan. ann. 1324, cap. 18 (Aguirre V. 257).

[4] Epist. Synod. Guillel. Episc. Cadurcens. circa 1325, cap. 14 (Martene Thesaur. IV. 692-3). His list includes all notorious sins which scandalize the people, also heresy, simony, irregularity, arson, enormous public blasphemy, commutation and breaking of vows, together with such cases as the bishops are accustomed to reserve, as in Rodez, namely, homicide, overlying children, sacrilege, forging and falsifying episcopal or papal letters, church-breaking, violation of ecclesiastical liberties, sorcery if grave (especially if with the Eucharist, the chrism and the like), unnatural crimes, bestiality, fornication with Jewess or Saracen, incest, defloration, seduction of nuns, perjury, clandestine marriage, promotion *per saltum* in orders, ordination by a bishop other than one's own, fornication in a church, palming adulterine children on a husband by his wife, abortion, false witness, marriage after betrothal to another, disturbance of divine service by excommunicates, burying excommunicates in consecrated ground, seduction by confessors, violence offered to parents, schism, carelessness leading to accidents at the altar, restitution or distribution of unclaimed ill-acquired gains amounting to more than forty *sous caourcins*, and all doubtful questions, especially respecting marriage.

Dr. Eck, in the Leipzig Disputation, admitted the abuse of reservation,

There was one limit to the exercise of this arbitrary discretion by the bishop, for as usual the Roman chancery turned to profitable account the supreme jurisdiction claimed by the Holy See. Plenary indulgences, with choice of confessors, of course overrode all episcopal reservations, and if these could be issued by the pope there was no reason why faculties enabling priests to set episcopal regulations at defiance should not be granted to those willing to pay for them. Accordingly letters of this kind were for sale to all applicants, empowering them for ten years to absolve for all cases save those reserved to the pope. For these, in 1338, the scrivener's fee was ten *gros tournois,* or one gold florin, besides two *gros* to the procurator for drawing up the petition, and whatever other charges might be made for engrossing, bullation, registering, etc.[1] It is not likely that these letters were issued in large numbers, for there can scarce have been motive on the part of many priests to procure them, unless some rich parishioner desired to escape his bishop, but there was at least occasional demand for them up to the sixteenth century.[2] It was probably through speculative motives only that Boniface IX., in 1402, revoked all which he had issued, on the ground of their abuse and of the scandal which they occasioned.[3] That priests occasionally emancipated themselves from the limitations imposed on them, without taking the trouble to procure these papal letters, is indicated by the severe penalty of suspension, leading in six days to excommunication, denounced for such offences, in 1389,

especially when it was dictated by avarice, in having pecuniary mulcts attached. —M. Lutheri Opp. Jenæ, 1564, T. I. fol. 276*b*.

[1] P. Denifle, Die älteste Taxrolle der Apost. Pönitentiarie (Archiv für Litt. und Kirchengeschichte, IV. 232, 235, 237).

By the end of the fifteenth century the price was raised to twenty-five *gros.* —White Hist. Library, Cornell Univ. A. 6124.

The form of application was "Supplicatur Sanctitati Vestræ a rectore parochiali etc. quatenus omnes homines utriusque sexus parochiæ suæ ab omnibus peccatis nisi talia sint de quibus merito sedes apostolica sit consulenda, valeat absolvere hinc ad decennium de gratia Vestra speciali."—Denifle, *loc. cit.*

[2] Jan. 16, 1514, one is issued to the Augustinian friar Geronimo, which excepts only the papal cases enumerated in the bull *in Cœna Domini.*—Hergenröther, Regesta Leonis X. n. 6303.

[3] Regulæ Cancellariæ Bonif. PP. IX. n. 73 (Ottenthal, p. 76).

by John, Bishop of Nantes, whose list of reserved cases was nearly as long as that of his brother of Cahors.[1]

In 1408, at the council of Reims, John Gerson pleaded earnestly against the extension of the system of reserved cases and pointed out not only the hardships which it inflicted on all penitents, but the infamy to which it exposed them, especially women, whose husbands and kindred were naturally led to suspect their virtue when they were often thus sent from a distance to procure episcopal absolution. Under this impulsion the council ordered visitors to be dispatched to all parishes with powers to absolve for reserved cases; if the parish priest was competent they were to give him a faculty for the purpose; if not, some fitting priest in the vicinage was to be selected as a local penitentiary.[2] The impression made by Gerson passed away, and, in the latter half of the century, the councils of Amiens and Tournay show the catalogue of episcopal cases to be enormously overgrown. In the former a list under forty heads embraces almost all offences, besides which all doubtful cases are to be sent to the bishop; in the latter, after a schedule of episcopal cases comes one of those reserved to the rural deans, and then follows an enumeration of the few that are left to the priest, while at the same time the bishop, Cardinal Ferry de Cluny, revoked all the faculties granted to deans and others to absolve for the episcopal cases.[3] In this, as we shall presently see, the bishops had a motive arising from their sempiternal conflict with the hated Mendicants, but none the less was it a severe hardship on the faithful. St. Antonino complains loudly of the result, and gives a list of thirty-six papal reserved cases followed by fifty-seven episcopal, which shows how narrow a field was left almost everywhere for the parish priest; nor was this all, for it surrounded the confessor with pitfalls from which the greatest care could scarce preserve him.[4] In 1528, Martin de

---

[1] Statut. Joh. Episc. Nannetens. ann. 1389, cap. 13 (Martene Thesaur. IV. 985).

[2] C. Remens. ann. 1408 (Gousset, Actes etc. II. 658, 661, 664). As early as 1260 a somewhat similar expedient was in force in Arles, as we have seen (p. 234).

[3] C. Ambianens. ann. 1454, cap. 5, § 4; C. Tornacens. ann. 1481, cap. 4 (Gousset, II. 709–11, 752–4).

[4] S. Antonini Confessionale, fol. 5–6, 14–15.—Bart. de Chaimis Interrog. fol. 5, 6, 10a.

Frias quotes approvingly John Gerson's assertion that the bishops by these reservations plunged innumerable souls into hell; it was difficult enough for the confessor to extract confessions, especially from bashful women and girls, and when they had to be sent a distance for a second confession and episcopal absolution they mostly refused to go.[1]

It is small wonder that Charles V., in his Formula of Reformation in 1548, desired to simplify the confessional, for both the confessor and the penitent, by abolishing all reserved cases,[2] but the bishops at the council of Trent were disposed to strengthen rather than to abandon a power of so much importance to them in their struggle with the Regulars. They therefore defined that bishops have authority, each in his own diocese, to reserve such sins as they see fit, that their action in this is good before God, the only exception being that in peril of death any priest can absolve for any sin.[3] The matter was thus placed beyond further discussion, and it rested with each bishop to use his prerogative wisely. Since then the only interference with it occurred in the proposed reforms of Leopold of Tuscany, in 1785, when, after pointing out the hardships to which penitents were exposed, he invited his bishops to grant faculties to all their parish priests to absolve for reserved cases, and Ricci, Bishop of Pistoia, promptly did so. The latter, in his synod of 1786, took no systematic action, but reservation was described as an improvident limitation of sacerdotal authority, and a hope was expressed that by a reformation of penitential processes it would become no longer necessary—criticisms which Pius VI. emphatically condemned as false, audacious, injurious to hierarchical power and derogatory to the authority of the council of Trent and of the Holy See.[4] Liguori is, therefore, safe in asserting that there is no limit to the exercise of this episcopal authority, although some doctors hold

---

[1] Martini de Frias de Arte et Modo audiendi Confessiones, fol. lxa. Martin proceeds to give a list of forty-seven cases regularly reserved to bishops by law and custom, which might be increased indefinitely, at the whim of the prelate.

[2] Formulæ Reformationis, cap. 13 (Le Plat, Monum. Conc. Trident. IV. 88).

[3] C. Trident. Sess. xiv. De Pœnit. cap. 7.

[4] Atti e Decreti del Consiglio di Pistoja, p. 154; Append. No. xi. xii.—Pii PP. VI. Bull. *Auctorem Fidei*, 1794, Prop. 44, 45.

that it cannot be carried to the point of morally incapacitating priests from the performance of their duty.[1]

The arbitrary exercise of this episcopal prerogative in each diocese necessarily introduces an element of uncertainty in the confessional which has its perplexities. Saulius, writing in 1578, instructs confessors to send every year to the Ordinary of the diocese to ascertain what changes have been made.[2] In 1579, S. Carlo Borromeo ordered his bishops to print lists annually and distribute them among their priests,[3] and in 1581 St. Toribio of Lima threatened with prosecution all priests who did not possess one.[4] In 1855 the council of Ravenna ordered that in every confessional there should be posted a copy of the bull *in Cœna Domini*, together with a list of the episcopal cases of the diocese,[5] and this, as a convenient mode of supplementing the memory of the confessor, may presumably be assumed to be a common practice. Where every bishop follows his own discretion, of course there can be no uniformity, and how slender was the discretion with which this arbitrary power was sometimes exercised is manifest when, in 1614, the Congregation of Bishops and Regulars felt obliged to decree that dancing in Lent ought not to be made a reserved case.[6] Usually, however, bishops have in modern times not pushed their authority so unreasonably. Father Gobat, in 1666, says that there are usually seven or eight cases—murder, arson, sacrilege, perjury and false witness, forgery, sorcery, blasphemy, adultery and other enormous crimes, but he adds that in the diocese of Constance there were forty-three.[7] La Croix, about 1715, enumerates those of a number of German bishoprics, varying from Munster, where violence to a cleric was the only one, and Mainz, where there

---

[1] S. Alph. de Ligorio Theol. Moral. Lib. VI. n. 519.

[2] Saulii Comment. in Confessionale Savonarolæ, Taurini, 1578, fol. 11.

[3] C. Provin. Mediolan. V. ann. 1579 (Acta Eccles. Mediolan. I. 229).

[4] Synod Liman. I. ann. 1581, cap. 10 (Harold. Lima Limata, p. 199). In consideration, however, of the "poverty and imbecility" of the Indians, St. Toribio empowered their confessors to absolve for all episcopal cases (C. Provin. Liman. I. ann. 1583, act. II. cap. 17). Paul III., about 1540, had authorized all confessors throughout the Indies to absolve for the papal cases contained in the bull *in Cœna Domini* (Harold, p. 112).

[5] C. Ravennat. ann. 1855, cap. 5 § 4 (Coll. Lacens. VI. 159).

[6] Pittoni Constitutiones Pontificiæ T. VII. n. 601. More significant in the same decree is the prohibition to reserve simple fornication by secular priests.

[7] Gobat Alphab. Confessar. n. 364-5.

were three—voluntary homicide, rape and arson—to Liége, where there were twenty.[1] Caramuel, in 1656, says, as a Spaniard, that he he had lived in Spain for many years and had never heard of a reserved case, and therefore he regarded it merely as a speculative matter,[2] but Corella, about 1700, tells us that he had taken infinite pains to gather correct information from all the Spanish sees, and gives, with appropriate comments, the reserved cases in all that he could obtain; they show for Pampeluna 31, Burgos 32, Calahorra 30, Tarazona 12, Toledo 10, Saragossa 9, Valencia 9, Sigüenza 13, Seville 8, Segovia 14, Salamanca 27, Valladolid 7, Palencia 13, Tarragona 19, Barcelona 14, Gerona 5, Vich 15, Tortosa 11, Lérida 12, Solsona 12 and Urgel 10.[3] In view of the assertion of the council of Trent that these somewhat eccentric proceedings of the bishops are ratified by God, one is somewhat puzzled by the assertion of Father Gobat that when a sin becomes especially prevalent it ceases *ipso facto* to be reserved; thus in Germany the reading of heretic books is so universal that it would be impossible to send all the offenders to Rome for absolution, and therefore in practice it is treated as not reserved—with what result to the salvation of the sinners he does not tell us.[4] When such laxity was recognized we need scarce wonder at the complaint of the council of Bordeaux in 1583 that some priests, disregarding the risk to themselves and their penitents, recklessly granted absolution for the gravest offences without caring whether they were reserved to pope or bishop.[5]

There are two classes of episcopal reserved cases—those which the bishop reserves of his own authority and those which he causes to be proclaimed in a diocesan synod. The doctors draw a distinction between them, the reservation of the former expiring with the death of the bishop, while the latter are perpetual until revoked. They argue that the synodal reservation is by Christ, who does not die;

---

[1] La Croix Theol. Moral. Lib. VI. P. ii. n. 1636–44.

[2] Caramuelis Theol. Fundament. n. 631.

[3] Corella Praxis Confession. P. I. Tract. xi. §§ 2–22. In the list of Seville there is a sin entitled *Renuevos*, which seems to be of doubtful significance, as it is explained by some to be stealing the shoots of mulberry trees and by others to be giving old wheat for new—a species of usury.

[4] Gobat Alphab. Confessar. n. 355.

[5] C. Burdegalens. ann. 1583, cap. 12 (Harduin. X. 1347).

it is he who reserves the cases to the bishop, not the bishop to himself.[1]

The matter is additionally complicated by the existence of another class of cases reserved to the Holy See for absolution, though these, with scarce an exception, are offences carrying with them *ipso facto* excommunication, the removal of which can only be effected by the pope or through powers delegated by him, after which absolution for the sin can be granted by any confessor.[2] The origin of the custom has been the subject of a good deal of discussion, more or less superfluous, for excommunication can only be removed by the power which imposes it, or by a superior one, and when censures are inflicted by the Holy See it alone can delegate authority to absolve for them.[3] It is true that, before the sacramental system and the power of the keys were thoroughly elaborated, cases of peculiar difficulty or atrocity, especially when ecclesiastics were the victims, were frequently referred to the pope for assessment of penance. Thus in one of the Penitentials there is a provision that the murderer of a cleric or of a near kinsman must make a pilgrimage to Rome and perform whatever penance may be prescribed by the pope,[4] though elsewhere there are innumerable other regulations setting forth the precise penance for every grade of such offences, and in some of them, as we have just seen (p. 312), in many places the murderer of a priest or bishop was sent to the king for judgment. There is ample store of examples in the papal letters of the decisions of the popes in cases thus sent to them, and the matter was regulated by the council of Limoges, in 1032, which provided that when, as often happened, bishops in

---

[1] Viva, Trutina Theolog. in Prop. xii. Alex. PP. VII. n. 14.

[2] Cabrini Elucidar. Casuum Reservator. P. I. Resol. 5. Simony in ordination was made an exception to this by Sixtus V. in 1588 (Ibid.). Liguori states (Theol. Moral. Lib. VI. n. 580) that there are only two papal cases without censures attached—accusing of solicitation an innocent confessor and accepting gifts of over ten Roman crowns from Regulars of either sex without making restitution.

[3] Ferraris (Prompta Biblioth. s. v. *Absolutio* Art. 1, n. 1) sees this, for he cites as authority for papal reservation only a decretal of Gregory IX., about 1229, which has nothing to do with the subject beyond an incidental assertion that the superior can bind and loose the inferior, not the latter the former (Cap. 16 Extra Lib. I. Tit. xxxiv.).

[4] Pœnit. Ps. Ecberti Lib. IV. cap. 6 (Wasserschleben, p. 333).

doubt sent penitents to Rome, the judgment of the pope should be respected, while it resolutely declared that no one should go to Rome for penance without the knowledge of his bishop.[1] Evidently as yet there were no special papal cases; the bishops considered the whole subject to be under their exclusive control, though they were frequently glad to have the benefit of the superior wisdom and learning of the Holy See in matters which puzzled them or when dealing with troublesome penitents.[2] In addition to this were cases in which popes themselves had intervened with excommunications, as when Philippe I. of France and the Countess Bertrade of Anjou, barefooted and humble, in the guise of penitents, appeared before Lambert of Artois, swore to renounce each other and were relieved from excommunication and reincorporated in the Church by him under commission from Paschal II.;[3] or when the Emperor Henry IV., in 1105, applied for release from excommunication to the Legate Richard of Albano, who refused on the ground that he had no power and that the pope alone could do it.[4]

All these were sporadic individual cases. The earliest general legislation creating a papal reserved case would appear to be that of the second Lateran council, in 1139, which decreed that whoever, at the instigation of the devil, should lay violent hands on a cleric or monk, incurred excommunication removable by no bishop, but must present himself to the pope and receive his sentence—a decree which was duly carried into the canon law.[5] Yet, when, in 1170, Thomas Becket was assassinated, and Bartholomew, Bishop of Exeter, applied to Alexander III. for instructions as to the punishment of those implicated, although the pope replied asserting his right to decide difficult cases, it was in a manner to show that he was glad to exercise a power that was by no means recognized as a matter of course.[6]

---

[1] C. Lemovicens. ann. 1032 Sess. II. (Harduin. VI. I. 890–1).

[2] See, for instance, Alex. PP. II. Epistt. 64, 115, 116, 117, 141 etc.

[3] Harduin. VI. I. 1799, 1877.

[4] Conr. Urspergens. Chron. ann. 1106.—Annal. Hildesheim. ann. 1105.—Annalista Saxo, ann. 1106.

[5] Cap. 29 Caus. XVII. Q. iv.—Quarrels in monastic life were frequent, leading to mutual violence, and it was found undesirable to send the culprits from their cloisters to Rome, wherefore Alexander III. (Post Concil. Lateran P. XIV. cap. 8) empowered the abbots to settle such matters at home, a regulation which continued in force.

[6] Alex. PP. III. Epist. 1014 (Migne, CC. 894).—Post. Concil. Lateran. P. XXXV. cap. 1.

The whole matter remained in the vaguest and most uncertain condition. During the remainder of the twelfth century the popes claimed exclusive jurisdiction over arson, spoliation of churches and entering a nunnery with evil intent,[1] while, in 1189, the council of Rouen added perjury to the list, and that of Paris, about 1198, included simony,[2] yet the latter in one clause specifies three papal cases and in another gives a current verse enumerating six, while, in 1217, Richard Poore, of Salisbury, only specifies two, violence to clerics and church-burning.[3] Still there seems as yet to have been no direct jurisdiction recognized; the culprit was sent to the bishop, and by him transmitted to Rome with letters,[4] and as late as 1235 St. Ramon de Peñafort merely mentions five episcopal cases, and adds that some of these are sent by the bishops to the Holy See.[5] Evidently thus far the papacy had not asserted any general claims, and each diocese followed its own customs. Even in 1252, Innocent IV., in granting a commission to the Bishop of Avignon to preach the crusade and absolve for papal cases only specifies two—violence to clerics and church-burning.[6] Soon after this Cardinal Henry of Susa contents himself with repeating the statement of St. Ramon de Peñafort,[7] but about the same period the council of Mainz, in 1261, specifies violence to clerics, church-burning and simony committed in orders as cases reserved to the pope.[8] Aquinas gives a list of six papal reserved cases, omitting simony and adding church-breaking, falsify-

---

[1] Post Concil. Lateran. P. xiv. cap. 2.—Cap. 1, 4, 5, 6, 9, 19, 22, 24 Extra Lib. vi. Tit. xxxix.

[2] C. Rotomagens. ann. 1189, cap. 26; Constitt. Synod. Odonis Paris. cap. vi. § 6 (Harduin. VI. ii. 1908, 1940).

[3] Constitt. Odonis cap. vi. § 4; Constitt. Richardi Episc. Sarum ann. 1217, cap. 28 (Ibid. VI. ii. 1940, VII. 97). The verse alluded to thus distinguishes episcopal and papal cases—

> Incestum faciens, deflorans aut homicida
> Pontificem quæras: Papam si miseris ignem,
> Sacrilegus, patris percussor, vel Sodomita,
> Si percussisti clericum, Simonve fuisti.

[4] C. Aquileiens. ann. 1184 (Harduin. VI. ii. 1883).—C. Rothomagens. *loc. cit.*—Post. Concil. Lateran. P. xiv. cap. 5.—Constitt. Odonis Paris. *loc. cit.*

[5] S. Raymundi Summæ Lib. iii. Tit. xxxiv. § 4.

[6] Raynald Annal. ann. 1252, n. 26.

[7] Hostiens. Aureæ Summæ Lib. v. De Pœn. et Remiss. § 14.

[8] C. Mogunt. ann. 1261, cap. 8 (Hartzheim III. 598).

ing papal letters, communicating with those excommunicated by name by the pope, and participating with excommunicates in their crimes.[1] About 1300 Boniface VIII. added a somewhat peculiar offence—disembowelling a corpse and boiling the bones, when those who died abroad desired to be buried at home.[2] Yet, almost immediately after this, an elaborate collection of the statutes of Cambrai makes no allusion to papal cases, but includes them all among episcopal; apparently, as St. Ramon had stated, it was still a matter wholly within the discretion of the bishop, and the same conclusion may be drawn from the silence of other councils of the fourteenth and fifteenth centuries when treating of reserved cases.[3] Indeed, Astesanus, after enumerating the episcopal cases, gives no list of papal ones, but says that the bishops send some of their own to Rome, when they are especially grave, in order to strike terror, but this is discretional and not a matter of law,[4] and Durand of S. Pourçain explains that Rome never reserved the direct absolution of any sins, but only the removal of certain excommunications and the granting of certain dispensations, commutations of vows and the like.[5] Meanwhile, in 1312, the council of Vienne had decreed three new papal reserved cases when committed by friars—administering sacraments, other than penitence, without the consent of the parish priest, illegally absolving excommunicates, and undertaking to absolve *a culpa et a pœna*.[6] Presumably the fact that all papal cases are " censures "[7]—that is, excommunications, absolution from which

---

[1] S. Th. Aquin. in IV. Sentt. Dist. xviii. Q. ii. Art. 5.

[2] Cap. 1 Extrav. Commun. Lib. iii. Tit. vi. This seems to be still in force in the seventeenth century, for Manuel Sa (Aphor. Confessar. s. v. *Excom. reser.* § 11) explains that it does not apply to kings, nor to those dying among the infidels, nor to anatomical pursuits.

[3] Statut. Eccles. Camerac. ann. 1300–1310 (Hartzheim IV. 68).—Epist. Synod Guillel. Cadurcens. circa 1325, cap. 14 (Martene Thesaur. IV. 693).—Statut. Johann. Nannetens. ann. 1389, cap. 13 (Ibid. pp. 985–6).—C. Ambianens. ann. 1454, cap. 5 § 4 (Gousset, Actes, etc. II. 709–11).—C. Tornacens. ann. 1481, cap. 4 (Ibid. pp. 752–3).

Yet, in 1409, we find Henry, Bishop of Nantes, ordering all parish priests to have written lists of both papal and episcopal cases (Martene Thesaur. IV. 994).

[4] Astesani Summæ Lib. v. Tit. xxxix. Q 3.

[5] Durand. de S. Porcian. in IV. Sentt. Dist. xvii. Q. 15.

[6] Cap. 1, Clement. Lib. v. Tit. vii.

[7] B. de Chaimis Interrog. fol. 110a.—Henriquez Summæ Theol. Moral. Lib. vi. cap. xiv. n. 1.—Jacobi a Graffiis Practica Casuum Reserv. Lib. i, cap. iv.

is a condition precedent to sacramental absolution—may partly explain this confusion, but evidently the whole subject was as yet imperfectly systematized.

It came up for consideration at the council of Constance, in 1414, where a *Collegium Reformatorium* was appointed to draft a project of reform. In this body it was proposed to commit these cases to the bishops or other official in the dioceses, but, after some debate as to secret sins, it was unanimously agreed that public cases should be left to the Holy See.[1] The list of papal cases was growing through the operation of the bull *in Cœna Domini,* or the anathema launched by the pope on certain solemnities at sinners of sundry kinds. The custom had commenced in the thirteenth century under Gregory IX. for the destruction of heresy, and had gradually grown and become an annual ceremony, embracing a considerable variety of offences specially obnoxious to the Holy See. Although, in the earlier formulas, there is no special reservation of absolution to the pope, this was assumed as a matter of course, and, in 1364, Urban V., referring to the earlier bulls, places the offences therein enumerated under the jurisdiction of his chamberlain.[2] When thus, about 1450, St. Antonino enumerates thirty-six papal cases, they are nearly all sins comprised in these bulls.[3] There was a speculative value in this, which the curia was not slow in improving, for the crusading and Jubilee indulgences contained a clause empowering the purchaser to select a confessor who could absolve him for these cases, and in addition confessional letters or *Beichtbriefe* were issued, granting special faculties for them. In 1466 Paul II. made a rule in his chancery, which, in 1469, was published in his bull *Etsi Dominici Gregis,* wherein, to diminish the facility of pardon that renders the faithful more prone to sin, he declares that no faculties heretofore granted shall avail to absolve for sins reserved to the Holy See, namely, infringements on ecclesiastical liberties, violation of papal interdict, heresy, conspiracy, rebellion or other offence against the person or

---

Reg. 5.—Corella, Praxis Confess. P. I. Tract. xi. § 1, n. 1.—Th. ex Charmes Theol. Univ. Dissert. v. cap. vi. Q. 4.

[1] Reformatorii Protocollum, cap. 30 (Von der Hardt, I. x. 631).

[2] Raynaldi Annal. ann. 1220 n. 23; ann. 1229 n. 37–41.—Nich. PP. III. Bull. *Noverit universitas,* 1280 (Bullarium, I. 156).—Urbani PP. V. Bull. *Apostolatus,* 1364 (Ibid. p. 261).

[3] S. Antonini Summa Confessionum, fol. 14–15.

state of the pope, presbytericide, personal offence of a bishop or other prelate, invasion or plunder of any State subject directly or indirectly to the Holy See, assault on pilgrims coming to Rome, prohibition of appeals to the curia, conveying arms or prohibited wares to the infidel, the imposition of new burdens on churches or clerics, simony in obtaining orders or benefices, and generally all the cases contained in the bull *in Cœna Domini.* Special licence was in future to be required in all these cases, and all general commissions were declared not to cover them.[1] Having thus cleared the market, there must have sprung up a lively demand for these special licences, for, in 1478, Sixtus IV. tried another similar stroke of trade. He deplored the stimulus to evil and the contempt for the power of the keys which he had caused by the reckless issue of indulgences, enabling the purchaser to select a confessor who could absolve him from reserved sins once in life and once *in articulo mortis,* and from other sins as often as required, thus exposing him to no little danger of perdition. To remedy this he repeats the enumeration of reserved sins made by Paul II., and declares that all absolution of them by virtue of his letters shall be invalid, and any confessor granting it shall be excommunicated, nor shall any future letters be held to convey such power unless they contain a clause derogatory of the present constitution.[2] Thus the market was cleared a second time, and the derogatory clause was easily inserted in the subsequent issue. These *Beichtbriefe,* authorizing absolution for all papal reserved cases, were sold in Germany for a quarter of a gulden apiece,[3] and it is no wonder that Dr. Eck, at the Leipzig disputation of 1519, admitted that he agreed with Gerson at the council of Constance in desiring a limitation put on the reservation of cases to the Holy See.[4]

---

[1] Cap. 3 Extrav. Commun. Lib. v. Tit. ix. The reservation of heresy to the pope shows the progress of the triumph of the Holy See over the episcopate, for this had, from time immemorial, been specially subject to the jurisdiction of the bishops.

[2] Cap. 5 Extrav. Commun. Lib. v. Tit. ix.

[3] Gröne, Tetzel und Luther, p. 196.

[4] Lutheri Opp. Jenæ, 1564, I. 256a.

As the progress of the Lutheran heresy grew alarming, Clement VII., in 1526, granted a faculty to all provincials and ministers of the Observantine Franciscans empowering them to absolve all Lutherans seeking to return to the Church, notwithstanding all previous constitutions and especially those of

At the council of Trent, in 1563, the bishops made an effort to withstand these papal encroachments by defining that the reservation should be limited to public offences, and that in all secret sins, even in those reserved to the pope, the bishop should have power to absolve his subjects in the forum of conscience, either personally or by deputy, except that in cases of heresy he must act personally.[1] Though the council was under the direct inspiration of the Holy Ghost and its decrees were promptly confirmed in January, 1564, by Pius IV., his imperious successor, St. Pius V., was not disposed to submit to this invasion of the papal prerogative, and in publishing the bull *in Cœna Domini* he not only retained the clause reserving to the pope the exclusive right of absolution, but added to it the defiant phrase " nor under pretext of any faculties conferred by the decrees of any council, by word, by letter, or by other writing," a formula which was rigidly maintained by his successors. As the council of Trent was the only one which had conceded to bishops this faculty of absolution, this clause was understood to be in direct derogation of it, and was so declared by Pius V., Gregory XIII., and Clement VIII., and repeatedly by the Congregation of the Council, August 21, 1609, July 7, 1617, and November 5, 1644.[2] The issue thus raised as to the supremacy of pope or council was a knotty

Leo X.—Bulario del Orden de Santiago, I. 97 (Archivo Histórico Nacional de España).

[1] C. Trident. Sess. XXIV. De Reform. cap. 6. Of course a debate arose as to the definition of *casus occultus.* Some held that the test was whether it could be proved or not in a court of justice; others that it was occult if it was not notorious to the whole community, though it might be known to three or four or seven or eight persons, and could be judicially proved. The Congregation of the Council of Trent decided rather vaguely that when the sin is known to two persons the penitent's conscience is not rendered safe by the episcopal absolution, because a crime can be proved by two witnesses.—Cabrini Elucidarium Casuum Reservator. P. I. Resol. cxi.—C. A. Thesauri de Pœnis Ecclesiast. P. I. cap. xxi —Barbosa Summa Apostol. Decis s. v. *Absolutio* n. 10.

There was also a fine distinction drawn between the forum of conscience and forum of penitence.—Cabrini, Resol. cxii.

[2] Ferraris Prompta Biblioth. s. v. *Absolvere* Art. 1.—Barbosa Summa Apost. Decis. s. v. *Absolvere* n. 3, 4.—C. A. Thesauri de Pœnis Ecclesiast. p. 335. In 1601 and 1602 Clement VIII. also forbade all priests to absolve for the *Cœna Domini* cases.—Jac. a Graffiis Practica Casuum Reservat. Lib. I. cap. 4, Reg. 18.

point concerning which the doctors differed, some inclining to one side and some to the other, and some discreetly avoiding committal.[1] Finally an assertion became current that the cardinals in consistory, on July 18, 1619, had pronounced in favor of the council of Trent and the episcopal power, an assertion which Alexander VII. condemned in 1665.[2] The condemnation was cleverly drawn so as only by implication to condemn the episcopal claim, and the controversy continued, the episcopal partisans asserting that it did not affect the main question, and the papalists arguing that if it did not do so there would have been no use in uttering it; that treated by the rules of probabilism it showed that the probability of the episcopal claims had been diminished by it and were consequently less worthy of respect in practice.[3] Thus the wrangle went on. In 1705 Wigandt asserts absolutely the validity of the Tridentine decree and makes no allusion to the papal attempts to override it.[4] Yet the popes continued to publish the bull *in Cœna Domini* with the derogatory clause, and Ferraris assumes that it is effective.[5] On the other hand, the Gallican Church asserted the power of the bishops to define and limit the number of papal reserved cases; this varied in the different dioceses, and in that of Paris only eight were recognized.[6] With the discontinuance of the annual publication of the *Cœna Domini* bull, in 1773, by Clement XIV., the immediate question ceased to be discussed, but that the papacy, with the disappearance of the Gallican pretensions, has been able to assert its supremacy is seen by the revision of the whole subject of censures *latæ sententiæ* made by Pius IX. in 1869, wherein he specifies thirteen offences, the absolution of which is specially reserved to the Holy See, seven others simply so reserved, three reserved to bishops, and four (together with nine prescribed by the council of Trent) which are not

---

[1] Em. Sa Aphorismi Confessar. s. v. *Absolutio* n. 4.—Summa Diana s. v. *Absolutio a reservatis* n. 3.—Henriquez Summæ Theol. Moral. Lib. VI. cap. xiv. n. 7.—Jacobi a Graffiis Practica Casuum Reservat. Lib. I. cap. 1, n. 15.—Escobar Theol. Moral. Tract. VII. Exam. iv. cap. 7, n. 37.—Gobat Alphab. Confessar. n. 370.

[2] Alex. PP. VII. Decret. 1665, Prop. 3.

Corella Praxis Confessionalis P. I. Tract. 1, cap. 1.—Viva Trutina Theol. in Prop. 3 Alexandri PP. VII.

[4] Wigandt Tribunal Confessar. Tract. XIV. Exam. ii. n. 71.

[5] Ferraris Prompta Biblioth. s. v. *Absolvere*, Art. I. n. 4.

[6] Héricourt, Loix ecclésiastiques de France, T. II. p. 14.

subject to any reservation. Not only is every one prohibited from absolving for those specially reserved, but any one attempting it under any pretext whatever thereby falls under excommunication reserved to the pope, and no distinction is recognized between public and secret sins.[1]

A system so artificial and so complicated inevitably gave rise to a large number of doubtful and puzzling questions, especially in the treatment of episcopal cases involving sacramental absolution. Ingenious as were the intellects which evolved the sacramental theory they were unable to make it fit at all points with the customs that had become traditional, and especially with the control which the bishops had always exercised over the reconciliation of sinners, a control which they were not willing to abandon. The doctrine of jurisdiction, however astutely thought out and applied, removed some of the incongruities but not all. It was self-evident that there could be no partial absolution; a man must be in a state of grace or of sin; he cannot be pardoned for one sin and not for all; he cannot at the same time be a friend and an enemy of God. It was, moreover, a corollary from this and an accepted rule that a confession to be valid must be complete; the *confessio dimidiata*, or imperfect confession, is invalid. It was also a rule that no man is to be obliged

---

[1] Pii PP. IX. Bull. *Apostolicæ Sedis*, 12 Oct. 1869.

There is no penalty for absolving knowingly for cases simply reserved to the Holy See or for those reserved to bishops.—Varceno Compend. Theol. Moral. Tract. XVIII. cap. vi. art. 4.

The bull of Pius IX. shows a great reduction and simplification of censures. In 1578, Saulius enumerates seventy-seven reserved papal cases; thirty-six from the *Corpus Juris* and forty-one from the bull *in Cœna Domini* (Saulii Comment. in Savonarolæ Confessionale, fol. 9–13). In 1692, Cabrino gives a list of twenty from the *Cœna Domini* and eighty-two from the *Corpus Juris* and papal decrees (Elucidar. Casuum Reservat. pp. 175–9), and not long afterwards Noël Alexandre catalogues 216 papal cases, besides thirty-four sometimes reserved to the pope and sometimes to bishops (Summæ Alexandrinæ P. II. n. 51–300).

Yet the theologians had little scruple in arguing away the papal reservations under the convenient plea of ignorance more or less invincible. This is especially manifested in the matter of duels, any participation in which was reserved by Clement VIII., in 1592, by the bull *Illius vices*, yet for which no one had any trouble in obtaining absolution from the local clergy.—Stadler, S. J. Tract. de Duello, cap. VIII. art. ii. § 6 (Ingolstadtii, 1751).

to confess the same sin twice, while sacramental confession must be made to the absolver, as otherwise the sacrament is incomplete, and it cannot be divided.[1] Now all these inviolable principles were incompatible with the practical treatment of a penitent guilty of both reserved and unreserved sins. At first the somewhat crude expedient was adopted of requiring the priest to whom the confession was made to bring the sinner to the bishop, or send him with letters detailing his sins and all their circumstances.[2] The former expedient entailed a labor on the priest which he was not likely to submit to; the latter was a violation of the seal of the confessional, which was beginning to be enforced, and yet it remained in use for centuries. Thus the solution, however illogical, generally adopted of the difficulty, lay in requiring the penitent to confess in full to his parish priest, receive absolution for such sins as were not reserved, and then be dispatched to the bishop to be absolved for the rest, with a letter, if he was too simple to explain the matter.[3] Yet this was not satisfactory in principle or wholly settled in practice, and Astesanus discusses at much length whether the first confession should be made to the priest and the second to the bishop, or *vice versa*, whether both confessions should be full or partial, whether both bishop and priest should impose penance and both absolve, in a manner to show how difficult and doubtful were the questions involved.[4] Pierre de la Palu describes four methods; he tells us that

---

[1] S. Th. Aquinat. in IV. Sentt. Dist. XVIII. Q. ii. Art. 5; Q. iii. Art. 3.—P. Lombard. Sentt. Lib. IV. Dist. XV. § 3.—Decr. Unionis in Concil. Florent. ann. 1439.

[2] Constitt. R. Poore Episc. Sarum ann. 1217, cap. 29; Constitt. S. Edmund. Cantuarens. ann. 1236, cap. 20; Concil. Anglican. *sine dato* (Harduin. VII. 97, 271, 308).

[3] S. Th. Aquin. in. IV. Sentt. Dist. XVII. Q. iii. Art. 4 ad 4.—Jo. Friburgens. Summæ Confessar. Lib. III. Tit. xxxiv. Q. 73 —Summa Pisanella. s. v. *Confessor* I. § 2.—S. Antonini Confessionale fol. 3*b*, 68*b*.—Bart. de Chaimis Interrog. fol. 107*b*.—Savonarolæ Confessionale fol. 63*a*.

The formula of letter as given by St. Antonino and Bart. de Chaimis shows us what was currently used towards the end of the fifteenth century—"Latorem vel latricem pro homicidio vel incestu in tali grado et hujusmodi commisso absolvendum vestræ paternitati transmitto ut absolutionis beneficio imponendo et ei pœnitentiam salutarem injungendo ipsum sanctæ ecclesiæ reconcilietis."

It will be seen how complete in this was the disregard of the seal of confession.

[4] Astesani Summæ Lib. v. Tit. xviii.

the one detailed above was that commonly practised, and he labors exhaustively to prove that the two absolutions are in fact only one.[1] Difficult as it was to devise a method of procedure, it was still more difficult to frame a line of argument that would reconcile any of them to the sacramental theory. Durand de St. Pourçain freely admits the impossibility of this; he presents and discusses four different solutions and then abandons the attempt in despair, saying that he is unable to explain it, for confession and absolution cannot be divided and parcelled out.[2] One solution that found considerable favor was rather damaging to the power of the keys; it was that all the sins were remitted by God through the preceding contrition, and that the successive absolutions of priest and bishop were merely reconciliations to the Church, which could be divided.[3] Angiolo da Chivasso in his discussion of the question only shows how incapable of resolution it was, and how its debate by the doctors only tangled it up more inextricably.[4] Prierias quotes approvingly the suggestion of Henry of Ghent that the superior, if first confessed to, does not absolve but only releases from the obligation of confessing to him; if the inferior is first confessed to, he absolves from all, but not from the obligation of confessing to the superior.[5]

The perplexity did not diminish with time. Domingo Soto dwells on the impropriety of dividing the confession and alludes to the diversity of opinion among the doctors as to the proper method to be pursued. The usual course, he says, is to make a full confession to the priest, who absolves for what he can and sends the penitent to the bishop for the rest, but whether he is then to make a second full confession is doubtful. Yet a better course is first to confess the reserved sins to the bishop, accept penance, and then make full confession to the priest and obtain absolution for all.[6] The council of Trent cautiously abstained from settling any of the doctrinal points involved and contented itself with telling priests that, as they can do

---

[1] P. de Palude in IV. Sentt. Dist. XVII. Q. 5, Art. 1. He states that this was the custom of the Papal Penitentiary, to absolve for the graver mortal sins and send the penitent home for absolution from the rest.

[2] Durand. de S. Porciano in IV. Sentt. Dist. XVII. Q. 15.

[3] Gab. Biel in IV. Sentt. Dist. XVII. Q. 1, Art. 3, Dub. 2.

[4] Summa Angelica s. v. *Confessio* v. §§ 9, 10.

[5] Summa Sylvestrina s. v. *Confessio* I. § 20.

[6] Dom. Soto Comment. in IV. Sentt. Dist. XVIII. Q. ii. Art. 5.

nothing with reserved cases, they must labor to send penitents to their superiors for absolution, but it did not even say whether the whole confession is to be repeated or not to the latter.[1] Bartolomé de Medina recommends that either the sinner or the priest should apply to the bishop for a faculty; if the bishop refuses, then the sinner should confess the reserved case to him and accept penance, getting a faculty for the priest to whom he then makes full confession and receives full absolution.[2] This preliminary recourse to the bishop seems to have been the ruling custom at the end of the sixteenth century, as it is recommended by both Saulius and Manuel Sa, though the latter asserts unqualifiedly that the sinner can divide his confession and receive absolution for each portion separately, in which he is supported by Escobar.[3] On the other hand, Chiericato and Viva declare with equal positiveness that if confession is made to the bishop he must give complete absolution; he cannot absolve for part and send the sinner to his confessor for the rest, nor can the confessor absolve him for the unreserved sins and send him to the bishop for the reserved ones. Tournely only states the conflicting opinions, and does not venture to decide the question. Noël Alexandre says that most theologians hold that the two absolutions are morally one, but he does not see how a man can be at the same time a friend and an enemy of God. Habert advises the priest not to absolve, but to send the penitent to the bishop for absolution for all his sins.[4]

In fact, how absolutely impossible it has proved to arrive at any certainty in a matter where man seeks arbitrarily to prescribe laws for the infinite, is seen in Liguori's discussion of it. He tells us that if a man has mortal sins, both reserved and unreserved, it is a disputed point whether he must confess before receiving the Eucharist.

---

[1] C. Trident. Sess. XIV. De Pœnit. cap. vii.

[2] Bart. a Medina Instruct. Confessar. Lib. II. cap. 1.

[3] Saulii Comment. in Savonarolæ Confessionale fol. 84b.—Em. Sa Aphor. Confessar. s. v. *Absolutio* n. 24, 25.—Escobar. Theol. Moral. Tract. VII. Exam. iv. cap. 5, n. 31.

[4] Clericati de Pœnit. Decis. XXIII. n. 15, 16; XLV. n. 14.—Viva Cursus Theol. Moral. P. VI. Q. 5, Art. 7, n. 6.—Tournely de Sacr. Pœnit. Q. VI. Art. iv.—Summæ Alexandrinæ P. I. n. 463.—Habert Praxis Sacr. Pœnit. Tract I. cap. 1, n. 12.

For further questions and details concerning these points see Henriquez Summæ Theol. Moral. Lib. VI. cap. xv. n. 4, 5.—Layman Theol. Moral. Lib. v. Tract. vi. c. 12, n. 7, 8.

A host of great authorities hold that he need not, if he has contrition, because the confession to a priest must be invalid, for as absolution cannot be divided, neither can confession. The other opinion, that he must confess, is more common and more probable, because as there is a divine precept that confession must precede communion, there should be confession *formaliter integra* if it cannot be *materialiter integra.* But there is also a disputed question whether, in such confession, the reserved sins should be included as well as the unreserved ones. The common opinion is in the affirmative, but the negative is equally and even more probable, as otherwise he would have to confess the same sins twice, which no one is required to do, nor is any one required to confess sins to one who has not jurisdiction over them.[1] Thus, after struggling with the problem for six hundred years the Church is still in the Serbonian bog of insoluble doubt.

These remarks of Liguori point to one of the most perplexing aspects of the question, for though reserved cases may give abundant annoyance to a layman he can generally afford to wait, while a priest obliged to celebrate mass must act at once or create "scandal" by admitting his unfitness. Anything is preferable to this, and an ingenious evasion of the difficulty has been devised by the discovery of what is known as indirect absolution. Thus, if the bishop hears the sinner first, he absolves directly for the reserved sins and indirectly for the unreserved; if the first confession is made to the priest he absolves directly for what is under his jurisdiction and indirectly for the rest. It is true that in the latter case the sinner is required subsequently to procure full absolution from one having authority, but it answers for the moment and serves the purpose of a guilty priest who has a confessor at hand in the sacristy. Liguori explains that the sinner must confess other mortal sins not reserved, or if he has none, then some venial sins or else some old mortal ones previously remitted, when, in receiving absolution for them, the reserved sin is indirectly absolved, though he must subsequently confess it to one having jurisdiction, nor do the moralists in recommending this course seem to recognize the incongruity of thus creating an artificial state of grace, sufficient for receiving and administering the sacraments, while yet there is a mortal sin awaiting absolution. It is not easy to

---

[1] S. Alph. de Ligorio Theol. Moral. Lib. VI. n. 265.

conceive how men who devise and suggest such practices can have any real belief in the sacredness and efficiency of the sacraments, and yet this course is approved by Benedict XIV.[1] One is tempted to inquire whether they believe that it was for such ends that Christ bestowed on the apostles the keys of heaven and hell.

While thus the question of reserved sins is of moment to priests compelled to celebrate, it has lost much of its importance in modern times as regards the laity. It is generally admitted that the bishop cannot absolve for a part and send the penitent to his confessor for the rest, and it is held that the confessor should absolve for what he can and send him for reserved sins to one having a faculty or apply for one himself.[2] It is true that this does not solve the doctrinal difficulties involved, but as they have proved themselves insoluble they are best passed over in silence. The easiest mode of cutting the Gordian knot is for the bishop to grant faculties for the absolution of reserved cases, and the only objection to it is that it is practically an acknowledgment of the impracticability of the time-honored system which grew up as a compromise in the struggle of bishop and priest for control over the confessional. Thus the general recommendation to confessors called upon to deal with a reserved case is to apply to the bishop for a faculty to absolve for it, which bishops are advised to grant with facility and gratuitously—in fact, the bishop commits sin who refuses, especially if he knows that the penitent cannot be induced to come to him.[3] We have seen that during the middle ages

---

[1] Eisengrein Confessionale Cap. iii. Q. 36 (Ingolstadii, 1577).—Layman Theol. Moral. Lib. v. Tract. vi. cap. 12, n. 7, 8.—Gobat Alphab. Confessor. n. 120, 369.—Cabrini Elucid. Casuum Reservat. P. I. Resol. xv.—Benzi Praxis Trib. Conscientiæ Disput. I. Q. ii. Art. 1, Par. 2, n. 12.—S. Alph. de Ligorio Theol. Moral. Lib. VI. n. 585.—Th. ex Charmes Theol. Univ. Diss. v. cap. vi. Q. 4.—Bened. PP. XIV. Cas. Conscient. Oct. 1736, cas. 3.

Similar in spirit is the trick recommended to a confessor who has a reserved sin and desires to avoid the shame of appearing before the bishop. He is told to apply for a faculty in blank to absolve for a reserved case, and then, if his name does not appear in it, he can get himself absolved by any other confessor. —Clericati de Pœnit. Decis. XLV. n. 15.—Cabrini Elucid. Casuum Reservat. P. I. Resol. xx.

[2] Varceno Comp. Theol. Moral. Tract. XVIII. cap. vi. Art. 4.

[3] S. Antonini Confessionale, fol. 3b.—Savonarolæ Confessionale fol. 63a.— Dom. Soto in IV. Sentt. Dist. XVIII. Q. ii. Art. 5.—Escobar Theol. Moral. Tract. VII. Exam. iv. cap. 5, n. 31.—Cabrini Elucid. Casuum Reservat. P. I.

it was customary in some dioceses for the bishop to constitute delegates in many places, so that penitents could have easy access to them, and this practice has been continued. S. Carlo Borromeo thus empowered all his *vicarj foranei*, who were further authorized to subdelegate their powers to proper persons, and when it was inconvenient to send penitents to them, the confessors were invited to apply for special faculties.[1] In 1601 the Sacred Congregation of Bishops and Regulars instructed bishops thus to provide for the convenience of their people.[2] That this was largely obeyed may be assumed from the complaint of the Jansenist Van Espen, about 1700, that the salutary influence of reserved cases in repressing serious sin is so largely neutralized in many places by the carelessness of bishops in granting faculties to improper persons.[3] While thus reducing the hardships attendant on the reservation of cases in a manner which demonstrates its conviction of the uselessness of the system, the Church has maintained the principle, as it is bound to do under the Tridentine decree, and we have seen how decisively Pius VI., in the constitution *Auctorem fidei*, condemned its proposed abandonment in the Tuscan reforms of the Grand Duke Leopold.

Resol. xxxvi.—S. Alph. de Ligorio Theol. Moral. Lib. vi. n. 586.—Kenrick Theol. Moral. Tract. xviii. n. 166.

The modern form of application for a faculty is—

"Illustrissime ac Reverendissime Domine,
   Titius (vel Titia) incidit in casum reservatum in Tabella Diœcesana sub N. Facti ipsum (vel ipsam) pœnitet et humiliter petit absolvi.
   Faveat rescriptum dirigere ad me confessarium,
                              Humilissimum Servum N.N."

The confessor signs his name and gives a fictitious one for the penitent. The sin is not described, but is designated by the number which it bears in the table of cases for the diocese. The correspondence is to be burnt.—Varceno Comp. Theol. Moral. Tract. xviii. cap. vi. Art. 4.

   [1] S. Carol. Borrom. Instructio (Ed. 1676, p. 57).

   [2] Jac. a Graffiis Pract. Casuum Reservat. Lib. i. cap. iii. n. 5.—Clericati de Pœnitent. Decis. xlv. n. 13.   Superiors of religious orders are likewise required to make similar provision for the local absolution of sins reserved within the Order (Bizzarri Collectanea Sacr. Cong. Episc. et Regular. pp. 275, 916).   In 1761 the General Minister of the Capuchins ordered that in each province or convent there shall be at least two penitentiaries with faculties for reserved cases (Bern. a Bononia Man. Confessar. Ord. Capuccin. cap. vi. § 3).

   [3] Van Espen Jur. Eccles. P. ii. Tit. vi. cap. 7, n. 25.

A further alleviation of the rigor of the system was granted in the admission of lawful impediments which may prevent the sinner from seeking absolution at the hands of the pope. This commenced almost as soon as papal reservation was established. It was manifestly impossible in many cases for the sinner to make the pilgrimage to Rome, and, from the time of Alexander III. onward, disabilities of many kinds were admitted to release him from its performance and to authorize his transfer to the bishop. Sickness, penury, age, youth, sex, danger, any impediment in fact, was thus allowed to justify the local absolution of those unable to apply in person to the pope, though they were obliged to promise or to give security to do so as soon as the impediment, if a temporary one, should disappear—except in the case of youth—under penalty of the revival of the censure.[1] Whether, under the circumstances, priests can absolve as well as bishops is a question which has excited much debate. Aquinas holds that they can, and so does Liguori, but Viva seems to incline to the negative.[2] The cases embraced in the bull *in Cœna Domini* have also given rise to prolonged discussion, as the only exception admitted in the bull itself is *in articulo mortis,* but the majority of authors seem to be of the opinion that impediments justify bishops in absolving for them also.[3] The thirteen cases specially reserved to the Holy See by the constitution *Apostolicœ Sedis* of 1869 replace those of the obsolete bull *in Cœna Domini.* A decision of the Congregation of the Inquisition in 1886, approved by Leo XIII., prohibits the absolution of

---

[1] Post Concil. Lateran. P. XIV. cap. 12, 13.—Cap. 3, 6, 11, 13, 33, 58 Extra Lib. v. Tit. xxxix.—Cap. 22 in Sexto Lib. v. Tit. xi.—Constitt. Coventriens. ann. 1237 (Harduin. VII. 286).—Summa Diana s. v. *Absolvere a censuris* n. 42. —Ferraris Prompta Biblioth. s. v. *Absolvere* Art. I. n. 5–8.

Ferraris gives this metrical enumeration of legitimate impediments—

> Regula, mors, sexus, hostis, puer, Officialis,
> Delitiosus, inops, ægerque, senexque, sodalis,
> Janitor, adstrictus, dubius, causæ, levis ictus,
> Debilis, absolvi sine summa sede merentur.

For clericide, however, women and monks were required to make the journey to Rome.—Libellus Taxarum, fol. 18*a* (White Hist. Library, A. 6124).

[2] S. Th. Aquin. in IV. Sentt. Dist. XVIII. Q. ii. Art. 5.—Summa Diana s. v. *Absolvere a reservatis* n. 3.—S. Alph. de Ligorio Theol. Moral. Lib. VI. n. 585.— Viva Trutina Theolog. in Prop. 3 Alex. PP. VII.

[3] Viva *loc. cit.* Ferraris *loc. cit.*—Clericati de Pœnit. Decis. XLV. n. 4, 5, 8.— Cabrini Elucid. Casuum Reservat. P. I. Resol. xcix.

these by either bishop or priest, but in cases of risking grave scandal or infamy the local confessor can remove the censure under pain of reincidence if the culprit does not within a month appeal to the Holy See by letter through his confessor.[1]

The question whether, in episcopal reserved cases, impediments enable the sinner to be absolved by his confessor is one on which opinions differ. The council of Trent specified that in them the only exception should be *in articulo mortis*, but priests assumed the power to absolve in such cases where there was an impediment. Clement VIII., in 1601 and 1602, strictly forbade this for the future, and Ferraris, about the middle of the eighteenth century, positively asserts that there is no rule permitting it.[2] On the other hand, practical writers of authority assume as a matter of course that if the penitent cannot go to the bishop without peril of life or reputation or the danger of creating "scandal" he can be absolved by a simple confessor; how this is accomplished however is not unanimously explained, for the moralists generally assert that it is done indirectly, while some hold that it is God who does it. Whether, after the impediment ceases, the penitent must present himself to one having authority and obtain absolution is a matter hotly disputed by the doctors.[3] In this shape, as we have seen, it affords a convenient outlet for a priest obliged to celebrate, in spite of the decrees of Clement VIII., for the pressure of necessity in such cases is universally recognized as justifying absolution on the spot.[4]

The question whether inculpable or invincible ignorance on the part of a penitent relieves him of the reservation of his sin has been variously argued. To admit it, as some authorities do, as a general principle, is putting a premium on avoiding knowledge of the list of reservations in a diocese, and the weight of opinion seems to be in favor of the distinction that, in reserved sins which are evils of themselves, ignorance grants no exemption, while it does in those which are merely statutory. Yet Roncaglia tells the confessor, to whom a reserved sin is confessed, to ask the penitent not only whether he

---

[1] Varceno Comp. Theol. Moral. Tract. XVIII. cap. vi. Art. 4.

[2] Jac. a Graffiis Pract. Casuum Reservat. Lib. I. cap. iv. Reg. 18.—Ferraris Prompta Biblioth. s. v. *Absolvere* Art. 1, n. 27–8.

[3] Clericati de Pœnit. Decis. XLV. n. 12.—Bernard. a Bononia Man. Confessar. Ord. Capuccin. cap. vi. § 5.

[4] Varceno Comp. Theol. Moral. Tract. XVIII. cap. vi. Art. 4.

knew the fact of the reservation, but also whether he thought of it at the time of commission, for, if he did not, what the moralists call "inculpable inadvertence" relieves him from the reservation and he can be absolved.[1]

Of course the death-bed is an insurmountable impediment, and the general rule that absolution is never to be refused to a repentant and dying sinner applies to reserved cases. This, however, was not admitted at first, for a bull of Clement III. to the dean of S. Pierre de Lille, about 1190, grants as a special privilege that he shall absolve *in articulo mortis* those of his clergy who have committed sins involving their applying to the Holy See for penance.[2] Absolution in peril of death, however, raises a question on which there has not been unanimity of opinion, for the penitent may survive, and in such case his condition has been the subject of debate. In 1304 Benedict XI. in his bull *Inter cunctas* decides that in such case the penitent must present himself to his bishop and obey his mandates both as to the sin and any excommunication involved.[3] As we have seen, this bull was revoked by the council of Vienne, but towards the end of the fifteenth century Bartholommeo de Chaimis repeats its prescription, and a century later Bartolomé de Medina holds that the sin is not remitted and absolution for it must be had of the bishop.[4] Later authorities however seem to be in accord that the penitent is fully absolved from his sin, but not from any excommunication incurred; for the latter he must apply to the bishop, unless indeed he has obtained a death-bed indulgence, in which case he is relieved from all.[5]

A more puzzling question is when a confessor, through design, inadvertence or ignorance grants absolution for a reserved case.

---

[1] Cabrini Elucid. Casuum Reservat. P. I. Resol. xxxi.—Roncaglia Univ. Moral. Theol. Tract. I. Q. ii. cap. 3, Q. 3.—Liguori at first taught that invincible ignorance of the reservation relieves the sinner from it, but he subsequently changed his opinion.—Theol. Moral. Lib. VI. n. 581. Cf. Elenchus Quæstionum Q. 83.

[2] Pflugk-Harttung, Acta Pontiff. Rom. inedd. I. n. 437.

[3] Cap. 2 Extrav. Commun. Lib. v. Tit. vii.

[4] Bart. de Chaimis Interrog. fol. 12.—Bart. a Medina Instruct. Confessar. Lib. I. cap. 10.

[5] S. Antonini Confessionale, fol 70.—Corella Praxis Confession. P. I. Tract. xi. § 1, n. 4.—Th. ex Charmes Theol. Univ. Diss. v. cap. vi. Q. 4.—Kenrick Theol. Moral. Tract. xviii. n. 161.

The earlier doctors were divided as to whether the absolution was valid; Aquinas only expresses himself doubtfully in favor of its nullity, while, at the close of the fifteenth century, Angiolo da Chivasso thinks that the penitent may be absolved in virtue of his good faith.[1] The opinion of its invalidity finally prevailed, and since the council of Trent it is considered to be settled in view of the decree that God ratifies the act of the bishop.[2] Such being the case the priest who has committed the mistake is placed in an awkward position. Bartholommeo de Chaimis advises him honestly to notify the penitent so that he may obtain valid absolution,[3] but the reputation of the confessor is too important to be exposed to such risk, and various deceits and evasions are recommended to avoid the damaging admission. St. Antonino, Baptista Tornamala and Angiolo da Chivasso suggest, in accordance with a discussion on the subject that took place at the council of Bâle, that, if it can be done without causing scandal, the confessor should quietly procure a faculty and then send for the penitent, pretend that he has not understood him, make him repeat his confession and absolve him; or, if this is likely to cause scandal, he may be absolved *in absentia* without knowing it, though others hold that he may be left to Christ, the high priest.[4] Azpilcueta and Zerola would prefer procuring a faculty and absolving the penitent personally, but, if there is danger of scandal or trouble, the absolution can be secretly given *in absentia*, nor need the penitent then be in a state of grace.[5] When Clement VIII. forbade absolution *in absentia* this became impracticable, and about 1620 Martin van der Beek recommends the method which has been continued in modern practice, namely, to procure a faculty and absolve if it can be done without risk of scandal; if not, to leave the penitent to the mercy of God,[6] which would seem to be an admission that,

---

[1] Jo. Friburgens. Summæ Confessor. Lib. III. Tit. xxxiv. Q. 74.—Summa Pisanella s. v. *Confessor* I. § 2.—Summa Angelica s. v. *Confessio* v. § 13.

[2] Astesani Summæ Lib. v. Tit. xxxix. Q. 3.—Weigel Clavis Indulgentialis cap. vii.—Bart. de Chaimis Interrog. fol. 92*a*.—Summa Sylvestrina s. v. *Confessio sacr.* I. § 20.—Palmieri Tract. de Pœnit. p. 180.

[3] B. de Chaimis, *loc. cit.*

[4] S. Antonini Summæ P. III. Tit. xvii. cap. 12.—Summa Rosella s. v. *Confessor* I. § 7.—Summa Angelica s. v. *Confessio* v. § 13.

[5] Azpilcueta Manuale Confessar. cap. xxvi. n. 14.—Zerola Praxis Sacr. Pœnit. cap. xxiv, Q. 16.

[6] Becani de Sacramentis Tract. II. P. iii. cap. 38, Q. 13.—Th. ex Charmes

after all, absolution is of less importance to the penitent than is his reputation to the priest. A still more perplexing question is when a nun confesses a reserved case and refuses to let the priest apply for a faculty to absolve her lest she or the convent should be exposed to loss of reputation ; this, as Chiericato assures us, makes the confessor sweat and shiver, and the moralists are much at a loss to advise what should be done.[1]

When absolution for a reserved case has been given in ignorance there is diversity of opinion among the authorities, some holding that it is good, others that it is invalid, while others draw a distinction between crass and invincible ignorance and argue that in the former it is invalid and in the latter good. Since the development of probabilism the ruling school of moralists consider that, if the confessor has a probable belief that the case is not reserved, whether it be so in reality or not, the absolution is good, for under such circumstances the Church is conveniently held to supply the deficiency of jurisdiction. Moreover, if the penitent has a probable opinion that the case is not reserved and the confessor a more probable opinion that it is reserved, the penitent's opinion must be followed and the confessor must absolve him. In cases of doubt the confessor can absolve if the doubt is positive ; if it is negative, opinions are divided—positive doubt in these matters being whether the penitent has committed the sin, negative being whether the sin is reserved.[2]

Another doubtful question is whether internal sins are included in the reservation ; that is, sins mentally conceived but not carried into effect by any external act. Thus, according to some authorities, if a

---

Theol. Univ. Diss. v. cap. vi. Q. 4.—Varceno Comp. Theol. Moral. Tract. XVIII. cap. vi. Art. 4.—The rule is now absolute that absolution must be given in the presence of the penitent, though there are nice questions as to the intervening distance allowable.—Varceno, Tract. XVIII. cap. iv. Art. 5.

[1] Clericato de Pœnit. Decis. XLI. n. 11–18.

[2] Summa Diana s. v. *Absolvere a reservatis* n. 21, 33.—Alph. de Leone de Off. et Potest. Confessar. Recoll. II. n. 120.—Cabrini Elucid. Casuum Reservat. P. I. Resol. xv.—Bernard. a Bononia Man. Confessar. Capuccin. cap. iv. § 2.— S. Alph. de Ligorio Theol. Moral. Lib. VI. n. 581, 596, 600.—Varceno Comp. Theol. Moral. Tract. XVIII. cap. vi. Art. 3, § 4.

If, in a doubtful case, a penitent is absolved by a simple confessor and afterwards learns that the case is reserved beyond doubt the absolution holds good. —Cabrini *loc. cit.* Resol. xi.

man thinks to himself, "There is no hell," or "Catholicism is no better than Calvinism," he can be absolved for the heresy by any confessor, but if he utters it aloud, even in solitude, it is reserved.[1] Others, however, say that the sin must be fully consummated to fall under the reservation, and that an unsuccessful attempt to commit it is not reserved unless the bishop has expressly so defined it in his decree. Whether, in fact, it is possible to reserve internal sins is a disputed question, some moralists holding that it is not, others that it is, but that to do so is not in accordance with custom.[2]

Another point of some practical importance that has caused considerable debate arises out of the difference in reservation in the various dioceses and the movement of penitents from one to the other. The sinner may have committed in one diocese a sin which is reserved there, and may confess it in another where it is not reserved, or *vice versa*, and the doctors are by no means in accord as to which jurisdiction should be considered as controlling the matter at the time of confession, though the general practice is to absolve or refuse absolution according to the reservation of the place of confession, provided the change of residence has been *bona fide* and not to escape severer regulations of the first domicile.[3] Even when the sin is reserved in both dioceses, the simpler question of what is to be done with strangers and travellers is not without its complications and difficulties.[4]

When a bishop commits a sin which he has reserved in his diocese, he can confess to any confessor, nor is it necessary for him to go through the form of granting a faculty for the purpose, although he is authorized to do so by a decision of the Congregation of Bishops and Regulars. An episcopal vicar-general, however, who commits

---

[1] Gobat Alphab. Confessar. n. 351.

[2] Bart. a Medina Instruct. Confessar. Lib. I. cap. 10.—Marchant. Tribunal Animar. Tom. I. Tract. II. Tit. iv. Q. 6, Concl. 2.—Cabrini Elucidar. Casuum Reservat. P. I. Resol. vii., viii.—Clericati de Pœnit. Decis. XLIV. n. 9.—Layman Theol. Moral. Lib. V. Tract. vi. cap. 12.—Bernardi a Bononia Man. Confessar. Capuccin. cap. iv. § 2.—Kenrick Theol. Moral. Tract. XVIII. n. 157.

[3] Martini de Frias de Arte et Modo audiendi Confess. fol. lxxia.—Escobar Theol. Moral. Tract. VII. Exam. iv. cap. 7, n. 38.—Tamburini Method. Confess. Lib. III. cap. vi. § 2.—Casus Conscientiæ Bened. PP. XIV. Dec. 1744, cas. 2.— S. Alph. de Ligorio Theol. Moral. Lib. VI. n. 588-9.—Varceno Comp. Theol. Moral. Tract. XVIII. cap. vi. art. 4.

[4] S. Alph. de Ligorio *loc. cit.* n. 590-3.—Varceno *loc. cit.*

such a sin must first grant the faculty and then make confession. Whether a parish priest who holds a general faculty for reserved cases can delegate this when he requires absolution for himself is a disputed question, with the probabilities in favor of the affirmative.[1] These are by no means the only doubtful and debatable points connected with the reservation of cases, but they will probably suffice to justify Rosemond's remark that reserved cases are snares for men which he declines to discuss and sends his readers to St. Antonino.[2] He could scarce have anticipated that these snares would be pronounced by the council of Trent to be a divine device.

In the prolonged struggle over the confessional between the secular and the regular clergy, reserved cases played a conspicuous part. The first allusion I have met concerning it occurs in 1289, when Nicholas IV., in permitting the Benedictine nuns of S. Paolo of Orvieto to confess to Dominicans, empowered the latter to absolve for episcopal cases.[3] There must have been a general claim on the part of the Mendicants to exercise such power, for, when Boniface VIII. endeavored to settle the quarrel by promising papal faculties to Mendicants whom the bishops refused to license, he added that they could only perform the functions of parish priests.[4] This denied them jurisdiction over episcopal cases, and when, in 1304, Benedict XI. enlarged their privileges, he maintained this restriction, but alluded to episcopal cases as consisting of arson, voluntary homicide, forgery, violation of the liberties and immunities of the Church, and sorcery.[5] Though Benedict's bull was revoked, in 1312, by the council of Vienne, the Mendicants claimed that his enumeration of the reserved cases was simply declaratory of existing law and was not affected by the revocation; they quoted him as defining four cases to be reserved *de jure*, viz., clerical sins involving irregularity, arson, sins requiring solemn penance and major excommunication, and also five *de consuetudine*, being the six enumerated above, excepting arson.[6] For these they admitted that

---

[1] Cabrini *op. cit.* P. I. Resol. xvi. xix. xxxiv.

[2] Godescalci Rosemondi Confessionale cap. xx. §§ 23, 24.

[3] Ripoll Bullar. Ord. Prædicator. II. 25.

[4] Cap. 2 Extrav. Commun. Lib. III. Tit. vi.

[5] Cap. 1 Extrav. Commun. Lib. v. Tit. vii.

[6] This is the enumeration given by St. Antonino (Summæ P. III. Tit. xvii.

the friars could not grant absolution; what else the bishops might reserve by decree or through their synods was binding on the parish priests, but not on the friars who were exempt from all episcopal control, who did not attend the diocesan synods and could not be expected to be familiar with the variations in the reserved cases. Besides, they added, the bishops were increasing enormously their lists of reservations, merely for the purpose of limiting the functions of the friars, which, as we have seen, was the truth, and they were not and would not be bound by such action.[1] Thus the quarrel went on, the Mendicants having the enormous advantage that nearly all the writers of authority were members of their Orders and asserted their claims, while, on the other hand, the bishops made what use they could of the power of reservation, at the expense of their own priests and people. The friars gained a decisive advantage when, in several bulls between 1545 and 1549, Paul III. granted to the Jesuits power to hear the confessions of all the laity and to absolve for all sins, even in papal cases, except those of the *Cœna Domini*— privileges of which the Mendicants speedily claimed the benefit.[2] The bishops had their turn at the council of Trent, where the terms of the decree respecting the episcopal reservation of cases were evidently framed to suppress this interference, but in spite of this the Mendicants and Jesuits continued to claim and exercise the right of disregarding their authority. At length the bishops obtained from Gregory XIII. a declaration of the Congregation of Bishops and Regulars that the privileges of the Regulars did not extend to episcopal cases, but, in 1583, the Jesuits had sufficient influence to procure from him a definition, *vivæ vocis oraculo*, that it was not his intention to derogate from the privileges of the Society, which he confirmed

---

cap. 11), who mingles Aquinas's list (supra p. 314) with that of Benedict. He probably only reflects the current views of the Mendicants, for he is followed by the other Summists.

[1] S. Antoninus *loc. cit. ;* Ejusd. Confessionale fol. 5, 6.—Summa Pisanella s. v. *Confessor* I. § 1.—Somma Pacifica cap. xxix.—Summa Tabiena s. v. *Dispensatio* § 15.—Bart. de Chaimis Interrogator. fol. 5, 6.—Summa Angelica s. v. *Confessio* III. § 28.—Summa Rosella s. v. *Confessor* II. *in corp.*

A statute of Soissons, about 1350, indicates the friction arising from the absolution of episcopal cases by the Mendicants.—Gousset, Actes etc. II. 578.

[2] Pauli PP. III. Bull. *Dilecti filii ;* Ejusd. Bull. *Licet debitum* (Litt. Apostol. Soc. Jesu, Antverpiæ, 1635, pp. 25, 48).

anew.[1] The struggle continued, and, in 1601 and 1602, Clement VIII. prohibited all Regulars in Italy, outside of Rome, from absolving for episcopal cases, together with those of the *Cœna Domini* and six others, viz., infraction of ecclesiastical immunity, violation of the cloisters of nuns, duelling, real simony, and *confidentia beneficialis*, which signifies procuring a benefice for a person, with an agreement that he will transfer it to the party procuring it, or will pay over the revenues or burden it with a pension. The Regulars were irrepressible, however, forcing at last Paul V., in 1617, to declare that, in spite of all prohibitions, many of them persisted in absolving for reserved cases, leading men to sin by the facility of absolution, wherefore he ordered the decrees of Clement VIII. to be inviolably observed. Yet, in spite of this, about 1620, the Jesuit Van der Beek asserts positively that his brethren have power to absolve for all sins save those of the *Cœna Domini*, and the practical use of these claims obliged Urban VIII., in 1629, to prohibit it again and declare that the Tridentine decree must be observed. Undaunted by this rebuff, they argued it away, by an ingenious series of technical reasoning, principally on the ground that it was only a decree of the Congregation of Bishops and Regulars, and had not the force of law, but only of a probable opinion ; in France especially they asserted that these decrees had never been received, and therefore were not binding. In 1647, the Congregation repeated the prohibition, but the Archbishop of Mechlin, in 1654, was obliged to complain to the Inquisition that the Regulars in his province paid no attention to it. Finally, in 1665, Alexander VII. formally condemned the proposition that the Mendicants can absolve for episcopal cases without a faculty from the bishop.[2] Yet a decision of the Congregation of the Council of Trent that the Jesuits could not absolve for episcopal

---

[1] The Mendicants made much use of *oracula vivæ vocis*—privileges which they claimed had been granted to them verbally by successive popes. Of course there could be no gainsaying such claims, and no limit to them until Urban VIII. was obliged to abolish all privileges based on this foundation.— Gobat Alphab. Confessar. n. 667–8.

[2] Jac. a Graffiis Pract. Casuum Reservat. Lib. I. cap. iv. Reg. 18.—Becani de Sacramentis Tract. II. P. iii. cap. 38, Q. 9, n. 3.—Compend. Privilegior. Soc. Jesu s. v. *Absolutio* § 1.—Ant. Arnauld, La Théologie Morale des Jésuites, pp. 193, 219.—Corella, Praxis Confession. P. I. Tract. xi. § 1, n. 6.—Viva Trutina Theol. in Prop. 12 Alex. PP. VII.—Clericati de Pœnit. Decis. XLV. n. 17.—Benzi Tribunal. Conscient. Disp. II. Q. 5 *ad calcem*.

cases except in virtue of privileges granted or confirmed subsequently to the council,[1] would indicate that they were quietly obtaining such privileges, and, in 1670, Clement X. felt it necessary to declare in the most authoritative way that the concessions to the Mendicants and Jesuits did not include the power to absolve for episcopal cases, that the confirmations obtained subsequent to the council of Trent did not revive them, and that the faculties granted for papal ·cases did not include episcopal ones.[2] So bitterly had this contest been carried on that the Regulars of Agen lodged with the Parliament of Bordeaux an *appel comme d'abus* against the bishop, and had influence enough to obtain an *arrêt* in their favor in 1666, but the case was appealed to the royal council, and Louis XIV. set the decision aside.[3] In spite of these repeated defeats, the Regulars still endeavored to maintain their ground, arguing that the old privileges of Pius III. were unaffected by the multitudinous subsequent legislation.[4] Curiously enough, Liguori reverses the view of the old Summists, and asserts the more probable opinion to be that Regulars can absolve for cases reserved to bishops *de jure*, though not for those which the bishops or synods reserve.[5]

As a whole, in the long struggle, the Regulars would seem to have been worsted by the bishops, although they still retained over the parish priests the advantage of being able to absolve for papal cases, except those of the *Cœna Domini* and the six reserved ones. This advantage, however, was taken away by Pius IX., in 1869, when he revised all the papal censures ; in doing so he revoked the privileges and faculties of all religious Orders to absolve for any of the papal cases still retained in vigor, and decreed that in future any concession granted must specifically state every case included in it.[6]

A considerable further inroad on episcopal reservation is made by the Jubilee indulgences, which commonly confer on those who obtain them the right to select a confessor, who, *ipso facto*, has faculty to absolve for all cases, however grave, and this has been decided by the Congregation of the Council of Trent to include all cases re-

---

[1] Barbosa, Summa Apostol. Decisionum s. v. *Absolutio* n. 6.
[2] Clement. PP. X. Constit. *Superna* §§ 6, 7 (Bullar. VI. 305).
[3] Juenin de Sacramentis Dist. VI. Q. vii. cap. 3, art. 3, § 4.
[4] Bernardi a Bononia Man. Confessar. Ord. Capuccin. cap. IV. §§ 2, 5.
[5] St. Alph. de Ligorio Theol. Moral. Lib. VI. n. 599.
[6] Pii PP. IX. Bull. *Apostolicæ Sedis*, 12 Oct. 1869.

served by bishops.[1] In a country like Spain, where the Cruzada indulgence is issued annually, and is largely taken by the pious, this must naturally neutralize to a great extent the episcopal power of reservation.[2]

---

[1] Barbosa, Summa Apost. Decis. s. v. *Absolutio* n. 5.

[2] Pii PP. IX. Bull. *Carissime* § 6, 4 Dec. 1877 (Salces, Explicacion de la Bula de la Santa Cruzada, p. 391).

CHAPTER XII.

THE CONFESSIONAL.

WHEN the Church had succeeded in establishing the necessity of sacramental confession, numerous questions of detail sprang up which required for their settlement long discussion by the theologians. Space will not here permit an exhaustive investigation of them all, but a cursory examination of some of the more important will show how the existing rules have been reached which govern the conduct of the confessional.

The schoolmen were not remiss in defining what are the requisites of a confession that shall entitle the penitent to absolution. Alain de Lille had contented himself with the three rudimentary conditions—contrition, confession, and the intention to sin no more.[1] S. Ramon de Peñafort advanced a step when he described valid confession as "amara, festina, integra et frequens"—bitter, speedy, complete and frequent.[2] When we reach Aquinas we find these qualifications expanded into a quatrain, which for centuries remained current among the theologians, all the points of which he tells us are requisite to the perfection of confession, though all are not essential to its validity—

> Sit simplex, humilis confessio, pura, fidelis,
> Atque frequens, nuda, discreta, libens, verecunda,
> Integra, secreta, lacrymabilis, accelerata,
> Fortis et accusans, et sit parere parata.[3]

These attributes divide themselves into the internal disposition of the penitent—the *dispositio congrua*—and his utterances to the confessor. The former group will be considered more conveniently hereafter, when we come to treat of absolution. At present we are more immediately concerned with the latter.

---

[1] Alani de Insulis Lib. de Pœnit. (Migne CCX. 300).
[2] S. Raymundi Summæ Lib. III. Tit. xxxiv. § 4.
[3] S. Th. Aquin. Summæ Suppl. Q. IX. Art. 4.

The *confessio integra*, the full and faithful confession of all mortal sins committed and not as yet remitted, is the most essential requisite, though full allowance is made for the imperfections of human memory, as we shall see in a subsequent chapter. Only what is confessed, or what is inculpably forgotten, can be the matter subjected to the keys, and no pardon can be granted for a portion of sins unless all are pardoned. There can be no partial reconciliation to God, and the wilful omission of a single mortal sin, constituting the *confessio informis* or *dimidiata*, renders the whole confession invalid and unsacramental; in fact, receiving the sacrament thus irreverently is a new sin.[1] No amount of contrition and of life-long penance self-imposed can wash away a sin thus concealed; every confession and communion is a fresh sin, and it were better for the penitent to live and die wholly without the sacraments.[2] As the council of Trent says, those who withhold anything knowingly submit nothing to God for pardon through the priest.[3] Even if a sin, withheld through shame, is drawn out by the questioning of the confessor, there have been rigid moralists who hold that the confession is fictitious and invalid.[4]

---

[1] Caietani Tract. v. De Confessione cap. 5.—There are plenty of marvellous stories illustrating this. Father Passavanti (Lo Specchio della vera Penitenza Dist. v. cap. iii.) tells us of a woman who kept back one sin in confession, and was condemned in consequence after death; at the intercession of St. Francis her soul was allowed to return to the corpse at her obsequies, when she confessed the omitted sin and was admitted to purgatory. Del Rio (Disquis. Magicar. Lib. ii. Q. xxvi. § 5) is authority for a tale, which was largely quoted by subsequent writers, of a baptized Peruvian slave-girl of dissolute life, who, on her death-bed, refused to confess her carnal sins, though she freely talked of them to others. She said that, when the priest came repeatedly and urged her to confess, a black dwarf appeared on one side of her bed and prevented her from making a full confession, though St. Mary Magdalen, on the other side, adjured her to do so. Her death was followed by the most terrifying evidences of her damnation. Chiericato (De Pœnit. Decis. xxiii. n. 5, 6) asserts that no holiness of life can save from perdition any one who consciously violates the sacrament by omitting a single mortal sin, and he adds that it was revealed to a holy hermit that there are three demons, one named *Claudens corda*, who closes the hearts of those listening to pious homilies; one named *Claudens crumena*, who leads penitents to evade making restitution; and one named *Claudens ora*, who induces them to make imperfect confessions, and each of these demons causes the ruin of multitudes of souls.

[2] Cherubini de Spoleto Quadragesimale Serm. lxii.

[3] C. Trident. Sess. xiv. De Pœnit. cap. 5.

[4] God. Rosemondi Confessionale, fol. 114.

Moreover, if the confessor knows that the penitent is guilty of a sin not included in the confession he sins in granting absolution, for he knows the sacrament to be invalid ;[1] to this, however, an exception is made when the confessor's knowledge comes from another confession, for then the seal prevents his making use of the knowledge, and he is perforce required to grant a sacrilegious absolution.[2]

In fact, the rule of completeness, like all other rules connected with the functions of the keys, was subject to exceptions rendered indispensable by human weakness, nor does the incongruity between this and the assumption that omissions are fatal to the sacrament appear to be recognized. Thus we are told that, if there is any danger to be anticipated from confessing a sin to the parish priest, either because he is known to be a solicitor to evil and the sin may excite his lust, or if it be a wrong committed against him or any of his kindred that may prompt him to vengeance, or if he be known as a revealer of confessions, or if it be feared that he may make a bad use of the knowledge to the injury of others, and if no other licensed priest is accessible, the penitent may prudently suppress the portion exposing himself or the priest or a third party to risk, and trust to God or to finding subsequently one to whom he may safely confide it.[3] Even shame, we are told, justifies suppression, especially on the part of women, and the confessor in such case may boldly absolve her, confiding in the mercy of God.[4] In fact, as Domingo Soto piously sums it up, a prudent and clement God does not require confession when it would involve grave peril, and therefore when there

---

[1] Jo. Sanchez Selecta de Sacramentis Disp. VIII. n. 6.

[2] Em. Sa Aphorismi Confessar. s. v. *Absolutio* n. 14.

[3] Bart. de Chaimis Interrog. fol. 10*b*.—Summa Tabiena s. v. *Confessio Sacr.* n. 14.—Summa Sylvestrina s. v. *Confessio Sacr.* I. §§ 4-6.—Mart. Eisengrein Confessionale, cap. iii. Q. 28-30.—Azpilcueta Man. Confessar. cap. viii. n. 5-6.—Em. Sa Aphorismi Confessar. s. v. *Confessio* n. 10.—Escobar Theol. Moral. Tract. VII. Exam. iv. cap. 5, n. 27.—Busenbaum Medullæ Theol. Moral. Lib. VI Tract. iv. cap. 1, Dub. 3, Art. 2.—Marchant Tribunal. Animar. Tom. I. Tract. II. Tit. vii. Q. 2. concl. 2; Tract. IV. Tit. vi. Q. 6.—Viva Trutina Theol. in Prop. 59 Innoc. PP. XI.—Layman Theol. Moral. Lib. V. Tract. vi. cap. 8.—Arsdekin Theol. Tripart. P. III. Tract. 1, cap. 1, Princip. 14.—Clericati de Pœnit. Decis. XXIII. n. 11, 14.—S. Alph. de Ligorio Theol. Moral. Lib. VI. n. 479-87.—Manzo Epit. Theol. Moral. P. I. De Pœnit. n. 35.—Gousset. Théol. Morale II. n. 433.— Varceno Comp. Theol. Moral. Tract. XVIII. cap. iv. Art. 5.

[4] Henriquez Theol. Moral. Lib. IV. cap. xxiv. n. 5.

is reason to dread risk to life or honor the sinner is not bound to confess.[1]

There are other causes of imperfect confession external to the penitent. Drowsiness or ignorance on the part of the confessor gives rise to perplexing questions, as we shall see hereafter. Ignorance of the language is likewise a recognized bar to perfect confession, but when the penitent does the best he can it is probable that the absolution is valid.[2] In a case of contagious disease the confessor can listen to a single sin and then hurriedly absolve the dying penitent.[3] The leading cause, however, of imperfect confession is when there are numbers to be heard and lack of time to give due attention to each. In case of battle or shipwreck this is inevitable, and the necessity of the circumstances is held to serve as a justification. A more frequent occasion, however, is the enormous afflux of penitents eager to gain some attractive indulgence to which confession is a condition precedent. When we read of the surging crowds flocking to the Roman Jubilees or to the Portiuncula indulgence of Assisi, we realize how impossible could have been any complete confession of the individual penitents. Father Gobat tells us that, at the Portiuncula, the Franciscans had the privilege of employing secular priests as temporary assistants, but this could only have been a partial remedy : he wishes that the Jesuits had the same advantage, for, on the three annual solemnities when their churches had an indulgence, the pressure was enormous. In the year in which he writes (1666), at Swiss Freiburg, on Quinquagesima Sunday, which was one of the indulgential days, they administered communion to over 9000 persons. In such case the confession could have been merely nominal, and his various allusions to the omissions necessary when there is a crowd of penitents show that it rendered the performance purely perfunctory.[4] From this

---

[1] Dom. Soto in IV. Sentt. Dist. xviii. Q. ii. Art. 5.—Summa Diana s. v. *Confessionis necessitas* n. 1–4. We shall see hereafter that modern theologians insist much more strongly on the necessity of complete confession, irrespective of the consequences to others.

[2] Em. Sa Aphorismi Confessar. s. v. *Absolutio* n. 9.

[3] Layman Theol. Moral. Lib. v. Tract. vi. cap. 13, n. 3.

[4] Gobat Alphab. Confessar. n. 105, 183, 325, 332. He tells us (n. 918) that he had heard much more (*longe plus*) than a hundred thousand confessions. He was then about sixty-five years old, and, assuming that he had been a priest for forty years, this would show an average of fifty confessions a week during a busy life-time. He further relates (n. 266) that the pious Father

necessity there naturally arose the general assertion that on such occasions imperfect confession suffices, but this was formally condemned by Innocent XI. in 1669.[1] Subsequent writers have accepted this as final, but it is presumable that the practice continues.[2] What is to be done under the circumstances is a point on which the authorities are by no means agreed.[3] Bishop Zenner, after insisting that each confession must be complete, no matter what may be the multitude waiting, adds that, after hearing some of the weightier sins, absolution can be given with the condition that the rest shall be confessed at another time,[4] which would seem to be an infraction of the rules condemning both partial and conditional absolutions, and indicates that in practice there is little respect for the elaborate theories on which rests the whole doctrine of the sacrament of penitence.

Yet it would in fact appear that confession must be complete, for the only reason given for its institution by Christ is the necessity that the priest should know all the sins on which he sits in judgment, specially and not merely in general, in order duly to apportion the penance.[5] Still, on the other hand, we are told that it is altogether unnecesary for the confessor to recall all the sins confessed, for in most cases this is morally impossible, and it suffices for him to bear in mind the general state of the penitent.[6] In spite therefore of the rigid doctrines of the theologians, doctrines inevitable under the

---

Bernardo Colnaghi, of Ancona, in a sermon on confession, invited any one who had not confessed for twenty years to come to him and be released of his sins. Two men presented themselves, of whom one had not confessed for twenty-five years and the other for forty, and the good father dispatched them duly absolved in a little over an hour apiece.

[1] Innoc. PP. XI. Decr. 1669, Prop. 59.

[2] Clericati de Pœnit. Decis. XXIII. n. 20.—Habert Praxis Sacr. Pœnit. Tract. II. cap. 1, n. 1.—C. Ravennat. ann. 1855, cap. V. § 10 (Coll. Lacens. VI. 160).

Cardinal Rezzonico, Bishop of Padua, in a visitation of his diocese, was scandalized at the tumultuous crowds on feast days struggling to get to the confessional, not only rendering them unfit for the solemn duty, but obliging them to hurry through it. He learned that the priests heard confessions only on such days, and he ordered that in future they should also sit in the confessional on the day previous.—Litt. Pastorale, 16 Dic. 1746.

[3] Cabrini Elucid. Casuum Reservat. P. I. Resol. cxlviii.

[4] Zenner Instructio Practica Confessar., § 76 (Viennæ, 1857).

[5] C. Trident. Sess. XIV. De Pœnit. cap. 5.

[6] Manzo Epit. Theol. Moral. P. I. De Pœnit. n. 53 (Ed. II. Neapoli, 1836).

theory of absolution, we may reasonably assume that imperfect confessions are by no means exceptional. Not only does this arise from the extraneous circumstances referred to, but the penitents themselves are to blame. Cherubino da Spoleto declares that many deceive themselves in thinking that they have made perfect confessions when they have not, and will find themselves plunged into hell while expecting to go to heaven.[1] Chiericato tells us that from long experience he knows that concealment of sins through shame is frequent;[2] Liguori admits that women who are acquainted with the confessor are apt not to make full confessions,[3] and a recent author assures us that perfect confession is the keenest torture that can be inflicted on the average man, and that there are very few who perform it thoroughly.[4] It is worthy of consideration whether the strain on the consciences of sinners, forced to make confession, with the consequent evasions and mendacity, do not, from a moral point of view, outweigh the possible benefit claimed for the practice.

We may fairly conjecture, indeed, that there must be a good deal of untruthfulness in the confessional, and the moralists condescend to human nature in admitting that a certain amount is permissible. It is only a venial sin to lie about venial sins, and even about mortal sins, provided they do not affect the present confession, and even this venial sin can be avoided by a skilful use of equivocation and mental reservation. The questions involved are delicate, however, and the exact degree and conditions of allowable mendacity afford ample field for nice distinctions by the casuists.[5] A sin that has been

---

[1] Cherubini de Spoleto Quadragesimale Serm. LXIII.

[2] Clericati de Pœnit. Decis. XXIX. n. 12.

[3] S. Alph. de Ligorio Praxis Confessar. n. 119.

[4] Müller, The Catholic Priesthood, IV. 147.—Yet Latomus (De Confessione secreta, Antverpiæ, 1525) in controverting the Lutheran assertion that confession is oppressive, assures us that it is only so to the impenitent: to say that it is so to the sinner desirous of salvation is too foolish to require refutation. In this he is oblivious of the older doctrine that so great is the suffering entailed by confession that its repetition can take the place of purgatory and enable the sinner to ascend directly to heaven.—Passavanti, Lo Specchio della vera Penitenza, Dist. V. cap. iii.

It is a habit of long standing, reproved by Aquinas (Opusc. lxiv.), for penitents to exonerate themselves by pleading that the devil tempted them beyond their strength, or that others led them into sin.

[5] Summa Angelica s. v. *Confessio* I. § 7.—Summa Tabiena s. v. *Confessio* II. n. 10.—Summa Sylvestrina s. v. *Confessio Sacr.* I. § 9.—Summa Rosella s. v.

confessed and pardoned can be denied because it is no longer existent, yet it exists sufficiently to form material for the sacrament in case the sinner chooses to confess it again,[1] as we have seen (p. 333) in the devices to obtain indirect absolution for reserved cases. All this is scarce in accordance with the theory that the confessional is the tribunal of God, to which the sinner resorts with an earnest longing to win pardon, and even more inconsequent is the deceit authorized by Benedict XIV. in deciding that a priest stained with impurity, who in confession represents himself as a layman bound by a vow of chastity, commits only a venial sin and makes a valid confession.[2]

Yet confessions may be too perfect and minute, and the terror of the confessional is the overscrupulous penitent, who is constantly tormenting himself with the dread that he has not secured pardon for the sins which he has confessed; that he has not confessed them properly and must repeat them again and again; that things are sins which are no sins. It suggests what an infinite amount of misery the system has caused to timid and conscientious souls, surrounded by multitudinous observances on which they rely for salvation, ever afraid of failing in some minute particular and seeing hell yawning before them as the penalty for some trifling omission. If they bore the confessor, it is only a slight return for the anguish of which he is the instrument, but he is not taught to sympathize with and compassionate them. Father Gury tells us that the way to treat them is to cut them short and dispense them from saying anything more —a power which the priest possesses—and then absolve them in spite of their entreaties to be heard.[3] Scarcely less severe as a trial

---

Confessio Sacr. II. § 15.—Em. Sa. Aphorismi Confessar. s. v. *Confessio* n. 12.—Layman Theol. Moral. Lib. v. Tract. vi. cap. 8, n. 15.—Busenbaum Medullæ Theol. Moral. Lib. vii. Tract. iv. cap. 1, Dub. 3, Art 3 —Tamburini Method. Confess. Lib. ii. cap. 10, § 2, n. 36-45.—Zuccherii Decis. Patavinæ Jan., 1707, n. 30-1.—Jo. Sanchez Selecta de Sacramentis Disp. ix. n. 7.—La Croix Theol. Moral. Lib. vi. P. ii. n. 1177-87—Gousset, Théol. Moral. II. n. 437.—Gury Casus Conscient. II. 441-5.

[1] Herzig Manuale Confessarii, P. ii. n. 52.

[2] Benedicti PP. XIV. Casus Conscientiæ, Apr. 1738, cas. 1.

[3] Alph. de Leone de Offic. et Potest. Confessar. Recoll. xxiii. n. 9-12.—Gobat Alphab. Confessar. n. 493-503.—Habert Praxis Sacr. Pœnit. Tract. i. cap. 7.—Gury Casus Conscient. I. n. 48-55.

The learned Carthusian, Joseph Rossell, wrote a book on the methods of dealing with over-scrupulous penitents, based to a large extent on the appli-

to the patience of the confessor is the habit of many penitents of expatiating on the sins of others, and the grave moralists repeat with glee the story of a parish priest, wearied with the persistent recital by a woman of her husband's failings, who gave her as penance three Paters and Aves for her own sins and three days' fasting on bread and water for her husband's, and on her expostulating told her that it was to teach her to confine herself in future to her own.[1]

In treating of reserved cases we have seen the question which naturally arose in them as to the practicability of dividing a confession—making part of it to one confessor and part of it to another. This is a point on which there has been considerable diversity of opinion and practice. Before the rise of the sacramental theory it was a matter of indifference, and there seems to have been no objection to it, or to confessing to several confessors at once. The latter custom of plural confession, indeed, continued to a comparatively late period. When, in 835, Ebbo was compelled to resign the archbishopric of Reims he made confession of his sins to Archbishop Ajulf and Bishops Badarad and Modoin and accepted penance from them for the salvation of his soul,[2] and when, in 991, Arnoul was obliged to vacate the same see he confessed to two archbishops and eleven bishops.[3] It shows how long was confession in reaching its final shape that this was considered to lend especial efficacy to the process. Peter Cantor asserts, at the close of the twelfth century, that the more the priests to whom confession is made the speedier is the pardon,[4] and from the number of instances in which the chronicles happen to report it at the death-bed of princes, it must have been a not uncommon proceeding. It is related at the death of Otho II., in 978, who confessed to Pope Benedict VII. and a number of bishops and priests; in 1089, William Rufus summoned several priests to hear his dying confession; in 1135, Henry I. confessed to

---

cation of the theories of probablism to their troubles. It is entitled *Praxis deponendi Conscientiam* (Bruxellæ, 1661) and found its way into the Roman Index.

[1] Clericati de Pœnit. Decis. xv. n. 20.—This is a common complaint of confessors—"la plûpart des confessions sont pleines des péchez d'autrui, ce qui est assez difficile d'empêcher."—Lochon, Traité du Secret de la Confession, p. 181 (Brusselle, 1708).

[2] D'Achery Spicileg. III. 336.   [3] Harduin. Concil. VI. i. 723.

[4] P. Cantor Verb. abbreviat. cap. 143.

his chaplains and then to Archbishop Hugo; in 1199, Richard I., dying before the castle of Chalus, had three Cistercian abbots to take his confession; while, in 1212, Philip of Namur had four Cistercian abbots, and in the same year Otho IV. confessed to an abbot and a number of priests.[1] In fact, among some orders of monks, this appears to have been the established custom,[2] and although Duns Scotus pronounces it unsacramental,[3] his disciple Astesanus thinks that the penitent thus receives sacramental absolution, though the priests commit sin in doing what is contrary to the customs and statutes of the Church.[4] His contemporary, the Dominican Pierre de la Palu, seems to know of no such statutes, for he says positively that confession can be made to a number of priests, either together or in succession, and absolution be received from each, and from his manner of allusion it would seem to have been at the time a not uncommon custom.[5] Prierias speaks doubtingly, saying that some doctors argue that such confession is not sacramental, but that Joan Andreas holds that if a sinner desires to confess publicly he can do so, though Aquinas says that public confession is allowable only for public crimes.[6] Latomus, Eisengrein and Martin van der Beek say unhesitatingly that it is permissible to confess to a number of priests and in the presence of auditors,[7] but the council of Trent only admits that Christ has not forbidden public confession as a means of humiliation and edification.[8] Chiericato, after weighing the opposing opinions, concludes that confession to a number of priests is sacramental, but it should only be done from necessity or from some sufficient

---

[1] Dithmari Merseburg. Chron. Lib. III.—Orderic. Vital. Hist. Eccles. P. III. Lib. viii. cap. 8; Lib. xiii. cap. 8.—Nic. Trivetti Chron. ann. 1199.—Cæsar. Heisterb. Dial. Dist. II. cap. 17.—Narrat. de Morte Othon. IV. (Martene Thesaur. III. 1374).

[2] P. de Honestis Reg. Clericor. Lib. II. cap. xxii.—Matt. Paris Hist. Angl. ann. 1196.

[3] Jo. Scoti in IV. Sentt. Dist. XVII. Q. unic.

[4] Astesani Summæ Lib. V. Tit. xviii.

[5] P. de Palude in IV. Sentt. Dist. XVII. Q. ii. Art. 1.

[6] Summa Sylvestrina s. v. *Confessio sacr.* I. § 23. Cf. Summa Tabiena s. v. *Confessio* II. § 37.

[7] Jac. Latomus de Confessione secreta, Antverpiæ, 1515.—Mart. Eisengrein Confessionale, cap. iii. Q. 56.—Becani de Sacramentis Tract. II. P. iii. cap. 37, Q. 4.

[8] C. Trident. Sess. XIV. De Pœnit. cap. 5.

motive.[1] Liguori adopts Busenbaum's assertion that secret confession to a priest is not of necessity, but is a usage of the Church.[2]

The sacramental theory was only developed by degrees and considerable time was required to reduce it to a uniform system. Towards the close of the twelfth century Peter Cantor mentions the custom in some convents of confessing to one of the monks and receiving absolution from the abbot, and that there was nothing irregular in this is manifest by the recommendation, towards the middle of the thirteenth century, by William of Paris, that, when the priest is ignorant, a learned deacon can hear the confession and determine the penance, after which the priest is to enjoin the penance and confer absolution.[3] Even at the end of the fifteenth century Baptista Tornamala alludes to the foolish monks who heard confessions and then sent the penitents to their priests for absolution.[4] In this uncertainty of practice it is no wonder that a custom arose of dividing a confession among several priests and relating a part to each—a custom reproved by the pseudo-Augustin and in a tract which passed current under the name of St. Bernard, as well as by Master Bandinus, who speaks of it as caused by shame.[5] It was difficult to repress, for Alexander Hales feels it necessary to explain that, except in reserved cases, confession must be made wholly to one priest, and Aquinas reiterates the assertion in a manner to show that he was combating a not infrequent custom on the part of those who feared human shame

---

[1] Clericati de Pœnit. Decis. XVI. n. 15.

[2] S. Alph. de Ligorio Theol. Moral. Lib. VI. n. 494.

[3] Morin. de Pœnit. Lib. X. cap. 15.—Guillel. Paris. de Sacr. Pœnit. cap. 19.

[4] Summa Rosella s. v. *Confessor* I. § 11.—It is related of the distinguished theologian Suarez that, in travelling near Coimbra, he confessed to a curate, who proceeded to absolve him by repeating the Ave Maria, when Suarez, finding him wholly ignorant of the absolution formula, was obliged to dictate it and have him follow it word by word. He sought the parish priest and pointed out to him the ruin of souls resulting from the ignorance of his vicar, when the good padre replied that he knew it and had ordered him only to hear confessions and then send the penitents to himself for absolution. This staggered Suarez still more, and he vainly endeavored to make the priest understand the nullity of the sacrament thus divided.—Clericati de Pœnit. Decis. XXXI. n. 17.

[5] Ps. Augustin. de vera et falsa Pœnit. cap. XV. n. 21.—Ps. Bernardi Meditatio de Conditione Humana cap. 9 (Migne, CLXXXIV. 500).—Bandini Sententt. P. IV. Dist. xvi.

more than offending God.[1] Of course such a practice was destructive of the jurisdiction of the parish priest and incompatible with the sacramental theory, yet its use in reserved cases tended to keep alive the idea that it was admissible, in spite of the animadversions of the doctors. Passavanti declares that not only is such confession invalid, but that it is a fresh mortal sin.[2] Gerson draws the distinction that, while it impedes the virtue of the sacrament if done through shame or hypocrisy, it does not if through ignorance, or in reserved cases, or when there is reasonable dread of scandal to arise from the confession of some special sin to the ordinary confessor.[3] Robert of Aquino is more rigid and explains that when a confession is divided between two priests the penitent is absolved by neither and must make a full confession to one.[4] Yet not long afterwards we are told by Prierias that these divided confessions were common, especially among loose women, who would confess their carnal sins to some priestly companion and then their lighter transgressions to one in good standing, in order to enjoy the fair repute thence accruing—a species of hypocrisy which some doctors considered to be a mortal sin, while others classed it as venial.[5] At the end of the fifteenth century, Manuel Sa shows how vague were still the conceptions on the subject when he tells us that to have two confessors and to confess grave sins to one and light ones to the other is a mortal sin, according to some doctors, because one of the confessors is deceived; others hold that it is not if done once or twice out of shame or modesty; others again define it to be a mortal sin if done for a sinful purpose, but not if it is done for a good purpose, such as to retain the favorable opinion of one of the confessors.[6] Half a century later Diana asserts that a man who desires to stand well with his ordinary confessor can reveal to him only his venial sins and then his mortals to another.[7] This divided confession had a quasi-recognition in the Jubilee indulgences, carrying with them the faculty of selecting

---

[1] Alex. de Ales Summæ P. IV. Q. XVIII. Membr. iv. Art. 5 § 2.—S. Th. Aquin. Summæ Suppl. Q. IX. Art. 3; Ejusd. Opusc. LXIV.

[2] Passavanti, Lo Specchio della vera Penitenza, Dist. V. cap. 5.

[3] Jo. Gersoni Regulæ Morales (Opp. Ed. 1488, XXI. G.).

[4] Rob. Episc. Aquinat. Opus Quadrages. Serm. XXIX. cap. 3.

[5] Summa Sylvestrina s. v. *Confessio sacr.* I. § 8.

[6] Em. Sa. Aphorismi Confessar. s. v. *Confessor* n. 16.

[7] Summa Diana s. v. *Confessionis requisita* n. 54.

one or more confessors to whom sins could be confessed as they were successively remembered, though it was recommended that the same confessor should be applied to if he could be had.[1] The more rigorous theologians, however, discountenanced the practice: Noël Alexandre, like Robert of Aquino, pronounces such confessions null and that they must be repeated,[2] and, in 1658, the priests of Paris included this device among the errors of the casuists.[3]

In modern practice we are told that there is nothing to prevent a penitent from confessing his mortal sins to a strange priest and getting absolution, and then his venials (which are not necessary matter for confession and absolution) to his ordinary confessor, unless he does so for the purpose of avoiding reproof and gaining fresh opportunity for sinning.[4] It is a mortal sin, however, purposely to seek out an unknown and ignorant confessor to whom to confess the graver delinquencies, and dividing mortal sins between two confessors renders the confessions invalid unless there are sufficient reasons why some sins should not be revealed to the ordinary confessor. In such case even the severer moralists see no objection to this, though they do not inform us how the difficulty as to partial absolution is evaded.[5]

The converse of this divided confession is gregarious confession, when the priest hears a multitude of penitents and absolves them in block. In battle or shipwreck or similar emergency this may be unavoidable; the Church accepts it as valid and assumes that the formula "I absolve you from your sins" grants a separate absolution to each one of those confessing.[6] In the old formulas for Holy Thursday reconciliation the use of the plural number shows that the penitents to be reconciled were thus restored to the Church in mass,[7]

---

[1] Marc. Pauli Leonis Praxis ad Litt. Magni Pœnitentiar. p. 16 (Mediolani, 1665).

[2] Summa Alexandrina P. I. n. 454.

[3] Ant. Arnauld, Théol. Morale des Jésuites, p. 377.

[4] Varceno Comp. Theol. Moral. Tract. XVIII. cap. iv. art. 4.

[5] Layman Theol. Moral. Lib. V. Tract. vi. cap. 8, n. 14.—Gury Comp. Theol. Moral. II. 475.—Gousset, Théol. Morale II. n. 440.—Zenner Instructio Pract. Confessar. § 78.—Summa Alexandrina P. I. n. 459-60.

[6] Ferraris Prompta Biblioth. s. v. *Absolvere* III. n. 15, 16.

[7] Martene de antiq. Eccles. Ritibus Lib. I. cap. vi. Art. 7, Ordo 1—"Absolvemus vobis vice beati Petri apostolorum principis, cui Dominus potestatem

and, though it was inconsistent with the practice of auricular confession, it survived the introduction of the sacramental theory, much to the disgust of the stricter sacerdotalists when it was applied to the ordinary parochial routine by ignorant or indolent pastors. A case of the kind, recorded by Cæsarius of Hiesterbach, is alluded to above (p. 248), and that it was by no means uncommon in the thirteenth century appears from the remonstrance of a layman to the Archbishop of Cologne, written probably about 1235, describing certain priests, learned and worthy enough, who, after divine service, were accustomed to order the congregation to raise their hands and confess their sins, after which absolution was granted with greater facility than they would forgive a debt of three farthings apiece. This he describes as a devilish snare for the ignorant multitude, who think no further confession necessary, deeming themselves as free from sin as when newly baptized, and in this deadly security they have no hesitation in sinning afresh.[1] Such a mockery of the sacrament could find no defenders, but Astesanus, in 1317, does not say that it is either unlawful or invalid, and he only condemns it as an infraction of the secrecy that should be observed in the confessional,[2] and two centuries later Giovanni da Taggia merely remarks that those who do it without necessity cause the penitents to disregard a precept of the Church.[3] The custom seems to have been an inveterate one, at least in Germany, for towards the close of the sixteenth century Sixtus V. ordered the Archbishops of Trier and Mainz to suppress it.[4] We do not hear of it elsewhere, except in the case of children, in dealing with whom this expeditious method seems to have continued in use, even to the present day, by careless pastors, reckless of the contempt for the sacrament thus induced in the plastic mind of youth. The moralists, of course, condemn it and generally assert that it is a mortal sin.[5]

---

ligandi atque solvendi dedit, sed quantum ad vos pertinet accusatio et ad nos pertinet remissio, sit Deus omnipotens vita et salus omnibus peccatis vestris indultor."

This is a transitional formula of probably the late eleventh century, and indicates how the old reconciliation merged into the scholastic absolution.

[1] Martene Ampl. Collect. I. 357.   [2] Astesani Summæ Lib. v. Tit. xviii.

[3] Summa Tabiena s. v. *Confessio* II. § 37.

[4] Maffei Hist. ab excessu Gregorii XIII. p. 16 (Bergomi, 1747).

[5] Summa Angelica s. v. *Confessio* I. § 29.—Summa Sylvestrina s. v. *Confessio Sacr.* I. § 23.—Synod. Verdunens. ann. 1598, cap. 51 (Harduin. VIII. 470).—

No penitent can be required to repeat a valid confession once made; if ordered to do so he can refuse, and indeed some doctors go so far as to say that even the pope cannot issue a precept to render it obligatory.[1] Yet before the details of the sacrament were understood, up to the middle of the thirteenth century, there was one occasion on which it was required. When a man confessed in peril of death the formula of the absolution administered to him contained a clause enjoining him, in case he escaped, to confess over again and accept penance,[2] which manifests a very vague conception as yet of the functions and efficacy of the sacrament and is a conditional absolution, which subsequent theologians held to be invalid. Even as late as 1317 Astesanus alludes to this, though in a manner to show that it was then falling out of use.[3]

The same nebulous conception as to the value of the sacrament is seen in the strenuous recommendations of repeated confession, as in the highest degree beneficial, though not obligatory. According to theory, confession, absolution and satisfaction, if valid, relieve the penitent from both *culpa* and *pœna*—his sins are remitted, the temporal punishment is atoned for, he is fully in a state of grace, and if he dies he is assured óf direct ascent to heaven. In spite of this he was told that the oftener he should repeat a confession, the quicker would be the remission and the less the *pœna*.[4] St. Antonino even assures us that, if repeated often enough, it may finally obtain exemption from the *pœna* when there is no contrition.[5]

A repetition of confession is requisite, however, when, from any cause, the original confession is invalid. This may arise either from defects in the penitent or in the priest, and leads to a considerable number of perplexing questions in which it would be vain to expect unanimity among the theologians. If the confession is made from

---

La Croix Theol. Moral. Lib. vi. P. ii. n. 1189.—Frassinetti's New Parish Priest's Practical Manual, pp. 366-7 (London, 1893).

[1] S. Antonini Summæ P. iii. Tit. xiv. cap. 19, § 4.—Summa Sylvestrina s. v. *Confessio sacr.* i. § 4.

[2] Johann. de Deo Pœnitentialis Lib. i. cap. 2.—Hostiens. Aureæ Summæ Lib. v. De Pœnit. et Remiss. § 45.

[3] Astesani Summæ Lib. v. Tit. xvi.

[4] Hostiens. Aureæ Summæ Lib. v. De Pœnit. et Remiss. § 56.—S. Th. Aquinat. in IV. Sentt. Dist. xvii. Q. iii. Art. 3.

[5] S. Antonini Summæ P. iii. Tit. xiv. cap. 19, § 4.

any other motive than that of obtaining absolution, if, for instance, to gain a good reputation, enabling one to cheat or to steal, it is invalid, and this motive may be either mortal or venial, affording to the moralists a wide field for debate. It is invalid, also, if the penitent has not sufficing attrition, though whether or not the absolution revives on his subsequently experiencing attrition is a question on which the authorities differ. Also, if there is not at least a formal or virtual resolve of amendment and of avoiding occasions of sin, which, as we shall see hereafter, is an equally fruitful source of discussion. Also, if the confession is incomplete through the omission of a mortal sin, and this may be intentional or through ignorance, with varying results. Also, if the penitent be under excommunication and does not mention it, though, if he is ignorant of it, it does not invalidate the absolution, even if the clause removing excommunication is omitted from the formula of absolution, as Gobat says is customary in Germany. Also, if the penitent forgets or neglects to perform the penance, some authorities require a repetition of the confession, while others hold it to be unnecessary. Also, if the confessor withholds his intention, or omits a necessary part of the formula of absolution, or is under excommunication, or is an intruder, or has not a licence from the bishop; but if this latter is not generally known and he is commonly reputed to be a confessor, some doctors hold that the absolution is good, while others, with customary lack of logic, say that the penitent is pardoned before God, but that if he finds out the truth he must repeat the confession. Also, if the confessor is sleepy, or inattentive, or deaf, some moralists require the confession to be repeated, or at least in so far as it was not heard, while others assert that the *bona fides* of the penitent supplies the defect in the confessor, and the same difference of opinion exists when the priest is too ignorant to be able to distinguish between sins.[1] For five hundred years and more these questions have

---

[1] Passavanti, Lo Specchio della vera Penitenza, Dist. v. cap. 5.—Weigel Claviculæ Indulgentialis cap. xv.—Somma Pacifica, cap. 1.—S. Antonini Confessionale fol. 45*b*; Ejusd. Summæ P. iii. Tit. xiv. cap. 19, §§ 4, 5.—Summa Angelica s. v. *Confessio* i. §§ 13, 14, 18, 20, 22.—B. de Chaimis Interrog. fol. 12–15.—Summa Sylvestrina s. v. *Confessor* i. §§ 9, 15.—Summa Tabiena s. v. *Confessio* ii. §§ 13–17, 22–25, 39.—Dom. Soto in IV. Sentt. Dist. xviii. Q. iii. Art. 3.—Clericati de Pœnit. Dist. xxxi.—Benzi Praxis Trib. Conscient. Disp. i. Q. ii. Art. 1, Par. 2, n. 4.—Varceno Comp. Theol. Moral. Tract. xviii. Cap. iv. Art. 6.

been agitated without the possibility of reaching absolute conclusions, and, indeed, a large portion of them depend upon shades of feeling so elusive and indefinable that certainty is unattainable. All that the theologians can do is to comfort themselves with the maxim *In dubio standum est pro valore actus*—in doubt, the validity of the act is to be assumed—but whether God is bound by this principle it might be hardy to affirm.

The question whether written confessions are allowable is one in which the custom of the Church has varied. A penitent, if there is sufficient cause, can write out the confession, in whole or in part, and hand it to the priest in the confessional, saying " I accuse myself of all the sins which you read here," and this apparently is sometimes done by women through sense of shame, when it is accepted as oral and she is of course subject to the usual interrogation,[1] but whether such writing can be sent to a confessor and absolution be returned by messenger has been the subject of some debate. We have seen (p. 182) that, in the early Church, *libelli*, or written confessions of sins, were read to the congregation ; and before the development of the power of the keys and the sacramental system there was no hesitation in sending a written confession and receiving such aids to forgiveness as were then held to be within the functions of the bishop. Thus in the ninth century Robert, Bishop of Le Mans, when sick unto death, sent a written statement of his sins to the bishops who were with King Charles besieging the Normans in Angers, and they sent to him from camp a quasi-absolution which was wholly precatory in character.[2] In the eleventh century, Gregory VII. had no hesitation in sending absolutions to persons at a distance, even without their confessing, and Paschal II. continued the practice in the next century.[3] As the scholastic theology began to take shape this came

---

[1] Escobar Theol. Moral. Tract. VII. Exam. iv. cap. 5, n. 36.—Varceno Comp. Theol. Moral. Tract. XVIII. cap. iv. Art. 5. Father de Charmes, however (Theol. Univers. Diss. V. cap. iv. Art. 2), says this is unlawful though valid.

[2] Martene de antiq. Ritibus Ecclesiæ Lib. I. cap. vi. Art. 7, Ord. 14.

[3] Gregor. PP. VII. Regest Lib. I. Ep. 34; Lib. II. Ep. 61; Lib. VI. Ep. 2. The deprecatory absolution sent by Paschal II. to Lambert of Arras is noteworthy—" Per merita beatæ Mariæ semper virginis et orationes sanctorum angelorum et beatorum apostolorum omniumque sanctorum, omnipotens Dominus te, carissime frater Lamberte episcope, ab omnibus peccatis absolvat

to be regarded as irregular, and the pseudo-Augustin, copied by Gratian, laid down the rule that confession must be auricular and not in writing or by messenger.[1] The uncertainty in which the matter rested is seen, about 1225, in Cæsarius of Heisterbach, who argues that written confessions are insufficient, although there are occasional instances of their sufficiency.[2] S. Ramon de Peñafort asserts positively that confession must be oral and not by messenger or letter,[3] and Alexander Hales soon afterwards takes the same position : when a priest is inaccessible, as with captives among the Saracens, it suffices to confess to God, with intention to confess to a priest.[4] Aquinas pointed out that the penitent must contribute to the sacrament ; the spoken words are a portion of it and are indispensable, except in case of insurmountable physical impediment.[5] This view became widely accepted ; as Peter of Tarantaise (Innocent V.) says, the act of confession is the material of the sacrament which without it is imperfect, therefore the confession must be oral and personal.[6] There were dissidents, however, and it was not until modern times that auricular confession became authoritatively recognized as essential to the sacrament and as a condition precedent to

---

et secundum fidem tuam gratiæ suæ tibi munus accumulet."—Löwenfeld. Epist. Pontiff. Roman. p. 73.

[1] Cap. 88 Caus. XXXIII. Q. iii. Dist. 1.

The schoolmen were in the habit of quoting the case of Thomas Becket, who was said to have confessed by letter to Alexander III. and to have received absolution in return, but the facts do not substantiate this. After Becket had accepted the Constitutions of Clarendon, he repented and abstained from his functions till he should be absolved by God and the pope. He therefore sent a messenger to Alexander, who replied in terms of consolation, telling him that God looked to the intention and not to the act. If he feels remorse he should confess in penitence to a priest, when God will dismiss the sin. Moreover, relying on the merits of Peter and Paul "te ab eo quod commissum est absolvemus et id ipsum fraternitati tuæ auctoritate apostolica relaxamus " and ordered him to resume his functions.—Baron. Annal. ann. 1164 n. 5, 6.

Thus confession was to be made to a priest, pardon was to come from God, and what Alexander did was virtually to absolve him from the oath taken at Clarendon.

[2] Cæsar. Heisterbach. Dial. Dist. III. cap. 27.

[3] S. Raymundi Summæ Lib. III. Tit. xxxiv. § 4.

[4] Alex. de Ales Summæ P. IV. Q. XVIII. Membr. iv. Art. 5, § 9.

[5] S. Th. Aquin. Summæ Suppl. Q. IX. Art. 3.

[6] Jo. Friburgens. Summæ Confessor. Lib. III. Tit. xxxiv. Q. 65, 76.

absolution. Duns Scotus does not say that confession and absolution by writing are unsacramental, and only deems them contrary to the secrecy characteristic of the confessional and dangerous through liability to publicity.[1] The Thomists and Scotists, however, did not divide upon the question. William of Ware, though a Franciscan, pronounces confession other than auricular to be unlawful, while Astesanus, François de Mairone, Pierre de la Palu and St. Antonino hold that it is allowable though inadvisable—if a penitent is lame and cannot walk, and the priest is sick and cannot come to him, confession and absolution can be exchanged by letter.[2] Cherubino da Spoleto advances only reasons of inexpediency against it and does not question its validity.[3] That it was not infrequently practised is apparent from a decree of the council of Strassburg, in 1435, which says that it was habitual with some priests when they were busy and that it is only permissible when there is legitimate cause, for sins are only remitted in oral confession.[4] Early in the sixteenth century Prierias seems to consider the question open, though personally he decides in the negative.[5] So Caietano says that if a confession is written it must be handed to the confessor, and that absolution can only be given verbally,[6] while Fumo holds that in case of necessity letters and messengers are allowable,[7] and Domingo Soto, on the other hand, follows Aquinas.[8] The council of Trent was silent on the subject, and the Tridentine Catechism objects to writing only on account of its interference with secrecy.[9] Several Spanish theologians of the highest character, such as Pedro Soto, Azpilcueta and Francisco Suarez pronounced in its favor, but when, in 1594, the Jesuit Juan Geronimo preached two sermons in support of the sacramental character of written confession and absolution, the Inquisition of Toledo prosecuted him, sentenced him to a severe reprimand and made him

---

[1] Jo. Scoti in IV. Sentt. Dist. xvii. Q. unic.

[2] Guill. Vorrillong in IV. Sentt. Dist. xvii.—Astesani Summæ Lib. v. Tit. xviii.—F. de Mayronis in IV. Sentt. Dist. xiv. Q. i.—P. de Palude in IV. Sentt. Dist. xvii. Q. ii. Art. 1.—S. Antonini Summæ P. iii. Tit. xiv. cap. 19, § 9.

[3] Cherubini de Spoleto Quadragesimale Serm. lxii.

[4] Statut. Eccles. Argentinens. ann. 1435, cap. 11 (Martene Thesaur. IV. 552).

[5] Summa Sylvestrina s. vv. *Confessio Sacr.* i. § 16 ; *Confessor* iv. § 7.

[6] Caietani Summula, s. v. *Confessio.*

[7] Fumi Aurea Armilla s. v. *Confessio* n. 23.

[8] Dom. Soto in IV. Sentt. Dist. xviii. Q. ii. Art. 6.

[9] Cat. Trident. De Pœnit. cap. 9.

sign an acknowledgment of his error and a pledge to teach the opposite thereafter.[1] Manuel Sa taught the validity of written confession and absolution, but, after the question had been adversely decided by Clement VIII., the Congregation of the Index ordered this passage struck out and a contrary one inserted.[2] Henriquez adopted a modified doctrine, that confession can be made by letter but absolution must be oral, and he too fell under the ban of the Index, his work being prohibited, *donec corrigatur*, by decree of August 7, 1603.[3]

The influence of Spanish theology at this period was preponderating and some emphatic decision was requisite to check the development of a doctrine so threatening to auricular confession. Accordingly, in 1602, Clement VIII. denounced the proposition as false, audacious and scandalous, and prohibited its being defended even as probable, under pain of excommunication removable only by the pope, as well as of other arbitrary punishment.[4] Still there were those who adhered to the position of Henriquez, that confession may be made by letter, though absolution requires personal presence, and they argued that the use of the particle *et* in place of *vel* in the papal decree allowed this doctrine to be taught. To put an end to this Paul V., in 1605, made a formal declaration in the Congregation of the Holy Office prohibiting it likewise.[5] Still the question refused to be settled and, in 1634, Urban VIII. was obliged to issue a decree forbidding the absolution, even by the Papal Penitentiary, of those who should teach or practise the doctrine of sacramental confession by letter.[6] Even this did not suffice, and a lively controversy on the subject continued throughout the seventeenth century,

---

[1] MSS. Universitäts Bibliothek of Halle, Yc, 20, Tom. I.

[2] Em. Sa Aphorismi Confessar. s. v. *Absolutio* n. 8.—Index Brasichellensis, I. 347.

[3] Henriquez Summæ Theol. Moral. Lib. I. cap. viii. n. 5; Lib. v. cap. ii. n. 7.—Index Brasichellensis I. 601.

[4] Clement PP. VIII. Decr. 20 June, 1602 (Bullar. III. 150).—Ferraris Prompta Biblioth. s. v. *Absolvere* Art. III. n. 14.

This gave rise to a question as to the lawfulness of death-bed absolution when, on the arrival of the priest, the penitent is speechless or senseless. Suarez wrote a tract on the subject in 1605 or 1606.—Döllinger u. Reusch, Moralstreitigkeiten in der römisch-katholischen Kirche, II. 266.

[5] Jac. Bayi Institt. Relig. Christ. Lib. II. cap. 91.—Viva Trutina Theol. Append. § 10.

[6] Pittoni Constitutiones Pontificiæ, T. VII. n. 786.

chiefly between the Dominicans and the Jesuits.[1] A case was cited as having occurred in England, during the persecution of the Catholics, in which one executed for his religion managed to transmit from prison a written confession to a priest, with a request to him to be present in disguise near the scaffold; he complied, their eyes met and he murmured the formula of absolution[2]—a somewhat superfluous ceremony, since the baptism of blood is as efficacious as that of water. Of course, the resistance of captious theologians was unsuccessful and the necessity of auricular confession and of presence in absolution is no longer disputed, though it rests only on the utterance of Clement VIII.[3] The definition as to absolution led to many nice speculations as to the distance which can intervene between priest and penitent without rendering the sacrament invalid, some doctors holding that twenty paces are allowable, while others contend for less; also, whether one must be able to see the other, or whether hearing suffices; also, when, from any cause, absolution is not given at the time of confession, how many days may elapse without affecting its validity[4]—speculations which are chiefly of interest as illustrating the difficulty of accommodating divine laws to the imperfections and accidents of human life. Modern science, moreover, has recently raised a new question, for the introduction of the

---

[1] La Croix Theol. Moral. Lib. VI. P. ii. n. 1195.—Morin de Pœnit. Lib. VIII. cap. 25.

In 1617 the Benedictine Pierre Milhard taught that both confession and absolution could be conveyed by messenger, a proposition which was promptly condemned by the Sorbonne (D'Argentré Coll. Judic. de novis Error. II. II. 116).—In 1643 the Franciscan Marchant (Trib. Animar. Tom. I. Tract. VI. Tit. ii. Q. 4, Concl. 2) maintained the theory of Henriquez, and after 1690 the Jesuit Arsdekin still taught the forbidden doctrine (Theol. Tripart. P. III. Tract. iii. cap. 3, § 6, Q. 3).

[2] Clericati de Pœnit. Decis. XXXV. n. 16.

[3] Th. ex Charmes Theol. Univers. Diss. V. cap. II. Q. ii. Art. 1.—Varceno Comp. Theol. Moral. Tract. XVIII. cap. iv. art. 5.

Tournely argues (De Sacr. Pœnit. Q. VI. Art. iv.) that there is nothing in the sacrament to prevent epistolary confession and absolution, but that the decree of Clement VIII. is final. La Croix (Theol. Moral. Lib. VI. P. ii. n. 1199) adopts the very conclusive reasoning that if absolution could be given *in absentia*, Clement VIII. could not have forbidden it.

[4] Marchant Trib. Animar. Tom. I. Tract. VI. Tit. ii. Q. 5.—Clericati de Pœnit. Decis. XXXV. n. 17–18.—Zenner Instruct. Pract. Confessar. § 80.—Mig. Sanchez, Prontuario de la Teología Moral, Trat. VI. Punto vii. n. 6.

telephone renders verbal communication possible at a distance, but it has been decided that, though telephonic confession may be oral, the absolution would be given *in absentia* and therefore would be invalid.[1]

Apart from the dogmatic questions respecting the integrity of the sacrament, it was impossible that the Church could consent to epistolary confession. Its theory is that the priest sits as a judge in the tribunal of conscience. The penitent is instructed, before coming to confession, to make diligent scrutiny of his memory and the council of Trent has rendered this *de fide*, but it is impossible to define the exact limits to which this self-examination should be pushed.[2] He is the only witness for and against himself, and in most cases, as the books tell us, an unwilling witness. To weigh the case properly, not only must every sin be revealed, but the circumstances connected with each one, and this can only be accomplished by a searching examination in which the confessor probes the conscience of the sinner to the bottom and ascertains all the facts requisite to enable him to reach an accurate judgment. We shall see, when we come to consider the subject of satisfaction, of how little real import all this is, but such is the basis on which the rule of confession is founded, and to abandon it would be to deprive the system of its *raison d'être.* It is true that in this, as in all other attempts to prescribe regulations in these matters, the doctors are by no means in accord as to the degree to which examination should be made into the modifying characteristics of a sin, some contenting themselves with generalities, while others insist on the minutest details. As a means of reducing to some kind of system the infinite variety of human actions and motives, circumstances have been classified as intrinsic or extrinsic, as modifying species or adding species, as aggravating or extenuating, and in conformity with this classification the council of Trent made it *de fide* that circumstances modifying species should be confessed,[3] as, for instance, theft may be either simple or sacrilegious, though in many cases the authorities admit the difficulty of distinguishing

---

[1] Marc Institt. Moral. Alphonsianæ n. 1663.

[2] C. Trident. Sess. xiv. De Pœnit. can. 7.—Benzi Praxis Trib. Conscient. Disp. i. Q. ii. Art. 1, Par. 2, n. 8.

[3] C. Trident. *loc. cit.*

between the classes.[1] As to the necessity of detailing merely aggravating circumstances, opinions appear to be about equally divided, with great names on either side. Liguori investigates the subject elaborately, states three opinions as current and pronounces that which denies the necessity to be the more probable.[2] As a general rule, the circumstances requiring to be investigated are recapitulated in the distich—

> Quid, quis, ubi, per quos, quoties, cur, quomodo, quando,
> Quilibet observet animæ medicamina dando—

but the practical application of this has been, from an early period, the subject of interminable and most intricate discussion. The questions involved show how completely the confessional has been transformed, from its original theory of a repentant sinner eager to cast the whole burden of his sins at the feet of the Saviour, into a criminal court in which the accused is expected to conceal his transgressions, and the truth has to be extorted from him by a series of carefully prearranged cross-questions. This was the inevitable result of enforced confession, and the theologians, accustomed to the established routine, appear utterly unable to appreciate the incongruity between the means and the ostensible end.

There was excuse for this in the older time when confession was voluntary and was scarce expected of a layman more than once or twice in a life-time. The accumulated sins of years might well require prompting of the memory to assist in their recollection, and in the

---

[1] Viva Cursus Theol. Moral. P. VI. Q. 5, Art. 2, n. 4.—Benzi Praxis Trib. Conscient. Disp. I. Q. ii. Art. 1, Par. 2, n. 2.

[2] S. Alph. de Ligorio Theol. Moral. Lib. VI. n. 458.

As an example of aggravating circumstances, Clericato (De Pœnit. Decis. XXVIII. n. 10) alludes to "Religiosis qui non verentur ingredi domus publicarium meretricum, et exire ex ipsis sine rubore, quamvis videantur ac observentur a transeuntibus et ab aliis in eodem vico habitantibus, qui omnes gravissimum scandalum ultra peccatum carnis committunt et deturpant bonum nomen sui Ordinis." Creating this scandal would seem superfluous, for Escobar tells us (Theol. Moral. Tract. VI. n. 66) that the excommunication decreed for religious who lay aside the habit is not incurred when this is done temporarily for the purpose of secretly stealing or fornicating. Pascal (Provinciales, Lett. VIe.) alludes to this with his customary caustic sarcasm, and Père Daniel (Entretiens d'Eudoxe et de Cléandre, Éd. 1828, P. II. pp. 68–71) vainly endeavors to explain it away. Apparently, according to Escobar, the motive for laying aside the habit in such cases is an extenuating circumstance.

Penitentials and compilations of canons we find rudimentary formulas to aid the priest in exploring the conscience of the penitent.[1] In 813, the council of Châlons complains that some penitents do not make full confessions and orders the confessor to push his enquiries through all the eight mortal sins,[2] while Benedict the Levite directs the priest to investigate all the details which may aggravate or extenuate the sin.[3] In the eleventh century, the indescribable nastiness of the questions which Bishop Burchard directs the confessor to put shows the custom completely established, and the contamination which it could not fail to bring on those who perchance were innocent and pure.[4] In the twelfth century, the pseudo-Augustin directs the confessor to extract both what the penitent conceals and what perhaps he is ignorant of, and then to push his investigations into all the circumstances, and this acquired the force of law when it was carried into Gratian.[5] As the system of the Penitentials passed away and the priest became clothed with the power of the keys and with discretion in the administration of penance, it grew still more important for him to ascertain all the details which might aggravate or mitigate the penalty to be imposed, and the instructions for his guidance assumed a more elaborate form. That which is alone possible to omniscience was sought for in framing rules for investigation and for weighing the information thus obtained. Alain de Lille, in his minute directions to the confessor, even endeavors to instruct him as to the conclusions to be drawn from the face of his penitent.[6] Yet already the dangerous suggestiveness of the process was recognized, and Eudes of Paris, about 1198, ordered priests to use the utmost caution—to inquire only about the customary sins and not about others unless some circumstances suggested the likelihood of their existence.[7]

When annual confession was enforced there was less to be apprehended from lapse of memory, but more from conscious suppression

---

[1] Ps. Bedæ Ordo ad dandam Pœnitentiam (Wasserschleben, p. 253).—Reginon. Discipl. Eccles. I. 300.—Garofali Ordines ad dandam Pœnitentiam, pp. 33-4.—Morin. de Pœnitentia Append. p. 23.

[2] C. Cabillonens. ann. 813, cap. 32 (Harduin. IV. 1037).

[3] Bened. Levit. Capitular. Lib. VII. cap. 379.—Isaac Lingonens. I. 39.

[4] Burchardi Decreti Lib. XIX.

[5] Cap. 1, § 3 Caus. XXXIII. Q. iii. Dist. 7.

[6] Alani de Insulis Lib. Pœnit. (Migne, CCX. 287).

[7] Constitt. Odonis Paris. cap. vi. § 1 (Harduin. VI. II. 1490).

by unwilling penitents, and the Lateran canon of 1216 is careful to prescribe diligent investigation into all circumstances of sin as part of the duty of the confessor. As enforced confession was gradually reduced to a system, the priest was accordingly instructed to interrogate the sinner seriatim on each of the precepts of the Decalogue, the seven deadly sins, the abuses of the five senses and the thoughts and lusts of the heart.[1] No loophole was to be left through which the penitent could escape the searching inquisition. Minute and suggestive lists were drawn up, hideous catechisms of sin, and though occasional caution was uttered, recommending reticence, especially as to lapses of the flesh, virginal purity and innocence could be no safeguard against foul and indecent questions. Women evidently were not expected to confess such matters willingly, so that inquiries had to be made to all, young and old; the usual instruction is to commence by asking about impure thoughts and whether they give pleasure, and if this is admitted the interrogations can be pushed from one step to another. Under such a method contamination can scarce be avoided at the hands of the most discreet of confessors, and if he chance to be brutal or coarse-minded the confessional becomes a source of demoralization. As the system developed under the busy hands of the scholastic theologians, the interrogations grew more elaborate. All sins were investigated in their minutest particulars to determine the exact amount of guilt involved in every supposable case—about which, however, the doctors were not by any means always in accord—and in order to perform his functions properly the confessor was required to push his inquiries into every detail. It was a mortal sin for him to omit this duty, and no more appalling summary of human wickedness and perversity is to be found than in the instructions drawn up for him in its performance.[2]

---

[1] Guillel. Parisiens. de Pœnit. cap. 24, 26.

[2] Constitt. Coventriens. ann. 1237 (Harduin. VII. 279 sqq).—C. Claromontens. ann. 1268, cap. 7 (Ibid. VII. 595).—Statut. Johann. Episc. Leodiens. ann. 1287, cap. 4 (Hartzheim III. 686 sqq).—Epist. Synod. Guillel. Episc. Cadurcens. cap. 14 (Martene Thesaur. IV. 694 sqq).—S. Bonaventuræ Confessionale Cap. II. Partic. 1.—Summa Angelica s. v. *Interrogationes.*

Among the questions to be asked of children of both sexes, from the age of seven to that of puberty, is "Si quoquomodo carnaliter peccavit per seipsum aut cum aliis maribus vel feminis et quomodo. Nam in hoc ætas anticipat. In hujusmodi tamen et in sequentibus confessor prudenter se habeat ne innocens quod ignorat addiscat, nec tamen oculis clausis pertranseat, cum in his hæc

These labors necessarily broadened the scope of the confessional; all possible lapses from rectitude in every sphere of human activity were investigated and estimated and catalogued and defined with a minuteness that had never before been attempted by moralists, and huge books were compiled to afford the priest the necessary aid in pushing his inquiries. The Ten Commandments, the seven deadly sins, the five senses, the twelve articles of faith, the seven sacraments, the seven works of temporal mercy and the seven spiritual, were ransacked to find objects of inquiry, and then all classes and callings of men were successively reviewed and lists of questions were drawn up fitted for their several temptations and habitual transgressions. Angiolo da Chivasso prints a series of about seven hundred inquiries as suggestions, and assures us that they are condensed as far as possible, and, in 1528, Martin de Frias cites it as a model, avoiding the extremes both of brevity and prolixity. Bartholommeo de Chaimis, after exhausting all the generalities of sins, gives instructions for the examination of children and married folk, princes and magistrates, lawyers, physicians, surgeons, courtiers, citizens, merchants, traders, bankers, partners, brokers, artizans, druggists, goldsmiths, tavern-keepers, butchers, tailors, shoemakers, lenders and borrowers, bakers, actors, musicians, farmers, peasants, tax- and toll-gatherers, rectors and administrators of hospitals and religious houses, clerics, simple priests, canons and incumbents of benefices, bishops and secular prelates, abbots and regular prelates, and finally monks and friars. These are only types of a class of works whose multiplication shows the demand existing for them, and the details into which they enter leave the impression that any penitent after undergoing such an examination as they suggest would have little to learn as to the sins which he might commit or the frauds and iniquities which he might perpetrate.[1]

ætas soleat multipliciter involvi," and then the author proceeds with a series of most suggestive questions for both sexes. These are decent, however, in comparison with the interrogatories prescribed for married folk.—Bart. de Chaimis Interrog. fol. 54–55, 61–62.

The caution to begin the inquiry as to carnal sins with women by asking about impure thoughts, and then proceeding gradually has remained the established formula.—Alph. de Leone de Off. et Potest. Confessar. Recoll. XVI. n. 27.

[1] Jo. Friburgens. Summæ Confessor. Lib. III. Tit. xxxv. Q. 82–4.—Manipulus Curatorum P. II. Tract. iii. cap. 9.—John Myrc's Instructions for Parish

Penitents thus were expected to conceal their sins as far as they could, and it was assumed that confessions were rarely complete without this searching course of examination, for few penitents, we are told, are found who use due diligence in revealing their transgressions.[1] At the same time there was no little complaint of the negligence and carelessness of so many priests, whom Pacifico da Novara calls confusers rather than confessors, those who simply listen to the penitent, grant invalid absolutions and plunge both themselves and their penitents into hell, whither the majority are hastening. This he attributes to their ignorance, for they scarce know how to read and have never looked into a book on confession, while Caietano says that the great mass of confessors defend their negligence by the time which attention to these details would consume, rendering them unable to attend to the number of penitents requiring their services, though it is a mortal sin to omit the necessary interrogation.[2]

Thus far the tendency had been to a constantly increasing demand

---

Priests, vv. 961–1414.—Casus Papales Confessorum (s. l. e. a. Hain 4675).—Somma Pacifica.—Confessionale Raynaldi (s. l. e. a. sed circa 1476).—S. Antonini Confessionale.—Summa Angelica s. v. *Interrogationes.*—Bart. de Chaimis Interrogat.—Martini de Frias de Arte et Modo audiendi Confessiones fol. xvi*a.*

John of Freiburg, among the instructions for the examination of secular priests, includes (*loc. cit.* Q. 83–4) " Item de luxuria et venatione et de irregularitate ac de incontinentia si est in sacris ordinibus. Item de advocatione et ludo alearum et similibus in quibus sæpius solent offendere Deum "—and this is moderate in comparison with the fearful list of inquiries given by St Antonino as necessary to be made of the clergy, suggesting the deplorable condition of the Church at the period. One significant point is the frequency with which matters are rated as mortal sins " nisi habet licentiam papæ," " nisi habet dispensationem papæ."—S. Antonini Confessionale, fol. 54–65.

It is observable that in rehearsing the ten commandments the second is run in with the first, and no questions are asked as to image-worship. The number of ten is made up by Bart. de Chaimis (Interrog. fol. 23, 43) by splitting the tenth into two. Father Habert (Praxis Sacr. Pœnit. Tract. II.) even reduces the commandments to eight, omitting the second and running together the seventh and tenth. For the various divisions of the Decalogue see Sayri Clavis Regia Sacerd. Lib. IV. cap. ii. n. 6. Cf. Catech. Trident. De I. Præcept. Decalogi cap. 4.

[1] S. Antonini Confessionale, fol. 20*b.*—Somma Pacifica cap. 2.—Bart. de Chaimis Interrog. fol. 16*a.*

[2] B. de Chaimis Interrog. fol. 16*a.*—Somma Pacifica cap. 2.—Caietani Opusc. Tract. v. De Confessione Q. 3; Ejusd. Summula s. v. *Interrogatio.*

for thoroughness of examination, accompanied by an euormous development in the enumeration of all possible sins and in the differentiation of their grades and varieties. The latter continued, but a reaction as to the former seems to have set in with the sixteenth century. Prierias discourages indiscriminate inquisitiveness. There are various opinions, he says, as to the duty of interrogation, but the safest seems to be that it should be let alone unless there is cause to suspect that the penitent is withholding sins through ignorance or forgetfulness or perversity, or when there are circumstances to be ascertained controlling the degree of guilt.[1] Domingo Soto even goes further, and in this he is followed by Fernando Rebello: Confession is voluntary and the truth is not to be extorted; all that the confessor should do is to assist the ignorant, and he warmly deprecates the manuals of confession in general circulation with a wealth of questions teaching the penitent much of which he had better be ignorant, especially as some priests deem it necessary to show their skill by omitting none of them.[2]

These protests had little effect. Warnings, of course, continued to be given as to prudence with youths and women, but they were accompanied with instructions that rendered them inoperative. S. Carlo Borromeo directs the confessor, after the penitent has finished, to interrogate on the basis of the Decalogue, and with those who rarely come to confession he is to go on with the seven deadly sins, the five senses, the precepts of the Church and the works of mercy; moreover he is to enquire closely into details and to address himself specially to the sins common in the class to which the peni-

---

[1] Summa Sylvestrina s. v. *Confessor* III. § 17.

[2] Dom. Soto in IV. Sentt. Dist. XVIII. Q. ii. Art. 4.—Rebelli de Obligationibus Justitiæ P. II. Lib. XVII. *De Officiis Confessarii.*

In one of these vernacular confessionals now before me (*Confessionario breve y muy provechoso,* without date) the penitent is required to go through the Decalogue *seriatim;* with each commandment he makes a general confession of its inobservance, followed by a special enumeration of all infractions; then the seven mortal sins are treated individually in the same duplicate manner; then the works of mercy and their neglect; then the sins of the five senses; then the three faculties of the soul; then the three theological and five cardinal virtues; then the sins against the Holy Ghost; then the seven gifts of the Holy Ghost and the seven sacraments. Finally each state and occupation of life is treated, with the sins to which it is likely to give occasion.

tent belongs.[1] Fornari gives virtually the same instructions and follows them with a long enumeration of the vices and failings of the several classes which are to be inquired into specially.[2] Henriquez commences by warning the confessor not to be too minute in sexual matters and to avoid indecent expressions, and then proceeds with a shocking catalogue of questions covering every possible species of impurity.[3] It was shortly after this that Paul V. issued the Roman Ritual still in use. This recognizes the use of interrogation, but gives a wholesome warning not to waste time in useless and curious inquiries, nor by imprudence to teach sin to the innocent, and especially to the young of either sex.[4] It is well to issue such warnings, but practically they can amount to little; the confessor must judge for himself, and his judgment will depend upon his temperament; he may spare the hardened and persistent sinner or he may leave an indelible stain on the soul of virginal innocence. Diana is profuse in his cautions not to enquire too minutely into the details of salacity, but it would not be easy to frame a series of more searching investigations into all the shades and complications of such sins than those which he compiles for the guidance of confessors.[5] Azpilcueta says that it is sufficient for a prostitute to confess that for so many years she admitted all comers, but Manuel Sa declares that he would not be content with so general a statement, though he prudently omits to specify what details he would enquire into.[6] Father Gobat reiterates the old prescriptions as to carrying the penitent through the Decalogue and the seven mortal sins and the precepts of the Church, but he cautions the priest not to render the confession too onerous and unpleasant to the penitent, and he virtually admits the superfluousness of it all when he concedes that an African slave in Brazil can be absolved if he makes known in-

---

[1] S. Caroli Borrom. Instructiones (Ed. 1678, p. 59).

[2] Fornarii Institt. Confessar. Tract. I. cap. 2; Tract. II. cap. 1–13, 19.

[3] Henriquez Summæ Theol. Moral. Lib. VI. cap. 29.

[4] Ritualis Roman. Tit. III. cap. 1. "Sed caveat ne curiosis aut inutilibus interrogationibus quemquam detineat, præsertim juniores utriusque sexus, vel alios de eo quod ignorant imprudenter interrogans, ne scandalum patiantur indeque peccare discant."

[5] Summa Diana s. vv. *Confessarius* n 30, 36; *Circumstantia.*

[6] Azpilcueta Comment. de Pœnit. Dist. V. cap. 1, n. 43.—Em. Sa Aphorismi Confessar. s. v. *Confessio* n. 43.

telligibly a single mortal sin, and that the deaf and dumb or those of a foreign tongue can be similarly shriven.[1]

As Father Gobat indicates, the principal restraint on excessive interrogation is the fear of rendering confession odious, which confessors are instructed always to bear in mind. This is apparent in the instructions of the shrewd Jesuit, Father Segneri, which go far to explain the success of the brethren of the Society of Jesus in the confessional. Interrogation, he says, ought not to be necessary, but it is, for few penitents will make a full confession without it. He counsels no brutal questioning, but a quiet insinuation, an assumption of the existence of sin, and when once a breach is made in the entrenchments of the penitent a little skill will make him surrender at discretion. Human nature and its weaknesses were never more closely and practically studied than by the children of Loyola.[2] In strong contrast with this dexterity is the straightforward business-like method of the Capuchin Corella. Written in the vernacular, and in the form of dialogue between the confessor and his penitent, his book lends a dramatic realism to the secrets of the confessional, which enables one to conceive thoroughly what occurs there. It carries the sinner through the Ten Commandments and then takes up each class and trade with the utmost minuteness, even to showing us a barber admitting that he had shaved customers on a feast-day. There is nothing quite so brutal as in Bishop Burchard and the older manuals, but the minuteness of detail which the confessor is represented as requiring of his female penitents is quite as indecent and dangerous, and, as an interchange of speech between man and woman, would seem incredible to any but a churchman.[3] The immense success which the work enjoyed throughout Europe during the first half of the eighteenth century and its translation into various languages show that it was recognized as a safe and practical guide. The average confessor cannot be expected to possess the cool dexterity of the trained Jesuit, and direct interrogation such as this must be a necessity, for the infinite detail with which every variety and degree of sin is examined and commented upon to decide exactly how much the penitent is bound to reveal and exactly of what he is required

---

[1] Gobat Alphab. Confessar. n. 296, 307, 335–7, 481–5.

[2] P. Segneri Instructio Confessarii (Dilingæ, 1699, pp. 20–33).

[3] Corella Praxis Confessionalis P. I. Tract. vi. cap. 8.

to accuse himself, is altogether beyond the capacity of the ordinary sinner. La Croix occupies sixty-three paragraphs in considering sexual offences alone, and this is simply to determine whether the confession is *integra* and has nothing to do with the puzzling questions as to mortals and venials or the simpler subject of the due amount of satisfaction.[1]

We may reasonably hope that this plainness and directness are not habitual in the confessional of to-day, but it rests entirely with the conscience and habits of the confessor. The tendency has undoubtedly been to a relaxation of the duty of interrogation, perhaps partly because of the increase in modern refinement and delicacy and partly in view of the steadily diminishing importance of penance. Chiericato, who was a contemporary of Corella, urges brevity and discretion, especially with regard to carnal sins, and tells the confessor that his penitents are not to be taken through all that is set down in the Moral Theologies.[2] The council of Rome, in 1725, in adopting a system of instruction for children at their first confession, is careful to warn priests not to teach them sins of which they may be ignorant.[3] Herzig passes over the subject briefly and cautiously, warning the confessor that it is as pitch which defiles whosoever touches it.[4] Liguori assumes that there is no need of interrogating those who are well instructed and ready to confess all details and circumstances; the confessor should not be over-zealous or render confession too onerous; ignorance, if conscientious, is to be respected, especially when enlightenment may do harm rather than good, and duties that would be burdensome are not to be officiously forced upon the penitent.[5] Guarceno in brief gives the same counsel.[6] The council of Ravenna, in 1855, orders the confessor to interrogate, but to abstain from trifling and irrelevant questions, and especially from dangerous ones which may teach the young sins of which they are ignorant.[7] Cardinal Gousset warns the confessor to be especially guarded in

[1] La Croix Theol. Moral. Lib. VI. P. ii. n. 1021–82.
[2] Clericati De Pœnit. Decis. XXXVI. n. 6.
[3] Acta Concil. Roman. Romæ, 1725, p. 139.
[4] Herzig Manuale Confessar. P. II. n. 51, Præcept. VI., IX. (Aug. Vindel. 1757).
[5] S. Alph. de Ligorio Theol. Moral. Lib. VI. n. 607, 610.
[6] Varceno Comp. Theol. Moral. Tract. XVIII. cap. iv. art. 5, Append.
[7] C. Ravennat. ann. 1855, cap. 5 § 6 (Coll. Lacens. VI. 159).

inquiries concerning carnal sins.[1] Bishop Healy quotes De Lugo and Liguori to show that the priest must interrogate only to supply deficiencies in the penitent's confession.[2] Father Müller enjoins the greatest caution in inquiring into sins against chastity, and instructs the confessor to be " very careful never to destroy, by any imprudent questions, the penitent's happy innocence of crime or the exalted idea the faithful usually have of priestly modesty and holiness."[3]

These utterances express the views of the laxist school, which, since Liguori and the bull *Auctorem Fidei*, has been the prevailing one. Rigorism, however, takes a stricter view of the duties of the confessor. What these are may be found conscientiously expressed, about the middle of the last century, by Father Habert. He directs that the penitent be first examined as to his knowledge of the faith; then the inquiry takes the widest possible range through the precepts of the Decalogue, which, as usual, are extended to cover all possible delinquencies, and every detail that may bear upon the character of a sin is to be minutely investigated. He does not conceal the difficulty of the delicate subject of lapses of the flesh. These are matters which penitents do not willingly reveal, and unless the confessor helps them with his inquiries they do not explain, and thus are left to putrefy in their filth from a mistaken sense of delicacy on the part of the priest. On the other hand, the utmost prudence is required to avoid teaching sin, for cases are not lacking in which the penitent leaves the feet of the confessor with the intention of experiencing what has been taught there. In this dilemma he can only suggest the old method of first inquiring about impure thoughts and whether they give pleasure, and on this being admitted he can push his inquiries further. The series of interrogations which follow are no more than the necessities of the confessional require, but to a layman they seem sufficiently shocking when addressed to a woman.[4] Alasia is somewhat more cautious in his directions as to

---

[1] Gousset, Théol. Morale, II. n. 454.

[2] Frassinetti's New Parish Priest's Manual, Append. p. 556.

[3] Müller's Catholic Priesthood, III. 142.

[4] Habert, Praxis Sacr. Pœnit. Tract. II. cap. xv.

So an official manual for the confessors of the diocese of Strassburg—"Sensim a cogitationibus simplicibus ad morosas, a morosis ad desideria, a desideriis levibus ad consensum, a consensu ad actus minus peccaminosos, et si illos fatentur ad magis criminosos ascendendo."—Monita Generalia de Officiis Confessarii ad Usum Diœcesis Argentin. cap. ii. § 3 (Argentinæ, 1722).

inquiries in these matters.[1]   Bishop Zenner, a very moderate rigorist, assumes that, with many penitents, the effort is to conceal rather than to confess their sins, and he emphasizes the necessity of interrogations, though they should be prudently conducted.[2]   Father Gury is a decided laxist, but he tells us that the confessor does not do his duty who grants absolution for a confession which gives only the species and number of each sin ; it is his business to interrogate and to learn all the details requisite to establish the grade of every sin ; at the same time he shows the difficulty of formulating any definite rule for practice and the impossibility of expecting uniformity among confessors.[3]

There is thus the widest latitude allowed to the discretion of the priest, who can adopt whatever practice his conscience may lead him to prefer.   What the customary method may be no one can pretend to say ; the confessor is responsible only to God ; there is no appeal from him and no one to call him to account.   The penitent is bound to silence by the " natural seal " as is the confessor by the " sacramental seal," and, save in cases of direct solicitation to evil, the secrets of the confessional must be revealed by neither.   What occurs there is to be known only to the parties concerned and to God.   The degree to which interrogations are to be pushed is a matter obviously surrounded by difficulties, if confession is to be more than a mere formality, and only the keenest knowledge of human nature combined with the loftiest spiritual gifts can guide aright the confessor in his arduous and responsible duty.

It has not been left to modern times to recognize the dangers attendant on interrogating the penitent.   Hardly had enforced confession been introduced when Bishop Poore of Salisbury cautioned his priests to so make their inquiries that the innocent should not be led into sin,[4] and Cæsarius of Heisterbach emphasizes this with the case of a nun who was led into sin by the beastly interrogation of her confessor and was saved only by the intercession of the Virgin.[5]

---

[1] Alasia Theol. Moral. T. II. p. 334 (Taurini, 1834).

[2] Zenner Instruct. Pract. Confessar. §§ 85, 96.

[3] Gury Casus Conscientiæ I. n. 31-2 ; II. 448-62.

[4] Constitt. R. Poore ann. 1217, cap. 27 (Harduin. VII. 97).

[5] Cæsar. Heisterb. Dial. Dist. III. cap. 47.—Passavanti, Lo Specchio della vera Penitenza, Dist. V. cap. 4.

A century later Guido de Monteroquer, in warning against too curious an investigation into carnal sins, speaks of the frequent instances in which both men and women have been led by it into guilt of which they had previously known nothing.[1] The teachers of the period admit that there were authorities who objected wholly to interrogation on this account; but, as perfect confession could be had in no other way, it had to be allowed, and they can only urge the greatest caution not to convert it into a source of infection for the innocent.[2] In the debased morality which we have seen prevailing among the medieval priesthood it was hardly to be expected that these warnings would receive much attention. Angiolo da Chivasso inveighs against those who are contaminators rather than confessors, who take delight in the opportunity afforded by the confessional of questioning women indecently, and he even hints that young men are not safe with them.[3] Savonarola's utterances indicate that salacious priests made use of the confessional to grope after the most prurient details.[4] Prierias warns the confessor that such curiosity injures himself as well as the penitent, and Rosemond asserts that numerous souls are daily imperilled through the lack of discretion of many priests.[5] Martin de Frias speaks of the frequency with which mortal sins are committed by the contaminators, who push their indecent inquiries on account of the delectation they experience in such details.[6] One very suggestive mode of teaching sin was a question used by ignorant priests—"If you should do this, or that, would you confess it?"—which the synod of Verdun, in 1598, forbids and characterizes as framed in the workshop of the devil.[7] Escobar reproves the indiscretion with which confessors are accustomed to push their questioning of women, and tells them that it would be

---

[1] Manip. Curatorum P. II. Tract. iii. cap. 9.

[2] S. Raymundi Summæ Lib. III. Tit. xxxiv. § 4.—Hostiens. Aureæ Summæ Lib. v. De Pœn. et Remiss. § 48.—Manip. Curator. *ubi sup.*—Jo. Gersonis Regulæ Morales (Opp. Ed. 1488, xxv. E.).

[3] Summa Angelica s. v. *Interrogationes.*—"Et quod stet [pœnitens] facie versa latere confessoris si est mulier aut juvenis, et non admittas quod aspiciat in faciem tuam, quia multi propter hoc corruerunt."

[4] Savonarolæ Confessionale, fol. 50.

[5] Summa Sylvestrina s. v. *Confessor* III. § 18.—Godschalci Rosemondi Confessionale cap. v. P. ii. § *De Conjugatis.*

[6] Martini de Frias de Arte et Modo audiendi Confessiones, fol. xv*a.*

[7] Synod. Verdunens. ann. 1598, cap. 51 (Hartzheim VIII. 470).

better for them to ascertain less exactly the grade of sin than thus to create scandal.[1] Gobat recognizes the extreme danger to both parties in these matters, and tells us that some moralists hold that they are not to be investigated as minutely as others deem to be necessary.[2] Tamburini, after a searching discussion of all possible sexual aberrations, cautions the confessor not to push his inquiries too far lest both parties be led into temptation,[3] and a manual of 1726 observes that a priest who seeks too curiously into details and uses expressions too free is a contaminator rather than a confessor.[4] The Jesuit rule was prudent, if not strictly logical—that it is better for the confessor to know less of the sins of his penitent than to create scandal for either party.[5] The learned Binterim, after a brief allusion to the brutalities of the Penitentials and discreet silence as to medieval and modern writers, observes "Past ages present much which modern times have changed. What has passed away belongs to history, not to the present."[6] Let us devoutly hope that it may be so.

It is not only the danger to the penitent that is acknowledged, but the risk of corruption to which the confessor himself is exposed. Already, at the end of the sixth century, Gregory the Great alludes to the perils incurred in receiving the confessions of the dying, when the recital of sins committed inflames with the desire to imitate them.[7] If thus the solemn atmosphere and repulsive details of the death-bed are insufficient to neutralize such incentives to sin, it is easy to imagine how great must be the strain on virtue when the priest, with all the passions of a man, has whispered in his ear from female lips the acknowledgment of lustful longings or of temptation unresisted. When St. Bonaventura tells the confessor that he must repress all feeling of pleasure at what he hears, it shows that he fully

---

[1] Escobar Theol. Moral. Tract. VII. Exam. iv. cap. 7, n. 38.

[2] Gobat Alphab. Confessar. n. 217, 539, 546.

[3] Tamburini Method. Confessionis Lib. II. cap. vii. § 10, n. 77.

[4] Istruzione per i novelli Confessori P. I. n. 149 (Roma, 1726).

[5] Lohner Instructio practica de Confessionibus P. I. cap. iii. § 2, Q. 4; P. II. cap. 1, Q. 3.

[6] Binterim, Denkwürdigkeiten, V. II. 234.

[7] S. Gregor. PP. I. Exposit. in I. Regum Lib. VI. cap. ii. § 4. "Nam dum cogitant quæ confitentes fecerunt, ad scelera quæ audiunt inardescunt; nam sæpe dum audiunt quibus se alii blandimentis obruerant, amare ipsi incipiunt quæ jam eorum exhortatione morientes illi confitentur."

appreciated the besetting danger of the confessional.[1] John of Freiburg recognizes it fully, and when Astesanus seeks to answer the
argument that details of carnal sin provoke delectation in the confessor he can only reply that they must be confessed and that the
grace of the sacrament annuls the inclination to sin—an argument
the futility of which he subsequently admits when cautioning the
priest not to be too curious lest he infect himself.[2] Passavanti considers the risk to both parties so great that he advises the penitent to
select a confessor and make a detailed confession, after which he or
she shall confess only in general terms, referring for particulars to
the first confession.[3] The very nasty discussions over the immediate
effects of the revelations of the confessional show how inflammable
is the material which the Church has furnished for functions so delicate, and penitents are instructed to use language as decent as possible
so as not to excite the sensuality of their pastors.[4] Habert gives a
most earnest warning to the confessor as to the dangers of the dis-
closures to which he must listen : the contagium of no infectious
disease is more deadly to the body than are the recitals of the confessional to the soul; only those in full spiritual vigor can hear them
without infection.[5] Theologians, in fact, differ on the question
whether a confessor who has realized by experience his own fragility
commits a mortal sin in exposing himself to the danger of listening
to the confessions of women.[6] As a palliative for this evil Benedict
XIV. suggests that a priest sins gravely who, after enjoying prolonged delectation from a confession of this kind, grants absolution
without first performing an act of contrition, and the council of

---

[1] S. Bonaventuræ Confessionale cap. 1, Partic. 2.

[2] Joh. Friburgens. Summæ Confessor. Lib. III. Tit. xxxiv. Q. 81, 83.—Astesani Summæ Lib. v. Tit. xii. Q. 1 ; Tit. xvii. See also S. Antonini de Audientia
Confess. fol. 10*b*.

[3] Passavanti, Lo Specchio della vera Penitenza Dist. v. cap. 4, 5.

[4] Caietani Opusc. Tract. xxii.—Summa Sylvestrina s. v. *Confessio Sacr.* §§ 2,
10.—Joh. Sanchez Selecta de Sacramentis Disp. x. n. 57.—Henriquez Summæ
Theol. Moral. Lib. xi. cap. xvi. n. 6.—Summa Diana s. v. *Pollutio* n. 3.—Zerola
Praxis Sacr. Pœnit. cap. xxv. Q. 17, 21.—Bonacinæ Compendium s. v. *Pollutio*
n. 2.—Gobat Alphab. Confessor. n. 543.—Clericati de Pœnit. Dist. XXXVI. n.
6.—S. Alph. de Ligorio Theol. Moral. Lib. III. n. 438.

[5] Habert Praxis Sacr. Pœnit. Tract. I. cap. ii. n. 2.

[6] Caramuelis Theol. Fundam. n. 506–10.—Summa Diana s. v. *Pollutio* n. 3.—
Zerola Praxis Sacr. Pœnit. cap. xxv. Q. 17, 21.

Suchuen, in 1803, directs that no confession is to be heard without offering a preliminary prayer to God to be preserved from infection if violations of the sixth commandment, which give rise to so many temptations, are to be listened to.[1]

In view of these admitted dangers, it cannot be a matter of surprise that the seduction of women in the confessional has always been a source of anxiety to the Church. I have been obliged to treat this unpleasant subject in some detail elsewhere,[2] and may be spared from examining it here as fully as its importance demands. It was a recognized evil prior to the enforcement of confession,[3] and it could not but increase when the whole population was driven annually to the confessional, regardless of the spiritual condition of the individual. That it was regarded as an ever-present probability is seen in the reiterated declarations that the parish priest who was known as a "solicitor" to evil forfeited his jurisdiction over women, who were then at liberty to seek another confessor,[4] or if this was not possible, even to omit confession altogether.[5] Council after council

---

[1] Benedicti PP. XIV. Casus Conscientiæ Sept. 1739, cas. 2.—Synod. Sutchuens. ann. 1803, cap. vi. § 7 (Coll. Lacens. VI. 608).

Akin to this is the prurient delight which the moralists seem to take in treating of sexual sins and their proneness to enter into the filthiest details, as well as to select them in presenting examples on which to argue. Chiericato remarks on this when he comes to treat of the sixth and ninth precepts, and promises to confine himself to what is strictly necessary, but he does not spare the reader much (De Pœnit. Decis. XXVII. n. 9). His good resolution does not endure, moreover, for he subsequently devotes an entire section to a wholly superfluous dissertation on hermaphrodite nuns, full of indecent details, related with quiet complacency (Ibid. Decis. XLIII.). It was a recognized fact that these grave theologians experienced delectation in treating of these subjects, and there was a question whether they thus commit sin, for it is for a good purpose.—Alph. de Leone de Off. et Potest. Confessar. Recoll. XIII. n. 24.

The most notorious example of the kind is Sanchez, *Disput. de S. Matrimonii Sacramento.* I have purposely avoided looking into it, but if it is worse than many of its congeners it must be indeed repulsive.

[2] History of Sacerdotal Celibacy, 2d Ed. pp. 350, 566 sqq., 632 sqq.

[3] C. Toletan. I. ann. 398, cap. 6.—P. Abælardi Serm. XXIX.—Cap. 8, 9, 10 Caus. XXX. Q. 1.—Calixti PP. II. Serm. I. de S. Jacobo (Migne CLXIII. 1390).

[4] Guido de Monteroquer, however, states (Manip. Curator. PP. II. Tract. iii. cap. 9) that when such a parish priest refuses a licence to confess elsewhere or there is no other priest accessible, there is nothing for the woman to do except to confess to him, first praying to God for strength to resist his importunities.

[5] Cherubini de Spoleto Quadragesimale, Serm. LXIV.

busied itself with devising futile measures to repress it. Bishop Poore
vainly threatened fifteen years' penance to be followed by imprisonment in a monastery,[1] while Bishop Pelayo shows his zeal for the
cloth by enumerating it among the customary sins of women.[2]
Cæsarius of Heisterbach speaks of the many examples which he
could adduce, but suppresses out of respect for religion; St. Bonaventura assures us that few parish priests are free from this or some
other vice that should incapacitate them ; and an anonymous contemporary writer alludes to the corruption of women in the confessional
as an ordinary and well-understood matter.[3] So well understood is
it, indeed, that it has led to an exception in the rule of perfect confession, and reticence on the subject of carnal sins is allowed to a
woman obliged to confess to a priest known as a solicitor to evil.[4]

The abuse was stimulated not only by the temptations and opportunities of the confessional, but it was virtually divested of all
spiritual terrors for the woman by the assurance of pardon. The
doctors of both the Dominican and Franciscan schools were unanimous in saying that a woman thus seduced ought not to confess to her
paramour and that he ought not to absolve her from their mutual
sin, but that if he did so the absolution is good, the only objection
urged against this being that it relieved the woman from the shame,
which is a wholesome concomitant of confession.[5] No other conclu-

---

[1] Constitt. R. Poore, ann. 1217, cap. 9 (Harduin. VII. 91).

[2] Alvar. Pelagii de Planctu Ecclesiæ Lib. II. Art. xlv. n. 84.

[3] Cæsar. Heisterb. Dial. Dist. III. cap. 41.—S. Bonavent. Quare Fratres
Minores Prædicent (Opusc. I. 405).—Collectio de Scandalis Ecclesiæ (Döllinger, Beiträge zur politischen, kirchlichen und Cultur-Geschichte, III. 186).

[4] S. Antonini Summæ P. III. Tit. xiv. cap. 19 § 8.—Bonal Institt. Theol.
T. IV. n. 246.

[5] Alani de Insulis Lib. Pœnit. (Migne, CCX. 298–299).—S. Th. Aquin. in
IV. Sentt. Dist. XIX. Q. 1, Art. 3 ; Ejusd. Summæ Suppl. Q. XX. Art. ii. ad 1.
—Jo. Friburgens. Summæ Confessor. Lib. III. Tit. xxxiv. Q. 65.—Astesani
Summæ Lib. V. Tit. xxxix. Q. 4.—Manip. Curator. P. II. Tract. iii. cap. 4.—
Cherubini de Spoleto Quadragesimale, Serm. LXIV.—Summa Sylvestrina s. v.
Confessio Sacr. I. § 17 ; III. § 9.

Domingo Soto (in IV. Sentt. Dist. XVIII. Q. iv. Art. 2) draws a distinction.
If granted without scandal and without incitement to sin the absolution is valid
and may be fruitful. But if it is known to others it causes scandal, which
can scarce be less than a mortal sin, and where there is danger of exciting
to evil it is an imprudent sacrilege, and is not only invalid but a mortal sin.
He adds that in some dioceses it was forbidden under pain of excommunica-

sion could be drawn from the carefully constructed theories of the keys, but somehow, as Alain de Lille says, the keys of heaven and hell have become strangely confused. Under such circumstances, in the popular mind, sin could scarce be reckoned as sin, while, so far as concerns the Church, if scandal could be avoided, it was good-naturedly tolerated as a necessary evil. Even after the outbreak of the Reformation, Bernal Diaz de Lugo argues that, unless married women or virgins are concerned, it is only a qualified fornication; although it is regarded with special horror by the people, it gives a handle to heretics and it leads men to keep their wives and daughters from the confessional, wherefore the punishment should be severe in proportion to the extent to which a case has become known and the scandal which it has caused.[1] As for the ordinary concubines of priests, there is no objection expressed to their confessing to their paramours unless they should fear that the confession itself might give occasion to sin and thus create an impediment to the sacrament.[2]

Solicitation in the confessional naturally afforded a fair mark for the heretics, of which, as Archbishop Carranza observes, they did not fail to take full advantage.[3] With the steady and alarming growth of heresy, it was full time for the Church to take effective steps for the suppression of the evil. The matter was clearly subject to episcopal jurisdiction, and there was ample store of statutes

---

tion. In fact it was so forbidden at Liége in 1287, and shortly afterwards at Cambrai (Hartzheim III. 686; IV. 68). In 1519 Rosemond tells us (Confessionale, fol. 117) that the prohibition was still nominally in force in the diocese of Liége, but that it was not observed, yet he wishes that the same rule were adopted elsewhere.

Doubtless one reason for the tolerance of an abuse so demoralizing was the dread of scandal caused by making the woman seek another confessor, and the implied violation of the seal. Even Benedict XIV., as we shall see, allowed this ever-present spectre of scandal to overcome his repugnance in this matter.

[1] Bern. Diaz de Luco Pract. Crim. Canon. cap. 75, 76. In a similar spirit Bishop Bernal Diaz cautions ecclesiastical judges not to inquire too curiously into secret cases of adultery, for the fragility of the clergy leads them to indulge in it on account of the little risk of discovery, and he emphasizes this by mentioning that, in the previous year, 1537, in the vicinity of Valladolid three priests had been castrated, within the space of eight months, in private vengeance for this offence.

[2] Angles Flores Theol. Quæstionum, P. I. fol. 148*a* (Venet. 1584).

[3] Carranza, Comentarios sobre el Catechismo, P. III. Tercera Sacramento, cap. vii.

for the exemplary punishment of offenders, but they had been allowed to become a dead letter, the bishops were inert, the crime was one not easily proved by the ordinary proceedings of the ecclesiastical courts, and the risk of scandal rendered all parties indisposed to action, although the seal of the confessional was relaxed in order that the penitent might speak if she saw fit.[1] Rome, however, had one instrumentality at its command which, by the secrecy of its methods, could avert unnecessary publicity, and, by the energy of its measures, could obtain conviction. This was the Inquisition, and though the crime of solicitation might seem to be beyond its cognizance, heresy has always been an elastic term, capable of being made to serve any desired end. Paul IV. therefore determined to employ the Holy Office; its organization in Spain was especially efficient, and tentative proceedings might safely be commenced there. Accordingly, on February 18, 1559, a brief was dispatched to the inquisitors of Granada, informing them that the pope was advised that sundry beneficed priests and confessors in their diocese were accustomed to solicit women in the confessional; such an abuse of the sacrament argued disbelief of the Catholic faith, and its perpetrators were therefore justiciable by the Inquisition, which was given full powers to try them and punish them at discretion, even relaxing them to the secular arm for execution; all exemptions and immunities of the religious Orders were moreover withdrawn, and they were all subjected to the jurisdiction of the Holy Office.[2] What was the immediate effect of the measure in Granada we have no means of knowing, but apparently it was sufficient to justify an enlargement of the field of experiment, for, in 1561, Pius IV. addressed a similar commission to the Inquisitor General rendering it operative throughout the Spanish dominions, and in Italy the Roman Inquisition was also set to work.[3] The Spanish Inquisition included the crime in its annual " Edict of Denunciations," which required all persons cognizant of the offences therein enumerated to denounce

---

[1] Rodriguez, Nuova Somma de' Casi di Coscienza, P. I. cap. 53, n. 9.

[2] Llorente (Hist. Critica, Cap. XXVIII. Art. 1, n. 4) places this brief in 1556, but a copy of it in the *Bulario del Orden de Santiago*, III. 322 (Archivo Historico Nacional de España) bears the date of 1559, in the fourth year of Paul IV.

[3] Pii PP. IV. Bull. *Cum sicut nuper* (Bullar. II. 48).—Tamburini, Storia Generale dell' Inquisizione, II. 238–48.

offenders forthwith to the Inquisition. This brought in an abundant harvest of accusations, and was suspended in 1571, but was resumed in 1576, on realizing that without it there was little hope of effective work.[1]

In some of the trials of the period, which I have had opportunity to consult, the brutal indecency of the confessor, as proved by the concurrent testimony of witnesses, almost passes belief and raises a curious question as to what could have been, in the minds of the victims, the conception of a religion which clothed such ministers of Satan with the awful power of the keys. That the Inquisition, however, regarded the offence as comparatively trivial is shown by the leniency of the punishments inflicted—detention in a monastery for a year or more, with perhaps a scourging, disability to hear confessions of women and similar penalties being the customary sentence, and these were always carried out in private, such culprits never being exposed to the humiliation of appearing in the public autos de fé.[2] The theologians, in fact, were not disposed to attach any peculiar importance to the crime, for it was a disputed question among them, with opinions equally divided, whether a guilty confessor, in making his sacramental confession, was required when revealing a carnal sin to specify whether it was simple fornication or committed with his penitent,[3] which forms an instructive contrast to their customary eagerness to require the acknowledgment of all aggravating circumstances. How much more the scandal was dreaded than the sin is exhibited in one or two Jesuit cases about this time. In 1583, Father Sebastian Briviesca was guilty of solicitation in Monterey, a town of Galicia. Another Jesuit father, Diego Her-

---

[1] Llorente, *ubi sup.* n. 7, 8.

[2] MSS. Universitäts Bibliothek, Halle, Yc. 20, T. I., XI. Similar clemency seems to have obtained in Naples. In one case a priest duly convicted by several witnesses was merely suspended.—Lenglet Du Fresnoy, Traité du Secret de la Confession, p. 303.

[3] Fumi Aurea Armilla s. v. *Circumstantia* n. 12.—Em. Sa Aphor. Confessar. s. v. *Confessio* n. 25.—Jo. Sanchez Selecta de Sacramentis Disp. XI. n. 3.—La Croix Theol. Moral. Lib. VI. P. ii. n. 1041.

In Spain the Cruzada indulgence afforded easy relief *in foro conscientiæ*, for it enabled offenders to select their own confessors, and these were authorized to absolve for all cases excepting heresy, and there was no heresy when the sinfulness of the act was admitted.—Escobar Theol. Moral. Tract. VII. Exam. iv. cap. 7, n. 37.

nandez, discovered it and desired to denounce the offender to the Inquisition, but was prevented and bitterly persecuted, while Briviesca was dismissed from the Order, was furnished with money and a companion to ship him from Barcelona to Naples, and was there provided for by being made confessor of the Hospital of Santiago. Cristóbal Trugillo, another Jesuit, similarly guilty, was conveyed away in the same manner. The facts, however, leaked out, and Francisco Marcen, Provincial of Castile, who had thus shielded his Order, was tried by the Inquisition of Valladolid in 1587, and was imprisoned for thus disobeying its edict. In the course of the affair the consultations between those engaged in it were carried on under a fictitious pretence of confession, thus parodying the sacrament in order to be able to claim the seal of the confessional for the communications made; while, by a refinement of casuistry, the women witnesses were persuaded that it was not their duty to denounce the offenders and were admitted to the Eucharist while thus under excommunication. A characteristic incident was that the question was submitted to the Jesuit professors at Salamanca, without stating that the Order was involved, when they pronounced that the offenders must be denounced to the Inquisition, but on being informed of the truth they promptly found arguments to reverse their decision.[1] In spite of the Inquisition the offence could not be suppressed in Spain. Towards the close of the seventeenth century Arbiol informs us that the perpetrators were mostly priests advanced in years; he denounces the offence as the scandal of the world, and seeks to discourage it by pointing out the disgrace attendant on an inquisitorial sentence.[2]

In 1608, Paul V. granted to the Portuguese Inquisition the same

---

[1] Bibl. Vatican. MSS. Ottobonian. Lat. 495.

How little the Society of Jesus trusted its members and how anxious it was to prevent scandal are visible in the rule that when a priest is hearing confessions of women there must always be a companion posted where he can see but not hear (S. J. Regulæ Sacerdotum n. 18). In addition to this the sacristan is directed to keep watch, and there must always be syndics observing the confessors and reporting to the superior any prolonged confessions or conferences outside of the confessional (Instructio pro Confessariis n. 5). Yet the Memoranda of a Visitor of the Order in the South German Province, in 1596, show that these salutary rules were neglected with the result occasionally of shocking scandals.—Reusch, Beiträge zur Geschichte des Jesuitenordens, p. 236 (München, 1894).

[2] Arbiol, Manuale Sacerdotum Lib. IV. cap. 23 (Cæsar-Augustæ, 1697).

jurisdiction over solicitation as that which had been conferred on the Spanish, and, in 1622, Gregory XV. extended its provisions over all the lands of the Roman obedience. Further, as there were many lands in which there was no Inquisition, and as the bishops had not jurisdiction over the regulars, who furnished so many confessors, he withdrew in this matter their privileges and exemptions and subjected them to the episcopal courts, on which he conferred power to punish at discretion, even including relaxation to the secular arm.[1] To emphasize this among the religious Orders, in 1633, Urban VIII. directed that this bull should be read annually, with a verbal warning, in the chapters of all Orders and sworn evidence of the fact be transmitted to the Roman Holy Office. He further issued an encyclical directing that when episcopal approbations were given to confessors they should be instructed to require all female penitents, who confessed to having been solicited, to denounce the offender.[2] Yet Gregory's bull was not published in either France or Germany, and there were few bishops who took the trouble to promulgate its provisions in their dioceses. In France the assemblies of the clergy refused to receive it as unsuited to the customs of the country and as infringing on the seal of the confessional, and an attempt to publish it early in the eighteenth century was promptly suppressed.[3] Father Gobat, writing in 1666, says that the German moralists have not commented upon the papal decrees, either because they have not been received and published in Germany, and there is no hope of its being done, or because the German women cannot be expected to go

---

[1] Gregor. PP. XV. Bull. *Universi Dominici Gregis* (Bullar. III. 484).

[2] Bened. PP. XIV. Bullar. I. 291.—Summa Diana s. v. *Denuntiare* n. 9.

[3] Pontas, Dict. de Cas de Conscience I. 872 (Ed. 1741).—Amort Dict. Select. Casuum Conscient. I. 704–5.—Lochon, Traité du Secret de la Confession, pp. 135, 144.

Yet in France the crime of solicitation was severely punished when detected. It was a *cas royal*, justiciable by the secular courts. June 23, 1673, a spiritual director of a convent, who had abused his position, was hanged and burnt in the Place Maubert, after trial and sentence by the Châtelet. Still, the arguments urged against Gregory's bull and the conditions proposed as necessary to prevent its provisions from working injustice would have reduced it to a nullity and show how little respect was entertained in France at the time for papal authority. People, in fact, had no hesitation in declaring that it afforded sufficient proof of papal fallibility.—Lenglet Du Fresnoy, Traité du Secret inviolable de la Confession, pp. 283, 304–20.

with complaints to such exalted personages as bishops and vicars-general, or because scandal was dreaded to the weak and comfort to the heretics; he adds that he can name a number of vicars-general who have never received such a complaint, save one in a single instance.[1]

In spite of this resistance of inertia the papacy did not abandon the struggle. It was not easy to define what constituted solicitation in confession, and advantage was taken of construing it in the strictest and most limited manner. In 1614, the Roman Inquisition had decreed that, as many priests used the confessional as a place of assignation, without hearing confessions, this should be considered as solicitation in confession and be liable to its penalties.[2] In 1666, Father Gobat argues that the most filthy conduct with a female penitent does not constitute a reserved case without the final act.[3] The casuists defended the proposition that for a confessor to hand a love-letter to a female penitent during confession is not solicitation, and this Alexander VII. condemned in 1665.[4] At the same time he struck a blow at a more important feature of the matter. We have seen it admitted by the theologians that the priest could grant valid absolution to his paramour for their common sin, and great authorities were found to argue not only that it was lawful but that it was expedient if it would quiet her conscience and avert defamation from her, even though the relations were notorious.[5] Alexander did not deny the validity of such absolution, but he condemned a proposition in circulation to the effect that it released the woman from the obligation of denouncing the priest, which was a perfectly fair deduction from the orthodox doctrine of the remission of the sin.[6] The comments of the moralists on the papal utterances show how ingenious were the devices employed to rob them of their efficiency and how difficult it naturally proved to induce women to undergo the labor

---

[1] Gobat Alphab. Confessar. n. 576–77.

[2] Mattheucci Cautela Confessarii Lib. I. cap. 5, n. 3.

[3] Gobat Alphab. Confessar. n. 358—"nisi copulam carnalem exerceat cum ea perfectione quam descripsi."

[4] Alex. PP. VII. Decr. 1665, Prop. 6.

[5] Summa Diana s. v. *Confessarius* n. 35.

[6] Alex. PP. VII. Decr. 1665, Prop. 7.—"Modus evadendi obligationem denunciandæ sollicitationis est si sollicitatus confiteatur cum sollicitante, hic potest ipsum absolvere absque onus denunciandi."

and mortification of denouncing those who had committed the offence on them, while confessors, to whom the knowledge came in subsequent confessions, were debarred by the seal of the confessional from the duty of denunciation without permission from the penitent.[1] Denunciation, in fact, is a thankless task on all hands. The confessor was warned, and the warning is repeated at the present day, that if he undertakes it he exposes himself to no little detraction and danger.[2] As for the woman, theologians argued that she was not bound to denounce if she had reasonable fear of grave injury to life, reputation or property, to herself or to her kindred to the fourth degree.[3] The Sorbonne went even further than this, for, with the support of the Faculty of Douai, in 1707, it declared, in spite of the bull of Gregory XV., that it was a mortal sin for a confessor to oblige a penitent to denounce a priest who had seduced her in the confessional. In 1698 it had already given an elaborate decision on the subject to the effect that the confessor should not be denounced until after he had received a fraternal admonition without abandoning his evil courses, nor even then if it would cause loss of reputation or danger to the woman, and in no case unless the prelate appealed to was known to be a man of wisdom and discretion, likely to manage the matter advisedly.[4] Under such limitations there was little danger of anything being done to check solicitation.

Moreover the reticence of Alexander VII., in not declaring invalid the absolution granted by the confessor to his victim, bore its natural fruits. It was left as an affair to be regulated in the several dioceses, and, acute as were the theologians, they do not seem to have recognized the absurd incongruity that salvation in such a matter could be

---

[1] Viva Trutina Theol. in Prop. 6 Alex. PP. VII.—Tamburini Method. Confess. Lib. III. cap. ix. § 4.—Mattheucci Cautela Confessar. Lib. I. cap. 5.—Jac. a Graffiis Pract. Casuum Reservat. Lib. II. cap. 12.

[2] Henriquez Summæ Theol. Moral. Lib. v. cap. x. n. 8.—Varceno Comp. Theol. Moral. Tract. XVIII. cap. viii. Append.

Fénelon, however, ordered all mission priests, to whom women confessed to have been solicited by confessors, to refuse absolution unless the penitent would authorize denunciation to be made to him, and he promised to avert all danger from both the woman and the priest.—Avis aux Confesseurs, v. (Œuvres, 1838, II. 349).

[3] Jo. Sanchez Selecta de Sacramentis Disp. XI. n. 55.—Viva Cursus Theol. Moral. P. VI. Q. viii. Art. 5, n. 8.

[4] Lochon, Traité du Secret de la Confession, pp. 197–217.

dependent on locality—that under precisely similar circumstances an absolution should be good before God if granted in one diocese and worthless across the boundary line. La Croix tells us that such absolutions, as a general rule, are lawful and sacramental, though some think them sacrilegious and provocative of fresh temptations, but they have been prohibited in certain dioceses, such as Liége, Milan and Cologne.[1] During the latter half of the seventeenth century it was the subject of considerable discussion in some local synods, where it was denounced as a frequent and intolerable abuse, and in some of them it was prohibited.[2] In 1709, Cardinal de Noailles, Archbishop of Paris, forbade it in future in his province,[3] but it remained valid and lawful throughout the Church at large until the accession of Benedict XIV.[4] In 1741, in the first year of his pontificate, he denounced the practice in the severest terms; he withdrew from confessors all power of absolving in such cases, absolution so given was declared invalid, except *in articulo mortis* when no other priest was accessible, and the attempt to grant it was subjected to *ipse facto* excommunication, reserved to the Holy See. Moreover, in confirming the constitution of Gregory XV., he sought to sweep away all the refinements and distinctions, through which casuists had evaded the papal decrees, by defining in the widest sense the act of solicitation, and he straitly commanded that absolution should be refused to one who had been solicited unless she would promise to denounce the offender.[5] In 1742 he extended these provisions to the

---

[1] La Croix Theol. Moral. Lib. VI. P. ii. n. 1204.

[2] Synod. Cameracens. ann. 1661, cap. 11; Synod. Namurcens. ann. 1698 cap. 28; Synod. Bisuntinens. ann. 1707, Tit. xiv. cap. 14 (Hartzheim IX. 888; X. 219, 323).—Synodicon Mechliniense, I. 559; II. 319.

[3] Pontas, Dict. de Cas de Conscience, I. 837.

[4] Benzi, writing in 1742 (Praxis Trib. Conscient. p. 253), says there is no general law prohibiting such absolutions, and they are good if not rendered invalid through lack of contrition and intention to abstain. Then to this he adds a postscript that he has received Benedict's bull *Sacramentum pœnitentiæ* and that it must be observed wherever published.

[5] Bened. PP. XIV. Const. *Sacramentum Pœnitentiæ*, 1 Jun. 1741 (Bullar. Bened. XIV. I. 23).

In spite of all the care with which this decree is drawn, the indefatigable commentators assumed that the "peccatum turpe" must be "copula consummata," but Liguori holds (Theol. Moral. Lib. VI. n. 554) that it applies to any external act of touch or speech. Yet Benedict himself gives color to such

Greek churches subject to Rome,[1] and in 1745 he took a retrograde step, which shows the pressure to prevent scandal, for he permitted absolution by an accomplice, *in articulo mortis*, when calling in another confessor might create suspicion.[2] In the same year, however, he promulgated a decree inflicting perpetual disability of administering the Eucharist on all guilty of solicitation, and he directed this, together with the legislation of his predecessors, in accordance with the decree of 1633, to be read annually in all the regular Orders, either at table or in a chapter specially assembled, and also in all general and provincial chapters, of which sworn evidence was to be forwarded to the Roman Inquisition.[3]

The Holy See has thus exhausted all the resources of its power; the legislation is ample if it can be enforced. Whether it is so or not must be a matter of conjecture, for scandal, as of old, is the most dreaded of all things. If solicitation were not regarded as an existing danger, the council of Venice, in 1859, would scarce have enjoined on all confessors to keep constantly before their eyes the papal decrees against it, nor would various other modern synods have deemed it necessary to repeat the prohibitions of absolving the accomplice in sin.[4] That Pius IX., in the bull *Apostolicæ Sedis*, in 1869, should maintain the excommunications *latæ sententiæ* against those who absolve their guilty partners and those who, when solicited, fail within a month to denounce the offending confessor, may be taken as a matter of course, but there is no little significance in an instruction issued, in 1867, by the Congregation of the Inquisition to all prelates in the Catholic world, pointing out that the papal constitutions were neglected, and that in some places abuses existed

---

casuistry when he decides (Casus Conscient. Jul. 1746, cas. 2) that if a confessor hands a love-letter to another confessor to be given to a penitent whom he knows will confess to the latter, and it is duly delivered as soon as the confession is ended, neither of them is guilty of solicitation.

For a discussion of the whole subject see his *De Synodo Diœcesana* Lib. VII. cap. xiv.

[1] Const. *Etsi Pastoralis* (Coll. Lacens. II. 518).

[2] Const. cxx. (Bullar. Bened. XIV. I. 219).

[3] Thesauri de Pœnis Ecclesiasticis P. II. s. v. *Solicitantes.*

[4] C. Venet. ann. 1859, P. III. cap. xxii. § 5 (Coll. Lacens. VI. 334).—C Australiens. I. ann. 1844, Decr. xii. (Ibid. III. 1052-3).—C. Tuamens. ann. 1817, Decr. xvii. (Ibid. III. 765).—C. Ravennat. ann. 1855 cap. v. § 9 (Ibid. VI. 160).—C. Remens. ann. 1857, cap. vi. n. 27 (Ibid. IV. 211).

which required greater energy on the part of officials to detect and punish. It further gave a summary of the procedure to be followed, by which it appears that three separate and independent denunciations against a confessor must be received before action is taken; the punishment, on conviction, is merely deprivation of the faculty to hear confessions and abjuration of the implied heresy, and even this trivial penalty may be diminished by confession before conviction. Every one concerned is sworn to the strictest silence, and when the case is ended it is to be regarded as forgotten.[1] These would seem but slender barriers to throw around temptations so severe to a celibate priesthood—temptations which lead Frassinetti to declare that "there cannot be the slightest doubt that to hear the confessions of women is the most dangerous and fatal rock which the minister of God has to encounter in the stormy sea of this world."[2] That the opportunities afforded by the confessional are not wholly thrown away would appear from Father Müller's remarkable summary of the seductions employed,[3] and from the space devoted in modern text-books to the various intricate questions and distinctions involved.[4]

In the recognized danger of confessing women it has always been the effort of the Church to reduce as far as possible the peril by

---

[1] Collectio Lacensis, III. 553–6. This leniency, doubtless attributable to the dread of scandal, offers an unfortunate contrast to the severity with which the offence was punished of old, including deposition, prolonged pilgrimage and life-long confinement in a monastery (Cap. 9, Caus. XXX. Q. 1).

[2] The New Parish Priest's Practical Manual, p. 361.

[3] Müller's Catholic Priesthood, IV. 158.—"Was it not he who taught them that such shameful deeds were innocent, that he meant no harm, that he intended only to cure them, to try them, or to sanctify them? Did he not assure them that he would take their sin upon his soul? Did he not tell them that every priest did such things? Did he not even threaten them with the vengeance of heaven if they refused?"
For another summary by St. Alphonso Liguori see Guarceno, Comp. Theol. Moral. Tract. XVIII. cap. viii. Append.

[4] Gury Comp. Theol. Moral. II. 590 sqq.—Varceno Comp. Theol. Moral. Tract. XVIII. cap. vi. art. 5; cap. VIII. append.—Mig. Sanchez, Prontuario de la Teología Moral, Trat. VI. Punto xi. The latter warns confessors that the greatest prudence is to be exercised in giving to solicited penitents the monition to denounce the offender, as otherwise it is apt to be the cause of scandal rather than of edification.

regulations which should render the confession as nearly public as is consistent with the preservation of its secrecy. At first these precautions seem to have been especially provided for nuns. The council of Paris, in 829, directs that when they confess it must be in church before the altar with witnesses not far off.[1] From that time onward there has been a perpetually recurring series of similar injunctions, the constant repetition of which, with trifling variations, shows how difficult it has been to secure their observance. In cases of sickness or other necessity, confession can be heard in the house of the penitent, but then the chamber-door must be open and some one be in sight, though not within ear-shot. Otherwise the confession is ordered to be in the open church, in some spot visible from around, it must be after sunrise and before sunset, and if the penitent is a female there must be some one else in the church, or she is not to be heard; the confessor, moreover, is directed to place her at his side, to avert his face or gaze upon the floor, and on no account to look at her.[2] These wholesome regulations, however, seem to have been but slackly observed, and the sterner moralists assume that their neglect led to abuses and disorders of the worst description.[3] It seems strange that it was not until the Counter-Reformation

---

[1] C. Parisiens. ann. 829, cap. 46 (Harduin. IV. 1323). This is virtually repeated, in 1279, by Archbishop Peckham of Canterbury (Ibid. VII. 788).

[2] Martene de antiq. Ritibus Eccles. Lib. I. cap. vi. art. 3, n. 8, 9.—Constitt. Odonis Paris. circa 1198, cap. vi. §§ 2, 3 (Harduin. VI. II. 1940).—Constitt. R. Poore ann. 1217, cap. 27 (Ibid. VII. 97).—Constitt. S. Edm. Cantuar. circa 1236, cap. 17 (Ibid. VII. 270).—C. Narbonnens. ann. 1227, cap. 7 (Ibid. VII. 146).—C. Claromont. ann. 1268, cap. 7 (Ibid. VII. 594).—C. Coloniens. ann. 1280 (Ibid. VII. 826).—C. Mogunt. ann. 1281, cap. 8 (Hartzheim, III. 664).— Statutt. Jo. Episc. Leodiens, ann. 1287, cap. 4 (Ibid. III. 686).—S. Bonaventuræ Confessionale Cap. I. Partic. 1, 3.—Raynaldi Confessionale.—Manipulus Curatorum, P. II. Tract. iii. cap. 8.—S. Antonini de Audientia Confess. fol. 13b; Ejusd. Summæ P. III. Tit. xvii. cap. 19.—John Myrc's Instructions for Parish Priests, vv. 880–895.

[3] Jo. Gersonis Orat. in C. Remens. ann. 1409 (Gousset, Actes etc. II. 657)— "Fiat confessio coram oculis omnium, in patente loco, ne subintroeat lupus rapax in angulis suadens agere quæ turpe est etiam cogitare. Væ aliter agentibus et sub familiaritatis specie in angulis vel camerulis res ignominia plenas exercentibus, easque deteriore sacrilegio sub devotionis specie palliantibus, excusantibusque."

So Bishop Robert of Aquino (Opus Quadragesimale Serm. XXIX. cap. 2). "Nam ego nescio laudare illos qui audiunt confessiones mulierum in locis

had commenced that the simple and useful device of the confessional was introduced—a box in which the confessor sits, with a grille in the side, through which the kneeling penitent can pour the story of his sins into his ghostly father's ear without either seeing the face of the other. The first allusion I have met to this contrivance is in the council of Valencia, in 1565, where it is ordered to be erected in churches for the hearing of confessions, especially of women.[1] In this same year we find S. Carlo Borromeo prescribing the use of a rudimentary form of confessional—a seat with a partition (*tabella*) to separate the priest from the penitent.[2] Eleven years afterwards, in 1576, he orders confessionals placed in all the churches of the province of Milan, and he alludes to their use in his instructions to confessors.[3] The innovation was so manifest an improvement that its use spread rapidly. In 1579, the council of Cosenza adopted it; in 1585, that of Aix; in 1590, that of Toulouse; in 1607, that of Mechlin; and in 1609, that of Narbonne. Some resistance was apparently expected on the part of the priests, for there are occasional threats of punishment for disobedience, and at Mechlin, where three months were allowed for compliance with the order, no one was permitted subsequently to hear a confession in any other way, except in case of necessity or by special licence from the Ordinary.[4] The Roman Ritual of 1614 orders the use of the confessional in all

secretis, in cameris, in angulis latebrosis in quibus etiam quandoque et sæpe qui boni et justi creduntur ad enormissima sacrilegia et vituperabiles dissolutiones labuntur."

[1] C. Valentin. ann. 1565, Tit. II. cap. 17 (Aguirre V. 417).

Binterim (Denkwürdigkeiten, V. II. 233) is in error in attributing to the council of Seville, in 1512, an allusion to confessionals. The allusion is to *confessionaria*—letters either papal or episcopal empowering the purchaser to be confessed in his own house, and also to have mass celebrated there; they had become so common as to be an abuse.—C. Hispalens. ann. 1512, cap. 19 (Aguirre, V. 370)). From the instructions given in 1528 by Martín de Frias (De Arte et Modo audiendi Confess. fol. vi.) as to the positions of priest and penitent, he evidently knows nothing of confessionals.

[2] C. Mediolan. I. ann. 1565, P. I. cap. 6 (Harduin. X. 653).

[3] C. Provin. Mediolan. IV. ann. 1576 (Acta Eccles. Mediolan. I. 146).—Instruct. Confessar. Ed. Brixiæ, 1678, pp. 51, 76.

[4] C. Consentin. ann. 1579 (Binterim, *loc. cit.*).—C. Aquens. ann. 1585, De Pœnit. (Harduin. X. 1550).—C. Tolosan. ann. 1590, cap. IV. n. 6–8 (Ibid. p. 1800).—C. Mechlin. ann. 1607, Tit. V. cap. 3 (Ibid. p. 1944).—C. Narbonn. ann. 1609, cap. 16 (Ib. XI. 17).

churches, and prescribes its position in an open and conspicuous place.[1] Yet, in 1630, Alphonso di Leone repeats the old injunctions that confessor and penitent shall not face or touch each other, and alludes to confessionals only as a device used in many dioceses, showing that as yet they were by no means universal.[2] Indeed, as late as 1709 the Spanish Inquisition found it necessary to issue an edict ordering priests to hear confessions in the body of the church and not in cells or chapels.[3] Yet in spite of the introduction of confessionals the necessity is felt of constant watchfulness to prevent abuses, and the modern councils, like those of old, are untiring in their admonitions of the precautions to be observed for the prevention of scandals.[4]

Akin to this, as connected with the morals of the confessional, is a question which has given rise to considerable discussion and difference of opinion—whether or not the penitent should mention, or the confessor should require him to reveal, the name of an accomplice in any sin. Although this would, of course, apply to robbery or crimes of violence, its special interest is connected with lapses of the flesh. In any case knowledge thus obtained might be put to evil uses, but in the latter class the temptation to a dissolute priest to take advantage of women whose weakness had thus come to his knowledge is peculiarly dangerous. Until the last century no authoritative expression of approval or condemnation was issued and the matter was left to the chance regulations of local synods and the conflicting opinions of the doctors. Lanfranc complains

---

[1] Rituale Roman. Tit. iii. cap. 1.

[2] Alph. de Leone de Off. et Potest. Confessarii Recoll. XVI. n. 20.

[3] Bibl. Nacional. de España, Seccion de MSS. P. v. fol. C. 17, n. 38.

[4] C. Baltimor. I. ann. 1829, Decr. xxv. (Coll. Lacens. III. 30–1).—C. Baltimor. V. ann. 1843, Decr. ix. (III. 90).—C. Australiens. I. ann. 1844, Decr. xii. (III. 1051).—C. Thurlesens. ann. 1850, Decr. xi. n. 41 (III. 782).—C. Rothomagens. ann. 1850, Decr. xvii. n. 3 (IV. 530).—C. Tolosan. ann. 1850, Tit. III. cap. 1, n. 70 (IV. 1054).—C. Casseliens. ann. 1853, Tit. iii. (III. 837).—C. Tuamens. ann. 1854, Decr. viii. (III. 860).—C. Quebecens. II. ann. 1854, Decr. ix. § 7 (III. 639). —C. Port. Hispan. ann. 1854, Art. iv. n. 1, 2 (III. 1098).—C. Halifaxiens. I. ann. 1857, Decr. xiv. (III. 745).—C. Viennens. ann. 1858, Tit. iii. cap. 7 (V. 169).—C. Coloniens. ann. 1860, Tit. ii. cap. 15 (V. 351).—C. Pragens. ann. 1860, Tit. iv. cap. 7; Tit. v. cap. 8 (V. 508, 543).—Synod. Ultraject. ann. 1865, Tit. iv. cap. 8 (V. 830).—C. Plen. Baltimor. II. ann. 1866, App. x. (III. 553).

that some penitents think that they cannot obtain pardon unless they betray the names of their accomplices and that some confessors make special inquiry after them, which he regards as exceedingly improper.[1] On the other hand, in the capitular confessions of the convents, the sinner was required to make a full statement, no matter whom it might implicate.[2] Occasionally a council would take note of the practice of over-curious confessors to prohibit it—perhaps the priest who made such inquiries was threatened with suspension, and the penitent who volunteered such information was ordered to be reproved.[3] It would seem to have been a common enough practice, of which Cæsarius of Heisterbach expresses his disapproval, for though it may occasionally be serviceable, priestly proclivity to sin renders it dangerous.[4] The schoolmen were divided on the question. Many held that such inquiries are proper when made with a good motive, such as to pray for the sinful accomplice, or to reprove her in secret, or to benefit her or the penitent in any way, and Aquinas asserts positively that the identity of the accomplice must be revealed if necessary to the completeness of the confession, which would infer the right of the confessor to require it.[5] Others deny that it should be done in confession, but suggest that subsequently the priest can properly ascertain the name.[6] Others again asserted that those confessors sin gravely who inquire curiously as to the persons with whom a penitent has sinned, but it is less when done outside of confession ; at the same time all necessary circumstances must be confessed, regardless of the consequences to others whom they may implicate.[7]

---

[1] Lanfranci Lib. de Celanda Confessione (Migne, CL. 629).

[2] Ps. Bernardi Documenta pie vivendi (Migne, CLXXXIV. 1173).

[3] Odonis Parisiens. Constitt. circa 1198, cap. vi. § 14 (Harduin. VI. II. 1941)· —R. Poore Constitt. ann. 1217, cap. 27 (Ibid. VII. 97).—Edmundi Cantuar. Constitt. ann. 1236, cap. 20 (Ibid. VII. 271).—Jo. Episc. Leodiens. Stat. ann. 1287, cap. 4 (Hartzheim III. 689).

[4] Cæsar. Heisterb. Dial. III. cap. 28–31.

[5] Jo. Friburgens. Summæ Confessor. Lib. III. Tit. xxxiv. Q. 87.—S. Antonini Summæ P. III. Tit. xiv. cap. 19, § 11.—Somma Pacifica cap. 2.—Rob. Episc. Aquin. Opus Quadrages. Serm. xxix. cap. 1.—S. Th. Aquin. Opusc. XII. Q. 6 ; In IV. Sentt. Dist. XVI. Q. iii. Art. 2 *ad calcem*.—Gab. Biel in IV. Sentt. Dist. XXI. Q. unic. ad 5, Dub. 2.

[6] S. Bonavent. in IV. Sentt. Dist. XXI. P. ii. Art. 1, Q. 3.—Astesani Summæ Lib. v. Tit. xii. Q. 5.—Cherubini de Spoleto Quadragesimale Serm. LXII.

[7] Durand. de S. Porciano in IV. Sentt. Dist. XVI. Q. xiv. § 8.—P. de Palude in IV. Sentt. Dist. XVII. Q. ii. Art. 1.—Joannis de Janua Summa quæ dicitur Catholicon s. v. *Confessio.*

Bartolommeo da S. Concordio forbids all inquiries and quotes S. Ramon de Peñafort in support,[1] and Bartolommeo Fumo, on the authority of Caietano, declares emphatically that nothing which will betray the name of another is to be confessed.[2] The tendency of opinion was decidedly in this direction. Bartolomé de Medina asserts that aggravating circumstances can be suppressed if necessary to prevent identification of an accomplice; if a confessor refuses absolution, unless a penitent will reveal his partner in guilt, he is to be denounced to the Inquisition as a heretic, and a subsequent confessor can refuse absolution until the penitent does so; when the accomplices, however, are heretics and robbers, absolution can be withheld until the penitent denounces them to the proper authorities.[3] Rodriguez quotes opinions to the effect that if a penitent desires to name his accomplice it is a most grave sin for the confessor to permit it.[4] On the other hand, Manuel Sa tells us that the older doctors held that sins implicating others must be confessed, but that many of the moderns consider that sins may even be suppressed which would harm or defame another; this opinion is probable, but he prefers the ancient one when mere loss of reputation is involved,[5] while Tamburini argues that the accomplice must be revealed if necessary to determine the character of the sin,[6] and Juan Sanchez suggests that the penitent may confess fully without betraying his accomplice by changing his dress and adopting a fictitious name and nationality, which will throw the confessor off of the scent.[7]

The theologians by this time were mostly agreed that it is a mortal sin to require the revelation of an accomplice without reasonable cause, but the definition of reasonable cause was somewhat elastic; the amendment of the accomplice was not regarded as a justification, but the revelation could be compelled if necessary to prevent the relapse of the penitent or to ascertain accurately the grade of the

---

[1] Summa Pisanella s. v. *Confessor* II. § 5.

[2] Fumi Aurea Armilla s. v. *Circumstantia* n. 11.

[3] Bart. a Medina Instruct. Confessar. Lib. II. cap. iv. De Complicibus § 1.

[4] Rodriguez, Nuova Somma de' Casi di Coscienza, P. I. cap. 53 § 9.

[5] Em. Sa Aphorismi Confessar. s. v. *Confessio* n. 17.

[6] Tamburini Method. Confess. Lib. II. cap. ix. § 2.

[7] Jo. Sanchez Selecta de Sacramentis Disp. IX. n. 10. For the authorities on either side of this long-vexed question, with the preponderance in favor of the revelation of the accomplice, see Benzi, *Praxis Tribunalis Conscientiæ,* Disp. I. Q. ii. Art. 1, Par. 2, n. 11.

sin.[1] These exceptions gave considerable latitude to evil-disposed priests, who could construe them as they saw fit with ignorant penitents, forcing the revelation of the identity of the accomplice, and the continued reprehension of the practice of making such inquiries outside of the confessional, where it would not be covered by the seal, shows that the desire for this forbidden knowledge was difficult to repress.[2]

It was not till 1745 that Benedict XIV., in a brief addressed to Portugal, finally prohibited absolutely, as scandalous and pernicious, the custom of inquiring the name of the accomplice; this did not suffice, and, in 1746, he subjected to excommunication *latæ sententiæ* reserved to the pope, all who should teach it as permissible. Even yet there were obstinate theologians who assumed that these decrees were restricted to Portugal and that the practice was still allowable elsewhere; a third decree was therefore requisite, which he issued within three months of the second, declaring that the prohibition was general and must be universally enforced. Yet so obstinately was the evil upheld that a fourth utterance was necessary, in 1749, placing in Portugal the offence under the jurisdiction of the Inquisition.[3] This settled the matter so far as direct demands by the confessor are concerned, though even this would seem to be by no means eradicated if we may judge from the necessity which several recent councils have felt of still prohibiting it[4] and from Pius IX., in the bull *Apostolicæ Sedis*, making special reference to the decrees of Benedict XIV. and confirming the reserved excommunication of all who shall teach it to be lawful for the confessor to inquire the name. Yet the prohibition can be virtually eluded, for the confessor, if he

---

[1] Escobar Theol. Moral. Tract. VII. Exam. iv. cap. 5, n. 32; cap. 7, n. 38, 41.—Gobat Alphab. Confessar. n. 244, 254.—Juenin de Sacram. Diss. VI. Q. 5, cap. 6, Art 3 § 3.—Viva Cursus Theol. Moral. P. VI. Q. 5, Art. 6, n. 5.—Summæ Alexandrinæ P. I. n. 479-86.—La Croix Theol. Moral. Lib. VI. P. ii. n. 1144.—Tournely de Sacr. Pœnit. Q. VI. Art. iv.

[2] Clericati de Pœnit. Decis. XXIII. n. 14.

[3] Benedicti PP. XIV. Constt. *Suprema*, 7 Jul. 1745; *Ubi primum*, 4 Junii 1746; *Ad eradicandam*, 28 Sept. 1746; *Apostolici ministerii*, 9 Dec. 1749. Cf. Ejusd. de Synodo Diœcesana VI. xi.

[4] C. Ravennat. ann. 1855, cap. V. § 6 (Coll. Lacens. VI. 159).—C. Venet. ann. 1859, P. III. cap. xxii. § 5 (Ibid. p. 334). In 1866 the Plenary Council of Baltimore (Acta p. 305) felt it necessary to print in the Appendix the constitutions of Benedict XIV.

sees fit, can ask questions which will enable him to identify the accomplice.[1] In addition to this the preponderating weight of modern authority does not regard the danger of exposing an accomplice as relieving the penitent from the obligation of confessing a sin. Father de Charmes, indeed, expressly says that he must reveal the name if necessary for the completeness of the confession, and this infers the right of the confessor to demand it.[2]

The age at which the obligation of annual confession should be enforced would appear to be a difficult point to decide. On the one hand, it seems a sacrilege to administer to children of tender years the awful sacrament of penitence, with its presumed requisites of contrition and charity and a conception of its significance as the means of averting the wrath of an offended God. On the other hand, according to the theory of the Church, as soon as a child is *doli capax*, is able to commit sin, to distinguish between right and wrong, and to be responsible for its acts, confession and absolution are the only means of rescuing it from perdition in case of death, and are therefore of the highest necessity. Besides this is the fact, of which the Church never loses sight, that the plastic period of childhood is the time in which the future man or woman is to be moulded and trained into implicit obedience to ecclesiastical formulas and authority and when the habits are to be formed which will render them docile and obedient subjects during life. These considerations naturally are quite sufficient to overcome any scruples as to bestowing the sacrament on those who are manifestly incompetent to deserve it or to understand what it means.

The question as to the age when responsibility commences has been variously answered. When, towards the end of the fourth century, it was put to Timothy of Alexandria, he declined to decide: Some, he says, are responsible when ten years old, others not till

---

[1] S. Alph. de Ligorio Praxis Confessarii n. 118.—Gury Casus Conscientiæ II. 467-70.

[2] Becani de Sacramentis Tract. II. P. iii. cap. 36, Q. 2.—Reiffenstuel Theol. Moral. Tract. XIV. n. 57.—S. Alph. de Ligorio Theol. Moral. Lib. VI. n. 489, 492.—Gousset, Théol. Morale II. n. 434.—Zenner Instructio Pract. Confessar. § 72, n. 2; § 96.—Bonal Institt. Theol. T. IV. n. 248-9.—Th. ex Charmes Theol. Univ. Diss. V. cap. iv. Q. 2, Art. 1, Concl. 3.

later, and Balsamon approves of the reply.[1] A phrase ascribed to Gregory the Great says that some persons attribute sin to no one under fourteen, as though there were none but sexual sins, while lying and perjury are also sins, and are frequent with children.[2] An ancient Ordo, probably not later than the ninth century, directs the priest to adapt the penance to the condition of the penitent, whether rich or poor, bond or free, infant, boy, youth, adult or aged,[3] which would infer that confession might be commenced at a very early age. We have seen (p. 196) that when the Empress Agnes made a general confession to St. Peter Damiani she is said to have included all sins committed since the age of five. While confession was yet voluntary and infrequent of course there could be no general regulation on the subject, and the Lateran canon of 1216 abstained (p. 229) from any more definite expression than requiring it after reaching years of discretion. The interpretation of this was necessarily variable. In 1227 the council of Narbonne fixed the age at fourteen.[4] When S. Ramon de Peñafort, in 1235, compiled the Decretals of Gregory IX. he seems to have found nothing bearing on the subject save the passage above quoted, ascribed to Gregory I. A quarter of a century later Cardinal Henry of Susa assumes seven to be the age of responsibility, when children should confess and receive penance,[5] and the Glossator on the Decretals says that at that age they are considered to be *doli capaces.*[6] On the other hand, various councils of the thirteenth and fourteenth centuries determine the age to be fourteen ;[7] and the systematic writers content themselves with prescribing the age of discretion.[8] In 1408, Gerson and the council of Reims, in stating that no cases are to be considered as reserved in children under fourteen, imply that confession and penance begin at

---

[1] Timothei Alexand. Responsa canonica cum Gloss. Balsamon. (Max. Bibl. Pat. IV. 1060).

[2] Cap. 1 Extra Lib. v. Tit. xxiii.   [3] Pez Thesaur. Anecd. II. II. 614.

[4] C. Narbonnens. ann. 1227, cap. 7 (Harduin. VII. 146).

[5] Hostiens. Aureæ Summæ Lib. v. De Delictis puerorum § 2; de Pœn. et Remiss. § 7.

[6] Summa Rosella s. v. *Confessio Sacram.* II. § 4.

[7] Statuta Johann. Episc. Leodiens. ann. 1287, cap. 4 (Hartzheim III. 688).— Statut. Synod. Cameracens. circa 1300 (Ib. IV. 69).—Statut. Synod. Remens. circa 1330 Sec. Locus, Præcept. IV. (Gousset, Actes etc. II. 540).

[8] Astesani Summæ Lib. v. Tit. x. Art. 2, Q. 3.—Manip. Curator. P. II. Tit. iii. cap. 2.

an earlier age,[1] and the tendency continued to lower the minimum, for, although Savonarola assumes that confession and communion are to begin simultaneously when the child can distinguish between common bread and the Eucharist, which, he says, is about the tenth or eleventh year, the other authorities of the Renaissance period specify seven as the age for the first confession ; Pacifico da Novara adds, however, that in some countries it is postponed until twelve or fourteen, and Cherubino da Spoleto quotes authorities for all ages from seven to fourteen.[2] After this, seven has continued to be the age usually prescribed for commencing confession, though S. Carlo Borromeo orders it to begin at five or six, and the Tridentine Catechism contents itself with merely designating the age of discretion, while it seems to be generally admitted that the penalties prescribed by the Lateran canon for neglect are not to be inflicted before the age of twelve.[3] In 1703, the council of Albania denounced forcibly the execrable custom prevailing there of not commencing confession before the age of sixteen, eighteen or twenty, leading to the eternal perdition of many souls, and, in 1803, the council of Suchuen blamed confessors who refuse to listen to children of nine or ten on account of their youth, and instructs them to urge all on reaching the age of seven, or at least of eight, to come forward.[4] To what extent these prescriptions are observed it would of course be impossible to state. In 1747 we find Cardinal Rezzonico, Bishop of Padua, expressing his astonishment on learning that many young people reached the age of sixteen or eighteen without receiving the sacraments, wherefore he ordered the enforcement of the rule of S. Carlo Borromeo ;[5]

---

[1] C. Remens. ann. 1408 (Gousset, Actes etc. 658, 664).

[2] Savonarolæ Confessionale fol. 7*b.*—Bart. de Chaimis Interrog. fol. 52*b,* 54*b.*—Rob. Episc. Aquin. Opus Quadrages. Serm. XXVIII. cap. 1.—Somma Pacifica cap. 12.—Summa Sylvestrina s. v. *Confessio Sacr.* II. § 4.—Cherubini de Spoleto Quadragesimale Serm. LXII.

[3] S. Car. Borrom. Instruct. Confessar. Ed. 1678, p. 55.—Em. Sa Aphorismi Confessar. s. v. *Confessio* n. 3.—Henriquez Summæ Theol. Moral. Lib. IV. cap. 5, n. 2, 3.—Summa Diana s. v. *Confessionis necessitas* n. 1.—Layman Theol. Moral. Lib. v. cap. vi. § 5, n. 7.—Clericati de Pœnit. Decis. L. n. 12.—S. Alph. de Ligorio Theol. Moral. Lib. VI. n. 665.—Cat. Trident. de Pœnit. cap. 8.

Liguori elsewhere (Istruzione Pratica, cap. ii. n. 37) assumes the age to be seven, although there may be cases in which it should commence earlier or later.

[4] C. Albanens. ann. 1703, P. II. cap. 4; C. Sutchuens. ann. 1803, cap. vi. § 6 (Coll. Lacens. I. 302; VI. 20).

[5] Lett. Pastorale, 14 Agosto, 1747.

and the utterance of recent councils on the subject is the measure of the importance attached to it by the Church and of the difficulty of enforcing obedience.[1]

While there has been, in modern times, this unanimity in commencing confession at the earliest possible age, there has been considerable uncertainty as to the administration of the sacrament of penitence. The incongruity of bestowing absolution on those incapable of understanding it or of fulfilling its requisite conditions did not prevent Pierre de la Palu from asserting that as soon as a child is *doli capax*, it is bound by the prescription of annual confession and communion, which, of course, implies absolution.[2] St Antonino is more cautious; the priest must decide from the confession of the child whether it has sufficient use of reason to be admitted to the Eucharist.[3] S. Carlo Borromeo, who wished confession to begin at the age of five or six, ordered absolution to be postponed until the confessor should judge the child to be capable of receiving the sacrament, which could scarce be before ten or twelve.[4] The synod of Verdun, in 1598, ordered that, after the age of eight, children should be heard singly in confession, while those younger should only receive an unsacramental benediction.[5] When Henriquez says that children younger than twelve are not subject to the Lateran canon and are not to be admitted to communion, the inference is that they are not to receive absolution; while, on the other hand, Juan Sanchez assumes that the precepts of annual confession and taking the Eucharist are in force as soon as the child is capable of distinguishing between right and wrong, which is in the sixth or seventh year.[6] .Gobat describes the perplexities of the conscientious confessor in determining whether children are capable of the sacrament or not; for himself, his rule is, when in doubt, to administer

---

[1] C. Ravennat. ann. 1855, cap. 5, § 11 ; C. Urbinatens. ann. 1859, P. I. Tit. viii. § 50 ; C. Baltimor. Plenar. II. ann. 1866, Tit. 5, cap. 5, n. 276 (Coll. Lacens. VI. 160, 20, III. 471).

[2] P. de Palude in IV. Sentt. Dist. XII. Q. 1 ad 5.

[3] S. Antonini Summæ P. II. Tit. ix. cap. 9, § 1. Yet St. Antonino elsewhere (P. III. Tit. xiv. cap. 12 § 5) quotes Pierre de la Palu without expressing dissent.

[4] S. Carol. Borrom. Instruct. Confessar. p. 55.

[5] Synod. Verdunens. ann. 1598, cap. 51 (Hartzheim VIII. 470).

[6] Henriquez Summæ Theol. Moral. Lib. IV. cap. 5, n. 2, 3.—Jo. Sanchez Selecta de Sacramentis Disp. XXVI. n. 4.

it conditioned on capacity.[1] Laymann suggestively tells us that children are not to be absolved if there is dread only of a whipping and not of hell; those who cannot comprehend the sacrament are to be dismissed with a benediction; when there is doubt, conditional absolution should be given.[2] This, which at best is a sort of make-shift to supplement human impotence in the exercise of superhuman attributes, has been eagerly accepted as a solution of the difficulty. Guarceno tells us that those confessors err gravely who do not administer absolution before the first communion, for the discretion differs widely which capacitates the child for the reception of the two sacraments; confession should begin at seven, and if there is doubt as to the capacity for absolution it should be given condition-ally.[3] From the earnestness with which Frassinetti argues against the practice of deferring absolution until the first communion, leaving unremitted the sins confessed meanwhile, this would appear to be a custom by no means eradicated; indeed, Gousset speaks of it as an abuse practised in some places.[4] There is a further question as to the applicability to children of the reservation of cases, which has been variously debated, but which seems to be settled by the prin-ciple that reservation is not a punishment inflicted on the sinner but a limitation of the jurisdiction of the confessor.[5] In view of the recognition of youth as an impediment in such cases (p. 336) the matter would appear to be academical rather than practical, but the modern custom of applying for faculties to absolve neutralizes the impediment, and we are told that in the last century Cardinal Hon-orati, as Bishop of Sinigaglia, removed from among reserved cases carnal sins in boys under fourteen and girls under twelve, for the reason that it would prevent their confession.[6]

In the spirit which pervaded medieval society it was inevitable that payment should be expected for administering the sacraments,

---

[1] Gobat Alphab. Confessar. n. 443–59.

[2] Laymann Theol. Moral. Lib. v. Tract. vi. cap. 5, n. 7.

[3] Varceno Comp. Theol. Moral. Tract. xviii. cap. iv. art. 2.—Marc Institt. Moral. Alphonsianæ n. 1663.

[4] Frassinetti's New Parish Priest's Manual, p. 367.—Gousset, Théologie Morale, II. 406.

[5] Cabrini Elucidar. Casuum Reservat. P. i. Resol. xxvii. xxviii.

[6] Fabri, Istruzione per i novelli Confessori, p. 311 (Jesi, 1785).

and that of penitence could be no exception. Even as early as the fifth century we see that fees were a matter of course for the exercise of such sacerdotal functions, for Leo I., in scolding the Italian bishops for baptizing on other days than Easter and Pentecost, threatened punishment for persistence, on the ground that they showed themselves to be seekers of filthy gain rather than of the advantage of religion.[1] In one of the earlier Penitentials the penitent is directed, before readmission to communion, to give a banquet to the priest who has prescribed the penance[2]—a practice doubtless conducive to a shortening of the penalty inflicted. That the custom of payment was general may be assumed from the effort to check it by the forgers of the False Decretals, who represent Pope Eutychianus as forbidding that anything shall be received for baptizing infants or reconciling sinners or burying the dead.[3] While exaction and extortion were thus prohibited, an exception was made in favor of the acceptance of fees voluntarily tendered.[4] That the priesthood of the period did not observe the distinction and for the most part withheld their services when their cupidity was not satisfied is manifested by a very curious passage in an *Ordo* of the period, in which a poor sinner, when invited to confess, protests that he is unable to pay for the service and that the priests will only oppress and persecute him for his poverty.[5] It was difficult to repress this, as is seen from the frequent injunctions to exact nothing but to take whatever may be

---

[1] Leonis PP. I. Epist. CLXVIII. cap. 1, Ad Episcopos.

[2] Pœnit. Columbani cap. 19 (Wasserschleben, p. 358).

[3] Ps. Eutychiani Exhortatio ad Presbyteros (Migne, V. 165).

[4] Reg. S. Chrodegangi Ed. D'Achery cap. 42 (Migne, LXXXIX. 1076); Ed. Harduin. cap. 32 (Concil. IV. 1196).

[5] Pez Thesaur. Anecd. II. II. 621.—" Ego homo sum ignoti nominis, obscuræ opinionis, infimi generis, modicæ substantiæ, cognitus nulli nisi soli mihi; non est mihi pecunia, nulli placere possum per servitia, desunt mihi præmia et dona et munera; hæc omnia perplurimorum sacerdotum requirit et desiderat cupiditas et avaritia; si hujusmodi confiteor scelera mea sacerdotibus sine his præfatis muneribus dedignantur me audire, et protectionem et defensionem et consilium exhibere vel aliquo modo succurrere, et ita deseror ab omnibus; quicunque me ex his aspiciunt fugiunt me aut persequuntur, et si qui de his mihi loquuntur venenum aspidum sub labiis eorum consideratur, occultam malitiam blandis sermonibus ornant, aliud ore promunt, aliud corde volutant, opere destruunt quod sermone promittunt, sub pietatis habitu velant malitias, calliditatem simplicitate occultant, produnt, culpant, objiciunt, ostendunt tantum vultu quod animo non gestant."

offered,[1] yet an offering was expected and was customary, forming part of the recognized revenue of the churches, divided monthly between the priests and the superior and known as *confessiones tricenariæ.*[2]

It was reserved for Innocent III. to give legality to the custom. The subject was somewhat delicate, for the demand of payment for the sacraments was undoubted simony, and yet without compulsion these so-called voluntary payments were liable to be not forthcoming. Innocent, however, accomplished the feat of facing both ways in a decree reciting that frequent complaints reach the Holy See that money is exacted for the sacraments and that fictitious difficulties are raised if the priestly greed is not satisfied, while, on the other hand, there are laymen inspired with heretical views who seek under the guise of scruples to infringe on the laudable custom which the piety of the faithful has introduced. Therefore depraved exactions are prohibited and pious customs are to be observed; the sacraments must be freely conferred, but the bishops shall coerce those who endeavor to change a laudable custom.[3] In this peculiar method of coercing voluntary payments, the sacrament of penitence is not specifically mentioned, but by common consent it was held to be included, and the laudable custom was firmly established, nor is it likely that many confessors were as scrupulous as one commemorated by Cæsarius of Hiesterbach for flinging the money after the penitent who refused to promise abstinence from sin.[4] The canonists of the thirteenth and fourteenth centuries show us that the custom was reduced to somewhat definite rules: the priest could not demand payment or refuse absolution in its absence; he was warned that he should not during the confession gaze wistfully and suggestively at the purse of the penitent, nor, if the latter was poor, ought he to exact a pledge to secure the payment; strictly speaking, the penitent was not legally bound to pay, unless the priest was poor or it was the custom of the diocese, but it was proper for him to do so in any case as an evidence of his devotion, and the decree of Innocent III. was freely cited in

---

[1] Ratherii Veronens. Synodica ad Presbyteros cap. 8.—Commonit. cujusque Episcopi cap. 15 (Martene Ampl. Collect. VII. 3).—C. Bituricens. ann. 1031 cap. 12 (Harduin. VI. I. 850).—C. Londiniens. ann. 1125, cap. 2; ann. 1138, cap. 1 (Ibid. VI. II. 1125, 1204).

[2] Du Cange, s. v. *Confessiones tricenariæ.*   [3] Cap. 42 Extra v. iii.

[4] Cæsar. Hiesterb. Dial. Dist. III. cap. 35.

support.[1] Cardinal Henry of Susa expresses a pious belief that the priest is not likely to be corrupted by such a trifle, but, as his power in the confessional was arbitrary, parishioners who had to appear before him annually doubtless felt that a reputation for liberality was desirable. St. Bonaventura in fact tells us that refusal to absolve without payment was common,[2] and this is confirmed by the utterance of the council of London, in 1268, under the Legate Ottoboni, which complains of the universal sale of the sacraments through the venality and greed of the clergy, and alludes specially to the practice of extorting fees before listening to confessions. It ordered diligent inquisition and punishment of offenders, significantly adding that custom should not be pleaded in defence.[3] The Mendicants were as deeply involved in this as the parochial clergy. Forbidden to handle money, the rule was to tell the penitent to make his payment to the procurator of the convent, but there seems to have been no prohibition to receive money's worth. A popular poem of the fourteenth century says of them

> Thai say that thai destroye sinne,
> And thai mayntene men most therinne.
> For had a man slayn al his kynne
> Go shrive him at a frere,
> And for lesse than a payre of shone
> He wyl assoil him clene and sone,
> And say the sinne that he has done
> His saule shal neuer dere.[4]

At the *Grands Jours* of Troyes, in 1405, the people complained of the exactions of the priests, and the court decided, capriciously enough, that eight *deniers tournois* could be charged for extreme unction, but that visiting the sick and hearing confessions must be performed

---

[1] Hostiens. Aureæ Summæ Lib. v. De Pœn. et Remiss. §§ 53, 54.—Jo. Friburgens. Summæ Confessor. Lib. III. Tit. xxxiv. Q. 84.—Astesani Summæ Lib. v. Tit. xxxi. Q. 2.

[2] S. Bonaventuræ Tract. Quia Fratres Minores Prædicent.

[3] C. Londiniens. ann. 1268, cap. 2 (Harduin. VII. 616).

[4] Hostiens. *ubi sup.*—Monumenta Franciscana, p. 604 (M. R. Series).

In 1482, when the Dominican Jean Angeli preached at Tournay that parish priests ought to receive nothing from their parishioners for confessions, but that it was otherwise with the Mendicants, the Sorbonne condemned the proposition as contrary to natural and divine law and consequently heretical.— D'Argentré, I. II. 305.

gratuitously.[1] This of course had no influence on the general practice, and there was an uneasy conviction underlying it that, in spite
of custom and of Innocent's decretal, it really was simony. The doctors endeavored to argue this away by the distinction between voluntary and coerced payments. If a bargain was made, or if absolution
was held dependent on money, it was simony in spite of custom; if
without this the object of the priest was to gain the fee and not to
save souls, it was mental simony; if such was not the object and the
money was tendered spontaneously, it could be accepted without sin.[2]
The priests themselves disregarded such niceties and collected their
fees from the willing and the unwilling alike. In the attempted
reformation with which Cardinal Campeggio, in 1524, endeavored to
stay the progress of the Lutheran heresy, at the assembly of Ratis-
bon, one provision was the prohibition of exacting anything from
unwilling penitents.[3] This was not effective for, in 1536, the council
of Cologne deplores that fines were imposed in place of the canonical
penances, and sinners were allowed to continue their evil courses to
the great scandal of the faithful,[4] and, in 1557, Georg Witzel, in a
memorial to the Emperor Ferdinand, includes the exaction among
the oppressions to be removed before a project for the reunion of the
Lutherans could be successful.[5] The payment of the fee, in fact, was
often the main thing. When, in 1564, Pierre de Bonneville, on trial
before the Inquisition of Toledo, admitted that he had not confessed or
communed for two years, in consequence of cherishing hatred against
a rival, the inquisitors immediately asked him whether his parish
priest had not looked after him, to which he replied that the priest
had called to inquire, when he had told him that he had confessed
and communed in the parish church, whereupon the priest collected
four maravedises from him and departed satisfied.[6]

When S. Carlo Borromeo forbade his priests from demanding fees
from penitents, he did not prohibit their acceptance, and he justified

---

[1] Preuves des Libertez de l'Eglise Gallicane, II. II. 91 (Paris, 1651).

[2] Weigel Claviculæ Indulgentialis cap. 76.—S. Antonini Confessionale fol.
31a.—Bart. de Chaimis Interrog. fol. 91b.

[3] Constitt. Ratisponens. ann. 1524, cap. 9 (Hartzheim VI. 200).

[4] C. Coloniens. ann. 1536, P. XIV. cap. 22 (Ibid. p. 310).

[5] Döllinger, Beiträge zur politischen, kirchlichen und Cultur-Geschichte,
III. 177.

[6] MSS. Universitäts Bibliothek, Halle, Yc. 20, T. V.

his action not on the ground of simony, but on the greater authority which the priest would have by manifesting his independence in such matters.[1] There was significance in the command of the council of Aix in 1585, when ordering the erection of confessionals in all churches, it prescribed that they should not be furnished with alms-boxes. This could not have been intended to preclude all payments, for the council of Narbonne, in 1609, while prohibiting all begging or demanding, permits the acceptance of whatever may be freely tendered, and Bishop Zerola, about the same time, informs us that this was the custom everywhere,[2] though there were rigorists who argued that payment cannot be accepted without simony.[3] The Jesuit Rule forbade it, though the prohibition seems to have been difficult of enforcement, and the Jesuit Giuseppe Agostino teaches that there is no simony in receiving payment for the labor of administering the sacraments.[4] Still less obedience was secured for the precept in the Roman Ritual, which prohibited confessors from either asking or receiving anything for the performance of their functions,[5] for not long afterwards Diana argues that, though it is a sin for the priest to refuse penance and the viaticum to the dying unless paid for, refusal to pay would also be a sin, since thus the departing soul would be condemned to damnation,[6] nor does he seem to realize how hideous is the conception which he thus conveys of his faith and its ministers. Various councils, about the year 1700, endeavored to suppress the custom of asking for payment, but were careful not to forbid its acceptance.[7] Chiericato admits that such payments are not truly "alms," as commonly expressed, but are wages for the labor per-

---

[1] S. Caroli Borrom. Instructio, pp. 69, 79.

[2] C. Aquens. ann. 1585, De Pœnit. (Harduin. X. 1530).—C. Narbonn. ann. 1609, cap. 16 (Ibid. XI. 18).—Zerola Praxis Sacr. Pœnit. cap. xxv. Q. 29.

[3] Rebelli de Obligationibus Justitiæ P. II. Lib. xvii. De Officio Confessarii.

[4] Reusch, Beiträge zur Geschichte des Jesuitenordens, p. 236 (München 1894).—Augustini Brevis notitia eorum quæ necessaria sunt confessariis, *De Simonia* n. 6.—But the Jesuit prohibition was rendered subject to the discretion of the superior (Regulæ Sacerdotum n. 22).

[5] Ritual. Roman. Tit. III. cap. 1.

[6] Summa Diana s. v. *Scandalum* n. 13.—Alph. de Leone de Off. et Potest. Confessoris, Recoll. XIII. n. 53.

[7] C. Neapolitan. ann. 1699, Tit. III. cap. 5 § 9; Synod. National. Albana ann. 1703 P. III. cap. 4; Synod. Bahiens. ann. 1707, Lib. II. Tit. 43 (Coll. Lacens. I. 186, 303, 851).

formed,[1] and Van Espen points out the danger of requiring priests to live on the fees of the confessional, whereby their temporal comfort is dependent on the number of their penitents.[2] Lochon, about the same period, speaks of the poor who give as a reason for not confessing that they are unable to pay for it, and sharply reproves the priests and vicars who boast that the confessional brings them in 100 or 150 livres a year, or that they have cleared so much at Easter or by the Jubilee.[3]

The first endeavor I have met with to enforce the prescriptions of the Roman Ritual occurs in the council of Avignon, in 1725, which orders bishops to be vigilant in preventing confessors from receiving anything, even under the pretext of alms.[4] This effort was sporadic and apparently produced no effect, and in one department of confessorial labor the Church was obliged to yield the point, for it recognized that confessors of nunneries must be supported. In 1589, the Congregation of Bishops and Regulars decreed that a proper "alms" should be paid to them, and, in 1605, it defined that this should be a stipend payable to the house of the confessor, sufficient to defray his expenses according to the custom of the country, the nuns themselves being wisely forbidden to pay anything.[5] In 1657, this stipend was fixed by the Congregation at two *giuli* per diem, to which the superior of the nunnery might add something if the confessor was especially assiduous, and regulations of this kind I presume are still in force.[6] If the stipend, however, is the principal motive of the confessor, he is guilty of grave mental simony whenever he thinks of it.[7]

In modern times the *Beichtpfennig*, or payment to the confessor, appears to be regulated by diocesan custom. Binterim, writing about 1840, labors strenuously to show that there is no simony in it, as there is no compulsion, but he admits that it is repulsive; the

---

[1] Clericati de Pœnit. Decis. X. n. 1.

[2] Van Espen Jur. Eccles. P. II. Tit. vi. cap. 4, n. 16.

[3] Lochon, Traité du Secret de la Confession, p. 297 (Brusselle, 1708).

[4] C. Avinionens. ann. 1725, Tit. XXX. cap. 4 (Coll. Lacens. I. 535).

[5] Clericati De Pœnit. Decis. XLII. n. 4.—Pittoni Constitutiones Pontificiæ, T. VII. n. 411, 557.

[6] S. Alph. de Ligorio Theol. Moral. Lib. VI. n. 577.—Pittoni, *op. cit.* n. 939. —The *giuli* was a coin of ten sous. In a decision of 1740 the stipend is fixed at fifty crowns a year.—Bizzarri Collect. S. Congr. Episc. et Regul. p. 388.

[7] Pittoni, *op. cit.* n. 411.

sinner may thus be deterred from unburdening his sins, and the priest does not venture to exhort to frequent confession lest he be suspected of seeking money rather than the salvation of his flock. In Germany he says the custom has long been abandoned, but in Holland, where the priests have no fixed incomes, it is still retained.[1] Since then the synod of Utrecht, in 1865, has forbidden wholly the asking or acceptance of fees on the ground of its appearing to be a redemption of sin and of its influence in preventing frequent confession.[2] On the other hand, in 1846, I find it spoken of as a legal and unobjectionable custom in those dioceses in which it is still retained,[3] and the council of Quebec, in 1863, prohibited the exaction of fees, but made no formal protest against their acceptance.[4]

---

[1] Binterim, Denkwürdigkeiten, V. III. 296–8.

[2] Synod. Ultraject. ann. 1865, Tit. IV. cap. 8 (Coll. Lacens. V. 831).

[3] Aschbach, Allgemeines Kirchen-Lexicon, s. v. *Beichtpfennig.*

[4] C. Quebecens. I. ann. 1863, Decr. III. § 10 (Coll. Lacens. VI. 402).

The Lutherans inherited the *Beichtpfennig* and long maintained it, as will be seen hereafter.

CHAPTER XIII.

THE SEAL OF CONFESSION.

It is a self-evident proposition that, if auricular confession is to be enforced, the penitent must be assured of the inviolable secrecy of his admissions of wrong-doing. To say nothing of the danger of punishment for graver crimes, his family relations and his reputation might be too nearly imperilled for him to venture on the unburdening of his conscience if there were risk that even his less grievous sins and weaknesses might be bruited abroad, and no man's life or honor would be safe against the stories that might be circulated by a malignant priest. The Church, in making confession a matter of precept, has therefore been obliged to give assurance to its children that they can repose absolute reliance on the impenetrable silence with which their utterances shall be covered.

Although the council of Trent is silent upon the subject, and though it was a disputed point among the schoolmen whether the seal of the confessional is of the essence of the sacrament,[1] the Church has had no hesitation in asserting it to be of divine law. The earlier theologians appear to have paid no attention to this point, and Aquinas only argues that, as the priest should conform himself to God, of whom he is the minister, and as God does not reveal the sins made known to him in confession, so the priest should be equally reticent,[2] but as he asserts it to be of the essence of the sacrament, and as the sacrament is of divine law, the conclusion is readily drawn that it must likewise be so.[3] Duns Scotus assents to this and holds that the confessor is bound to silence by the law of nature, the positive

---

[1] Aquinas (In IV. Sentt. Dist. XXI. Q. iii. Art. 2) asserts the seal to be of the essence of the sacrament, and is followed by Angiolo da Chivasso (Summa Angelica s. v. *Confessio*, ult. § 1), whence he draws the natural but self-destructive conclusion that its violation renders the sacrament null. Pierre de la Palu says that it is not of the essence (Summa Tabiena s. v. *Confessionis celatio in corp.*), and so does Domingo Soto (In IV. Sentt. Dist. XVIII. Q. ii. Art. 6).

[2] S. Th. Aquin. in IV. Sentt. Dist. XXI. Q. iii. Art. 1.

[3] Ejusd. Summæ Suppl. Q. XI. Art. 1.

law of God and the positive law of the Church.[1] His disciple,
François de Mairone, admits that the seal is of divine law, though
it would not be easy to prove it, but it has been so decreed by the
Church.[2] Astesanus accepts it without question or argument.[3] That
the point, however, was under debate in the schools, without entire
agreement as to the proof, is seen in the remark of Durand de S.
Pourçain, that the common argument is that confession and its
seal proceed from the same law, and as one is divine the other must
be, but he rejects this reasoning and prefers to argue that the seal is
part of the sacrament, and is therefore of divine law.[4] Guido de
Monteroquer seems to know nothing of divine origin and bases the
seal wholly on the positive law of the Church as expressed in Gratian
and the Lateran canon.[5] Passavanti says nothing of the divine origin
of the seal and only urges in its support reverence for the sacrament,
the heavy punishment for violation, and the interference with confession which disregard of secrecy would cause.[6] Piero d'Aquila
proves the divine origin by a new line of argument—revealing confessions would deter men from confessing; confession is of divine
law, and consequently the prohibition of what would interfere with
it must also be of divine law.[7] Subsequent authorities, as a rule,
came to admit the divinity of the seal as a matter of course, though
as late as the close of the fifteenth century Gabriel Biel considers it
to be only of natural law and confines his argument wholly to its
utility.[8] Of course no evidence is furnished beyond Melchor Cano's
argument that Sixtus IV. condemned as heresy Pedro de Osma's
denial of the obligation of the seal, and that if it were not divine
its denial would not be heretical, or Gobat's reasoning that Christ
could not have imposed on man the heavy burden of confession
unless he had lightened it by explicitly or implicitly adding the

---

[1] Jo. Scoti in IV. Sentt. Dist. xxi. Q. unic.

[2] Fr. de Maironis in IV. Sentt. Dist. xxi. Q. iii.

[3] Astesani Summæ Lib. v. Tit. xx. Q. 2.

[4] Durand. de S. Porciano in IV. Sentt. Dist. xxi. Q. iv. § 6.

[5] Manip. Curator. P. ii. Tract. iii. cap. 11.

[6] Passavanti, Lo Specchio della vera Penitenza, Dist. v. cap. 4.

[7] P. de Aquila in IV. Sentt. Dist. xx. Q. iii.

[8] Gab. Biel in IV. Sentt. Dist. xxi. Q. unic. Art. 1.—S. Antonini Summæ
P. iii. Tit. xvii. cap. 22.—Summa Sylvestrina s. v. *Confessio* iii. § 1.—Summa
Tabiena s. v. *Confessionis Celatio* § 1.—Dom. Soto in IV. Sentt. Dist. xviii.
Q. iv. Art. 5.

seal.[1] Benzi relies for evidence on tradition and the practice of the Church, while Gury and Marc beg the question by saying that it is implicitly of divine law, for, by the institution of Christ confession ought to be secret, and therefore the obligation of the seal was imposed on confessors by Christ.[2] Of course, all modern writers assert its divine origin, and of course no one pretends to offer evidence, while Guarceno even asserts that it is heresy to doubt the obligation, in spite of the discreet reticence of the council of Trent on the subject.[3] Binterim, in fact, assures us that evidence would be superfluous : Christ guaranteed to the faithful impenetrable silence on the part of his deputies, and it was wholly unnecessary that he should express it in words.[4] Yet the theologians are blind to the fact that when they give as a reason for the disuse of public penance for private sins, that it would indirectly violate the seal, they admit that the latter is of comparatively recent introduction.[5]

As the matter has thus passed wholly out of the domain of reason into that of faith, it is perhaps not surprising that presumptuous ignorance should assume not only that the seal is a divine ordinance but that in fact, in the whole history of the Church, there has never occurred an instance of its violation. Thus Guillois tells us that it has never been broken, and that it is said that even the unfrocked *insermentés* priests of the French Revolution, some of whom sank to the depths of degradation, never revealed anything that they had heard in confession.[6] Cardinal Gibbons even goes further, and with customary theological logic finds in this alleged fact a proof of the divine origin of the sacrament.[7] Such assertions may strengthen

---

[1] Melchior. Cani de Pœnit. P. v. (Ed. 1550, p. 80).—Gobat Alphab. Confessar. n. 837.

[2] Benzi Praxis Tribun. Conscientiæ Disp. II. Q. vii. Art. 1, n. 1.—Gury Comp. Theol. Moral. II. 647.—Marc Institt. Moral. Alphonsianæ n. 1860.

[3] S. Alph. de Ligorio Theol. Moral. Lib. VI. n. 634.—Palmieri Tract. de Pœnit. p. 393.—Varceno Comp. Theol. Moral. Tract. XVIII. cap. iv. art. 7.

[4] Binterim, Denkwürdigkeiten, V. III. 312.

[5] S. Alph. de Ligorio Theol. Moral. Lib. VI. n. 512.

[6] Guillois, History of Confession, translated by Bishop de Goesbriand, p. 183.—Guillois probably derives the assertion as to the Revolutionary priests from Grégoire, Hist. des Confesseurs des Empereurs etc. p. 99.

[7] Cardinal Gibbons says that he does not know " of any instance under my observation, nor of any recorded in history, where the seal of the confessional has been violated. This fact can be affirmed, not only of those priests who

the confidence of those inclined to suspect the discretion of their pastors. We shall presently see on what basis they are founded.

Yet with all this confident assertion of the divine origin of the seal it is instructive to observe that, when the theologians settle down to facts and to details, the reason they allege for the secrecy of the confessional is the very human one that without it confession would be too odious to be successfully enforced, and, in debating the innumerable questions to which the application of the rule gives rise, the sole test which they apply is not in conformity with the presumed command of Christ, but whether a decision in this sense or that will render confession odious.[1] The whole matter is customarily treated on the basis of the most naked expediency.

Of course, in the early centuries, when the only form of penitential confession recognized by the Church was public, there could be no injunction of secrecy. If evidence of this be wanted it can be found in the early codes prescribing the functions of the priesthood and the penalities imposed for derelictions—the canons of Hippolytus and the Apostolic Constitutions, the so-called Canons of the Apostles and the canonical epistles of Gregory of Nyssa and Basil the Great, the penitential decrees of such councils as those of Elvira, Nicæa and Ancyra and the collections of the African Church. All

---

have remained faithful to their sacred calling, but even of those who from time to time have proved unfaithful. This inviolability may, without presumption, be regarded as an additional proof, not only of the divine institution of the sacrament of penance, but also of the special protection of God over those who are charged with the important duty of hearing confessions."— Letter in N. Y. Herald, Feb. 7, 1892.

In this the Cardinal only exaggerates somewhat an assertion in Aschbach's *Allgemeines Kirchen-Lexicon* s. v. *Beichtsiegel.*

[1] Alex. de Ales Summæ P. IV. Q. XIX. Membr. ii. Art. 1.—S. Bonavent. in IV. Sentt. Dist. XXI. P. ii. Art. 2, Q. 1.—S. Th. Aquin. in IV. Sentt. Dist. XXI. Q. iii. Art. 1 ad 1.—S. Antonini Summæ P. III. Tit. xvii. cap. 22, ? 3.— Rob. Aquinat. Opus Quadrages. Serm. XXIX. cap. 2.—Summa Tabiena s. v. *Confessionis Celatio* ? 5.—Eisengrein Confessionale, cap. vii. Q. 14–17.—Dom. Soto in IV. Sentt. Dist. XVIII. Q. ii. Art. 5, 6.—Summa Diana s. v. *Sigillum sacrament.* n. 16, 21, 38, 43, 46, 47.—Layman Theol. Moral. Lib. V. Tract. vi. cap. 14, n. 14.—Gobat Alphab. Confessar. n. 873.—Benzi Praxis Trib. Conscient. Disp. II. Q. vii. Art. 1, n. 1, 2; Art. 3, n. 3, 23.—S. Alph. de Ligorio Theol. Moral. Lib. VI. n. 634.—Gury Comp. Theol. Moral. II. 647, 651, 654, 655, 671.—Varceno Comp. Theol. Moral. Tract. XVIII. cap. iv. Art. 7 ?1.

these together form a tolerably extensive body of canon law, representing the doctrine and practice of the different churches up to the close of the fourth century, and had there been any duty incumbent on priests to listen to the confessions of sinners and to veil them in impenetrable silence there would unquestionably have been some allusion to it and some penalty prescribed for its violation. The absolute ignorance of any such duties manifested by all these lawgivers is sufficient evidence of their non-existence.[1] At the same time the danger to which a penitent might be exposed by the public knowledge of his sins is seen in the exception made by St. Basil the Great in favor of a wife who confesses to adultery and from some remarks of St. Augustin.[2] The first allusion to the advisability of secrecy, when sinners sought counsel in private of holy men, in place of confessing before the congregation, occurs in the life of St. Ambrose by his disciple Paulinus, and this shows that it was a voluntary silence, considered remarkable at the time, for the biographer refers to the reticence of the saint in such matters as a praiseworthy trait, rendering him an example for subsequent priests, that they should rather be intercessors with God than accusers before men.[3] When, in the fifth century, Sozomen relates the tradition that after the Decian persecution, the excessive number of penitents caused bishops to place in the churches holy priests known for their wisdom and taciturnity to listen to their confessions, the details into which he enters show that such customs were unknown to his contemporaries.[4] In the West, it was not till 459 that Leo the Great forbade the public reading of confessions before the congregation, for the reason that it deterred sinners from unburdening their consciences through the attendant humiliation and danger of prosecution for their crimes.[5] Secret confession being thus recognized as lawful,

---

[1] In the dearth of other evidence of antiquity, the Carthaginian canon (p. 15) prohibiting a bishop from denying communion for a sin privately confessed, has been cited as proof (Lenglet Du Fresnoy, Traité du Secret inviolable de la Confession, p. 14. Paris. 1707). Those who do so forget that in early times the penitent was not admitted to communion until his prolonged penance was completed, and we shall see that it was a concession in his favor when the Penitentials allowed it midway.

[2] S. Basil. Epist. Canon. II. cap. xxxiv.—S. Augustin. Serm. LXXXII. cap. 8.

[3] Paulini Vit. S. Ambros. n. 39.   [4] Sozomen H. E. VII. 16.

[5] Leonis PP. I. Epist. CLXVIII. cap. 2.

the advisability of making it only to those who would not betray the confidence naturally followed. In the sixth century St. Benedict tells his monks that any sins of the soul should be made known to the abbot or to some one else who can cure their wounds without making them public.[1] About the same period, in the East, St. John Climacus shows that there was no recognized rule on the subject by arguing, in anticipation of Aquinas, that God does not reveal the sins confessed to him, and the confessor should follow the example.[2]

During the succeeding centuries, as the practice of auricular confession gradually spread, the matter of secrecy remained in this shape—a sort, of vague moral obligation, without any definite expression or liability to any penalty. In the vast body of the Penitentials, ransacking every sin and dereliction to affix to it an appropriate punishment, there is none prescribed for violation of the seal, and in the numerous *Ordines* which have reached us there is no allusion to it. At length, in 813, we have a recognition of the duty and of its disregard in an investigation ordered by Charlemagne into the truth of a report that priests for bribes would betray robbers who had confessed to them[3]—the Frankish law-giver could readily see that no man's life would be safe if such practices were allowed and such testimony were admitted. At the same time there was no obligation when a penitent could be benefitted, for he encouraged his Saxon converts to confess by a law providing that any one guilty of a mortal crime, who would voluntarily confess to a priest and accept penance, should escape death on the testimony of the confessor.[4] Towards the close of the ninth century, the council of Douzy informs priests that sins confessed to them are to be made known only to God in their prayers, but it names no penalty, and the only authority it can quote for this is the passage in the Rule of Benedict.[5]

The tenth century affords us no material for tracing the development of the seal, but in the awakening of the eleventh it makes its

---

[1] S. Benedicti Regulæ cap. xlvi. Towards the close of the sixth century this injunction is repeated by St. Paulinus of Aquileia, *De Salutaribus Documentis* cap. 52.

[2] S. Jo. Climaci Lib. de Pastoris Officio.

[3] Capit. Car. Mag. I. ann. 813, cap. 27.

[4] Capit. de Partibus Saxoniæ ann. 879, cap. 14.

[5] C. Dusiacens. II. ann. 874 cap. 8 (Harduin. VI. I. 157).

appearance as one of the incidents in the growth of sacerdotalism. An *Ordo* of the period manifests a solicitude for the penitent in ordering that no fasts shall be prescribed which will betray his sin, but prayer and almsgiving shall be imposed in their place.[1] About the same time there appears the first prescription of a penalty for revealing a confession, the extreme severity of which shows profound conviction of the difficulty of enforcing the rule, for it orders the offender to be deposed and to spend the rest of his days in pilgrimage.[2] The form in which this is drawn gives it the appearance of being an innovation, and though it was copied into the collection of Anselm of Lucca,[3] it seems at the time to have remained generally unknown and inoperative. Some Norman canons of the period contain simply a precept that sins made known in confession are to be revealed to no one.[4] It was about this period that Lanfranc felt it necessary to argue elaborately that the confessor should preserve silence as to what he learned in confession ; he has no established rule to cite in support of his appeal, no authoritative decision of the Church ; he is able to threaten no penalties, and can only say that the priest who does otherwise is guilty of a mortal sin.[5] The absence of any recognized prescription on the subject could not be more clearly indicated. Similar evidence is afforded in the struggle of St. Anselm to reform the concubinage of the clergy ; those who confess their sin in secret and repent are not to be deprived of their functions, and for this he alleges only reasons of expediency without invoking any prohibition of revealing what had passed in the confessional.[6] Equally significant is the treatment of the subject by St. Ivo of Chartres. He says that there are canons forbidding the

---

[1] Morin de Pœnitent. Append. p. 25.

[2] Corrector Burchardi cap. 244 (Wasserschleben, p. 678)—"Caveat ante omnia sacerdos ne de his qui ei confitentur peccata sua alicui recitet ; quod ei confessus est non propinquis non extraneis, nec, quod absit, pro aliquo scandalo, nam si hoc fecerit deponatur et omnibus diebus vitæ suæ peregrinando pœniteat. Si quis sacerdos palam fecerit et secretum pœnitentiæ usurpaverit, ut populum intellexerit et declaratum fuerit quod celare debuerit ab omni honore suo in cunctum populum deponatur et diebus vitæ suæ peregrinando finiat."

[3] Anselmi Lucens. Collect. Canon. Lib. XI. cap. 25.

[4] Post Concil. Rotomagens. ann. 1074, cap. 8 (Harduin. VI. I. 1520).

[5] Lanfranci Lib. de Celanda Confessione (Migne, CL. 625–8).

[6] S. Anselmi Cantuar. Epistt. Lib. I. Ep. 56.

revelation of confessions, and proceeds to quote a few from the earlier
councils and St. Augustin which have no relation to the question.[1]
Evidently he had no authority to cite and knew of no penalty to
prescribe. When Abelard says that there may be cases in which
prudence prevents confession to avert scandal, he shows how little
reliance was placed on the reticence of confessors, and in another
passage he asserts that there are many prelates to whom it is not
only useless but injurious to confess, in consequence of their readi-
ness to reveal what is confessed, thus scandalizing the Church and
exposing penitents to great peril.[2] Cardinal Pullus feels obliged to
argue that the confessor is not to deprive of communion or to shame
by public accusation those whose sins he knows only through secret
confession.[3]

Soon after this the canon of the *Corrector Burchardi* emerges in a
somewhat abbreviated form, with the name of "Gregorius" attached
to it, in the compilation of Gratian, who, on the strength of it, asserts
that the confessor who reveals the sins of his penitent is to be deposed.[4] Gratian was promptly followed by Peter Lombard;[5] it was
easy to identify the "Gregory" with Gregory I. or Gregory VII.,
and the tremendous punishment prescribed by the canon, having
thus obtained lodgment in the two most authoritative works of the
twelfth century, became a fixture in canon law, branding the offence
as one of the deepest dye and exaggerating to the utmost the inviolable character of the seal. With the development of the sacramental
theory, and the increasing importance attached to auricular confession,
it was inevitable that the impenetrable secrecy of the confessional
should be more and more insisted upon. Not only was the priest
forbidden to speak of the sins thus made known to him, but he was
told that he could make no use of the knowledge thus acquired.
Peter of Blois sharply reproves an abbot for treating his penitents
with contempt and thus exposing them to suspicion, while Alexander
III. decreed that a confessor had no right publicly to objurgate a
penitent for his sins or to excommunicate him by name, thus giving
the force of law to the warnings uttered a quarter of a century be-

[1] Ivon. Carnotens. Epist. CLVI.; Decreti P. v. cap. 363–4.
[2] P. Abælardi Epit. Theol. Christ. cap. xxxvi.; Ethicæ. cap. xxv.
[3] Rob. Pulli Sententt. Lib. VI. cap. 51.
[4] Cap. 2 Caus. XXXIII. Q. iii. Dist. 6.
[5] P. Lombardi Sentt. Lib. IV. Dist. xxi. § 7.

fore by Cardinal Pullus.[1] Towards the close of the century Bishop
Eudes of Paris accepted the principle in its fullest sense and decreed
that no one through anger, hatred or fear of death must reveal,
directly or indirectly, by word or sign or allusion, anything heard
in confession, and in 1199 a council of Dalmatia includes the offence
among those entailing degradation[2]—evidently the extreme severity
of the *Corrector Burchardi* was unknown or disapproved. Innocent
III. expressed his sense of the importance of the seal when he declared that the confessor who reveals a sin is more guilty than the
penitent who commits it;[3] but he did not consider it as absolutely
inviolable if there is truth in a story told by Cæsarius of Heisterbach, who, as a Cistercian, is not likely to be misinformed. A
Cistercian not in priests' orders was in the habit of celebrating mass;
on confessing to his abbot he was ordered to discontinue the sacrilege, but disobeyed, fearing detection. The abbot, perplexed, stated
the case in the next general chapter and asked advice. The assembled abbots were equally at a loss and referred the matter to Innocent III., who laid it before the Sacred College, when the cardinals
were of opinion that the seal of confession must not be broken, but
Innocent declared that such a confession was not a confession but
blasphemy, and was entitled to no respect. To this his cardinals
finally assented, and the decision was conveyed to the next Cistercian
chapter.[4]

Finally, as we have seen (p. 229), when the Lateran council, in
1216, rendered annual confession obligatory, care was taken to assure
the people of its secrecy by a clause which gave the sanction of positive law to the penalty provided by the *Corrector Burchardi*, with
the substitution of life-long reclusion in a monastery for perpetual
pilgrimage. Still there was no thought of claiming divine origin
for the purely human prescription, nor was its binding force clearly
recognized among churchmen, for, a few years afterwards, John,

---

[1] P. Blesens. de Pœnit. (Migne, CCVII. 1091).—Post Concil. Lateran. P.
XLIX. cap. 55 (Cap. 2 Extra I. xxxi.).

[2] Odonis Paris. Synod. Constitt. circa 1198, cap. 6; Concil. Dalmat. ann.
1199, cap. 4 (Harduin. VI. II. 1941, 1953).

[3] Innoc. PP. III. Serm. I. de Consecratione (Migne, CCXVIII. 652).

[4] Cæsar. Heisterb. Dial. Dist. III. cap. 32.—Cæsarius relates another story
(Ibid. cap. 42) of a priest who endeavored to seduce a female penitent by
threatening to reveal her sins, and on her proving firm fulfilled his threat.

priest of S. Thomas de Portione of Rome, was sentenced to interdict, with the alternative of making good the amount stolen, because
he refused to reveal the author of some thefts which he had learned
in confession.   He appealed to Honorius III., who ordered the
interdict removed, merely remarking that it would be pernicious to
force the priest to make known what he had heard in confession or
to pay for what he had not stolen.   Neither surprise nor indignation
is expressed at such an attempt by ecclesiastical judges, and the inclusion by S. Ramon de Peñafort, in 1235, of this decision in the
Decretals of Gregory IX. shows that up to that time the matter was
regarded as purely a disciplinary regulation.[1]   How completely,
indeed, it was still considered to be merely a human institution—a
privilege provided for the benefit of penitents—is manifested by S.
Ramon, who states that a heretic confessing his heresy and refusing
to abandon it or to betray his associates is not entitled to the seal,
for, as an infidel, faith is not to be kept with him.[2]   This, in fact,
continued for some time to be the doctrine of the Church, as condensed in the verse " Est hæresis crimen quod nec confessio celat."
and gave infinite trouble to later canonists who, till the end of the
fifteenth century, felt obliged to controvert it and to argue that the
most the confessor could do was to warn the bishop to look after his
flock, without mentioning names.[3]   Moreover, William of Auxerre,
about 1220, reports three cases submitted to the Paris doctors, in
two of which confessors learned of impediments to approaching marriages and in the third of the irregularity of a cleric about to be
ordained, when the doctors decided that to reveal them would not
be an infringement of the seal ; infringement, they said, was the improper divulging of confessions, and this was merely " opening " the
seal, for evil must be prevented as far as possible.[4]   Matthew Paris
utters no word of comment when he relates how a conspiracy against

---

[1] Cap. 13 Extra y. xxxi.

[2] S. Raymundi Summæ Lib. III. Tit. xxxiv. § 4.

[3] Hostiens. Aureæ Summæ Lib. v. de Pœn. et Remiss. § 53.—S. Th. Aquin.
in IV. Sentt. Dist. XXI. Q. iii. Art. 1 ad 1 ; Ejusd. Summæ Supplem. Q. XI.
Art. 1.— J. Scoti in IV. Sentt. Dist. XXI. Q. unic.—Astesani Summæ Lib. v.
Tit. xx. Q. 2.—Durand. de S. Porcian. in IV. Sentt. Dist. XXI. Q. iv. § 12.—
Manip. Curator. P. II. Tract. iii. cap. 11.—Summa Pisanella s. v. *Confessionis
Celatio.*—Rob. Aquin. Opus Quadrages. Serm. XXIX. cap. 2.—Gab. Biel in IV.
Sentt. Dist. XXI. Q. unic. Art. 3, Dub. 1.

[4] Tournely de Sacr. Pœnit. Q. VI. Art. iv.

Innocent IV., in 1247, was revealed by a priest who had learned it from the death-bed confession of one of the accomplices.[1] Evidently it required considerable time to elaborate the divine origin and supreme importance of the seal, and even after these had long been accepted there were French canonists in the seventeenth century who argued that in France high treason was not protected by it.[2]

To supplement the seal, in the effort to popularize confession, there was a persistent attempt made to remove the dread naturally felt as to the discretion of the confessor by persuading people that a supernatural power immediately effaced from the memory of the priest all the sins confided to him. We have seen (p. 235) that this belief was emphatically asserted in the *Sermones ad Fratres in Eremo* forged in the name of St. Augustin. Even Peter Cantor declares that when men in danger of shipwreck confess their sins publicly, they are obliterated from the memory of those who are saved.[3] The punishment decreed by the Lateran canon sufficiently contradicted this superstition, and William of Paris does not repeat it, but he ventures on a statement, of which there was no danger of disproof, by assuring us that such is the power of sacramental confession that even the omniscient God forgets the sins confessed.[4]

The Lateran canon, relying wholly on human means, slowly produced its effect. The local councils held during the next two centuries repeated its provisions with more or less emphasis and gradually impressed the priesthood with the idea of the heinousness of revealing confessions.[5] In 1302, indeed, the council of Toledo felt obliged to threaten deportation to the mines or perpetual imprisonment on

[1] Matt. Paris. Hist. Anglic. ann. 1247 (Ed. 1644, p. 486).

[2] Lenglet Du Fresnoy, Traité sur le Secret de la Confession, p. 127. Henry IV. put the question to his confessor, the Jesuit Coton, who courageously replied that, sacred as was the life of the king, the seal was even more sacred.—Ibid. p. 129.

[3] P. Cantor. Verb. Abbreviat. cap. 144.

[4] Guillel. Paris. de Pœnitentia cap. 21.

[5] Statuta Rich. Poore ann. 1217, cap. 29 (Harduin. VII. 97).—C. Rotomagens. ann. 1223, cap. 9 (Ibid. p. 128).—C. Mogunt. ann. 1261, cap. 8 (Hartzheim III. 598).—C. Mogunt. ann. 1281, cap. 8 (Ibid. p. 664).—C. Coloniens. ann. 1280, cap. 8 (Ibid. p. 828).—Synod. Nemausens. ann. 1284 (Harduin. VII. 912).—Statutt. Joh. Episc. Leodiens. ann. 1287, cap. 4 (Hartzheim III. 689).—Statutt. Synod. Remens. circa 1330, Sec. Locus, Præcept. iv. (Gousset, Actes etc. II. 540).—C. Suessionens. ann. 1403, cap. 45 (Ibid. p. 631).

bread and water to restrain the practice of violating the seal,[1] and Astesanus is inclined to laxity respecting it, when the questions were involved of the promotion of unworthy sinners or the marriage of those who had contracted spiritual affinity through sin.[2] Meanwhile the schoolmen were busily at work elaborating their theories of its divine origin, and exhausting their ingenuity in devising cases to illustrate the rigor of its observance. All this became universally accepted as doctrine, so that when Pedro of Osma, in 1479, in denying the necessity of confession, likewise denied the obligation of the seal, Sixtus IV. had no hesitation in condemning his opinions as heretical.[3] Still, as late as 1524, the council of Sens felt it necessary to explain at considerable length that the priest who breaks the seal violates the divine, the natural and the ecclesiastical law, and that such a practice renders confession impossible, to which it added, by way of warning, the clause of the Lateran canon threatening degradation and monastic reclusion.[4] Even in 1605 the synod of Coire, in ordering priests to be examined as to their knowledge respecting the seal, shows by the questions which it prescribes that they were expected to be almost wholly ignorant on the subject.[5] Yet at this period many doctors still held that knowledge obtained in confession could be used to prevent a greater evil than the infraction of the seal, if it could be done without direct or indirect revelation or injury to the penitent[6]—a doctrine which was not condemned until 1682, when it was submitted to the Congregation of the Inquisition as one of the errors of the Jansenists.[7] The beginning of the eighteenth century witnessed considerable trouble at Arras, arising from the indiscretion of some confessors and leading to scandals which had to be settled by the secular tribunals. They seem to have been caused by efforts to enforce the papal bulls against solicitation, which were so energetically resisted by the Gallican clergy, and they culminated in

---

[1] C. Penna-Fidelis ann. 1302, cap. 5 (Aguirre, V. 227).

[2] Astesani Summæ Lib. v. Tit. xx. Q. 2.

[3] Alph. de Castro adv. Hæreses Lib. iv. s. v. *Confessio.*

[4] C. Senonens. ann. 1524 (Bochelli Decr. Eccles. Gallic. Lib. ii. Tit. vii. cap. 171).

[5] C. Curiens. ann. 1605, *De Sigillo* (Hartzheim VIII. 642).

[6] Vittorelli not. in Tolet. Instruct. Sacerd. Lib. iii. cap. 15.

[7] Le Tellier, Recueil Historique des Bulles, Mons (Rouen), 1704, p. 428.— Viva Trutina Theol. Append. ¿ 6.

the publication of a tract which asserted that the confessor can reveal indirectly a confession when there is a good object to be gained; that he can force a penitent to reveal the name of an accomplice, whom he can then interrogate both sacramentally and otherwise, denounce him to the bishop for prosecution, furnish the names and facts, summon the witnesses and interrogate them; that the confessor can also oblige the penitent to repeat the details of his sins outside of the sacrament and thus be relieved from the obligation of the seal. The Bishop of Arras, Gui de Rochechouart, in 1708, condemned twenty-two propositions drawn from this tract and forbade it to be read or taught.[1] It was in all likelihood the production of an opponent of the papal measures, framed to point out the practical conclusions which might be drawn from them.

During the course of this development the Church claims several martyrs who sealed with their blood their fidelity to the obligation of secrecy. It is related that Wenceslas of Bohemia, in 1383, angered with his Queen Johanna, ordered her confessor, John of Nepomuk, then a canon of Prague, to reveal her confessions, and on his refusal after threats and incarceration, caused him to be thrown from the bridge into the Moldau. His holiness was manifested by the river promptly drying up, leaving his body exposed, which after three days was buried in the church of St. Vitus, and thenceforth we are told that whosoever insulted his memory came to a speedy end. His merits were long in meeting recognition in Rome, for he was not canonized until 1729.[2] The Jesuit, Henry Garnet, is also claimed

---

[1] Lochon, Traité du Secret de la Confession, Brusselle, 1708, pp. 331–42.

[2] Dubrav. Hist. Bohem. Lib. XXIII. No saint can be considered safe from the attacks of iconoclasts. In 1677 the Jesuit Balbinus (Epit. Rer. Bohemicar. ann. 1383) tells us that there were even then ignorant men who detracted from the memory of the holy martyr. Modern research has shown that there was a John of Nepomuk, notary, canon and vicar of John of Genzenstein, Archbishop of Prague, who was drowned by order of Wenceslas in 1393, in consequence of a quarrel over the abbey of Klabran.—Abel, Die Legende vom heiligen Johann von Nepomuk, Berlin, 1855.

The evidence in favor of the martyrdom will be found in the *Acta in Causa Canonizationis Beati Joannis Nepomuceni Martyris* (Viennæ, 1722, pp. 318 sqq.) where it is interesting to trace the growth of the legend. The earliest reference to the matter is a cursory one by Paul Zidek, who wrote in 1471, nearly ninety years after the date assigned to the martyrdom. The silence of all previous and contemporary writers is customarily explained by the Hussite heresy, but

as a martyr, though doubtfully. Catesby is said to have revealed in confession the Gunpowder Plot to Father Oswald Tesmond or Greenway and asked Tesmond to consult Garnet under seal; Garnet endeavored unsuccessfully to dissuade Catesby, and on his trial admitted his knowledge of the plot under the seal of confession.[1] To this is doubtless attributable the controversy on the subject between Isaac Casaubon and Cardinal Duperron. Casaubon argued that confessors were bound to reveal projected crimes against the state and asserted that the Sorbonne had so declared, while Duperron in reply produced a declaration from the chief doctors of the Sorbonne that they would rather endure the stake than teach such a doctrine.[2] Another martyr is reputed to be Johann Sarcander, pastor of Holleschau in Moravia, who, in 1620, during the troubles of the Winter King's short reign, was put to death, the chief cause assigned being his refusal to violate the seal.[3]

The confessor, in fact, was the repository of too many secrets not to be subjected to pressure for their disclosure, while as yet the seal was imperfectly respected and had not been recognized as justifying a refusal to testify. The case mentioned above, in which Honorius III. intervened to protect a priest threatened by a Roman ecclesiastical court for not revealing the authors of a robbery, shows how difficult it was at first for even churchmen to acknowledge the supreme obligation of silence, and in the secular courts there must have been frequent instances of similar efforts at coercion. The course for the priest to pursue in such cases was not determined for some time. S. Ramon de Peñafort contented himself with introducing the decree of Honorius in the compilation of Gregory IX., and in his *Summa*

---

this did not break out till more than thirty years after the date assigned to the occurrence. When Sigismund for a time restored Catholicism after he regained Prague, in 1436, had there been any such belief among the people it would have been exploited to the utmost. Besides, the Calixtins, who were the dominant sect among the Hussites, retained auricular confession and the sacrament of penitence, and could have had no possible objection to reverencing a victim of Wenceslas.

[1] Bartoli, dell' Istoria della Compagna di Giesù in l'Inghilterra, pp. 495, 545 (Roma, 1667).—Clericati de Pœnitent. Decis. XLIX. n. 2.—R. Bellarmini Apologia pro sua Responsione, Mendacium XV. (Opp. IV. 408, Neapoli, 1858).

[2] Lochon, Traité du Secret de la Confession, Préface.

[3] Guillois, History of Confession, p. 187. Proceedings for the beatification of Sarcander were commenced in 1836.

prudently avoids touching the question, but his *postillator* refers to it. It is a convincing proof of the novelty of the seal and of the difficulty of enforcing its recognition, that the priest when interrogated in court is not told to plead the privilege of the confessional but is at once instructed to resort to lying and perjury and mental reservation; he is to say "I know nothing whatever" with the reservation "as man," or "I know nothing through confession" with the reservation "to tell you."[1] Alexander Hales explains this: what the priest knows by confession he knows as God, not as man, and he can deny the knowledge under oath.[2] This slightly blasphemous device of knowing as God seems to have been invented in the previous century by Alexander III.,[3] and the schoolmen seized upon it to relieve the confessor from all responsibility to man, for they argued that what he knew as God he could not know as man; to deny such knowledge under oath was therefore not perjury, and some even went so far as to assert that it would be a lie to admit of knowledge. To this demoralizing system of equivocation Aquinas and Bonaventura lent the sanction of their great authority.[4] Duns Scotus easily exploded it by pointing out that the confessor in the sacramental function is not God but God's minister, and his knowledge as man is daily proved by his consulting experts in difficult cases, by allusions in sermons to matters learned in the confessional and by the received practice that a confessor can speak of a sin thus made known to him provided it is done in such a manner as not to implicate the penitent.[5] Durand de S. Pourçain endeavored to get around the difficulty by arguing that a witness in court speaks as a subject, while a confessor, *qua* confessor, is not a subject, but, if he appears as a voluntary witness, denial of knowledge is a lie.[6] The long argument which Pierre de la Palu devotes to the subject shows how difficult it was for the schoolmen to satisfy themselves with regard to it.[7] The fiction of

---

[1] Guill. Redonens. in Raymundi Summæ P. III. Tit. xxxiv. § 4.

[2] Alex. de Ales Summæ P. IV. Q. xix. Membr. 2, Art. 1.

[3] "Quia non ut judex scit sed ut Deus."—Post Concil. Lateran. P. xlix. cap. 55.—Cap. 2 Extra, I. xxxi.

[4] S. Th. Aquinat. in IV. Sentt. Dist. xxi. Q. iii. Art. 1 ad 1, 3; Summæ Supplem. Q. xi. Art. 1.—S. Bonavent. in IV. Sentt. Dist. xxi. P. ii. Art. 2, Q. 1.

[5] J. Scoti in IV. Sentt. Dist. xxi. Q. unic.

[6] Durand. de S. Porcian. in IV. Sentt. Dist. xxi. Q. iv. § 10.

[7] P. de Palude in IV. Sentt. Dist. xxi. Q. iii. Art. 3, Concl. 1.

knowing as God, however, was too flattering and too convenient to be abandoned ; it won its way in spite of the opposition of Scotist doctors,[1] and became a commonplace in the manuals and systems, which instruct the priest to commit perjury and quiet his conscience with the figment that he does not know as man.[2] Even the secular lawyers finally accepted it and admitted that there is no sin in thus swearing.[3]

With the seventeenth century there came for a time a tendency to a more honest and straightforward course. Willem van Est instructs the priest that he cannot deny knowledge, but must say that such inquiries are impious and that it is not right for him to answer them, and Maldonado asserts that he should state that he has nothing to say, for he cannot reveal on one side or the other what he has learned in confession.[4] They had few followers, however, and some moralists, like Berteau, Busenbaum and Gobat, suggest ingenious and barefaced equivocation and mental reservation, while others, like Laymann and Diana, adhere to the old formula of perjury under the assumption of knowing only as God.[5] Modern moralists of all schools unite in the instruction that the priest is to deny unequivo-

---

[1] Astesani Summæ Lib. v. Tit. xx. Q. 1. Angiolo da Chivasso (Summa Angelica s. v. *Confessio* ult. § 4) advises mental reservation "quia non possit negare quin sciat ut homo."—Gabriel Biel (In IV. Sentt. Dist. xxi. Q. unic. Art. iii. Dub. 1, ad 3) instructs the confessor to refuse to answer, and if this is construed against an accused person he is not responsible.

[2] Jo. Friburgens Summæ Confessor. Lib. iii. Tit. xxxiv. Q. 91-7.—Manip. Curator. P. ii. Tract. iii. cap. 11.—P. de Aquila in IV. Sentt. Dist. xx. Q. iii. —Passavanti, Lo Specchio della vera Penitenza Dist. v. cap. 4.—Summa Pisanella s. v. *Confessionis Celatio* n. 2.—S. Antonini Summæ P. iii. Tit. xvii. cap. 22.—Summa Sylvestrina s. v. *Confessio* iii. § 6.—Caietani Summula s. v. *Confessori necessaria.*—Summa Tabiena s. v. *Confessionis Celatio* § 1.—Eisengrein Confessionale, cap. vii. Q. 11.—Fr. Toleti Instructio Sacerdotum, Lib. iii. cap. xvi. n. 4.

Eisengrein, however, subsequently says (Q. 19) that the confessor is to protest against all inquiries as sacrilegious.

[3] Damhouder Rerum Criminal. Praxis cap. liii. n. 8.

[4] Estius in IV. Sentt. Dist. xvii. § 14.—Tournely de Sacr. Pœnit. Q. vi. art. 4.

[5] Berteau, Director Confessar. p. 494.—Busenbaum Medulla Theol. Moral. Lib. vi. Tract. iv. cap. 3, Dub. 1.—Gobat Alphab. Confessar. n. 840.—Jac. a Graffiis Practica Casuum Reservator. Lib. ii. cap. xxxvi. n. 23,—Layman Theol. Moral. Lib. v. Tract. vi. cap. 14, n. 12.—Summa Diana s. v. *Sigillum Sacram.* n. 30.—Arsdekin Theol. Tripart. P. iii. Tract. 1, cap. 3, Q. 1.

cally under oath all knowledge of what he has heard in confession, although some of them do not take the trouble to explain it by the fiction of knowing only as God.[1]   The retention to the present day and insistance on this are presumably for the benefit of priests on distant missions, for it can hardly be possible that any civilized nation can refuse to recognize the privileged nature of communications between penitent and confessor, like those between client and counsel.   It is true that, as recently as 1810, at Jemappes, a court insisted on a priest revealing the name of a thief which he had learned in confession, but on appeal the decision was set aside by the Court of Cassation.   In 1822, before a court at Poitiers, the prosecuting officer made a similar demand, but it was refused.   In 1813 the question was settled in New York, in the case of a priest named Kohlmann, who had returned some stolen articles which he had caused a thief to restore.   He refused to reveal the name and was prosecuted, but a Protestant jury acquitted him on the reasonable ground that to destroy the seal of confession is equivalent to denying the sacrament to Catholics.[2]

The extreme rigor of the penalties decreed by the canon in the *Corrector Burchardi* and in the Lateran Council—deposition and life-long penance either in pilgrimage or in a monastery—marks the sense of the importance attached to the preservation of the seal. The Lateran canon became the received law of the Church and continued to be cited by all writers as in force until the eighteenth century was well advanced.[3]   Yet it had few terrors for gossiping or

---

[1] Habert Praxis Sacr. Pœnit. Tract. I. cap. 8.—S. Alph. de Ligorio Theol. Moral. Lib. VI. n. 646.—Benzi Praxis Trib. Confess. Disp. II. Q. vii. Art. 1, n. 4.—Concina Theol. Christ. contracta, Lib. XI. cap. iv. n. 11.—Th. ex Charmes Theol. Univ. Diss. v. cap. iv. art. 2.—Zenner Instruct. Pract. Confessar. § 60.—Gury Comp. Theol. Moral. II. 650.—Varceno Comp. Theol. Moral. Tract. XVIII. cap. iv. art. 7, § 1.—Gousset, Théol. Morale III. 512.—Mig. Sanchez, Prontuario de la Teol. Moral. Trat. VI. Punto xiii. § 21.

[2] Grégoire, Hist. des Confesseurs des Empereurs etc. pp. 92–4.

[3] Hostiens. Aureæ Summæ Lib. v. De Pœn. et Remiss. § 53.—Summa Pisanella s. v. *Confessionis Celatio* § 1.—S. Antonini Summæ Lib. III. Tit. xvii. cap. 22.—Summa Sylvestrina s. v. *Confessio* III. § 5.—Eisengrein Confessionale cap. vii. Q. 18.—Toleti Instruct. Sacerd. Lib. III. cap. xvi. n. 4.—Em. Sa Aphorismi Confessar. s. v. *Confessio* n. 31.—Summa Diana s. v. *Sigillum sacram.* n. 51.—Héricourt, Loix ecclésiastiques de France T. II. p. 14.

evil-disposed priests, for in the forum of conscience the penance to be imposed was discretional, like that for any other sin,[1] and in the external forum the punishment could only be inflicted after trial and conviction, of which the chances were remote. Few penitents whose sins had been betrayed would care to undergo the labor and expense of such a prosecution before the offender's bishop or superior, with the prospect of a result doubtful as to success but certain to extend and intensify the knowledge of his crimes or failings. It was a debated point whether an official prosecution could be instituted without the penitent's assent. Proof was difficult, because those to whom a priest might unlawfully reveal the secrets of the confessional were equally bound by the seal, and it was a disputed question how far the penitent himself could release anyone from its obligation. So sacred, indeed, was the seal that Gobat points out that any attempt by a judge to inquire into such a case would be sacrilegious, as no one could talk or give evidence about the matter, and Lenglet Du Fresnoy argues that the confessor himself cannot be examined because his admission would be a second violation of the seal, worse than the first. The matter was thus surrounded with difficulties, and the doctors were by no means in accord as to where lay the burden of proof. Niccolò da Osimo says, in 1443, that, if the confessor denies the accusation and the penitent cannot prove it, nor the priest show where else he learned the crime, nor prove it on the penitent, then the punishment is discretional. Prierias and Giovanni da Taggia tell us that if the priest asserts that he heard the crime outside of the confessional, some doctors decide that he must be believed, while others hold that he must show where he heard it, otherwise the presumption is against him, but still the punishment is discretional, as he is not fully convicted, in which somewhat irrational conclusion Henriquez concurs. Chiericato says that unless the permission of the penitent is procured for the prosecution it is null and void, and that all the witnesses are bound by the seal and cannot testify without his licence. Benzi, on the other hand, declares that

---

[1] S. Antonini Summæ P. III. Tit. xvii. cap. 22. The Papal Penitentiary charged seven *gros tournois* for absolution for violation of the seal, but it marked the sense of the heinousness of the offence by adding that the severest punishment must also be inflicted, a clause not found in any other item of the Taxes.—Libellus Taxarum fol. 17*b* (White Historical Library, Cornell University, A. 6124).

the prosecution can be carried on without a faculty from the penitent, and that the crime can be proved by witnesses. Tournely points out that, if the accused pleads that he had permission from the penitent to reveal the sin, the burden of proof is on him, which is an impossibility for him, and that therefore great caution should be used in undertaking such trials. These were not all the questions involved, but they will suffice to justify the remark of Lenglet Du Fresnoy, that few prosecutions are so difficult to carry on as those for violations of the seal.[1]

In view of these uncertainties and of the anxiety of the Church to avoid a scandal so dangerous it is evident that trials for this offence must have been rare, and rarer still the infliction of the canonical punishment. Gobat, in fact, mentions a case in which a parish priest in a sermon scolded two of his parishioners, for sins made known to him in confession, in a manner enabling them to be identified, and yet the ecclesiastical judge only inflicted on him a heavy fine. He adds that at this period (1666) it would be impossible to enforce the penalty of perpetual imprisonment in a monastery, and that, moreover, all punishments are subject to the discretion of the judge.[2] By this time, indeed, the canonical punishment was admitted to be obsolete, and it would seem that in some places, at least, it was customary on conviction to degrade the offenders and hand them over to the secular arm, which sometimes, as in Venice, put them to death, and sometimes sent them to the galleys.[3] At the present day there is not the resource of calling in the secular arm, and the offence is doubtless treated with less harshness. It can hardly be regarded as

---

[1] Gobat Alphab. Confessar. n. 847.—L. Du Fresnoy, Traité du Secret, p. 264. —N. de Auximo in Summam Pisanellam s. v. *Confessionis Celatio* n. 1.—Summa Sylvestrina s. v. *Confessio* III. § 5.—Summa Tabiena s. v. *Confessionis Celatio* § 16.—Henriquez Summæ Theol. Moral. Lib. VI. cap. xiv. n. 10.—Summa Diana s. v. *Sigillum Sacram.* n. 51-55.—Clericati de Pœnit. Decis. XLIX. n. 6, 17.—Benzi Praxis Trib. Confess. Disp. II. Q. vii. Art. 1, n. 6.

Diana remarks (*ubi sup.*) that when infractions of the seal were denounced to the Inquisition it was accustomed to hand them over to the episcopal courts, as it had no jurisdiction unless the culprit thought it lawful or held some other heresy concerning the sacrament.

[2] Gobat Alphab. Confessar. n. 843-5.

[3] Henriquez Summæ Theol. Moral. Lib. VI. cap. xix. n. 9.—Gobat Alphab. Confessar. n. 842.—Clericati de Pœnit. Decis. XLIX. n. 18.—Benzi Praxis Trib. Confess. Disp. II. Q. vii. Art. 1, n. 6.

deserving of extreme punishment seeing that the Congregation of Bishops and Regulars prescribes for it, when committed by a member of a religious Order, the comparatively light penalty of fasting thrice a week on bread and water, to be eaten on the floor of the refectory, and then to lie at the entrance and be trodden on by the outgoing brethren.[1]

When once the seal of confession was established, the schoolmen naturally busied themselves with developing it in every direction and exalting its inviolability. There arose of course the question whether the priest could be released from its obligation by a dispensation from his bishop or from the pope, for the habit was growing of regarding the dispensing power as superior to all law. Some doctors held the affirmative, or that the point was at least doubtful,[2] but the great mass of authorities decided in the negative, alleging various reasons—that the confessor knows only as God, that the Church cannot alter what God has ordered, that in the confessional the priest is the special delegate of God, and as such is superior to the pope, who is only a general delegate. Thus the principle became established, and it was agreed that if a priest should be excommunicated by bishop or pope for refusing to reveal a confession the excommunication would be void.[3]

The definition of violation of the seal was speedily enlarged, so as to cover not only the publication or revelation to any one of sins confessed, but also any hint or sign which might raise suspicion or convey knowledge of what has occurred in the confessional—even if a priest should say of a thief about to be hanged that he had shown great contrition in confessing his thefts. What the priest knows as God he is held not to know as man; it is not to influence his action

---

[1] Pittoni Constitutiones Pontificiæ T. VII. n. 963.

[2] F. de Mairone (in IV. Sentt. Dist. xxi. Q. iii.) mentions this opinion, but decides against it. Piero d'Aquila (in IV. Sentt. Dist. xx. Q. iii.) inclines to the negative, but says "ideo illud non assero sed pro nunc suspensum relinquo."

[3] S. Th. Aquin. in IV. Sentt. Dist. xxi. Q. iii. Art. 3; Summæ Suppl. Q. xi. Art. 1.—Astesani Summæ Lib. v. Tit. xx. Q. 2.—Durand. de S. Porciano in IV. Sentt. Dist. xxi. Q. iv. § 8.—S. Antonini Summæ P. iii. Tit. xvii. cap. 22.—Rob. Aquinat. Opus Quadrages. Serm. xxix. cap. 2.—Summa Sylvestrina s. v. *Confessio* iii. §§ 1, 2.—Summa Tabiena s. v. *Confessionis Celatio* § 1.

in any manner—at least in any manner which, by redounding to the
injury of the penitent, might tend to render confession odious. If
he is an abbot and learns in confession from a prior that the latter
is unfit for his post, he cannot remove him ; if he discovers that his
servant is a thief he cannot discharge him, and the degree of precau-
tion which he can adopt, as, for instance, with regard to the custody
of keys, is a disputed point ; if he discovers that his church has been
polluted he cannot inform the bishop and have it reconciled ; if he
finds that his usual confessor is not a priest he cannot cease confessing to him, if this would cause him disrepute, but should confine himself to venial sins and seek another for mortals ; he cannot refuse
the Eucharist, even secretly, to one whom he has thus learned to be
unfitted for it ; he cannot refuse to celebrate a marriage of which he
has thus learned an absolute impediment ; he cannot baptize or save
the life of an unborn child of a dying mother who has confessed to
him its existence ; he cannot prevent the execution of one whom he
thus knows to be innocent ; he cannot avoid the society of one whom
he thus learns to be excommunicate. There is no limit to the extravagance of the theologians in defining the infinite importance of
the seal. Its violation is not permissible to save the life of the pope,
or to avert the overthrow of the state, or even, as some declare, to
gain the salvation of mankind, or to prevent the conflagration of the
world, or the perversion of religion, or the attempted destruction of
all the sacraments.[1] Such being the case, the integrity of the sacrament of penitence itself must yield to the supreme importance of the
seal : if a confessor when confessing cannot include a sin without
mentioning matters heard in confession he can omit it and leave it

---

[1] Summa Tabiena s. v. *Confessionis Celatio* § 1.—Fumi Aurea Armilla s. v.
Confessor n. 7.—Dom. Soto in IV. Sentt. Dist. XVIII. Q. iv. Art. 5.—Toleti Instruct.
Sacerd. Lib. III. cap. xvi. n. 3, 6.—Em. Sa Aphorismi Confessar. s. v. *Confessor* n·
27, Addit.—Henriquez Summæ Theol. Moral. Lib. VI. cap. xix. n. 5.—Summa
Diana s. v. *Sigillum Sacram.* n. 1, 27.—Clericati de Pœnit. Decis. XLIX. n. 2,
16.—Gobat Alphab. Confessar. n. 790, 894, 899, 904.—Berteau Director. Con-
fessar. p. 492.—Benzi Praxis Trib. Conscient. Disp. II. Q. vii. Art. 1, n. 2 ; Art.
3, n. 23.—Tournely de Sacr. Pœnitent. Q. VI. Art. iv.—Bened. PP. XIV. Casus
Conscient. Maii, 1737, cas. 2.—S. Alph. de Ligorio Theol. Moral. Lib. VI. n.
634, 657–8.—Th. ex Charmes Theol. Univ. Dissert. v. cap. iv. Q. 2, Art. 2.—
Gury Comp. Theol. Moral. II. 667.—Varceno Comp. Theol. Moral. Tract.
XVIII. cap. iv. Art. 7.—Mig. Sanchez, Prontuario de la Teol. Moral. Trat. VI.
Punto xii. n. 4.

unconfessed.[1] Similarly, if a penitent reveals the name of a partner in guilt and she comes to confession and does not include that sin, the confessor cannot question her about it, but must give her absolution, though he knows that she still has a mortal sin upon her soul and will commit another by taking communion while in that state.[2] This trifling with the sacrament shows so little respect for the functions of the keys that Reuter, to avoid it, suggests the trick of repeating the *Misereatur tui* etc., omitting the sacramental words of absolution, and letting her depart unhouselled yet thinking herself absolved.[3] It is not the only case in which divine laws humanly interpreted contradict each other.

Of course the confessor is instructed that he must at any moment be prepared to endure death in preference to violating the seal in any manner. As the use, in any way, of knowledge gained in confession is strictly prohibited, it is even a question whether he can take any steps however simple to avoid a snare prepared for him of which he has learned in confession. To illustrate this the theologians have constructed many cases that have been debated for centuries, of which two will suffice. A priest travelling with some casual companions learns from one of them in confession that a plot has been laid to

---

[1] Gab. Biel in IV. Sentt. Dist. XXI. Art. 3, Dub. 1 ad 5.—Summa Sylvestrina s. v. *Confessio* III. § 8.—Toleti Instruct. Sacerd. Lib. III. cap. xvi. n. 3.—Gobat Alphab. Confessar. n. 838.—Layman Theol. Moral. Lib. V. Tract. vi. cap. 14, n. 13.—Benzi Praxis Trib. Conscient. Disp. II. Q. vii. Art. 3, n. 10.—Th. ex Charmes Theol. Univers. Diss. V. cap. iv. Q. 2, Art. 1, concl. 5.—Varceno Comp. Theol. Moral. Tract. XVIII. cap. iv. Art. 7.

This point was not settled without some discussion. The case is put of a priest who absolves a penitent in a reserved case without authority. Can he confess the fact if his confessor will recognize the sinner, as, for instance, if it is a bishop who has obtained his see simonically? Duns Scotus (In IV. Sentt. Dist. XXI. Q. unic) says that he cannot, but must confess to God; François de Mairone (In IV. Sentt. Dist. XXI. Q. iii.) says that he can, for it only goes from one confession to another and is still covered by the seal.

[2] Summa Diana s. v. *Sigillum Sacr.* n. 49.—Habert Praxis Sacr. Pœnit. Tract. iv.—Some authorities say that in this frequent case the confessor can make a general inquiry, but on denial must absolve.—Gobat Alphab. Confessar. n. 241–5; Benzi Praxis Trib. Conscient. Disp. II. Q. vii. Art. 3, n. 8.— Manzo says (Epit. Theol. Moral. P. I. De Pœnit. n. 94) that if he cannot indirectly induce confession and cannot avoid absolving, he must grant the sacrilegious absolution rather than violate the seal.

[3] Reuter Neoconfessarius instructus n. 36.

murder him in a wood through which their journey lies : must he advance unflinchingly to his doom or is it allowable for him to evade it if he can do so without betraying the penitent? Again, a penitent confides in confession to a priest about to celebrate mass that the chalice is poisoned : must he perform the service and die, or can he devise some excuse for not celebrating? There were rigorists who insisted that in these cases the priest must calmly proceed as though in ignorance ; there were others who argued that evasion is justifiable if it can be accomplished without exciting suspicion as to the penitent, but all agree that death must be welcomed in preference to violating the seal.[1]

Whether a confessor can allow his knowledge of the unworthiness of a penitent to influence his vote in secret ballot, when that penitent is a candidate for office, is a disputed question, with great names on either side. In fact the degree, if any, in which a confessor can permit his actions to be governed by the knowledge gained in confession has been the subject of interminable debates and forms, in the words of Tamburini, the most important and most vexatious of questions, and though there has been a tendency on the part of some to teach a lax doctrine respecting it, the weight of authority leans to that which will most avoid rendering confession odious.[2]

---

[1] Jo. Scoti in IV. Sentt. Dist. XXI. Q. unic.—Astesani Summæ Lib. V. Tit. XX. Q. 2.—Rob. Aquinat. Opus Quadrages. Serm. XXIX. cap. 2.—Summa Angelica s. v. *Confessio* ult. § 7.—Summa Sylvestrina s. v. *Confessio* III. §§ 9-13.— Summa Tabiena s. v. *Confessionis celatio* § 12.—Dom. Soto in IV. Sentt. Dist. XVIII. Q. iv. Art. 5.—Henriquez Summæ Theol. Moral. Lib. VI. cap. xxiv. n. 5.—Layman Theol. Moral. Lib. V. Tract. vi. cap. 14, n. 20.—Summa Diana s. v. *Sigillum sacram.* n. 28, 29.—Gobat. Alphab. Confessar. n. 897.—Tamburini Method. Confess. App. cap. vi.—Arsdekin Theol. Tripart. P. III. Tract. iii. cap. 4, n. 17.—Clericati de Pœnit. Decis. XLIX. n. 14.—Tournely de Sacr. Pœnit. Q. VI. Art. iv.—Benzi Praxis, Trib. Conscient. Disp. II. Q. vii. Art. 3, n. 23.—S. Alph. de Ligorio Theol. Moral. Lib. VI. n. 659.—Th. ex Charmes Theol. Univ. Diss. V. cap. iv. Art. 2.—Gury Comp. Theol. Moral II. 669.—Varceno Comp. Theol. Moral. Tract. XVIII. cap. iv. Art. 7, n. 1.

[2] S. Antonini Summæ P. III. Tit. xvii. cap. 22, § 1.—Escobar Theol. Moral. Tract. VII. Exam. iv. cap. 7, n. 41.—Tamburini Method. Confess. Append cap. vi. § 2, n. 1.—Arsdekin Theol. Tripart. P. III. Tract. 1, cap. 3, Q. 15.—Summæ Alexandrinæ P. I. n. 577.—Lenglet Du Fresnoy, Traité du Secret, p. 203, Append. p. 38.—S. Alph. de Ligorio Lib. VI. n. 655-7.

The Jesuit Tanner taught that the confessor can use the knowledge gained in the confessional for a good end, provided he does not reveal it ; he can urge

It is a violation of the seal to decline to give a certificate of confession, though absolution has been refused, when such certificates are required, as in schools and seminaries and convents, even though they may be abused to obtain sacrilegious communion; but when such certificates are not obligatory and an unabsolved penitent may ask it for a wrong purpose—as, for instance, to get married—it can be refused. These certificates are never to specify whether absolution has been given or withheld, for that would be a violation of the seal.[1] In fact, to mention that absolution has been denied is a violation, and when parents, teachers or masters ask whether their children, pupils or servants have been absolved they are to be referred to the penitents for information, and the same answer is to be given to sisters of charity who are apt in hospitals to seek such information in order that they may prepare for the viaticum.[2] Even conversation with the penitent, outside of the confessional concerning sins confessed, is a violation of the seal, unless the penitent freely and voluntarily accords permission. Toletus tells us that if a confessor finds that he has improperly conferred absolution (as in a reserved case or by not insisting on restitution) he cannot inform the penitent of it, but should say to him " I pray you to confess again, for I was deceived in your confession," and then the penitent ought to obey, when the impediment can be stated, but if the penitent refuses he cannot be compelled, and if there is danger of scandal it is better not even to approach him. Even if the confessor knows that the penitent has not performed his penance he cannot allude to it in a subsequent confession.[3]

---

the public authorities to vigilance, he can dismiss unworthy persons or prevent their promotion, etc., but the General Aquaviva prohibited action on this opinion or its teaching in the schools.—Summa Diana s. v. *Sigillum Sacram.* n. 43.

[1] Summa Diana s. v. *Sigillum Sacram.* n. 32.—Benzi Praxis Trib. Conscient. Disp. II. Q. vii. Art. 3, n. 7.—S. Alph. de Ligorio Theol. Moral. Lib. VI. n. 639.—Gury Comp. Theol. Moral. II. 661.—Varceno Comp. Theol. Moral. Tract. XVIII. cap. iv. Art. 7, n. 2.

This, however, is denied by some high authorities such as De Lugo, Bonacina and others (Benzi, *loc. cit.*), and in the seventeenth century the practice was not uniform (Du Fresnoy, p. 253).

[2] Benzi, *loc. cit.*—Varceno, *loc. cit.*—Gury Comp. Theol. Moral. II. 659.

Caietano (Summula s. v. *Confessori necessaria*) denies that to give such information is a violation, but says that it ought not to be done.

[3] Toleti Instruct. Sacerd. Lib. III. cap. xvi. n. 5.—Summa Diana s. v. *Sigillum Sacram.* n. 40, 41.—Escobar Theol. Moral. Tract. VII. Exam. iv. cap. 7, n

The supreme importance attached to the seal is shown in the rule that if in any case involving it there are two probable opinions the one to be followed is that which favors the seal, to the exclusion of the other, for the violation is a danger to be averted at all risks.[1] This indicates that here, as everywhere else in our subject, every attempt to establish a rule of conduct only raised a cloud of doubtful problems which taxed to the utmost the ingenuity of the moralists, and were often incapable of a solution commanding universal assent. A few of these are worth brief consideration, if only to show the difficulty of handling questions so intangible.

We have seen (p. 362) that it is allowable for a penitent to write out his confession and hand it to the priest. If, through accident or carelessness, such a paper should fall into other hands, is the finder bound by the seal or not? Some doctors hold that he is; the paper is an inchoate confession, and if it comes into the possession of a judge he cannot use it, but must bury it in impenetrable silence. The matter came up in a practical shape during the trial of the celebrated Dame de Brinvilliers, in 1676. Among her papers was found a recital of the crimes of which she was accused and of many others equally atrocious; it was in the form of a sacramental confession, commencing " Je me confesse à Dieu et à vous, mon père," and, after considerable discussion, it was not received as evidence, though it could not but influence the minds of the judges.[2] More recent writers, however, are at odds on this point, the commoner opinion

---

41.—S. Alph. de Ligorio Theol. Moral. Lib. VI. n. 652-3.—Th. ex Charmes Theol. Univers. Diss. v. cap. iv. Art. 2.—Varceno Theol. Moral. Tract. XVIII. cap. iv. Art. 7, n. 1.

All this gives rise to a host of questions on which the authorities are by no means unanimous. See Gobat Alphab. Confessar. n. 825-35; Clericati de Pœnit. Decis. XLIX. n. 10.—Benzi Praxis, Disp. II. Q. vii. Art. 3, n. 14.—Arsdekin Theol. Tripart. P. III. Tract. iii. cap. 4, n. 13.

[1] Benzi, Praxis Disp. II. Q. vii. Art. 1, n. 5.—Gury Comp. Theol. Moral. II. n. 650.—Guarceno states (Comp. Theol. Moral. Tract. XVIII. cap. iv. Art. 7) that probable opinions cannot be used in matters relating to the seal, but it is impossible to exclude probabilism altogether, for Tamburini (Method. Confess. Append. cap. vi. n. 16) cites two probable and opposite opinions on the question of celebrating in a polluted church.

[2] Em. Sa Aphorismi Confessar. s. v. *Confessio* addit. ad calcem.—Summa Diana s. v. *Sigillum Sacram.* n. 11.—Lenglet Du Fresnoy, Traité du Secret, p. 150.

being that it is not covered by the seal but only by the natural law of secrecy ; all agree that to use the information thus obtained is a mortal sin, if the sins detailed in the writing are mortal, while some hold this even if they are only venial. Gury says, however, that if the paper has been used in confession by handing it to the confessor it thus becomes part of the confession and is covered by the seal.[1]

The question as to the confessor's consulting with experts involves some intricate points. So many doubtful and difficult matters must come for decision before a confessor that even the most experienced must at times feel the need of advice, and in the Lateran canon the priest is directed when in doubt to seek the assistance of those more learned, carefully suppressing the name of the penitent.[2] Previous to the enforcement of confession there had been no scruples of this kind. About 1190, we find details of confessions sent to Clement III., with the names of the penitents, in seeking his advice : his answers repeat them and are embodied in the legal compilations of the period, thus rendering them *publici juris*.[3] Of course, when the seal became established, this was impossible, and the schoolmen had no difficulty in proving that it covered the consultation by arguing that this in fact was only a portion of the confession.[4] Yet Guido de Monteroquer not unnaturally seems to regard the very act of consultation as in some sort a violation of the seal, for he instructs the confessor, when seeking advice, not to say " I have heard such a crime in confession," but to put it hypothetically " If such a case happens, what ought to be done?" and he explains that the confessor cannot say that he has heard it because he was acting as the vicar of God.[5] St. Antonino does not go quite so far, but he insists on the utmost caution, so that the consultant may not be able to form a suspicion as to the penitent, and finally the confessor is told that he must not leave the confessional to consult an expert and return,

---

[1] Clericati de Pœnit. Decis. XLIX. n. 7.—S. Alph. de Ligorio Theol. Moral. Lib. VI. n. 650.—Benzi, Praxis Disp. II. Q. vii. Art. 4, n. 3.—Gury Comp. Theol. Moral. II. 653.

[2] Cap. 12 Extra v. xxxviii. "Sed si prudentiori consilio indiguerit illud absque ulla expressione personæ caute requirat."

[3] Compilat. II. Lib. IV. Tit. xiii. cap. 2; Lib. v. Tit. xviii. cap. 2 (Friedberg, Quinque Compilationes Antiquæ, pp. 96, 102).

[4] Jo. Scoti in IV. Sentt. Dist. XXI. Q. unic.

[5] Manip. Curator. P. II. Tract. iii. cap. 11.

because this would lead the bystanders to infer that the penitent has confessed some mortal sin.[1] Curiously enough, with all this zeal for the preservation of secrecy, it is a disputed point whether or not the consultant is bound by the obligation of the seal. Some moralists argue that, as he can only be consulted with the permission of the penitent, he is the latter's agent, the communication to him is not sacramental, and he is only bound by natural secrecy; others hold that, as the consultation is pertinent to the administration of the sacrament, he is subject to the sacramental seal.[2] If the penitent declines to assent to the consultation, the confessor is instructed to refuse absolution and tell him to seek some one more learned.[3]

We have seen what trouble reserved cases have given in dividing confession and absolution, and they naturally formed an equally vexatious problem with regard to the strict obligation of the seal. In fact, it shows how completely the seal, in its modern acceptation, is a consequence and outgrowth of enforced confession, that the practice of sending penitents with reserved cases to the bishop continued so long, for it was an advertisement to the world that they had committed a reserved sin. In 1408, John Gerson complains of the infamy to which it exposed sinners, especially women, to be thus sent to the bishop.[4] The schoolmen found some difficulty in reconciling the incongruity. William of Ware quotes William of Auxerre as saying that the seal does not prevent the confessor from referring cases to his superior, but he pronounces this to be a mistake, as it reduces the confessor to the functions of an interpreter. Yet Duns Scotus accepted this; he argued that in such cases the confessor is merely an interpreter or medium of communication, and thus the whole is one confession and is covered by the seal.[5] This, in fact, was the simplest explanation when the penitent was sent to the bishop

---

[1] S. Antonini Summæ P. III. Tit. xvii. cap. 22, § 3.—Toleti Instruct. Sacerd. Lib. III. cap. xvi. n. 2.—Benzi, Praxis Disp. II. Q. vii. Art. 3, n. 5.

[2] Escobar Theol. Moral. Tract. VII. Exam. iv. cap. 7, n. 10.—Layman Theol. Moral. Lib. V. Tract. vi. cap. 14, n. 18.—Liguori, in the earlier editions of his Moral Theology (Lib. VI. n. 648. Cf. Elenchum Quæstionum, Q. 77), considered that the consultant is not bound by the seal, but subsequently he concluded that the affirmative is more probable.

[3] Lenglet Du Fresnoy, Traité du Secret, p. 210.

[4] C. Remens. ann. 1408 (Gousset, Actes etc. II. 658).

[5] Vorrillong in IV. Sentt. Dist. XXI.—Jo. Scoti in IV. Sentt. Dist. XXI. Q. unic.

with a letter stating that he required absolution and penance for incest or homicide, or whatever the reserved sin might be, a practice which, as shown above (p. 330), continued at least until the eve of the Reformation, and probably longer. Doubtless the increasing rigor in the construction of the seal contributed to discourage the custom, for, about 1690, Arsdekin asserts that for a confessor to give to his penitent, without his permission, a letter to the bishop, simply stating that he has a reserved case, is an infraction of the seal.[1] The modern system of applying for a faculty eludes the difficulty by removing the reservation, and the formula of application (p. 335) is carefully drawn to reduce the violation of the seal to a minimum, though it cannot wholly avoid what amounts to an infraction under the more rigid definitions. To escape it as far as possible, Gobat instructs the priest, when he receives the faculty, not to send for the penitent but to wait till he meets him casually; then tell him to say " I accuse myself again of such a sin," and absolve him on the spot, without making the sign of the cross—presumably to avoid attracting attention.[2] This would seem to rate the importance of the seal higher than that of the sacrament, as it renders the latter wholly a matter of chance.

The subject of restitution of ill-gotten gains and reparation for injuries, which forms an important portion of the duties of the confessional, is somewhat difficult to reconcile with the strict obligations of the seal, for the confessor is the natural channel through which such payments can be made by penitents desirous of escaping the humiliation of acknowledging their offences, and it is a debated question whether, in serving in that capacity, he is violating the seal or not. The weight of authority is in the negative, but the utmost caution is enjoined to prevent suspicion as to the source of payment.[3]

A question which gave rise to considerable discussion, in establishing the inviolability of the seal, is whether a priest can make use of knowledge gained both inside and outside of confession. On the one hand it was urged that malicious priests might reveal sins confessed to them, on the plea that they knew of them otherwise: on

---

[1] Arsdekin Theol. Tripart. P. III. Tract. iii. cap. 4, n. 6.

[2] Gobat Alphab. Confessar. n. 700.

[3] Benzi, Praxis Disp. II. Q. vii. Art. 3, n. 21.—Gury Comp. Theol. Moral. I. 708.

the other, that sinners might close the mouths of priestly witnesses by promptly confessing to them their misdeeds. Alexander Hales thinks this latter argument the stronger, and puts the case of four priests journeying together, of whom one commits a crime in the sight of his companions and confesses it to one of them. The other two denounce the culprit and summon the confessor as a witness, when, on his refusing to testify, his bishop can rightfully punish him.[1] Some doctors drew a distinction and taught that the lips of the confessor were sealed by the confession if he had prior knowledge of the fact, but not if he acquired it subsequently. Aquinas refutes these arguments and holds that knowledge obtained elsewhere releases the seal, irrespective of time, but the confessor must not mention the corroborative fact of the confession.[2] Bonaventura agrees with this and adds that the confessor should warn the penitent of the fact of his knowledge and should not volunteer his testimony, but wait to be summoned as a witness by due authority.[3] The use of knowledge thus gained extrinsically has become the received practice of the Church, with comparatively few dissidents, but the elaborate and intricate arguments necessary to establish it show the inherent difficulties of the questions involved and the nervous anxiety to avoid rendering confession odious.[4]

Another question which has provoked endless controversy, not even yet positively settled, is the apparently simple and elementary one whether or not the penitent can authorize the confessor to make known any sins which he has confessed to him. Alexander Hales and Bonaventura argued that such authorization must be invalid, because the confessor knows only as God and is ignorant as man; therefore, if the penitent wishes to release the priest from silence, he must relate the facts again outside of confession. Other doctors advanced another reason; the pope cannot authorize violation of the seal and much less can a layman. Aquinas brushes aside these dialectics and asserts the power of the penitent to permit the con-

---

[1] Alex. de Ales Summæ P. IV. Q. xix. Membr. 2, Art. 2.

[2] S. Th. Aquinat. in IV. Sentt. Dist. xxi. Q. iii. Art. 2; Summæ Suppl. Q. xi. Art. 5.

[3] S. Bonaventuræ in IV. Sentt. Dist. xxi. P. ii. Art. 2, Q. 3.

[4] Eisengrein Confessionale cap. vii. Q. 27.—Arsdekin. Theol. Tripart. P. iii. Tract. iii. cap. 4, n. 2.—Benzi, Praxis Disp. ii. Q. vii. Art. 3, n. 12.

fessor to reveal what he pleases to whom he pleases.[1]   Then Durand
de S. Pourçain advanced a reason of expediency, pointing out that
if such authorization were recognized a prisoner on trial might be
commanded by the judge to release his confessor from the seal, when
a refusal would expose him to justifiable suspicion.[2]   William of
Ware assumes the power of authorization as an accepted fact, for
every one can renounce a right.[3]   Guido de Monteroquer says that
it is a disputed question, and Angiolo da Chivasso denies the power.[4]
So the debate went on, some authorities affirming, others denying,
and some contenting themselves with stating that the question is
doubtful and disputed; nor has it ever been authoritatively settled,
though the common opinion of modern authorities is in the affirmative, and the priest is warned to be exceedingly cautious in the use
of such authorization, for any indiscretion tends to render confession
odious, and he is not to extort it by threats of withholding absolution.[5]

We have seen above (p. 220) how persistently the custom of confession to laymen lingered and how difficult it proved to establish
the exclusive right of the priesthood to hear confessions.   The question as to the obligation of the seal in such confessions was a delicate
one, for the denial of it would, on the one hand, assist in breaking
down the practice and, on the other, would tend to diminish the
reverence inculcated for everything connected with the sacrament.
Aquinas, who admitted the quasi-sacerdotal character of lay confession, argues that in it the seal, strictly speaking, cannot exist, but

---

[1] Alex. de Ales Summæ P. IV. Q. xix. Membr. ii. Art. 2.—S. Bonaventuræ
in IV. Sentt. Dist. xxi. P. ii. Art. 2, Q. 2.—S. Th. Aquin. in IV. Sentt. Dist.
xxi. Q. iii. Art. 2; Summæ Suppl. Q. xi. Art. 4.

[2] Durand. de S. Porciano in IV. Sentt. Dist. xxi. Q. iv. § 9.

[3] Vorillong in IV. Sentt. Dist. xxi.

[4] Manip. Curator. P. ii. Tract. iii. cap. 11.—Summa Angelica s. v. *Confessio*
ult. § 5.

[5] Summa Sylvestrina s. v. *Confessio* iii. § 2.—Summa Tabiena s. v. *Confes-
sionis Celatio* § 11.—Eisengrein Confessionale cap. vii. Q. 23-5.—Em. Sa
Aphorismi Confessar. s. v. *Confessor* n. 30.—Mart. Fornarii Instit. Sacerd. p.
93.—Toleti Instruct. Sacerd. Lib. iii. cap. xvi. n. 4.—Zerola, Praxis Sacr.
Pœnit. cap. xxv. Q. 34.—Marchant Trib. Animar. Tom. I. Tract. iv. Tit. vi.
Q. 6. Append. 2, Concl. 3.—Busenbaum Medullæ Theol. Moral. Lib. vi. Tract.
iv. cap. 3, Dub. 1.—Arsdekin Theol. Tripart. P. iii. Tract. iii. cap. 4, n. 12.—
Lenglet Du Fresnoy, Traité du Secret, p. 173.—Tournely de Sacr. Pœnit. Q.
vi. Art. 4.—Benzi, Praxis Disp. ii. Q. vii. Art. 1, n. 3.—S. Alph. de Ligorio
Theol. Moral. Lib. vi. n. 651.—Marc Institt. Moral. Alphonsianæ n. 1866.

nevertheless the recipient of the confession is bound to the most rigorous secrecy.[1] Astesanus says that he participates in some sort in the seal and is subject to punishment at discretion for violation of it.[2] This view long prevailed. Prierias quotes various authorities to the same effect, and insists that the lay confessor, when interrogated, must deny and swear, the same as a priest, which infers that he too receives the confession as God.[3] Domingo Soto even says that the layman is more bound by the seal than a priest, and its violation by him is a mortal sin, deserving of severe punishment, while Cardinal Toletus asserts that such confessions are covered by the seal.[4] Diana considers it a disputed question, while Chiericato affirms that the layman is bound.[5] Later doctors take the view that if confession is made knowingly to a layman under necessity it is not covered by the seal; if under the mistaken belief that the confessor is a priest, it is, but it is admitted that the question is one on which opinions are not unanimous.[6]

In treating of satisfaction we shall see hereafter the influence exerted by the rigid definition of the seal in mitigating the severity of penance, for it became a received axiom that the inflictions imposed should in no way expose the penitent to suspicion as to the sins which he had confessed. It required some time to develop this idea and render it dominant. Aquinas remarks that confessions are to be secret and not public on account of the scandal and incitement to evil caused by the recital of sins, but there is no scandal in penitence, for works of satisfaction are performed for trifling sins and even for none.[7] Penance however was diminishing so rapidly that its manifestation could not fail to imply that the penitent had been guilty of mortal sin, and the desire to avoid rendering confession odious was sufficient motive for the prescription that penance, like confession

---

[1] S. Th. Aquin. in IV. Sentt. Dist. XXI. Q. iii. Art. 1 ad 3.

[2] Astesani Summæ Lib. v. Tit. xx. Q. 2.

[3] Summa Sylvestrina s. v. *Confessio* III. §§ 1, 4. See also Petri Hieremiæ Sermones, De Pœnitentia Serm. xvii. (Brixiæ. 1502).

[4] Dom. Soto in IV. Sentt. Dist. XVIII. Q. iv. Art. 1, 5.—Toleti Instruct. Sacerd. Lib. III. cap. xvi. n. 6, 7.

[5] Summa Diana s. v. *Sigillum Sacram.* n. 3.—Cliericati de Pœnit. Decis. XLIX. n. 6.

[6] Benzi, Praxis Disp. II. Q. vii. Art. 4, n. 2.—Varceno Comp. Theol. Moral. Tract. XVIII. cap. iv. Art. 7.

[7] S. Th. Aquin. in IV. Sentt. Dist. XVII. Q. iii. Art. 4 ad 4.

itself, should be secret. Astesanus lays down the rule that the penitent is bound to keep his penance secret, when the knowledge of it would tend to injure his reputation or that of the confessor, which infers that the latter should only inflict what can be kept from observation.[1] So completely was this principle accepted that Durand de S. Pourçain inquires whether the papal penitentiaries are not making public the sins confessed to them when, for clericide and other heinous offences, they are accustomed to strip the penitent and scourge him around the church, and he replies that he had asked the penitentiaries and had been told that they only did this when the crime was notorious at the home of the penitent, and moreover that his face was always so covered as to be unrecognizable.[2] In modern times it is asserted to be a violation of the seal to impose a penance which may arouse suspicion of the commission of mortal sin, but in this, as in so much else, contradictory necessities cannot be reconciled, and it is admitted that certain adjuncts of penance must be excepted when required for the restitution of debts, reparation of reputation, saluting an enemy and the avoiding of approximate occasions of sin in abandoning a trade, dismissing a concubine, leaving a certain house etc.[3] It would appear moreover that a form of conditional penance, which is a favorite with some writers, such as kissing the ground whenever the penitent utters a blasphemy[4] cannot be carried out without at least an implied violation of the seal. The penances customary among the Regulars also gave rise to troublesome questions. After the capitular penances had been discontinued, through the introduction of auricular confession, penances were frequently prescribed to be performed in the chapter or the choir or the refectory, and this, with the growth of the strict observances of the seal, was denounced as an infraction.[5]

---

[1] Astesani Summæ Lib. v. Tit. xx. Q. 2.

[2] Durand. de S. Porciano in IV. Sentt. Dist. xiv. Q. iv. §§ 12-13.—Cf. Jo. Friburgens. Summæ Confessor. Lib. iii. Tit. xxxiv. Q. 12.

Yet Pontas asserts (Dict. de Cas de Conscience s. v. *Confesseur* ii. cas 3) that a penitent must not be absolved who refuses to accept a penance of Friday fasting for a year because it will expose him (or her) to the suspicion of family and friends, and who declares that he prefers to accept a longer time in purgatory.

[3] Tournely de Sacram. Pœnit. Q. vi. Art. 4.—Benzi, Praxis Disp. ii. Q. vii. Art. 3, n. 5.

[4] Th. ex Charmes Theol. Univ. Diss. v. cap. 5, Q. 2, Concl. 2.

[5] Jo. Sanchez Selecta de Sacramentis Disp. vi. n. 18.

While, rigidly speaking, the penitent is perhaps not bound by the seal of the confessional, whatever occurs there is covered with the veil of impenetrable secrecy, except, indeed, any solicitation to evil of which the confessor may be guilty. Saving this, it is a mortal sin for the penitent to speak of what the priest has said to him, especially, we are told, if it would tend to the discredit of the latter or expose him to ridicule. Some authorities are inclined to ascribe this to the sacramental seal, but the majority construe it as what is called the natural seal.[1] Morally the distinction between the two would not seem to be great if the authorities are correct in stating that the penitent can deny under oath any confession which he has made, because he has made it to the confessor as God and not as man,[2] but apparently there is the practical difference that no special punishment is decreed for infraction on the part of the penitent. His offence is a mortal sin to be wiped out by confession and satisfaction.

The seal would be an exception to the divine laws confided to the care of the Church if the Church had not found itself under the necessity of admitting limitations to its operation. We have seen that at first it was held not to cover heresy, because faith was not to be kept with heretics, and this possibly led to the theory held by some authorities that all sins of which the penitent did not promise amendment were deprived of its protection and could be revealed. Aquinas feels it necessary to disprove this elaborately, and was followed by the leading doctors, but it still had supporters up to the sixteenth century.[3]

---

[1] Jo. Gersonis Regulæ Morales (Opp. Ed. 1488, XXV. F.).—Jo. Nider Præceptorium, Præcept. III. cap. ix.—Eisengrein Confessionale cap. vii. Q. 19.—Gobat Alphab. Confessar. n. 862.—Henriquez Summæ Theol. Moral. Lib. VI. cap. xxi. n. 6.—Layman Theol. Moral. Lib. VI. cap. xiv. n. 20.—Reginald. Praxis Fori Pœnit. Lib. III. n. 35.—Busenbaum Medullæ Theol. Moral. Lib. VI. Tract. iv. cap. 3, Dub. 1, Resp. 2.—Tamburini Method. Confess. Append. cap. iv. n. 1.—Benzi Praxis, Disp. II. Q. vii. Art. 4, n. 4.—Gury Comp. Theol. Moral. II. 652.—Varceno Comp. Theol. Moral. Tract. XVIII. cap. iv. Art. 7 § 1.

Apparently at times irreverent penitents have complained of their confessors to their superiors, have talked disrespectfully of what was said to them in confession, and have generally given a good deal of unpleasant trouble.—Lochon, Traité du Secret de la Confession, pp. 54-8.

[2] Em. Sa Aphorismi Confessar. s. v. *Confessor* n. 24.—Alabardi Tyrocinium Confessionum P. I. cap. xxxvii. (Venetiis, 1629).

[3] S. Th. Aquin. in IV. Sentt. Dist. XXI. Q. iii. Art. 1 ad 1; Summæ Suppl.

A more doubtful controversy occurred on the question of future sins—sins which the penitent confessed an intention of committing and refused to abandon. Many reasons seemed to urge that the confessor should not be debarred from giving notice of them to the individual or authorities threatened, and the earlier doctors, as S. Ramon de Peñafort and Alexander Hales, argue that they are not entitled to the protection of the seal.[1] The object, however, of rendering confession attractive overcame this reasoning, and subsequent authorities insisted that such future sins should be kept secret, but that when the danger to be anticipated from them was urgent the confessor could give a general warning to prelates or rulers to be on their guard[2]—which in itself was an infraction of the rule that no use of any kind should be made of knowledge thus obtained. Yet late in the fifteenth century Angiolo da Chivasso argues that if the future crime threatens injury to others it is not *in foro pœnitentiæ,* and may be revealed, though he admits that most of the doctors think otherwise.[3] Not long afterwards Caietano pronounces uncompromisingly in favor of the seal, while Prierias gives a typical example of the conscienceless ease with which everything can be made to yield to expediency. He states both sides of the question and gives the reasons for each, and then concludes that if the evil to be prevented is greater than the scandal of breaking the seal, the priest should reveal the sin ; this is especially the case when an individual or the community is threatened, for then he is bound to reveal it if he can conveniently do so without danger to himself and advantage to others, including the penitent.[4] Subsequent authorities seem substantially unanimous that all such intended crimes are covered by the seal, but that warnings and cautions in general terms can be given to the parties threatened.[5]

Q. XI. Art. 1.—Durand. de S. Porciano in IV. Sentt. Dist. XXI. Q. iv. § 12.—Summa Tabiena s. v. *Confessionis Celatio* § 2.

[1] S. Raymundi Summæ Lib. III. Tit. XXXIV. § 4.—Alex. de Ales Summæ P. IV. Q. XIX. Membr. ii. Art. 2.

[2] S. Bonaventuræ in IV. Sentt. Dist. XXI. P. ii. Art. 2 § 1.—Astesani Summæ Lib. V. Tit. XX. Q. 2.—Summa Rosella s. v. *Confessionis Celatio.*

[3] Summa Angelica s. v. *Confessio* ult. § 7.

[4] Caietani Opusc. Tract. XXI.—Summa Sylvestrina s. v. *Confessio* III. § 2.

[5] Summa Tabiena s. v. *Confessionis Celatio* § 2.—Eisengrein Confessionale cap. vii. Q. 15.—Toleti Instruct. Sacerd. Lib. III. cap. xvi. n. 6.—Summa Diana s. v. *Sigillum sacram.* n. 16.—Juenin de Sacramentis Diss. VI. Q. 5, cap. 6, Art.

A somewhat curious distinction is drawn in the case of debts and deposits mentioned by the penitent in the course of his confession. If these are connected with theft, fraud or usury on his part, the knowledge is protected by the seal; if not, they are not regarded as part of sacramental confession, and the confessor is required to reveal what he knows about them when summoned by proper authority to give evidence, even though he may have sworn to keep silence.[1] We may perhaps regard this as part of a subject which has caused a vast amount of discussion—the exact position of matters mentioned casually or otherwise by the penitent in confession and relating more or less directly to his sins. This is evidently a very wide and obscure question, in the intricate variations of which the casuists can revel to their hearts' content. Aquinas would appear to have settled it when he said that, although the seal only extends as far as the sacrament, still all things uttered in the confessional are to be strictly held secret, on account of the danger of scandal, yet not long afterwards John of Freiburg tells us that the obligation of secrecy only covers the sins confessed.[2] The debate on this point centred chiefly on what are known as natural defects, such as diseases, illegitimacy, ignoble birth, Jewish descent and other similar matters which the penitent may chance to mention in confession, and the degree to which they are covered by

---

4, § 3.—Tamburini Method. Confess. Append. cap. iii. n. 9.—Clericati de Pœnit. Decis. XLIX. n. 15.—Tournely de Sacr. Pœnit. Q. VI. Art. iv.—Benzi, Praxis Disp. II. Q. vii. Art. 3, n. 2.

Lochon (Traité du Secret, p. 96) objects to giving warning. The strictness with which the seal was construed in these matters is shown in a case related by Damhouder (Praxis Criminalis, cap. clii. n. 9) as occurring at Bruges in his time. A sick man confessed to his priest that he and a number of accomplices proposed in about a week to set fire to several parts of the town. The priest reported it in general terms to a magistrate, who caused him to be shadowed and thus identified the penitent and his confederates. On deliberation, however, it was concluded that they could not be punished in view of the source of information.

[1] Jo. Friburgens Summæ Confessor. Lib. III. Tit. xxxiv. Q. 98.—S. Antonini Summæ P. III. Tit. xiv. cap. 19, § 12.—Summa Pisanella s. v. *Confessionis Celatio* n. 8.—Jac. a Graffiis Practica Casuum Reservat. Lib. I. cap. xxxvi. n. 36.

The Summa Tabiena, however (s. v. *Confessionis Celatio* § 9), says that although such matters are not under the seal they must not be revealed.

[2] S. Th. Aquinat. Summæ Suppl. Q. XI. Art. 2.—Jo. Friburgens. *ubi sup.*

the seal constitutes what Tamburini calls a *celebris difficultas*, some doctors arguing that they are protected and others not, though the tendency in modern times has been to construe them as covered for the very cogent reason that to reveal them is to render confession odious. Yet personal defects, which the confessor can observe for himself, are by many regarded as not entitled to secrecy, and there is a tolerably equal division on the question whether a confessor can say of a penitent that he is over-scrupulous or long-winded, though it is admitted to be indiscreet. Circumstances not displeasing to the penitent, as that he is married or a priest or a soldier or a trader are held not to be covered by the seal.[1] There are some high authorities moreover who teach that venial sins confessed are not covered by the seal, and that it is only a venial sin for the confessor to talk about them through inadvertence or lack of thought.[2]

An exception to the seal has likewise been admitted with regard to the virtues and spiritual gifts of penitents as revealed by them in confession. It is true that Diana asserts that the confessor, to obtain Christian burial for a public prostitute, cannot inform the parish priest that she died contrite and that he had absolved her,[3] but the testimony of confessors is an important factor in obtaining the beatification of saints, and although the seal is not removed by death,[4] it has been held not to preclude their revealing the virtues which they may have learned in confession, such as the virginity preserved by St. Thomas Aquinas, St. Francis Xavier, St. Pius V. and St. Luigi Gonzaga. So a confessor in writing the life of a pious penitent may say that he never committed a mortal sin. The extension of this to the living has been the subject of considerable discussion, in which the

---

[1] Toleti Instruct. Sacerd. Lib. III. cap. xvi. n. 2.—Jos. Augustini Brevis Notitia Necess. Confessionar. De Sacr. Pœnit. n. 54.—Gobat Alphab. Confessar. n. 792.—Tamburini Method. Confess. App. cap. iii. n. 13.—Benzi, Praxis Disp. II. Q. vii. Art. 3, n. 1, 3.—Gury Comp. Theol. Moral. II. 657.—Varceno Comp. Theol. Moral. Tract. XVIII. cap. iv. art. 7, § 1.

Gobat (*loc. cit.*) quotes in this connection from Cardinal de Lugo the very significant remark "Si tamen circumstantiæ sunt publice notæ, et simul careant probro, potes innoxie de illis loqui, ut quando quis confessus est se peccasse cum aliqua, cum tamen sit clericus in majoribus aut conjugatus."

[2] Clericati de Pœnit. Decis. XLIX. n. 5.

[3] Summa Diana s. v. *Sigillum Sacram.* n. 50.

[4] Juenin de Sacramentis Diss. VI. Q. 5, cap. 6, Art. 4, § 3.—S. Alph. de Ligorio Lib. VI. n. 634.—Varceno Comp. Theol. Moral. Tract. XVIII. cap. iv. Art. 7.

majority of the moralists claim that, when visions and ecstasies and revelations and other spiritual graces have been related in confession, to obtain direction and not as connected with some sin, they are not covered by the seal unless the penitent objects to their being talked about, in which case they are covered.[1]

Whether knowledge gained in confession can be used for the benefit of penitents is a disputed question. It is nearly akin to the Jansenist proposition condemned by the Inquisition in 1682 (sup. p. 423), but subsequent to that decision Chiericato asserts it. Such use would seem to have much to recommend it, but the admission is fraught with inevitable dangers and more recent authorities reject it.[2] Closely related to this was the practice (p. 396) recommended by some of the earlier doctors, of obtaining the name of a partner in sin in order to administer what is called fraternal correction. The energy with which, in 1708, Lenglet Du Fresnoy argues against this infraction of the seal shows how stubborn was the custom.[3]

Human nature being what it is, there is a manifest impossibility in preventing priests from talking about the sins which they learn in confession. At the best, the interchange of experience may be wise, and it may be an indispensable ingredient in the ghostly counsel bestowed on penitents. On the other hand, it may degenerate into gossip, hurtful to all parties and liable to lead to suspicion as to the sinners concerned. Recognizing it as inevitable the Church permits it, provided abundant caution is used to avoid all danger of identifying the individuals concerned, though absolute silence is recommended as preferable, especially before laymen, and the books as a warning give instances in which, without intentional indiscretion, penitents have been identified and the seal has been broken.[4]

The extent to which a preacher in his sermons may use or refer to the knowledge gained in confession has naturally been the subject of no little discussion. To prevent all such use is impossible and

---

[1] S. Antonini Summæ P. III. Tit. xvii. cap. 22, § 3.—Gobat Alphab. Confessor. n. 795.—Clericati de Pœnit. Decis. XLIX. n. 8.—Benzi, Praxis Disput. II. Q. vii. Art. 3, n. 4, 18.—Varceno Comp. Theol. Moral. Tract. XVIII. cap. iv. Art. 7, § 1.

[2] Clericati de Pœnit. Decis. XLIX. n. 11.—Varceno Comp. Theol. Moral. Tract. XVIII. cap. iv. Art. 7.

[3] Du Fresnoy, Traité du Secret, pp. 231-40.

[4] Berteau Director Confessar. p. 491.—Clericati de Pœnit. Decis. XLIX. n. 8.— Gobat Alphab. Confessar. n. 816, 820.—Gury Comp. Theol. Moral. II. 664.

equally so is it to lay down rules for safe guidance. It is generally agreed, of course, that it is an infraction of the seal for a parish priest to speak of having in confession heard certain sins and to do it in a manner enabling the congregation to identify the sinners, and even more general references are not allowable when the assemblage is small, as in a nunnery or to a group of novices. Even to say, in conversation or otherwise, that certain sins are prevalent in a place, is a violation or not, according to the size of the place, and as absolute definition is sought in all things, the delimitation, by a sort of common consent, has been fixed at three thousand inhabitants, the divine law of the seal being operative below that number and not above it.[1] It is easy to imagine how, in small country parishes where the failings of each are known to all, any allusions by the priest that can be construed as applicable to any of his parishioners will be attributed to knowledge acquired in the confessional and will cause scandal and heart-burnings.

Perhaps the most notable exception to the inviolability of the seal, standing in curious contrast to the effusive declamation that it must not be infringed to prevent the conflagration of the world, is that in times of pestilence the confessor can consult his own safety by having the dying sinner brought to a window, or can keep aloof from the bed, when the penitent must speak aloud and others can hear his confession. In such cases, however, the confession of a single sin suffices and absolution can be given from a safe distance.[2]

To be entitled to the protection of the seal, confessions must be genuine and sacramental, uttered for the purpose of obtaining absolution. Confession may be made from other motives, and in such case the seal does not operate. The test is the intention of the penitent, and this affords a wide field for the fine-drawn distinctions of

---

[1] Gobat Alphab. Confessar. n. 877–80.—Benzi Praxis, Disp. II. Q. vii. Art. 3, n. 22.—Casus Conscient. Bened. PP. XIV. Jun. 1737, cas. 3.—S. Alph. de Ligorio Theol. Moral. Lib. VI. n. 654.—Gury Comp. Theol. Moral. II. 667-8.—Varceno Comp. Theol. Moral. Tract. XVIII. cap. iv. Art. 7, § 2.

Somewhat similar is the answer of Benedict XIV. (Casus Conscient. Aug. 1739, cas. 3) to the question whether a priest violates the seal if he asks a friend going to the cathedral city to procure for him a faculty to absolve for incest. He says it depends on the size of the town or village, so that the friend may or may not be led to suspect the penitent.

[2] Laymann Theol. Moral. Lib. V. Tract. VI. cap. 13, n. 3.

the casuists.[1]   The confessional was occasionally resorted to for the purpose of securing secrecy, as we have seen (p. 387) done by the Spanish Jesuits, who, as theologians, must have known that the device was not only sacrilegious but ineffective in so far as their own consciences were concerned.   This device, however, was not of their invention, but was resorted to almost as soon as the seal was established, for, in 1279, Archbishop Peckham of Canterbury, seeking aid from Rome to discipline a licentious bishop, who had five children by a concubine, writes that the offender had admitted his guilt in a private interview and had then claimed for it the seal of the confessional.[2] All this naturally led to the practice of confiding secrets to priests under the seal, though not in confession.   It is generally, though not universally, admitted that such confidences are not entitled to the protection of the seal, but there has been considerable diversity of opinion as to the precise degree of obligation incurred by the priest who listens under such a condition, expressed or implied.   Some moralists hold that although it is not the seal it is as binding as the seal, others that it is entitled to the natural seal, others that it is less effective than an oath of secrecy and can be revealed in case of necessity or at the command of a superior.   Father Sayre tells us that in his time (1605) it was a common practice, even between laymen, and that the belief in its sanctity was a widely spread vulgar error.[3]

In a priesthood like that of the middle ages, so largely composed of men corrupt and ignorant of their duties, it was manifestly impossible that violations of the seal should not be of frequent occurrence. Carelessness, malice, intoxication, garrulity—numerous motives more or less innocent—rendered the enforcement of the precept a difficult

---

[1] Durand. de S. Porciano in IV. Sentt. Dist. XXI. Q. iv. § 12.—N. de Auximo in Summ. Pisanellam s. v. *Confessionis Celatio.*—Vittorelli in Toleti Instruct. Sacerd. Lib. III. cap. xvi. n. 7.—Juenin. de Sacramentis Diss. VI. Q. 5, cap. 6, Art. 4, § 3.—Gobat Alphab. Confessar. n. 798.—Benzi, Praxis Disp. II. Q. vii. Art. 2.—Gury Comp. Theol. Moral. II. 648.

[2] Wilkins Concilia II. 40.

[3] S. Th. Aquin. in IV. Sentt. Dist. XXI. Q. iii. Art. 1.—Summa Pisanella s. v. *Confessionis Celatio* n. 6 cum not. Nich. de Ausimo.—Summa Tabiena s. v. *Confessionis Celatio* § 3.—Caietani Summula s. v. *Confessori necessaria.*—Toleti Instruct. Sacerd. Lib. III. cap. xvi. n. 7.—Henriquez Summæ Theol. Moral. Lib. VI. cap. xxi. n. 3.—Varceno Comp. Theol. Moral. Tract. XVIII. Art. iv. n. 7.—Sayri Clavis Regia Sacerd. Lib. XII. cap. xvi. n. 15.

matter, to be effected only by effort extending through centuries. For this conclusion we are not left wholly to *a priori* reasoning, though cases of infraction were rarely of a nature to find place in the chronicles of the period. Ample evidence exists in the complaints of those who were busied in introducing and enforcing the rule. Prior to the Lateran canon, Alain de Lille advises penitents not to confess to priests notorious for revealing the sins confessed to them ; if the parish priest is one of these, his licence should be obtained to seek another confessor.[1] The threats embodied in the Lateran canon did not mend matters speedily. William of Paris says that no one is bound to confess when the confessor is a traitor and publisher of confessions ; at the most, when the parish priest is such, only those sins should be confessed to him of which the knowledge can work no evil to his subjects, and a licence be sought from him or from the bishop to confess elsewhere.[2] Not long after this occurred a notorious case, well-known to theologians and historians. The Dominican Berenguer de Castel-Bisbal, Bishop of Gerona, was confessor to Jayme I, *el Conquistador*, of Aragon, and, according to the latter's statement to Innocent IV., treacherously betrayed him by revealing a secret learned in the confessional. The royal wrath was savagely gratified by cutting out a part or the whole of the culprit's tongue and banishing him, a violation of clerical immunity which subjected the king to excommunication, when, like Henry II. of England, he was glad to purchase absolution by conceding partial exemption from secular law to ecclesiastics and by making enormous gifts to the monastery of Bonifaza and to the hospital of S. Vicente at Valencia.[3]

Even when there was sufficient reticence to withhold the names of penitents, Cardinal Henry of Susa complains that many priests gossiped so recklessly about confessions made to them that identification of individuals was easy and that sinners were thus largely deterred from confession.[4] This dread of priestly garrulity was a considerable factor in the success as confessors of the intruding Mendicants, for, at least in the earlier period, they were regarded

---

[1] Alani de Insulis Lib. de Pœnit. (Migne CCX. 304).

[2] Guill. Parisiens. de Sacr. Pœnit. cap. 2.

[3] España Sagrada, XLIV. 22-27, 279-87.—Concil. Ilerdense ann. 1246 (Aguirre, V. 194).—Raynald. Annal. ann. 1246, n. 43-48.—Caramuelis Theol. Fundam. n. 1841.

[4] Hostiens. Aureæ Summæ Lib. v. De Pœn. et Remiss. § 52.

as more strict than the secular clergy in the observance of the rule.[1] That it was not a mere presumptive fear of indiscretion, but a well-founded apprehension based on experience, is seen by the efforts of the local councils during the thirteenth and fourteenth centuries to enforce the observance of the precept (p. 422), while even until the sixteenth century the list of interrogations drawn up for the examination of priests in the confessional contain an inquiry as to the violation of the seal[2]—evidently it was one of the offences customarily expected of them. Erasmus alludes to the garrulity of confessors as a matter of common notoriety,[3] and this is confirmed by the constant reiteration in the manuals and text-books down to the present time, of the dictum of William of Paris—that the penitent who knows by experience that his parish priest is a revealer of confessions, or has a reason to fear it in his own case, is excused from confessing to him; if he can find another priest to shrive him he can do so; if not, let him confess only such matters as will not injure him or others if divulged.[4] La Croix emphasizes it by saying that a penitent feeling certain that his confessor will reveal his sins to a single person is not bound to confess to him even on the death-bed, when, if assured of his own contrition, he can confess some venials, and thus receive indirect absolution.[5] There is ample evidence that these provisions were not framed merely to meet a speculative difficulty. Bartolomé de Medina speaks of the evils wrought in Spain by immodest confessors who violate the seal and bring shame upon the ministry and contempt for its functions.[6] In 1604 the council of Cambrai felt it necessary to prohibit priests from gossiping together about the confessions which they had heard, and, in 1699, the council

---

[1] S. Bonaventuræ Tract. Quare Fratres Minores prædicent.

[2] B. de Chaimis Interrog. fol. 92*b*.—Somma Pacifica cap. xxii.—Confessionario breve y muy provechoso, cap. xii.

[3] "Sunt enim permulti, quod compertum est, qui, quod accipiunt in confessionibus effutiunt."—Erasmi Colloq. Confab. pia.

[4] S. Bonaventuræ Confessionale Cap. iv. Partic. 1.—Manip. Curator. P. ii. Tit. iii. Cap. 4.—Joannis de Janua Summæ s. v. *Confessio.*—Summa Pisanella s. v. *Confessio* iii. n. 4.—S. Antonini Summæ P. iii. Tit. xiv. Cap. 19, ? 8.—Saulii Comment. in Savonarolæ Confessionale fol. 85*a*.—Clericati de Pœnit. Decis. xxiii. n. 11.—S. Alph. de Ligorio Theol. Moral. Lib. vi. n. 673.—Bonal Institt. Theol. T. IV. n. 246.

[5] La Croix Theol. Moral. Lib. vi. P. ii. n. 1190.

[6] Bart. a Medina Instruct. Confessar. Lib. ii. cap. 4.

of Naples tried to restrain the evil by cautioning them not to reveal confessions.[1] That these efforts were not uncalled for may be guessed from the rebuke uttered by S. Leonardo da Porto Maurizio of the indiscretion of those priests who freely chatter about matters heard in confession as though they were the current talk of the streets.[2] Lochon, in 1708, tells us that he is induced to write his book by the indiscretion of many priests and the uncertainty felt by the faithful whether their confessions will be held secret—in fact, he says, that many priests make confessions the staple of their talk, speaking without reticence at table and elsewhere of their granting or withholding the absolution of individuals, gossiping about the family affairs and defects of their penitents and violating the seal without scruple, even though not revealing the sins confessed, besides which they often take when preaching the opportunity of humiliating those against whom they have a grudge.[3] Matters were no better in Italy, for Pittoni states that the imprudent garrulity of confessors is the cause of constant scandals.[4] The action of several recent councils would appear to justify the inference that even yet the seal of the confessional is not observed as rigorously as might be desirable.[5]

Apart from these generalities, individual cases, from the very nature of the offence, are not apt to be known or recorded, but I have met with a few which serve to indicate that they are by no means unexampled. One which, by its public nature, attracted some attention at the time, occurred in 1331 as an incident of the affair which drove to England Robert d'Artois, brother-in-law of Philippe de Valois, and thus contributed to the hundred years' war. In the endeavor to bolster up claims to Artois, which he had renounced, Robert produced sundry forged documents. They were pronounced fraudulent, a woman who had fabricated them for him was burnt,

---

[1] C. Cameracens. ann. 1604, Tit. VIII. cap. 8 (Hartzheim VIII. 594).—C. Neapolit. ann. 1699, Tit. III. cap. 5, n. 6 (Coll. Lacens. I. 185).

[2] S. Leonardo da P. M., Discorso Mistico e Morale, ≀ xxx.

[3] Lochon, Traité du Secret, Préface, pp. 59–60, 63, 71.—See also Summæ Alexandrinæ P. I. n. 570.

[4] Pittoni Constitutiones Pontificiæ, T. VII. n. 345.—"Confessarii igitur omnino linguam contineant, quia ex eorum imprudenti loquacitate sæpissime gravissima oriuntur scandala."

[5] C. Senonens. ann. 1850, Tit. III. cap. 5; C. Lauretan. ann. 1850, Sect. IV. n. 25; C. Venet. ann. 1859, P. III. cap. xxii. ≀ 5 (Coll. Lacens. IV. 892; VI. 334, 785).

and he fled to the Duke of Brabant.   In the course of his trial his
confessor, a Dominican named Jean Aubery, was seized and refused
to reveal what he had learned in confession, but on being pressed
consented to speak if he could be assured by masters in theology that
he could do so with a good conscience.   An assembly of theologians
was held in the palace of the Bishop of Paris, presided over by Pierre
de la Palu, the foremost theologian of France, then recently created
Patriarch of Jerusalem.   In his writings Pierre construes rigidly the
obligations of the seal, but on this occasion he argued that the confessor could and ought to reveal what he knew; only sins are covered
by the seal, but this was not a sin but the manifestation of the truth,
necessary for justice and the peace of the realm, for which he would
deserve reward.   All the masters present assented, Jean promised to
testify and was assured that he would be recommended to the king.
He was carried before the officials and revealed all he knew, after
which he was remanded back to prison and was never seen again—a
martyr of the system if not of the seal.[1]

The next century affords an example in which there was even
higher authority for the violation of the seal, for the confessor in
this case was a cardinal, who, under dispensation from Eugenius IV.,
revealed a confession the knowledge of which was important to the
papal policy of the moment.   In this case Prierias is the apologist,
and argues that it was for legitimate cause and beneficial to some one,
even though not to the penitent—and, besides, the penitent could
also have revealed it himself.[2]   Several cases occurring in the sixteenth century may be noted.   The plot of the Constable Bourbon
against Francis I. is said to have been discovered through the revelation of a confessor to whom it was confided, though the story is
told in different ways.[3]   In Spain, St. Thomas of Vilanova, when
Archbishop of Valencia, interfered to save a murderer who had by
mischance confessed to a brother of his victim and had consequently

---

[1] Guillel. Nangis Contin. ann. 1331.

[2] Summa Sylvestrina s. v. *Confessio* III. § 2.

[3] De Thou (Hist. Universelle Liv. III.) states that the Seigneur de S. Valier,
father of Diane de Poitiers, was concerned in the plot and was betrayed by
his confessor.   Pasquier (Recherches de la France, Liv. VIII. ch. 39) says that
two gentlemen of Normandy were solicited to join and refused; they confessed
to a priest who revealed the matter to Brézé, Seneschal of Normandy.

been betrayed ; in this case the confessor was leniently punished.[1]
Offending priests did not always escape so easily. At Toulouse, in
1579, an innkeeper murdered a guest and buried the body in the
cellar : he confessed the crime to a priest who, seduced by a reward
offered for the detection of the murderer, denounced the criminal to
the magistrates ; under torture the culprit confessed the crime, adding that no one but the confessor could have betrayed him ; an
investigation ensued, which resulted in the Parlement of Toulouse
releasing the criminal and hanging the priest, after he had been
degraded by the bishop.[2] In this the example was followed of a
case occurring at Padua about 1530, when the murderer was discharged and the priest executed in Venice.[3]

In the seventeenth century Gobat happens to relate two cases of
recent occurrence. In one of these a man poisoned his two children,
of whom one died. Suspicion arising he fled, but meeting a Dominican of his town, he relieved his conscience by confession. The
Dominican reported it ; the man was arrested, tried and executed.
In another case a woman tried for a crime could not be induced to
admit her guilt. A Dominican visited her in prison ; she confessed
to him, he revealed it to the judge, and she was duly put to death.[4]
As no punishment seems to have awaited the friars it would appear
that the Teutonic practice in these matters differed from the Latin,
though perhaps it may be attributed rather to a growing indifference
to the sanctity of the seal, for this is manifested in a curious case
which occurred, in 1705, in the diocese of Carcassonne. A parish
priest revealed a confession to the wife of a man whom the penitent
had injured. The affair became public and the syndic of the place
denounced the priest to the episcopal official, who, on conviction,

---

[1] Lenglet Du Fresnoy, Traité du Secret, pp. 101–104.
[2] Clericati de Pœnitent. Decis. XLIX. n. 19.   [3] Du Fresnoy, *op. cit.* p. 108.
[4] Gobat Alphab. Confessar. n. 778–9. As a Jesuit, Gobat naturally was not
averse to making known the derelictions of Dominicans, but he himself did
not observe the prescriptions of the seal, for he tells us of a peasant with whom
he had trouble in getting him to define the number of his sins. The man's
parish priest was a penitent of Gobat, who thus knew that he was equally
negligent in confessing, so he instructed the rustic on his return to the priest
to say to him that it was no wonder his parishioners confessed so badly since
he confessed so imperfectly himself (Ibid. n. 444). As Gobat was a trained
theologian and an unusually experienced confessor, his story makes one doubt
the observance in practice of the rigid definitions of the books.

sentenced him to three years' residence in a seminary. The punishment was uncanonically light, but the priest appealed to the court of the metropolitan, which set the sentence aside and put the costs on the syndic, who then interjected an *appel comme d'abus* to the Parlement of Toulouse, which decided that it had no jurisdiction except to relieve the syndic.[1] It was not many years after this that Père d'Aubenton is said to have revealed to the Regent Orleans a confession of Philip V. of Spain.[2]

In view of these cases it is somewhat remarkable that violation of the seal is so rarely included among the heinous sins reserved to episcopal jurisdiction *in foro pœnitentiæ*. I have met with but one instance of it—that of the Abbot of Monte Cassino, who possessed diocesan rights over a considerable territory.[3] As the list of reserved sins is public, perhaps it is thought indiscreet to let it be known that such cases are possible. At the same time it is admitted that they belong to the class in which *parvitas materiæ* cannot be pleaded in defence—that is, that the trifling nature of an infraction will not serve in extenuation. Recent authorities, however, tell us that if the danger of indirect revelation is very remote *parvitas* may be urged.[4]

The most persistent violators of the seal were the regular Orders. We have seen how emphatically monastic superiors were forbidden to make use in any way of knowledge gained in confession. Yet already in the thirteenth century the complaint was made that they arranged surreptitiously to obtain information as to the sins of their subjects by establishing a code to be used by confessors under which every offence had its special penance, so that they knew at once of what each member of the house had been guilty.[5] Of course, knowledge thus gained by violating the seal would be used without scruple as to further violation. The temptation of exploiting the confessional for the government of the large and sometimes insubordinate

---

[1] Du Fresnoy, *op. cit.* Append. p. 105.

[2] Grégoire, Histoire des Confesseurs des Empereurs etc. p. 99.

[3] Jac. a Graffiis de Casuum Reservat. Lib. II. cap. xxxvi. n. 1.

[4] Alph. de Leone de Off. et Potest. Confessar. Recoll. VII. n. 43.—Gury Comp. Theol. Moral. II. 649.—Varceno Comp. Theol. Moral. Tract. XVII. cap. iv. art. 7.

[5] Collectio de Scandalis Ecclesiæ (Döllinger, Beiträge zur politischen, kirchlichen und Cultur-Geschichte, III. 194).

bodies of men assembled in the religious Orders was sufficient to overcome, all reverence for the sanctity of the seal. Its use continued and was reduced to a system among the Jesuits as one of the means whereby the ironclad discipline of the Society was maintained and enforced. An inside view of it is afforded by a very curious memorial from some Spanish Jesuits to the Inquisition, forwarded about 1590 by the Holy Office to Sixtus V. Among various complaints is one that the Company of Jesus is governed through the confessional. The ordinary confessor, it is stated, can absolve only for venial and mental sins. All actual and mortal sins are reserved for the Rector of the College or his superior; to this superior every member has to confess once in six months, and then repeat it yearly to the provincial when he comes, and again to the visitor when he makes his rounds. All this is in order that the superiors may know the character of every member and govern them accordingly. This renders the sacrament odious, it leads to imperfect confession, for they argue that when the seal is thus violated there is no sin in concealing sins, and that it is a sacrilege thus to abuse the sacrament. Besides, many take advantage of this when confessing to poison the ear of the superior with false witness concerning their comrades, and as it is all written down and sent to the General there result many unjust punishments; men are dishonored and debarred from advancement. It is no unusual thing for a man to be kept in the novitiate for twenty or thirty years without being admitted to profession.[1]

---

[1] Bibl. Vatican. MSS. Ottobonian. Lat. n. 495. As I believe this remarkable document is inedited, a short extract from it may serve as a contribution to the history of the Company of Jesus, which is still to be written.

"Con lo qual dizen hacerse el santo sacramento de la confesion odioso, pues hazen que totas sus flaquezas y miserias los ayan los subditos de manifiestar muchas vezes y a muchas personas, y para governarlos exteriormente, y que desto procede el detener a muchos religiosos veinte y treinta años sin admitirlos á la profesion, y que el que entre mozo novicio se vee viejo y novicio. Dizen tambien hazerse esto santo sacramento pernicioso, porque da ocasion á que no se haga la confesion entera y que se callen en ella muchas faltas, y aun dizen que con tanto perjuicio y daño de sus honrras y famas no les obliga el precepto de la integridad de esto santo sacramento, y que no peccan en dimidiar sus confesiones. Demas desto dizen este santo sacramento se haze sacrilego de parte de los superiores confesores, pues usan del para sus designias y gobierno exterior, y de parte de los que confiesan pues dividen la confesion, no se conesando enteramente con escrupulo de sus consciencias, y que ay muchas quef

Sixtus V. apparently took no action on this memorial, but it may reasonably be regarded as a factor in inducing his successor, Clement VIII., to take the subject into serious consideration. There were, indeed, theologians of authority who openly taught that a prelate could use for the government of his diocese or convent information obtained in confession from his subjects.[1] Nothing was more conducive than this to render confession odious among ecclesiastics, and for this reason conscientious prelates, like S. Carlo Borromeo, were accustomed to refuse to hear the confessions of their subordinates.[2] It was not an easy matter for even a pope to handle, in view of the powerful influence of the religious Orders, together with the scandal to be caused by proclaiming that the seal was habitually violated by those who were regarded as the bulwarks of the Church, and nothing but a profound sense of the necessity could have prompted Clement to action. Yet, in 1593, he took the decisive step of forbidding superiors, and all confessors who might be promoted, from using in any manner whatsoever the knowledge gained in confession for the external government of their Orders. It argued a lack of confidence in their obedience that to check the abuse of which the Spanish Jesuits complained—that the ordinary confessor was practically divested of authority in the confessional by the extension of reservations—that he moreover limited the power to decree reserved cases. Of these he prescribed eleven and forbade their increase save by general chapters, and soon afterwards he practically abolished even these by decreeing that if the superior refused to grant a faculty for a reserved case, the confessor could absolve without it.[3] That Urban VIII. was obliged to publish anew

---

so color de confesiones dizen de otros al superior quando se confiesan testimonios falsos, como saben que su gobierno es de confesiones y que el superior los a de creer y escriverlo al General, y que asi se an visto muchos testimonios lebantados y muchos castigos sin culpa, de donde se sigue que las faltas y caydas en la dicha compañia perpetuamente estan en pie y dexan el hombre sin credito."

For an account of these troubles and of those alluded to above (p. 386), from the Jesuit point of view, see Carlo Borgo's *Memoria Cattolica*, pp. 91 sqq., Cosmopoli (Roma) 1780.

[1] Juenin de Sacramentis Diss. VI. Q. 5, cap. 6, art. 4, § 3.

[2] Clericati de Pœnit. Decis. XXXIX. n. 3.

[3] Clement PP. VIII. Decr. 26 Maii, 1593 (Bullar. IV. 68, inter Constitt.

Clement's legislation shows how stubborn was the opposition which it excited, but it has remained since then the law of the Church, and the prohibition to use knowledge gained in confession is construed as applying to secular prelates as well as to regular.[1]

Urbani VIII.).—Bernardi a Bononia Man. Confessar. Ord. Capuccin. cap. 5, § 2.—La Croix Theol. Moral. Lib. VI. P. ii. n. 1600, 1602 sqq.

The eleven specified reserved cases are apostasy, furtively leaving the house at night, sorcery, mortal theft of property of the house, ownership in violation of vow of poverty, consummated carnal sin, perjury in court, complicity in procuring abortion, homicide or wounding, forgery of the signature or seal of the house, and interfering with letters between the superior and his subjects.

The Jesuits, in their fifth general congregation, held in 1595, forthwith added nine more cases.—Quintæ Congr. Gen. Decr. 51, 57, 64 (Decreta Congr. Gen., Antverpiæ, 1635, pp. 311, 322, 328). Cf. La Croix Theol. Moral. Lib. VI. P. ii. n. 1668).

Human perversity could always be relied upon to turn to its account whatever measures were taken to check disorder. The system of reserved cases which Clement VIII. thus virtually abrogated had been adopted by Martin V. in 1430, as one of the means of enforcing the much needed reform of the Conventual Franciscans, when he declared contumacious disobedience, holding of private property, lapses of the flesh, violence, false witness, libelling, forgery of seals and false accusations to be reserved to the provincial ministers.—Martini PP. V. Bull. *Cum generale*, Regulæ cap. 7 (Bullar. I. 311).

[1] Gury Comp. Theol. Moral. II. 670.

CHAPTER XIV.

ABSOLUTION.

ALTHOUGH, in a general way, absolution has been referred to in preceding chapters, there is much concerning it which requires further consideration if we would understand the evolution of sacerdotalism leading to the existing theory and practice of the Church.

We have seen that in primitive times there was nothing to correspond with the modern conception of absolution—the pardon or remission of sin by one human being to another. There was reconciliation to the Church, but there was no assumption that this reconciliation included or inferred justification—the reconciliation of the sinner to God. Yet penitence entitled the repentant sinner to the mediation of the Church, including its ministers and the congregation, and this mediation was held to be an efficient factor in placating the Deity. From an early period the prayers of the just were regarded as the most available means of supplementing the repentance of the sinner and of inducing God to avert from him the sentence of perdition. The congregation joined in prayer over the penitents during the term of penance and at the ceremony of reconciliation. The intercession of all was sought, but that martyrs and saints and finally priests came to be regarded as peculiarly efficient mediators was a natural development of a religion which was constantly becoming more contaminated with pagan elements and more anthropomorphic in its conception of the Divine Being.

We have already seen how gradual was the growth of belief in the power of the keys and that, whatever may have been the pretensions of the priests reproved by St. Jerome and St. Isidor of Pelusium, the Church through its authoritative expositors for a long while thereafter made no positive claim for its ministers of the power of remitting sin. That was a heresy of the Donatists, fittingly rebuked by St. Augustin. When they presumed to use the "indicative" form of absolution, which Latin Christianity adopted only in the thirteenth century, he declared it to be fatuous and heretical, for it is

God who pardons and not the priest.[1] Priests could pray over the repentant sinner and implore for him the mercy of God, but that was all, and no one ventured to define the exact value of their prayers: they simply did all that they could and the penitent could ask no more. So careful, indeed, were the Fathers from usurping the functions of God that even the formula of baptism was purely deprecatory, and the words " I baptize thee " do not make their appearance until the seventh century.[2]

Leo I. only knows a supplicatory power as belonging to the bishops, though he assumes that the prayers of the Church procure reconciliation to God.[3] The biographer of St. Hilary of Arles de-

---

[1] S. Augustin. Serm. xcix. cap. 8.

[2] The oldest Sacramentary dates from the close of the fifth century : it does not give the details of the baptismal rite, but, in the mass following, the remission of sins in it is ascribed wholly to God—" quos ex aqua et Spiritu sancto regenerare dignatus es tribuens eis remissionem omnium peccatorum."—Sacram. Leonianum (Muratori Opp. T. XIII. P. i. p. 522).

The next, which is of the sixth or seventh century, gives the whole ritual. It contains no " Ego te baptizo," but as the neophyte emerges from the third plunge the priest utters the prayer " Deus omnipotens, pater Domini Nostri Jesu Christi, qui te regeneravit ex aqua et Spiritu sancto quique dedit tibi remissionem omnium peccatorum, Ipse te lineat Chrismate salutis in Christo Jesu in vitam æternam."—Sacram. Gelasianum, Lib. i. n. lxxv. (Muratori XIII. ii. 169).

In the subsequent *Sacramentarium Gregorianum* (Muratori, *loc. cit.* pp. 745, 914) the priest, when making the immersion, says " Ego te baptizo in nomine Patris et Filii et Spiritus sancti " while retaining the rest of the formula, and this incongruous mixture of indicative and deprecatory elements is still retained (Rituale Romanum, Tit. ii. cap. 2), as we shall see is also the case in the absolution formula.

The parallel has its interest, for when Aquinas was battling with the opponents of the newly-introduced indicative formula of absolution, he argued (Opusc. xxii.) that as in baptism the priest says " Ego te baptizo," so in absolving he should say " Ego te absolvo," ignorant that both were equally destitute of early authority.

In the sacrament of extreme unction the deprecatory form has been preserved, in spite of some attempts to modify it in the same way (Rit. Roman. Tit. v. cap. 2—Concil. Trident Sess. xiv. De extrema Unctione cap. 1.—Bened. PP. XIV. De Synodo Diœcesan. Lib. viii. cap. 2). There is good reason for this in the fact that part of the function of this sacrament is to restore the sick to health in fulfilment of the promise in James v. 14, and, as in this case the result is known, it is manifestly wiser to leave the whole responsibility with God

[3] Leonis PP. I. Epist. cviii. cap. 2 (Ad Theodor.)—" indulgentia Dei nisi

scribes him only as praying over his penitents.[1] A sermon attributed to St. Cæsarius of Arles argues that private penance is much less efficient than public because in the latter the penitent attains remission of sins through the prayers of the congregation moved to pity by the sight of his humiliation; it would be a doubt of God's mercy to suppose that such prayers are ineffectual.[2] Evidently the good saint had never heard of priestly absolution or any formula for its ministration.

We have seen that with the introduction of the Penitentials there came closer relations between priests and their penitents, accompanied with the gradual invasion of private confession and penance upon the public ceremonies with which the Church had been accustomed to administer reconciliation. Further details of this change will be more conveniently considered hereafter; for our present purpose it suffices to allude to the struggle between the bishops and the priests, in which the former retained jurisdiction over public and notorious crimes and abandoned to the latter private sins made known only through secret confession, except in such cases as came to be known as reserved. Yet as the priests had not yet received in ordination the power to bind and to loose, they were merely at liberty to give

---

supplicationibus sacerdotum nequeat obtineri." So again (Epist. CLXXI. cap. 1, ad Timoth.) "reconciliandos Deo per Ecclesiæ preces instanter acquiras."

[1] Vit. S. Hilar. Arelatens. cap. xiii. (Migne, L. 1233).

[2] S. Augustin. Sermones, Append. Serm. CIV. n. 7; CCLXI. n. 2 (Migne, XXXIX. 1948, 2228).

A bull of Boniface IV. (608–615) has been customarily cited to prove the early existence of sacramental absolution. It runs "Sunt nonnulli fulti nullo dogmate, audacissime quidem zelo magis amaritudinis quam dilectione inflammati asserentes Monachos, qui mundo mortui sunt et Deo vivunt, sacerdotalis officii potentia indignos, neque pœnitentiam neque Christianitatem largiri, neque absolvere posse per divinitus injunctam sacerdotali officio potestatem. Sed omnino labuntur." It is attributed to a synod which Bede (H. E. Lib. II. cap. 4) says was held by Boniface IV. "de vita monachorum et quiete ordinaturus," and is given as such in the collections (Harduin. III. 585; Migne, LXXX. 104) and the later canonists (Ivon. Decr. VII. 22; Gratian. cap. 25, Caus. XVI. Q. 1). It is, however, a manifest forgery (Jaffé, p. 939); no other acts of the council have reached us, and this is only found in two MSS. the recensions of which differ considerably. It is borrowed from a canon of the council of Nîmes, held by Urban II. in 1096 (Harduin. VI. II. 1749) as part of the struggle alluded to (p. 298) between the regulars and seculars, and its attribution to Boniface IV. to give it greater antiquity was doubtless suggested by the passage in Bede.

such comfort as they could to penitents by praying over them and interceding for them with God. The formulas of so-called absolution in the rituals and Pœnitentials and Ordines have been preserved in great numbers and, until the eleventh century was well advanced, are all merely prayers to God to grant pardon to the sinner,[1] nor did they restore him to communion, for that was regulated by the length of penance imposed. Some of them are elaborate, in others the ceremony is exceedingly simple, after the prolonged preliminaries had been performed; priest and penitent prostrated themselves and prayed; then they consulted together as to the penitence to be imposed; the priest merely said "May God guard thee from all evil," etc., and dismissed the sinner.[2] Prayer is the only means of obtaining pardon for the sinner alluded to in the statutes which pass under the name of St. Boniface and in the Rule of St. Chrodegang;[3] Alcuin alludes only to it,[4] and even Benedict the Levite knows of nothing else, except the imposition of hands for public sinners reconciled and absolved from excommunication.[5] So thoroughly was this

---

[1] Sacramentarium Gregorianum (Muratori Opp. T. XIII. P. ii. pp. 882-9, 833-4, 916).—Sacramentarium vetus (Migne CLI. 865-8).—Liturg. Fontanellens (Ibid. p. 914).—Wasserschleben, Bussordnungen, pp. 252, 302, 349, 363, 376, 389, 411, 423, 426, 437, 551, 666.—Morin. de Pœnitentia, Append. pp. 19, 25, 51, 55.—Martene de antiq. Eccles. Ritibus Lib. i. cap. vi. Art. 7.—Pez, Thesaur. Anecd. II. ii. 661.—Burchardi Decreti Lib. xix. cap. 7.

It was the same in the Greek Church. See the *Libellus Pœnitentialis* ascribed to John the Faster (Morin. Append. pp. 80-2, 94). A Greek *Ordo* of uncertain date expressly disclaims all power to remit sins—"Ego humilis et peccator sum: illius qui meæ humilitati confitetur peccata super terram dimittere non valeo. Nullus est qui peccata dimittere possit nisi solus Deus . . . Deus tibi dimittat in hoc sæculo et in futuro. Vade in pace." (Ibid. p. 120).

[2] "Et dicitur ei capitulum: Dominus custodiat te ab omni malo et reliqua, et relinquas eum."—Pœnit. Sangallens. (Wasserschleben, p. 426)—Pœnit. Floriacens. (Ibid. p. 423).

[3] S. Bonifacii Statuta cap. 31 (D'Achery Spicileg. I. 509).—Reg. S. Chrodegangi cap. 32 (Migne, LXXXIX. 1073)—"Tunc da illi pœnitentiam canonice mensuratam et postea effunda super eum orationes et preces."

[4] Alcuini Epist. cxii.—"Quatenus orationibus illius nostræ confessionis oblatio Deo acceptabilis fiat et remissionem ab eo accipiamus cui est sacrificium spiritus contribulatus."

[5] Bened. Levitæ Capitul. Lib. v. cap. 116.—"Ut divinis precibus et miserationibus absolutus a suis facinoribus mereatur; quoniam sine manus impositione nemo absolvitur ligatus."

Here imposition of hands absolves from excommunication; the absolution from sin comes from God.

understood that after confession the penitent was instructed to ask
not for absolution but for prayer and intercession, so that God might
deign to grant him pardon.[1] The function thus performed was sometimes called "repropitiation" to indicate that, by the efforts of the
priest, God was again rendered propitious to the sinner.[2] Theodulf
of Orleans treats confession merely as an appeal to the priest for
counsel and aid, so that by mutual prayer or the performance of
penance the stains of sin may be washed away.[3] When, in 850, the
council of Pavia denied that priests had any power of the keys it did
not forbid them to continue praying over their penitents as they had
been doing for two centuries, thus assuming that the prayers were
only intercessory,[4] and this is emphasized by the synod of Douzi, in
874, which asserted that the priest has no more power over the sins
of others than over his own—he can only pray alike for either.[5] So
little importance, indeed, was ascribed to these ceremonies, and so
foreign as yet was the idea that they were essential to the pardon of
sin, that Charlemagne, in ordering a general fast and prayer for
famine, pestilence and war, orders his subjects to fit themselves for
it, not by confession and absolution, but by cleansing their souls for
themselves by repentance and tears and abstaining from sin here-

---

[1] " Domino Deo confessus sum et tibi Deo amico et sacerdoti, et rogo te cum
humilitate ut digneris orare pro me infelici et indigno ut mihi dignetur per
suam misericordiam Dominus dare indulgentiam peccatorum meorum.—Oth-
mari Abbatis Instructio (Wasserschleben, p. 437).

This continued until the eleventh century. Bishop Burchardt (Decr. XIX.
7) gives a similar formula, which is likewise in the *Corrector Burchardi* cap.
182 (Wasserschleben, p. 666), and in an *Ordo* printed by Garofalo from a Farfa
MS. of the eleventh century (Garofali Ordo ad dandam Pœnitentiam, Romæ,
1791, p. 37). See also Morini Append. p. 56.

[2] Pœnit. Cummeani Prolog. (Wasserschleben, p. 462).—"Quid est autem
repropitiare delictum nisi cum adsumpseris peccatorem et monendo, hortando,
docendo adduxeris eum ad pœnitentiam, ab errore correxeris, a vitiis emunda-
veris, et feceris eum ut ex tale converso propitius sit Deus, pro delicto repropitiare diceris."

[3] Theodulphi Capitulare, cap. 30 (Harduin. IV. 919)—" Quia confessio quam
sacerdotibus facimus hoc nobis adminiculum affert, quia accepto ab eis salutari
consilio, saluberrimis pœnitentiæ observationibus sive mutuis orationibus, peccatorum maculas diluimus."

[4] Synod. Regiaticina ann. 850, cap. 7 (Harduin. V. 27).

[5] C. Duziacens. II. ann. 874, cap. 8 (Harduin. VI. I. 157).—"In secreta oratione pro quibus sicuti et pro suis jugiter intercedat peccatis."

after.[1] Even at the end of the eleventh century so indefinite as yet
was the value assigned to these sacerdotal ministrations that Urban
II. at the council of Nîmes, in 1096, promulgated a canon asserting
that the prayers of monks had more power to wash away sins than
those of secular priests and that they were not to be prevented from
administering absolution[2]—showing how vague was still the conception embodied in the latter term, and that the power of the intercessor
depended on his holiness and not on his ordination. Moreover, the
collections of canons of the period continue to contain those which
treat the priest as merely counselling his penitent.[3] Even as late as
1117, when Queen Urraca of Castile and Bishop Gelmirez of Compostella were besieged by a rebellious mob and were in momentary
expectation of death, there was no talk of the bishop absolving his
companions ; he simply proposed that they should mutually confess
their sins and join in prayer to God for their remission.[4] Nor was
the purely intercessory character of the rite confined to private
reconciliation ; it was the same with the ceremonies of public reconciliation administered by bishops when receiving the repentant sinner
back into the Church after he had performed the penance assigned to
him, the only essential difference being that on these occasions the
whole congregation was assumed to join in the prayer.[5]

Yet during the period under consideration, there came a change,
not distinctly traceable in successive development, but confused and
irregular, out of which was ultimately evolved the power of the keys
and sacramental absolution. It is impossible to give a connected

---

[1] Ghaerbaldi Instruct. Pastoralis (Martene Ampl. Collectio VII. 23).

[2] C. Nemausens. ann. 1096, cap. 2, 3 (Harduin. VI. II. 1750).

[3] Burchard. Decr. XIX. 30 (Corrector Burchardi cap. 205).—Burchardi XIX.
36 (Ivon. Decr. XV. 53).—Ivon. Decr. XIII. 43.

[4] Historia Compostellana, Lib. I. cap. cxiv. n. 4 (Hispaña Sagrada XX. 231).
—"Confiteamur alterutrum peccata nostra et oremus pro invicem ut salvemur;
invocemus misericordiam Dei ut peccata nostra dimittat et misericordiam suam
præstare nobis dignetur."—Evidently the contemporary Bishop Munio who
relates this knew nothing of absolution.

[5] Sacrament. Gelasianum, Lib. I. n. 15, 59 (Muratori Opp. T. XIII. P. II. pp.
20, 91).—Pœnit. Ps. Roman. (Wasserschleben, p. 376).—Pez, Thesaur. Anecd.
II. II. 631.—Pœnit. Bobiens. (Wasserschleben, p. 411).—Pœnit. Ps. Bedæ (Ibid.
p. 256).—See also a very elaborate *Ordo* for public penance, of the late ninth
century in Morin, Append. pp. 60-68.

account of this, as the scattered indications concerning it are incapable of resolution into symmetrical chronological sequence. Thus far we have dealt with reconciliation, a term which, in spite of the bishops, came to be employed as designating the result of private confession followed by priestly prayers and the imposition of penance;[1] it could be administered at any time, while the public reconciliation was reserved for bishops on Holy Thursday, and it was the ceremony which soothed the last moments of the dying penitent.[2] Gradually, as the belief in the power of the keys developed, this reconciliation came to be regarded as in some way reconciling to God as well as to the Church. We have seen (p. 128) the audacious interpolations by which Benedict the Levite interjected into ancient formulas the idea that absolution was wrought by the prayers of the priest, and the word "absolution" began quietly to be used as well as reconciliation.[3] To the older writers, pardon was gained by the efforts and good works of the repentant sinner, as we have seen in the numerous lists of the seven methods of obtaining it, and in this he could be assisted by the prayers of the priest and of the congregation, but now, in an indistinct and hazy manner, absolution became associated with reconciliation in some minds, while others kept the ideas distinct. Alcuin uses the words interchangeably, and so does Benedict the Levite.[4] About the year 900 Abbo of S. Germain employs absolution in place of reconciliation, and so does a Penitential of about the same period.[5] Yet the synod of St. Macra, in 881, attributes absolution to God and reconciliation to the priest or bishop,

---

[1] Pœnit. Ps. Theodori cap. 41 § 1 (Wasserschleben, p. 610).—Pœnit. Ps. Ecberti (Morin. Append. p. 19).—Pez, Thesaur. Anecd. II. II. 56.—Ps. Alcuin. Lib. De Divinis Officiis cap. 13.—Bened. Levitæ Capitular. Lib. v. cap. 116.—Statuta S. Bonifacii, cap. 31 (D'Achery I. 509).—Commonitor. cujusque Episcopi cap. 47 (Martene Ampl. Collect. VII. 5).

[2] Morin. Append. pp. 29–31.— Ps. Eutychian. Exhort. ad Presbyteros (Migne, V. 165–8).—Ps. Evaristi cap. iii. (Burchardi Decr. Lib. XVIII. cap. 16; Ivon. Decr. P. XV. cap. 38; Gratian. cap. 4 Caus. XXVI. Q. vi.).

[3] Curiously enough, from a comparatively early period, the Church claimed power to absolve the soul after death, a claim which it subsequently abandoned. The subject will be more conveniently considered hereafter when we come to examine the varying doctrines as to the future life.

[4] Alcuini Epist. CXII.—Bened. Levitæ Capitular. Lib. v. cap. 129, 134, 136 (Isaac. Lingonens. Tit. I. cap. 13, 16, 17).

[5] Abbon. Sangerman. Serm. III. (D'Achery I. 339). — Pœnitent. Vindobonens. (Wasserschleben, p. 418).

and so does Bishop Riculfus of Soissons.[1] This conception possibly explains the use of the word absolution in Urban II.'s decree of 1196, mentioned above, but the exceedingly vague sense attached to it, even in the twelfth century, is visible in the rule that when a monk was dangerously sick he was to receive the benediction and absolution from all his brethren; if he grew worse extreme unction and the Eucharist were given, after which all united in prayer to God for his absolution.[2] A distinction between absolution and reconciliation, not easily intelligible, is expressed in one of the False Decretals, which says that priests can absolve the sick but require episcopal permission to reconcile for secret sins,[3] and it was probably on the authority of this, which was carried through all the collections of canons, that, about 1130, Honorius of Autun reserves to the bishop the power of reconciliation while including absolution among the duties of the priest.[4] By this time there was no practical difference between the terms. Herbert de Losinga, in his prayer to St. John, does not ask for absolution or remission of sins, but for reconciliation.[5] Yet the schoolmen were beginning their labors in defining everything, and some distinction, if only verbal, must be found for the terms which were virtually synonymous. They were evidently puzzled by the use of both words for the same thing, and St. Ivo of Chartres, the leading authority of the early twelfth century, attempted to show that although the act was one it had two results, when he ex-

---

[1] Concil. apud S. Macram ann. 881, cap. 7 (Harduin. VI. I. 361-2). "Quoniam aliter nec a Deo salvetur nec sacerdotali ministerio reconciliari potest."—Riculfii Suessionens. Constitt. cap. 9, 11 (Ibid. pp. 416-17).

[2] P. de Honestis Regulæ Clericorum Lib. II. cap. 22. Some twenty years later we find death-bed absolution among the Carthusians—Guigonis I. Consuetud. cap. xii. § 2.

The word absolution is used as a priestly function in a council held in Rome by Gregory VII. about 1075 (Pflugk-Harttung, Acta Pontiff. Roman. II. 126). Corresponding canons of a council of Poitiers, in 1100, employ the phrase *pœnitentiam dare* (Harduin. VI. II. 1860). The exceeding vagueness of the conception of "absolution" at this period is seen in Gregory's undertaking to absolve his correspondents at a distance (p. 362), and we shall encounter further examples of this when we come to treat of the development of indulgences in the eleventh century.

[3] Ps. Evaristi cap. iii. (Burchardi Decr. Lib. XVIII. cap. 16).

[4] Honorii Augustodun. Gemmæ Animæ Lib. I. cap. 181, 185.

[5] Herberti de Losinga Epist. XVIII. (Bruxellis, 1836, p. 36).—"Veniam, tandem veniam, O beate Johannes tuis meritis ad reconciliationem."

plained that priests in absolving reconcile penitents, even as Christ in his humanity reconciled the world and in his divinity absolved it.[1] This, which shows the complete identity of absolution and reconciliation, would seem to have become the accepted view, for Alexander Hales defines sacramental confession as that which is provided for reconciliation by absolution, and the power of which is confided to priests alone.[2] Yet the meaning of the word absolution continued to be vague. In 1134 we are told in the Cistercian Rule that on stated occasions absolutions were pronounced on all dead kindred of the brethren by name, the absolutions consisting simply of the phrase *requiescant in pace.*[3] Any prayer, whether for the dead or living, was thus termed an absolution ; for the living it consisted of nothing more, for, in the middle of the century, Gratian, in arguing for the necessity of confession, asks how a priest is to pray for a sin which he does not know.[4]

---

[1] Ivon. Carnot. Serm. II. (Migne, CLXII. 518). Yet St. Ivo gives a canon (Decr. xv. 28) in which the priest only reconciles the dying according to the old rule by which the penitent, if he survives, is to perform due penance.

[2] Alex. de Ales Summæ P. IV. Q. xix. Membr. 1, Art. 1.—" Confessio sacramentalis . . . quæ ordinata est ad reconciliationem quæ fit per absolutionem."

Hales here evidently distinguishes the reconciliation in the *forum internum* from the reconciliation in the *forum externum,* which was entirely independent of absolution. It would lead us too far from our subject to discuss this matter in detail, and a single instance will illustrate the difference as well as the advantage resulting to the Church from extending its jurisdiction over both worlds. In 1240 the Duke of Lenezycz hanged John the Scholasticus of Ploczk and Breslau, whereupon Peter, Archbishop of Gnesen, excommunicated him and laid his dominions under interdict. He purchased reconciliation by surrendering to the archbishop the town and district of Lovicz and conferring certain franchises and property on the churches of Breslau, Ploczk and Cujavien, in addition to which he was required to supplicate Gregory IX. to confirm his absolution. A war with the pagans served to excuse his personal appearance in Rome, and Gregory sent a commission to the Bishop of Breslau and to a canon of Cracow to absolve him after imposing such a penance as should . serve to deter others from similar crimes.—Raynald. Annal. ann. 1240, n. 36, 37.—See also the case of Ruggiero da Bonito, penanced, in 1319, by John XXII. for the murder of the Bishop of Fricento (Raynald. ann. 1319, n. 13), and the formula for such cases in the " Formulary of the Papal Penitentiary," p. 30 (Philadelphia, 1892).

[3] Usus Antiquiores Ord. Cisterciens. cap. 100 (Migne, CLXVI. 1480).—" In quibus tamen absolutionibus dicetur tantum *Requiescant in pace.*" Cf. Du Cange s. vb. *Absolvere* 4; *Absolutio* 5.

[4] Post Cap. 87 De Pœnitentia Dist. I. § 9.

In the growth of the simple priestly prayer over the penitent into an absolution or pardon of his sins before God, we can trace the practical result of the development of the power of the keys, but it derived its completeness from the new factor of the cognate theory of the sacraments invented by the tireless brains of the schoolmen of the twelfth century. Few things illustrate more instructively the evolution of sacerdotalism than the manner in which the sacraments grew and multiplied and became invested with the power to determine human salvation. Originally the word was used with a very vague and general signification. To Tertullian it had merely the sense of mystery (μυστήριον).[1] It is true that in the fourth century Hilary of Poitiers speaks of the sacrament of baptism, but he also speaks of faith as a sacrament; so the cross is a sacrament and likewise the crucifixion, and even prayer.[2] St. Augustin defines a sacrament as anything in a ceremony which signifies something holy; the celebration of Easter is a sacrament; even a number may be a sacrament; in baptism the word transforms the water into a sacrament;[3] but he is not quite consistent when he alludes to Noah's ark as a sacrament, and says that the sacraments of the Old Law were prefigurations of the advent of Christ, after which they were abolished and were succeeded by those of the New Law, fewer in number, greater in influence, and easier in performance[4]—evidently to him the hard life-long penance of the period had about it nothing of a sacramental character. Occasionally, moreover, he uses the word in its original sense of mystery.[5]

The subject was regarded as of no special interest or importance, and allusions to sacraments are comparatively few in the writers of the succeeding centuries.[6] St. Isidor of Seville found himself obliged

---

[1] Tertull. adv. Marcionem Lib. v. cap. 16; De Anima cap. 9; De Jejuniis cap. 7.

[2] S. Hilar. Pictaviens. Tract. in Ps. CXVIII. n. 5; Comment. in Matt. cap. V. n. 1; cap. VI. n. 1; cap. XI. n. 25; cap. XIII. n. 6; cap. XXX. n. 2; cap. XXXIII. n. 5.

[3] S. Augustin. Epist. LV. ad Januarium, cap. 1, 4, 17; In Joannem Tract. LXXX. n. 3.

[4] S. Augustin. contra Faustum Lib. XIX. cap. 12, 13.

[5] Ejusd. Epist. CXL. cap. 14.—"Aut certe profundum sacramentum nos intelligere voluit."

[6] It seems to have been reserved to Father Tournely to discover that the reason why the sacraments are so rarely alluded to by the Fathers is that they

to define the word, which he did by borrowing the definition of Augustin and adding that the sacraments are baptism, chrism and the Eucharist, which are so called because, under cover of material things, the divine virtue operates secretly.[1] It was probably to these that Gregory the Great referred when he tells us that we receive the sacraments externally that we may be filled internally with the grace of the spirit.[2] This limitation of the term to material objects did not prevent the use of the word in its old vague and general significance. In liturgies of the seventh century we find Lent spoken of as a sacrament, the cross is a sacrament and so are the advent of Christ, the articles of the creed and even the Virgin.[3] The exorcised salt used in baptism is also a sacrament.[4] The definition given by St. Isidor, however, gradually made its way. In the ninth century we find it copied by Rabanus Maurus, who adds that there are several kinds of baptism besides that of water, for there are the baptisms of the Holy Ghost and of martyrdom; there are other modes also, he says, of purging away sins, and among them he enumerates repentance and confession, which shows that thus far the latter were excluded from the list of sacraments.[5] His contemporary, Walafrid Strabo, takes the same view; the only sacraments he knows are baptism, the Eucharist, and chrism.[6] Early in the eleventh century Fulbert of Chartres enumerates as the sole requisites for salvation belief in the Trinity, baptism and the Eucharist;[7] he knows no other sacraments. In 1025 we have a long discourse on repentance addressed by Gerard, Bishop of Arras, to some Cathari whom he endeavored to convert. The good bishop evidently had no conception that there was anything sacramental about penitence; he says nothing about confession, absolution or satisfaction, but

---

did not desire to expose them to the ridicule of the pagans.—Th. ex Charmes Theol. Univ. Diss. v. cap. ii. Q. 2, art. 2.

[1] S. Isidor. Hispal. Etymolog. Lib. VI. cap. xix. n. 39, 40.

[2] S. Gregor. PP. I. in I. Regum Expos. Lib. v. cap. iii. n. 21.

[3] Missale Gothicum (Muratori Opp. T. XIII. P. III. pp.; 292, 355).—Sacramentum Gallicanum (Ibid. pp. 635, 674, 676, 706).

[4] Sacramentar. Gelasianum (Ib. T. XIII. P. I. p. 67). A survival of this is still preserved in the Roman Ritual (Tit. II. cap. 2), where the blessed salt is spoken of as a sacrament.

[5] Rabani Mauri de Universo Lib. v. cap. 11.

[6] Walafridus Strabo de Rebus Ecclesiasticis.

[7] Fulberti Carnotens. Epist. 5 (Migne, CXLI. 197).

teaches that simple repentance obtains forgiveness without formulas or priestly ministration.[1] On the other hand, towards the close of the century, Lanfranc speaks of three sacraments of confession; he defines a sacrament by quoting St. Augustin, and adds that it also means an oath because taken on sacred things, and that the consecration of anything is called a sacrament.[2] St. Anselm of Lucca seems to have a more definite idea of the subject, but he only knows four sacraments—baptism, the chrism, imposition of hands and the Eucharist.[3] The contemporary Bonizo, in his little treatise on the subject, only describes three—the Eucharist, blessed salt and the three forms of consecrated oil, but he says there are other sacraments now used by the Church, such as breathing in exorcism, *effetatio* for catechumens, and the imposition of hands by which the Holy Ghost is given in baptism, penitents are reconciled and the functions of their ministry are conferred on bishops, priests and deacons.[4] St. Ivo of Chartres soon afterwards shows an equally vague conception of the significance of the word. So far from attributing the institution of the sacraments to Christ, he says that they have been used since the creation of the world. When he enumerates them he only mentions baptism, the Eucharist and the chrism, but he adds that everything which is done in exorcisms, such as prayers and insufflations, is a sacrament; the sacraments common to bishop and priest are catechising, celebrating mass and preaching; if he alludes to the sacrament of penitence, it is an infliction to be borne like the knife of the surgeon; in the portion of his Decretum devoted to the sacraments the only ones treated are the Eucharist, baptism, the chrism and holy water.[5] The Gloss. of Monte Cassino, which is probably attributable to this period, gives only the customary enumeration of baptism, the chrism and the Eucharist.[6]

When the schoolmen undertook the reconstruction of theology it was not to be expected that this subject would be passed over in

---

[1] Synod. Atrebacens. ann. 1025, cap. 8 (Gousset, Actes etc. II. 32–6).

[2] Lanfranci Lib. de Celanda Confessione; Ejusd. Lib. de Corp. et Sang. Domini cap. 12, 13.

[3] S. Anselmi Lucens. Collect. Canonum Lib. IX.

[4] Bonizonis Placentini Lib. de Sacramentis.

[5] S. Ivon. Carnotens. Serm. I., II., IV., XIII.; Ejusd. Decreti P. I., II. cap. 73, 75, 118.

[6] Du Cange s. v. *Sacramentum* I.

their universal passion for exploration and definition. The first to attack it systematically seems to have been Hugh of St. Victor, who devoted an elaborate treatise to it. The only sacraments that he mentions as essential to salvation are baptism and communion. There are others, however, which are aids to sanctification, because through them virtue may be exercised and greater grace acquired, such as holy water and the blessed ashes placed on the head on Ash Wednesday; and again there are others which seem to have been instituted only because they are requisite for the sanctification of other sacraments.[1] He describes at length the three great sacraments of baptism, of confirmation and the chrism, and of the Eucharist, devoting a chapter to the question whether baptism or the imposition of hands is the greater sacrament. As for the lesser sacraments, he says they cannot all be enumerated, but he classifies them in three divisions—those consisting of things, such as holy water, blessed ashes, the blessing of palms and wax candles and the like; others in acts, as the sign of the cross, the breathing in exorcism, spreading the hands, bending the knees etc.; others again in words, as the invocation of the Trinity and similar formulas. In another treatise he tells us that matrimony is a sacrament and so is penitence, but it has no sacramental virtue in itself, and its effects depend on the character of the ministrant.[2] These indefinite and somewhat contradictory views show how unexplored as yet was the field through which he was tentatively groping his way. In 1139 the second council of Lateran, in speaking of the sacraments, makes no allusion to penitence, though it could scarce have been omitted had it been recognized as one of them.[3] It is true that about the same time St. Bernard makes

---

[1] Hugon. de S. Vict. de Sacramentis Lib. I. P. ix. cap. 7.

[2] Ibid. Lib. II. P. vii. ix., xi., xiv. Ejusd. Summæ Sententt. Tract. IV. cap. 1; Tract. VI. cap. 12.

In a very significant passage he says "How can I feel certain of pardon if I complete the penance and satisfaction prescribed for me by a man who may be ignorant or negligent? Do what you are ordered. God will know your devotion. If you have a priest who does not tell you what is necessary it is because your sins have deserved this misfortune."—De Sacramentis Lib. II. P. xiv. cap. 3.

[3] C. Lateran. II. ann. 1139, cap. 2, 22 (Harduin. VI. II. 1208).

In the life of St. Otho, the apostle of Pomerania (Canisii Thesaur. III. II. 62), who died in 1139, he is represented as preaching to his new converts a sermon in which he develops the whole system of the seven sacraments, of

a passing allusion to the "sacrament of confession,"[1] but this is evidently but the use of the word in its customary sense of something holy, for the *Liber de Vera et falsa Pœnitentia* of the Pseudo-Augustin, which so exaggerated the sacerdotalism of penitence, knows nothing of it as a sacrament, and Hugh Archbishop·of Rouen seems to regard baptism and the Eucharist as the only sacraments.[2]

The speculations of the theologians of Paris had thus far met with no response. In Rome they attracted no attention, for Gratian quotes without dissent St. Isidor's enumeration of the three sacraments—baptism, the chrism and the Eucharist—and he treats only of baptism, confirmation and the Eucharist.[3] Elsewhere he classifies sacraments into those which are of necessity and those which are of dignity; the necessary ones cannot be repeated, for they are indelible, and if administered by heretics are valid (thus excluding penitence), while those of dignity must be worthily administered by the worthy to the worthy.[4] Evidently up to the middle of the twelfth century there was no conception of the sacramental theory, such as it soon afterwards became under the fashioning hands of the Paris theologians. Of this we have the earliest description in Peter Lombard, who doubtless only threw into shape the ideas which were becoming dominant in the French schools and were finally accepted by the Church as embodying its aspirations to control the spiritual destinies of man. In fixing the number of sacraments at the mystic figure of seven—baptism, confirmation, the Eucharist, penitence, extreme unction, orders and matrimony—he wastes no time in arguing whether these or others shall be admitted, but states it as an accepted fact, as it doubtless was by this time in the University of Paris, the source and creator of modern theology.[5] It was

---

which the fifth is that of penitence. The date of this life is unknown and has been placed as late as 1500, but it probably was a little anterior to 1189, when St. Otho was canonized, as his canonization is not mentioned in it. The sermon of course is a pious fraud, entitled to no weight as historical evidence.

[1] S. Bernardi Lib. ad Milites Templi cap. 12.

[2] Hugon. Archiep. Rotomagens. Dialogor. Lib. v. (Martene Thesaur. V. 947).

[3] Cap. 84 Caus. I. Q. 1.—P. III. De Consecratione.

[4] Post cap. 39, 106, Caus. I. Q. 1.

[5] P. Lombard. Sentt. Lib. IV. Dist. ii. ¿ 1.—"Jam ad Sacramenta novæ legis accedamus quæ sunt Baptismus, Confirmatio, panis benedictio, id est Eucharistia, Pœnitentia, Unctio extrema, Ordo, Conjugium."

Probably to this period may be attributed a forged decretal assigned to

easy to make the assertion, but the schoolmen could not fail to recognize the difference between the three long recognized sacraments and the new ones thus classed with them, now that the mass of observances, such as holy water, blessed salt, the sign of the cross etc., were separated from them and relegated to the inferior position of mere "sacramentals." It was evidently necessary to assign to them a new and distinct efficacy, akin to the mysterious power ascribed to the oldest of all, the rite of baptism. How difficult was this, and what endless debates were yet required before the theory of the supernatural efficacy of the seven sacraments could be defined and established may be seen in Peter Lombard's laborious endeavor to explain the sacramental character of penitence. A sacrament, he says, is a sign of a sacred thing. But what is this sign here? Some, as Grandulfus, say that the sacrament is only what is shown externally, namely, the exterior penitence which is the sign of the interior contrition and humility. If this be so, then not every evangelical sacrament accomplishes what it figures, for exterior penitence does not cause interior, but rather interior is the cause of exterior. But they say this is only to be understood of the sacraments of the New Testament, such as Baptism, Confirmation and the Eucharist. But the

---

Alexander I. (A. D. 108–116), evidently fabricated for the purpose of establishing the sacramental character of matrimony.—Collectio Lipsiensis, Tit. LIX. cap. 6 (Friedberg, Quinque Compilationes Antiquæ, p. 205).

How little idea was entertained by the primitive Church that there was any sacramental character in marriage is indicated in one of the canons of Hippolytus (XVI. 80, Achelis p. 85), which denounces as a homicide a man who abandons a concubine and marries a wife, unless the concubine has been unfaithful. The Apostolic Constitutions however (VIII. 38) take a different view of the matter.

The sacrament of orders was equally unknown. Hippolytus tells us (V. 43–7, pp. 67–8) that, if a believer has suffered prison or torture for Christ, he is a priest before God "immo confessio est ordinatio ejus," but to become a bishop he must be ordained; if he has confessed the faith but not suffered, he is worthy of priesthood, but must be ordained by the bishop. A slave punished for Christianity has the spirit of a priest, and the bishop in ordaining him is to omit the clause in the prayer respecting the Holy Ghost. All this is changed in the Apostolic Constitutions, VIII. 29.

Baptism likewise was not essential (X. 63–4, p. 76). A slave is not to be baptized without his master's consent. He must be content to be a Christian, and if he dies without baptism he is not to be separated from the flock. The Apostolic Constitutions (VIII. 38) forbid the baptism of a slave without the owner's consent, but omit the rest.

sacraments of Penitence and Matrimony date from the beginning of
the human race, and before the time of grace, for they were both
instituted for our first parents.[1] Again, if exterior penitence is the
sacrament and interior the thing of the sacrament, the thing precedes
the sacrament oftener than the sacrament the thing; but there is no
inconvenience in this, for it often happens in the sacraments which
cause what they figure. Again, some say that exterior and interior
penitence are one sacrament and not two, as the bread and wine are
one; and, as in the sacrament of the Body, so in this, they say, there
is a sacrament only, namely, of exterior penitence; a sacrament and
a thing, namely, interior penitence, and a thing and not a sacrament,
namely remission of sins. For exterior penitence is both the thing
of the sacrament (that is, of exterior penitence) as well as the sacrament of the remission of sins, which it figures and accomplishes.
Also, exterior penitence is the sign of both interior penitence and
the remission of sin.[2] This passage will probably suffice to indicate
the kind of reasoning by which, through the subtile debates of the
schools for centuries, the theory of the sacraments, their nature and
power, was gradually evolved and assumed the definite shape which
has become a matter of faith. It also shows how, in the case of
penitence, the absolute remission of sin came to be accepted as effected
by sacramental confession and absolution.

Although Peter Lombard's doctrine of the seven sacraments eventually was adopted, it did not by any means meet with immediate
acceptance. We have seen (p. 57) how long the custom of deacons
receiving penitents to communion continued, showing that the sacramental character of penance only penetrated gradually through the
Church, and the same indication is found in the persistence of confession to laymen and women (pp. 221 sqq.) and of dividing confes-

---

[1] In this Peter Lombard and many another schoolman engaged in building
up the sacramental theory unconsciously taught heresy. Even in the fourteenth century Durand de S. Pourçain, while admitting (In IV. Sentt. Dist.
II. Q. 1 § 6) that penitence is a sacrament of the New Law, holds that that of
matrimony dates from Adam. Unfortunately for their orthodoxy, the council
of Trent (Sess. VII. De Sacramentis in genere can. 1) declared it to be *de fide*
that Christ instituted all the seven sacraments.

[2] P. Lombard. Sentt. Lib. IV. Dist. xxii. § 3. He had previously (Dist. XIV.
§ 1) defined exterior penitence to be a sacrament, and interior penitence to
be a virtue of the mind, and either of them is a cause of justification and
salvation.

sion from absolution (p. 356). Cardinal Pullus freely admits the sacrament of penitence, but is wholly unable to explain how it works absolution ; in fact he cannot frame an intelligible definition of absolution itself; he admits that it is God who pardons, and the priest only comforts the penitent by revealing that pardon in the sacrament, but as God does not pardon until due penance has been performed, and no one can tell when this time arrives, the absolution given in the confessional is reduced to a promise which may never be performed.[1] Evidently the shrewdest intellects were at fault in adapting the old theories to the new, and the new was as yet imperfectly understood even by its founders, as is seen in the teaching which so long held its place in the schools (p. 145), that the priest in the sacrament only made manifest the pardon by God. In this half-developed condition the importance of the consequences that might be deduced from it were not recognized, and it was treated with little respect. Stephen of Tournay pays no attention to it—to him penitence was no more a sacrament than it was to his master Gratian, and the same may be said of Master Roland, afterward Alexander III., though the latter, as a matter of convenient nomenclature, speaks of penitence as a sacrament in his bull *Omne datum optimum*, issued to the Templars several times between 1163 and 1183.[2]

Even Richard of St. Victor, who did so much to define the power of the keys and to establish its exercise in priestly hands, seems to regard the sacramental question as a theological subtilty of no practical importance ; absolution is a condition precedent to receiving the sacraments, but then absolution cannot be denied to any one who repents because he has been pardoned by God the moment he repents.[3] Peter of Poitiers shows still more significantly the hesitation with which the new theory was received when he tells us that some doctors assert penitence not to be a sacrament but only a sacramental, like holy water and blessed bread ; he thinks it, however, more likely to be a sacrament—not a sacrament of the New Testament but of the Old, for it is not the work of God but of man, and its only power is

---

[1] R. Pulli Sentt. Lib. v. cap. 15, 24; Lib. vi. cap. 61.—" Peracta, inquam, pœnitentia reus per Deum absolvitur . . . . Hujusmodi absolutionem homo non facit, quia quando eam fieri conveniat nemo novit."

[2] Steph. Tornacens. Summa Decr. Gratiani, Caus. xxxiii. Q. 3.—Rolandi Summa, Caus. xxxiii. Q. 3.—Rymer, Fœdera, I. 30, 54.

[3] R. a S. Victore de Potestate ligandi et solvendi, cap. 21, 22.

derived through charity : remission of sin certainly precedes it, but still it is necessary lest the pardoned sins return through contempt.[1] The council of London, in 1175, omits penitence from among the ministrations for which no money is to be charged, as though it formed no part of priestly functions.[2]   Alain de Lille accepts only six sacraments, including penitence among them, and omitting orders, which is replaced by dedication of churches, while confirmation and extreme unction are run together under chrism, as of old, showing how hazy and uncertain as yet, was the whole subject.[3]   Adam de Perseigne admits penitence to be a sacrament and explains that the contrition of the penitent is the *res sacramenti*, while his labor in penance is its external visible species, which shows how blindly the theologians were yet groping for some working hypothesis to explain the new doctrine.[4]   The same vagueness is exhibited by Master Bandinus who explains the use of confession because the sacrament manifests advantageously the union between Christ and the Church.[5] Evidently the theologians as yet did not know exactly what to do with their new acquisition.   Its spread through the Church was slow.   As late as 1217 Bishop Poore of Salisbury feels obliged to enumerate the seven sacraments and explain them to his clergy, showing how novel and unfamiliar they as yet were in England, and in 1255 Walter of Durham felt it necessary to insist that all priests should know the seven sacraments.[6]   This, however, proves that Peter Lombard's catalogue had triumphed in the schools, and thenceforth theologians revelled in the subtilties by which they exhibited their dialectic skill and ingenuity in determining the nature, relations and operations of the several sacraments.[7]

In this development a complete revolution was effected in the

---

[1] Pet. Pictaviens. Sentt. Lib. III. cap. xiii.

[2] Concil. Londiniens. ann. 1175, cap. 7 (Harduin. VI. II. 1637).

[3] Alani de Insulis de Artic. Cathol. Fidei Lib. IV. (Pez, Thesaur. Anecd. I. II. 487).

[4] Adami Persenniæ Abbatis Epist. XXVI. (Migne, CCXI. 672).

[5] Mag. Bandini Sentt. Lib. IV. Dist. xix.

[6] Richardi Poore Constitt. cap. 13; Walteri de Kirkham Constitt. ann. 1255 (Harduin. VII. 92, 487).

[7] See, for instance, the infinite distinctions and arguments of Alexander Hales (Summæ P. IV. Q. xiv. Membr. 1, Art. 3) on the sacrament of penitence, which he tells us was instituted by Christ at the commencement of his teaching but not in its formal shape until he delivered the keys to St. Peter.

whole economy of the Church as the efficient instrument of human salvation. It was permanently and irremovably interposed between God and man, for it was the sole custodian and ministrant of the sacraments, and these were essential to all who would seek eternal life. Aquinas tells us that they flowed from the side of the crucified Christ, that the whole Church is founded on them, and that it has no power to institute new ones.[1] The three that are indispensable are baptism for all, penitence for sinners, and orders for churchmen; the rest are only important aids to salvation, and thus the Eucharist, which had ranked the highest, was relegated to the second class.[2] As for the sacrament of penitence, without it there can be no remission of sin—or at least without a vow of receiving it when circumstances shall permit; it is the only channel through which the sinner obtains the benefit of the Passion, and thus is necessary to salvation. It is true that infused grace suffices for the remission of sin, but infused grace is not to be had without the sacrament.[3] The Scotists were not behind the Thomists in their definition of its power. Duns Scotus taught that this is so great that it suffices for the recipient not to impose an obstacle by desiring to commit sin at the moment when the words of absolution are uttered, and Astesanus declares that there is no pardon for sin except by means of the sacrament.[4] Its exact constitution however was not yet satisfactorily determined; all sacraments consist of matter and form, and Durand de S. Pourçain defines that in penitence the matter consists in the words of the confession, the form in the words of absolution; thus contrition and penance become mere accidents, though they are essential to the enjoyment of its benefits.[5]

It is true that all this, like the rest of scholastic theology, was merely the speculation of the schools, without any authoritative definition by the Church at large, but it became the universal teaching in which theologians were trained, and was accepted everywhere as a

---

[1] S. Th. Aquin. Summæ P. III. Q. lxiv. Art. 2; Suppl. Q. xvii. Art. 1.

[2] S. Th. Aquin. Summæ P. III. Q. lxv. Art. 4. Still Aquinas somewhat inconsequently endeavors (Ibid. Art. 3) to overcome this practical discrimination against the Eucharist by declaring it to be "sacramentorum omnium potissimum."

[3] Ejusd. Summæ Suppl. Q. VI. Art. 1.

[4] Jo. Scoti in IV. Sentt. Dist. XIV. Q. 4.—Fr. de Maironis in IV. Sentt. Dist. XIV. Q. 1.—Astesani Summæ Lib. V. Tit. ii. Art. 2.

[5] Durand. de S. Porciano in IV. Sentt. Dist. XVI. Q. 1 § 4.

whole, though details continued to excite debate. When, at length, at the council of Florence, in 1439, the occasion offered to define the faith of the Church in the Decree of Union with the Armenians, the work of the schoolmen was ratified and the new theology became the standard of Latin Christianity. As regards the sacraments, Peter Lombard's seven were assumed to be necessary articles of faith, and the views of Aquinas were unreservedly accepted, representing their three integral parts as matter, form, and the intention of the ministrant. In the sacrament of penitence the matter was declared to be the acts of the penitent—contrition, confession and satisfaction—the form is the words of absolution, the minister is the priest having due jurisdiction, and the effect is absolution from sin.[1] So completely was salvation dependent on the sacrament that it became a received maxim of the schools that even the pope cannot grant a dispensation which will enable a sinner to be saved without absolution.[2] Finally, when, in the sixteenth century, the reformers called in question the whole scholastic theory of the seven sacraments, the council of Trent was of course obliged to emphasize their necessity and power by defining it to be a matter of faith that all seven were instituted by Christ and are necessary for salvation.[3] As for confession, it was declared *de fide* that it was instituted by Christ and had been observed by the Church from the beginning; the sacrament of penitence is as necessary to the sinner as baptism, for without it he cannot attain to justification, although, in case of necessity, the vow to accept it, which is an essential part of contrition, suffices.[4] This settled the matter, while the importance attached to the doctrine of the sacraments and the prevailing ignorance respecting it are reflected in the labored explanations of the Catechism prepared for the instruction of parish priests.[5]

---

[1] C. Florent. ann. 1439, Decret. Union. (Harduin. IX. 440).

[2] Summa Tabiena s. v. *Absolutio* I. n. 1.

[3] C. Trident. Sess. VII. De Sacramentis in genere, can. 1, 4.

[4] C. Trident. Sess. VI. De Justificatione cap. 14; Sess. XIV. De Pœnitentia cap. 2, 4 ; can. 6.

In view of the Tridentine definition it is not easy to understand the condemnation by Pius V., Gregory XIII. and Urban VIII. (Bull. *In eminenti* Prop. 70, 71) of the Baian and Jansenist proposition that, except in case of necessity or of martyrdom, contrition with perfect charity and the vow to confess will not remit sin without the actual reception of the sacrament.

[5] Catechismi Trident. Lib. II. De Sacramentis in generi (Colon. 1572).

The Greek Church has adopted the seven sacraments of the Latin. That of

In reviewing the successful labors of the schoolmen to define and establish the power of the keys and the doctrine of the sacraments, it is easy to understand how the intercessory prayers of the priest gradually grew into absolution and how the distinction between the reconciliation of the bishop and the absolution of the priest faded away in the sacramentary power ascribed to both. As a necessary complement to this came the change (p. 122), gradually introduced through the twelfth and thirteenth centuries, in the ordination formula of the priest, by the interpolation of the clause "Receive the Holy Ghost, whose sins thou shalt forgive they are forgiven, and whose sins thou shalt retain they are retained." When these enlarged functions were finally established it was not to be expected that bishop or priest would remain content with the deprecatory formulas of absolution which ascribed to them only the intercessory power enjoyed by their predecessors. When the penitent was told that confession and penance were to win for him remission of sins, he would naturally ask for some more definite assurance than a few prayers to God muttered over his head, and it was inevitable that they should be modified to correspond with the change in doctrine. As in the latter, so in the former, the change was gradual. It was natural that the claim of more than intercessory power should show itself first in the formulas of public reconciliation by the bishops. An *Ordo Romanus*, of uncertain date, but probably early, among a number of purely intercessory prayers, has one which is fairly "indicative"—that is, which claims the power of absolution—although it refers to this power as a delegation from God. The plural form shows that it was addressed to a number of penitents, who were thus relieved of their sins by wholesale.[1] The changes shown in the

penitence works its effect when absolution is granted by the priest, according to the rules and customs of the Church. Then immediately all sins are forgiven to the penitent by God, in accordance with the promise of Christ in John xx. 23.—Liber Symbolicus Russorum, oder der grösserer Catechismus der Russen, pp. 67, 78 (Frankfort u. Leipzig, 1727).

[1] "Nos etiam, secundum auctoritatem nobis indignis a Deo commissam absolvimus vos ab omni vinculo delictorum vestrorum ut mereamini habere vitam æternam."—Mag. Biblioth. Patrum. T. VIII. pp. 423–4 (Ed. Colon. 1618). This may possibly be an interpolation of later date. The same *Ordo* contains prayers deprecatory in character—"Ipse vos largifluo pietatis suæ dono, ac meæ simul parvitatis ministerio absolvere dignetur ab omnibus fragilitatis vestræ excessibus."

formulas used by priests in private confession are more tentative, indicating how timidly at first the claim was made that the priest could do anything save intercede with God. The old prayers were retained, but there was injected into them an assertion that the priest as far as he could, or as far as was granted to him, or as far as was permitted to him, absolved the sinner, or he associated himself with the saints, to whom, curiously enough, a power of absolution was ascribed, showing how crude as yet were the conceptions as to the functions of God and his creatures.[1]

---

[1] Numerous formulas of this transitional kind will be found in the collections of Fathers Martène and Morin, presenting the subject in every variety of expression that the imagination of the scribe could suggest. Several interesting ones were also printed by D. Vincenzo Garofalo in Rome, in 1791, from among which I extract the following examples:

In one, after prayers in the older fashion, there occurs the formula "Ipse te absolvat ab omnibus peccatis et de istis peccatis quæ modo mihi coram Deo confessus es . . . cum ista pœnitentia quam modo accepisti, sis absolutus a Deo Patre et Filio et Spiritu sancto et ab omnibus sanctis ejus et a me misero peccatore, ut dimittat tibi Dominus omnia delicta tua et perducet te Christus ad vitam æternam." This is followed by a prayer in which we find "absolvat te sanctus Petrus et beatus Michael archangelus, et nos in quantum data est nobis potestas ligandi et solvendi absolutionem damus, adjuvante Domino nostro Jesu Christo."—Garofali p. 15.

Then there is another formula, perhaps a little more assured—"In ea potestate vel auctoritate fidentes quam Dominus nobis in beato Petro apostolo tribuit . . . . quantum nobis permissum est, ab omni vinculo peccatorum absolvimus: et quidquid voluntate propria, suadente Diabolo, commisisti, quantum possumus pro divina gratia indulgemus."—Ibid. p. 16.

Somewhat more assertive is this: "Tu homo qui me confessus es peccata tua coram Deo et omnibus sanctis, qui fidem sanctæ Trinitatis et remissionem peccatorum credis, in hac potestate ligandi atque solvendi quam tradidit Deus beato Petro apostolo aliisque apostolis et quæ pertinet ad successores illorum pontifices et sacerdotes, et tantum quantum nobis concessa est et de his peccatis [quæ] mihi confessus es, absolutus sis per misericordiam Dei, ut diabolus tibi nec nocere nec te dampnare possit."—Ibid. p. 37.

When dealing with clerical penitents there would seem to be no such claim made. The absolutory formula is purely deprecatory, calling upon all the archangels and angels, the patriarchs, prophets, apostles, martyrs, confessors and virgins to intercede for the sinner.—Ibid. p. 24.

Muratori prints (Antiq. Ital. Diss. LXVIII. T. XIV. p. 61) a curious formula which assumes a quasi-prophetic power operative at future death. It also shows the use of "mystery" for sacrament and the confused idea of the period, vacillating between absolution and reconciliation, and including both for greater certainty—"Tu qui es nostri mysterii vinculo alligatus, si forte tibi

At what period these transitional formulas came into use it would be impossible now to determine with accuracy. About 1020, Bishop Burchard in his *Decretum*, which long continued authoritative, knows only the strictly deprecatory form.[1] The change probably commenced during the eleventh century and continued through the twelfth, growing step by step more decided, as the schoolmen worked out their theories of sacerdotalism and the priesthood reduced them to practice. It was long, however, before anything more than this tentative form was ventured upon. A formula for the reconciliation of public penitents, used in the church of Reims in the early thirteenth century, only represents the bishop as acceding as far as he can in the pardon granted by God, and calls for the intercession of the Virgin Mary and the saints.[2] Another of about 1250 is even less assertive,

---

contigerit, me absente, in aqua seu in itinere vel in quocumque loco ut ab hoc sæculo migrare cogeris, quantum nostræ est potestati absolutus et reconciliatus sis a nobis et a Domino Deo ejusdemque misericordiæ commendatus."

[1] There is a transitional formula in Regino, de Discipl. Eccles. Lib. I. cap. 295, but it is recognized as an interpolation.

In the formula given by Burchard (Decr. Lib. XIX. cap. 7) the priest, after reciting Psalms 102, 50, 53 and 51, addresses a long prayer to God—" ut famulo tuo N. peccata et facinora sui confitenti, debita relaxare et veniam præstare digneris et præteritorum criminum culpas indulgeas," and finally he dismisses the penitent with the adjuration " Deus omnipotens sit adjutor et protector tuus et præstet indulgentiam de peccatis tuis præteritis, præsentibus et futuris. Amen." The whole rite is purely deprecatory.

Not long after this, in 1032, we have a very curious transitional formula, which illustrates the vague and confused conceptions as yet current on the subject. The Archbishop of Bourges, in proclaiming peace and insisting on its observance, said " Hæc qui observaverit, tanquam filio pacis immo Dei, a Domino nostro Jesu Christo et sanctis apostolis ejus, absolutionem conferimus peccatorum et benedictionem æternam : ut sicut Dominus beato Petro et huic beato Martiali, ad cujus sanctissimum corpus assistimus, ceterisque apostolis, virtutem atque potestatem ligandi atque solvendi tribuere dignatus est; ita a peccatorum nexibus absolvere dignetur eos qui de pace et justitia Deo et nobis qui ejus vice licet indigni fungimur, obedire festinaverint."—C. Lemovicens. ann. 1032, Sess. I. (Harduin. VI. I. 874).

If this is an absolution it is conditioned on future action, and therefore, as we shall see, is invalid, according to the received doctrine of the Church.

[2] "Omnipotens Deus, qui beato Petro apostolo suo cæterisque discipulis suis suam licentiam dedit ligandi atque solvendi, ipse vos absolvat ab omni vinculo delictorum. Et quantum nostræ fragilitati permittitur sitis absoluti ante tribunal Domini nostri Jesu Christi, habeatisque vitam æternam et vivatis in

as it only introduces the bishop as one through whose ministry God pardons the penitents.[1] Still another manifests the prevailing confusion of thought, since it represents the bishop as absolving in order that God may remit the sins of the penitents, both past and future.[2] Many of the *Ordines* of the period, moreover, contain a number of formulas, some deprecatory and some transitional, showing that it was left to the choice of the bishop or priest which of them he should select, and that all were held to be equally effective. In fact, as the prevailing theory during the thirteenth century was that the priest only made manifest the absolution by God (p. 146), the exact phraseology in which he might do this was evidently of minor importance.

It is to this that we may probably attribute the introduction, about the year 1240, of what is known as the "indicative" formula—the interpolation of the phrase *Ego te absolvo*, "I absolve thee" among the intercessory prayers with which it forms so strange and incongruous a contrast.[3] However little real importance this might have at the time, under the current theories of the function of the priest in absolution, it could scarce fail to excite animadversion and opposition as an assumption of power for which the Church was not as yet prepared. But a few years earlier William of Paris, one of the fore-

---

sæculo sæculorum, intercedente beata Dei genitrice Maria cum omnibus sanctis."—Morin. de Pœnit. App. p. 48.

[1] "Ipse vos absolvat per ministerium nostrum ab omnibus peccatis vestris . . . atque a vinculis peccatorum vestrorum absolutos perducere dignetur ad regnum cœlorum. Amen. Absolutionem et remissionem omnium peccatorum vestrorum percipere mereamini hic et in ævum."—Ibid. p. 71.

[2] Procedente pietate divina, ad quem propria remissio pertinet peccatorum, vos fratres invocato nomine Domini nostri Jesu Christi absolvimus ut dimittat vobis Dominus omnia peccata vostra, tam præterita quam futura.—Martene de antiq. Ecclesiæ Ritibus Lib. I. cap. vi. Art. 7, Ordo 14.

It will be observed that in this, as in two of those previously cited, there is an attempted remission of future sins.

[3] The date of 1240 may be assumed as a probable approximation, as the indicative formula begins to make its appearance soon afterwards. Aquinas in a tract (Opusc. XXII. cap. 5), which we may suppose to be written about 1270, represents his disputant as asserting that thirty years before the deprecatory formula alone was known; this Aquinas does not deny except by citing the text of Matthew as a proof of greater antiquity.

In 1247 we have an example of the new formula, somewhat diluted by the invocation of Christ and St. Peter—"Ego absolvo te auctoritate Domini Dei nostri Jesu Christi et beati Petri apostoli et officii nostri."—Joann. de Deo Pœnitentiale, Lib. I. cap. 2.

most theologians of the day, had chanced to use as an illustration the fact that the priest does not, like a secular judge, absolve or condemn, but only prays to God to grant absolution, thus showing that the indicative formula was wholly unknown to him.[1] It therefore came as a surprise, and the conservative view found expression in a remonstrance addressed to the Archbishop of Cologne by a learned layman of Spires, in which he argued that no man can say to another " ' I remit thy sins to thee :' even Christ did not say this but ' Thy sins be forgiven thee.' No one should even say ' May God pardon thy sins and I pardon them ' unless for offences committed against himself."[2] The earliest defence of the new formula that has reached us is that of Alexander Hales, in 1245. He speaks of it as received in use, and proceeds to prove that it is properly added to the deprecatory prayers of the absolution by arguing that the prayers obtain grace for the penitent, and the absolution only assumes that the grace is bestowed, for no priest would absolve any one whom he did not believe to be absolved by God[3]—thus apologizing for it and assuming

---

[1] Guillel. Parisiens. de Sacram. Pœnit. cap. 19. " Neque more judicum forinsecorum pronuntiat confessor Absolvimus te, non condemnamus, sed magis orationem facit super eum ut Deus absolutionem et remissionem atque gratiam sanctificationis tribuat," and he adds " Unde in absolutione confitentium non consueverunt dicere sacerdotes : dimittat tibi Deus peccata quæ confessus es mihi, sed potius omnia."

Yet with an inconsistency which shows how vague were the ideas of this period of development, he attributes to the deprecatory formula the powers of the indicative, even to the infusion of grace and release from hell and purgatory ; it is the sacrament that effects it all (Ibid. cap. 21).

[2] Martene Ampl. Collect. I. 357. The remonstrance is addressed to H., Archbishop of Cologne, whom Dom Martène suggests may be Heribert, archbishop from 999 to 1021. This is evidently impossible, for no indicative formula had been imagined at that period. A more probable recipient was Heinrich von Molenarken, archbishop from 1225 to 1238.

[3] Alex. de Ales Summæ P. IV. Q. XXI. Membr. 1. Cf. Membr. 2, Art. 1.

Modern apologists, of course, find the change from deprecatory to indicative absolution difficult to reconcile with the inherent power to bind and to loose transmitted through the apostles. Binterim (Denkwürdigkeiten, V. III. 231–7), after invoking a distinction between public and private penance, and disputing the conclusions of Fathers Morin and Martène, that originally the bishop and priest were mere intercessors, endeavors to prove that the deprecatory and indicative forms are virtually the same. " Das Gebet der Kirche um der Sündervergebung ist zugleich der Ausspruch das einer der Sündervergebung würdig ist." However this may have been in the middle of the thirteenth

that in reality it meant nothing more than the current doctrine that the priest only made manifest the pardon by God.

Discussion continued, and the matter naturally came before the University of Paris, which debated the question, probably at some time between 1250 and 1260. As the champion of sacerdotalism it could only reach one conclusion, and it pronounced in favor of the *Ego te absolvo*, without which the mere deprecatory absolution was invalid.[1] The objectors were not silenced; some doctor, whose name has not reached us, wrote a tract in defence of the time-honored form which attracted so much attention that the Dominican General summoned the great disputant of his Order, St. Thomas Aquinas, to refute it. This, of course, was an easy task for the dialectics of the Angelic Doctor. The grant of the power of the keys was absolute, and must be so expressed; the older authorities alleged in favor of the deprecatory formula were brushed aside as incompetent to decide so great a question: if the Master of Sentences did not adopt the indicative form, he at all events did not express an objection to it—which he could scarce have done, seeing that he had never heard of it; the incongruous retention of the preliminary prayer for forgiveness is explained by its being intended to obtain for the penitent fitness to receive the sacrament, though it expresses nothing of the kind.[2] In his latest work Aquinas discusses the question elaborately and replies to all the arguments which continued to be brought against the innovation, but in the end he admits that a qualificatory explanation would be desirable, and that a more perfect form would be "I absolve thee, that is, I grant thee the sacrament of absolution"[3] —a concession which shows how indefinite as yet were the conceptions of the theologians.

In spite of the University of Paris and the Angelic Doctor, the use of the indicative formula spread but slowly. The uncertainty of the period is visible in the authoritative work of Cardinal Henry of Susa, who in one place gives a qualified indicative, and in another a transitional form, while purely deprecative ones continued to be used.[4] Ap-

---

century, it assumed a very different complexion when the absolution subsequently was held to confer pardon.

[1] S. Th. Aquin. Opusc. XXII. cap. 2.   [2] Ibidem.

[3] "Ego te absolvo, *i. e.* sacramentum absolutionis tibi impendo."—S. Th. Aquin. Summæ P. III. Q. lxxxiv. Art. 3.

[4] Hostiens. Aureæ Summæ Lib v. De Pœn. et Remiss. §§ 45, 60.—Martene de Antiq. Eccles. Ritibus Lib. I. cap. vi. Art. 7, Ord. 15, 17.

parently the Holy See lent its influence in favor of the innovation, for, at the council of London, in 1268, held by the Cardinal legate Otto-boni, a canon was adopted specially ordering all confessors to employ it.[1] Towards the end of the century John of Freiburg discusses the question in a manner to show that it was as yet by no means settled. He quotes Albertus Magnus, Aquinas, and John of Varzy—all Dominicans—in favor of the indicative form, but adds that, as the priest does not absolve by his own authority, but only ministerially, it is well to append some phrase such as "In the name of the Father, Son and Holy Ghost," or "By the virtue of the Passion of Christ," or "By the authority of God"[2]—all qualifications which show that the absolute assumption of power was still repugnant to many pious souls. The Franciscans were not as prompt as the Dominicans to approve the change. St. Bonaventura accepts the indicative formula, but explains that the initial prayer obtains grace, and when God has pardoned the *culpa* the words *Ego te absolvo* obtain remission of part of the purgatorial *pœna*, and enable the priest to commute the rest into appropriate penance, thus reducing the formula to a wholly subordinate position.[3] Duns Scotus treats the phraseology as a matter of indifference; the words *Ego te absolvo* answer well enough, and in the rest of the formula each church can follow its own custom.[4] Astesanus, in 1317, argues that the indicative form is requisite to distinguish sacramental absolution from the general absolution in the mass, which is deprecatory and not sacramental.[5] William of Ware soon afterwards adopts the somewhat grudging admission of Duns Scotus, and adds that the words "In the name of the Father etc." should follow in order to show that the priest acts as a commis-sioner and not as a principal.[6] Even the Dominican, Durand de S. Pourçain, considers the plain *Ego te absolvo* too absolute, when the real agent is God, and urges some clause recognizing God in the matter.[7]

If there was hesitation in the schools to accept the naked *Ego te*

[1] C. Londiniens. ann. 1268, cap. 2 (Harduin. VII. 617).

[2] Joh. Friburgens. Summæ Confessor. Lib. III. Tit. xxxiv. Q. 89.

[3] S. Bonavent. in IV. Sentt. Dist. XVIII. P. 1, Art. 2, Q. 1, 2.

[4] Jo. Scoti in IV. Sentt. Dist. XIV. Q. iv.

[5] Astesani Summæ Lib. V. Tit. ii. Art. 2.

[6] Guiller. Vorrillong in IV. Sentt. Dist. XIV.

[7] Durand. de S. Porciano in IV. Sentt. Dist. XXII. Q. ii. § 6.

absolvo, there was equal uncertainty among the churches. In 1284 the council of Nîmes prescribes a formula of a diluted character.[1] Early in the fourteenth century some churches of Provence still used the form " May God the Father, God the Son and God the Holy Ghost absolve thee ! "[2] About 1325 William, Bishop of Cahors, employs a formula somewhat hesitating in character, and, about 1350, Pierre, Bishop of Senlis, prescribes one which is deprecatory.[3] The form current in England in the fifteenth century shows that it was still held to be proper to disclaim inherent personal power,[4] and Thomas of Walden is indignant at the audacity of those who added " and I restore thee to baptismal innocence."[5] John Gerson, about the same time, requires the addition of " In the name of the Father etc."[6] By this time the phrase *Ego te absolvo* had come into general use, though the sentences with which it was linked varied with the customs of the local churches, and the council of Florence, in 1439, impliedly declared it to be the essential part of the absolution formula when it defined it to be the " form " of the sacrament of penitence.[7]

Even this did not wholly settle the question. Dr. Weigel, who, it is true, was an adherent of the council of Basle, accepts it, with the explanation that it only means that the priest acts as the minister of God in absolving what God had already absolved, and in reconciling the penitent to the Church,[8] and Robert, Bishop of Aquino, who died in 1475, gives us a very curious formula, which shows that the transitional forms still lingered in use.[9] In the schools

---

[1] Synod. Nemausens. ann. 1284 (Harduin. VII. 911).

[2] Fr. de Mairone in IV. Sentt. Dist. xiv. Q. 1.

[3] Epist. Synod. Guill. Episc. Cadurcens. cap. 14 (Martene Thesaur. IV. 694). —Martene de antiq. Eccles. Ritibus Lib. iv. cap. xxii. Ordo 4.

[4] Ego auctoritate Dei patris omnipotentis et beatorum apostolorum Petri et Pauli et officii michi commissi in hac parte, absolvo te ab hiis peccatis michi per te confessis et ab aliis de quibus non recordaris. In nomine Patris etc. Amen.—John Myrc's Instructions to Parish Priests, v. 1801.

[5] Thomæ de Walden de Sacramentis cap. CLVII. § 6.

[6] Jo. Gersonis Opusc. Tripart. P. II. *ad calcem.*

[7] C. Florent. ann. 1439, Decr. Union. (Harduin. IX. 440)—" Forma hujus sacramenti sunt verba absolutionis quæ sacerdos profert cum dicit *Ego te absolvo* etc."

[8] Weigel Claviculæ Indulgentialis cap. 9.

[9] Rob. Episc. Aquinat. Opus Quadragesimale, Serm. xxix. cap. 1.—The priest informs the penitent that his sins deserve so much penance—" Sed forte vita tua ad hoc agendum tantum non extenderetur. Injungo tamen tibi

however it was universally admitted that the one essential and indispensable clause was the *Ego te absolvo,* however the Thomists and
Scotists might debate as to the value of additional and supplementary
sentences.[1] It was inevitable that the council of Trent, when it came
to define the doctrines of the Church against heretic assault, should
accept this position. Its theologians had been trained in this belief,
and for two centuries and a half the tradition had been almost uniform. It did not pause to look further back or to realize that it was
proclaiming as orthodoxy what St. Augustin had stigmatized as a
Donatist heresy, but it accepted the custom, and in serene uncon-
sciousness it declared that the words *Ego te absolvo* are the sole
essential part of the formula from which its power is derived, and
that the adjuncts, while laudable, are superfluous.[2] As thus without
these words the absolution is null, the council unknowingly proclaimed to the world that, prior to the middle of the thirteenth century, an infallible Church had never administered to its children a
valid absolution, although such absolution is indispensable to their
salvation.

The Tridentine decree was final, and wherever the older formulas
may have remained in use they were speedily rooted out.[3] Yet, in
1584, Bishop Angles, after reciting the various opinions on the sub-

---

talem pœnitentiam pro omnibus, et eleemosynas quibus peccata redimentur, et
omnia alia bona quæ feceris et mala quæ pro Christo sustinueris accepta loco
pœnitentiæ et quod prosint tibi in remissionem peccatorum tuorum. Et si
interim moriaris, auctoritate Dei et beatorum apostolorum Petri et Pauli et
sanctæ ecclesiæ et nostratæ, absolvimus ab omnibus his quæ confessus es et
ab aliis de quibus non recordaris in quantum possumus et debemus. Et si
quidquid purgandum remanserit in purgatorio purgetur juxta misericordem
Dei voluntatem."

[1] Summa Angelica s. v. *Confessio* v.—Summa Rosella s. v. *Absolutio* v.—Gab.
Biel in IV. Sentt. Dist. xiv. Q. ii. Art. 1, not. 1.—Bart. de Chaimis Interrog.
fol. 107-8.—Savonarolæ Confessionale fol. 65*b*.—Summa Sylvestrina s. v. *Absolutio* vi. § 2.—Summa Tabiena s. v. *Absolutio* i. n. 4.

[2] C. Trident. Sess. xiv. De Pœnit. cap. 3.—" Docet præterea sancta synodus
sacramenti pœnitentiæ formam, in quâ præcipue ipsius vis sita est, in illis
ministri verbis positam esse: *Ego te absolvo, etc.*, quibus quidem de ecclesiæ
sanctæ more preces quædam laudabiliter adjunguntur; ad ipsius tamen formæ
essentiam nequaquam spectant; neque ad ipsius sacramenti administrationem
sunt necessariæ."—Cf. Catechis Trident. De Pœnitentia cap. 3.

[3] C. Leovardiens. ann. 1570, cap. 6; C. Wratislaviens. ann. 1592, cap. 8; C.
Cameracens. ann. 1604, cap. 18 (Hartzheim VII. 317; VIII. 392, 595).

ject, concludes that the priest as judge is at liberty to formulate the sentence as he pleases, provided only that it is an authoritative remission [1] A curious episode not long afterwards, however, suggests a conjecture as to the real importance attached to this point by the Holy See. It had under its direction in southern Italy a hundred or more parishes of Greek Catholics, who were allowed to employ their own rites, among which was a purely deprecatory form of absolution. In 1595, Clement VIII. permitted, in case of necessity, these Greek priests to administer absolution to Latins, but required that they should use the formula prescribed by the council of Florence, to which they might, if they chose, append their own, and it seems to have escaped his attention that he was assuming the slightly absurd position that a Greek could be saved by a deprecatory absolution while for a Latin an indicative one is necessary.[2]

Hitherto the local churches had maintained to a great degree their independence as to ritual, but the council of Trent had profoundly altered the situation. It had established more firmly than ever the supremacy of the Holy See, it had embodied the speculations of the schoolmen as points of faith and it had enabled the Latin Church to organize itself as a compact theocracy to resist the alarming progress of heresy. To take full advantage of this it seemed advisable to introduce uniformity of observance everywhere. In furtherance of this St. Pius V. promulgated a Missal, Clement VIII. a Pontifical and Ceremonial, and, in 1614, Paul V. issued a ritual which he rendered obligatory throughout the Roman obedience. In this was comprised a formula for absolution, containing the indispensable clause "I absolve thee" with various strangely incongruous prayers and adjurations, survivals of the old deprecatory formulas, and this

---

[1] Angles Flores Theol. Quæstionum, P. I. fol. 99b (Venet. 1584). For subsequent slightly varying formulas see C. Aquens. ann. 1585 *De Pœnitentia,* and C. Narbonn. ann. 1609, cap. 16 (Harduin. X. 1532; XI. 17).

[2] Clement. PP. VIII. Decr. 31, Aug. 1595, § 3 (Bullar. III. 52).

Morin (De Pœnit. Lib. VIII. cap. xii. n. 7) tells us that in Rome he asked the learned Chian Ligarinus, who was principal of the Greek college, maintained at papal expense, what was their customary formula of absolution, when he wrote out in Greek a sentence which Morin translates "Ipse Domine remitte, dimitte, condona peccata hujus N. quia tua est potentia et tuum regnum, Patris etc.

has since then remained in force.[1]　A considerable period was required to establish the desired uniformity everywhere, but it was

---

[1] "Misereatur tui omnipotens Deus, et dimissis peccatis tuis, perducat te ad vitam æternam. Amen.

"Indulgentiam, absolutionem et remissionem peccatorum tuorum tribuat tibi omnipotens et misericors Dominus. Amen.

"Dominus noster Jesus Christus te absolvat: et ego auctoritate ipsius te absolvo ab omni vinculo excommunicationis, suspensionis et interdicti in quantum possum et tu indiges. Deinde ego te absolvo a peccatis tuis in nomine Patris et Filii et Spiritus Sancti. Amen.

"Passio Domini nostri Jesu Christi, merita beatæ Maria Virginis et omnium sanctorum, quidquid boni feceris et mali sustinueris sint tibi in remissionem peccatorum, augmentum gratiæ et premium vitæ æternæ. Amen."—Rituale Romanum, Tit. III. cap. 2.

In this the only necessary words are *absolvo te,* though it is better to add *a peccatis tuis,* and this suffices in cases of urgency. Other forms are valid but illicit, because not in accordance with the prescriptions of the Church. Such are *Ego tibi remitto vel condono peccata tua; Solvo te a peccatis tuis; Jubeo volo te absolutum a peccatis tuis,* etc.—Ferraris Prompta Biblioth. s. v. *Absolvere* III. n. 1–9. Cf. Em. Sa Aphorismi Confessar. s. v. *Absolutio* n. 1; Summa Diana s. v. *Absolutio* n. 1.

While the omission of the invocation of the Trinity does not invalidate the absolution, some doctors hold that to omit it is a mortal sin, while others regard it as only venial.—Mig. Sanchez, Prontuario de la Teologia Moral. Tract. VI. Punto vii. n. 2.

Absolution from excommunication is foreign to our subject, but its occurrence in the above formula suggests the remark that it has formed by no means the least perplexing duties of the confessor. In the middle ages excommunications *latæ sententiæ* and *ipso facto* became so multiplied, and so intricate in consequence of their being reserved to bishop or pope, that no man could know whether he was under excommunication or not and no confessor whether he had power to absolve. In 1418, Martin V. described the situation "et sint multiplices et inexplicabiles sententiæ excommunicationis in Corpore Juris quarum nonnullæ etiam a peritissimis ignorantur," wherefore he makes provision for the absolution and dispensation of priests who have ignorantly granted absolution without authority (Pittoni Constitutiones Pontificiæ T. VII. n. 47). The question whether, under these circumstances, the penitent is absolved is a knotty one on which the doctors were not in accord (Jo. Friburg. Summæ Confessor. Lib. III. Tit. xxxiv. Q. 75). There was the same doubt and difficulty when the penitent was unaware that he was under excommunication (Summa Angelica s. v. *Confessio* I. § 20; Bart. de Chaimis Interrog. fol. 14–15). In modern practice the doctrine of invincible ignorance renders absolution in such cases valid, even though the excommunication is not removed (Bened. PP. XIV. Casus Conscient. Feb. 1736, cas. iii.).

When in hasty absolutions the clause *ab omni vinculo excommunicationis,* etc.,

ultimately accomplished. In 1703, the synod of Albania ordered all the priests of the province to learn the Roman formula within two months under pain of deprivation of functions.[1]

The final clause "Whatever of good thou mayest do and of evil thou mayest endure be to thee in remission of sins, in increase of grace, and reward of eternal life" was no novelty. Already in the thirteenth century the doctors instructed the confessors that it was highly beneficial to the penitent to impose on him as penance whatever good works he might do and tribulations he might suffer. Sacerdotalism grasped so eagerly at control of every action of life that the schoolmen argued that good works performed by command of the confessor acquire a double value through the power of the keys and that by the simple utterance of this formula the penitent's charities, piety and misfortunes, past as well as future, would be reckoned for him as penance performed in satisfaction of his sins: apparently man throughout life was never to be allowed to deal directly with his God. Thus, although this clause was not indispensable, it was highly beneficial to the penitent, and the confessor was advised never to omit it. It thus became a recognized portion of the formula, and it served, according to some authorities, to justify the imposition of trifling penance for the gravest sins.[2] Yet in this, as in almost everything else, the doctors are at odds, for some argue that as the clause is merely deprecatory it has no effect in elevating the good works of the penitent to sacramental efficacy.[3]

---

is omitted the question is a nice one whether absolution from censures is conferred. Tamburini (Method. Confess. Lib. II. cap. x. n. 57) argues in the affirmative because absolution from sin involves release from all the bonds imposed by it, though this reasoning would prove the clause to be useless.

[1] Synod. Albana, ann. 1703, P. II. cap. 4. (Coll. Lacens. I. 302).

[2] Hostiens. Aureæ Summæ Lib. v. De Pœn. et Remiss. §§ 51, 60.—Jo. Friburgens Summæ Confessor. Lib. III. Tit. xxxiii. Q. 108–10.—Astesani Summæ Lib. v. Tit. xxxi. Q. 2.—S. Antonini Summæ P. III. Tit. xvii. cap. 21, § 1;|Ejusd. Confessionale, fol. 69*a*, 71*b*.—Summa Angelica s. v. *Confessio* VI. § 4.—Savonarolæ Confessionale, fol. 65*b*.—Summa Sylvestrina s. v. *Confessor* IV. § 2.—Zerola Praxis Sacr. Pœnit. cap. xxiv. Q. 10, 12.—Summa Diana s. v. *Absolutio* n. 2.

It is possibly because it seems to invalidate somewhat the importance of this clause in the formula that Clement XI. (Bull. *Unigenitus* Prop. 70) condemned as a Jansenist error the proposition that temporal afflictions always serve either to punish sin or to purify the sinner.

[3] S. Alph. de Ligorio Theol. Moral. Lib. VI. n. 507.

Of course, the decision at Trent, confirming that at Florence, was accepted unconditionally by the theologians, and it was not difficult to prove that the deprecatory portions of the formula have no absolutory power whatever, because, as Willem van Est says, it would be absurd to repeat the form of the sacrament in the words "I absolve thee" if it had already been uttered in different phrase.[1] Juan Sanchez is even more emphatic: the absolution is effected by the priest, not by Christ, even as in the mass it is the priest, not Christ, that consecrates, and hence it is useless to represent the priest as praying —an argument which sufficiently illustrates the complete revolution effected by the sacramental theory in the doctrine of the forgiveness of sin.[2] Hardly, however, had this been satisfactorily established, when the labors, among the ancient records, of scholars of undoubted orthodoxy, brought to light the forgotten rituals and furnished incontrovertible evidence that the indicative clause was a late interpolation. It was a cruel dilemma. Father Morin placed the matter in a shape which admitted of no dispute, but he treated the subject historically, not theologically, and while he showed how and when the change came about he did not venture to speculate how the old doctrine was to be reconciled with the new.[3] Father Juenin could not escape so easily. He admitted the fact that anciently all absolutions were deprecatory and that the council of Trent had made it *de fide* that they must be indicative; to explain this he can only argue that the Church can define the conditions requisite to the validity of its sacraments; it is a judicial proceeding and courts can frame new rules to supersede the old[4]—discreetly forgetful that it is a matter of faith, not of discipline; that man is here dealing not with man but with God, and was just as certain in 1230 that he was following the divine law as he was in 1300 when he had changed that law, not through a revelation but through the dialectics of a few schoolmen. Father Tournely admits the change, and in disregard of the Tridentine decree, asserts that it makes no difference for the Greeks absolve validly with a deprecatory formula.[5] Liguori is more prudent in calmly remarking that some doctors assert that the ancient form was deprecatory, but

[1] Estius in IV Sentt. Dist. XV. § 3.
[2] Jo. Sanchez Selecta de Sacramentis, Disp. VI. n. 13.
[3] Morin. de Pœnit. Lib. VIII. cap. 8-12.
[4] Juenin de Sacramentis Diss. VI. Q. vii. cap. 1, Art. 1; cap. 2, Art. 2, § 2.
[5] Tournely de Pœnit. Q. VI. Art. ii.

there are some who deny it; it is "common" among theologians that the deprecatory form is invalid, and there can be no doubt that the council of Trent has rendered the use of the indicative *de fide.*[1] Palmieri is bolder; he assumes that the old deprecatory form was used in public penance, which he says was not sacramental, and there may have been another form in private penance—though how it should have left no trace he does not explain : besides, he argues with Tournely, that there is no essential difference between the two forms, and that the deprecatory suffices, and in this he does not hesitate to take issue with Liguori, though he abstains from a positive affirmation.[2] When St. Alphonso Liguori asserts a matter to be *de fide* on the unquestioned authority of Trent, and a theological teacher in Rome calls it into question, what certainty can the faithful feel in any dogma?

I have dwelt thus in detail on these questions because they shed much light on the evolution of the priestly power to remit sins on which the spiritual authority of the Church is so largely based, and a brief recapitulation of the process may not be amiss. The primitive reconciliation to the Church was accompanied by the prayers of priest and people, through which it was hoped that the penitent would likewise enjoy reconciliation with God. The bishop alone had the power of reconciliation, and he alone in ordination received the Holy Ghost with the grant of the keys, such as it was. The constant reiteration of the command that the priest should not admit

---

[1] S. Alph. de Ligorio Theol. Moral. Lib. vi. n. 430.

A recent Spanish theologian quotes Liguori as saying that the existence of ancient deprecatory formulas is almost universally (*communissime*) denied, and Concina to the effect that the evidence is inconclusive, and there he leaves it. —Mig. Sanchez Prontuario de la Teología Moral, Trat. vi. Punto vii. n. 9.

Father de Charmes furnishes the most characteristic specimen of theological imperviousness. He does not blush to say (Theol. Univ. Diss. v. cap. ii. Q. 2, Art. 2) "Forma sacramentalis absolutionis ex institutione Christi debet esse indicativa; ita nec unquam fuerit nec possit esse deprecativa," and he dismisses all the evidence of the Penitentials and *Ordines* "Tum quia nullius est momenti illa probatio negativa contra expressa clavium concessione a Christo facto ecclesiæ."

[2] Palmieri Tract. de Pœnit. pp. 127–41. "Nos rem in medio relinquimus, quamvis, ut quod est fateamur, verisimilior nobis appareat sententia affirmans sufficientiam per se formæ deprecativæ."

to reconciliation without the authority of the bishop shows that the priests were constantly infringing on the episcopal prerogatives, which the bishops were as jealously maintaining. With the rise of the system of the Penitentials in the extensive dioceses of the missionary lands, the bishops were content to allow their priests to pray over their penitents, a ceremony in which they recognized no exercise of the power to bind and to loose, for, as we have seen, in the synod of Pavia, in 850, they expressly declared that this power was exclusively episcopal and was not shared by the priests except when specially delegated, for the bishops alone were the representatives of the apostles. In this way the so-called absolution of the Penitentials established itself, comforting to the penitent without any definite determination of its value as an intercession with God. With the growth of belief in the power of the keys, both priest and penitent cheerfully united in ascribing increased importance to this deprecatory ceremony, as advantageous to both, and, as reconciliation to the Church gradually was assumed to be reconciliation to God, so the formula of the priest was held to infer that the pardon prayed for was granted. When the power of the keys was finally established, when auricular confession was elevated into a sacrament, and when the Holy Ghost and the power to bind and to loose were conferred on the priest in ordination, there could no longer be any distinction between reconciliation and absolution; both were equally sacramental, and both secured pardon for the sinner who threw no obstacles in the way. Reconciliation thus became absolution, and, as it was the recognized function of the priest to administer the sacraments, this one could not be withheld from him. Yet in making this concession to the priest the bishop retained control; though in theory the power of the keys was granted by God, in practice it was merely a delegated power, for it could only be exercised by episcopal consent, and under the name of reserved cases the bishop retained exclusive jurisdiction over such sins as he saw fit. Thus, towards the end of the twelfth century, Peter of Poitiers tells us that, although the power of binding and loosing is incident to ordination and is possessed by every priest, it is only potential and not active unless he has a cure of souls or a delegation from the bishop.[1] For awhile

---

[1] P. Pictaviens. Sentt. Lib. III. cap. 16.

The forged decretal of Evaristus, already quoted, shows that the reconciliation for secret sins by priests was recognized as a delegated power—"Ut pres-

the deprecatory formula of reconciliation and absolution continued to satisfy the conscience, but, as the value ascribed to the ceremony was enhanced by scholastic dialectics, it gradually assumed more and more an indicative form, until at last the "I absolve thee" was boldly injected in it. That the priestly class should welcome this recognition of their authority was natural; that penitents, when once they had heard of it, should demand it for the repose of their consciences was inevitable; the opposition excited by the innovation was gradually silenced, and finally the council of Trent placed the stigma of nullity on what had been the universal practice of the Church up to the middle of the thirteenth century.

No sooner had the fact of sacramental absolution been established to the satisfaction of the schoolmen than debates arose as to its nature, extent, and mode of operation. The more important of these questions have been referred to in Chapter VII., but there are a few more which merit brief notice.

The validity of priestly ministrations in sinful hands was a subject which had long exercised the Church : it had caused the persistent and dangerous heresy of the Donatists, and, at the period when the scholastic theology was assuming shape, the Waldenses revived the theory that a wicked priest could not administer valid sacraments. Hugh of St. Victor, in a passage quoted above (p. 472) had been disposed to concede that the virtue of the absolution was dependent upon the capacity of the minister, but the complaints of Peter Lombard and Alain de Lille of the ignorance and vice of a large portion of the sacerdotal body show how fatal to the sacramental theory would have been such an admission, and it was accepted in the schools that a bad priest in virtue of his office could grant absolution as valid as a good one; like the consecration of the Host, the sacrament of penitence is effected *ex opere operato* and not *ex opere operantis*.[1] Whether this applies to a heretic priest administering absolution *in articulo mortis* to a true believer, is, however, a question which the Church has never been able to determine positively.

---

byteri de occultis peccatis jussione episcopi pœnitentes reconcilient."—Ps. Evaristi cap. iii. (Burchard. Lib. xviii. cap. 16; Ivon. Decr. xv. 38; Cap. 4 Caus. xxvi. Q. vi.).

[1] Hostiens Aureæ Summæ Lib. v. De Remiss. ℥ 3.—Estius in IV. Sentt. Dist. xv. ℥ 2.

In the cognate case of baptism, where also the salvation of a human soul is at stake, any one, heretic or pagan, male or female, can administer a valid sacrament, but Aquinas declares that this applies to no other.[1] St. Antonino affirms that heretic absolution is good if the penitent is ignorant of the heresy or is firm in the faith and is pressed by necessity.[2] The council of Trent says that for the dying there is no reservation of cases and that all priests can absolve all sinners,[3] and though the good fathers were probably thinking of papal and episcopal cases, the incautious phrase has been used to support the validity of heretic absolution, while to render the confusion worse a private decision of the council is cited in support of the negative, and one of Innocent XI. in that of the affirmative. Liguori tells us that prior to the council the common opinion was adverse, but since then it has been in favor of the validity of such absolution.[4]

It was an old rule that reconciliation should never be refused to the dying who sought for it,[5] and when reconciliation became absolution the same charitable custom gradually established itself, and was finally recognized as a universal rule expressed in the above utterance of the council of Trent. If the dying man has asked for a confessor, or has shown signs of contrition, and is speechless on the arrival of the priest, he is still to be absolved conditionally without confession ; even in the absence of such indications, if he has been regular in religious observances, the same holds good, in the opinion of the majority of doctors, although there are great names ranged in the negative. It is related of Clement VIII. that, when he chanced to see a workman, employed on St. Peter's, fall from a great height, he exclaimed, with rare presence of mind, while the poor wretch was still in the air, " If thou art capable, I absolve thee from thy sins."[6] There are, however, multitudes of cases, as in battle and ship-

---

[1] S. Th. Aquin. Summæ P. III, Q. lxxxii. Art. 7 ad 2.

[2] S. Antonini Summæ P. III. Tit. xiv. cap. 19 § 16.

[3] C. Trident. Sess. XIV. De Pœnit. cap. 7.

[4] S. Alph. de Ligorio Theol. Moral. Lib. VI. n. 560.—Ferraris Prompta Biblioth. s. v. *Moribundus* n. 32–35.

[5] Innoc. PP. I. Epist. vi. cap. 2.—Rodolphi Bituricens. Capit. cap. 44.

[6] Em. Sa Aphorismi Confessar. s. v. *Absolutio* n. 10.—Juenin de Sacramentis Diss. VI. Q. vii. Art. 4, § 3.—Ferraris Prompta Biblioth. s. v. *Moribundus* n. 3, 4.—S. Alph. de Ligorio Theol. Moral. Lib. VI. n. 482.

Yet the proposition that a man of Christian life, if bereft of his senses or of

wreck, when men die without the chance of ghostly consolation. The Church boasts that it never requires the impossible of its children, and however much it may invalidate the assumed necessity of the sacrament for salvation, it is conceded that in such case contrition embracing desire for the sacrament procures pardon.[1] What exact degree of contrition obtains remission under these circumstances it would not be easy to define, but a case on record would seem to indicate that a mere impulse suffices, for a knight slain in a tournament was buried in unconsecrated ground, under the papal bulls excommunicating all participants in such sports, but his friends appealed to the pope and proved that his right hand was raised to his face as though to make the sign of the cross; this was admitted as sufficient evidence of repentance, and the pontiff authorized his burial with the rites of the Church.[2] The grant of the plenary indulgence of the *Cruciata*, moreover, contained a clause that the absence of a confessor at death should not deprive the recipient of its benefit provided he was contrite and had duly confessed at the prescribed time.[3] When in cases of sudden death a confessor is sent for and arrives after life is extinct, he cannot absolve, for his jurisdiction is only over the living. There are some, indeed, who hold that the soul does not

---

speech, is to be absolved, when enunciated by the Jesuit Moya, was condemned as dangerous by the Sorbonne (D'Argentré, III. I. 113) and Pontas is even more decided in rejecting it (Dict. de Cas de Conscience s. v. *Absolution* cas. 4). The Jesuits ordered that it should not be taught in the schools, but their priests argued that prohibition of teaching did not infer prohibition of the practice (Gobat Alphab. Confessar. n. 602–5). For the conflicting opinions on the subject see La Croix Theol. Moral. Lib. VI. P. ii. n. 1140.

[1] Dom. Soto in IV. Sentt. Dist. XVIII. Q. iv. Art. 4.—Palmieri Tract. de Pœnit. p. 279.

[2] Döllinger, Beiträge zur Sektengeschichte des Mittelalters, II. 622.

Caramuel relates (Theol. Fundam. n. 1876) as an example to be followed that when Don Balthasar de Morradas lay insensible and dying in Prague, some priests, hastily summoned, dared not to absolve him. Then came a Jesuit P. N., of high repute for learning and piety, who turned out the others, and after an interval left the room saying "He exhibited sufficient signs of sorrow and I absolved him," though there had been no change in the condition in the moribund. As Caramuel remarks, thus Don Balthasar was saved and scandal was averted.

[3] Nogueira Exposit. Bullæ Cruciatæ, Coloniæ, 1744, p. 3.—In the modern bull of the Cruciata this privilege is not confined to the dying, but is enjoyed by the living if from any cause they are debarred from confession.—Pii PP. IX. Bull *Dum Infidelium*, 30 Apr. 1861, § 1.

leave the body until a certain time after apparent death, and that during this interval the priest should grant conditional absolution, but this belief is only of doubtful probability, and the practice is not to be recommended.[1]

In treating of the power of the keys we have seen the different theories successively current as to the value of the absolution conferred in the sacrament. In addition to these general views there necessarily arose questions affecting individual cases. As far as these originate in the penitent, they will be considered in the next chapter, but there are some which depend on the confessor, and may be briefly referred to here. The limitation of jurisdiction, as we have seen, introduces a multitude of uncertainties, for the sacrament is invalid if a priest absolves a penitent of a different diocese, or for a sin which his bishop has reserved, and, though modern liberality has somewhat diminished these difficulties, it is impossible for the unlearned penitent to be familiar with all details, and he is liable to be deceived into imagining himself absolved when he is not—a liability which we are told was formerly largely abused by designing priests for purposes of gain.[2] Another source of uncertainty lies in the confessor misunderstanding the penitent through deafness, inattention, abstraction or drowsiness, for the theory is that he must have a clear perception of all the sins confessed in order that his intention may be brought to bear upon them all, otherwise the absolution is invalid. This is a subject which has evoked considerable discussion and many conflicting opinions, as we have seen above (p. 165). Ignorance on the part of the confessor as to his duties is another source of doubt which has been alluded to above (p. 164). The theologians are never weary in expatiating on the immense and varied range of knowledge requisite to perform properly the duties of the confessional, but as this knowledge is mostly conspicuous by its absence, the question as to whether God will ratify the judgments of an ignorant priest is one on which the moralists have found it hard to agree, some holding that he will, others that he will not, and others again contenting themselves with saying that it is a dis-

---

[1] La Croix Theol. Moral. Lib. VI. P. ii. n. 1164.

[2] Astesani Summæ Lib. v. Tit. xxxviii. Q. 3.—Weigel Claviculæ Indulgentialis cap. 7.—Bart. de Chaimis Interrogatorium, fol. 13*b*, 92*a*.

puted question, with probabilities on both sides.[1] The matter, however, is one which affects so intimately the value of the whole system, that to render the validity of the sacrament dependent upon the learning or wisdom of the ministrant is to destroy all confidence in it, and, as we shall see hereafter, the tendency in modern times is to assure the penitent that the absolution is good, independent of the fitness of the confessor. It can readily thus be seen how manifold and intricate are the questions concerning the validity of absolution, turning in many cases upon delicate shades of feeling on the part of either penitent or confessor. The salvation of the former may depend upon his rightful appreciation of them and on his repeating, if necessary, his confession, but it is in many cases beyond his power even to know the facts, or, if he knows them, to understand their correct legal application.[2]

In addition to all this there comes the impenetrable question of the intention of the ministrant, which is indispensable to the validity of all sacraments. In the development of the sacramental theory this at first received no attention, but it gradually suggested itself as a sort of counterpoise to the doctrine of *ex opere operato*, to afford to the priest a share in the operation. Through the labors of the schoolmen it gradually assumed a more definite shape until Aquinas finally defined the sacraments to consist of matter, form, and the intention of the ministrant, of which the last is as indispensable as either of the others.[3] This definition was formally accepted by the Church in the council of Florence in 1439, and confirmed in that of Trent.[4] It is thus *de fide* that the intention of the confessor to do what the Church does is essential to the validity of the absolu-

---

[1] Astesani Summæ Lib. v. Tit. xxxviii. Q. 2.—Estius in IV. Sentt. Dist. xvii. ? 3.—Summa Diana s. v. *Confessarius* n. 25.—La Croix Theol. Moral. Lib. VI. P. ii. n. 1213.

[2] See Dom. Soto in IV. Sentt. Dist. XVIII. Q. ii. Art. 5; Q. iii. Art. 3.

[3] Alex. de Ales P. IV. Q. VIII. Membr. iii. Art. 1, ? 1.—S. Bonavent. in IV. Sentt. Dist. VI. P. ii. Art. 3, ? 1.—Hostiens. Aureæ Summæ Lib. III. De Baptismo ? 8.—S. Th. Aquin. in IV. Sentt. Dist. VI. Art. ii.; Opusc. V. De Artic. Fidei et Sacram.; Summæ P. III. Q. lxiv. Artt. 8, 10.—Durand. de S. Porciano in IV. Sentt. Dist. VI. Q. ii. ?? 8–10.

[4] C. Florent ann. 1439, Decr. Union. (Harduin. IX. 438).—C. Trident. Sess. VII. De Sacramentis in genere can. 11.

tion.[1] As usual, there has been dissent, and some theologians have maintained that the intention to perform the external ceremony suffices, but Alexander VIII. condemned this opinion in 1690.[2] This casts a doubt upon the validity of all absolutions, which the theologians admit, but which they are unable to rectify,[3] and, in reply to the argument that it is contrary to divine justice that penitent sinners or helpless infants should be damned through the malice of a priest, Ferraris can merely say that they are damned for their sin, actual or original: God has duly provided the means for their salvation, and is not bound, even if he could, to prevent the malice of his minister.[4]

It is evident from all this that there can be no assurance that the absolution granted in the confessional is of any value, even to a penitent properly disposed, but however freely this may be admitted among themselves by theologians, it is not allowed to affect the positive assurances which they give to the people that their sins are remitted by the sacrament. We have seen (p. 156) how absolute are the promises uttered by Cardinal Bellarmine and others, and the same assertions continue to be made in the popular manuals of instruction. In one widely circulated under the highest authority the penitent is told that the confessor will, "if he finds you properly disposed, give you in God's name absolution for your sins . . . and this absolution will be made good by God in heaven,"[5] and another

---

[1] Ferraris Prompta Biblioth. s. v. *Intentio* -- S. Alph. de Ligorio Theol. Moral. Lib. VI. n. 16, 17, 18, 25.

[2] Alex. PP. VIII. Constit. *Pro pastorali cura* Prop. 28 (Bullar. XII. 67).

This is one of the matters of which the discussion is prudently forbidden by Benedict XIV. *De Synodo Diocœsan.* Lib. VII. cap. iv. n. 9.

[3] Durand. de S. Porciano in IV. Sentt. Dist. XIX. Q. ii. § 7.—Dom. Soto in IV. Sentt. Dist. XVII. Q. ii. Art. 5.—Pallavacini Hist. Concil. Trident. IX. vi. 4-6.

[4] Ferraris Prompta Bibl. s. v. *Intentio* n. 30. For some of the intricate questions concerning the precise intention of the priest as he recites the successive clauses of the absolution, see Gobat, *Alphab. Confessarior.* n. 146-57. It is only a venial sin for the priest to utter the formula without thinking about it, provided he makes no mistakes. Ib. n. 177.

[5] Jos. Faà di Bruno, Catholic Belief: or a short and simple exposition of Catholic Doctrine, p. 310. As this work has the imprimatur of Cardinal Manning (1883), of Archbishop McCloskey (1884), and an introduction by Bishop Ryan of Buffalo (1884), and as the copy before me is of the eightieth thousand, I presume that it presents the current authorized teaching.

recent work asserts that "the absolution of the priest will be just as valid, just as powerful as the absolution of Jesus Christ himself."[1]

Allusion has been made above (pp. 329, 348) to the principle that pardon cannot be partial—that remission must be for all sins or for none, since absolution restores the state of grace which is incompatible with the coexistence of a mortal sin, and there can be no divided reconciliation with God. Besides, as a single mortal sin unremitted casts the sinner into hell for eternity, it could practically make no difference how many others might be remitted. All this, in the perfected theory, is self-evident enough, but before the theory was worked out by the schoolmen the conception of these matters was so vague that there was a common abuse in which priests received sinners to penitence for individual sins. Urban II. condemned this at the council of Amalfi, in 1089, as leading souls to perdition, and the warning had to be repeated more than once[2] Peter Lombard easily saw the fallacy of such partial absolution, and laid down the rule that confession to be valid must be complete; if the sinner omits any mortal sin the absolution granted is ineffective even for those confessed.[3] Notions on the subject, however, were still too confused for this to be universally accepted, and towards the close of the twelfth century Master Bandinus argues that confession of a single sin is valid if satisfaction and amendment follow, otherwise it is not.[4] The later schoolmen saw clearly the error of this, and the principle became established that the penitent must confess all the mortal sins that he can recollect and receive absolution for all, since God does not remit one without the rest, and the priest must absolve for all or none.[5] Yet immutable as the rule appears to be by its very nature, we have seen the exceptions forced upon it by the principle of jurisdiction and the practice of reserved cases, and Father Segneri leaves

---

[1] Müller's Catholic Priesthood, I. 49.—See also the "Catechism of the Third Plenary Council of Baltimore" (1884), p. 32.

[2] C. Melphitan. ann. 1089, cap. 16; C. Claromont. ann. 1095; C. Lateranens. II. ann. 1139, cap. 22 (Harduin. VI. II. 1687, 1736, 2212).—Cap. 8 Caus. XXXIII. Q. iii. Dist. 5.

[3] P. Lombard. Sentt. Lib. IV. Dist. xv. § 3.

[4] Mag. Bandini Sentt. Lib. IV. Dist. xv.

[5] Alex. de Ales Summæ P. IV. Q. XVIII. Membr. vi. Art. 5, § 6.—S. Bonavent. in IV. Sentt. Dist. XX. P. ii. Art. 1, Q. 1.—S. Th. Aquinat. Summæ P. III. Q. lxxxvi. Art. 3.—Catech. Trident. De Pœnitentia cap. 9.

it to the discretion of the confessor by telling him that if hurried he can listen only to the graver sins and grant absolution for them, with the command to the penitent to confess the rest at the next time.[1] There is also an admission of partial absolution in the rule that if an invalid absolution is followed by one or more confessions, and the prior invalidity is then discovered, the first confession must be repeated, but the subsequent ones are valid and need not be.[2] Partial absolution, in fact, came to be known as *absolutio dimidiata*, and could occur when the priest restricted his attention to only a portion of the sins confessed to him.[3] Another illustration of it is seen in the rule that if a penitent confesses to having committed a sin ten times, and subsequently remembers that the number was fifteen or twenty, he must, in his next confession, include the overplus, which infers that those first confessed were pardoned while the rest were not.[4] These petty details are not without interest as showing the difficulty of applying in practice the principles which seem in theory so clear and well-constructed.

Even as there can be no partial absolution so it would appear that there must be no gradations or differences in its quality, especially in view of the current assurances that the pardon granted by the priest is as complete as though granted by Jesus Christ himself. Yet ingenuity has devised even this, and an absolution granted by the pope would seem to be regarded as more effective than that of an ordinary confessor. An indulgence conceded to the Clares authorizes the priest to absolve them and restore them to baptismal innocence as thoroughly as the pope would do if he heard them in confession. In 1855, the Clares applied to learn whether this was still in force or whether it had been included in the abrogation of monastic indulgences by Paul V., in 1606, and were told that it was no longer available for the living but was still effective on the death-bed.[5]

---

[1] Segneri Instructio Confessarii, p. 85 (Dilingæ, 1699).

[2] Escobar Theol. Moral. Tract. VII. Exam. iv. cap. 7, n. 36.—Clericati de Pœnit. Decis. XXXI. n. 3-5.

[3] La Croix Theol. Moral. Lib. VI. P. ii. n. 1148.

[4] Cabrini Elucidar. Casuum Reservator. P. I. Resol. xiv.

[5] Ferraris Prompta Biblioth. s. v. *Indulgentia* Art. v. n. 66.—Decr. Authent. Sacr. Congr. Indulgent. n. 691, 12 Mart. 1855.—"Quomodo Sanctitas Domini nostri N. Papæ faceret si ipsemet in confessione peccata vestra auscultaret."

A subject which has led to considerable debate and variety of opinion is the validity of conditional absolutions—that is, absolutions conditioned on some future event. In the early development of the sacramental theory absolutions of this kind were the rule,[1] for the penitent had to earn his pardon by penance and amendment. As the theory became perfected it was recognized that such absolution was incompatible with the absolute effectiveness claimed for the sacrament and the application of the treasure of the Church, and consequently it was pronounced invalid,[2] although as late as the close of the thirteenth century, Henry of Ghent, the *Doctor Solennis*, argued that a bishop might commit to a priest the shriving of a penitent conditioned on his confirming the absolution.[3] When, however, the dependence is on past or present conditions that are uncertain, as *si tu es capax, si ego possum*, there is no question as to the validity of the sacrament if the conditions are fulfilled, and the probabilities are in favor of this validity even when the condition is only formulated mentally, as we are told is generally the habit with timid and inexperienced confessors.[4]

There is one burning and much debated question connected with the efficiency of absolution—the reimputation of sin. Are sins so thoroughly remitted by the sacrament that they are destroyed, or are they merely suspended, ready to return with all their consequences if the pardoned sinner proves his unworthiness of God's mercy by again relapsing into mortal sin? To the rigid virtue of the earlier Church, which knew nothing of the sacrament and required life-long penitence in expiation of sin, it seemed a matter of course that the ingratitude of relapse brought back the pardoned offences and their responsibilities, and the parable in Matthew xviii. 23–35 was regarded as proving it conclusively. So St. Augustin gives us to understand, and it is assumed in the Gelasian Sacramentary.[5] St. Ivo of Chartres

---

[1] Rich. a S. Victore de Potestate, etc., cap. 8.

[2] Jo. Friburgens. Summæ Confessor. Lib. III. Tit. xxxiv. Q. 136.—Marc, Institt. Moral. Alphonsianæ n. 1414.

[3] Summa Rosella s. v. *Absolutio* 5.—Summa Tabiena s. v. *Absolutio* I. n. 6.

[4] Clericati de Pœnit. Decis. xxxv. n. 12.—S. Alph. de Ligorio Theol. Moral. Lib. VI. n. 431.—Marc. Institt. Moral. Alphonsianæ n. 1663.

[5] S. Augustin. de Baptismo contra Donatistas Lib. I. cap. 12.—Sacramentar. Gelasian. Lib. I. n. xxxix. (Muratori Opp. T. XIII. P. II. p. 93).

gives the passage from St. Augustin without qualification, showing that it was still the current theory in the early twelfth century.[1] When the schoolmen commenced their labors they began to call it into question, for it was a serious blot on the power of the keys and the efficacy of the sacrament which they were seeking to establish, but it was too deeply rooted in tradition to be easily overthrown. Hugh of St. Victor, in one passage, argues in favor of reimputation, though as one of the hidden ways of God it cannot be positively asserted; in another, he argues against it, because God does not judge twice, but he is uncertain.[2] Gratian devotes a long section to the subject and loses himself in speculations on its connection with predestination, but seems finally to incline to the affirmative.[3] Peter Lombard states that the question is obscure and perplexed, authorities are divided upon it, and he prudently leaves it to the judgment of the reader without expressing an opinion of his own.[4] It was not a matter of merely speculative interest, but of no little practical importance. So long as confession was rare and mostly postponed to the death-bed, it made little difference in practice whether or not relapse brought reimputation, but when annual confession was urged and was becoming frequent, the affirmative belief entailed the necessity of confessing anew all the sins that had been pardoned and of assuming fresh penance for them. Experience showed that few penitents enjoyed a change of heart and abstained from sin, and this cumulative reduplication of penance was a fearful burden which might well seem to threaten the promising progress of annual application for the sacrament. What, in fact, was the worth of the remission claimed for the keys if it lasted only until the commission of a new sin? The interest of theologians therefore was enlisted on the negative side of the question, but notwithstanding this the new views made slow progress. Peter of Poitiers adheres to the old doctrine and resolutely faces the consequences, saying that it is safer to confess the pardoned sins again.[5] On the other hand, Adam of Perseigne asserts that they need not be, unless as an exercise of

---

[1] S. Ivon. Decr. P. xv. cap. 21.

[2] Hugon. de S. Victore de Sacramentis Lib. ii. P. xiv. cap. 9; Summæ Sentt. Tract. vi. cap. 13.

[3] Gratian. Caus. xxxiii. Q. iii. Dist. 4.

[4] P. Lombard. Sentt. Lib. iv. Dist. xxii. § 2.

[5] P. Pictaviens. Sentt. Lib. iii. cap 12.

humility,[1] while Master Bandinus contents himself with saying that either opinion may be held, for the doctors are divided.[2] Innocent III. had no hesitation in assuming as a gospel truth that a single sin will work the reimputation of all pardoned ones,[3] but his authority was insufficient to settle the question, and it continued to be argued ; in fact, the introduction of enforced annual confession inferred that all Christians relapsed promptly into sin, and if this required a constantly growing length of confession, like the house that Jack built, with reduplication of penance, reimputation was rendered a practically impossible doctrine which had to be got rid of, directly or indirectly. Yet the task was not easy ; S. Ramon de Peñafort admits his inability to form a definite opinion and states four theories as current at the time without pronouncing between them.[4] His contemporary, William of Paris, states that reimputation is one of four questions which greatly agitate the schools; he argues against it, but he reaches practically the same result by urging that the sin of ingratitude subjects the relapsed sinner to all the punishment of the remitted sins.[5]

This device of shifting the burden from reimputation to ingratitude was a compromise eagerly accepted. Cardinal Henry of Susa, who does not venture positively to deny the return of sin, and St. Bonaventura, who does deny it, both assert that the relapsed sinner is damned for his ingratitude.[6] Aquinas puts it into attractive shape to save the honor of the sacrament ; he argues that man cannot undo the work of God, and that no subsequent act can recall what God has taken away, but the guilt of the sins returns, inasmuch as the relapse is aggravated by the previous pardon and the sin of ingratitude virtually causes reimputation.[7] This view, which was destined to become dominant, by no means won general acceptance at the time. John of Freiburg does not venture to do more than to cite the con-

---

[1] Adami Perseniæ Abbatis Epist. xxvi. (Migne, CCXI. 683).

[2] Mag. Bandini Sentt. Lib. iv. Dist. xxi.

[3] Innoc. PP. III. Serm. i. De Consecr. Pontif. (Migne CCXVII. 652).

[4] S. Raymundi Summæ Lib. iii. Tit. xxxiv. § 4.

[5] Guillel. Parisiens. de Sacram. Pœnit. cap. 19.

[6] Hostiens. Aureæ Summæ Lib. v. De Pœn. et Remiss. § 57.—S. Bonavent. in IV. Sentt. Dist. xxii. Art. 1, Q. 1, 2.

[7] S. Th. Aquin. Summæ P. iii. Q. lxxxviii. Artt. 1, 2, 3. He quotes a couplet current in the schools—

Fratres odit, apostata fit, spernitque fateri,
Pœnituisse piget, pristina culpa redit.

flicting opinions of the doctors.[1] Duns Scotus went a step further; the penitent has given to God an equivalent satisfaction, the transaction is closed and cannot be reopened; at most the pardoned sin can return only in the sense of an aggravating circumstance—a view of the matter in which he was naturally followed by his disciples, François de Mairone, Astesanus and Piero d'Aquila.[2] The Franciscans having thus cleared the way, the Dominican Durand de S. Pourçain followed with the universal solvent of the treasure of salvation; in the sacrament the priest applies an equivalent of the merits of Christ; the debt is settled and cannot be claimed anew.[3] Guido de Monteroquer states both opinions without venturing to decide between them.[4] Gabriel Biel inclines towards the views of Aquinas; the pardoned sins may be said to return through the ingratitude of relapse, and thus form an aggravating circumstance, meriting increase of punishment.[5] The question was one which, in in view of its supreme importance, its uncertainty and the long debate over it, would seem to have especially invited an authoritative definition from the council of Trent, but that body maintained a discreet silence upon the subject, and it has never been settled. Post-Tridentine theologians mostly teach a doctrine based on that of Aquinas— that reimputation does not occur *simpliciter* but *secundum quid*, for subsequent sins are rendered graver in consequence of the ingratitude, but the subject still remains open and is matter for debate.[6]

Another question relating to absolution, in which the altered custom of the Church has aroused a certain amount of discussion, is whether it should be conferred before or after the performance of penance. The proposition would seem to be self-evident that pardon and restoration to standing in the Church, with participation in its

---

[1] Jo. Friburgens. Summæ Confessor. Lib. III. Tit. xxxiv. Q. 143.

[2] Jo. Scoti in IV. Sentt. Dist. XXII. Q. 1.—Fr. de Maironis in IV. Sentt. Dist. XXII. Q. 1.—Astesani Summæ Lib. v. Tit. iv. Art. 3.—P. de Aquila in IV. Sentt. Dist. XXII. Q. 1.

[3] Durand. de S. Porciano in IV. Sentt. Dist. XXI. Q. 1, § 7.

[4] Manip. Curator. P. II. Tract. iii. cap. 7.

[5] Gab. Biel in IV. Sentt. Dist. XXII. Q. unic. Artt. 2, 3.

[6] Estii in IV. Sentt. Dist. XXII.—Juenin de Sacramentis Dist. VI. Q. iv. cap. 2, Art. 4.—Th. ex Charmes Theol. Univ. Diss. v. cap. vii. concl. 2.—Palmieri Tract de Pœnit. pp. 195-203.—Varceno Comp. Theol. Moral. Tract. XVIII. cap. 8.—Scheffer S. J. in *Zeitschrift für katholische Theologie*, 1891, B. XV. S. 241.

mysteries, should not be granted until expiation had been made for
the offence, and this, as we have seen, was the universal rule in the
earlier times, when admission to the Eucharist was the sign of reconciliation. The successive stages of penance were steps leading to the
final restoration to communion, and a tract in opposition to the Novatians assumes as a postulate that the penitent cannot be admitted to
the Lord's Supper until his penance is completed.[1] Sinners who had
not applied for public penance followed the dictates of their own
consciences and determined for themselves whether or not they were
worthy to receive the body and blood of the Lord,[2] but St. Ambrose
rebukes severely those who applied for penance and expected to be at
once admitted to communion.[3] As private confession gradually
established itself in the Greek Church, the confessor when it was concluded prayed over the penitent, who again presented himself when
the prescribed penance had been performed, and a second prayer,
or deprecatory absolution was offered over him.[4] In the seventh
century, Theodore of Canterbury enunciates the absolute rule that
the Holy Thursday reconciliation by bishops is performed after the
period of penance is completed, and these periods were frequently

---

[1] Ps. Augustin. Quæstt. ex Vet. et Nov. Testam. cap. 102 (Migne, XXXV.
2308).

[2] S. Augustin. Serm. CCCLI. cap. 4; Append. Serm. CXV. cap. 4; Serm.
CCLV.—Socrat. H. E. v. 19.
Unless a man felt himself guilty of that which deserved excommunication
he was not to deprive himself of the daily medicine of the Eucharist (S.
August. Epist. LIV. cap. 3, ad Januarium) showing that daily communion was
still practised and that the sinner would tacitly admit his sin by abstention.
In the seventh century, Theodore of Canterbury tells us that the Greeks took
communion every Sunday, and three weeks' absence incurred excommunication. Among the Latins the custom was the same, except that it was not
enforced with a penalty.—Theodori Pœnit. I. xii. §§ 1, 2 (Wasserschleben, p.
196).

[3] S. Ambros. de Pœnit. Lib. II. cap. 9.—Carried into Gratian, cap. 55, Caus.
XXXIII. Q. iii. Dist. 1.

[4] Johann. Jejunator. Libellus Pœnitent. (Morin de Pœnitent. Append. pp.
80, 94).
Morin endeavored to obtain an explanation of this double absolution from
Leo Allatius, who assured him that the second formula had been intended to
absolve from excommunication. As this did not tally with the text, he made
inquiries of the Archbishop of Trebizond, when in Paris, and was told that it
was then used when the penance was reduced in order to compensate for
insufficient satisfaction (Ibid. pp. 139–40).

long. Thus an apostate returning to the faith is excluded from the
church for three years, after which he is allowed to enter, but is not
admitted to communion for seven years more.[1] It was difficult to
maintain the rigor of these rules and the progressive relaxation of
discipline appears in the concession that, although penitents ought not
to be admitted to communion before the completion of their penance,
yet, out of compassion, they could be allowed to partake of the Eucharist after six months or a year.[2]

At the same time, in the *Ordines ad dandam Pœnitentiam* which
accompany the Penitentials, it would appear that the prayers, which
in private confession constituted the so-called absolution, were uttered
immediately on the conclusion of the confession. They had, as we
have seen, no sacramental character, and they did not restore the
penitent to communion till his penance or a portion of it was performed, but doubtless they comforted him and led him to accept
more cheerfully the penance imposed or to commute for it more
liberally. With the further progress of relaxation a custom sprung
up rendering it in some degree discretional with the priest whether
to admit the penitent at once to reconciliation or to make him await
the performance of this penance ;[3] instructions even are found that
reconciliation is to be granted at once ; or the distinction is drawn
that for secret sins immediate reconciliation shall be given, while for
public ones it is to be postponed till Holy Thursday—thus showing
that, as we shall see hereafter, there was no difference in character
between public and private reconciliation and penance, but merely
that where public scandal had been caused there must be public
manifestation of repentance.[4] This increasing laxity did not suit
the views of the more rigorous sacerdotalists, who sought to check it
by the current device of forgery. Halitgar of Cambrai attributes to
Pius I. (A. D. 141–151) a command that penitents are not to be ad-

---

[1] Theodori Pœnitent. I. xiii. § 2 ; Canones Gregorii cap. 45 (Wasserschleben,
pp. 197, 165).

[2] Theodori Pœnitent. I. xii. § 4 ; Theodori Capitula cap. 26 ; Canones Gregorii
cap. 123 ; Pœnitent. Merseburg, cap. 117 ; Pœnitent. Vindobonens. cap. 86 ;
Judicii Clementis cap. 11 ; Pœnitent. Cummeani XIV. 6 (Wasserschleben, pp.
196, 147, 174, 403, 421, 434, 492).

[3] Ps. Alcuin. Lib. de Divinis Officiis cap. 13.—Morin. de Pœnit. Append. p. 55.

[4] Pœnit. Vindobonens. cap. 46 ; Ps. Theodori Pœnit. cap. 41 § 1 (Wasserschleben, pp. 420, 610).

mitted to communion until the completion of their penance.[1] Benedict the Levite lays down the positive rule that, whether the penance be public or private, the reconciliation must be postponed till after the performance of penance.[2] It was difficult to tighten the bonds of discipline among the wild converts whose subordination had been purchased by laxity. Jonas of Orleans complains that confessed homicides intruded themselves irreverently in the congregations of the faithful,[3] and Nicholas I., in prescribing penance for a matricide, admits him to communion after the third year, although for seven years more his oblations are not to be received and he is to undergo severe penance.[4] In 895, the council of Tribur endeavored to return to the ancient rigor, and in cases of voluntary homicide prescribed that the seven years of penance shall elapse before the sinner is reconciled and admitted to communion;[5] and not long afterwards Abbo of S. Germain states positively that no bishop can grant absolution before the penance has been completely performed.[6]

The effort to restore the old discipline was unsuccessful, and its failure may perhaps be partially ascribed to the system of redemption of penance which, as we shall have occasion to see hereafter, was destined to exercise a sinister influence on Church and people alike. The process of relaxation is illustrated by a sentence imposed, in 1065, by Alexander II. for church-burning, where five years' penance

---

[1] Halitgari Pœnit. Roman. cap. 10 (Canisii Thesaur. II. II. 130).

[2] Bened. Levit. Capitular. Lib. v. cap. 116, 127. During public penance the penitent, while denied the Eucharist, was allowed to receive blessed salt, which, as we have seen, was then reckoned as a sacrament.—Ibid. Lib. VII. cap. 263; Addit. IV. cap. 63, 76.

The case of Ebbo, Archbishop of Reims, illustrates the principle of reconciliation after penance as well as the political use of the disciplinary machinery of the Church in the prevailing disorder. After the restoration of Louis le Débonnaire, in 835, he was forced to acknowledge his complicity in the rebellion of the emperor's sons and to resign his see as a penance. When, after the death of Louis, in 840, Ebbo returned to France in the train of the Emperor Lothair and took possession of his former see, he argued that his banishment for nearly seven years had served as the customary penance, and that he was entitled to restoration in sign of reconciliation.—Ebbonis Apologeticum (Migne, CXVI. 15).

[3] Jonæ Aurelianens. de Instit. Laicali Lib. I. cap. 10.

[4] Nicholai PP. I. Epist. CXXXIII.—Gratian. cap. 15, Caus. XXXIII. Q. ii.

[5] C. Triburiens. ann. 895, cap. 58 (Harduin. VI. I. 456).

[6] Abbon. Sangerman. Serm. II. III. (Migne, CXXXII. 765, 769).

is prescribed, but the offender is admitted to communion after the expiration of the current year.[1] In the second quarter of the next century Hildebert of Le Mans shows us that although formal reconciliation was postponed to the end of penance, as a matter of favor penitents were allowed to take communion at Easter.[2]

When reconciliation developed into absolution in its sacramental sense, the power thus assumed should have aroused greater discretion as to its exercise, but the desire to render confession attractive was too strong, and concessions were made to bring penitents to seek the sacrament. While the sacramental theory was developing, Cardinal Pullus, as we have seen above (p. 476), asserts that God does not pardon until due penance has been performed; when it was assuming shape, there was a saving clause that absolution conferred at confession was conditioned on performance of the penance enjoined; if this was neglected, the sinner fell back into the state of eternal damnation.[3] Conditional absolution, however, as we have seen, passed out of fashion, and the custom became general of administering absolution as soon as the confession was concluded, for which the argument was adduced that the works of penance are greatly more meritorious when performed in the state of grace conferred by absolution than they could be before.[4] Indeed, it became usual to grant the absolution even before imposing the penance; St. Antonino tells us that it is a matter of indifference which precedes the other,[5] while subsequent authors differ between themselves, some agreeing with him, while others hold that absolution should have precedence, and others again that the penance should first be imposed, for which Chiericato adduces the practical argument that the penitent, if he desires the sacrament, cannot then refuse to accept the pen-

---

[1] Löwenfeld Epistt. Roman. Pontiff., p. 53.

[2] Hildeberti Cenomanens. Serm. xxxiv. (Migne, CLXXI. 509). Morin (De Pœnit. Lib. ix. cap. xxix. n. 17) gives an example of this from a ritual of Rouen in the fourteenth century. On the other hand, in the thirteenth century, Alexander Hales says (Summæ P. IV. Q. xiv. Membr. vi. Art. 3) that unreconciled penitents can remain in the church until the octave of Easter, without however being admitted to communion.

[3] Rich. a S. Victore de Potestate etc. cap. 8.

[4] Estii in IV. Sentt. Dist. xv. §§ 10, 15. When performed after absolution the works of penance are *de condigno*, when performed before they are only *de congruo*.

[5] S. Antonini Summæ P. iii. Tit. xvii. cap. 20, § 1.

ance.[1] Yet the old custom of delaying absolution to the end of penance
was long in dying out. Father Morin adduces from various rituals,
up to the fourteenth century, that on Holy Thursday the penitents
were examined and classified into those entitled to reconciliation and
those whose penance was still to be continued.[2] He attributes the
innovation of immediate absolution to the crusades, the innumerable
members of which had a right to claim the benefit of the sacrament,
while Father Juenin ascribes it to the multiplication of indulgences,
which is virtually the same thing.[3] This doubtless contributed to
familiarize the popular mind with the custom, but there were occasional remonstrants. Dr. Weigel, whose adhesion to the council of
Bâle shows his tendency to rigorism, quotes an old formula postponing reconciliation to the end of penance, and deplores the prevailing laxity which occasions so many evils.[4] Yet when Pedro de
Osma taught at Salamanca that absolution should be deferred till
the conclusion of penance, the council of Alcalá, in 1479, pronounced
it a heresy, and Sixtus IV. confirmed the decision after consultation
in due form with his cardinals.[5]

Thus a practice which had at first been universal and had continued until within little more than a hundred years was pronounced
a heresy by the Holy See in the most formal manner. The affair,
however, was scarce heard of outside of Spain, and we may reasonably assume that its memory was speedily buried, for, when, in
1517, Luther, in his twelfth proposition, asserted that of old the
canonical penances were imposed prior to absolution, as a trial of
true contrition, Prierias in his rejoinder not only assented to this,
but added that even now this is the proper course unless there is
certainty that the penitent will perform them, and, in 1525, Latomus

---

[1] Summa Sylvestrina s. vv. *Absolutio* VI. § 2; *Confessor* IV. § 1.—Aurea
Armilla s. v. *Absolutio* n. 7.—Azpilcueta, Comment. de Pœnit. Dist. VI. cap. 1,
In Princip. n. 35.—Zerola Praxis Sacr. Pœnit. cap. xxiv. Q. 13.—Summa Diana
s. v. *Pœnitentiam imponere* n. 8.—Reginaldi Praxis Fori Pœnit. Lib. VII. n. 19.
—Clericati de Pœnit. Decis. XXXIV. n. 4.—Ferraris Prompta Biblioth. s. v.
Pœnit. Sacram. n. 39.

[2] Morin. de Pœnit. Lib. IX. cap. xxix. n. 15–17. See also Binterim, *Denkwürdigkeiten*, V. III. 202–3.

[3] Morin. de Pœnit. Lib. X. cap. xxii.—Juenin de Sacramentis Diss. VI. Q.
vi. cap. 5, Art. 2.

[4] Weigel Claviculæ Indulgent. cap. 19.

[5] Alfonsi de Castro adv. Hæreses Lib. IV. s. v. *Confessio.*

admits that of old absolution was deferred until after the performance of penance.[1] In the seventeenth century the high authority of
Cardinal Lugo is on record to the effect that the confessor can require the penance to be performed prior to conferring absolution,
but that in such case it loses the merit derived *ex opere operato*,[2] and
not long afterwards Cardinal Aguirre, who was inclined to rigorism,
urged the propriety of delaying absolution till the completion of
penance, and scolded the penitents who demand it at once, and who
abuse the pious confessors for postponing it until penitential observances shall render them fit to receive it.[3] These theologians of
the purple had no conception how nearly they were trenching on an
heretical teaching of Jansenism. In 1678 there appeared an anonymous book on the subject, under the title of *Pentalogus Diaphoricus*,
arguing that immediate absolution is an abuse, and, in 1685, it was
duly condemned by the Congregation of the Index.[4] Antoine
Arnauld, in his *Traité de la fréquente Communion*, argued in the
same sense, and so did John, Bishop of Castoria, in his *Amor pœnitens*, for which his book was duly suspended, *donec corrigatur*.
Other rigorists, such as Huyghens, Opstraet, Gabriel and others,
were equally earnest, and their opinions were condemned by Alexander VIII. in 1690.[5] Noël Alexandre more cautiously asserted
the power of the confessor to defer absolution, when he deems it
judicious, until the penance has been partly or wholly performed,
especially in the case of habitual sinners.[6] The later Jansenists,
Pasquier Quesnel and his followers, scarce went further than this

---

[1] Dial. Sylvest. Prieriat. Art. 12 (Lutheri Opp. Jenæ 1564 fol. 17*b*).—Jac. Latomus de Confessione Secreta, Antverpiæ, 1525.

[2] Gobat Alphab. Confessar. n. 756.

[3] Aguirre Dissert. in Conc. Toletan. III. n. 158, 164–5 (Concil. Hispan. III.
255).

[4] Père Le Tellier assumes (Recueil Historique des Bulles etc. p. 430) that
the *Pentalogus* was a Jansenist production, but Dr. Reusch (Der Index der
verbotenen Bücher, II. 520) informs us that it was written by Charles de Brias,
a Carmelite Provincial and antagonist of the Jansenists, and that Antoine
Arnauld pronounced it to be a monstrous mass of truth and error.

[5] Arnauld, Traité de la fréquente Communion, Ch. XI. XII.—Alex. PP. VIII.
Decr. 7 Dec. 1690, Prop. 16, 17, 18, 20, 22.—Viva Theol. Trutina in easdem
Propp.—La Croix Theol. Moral. Lib. VI. P. ii. n. 1205, 1230.—Index Innoc.
PP. XI., Append. p. 3.

[6] Summæ Alexandrinæ P. I. n. 598.

when they urged that it is wholesome for penitents to endure for awhile the burden of their sins before reconciliation, and that immediate restoration destroyed all sense of sin and of true penitence, but by this time the Holy See was wholly under Jesuit influence, and even propositions so moderate as these were included by Clement XI. in his sweeping condemnation of Jansenist errors and heresies.[1]

The final struggle over the question was an incident in the attempted reform of the Tuscan Church, towards the close of the eighteenth century, by the Grand Duke Leopold. We shall have occasion hereafter to refer more fully to this movement, and need only mention here that his *protégé*, Scipione de' Ricci, Bishop of Pistoja and Prato, in 1786, assembled a diocesan synod to commence the work. Prominent among the evils to be cured, according to the synod, was the unbridled facility of absolution, which was the most fruitful cause of demoralization, reducing Christian virtue to an empty name, and rendering the administration of penitence a confused Babel of capricious rules.[2] The neglect, it added, of the true functions of the sacrament was the deplorable cause of the abuses and disorders prevailing in it, so that we see multitudes of pretended penitents and scarce a single conversion.[3] Among the reforms suggested to remedy these deplorable conditions, that which pertains to our present subject was simply that while the synod said that it did not disapprove the practice of imposing penance to be performed after the absolution, there should also be acts preceding it of peni-

---

[1] Clement PP. XI. Bull. *Unigenitus*, Prop. 87, 88 (Bullar. VIII. 121).

[2] "Si è introdotta quella sfrenata facilità di assolvere che è la cagione più feconda dei mali che soffra la chiesa. Si è perduta la vera idea della giustizia cristiana ed estinto lo spirito della religione, il quale consiste nella carità, non è rimasto che un vano simulacro di giustizia farisiaca, ed il puro nome della cristiana virtù. Colle varie immaginazioni degli uomini . . . si è introdotta uno Babilonia ed una confusione di massime capricciosi in ogni parte della morale e particolarmente nell' amministrazione della Penitenza."—Atti e Decreti del Concilio di Pistoia dell' Anno de 1786, p. 95.

This decree was signed by Ricci and 236 members of the synod. Six refused to sign and one signed conditionally.—Ibid. p. 100.

[3] "È l'origine funesta di tanti abusi e disordini che regnano per tuttavia in un così augusto Sacramento, e per cui, come piansero tante volte i Romani Potifici e i sacri pastori, noi vediamo una moltitudine grande di pretesi penitenti e quasi nessuna conversione."—Ibid. p. 141.

tence and humiliation.[1] This would appear to be a very moderate measure of reform, but the hardy utterances of the synod aroused a storm of objurgation which did not spare even this, and Ricci was told that in it he was reviving the condemned errors of St. Cyran, Arnauld and the Jansenists.[2] The projected reforms of Leopold were far-reaching; they included the reduction of the authority of the Holy See to its ancient limits and the independence of the State, and they necessarily excited the bitterest antagonism. An assembly of his prelates, convened in Florence in 1787, manifested an indisposition to support him, but he might have accomplished permanent results had he not been called by the death of his brother Joseph II., in 1790, to the imperial throne, where his own speedily followed, in 1792. Thus deprived of its protector, the synod of Pistoia could safely be condemned, and, in 1794, Pius VI. issued the bull *Auctorem fidei*, in which eighty-five distinct errors in its utterances were qualified in carefully measured terms of disapprobation. Of these the one requiring acts of humiliation and penitence prior to absolution is stigmatized as false, audacious, insulting to the common practice of the Church and leading to the error condemned in Pedro de Osma.[3] At the same time this is not construed as depriving the confessor of the discretion of requiring satisfaction to be performed before absolution is conferred, which some moralists recommend to be done with certain penitents.[4]

---

[1] Ibidem, p. 148.

[2] Istruzione per un' Anima fedele, p. 230 (Finale, 1787).

[3] Pii PP. VI. Bull. *Auctorem fidei*, Prop. xxxv.

[4] Palmieri Tract. de Pœnit. p. 460.

Palmieri asserts (p. 425) in contradiction to all the evidence, that in the early Church absolution was generally performed before satisfaction, and in support of this he quotes (p. 462) an irrelevant passage from the Apostolic Constitutions, Lib. II., and omits the decisive one—"idem nos facere debemus et eos qui se peccatorum pœnitere dicunt, segregare per certum tempus secundum proportionem peccati; deinde, pœnitentia peracta, recipere tanquam patres filios" (Lib. II. cap. 19).

The point is not without importance in view of the modern theories which, as we shall see hereafter, seek to find some support for the assertion of the council of Trent that the sacrament of penitence and indulgences existed in the primitive Church.

Although not strictly a part of our subject, a rapid glance at the theories and practice of the early Reformers with regard to confession and absolution may not be without interest. It was naturally difficult for those trained in the doctrines of the Church to renounce at once absolutely its consolations; the idea that confession was a safeguard of morality was generally entertained, and the people would scarce have been satisfied to abandon wholly the rites which they had been taught to consider as essential to salvation. Luther, in 1520, expressed his emphatic approval of auricular confession as useful and indeed necessary, though it was not divinely instituted, it should be wholly voluntary, and need not be made to the priest.[1] The Augsburg confession lays stress on the fact that confession is strictly enforced among the Lutherans and that communion is given only to those examined and absolved. Great merit is claimed for the insistance with which faith in absolution is taught; it is believed as a voice from heaven, and the believer is not tortured with doubts and distinctions, as in the Catholic Church. Penitential works are superfluous; faith is the one thing needful, and the believer is justified by his belief.[2] Jurisdiction is admitted in the bishops to remit sins and examine the faith of those applying for communion in order to reject the unfit.[3] As Melanchthon says in his Apology, the Reformers had so improved the benefits of absolution and the power of the keys that many afflicted consciences gained consolation; they believed in the gratuitous remission of sin through Christ, and felt themselves fully reconciled to God through faith, while formerly all the strength of absolution was weakened by the doctrine of works and the sophists and monks never taught gratuitous remission. There is no definite period fixed for confession, which is wholly voluntary; all are not fit for it at any stated time, and at the end of a year it is impossible to recall all sins committed; to prescribe

---

[1] M. Lutheri de Captiv. Babilonica cap. de Pœnit.

[2] Confessio Augustana, Abusus Artic. IV. (Lutheri Opp. Jenæ, 1570, T. IV. fol. 198a.—Goldast. Constitt. Imperial. II. 164).

The examination required previous to absolution was not into sins, but into the applicant's knowledge of the faith, the Paternoster, the Commandments and the Catechism. Luther held this to be the chief object of confession to the priest. It became known as the *Verhör.*—Steitz, Die Privatbeichte und Privatabsolution der Lutherischen Kirche, I. § 31 (Frankfurt a. M. 1854).

[3] Confessio Augustana, Abusus Artic. VII.; De Potestate Ecclesiastica.

this is a slaughter-house of conscience, which has driven many to despair.[1]

Luther's conception of the power of the keys was that it is granted to the Church at large and to every member. Absolution can be had from anyone, a brother or a neighbor, at any time and in any place, in the house or in the fields, and he who is asked for it has no right to refuse it. But the private man must not presume to exercise this power in public, for that is reserved to him who is selected by the congregation, which confers this right upon him ; in private, both are equally effective, for this effectiveness depends upon the faith of the penitent. The best satisfaction is to sin no more and to do good to your neighbor, be he friend or enemy.[2]

The Lutheran Church regulations naturally tended to attach more importance to absolution from the priest than from laymen ; no one was to be admitted to communion unless he had been absolved by a minister ; those not known to him underwent the *Verhör*, or examination into their familiarity with the articles of religion, and in addition to this there was a *Rechenschaft* in which they were asked whether they lived in hatred or sin, but all special interrogation was forbidden, and it was at the option of the penitent whether he should mention any sins troubling his conscience. Both *Rechenschaft* and *Verhör* took place openly in the choir, while the seal of confession was as strictly preserved as among Catholics—what was confessed to the pastor was confessed to Christ.[3] As regards absolution, it is instructive to note that the Lutheran Church at once fell into nearly the same difficulties as the Catholic in seeking to formulate the supernatural powers claimed. The *Sächsische Kirchenordnung* of 1539 instructs the penitent to revere the absolution as though it were spoken by God himself from heaven.[4] Other formulas show how perplexing it was to avoid the indicative form while granting the absolute forgiveness of sins assumed in the Lutheran theory.[5]

---

[1] Ph. Melanchthonis Apologia (Lutheri Opp, T. IV. fol. 229).

[2] Steitz, *op. cit.* I. §§ 7, 8, 9, 10, 11, 12, 16, 19. 34.

[3] Ibid. II. § 37 (pp. 111, 112, 115, 121, 122, 132); § 38 (p. 133).

[4] The absolution formula says "Und mein lieber Freund, dies Wort der Absolution so ich auf Gottes verheissung die mittheile, sollst du achten als ob dir Gott durch eine Stimme von Himmel Gnade und Vergebung deiner Sünden zusagt, und sollst Gott herzlich danken der solche Gewalt der Kirche und den Christen auf Erden gegeben hat."—Steitz, II. § 39.

[5] Some specimen formulas are—

"Der allmächtige Gott . . . vergiebt er die alle deine Sünde, und ich

Luther's teaching that all Christians could grant absolution was gradually forgotten. Already, in 1615, the Brunswick-Lunenburg *Kirchenordnung* alludes only to its ministration by the pastors.[1] In the same way personal absolution became reserved for special cases, while general absolution from the pulpit to the congregation was retained. This was held to pardon sin as effectively as private absolution for all who had faith and were duly prepared. Those who desired its benefits were .expected to undergo the *Verhör*, in which they individually expressed their repentance and received whatever instruction was requisite.[2] At the present time, in most of the German churches, even the *Verhör* is merged into a general formula. The pastor asks three questions : if every one has confessed to God and seeks his grace ; if every one has faith ; if every one renounces all sin and hatred ? These are answered in the affirmative, when he announces that those who observe these things in their hearts need not doubt that their sins are forgiven through the passion of Christ.[3]

In inheriting confession the Lutheran Church likewise inherited the *Beichtgeld* or *Beichtpfennig*—the fee paid by the penitent to the confessor. The Lutheran pastor stepped into the place of the parish priest without his temporalities or the source of income derived from the celebration of mass, and he not unnaturally, though unadvisedly, maintained his hold on what means of support he could. Towards the end of the seventeenth century the jurisconsult, Peter Müller, printed a little tract on the subject, from which we learn that the Theological Faculty of Leipzig decided that there was no law pre-

---

als berufener Diener der christlichen Kirche, auf Befehl unseres Herrn Jesu Christi verkündige die solche Vergebung aller deiner Sünden in Namen des Vaters, etc."

"In Namen desselbigen unsers Herrn Jesu Christi, auf seinem Befehl und in kraft seiner Worte, da er sagt: Welchem ihr die Sünde erlasset etc. spriche ich dich aller deiner Sünde frei, ledig und los das sie dir allgemahl sollen vergeben sein so reichlich und vollkommen also Jesus Christus dasselbige," etc.

"Und ich aus Befehl unsers Herrn Jesu Christi, anstatt der heilige Kirche sage dich frei ledig und los aller deiner Sünden in Namen," etc.—Steitz, II. § 40.

[1] Steitz, II. § 41 (pp. 149-50).

[2] Steitz, II. § 42 (pp. 153-4). In 1666 the Jesuit Gobat (Alphab. Confessar. n. 619) states that in many Lutheran towns the custom of auricular confession was still observed.

[3] Steitz, p. 160.

scribing it, and the sinner was not obliged to pay it, but that it was
simply a matter of good-will. Of course, it was argued not to be a
payment for the forgiveness of sins, but an exhibition of obedience
and love of God, while experience showed that many more withheld
it than paid it. At that period it was not by any means universal.
In Würtemberg and Upper Hesse it had been discontinued; in the
duchy of Altenburg its retention was apologized for on the plea of
the hard times and the increased cost of the necessaries of life.[1] The
custom was felt to be a scandal, but was difficult to shake off. It
was admitted that many thought the payment necessary, and abstained
from confession in consequence; the pastors incurred deserved odium
by demanding and exacting it; where there were several ministers
in a parish they competed with each other for the fees; when confined to bed by sickness they would cause penitents to be brought
before them so as not to lose the money. Quarrels over penitents
would occur, quarrels which the Leipzig faculty declared to be a disgrace to the Church, and it decided that no one should be subject
to constraint in the choice of a confessor. Already, in 1628, the
Supreme Consistory of Dresden threatened dismissal from benefice
and function for those who collected the *Beichtpfennig* as a debt, and
it inflicted this penalty in some cases brought before it. Scandals
and lawsuits seem to have been not infrequent, and the rival Cal-
vinists described how the Lutheran pastors sold for half a thaler
pardons for the sins of a lifetime.[2]

These troubles continued. In the middle of the eighteenth century Böhmer deplores the *jus bannarium parochiale*, which existed
almost everywhere, and under which the sinner could confess nowhere save in his own parish—a survival of the old "jurisdiction"
of the Roman Church. If there were two pastors in the parish he
could confess to either, leading to contentions between them and
sometimes to the denial of the sacraments to a parishioner who had
transferred his confession—an outrage punishable by suspension.
All this he says arose from the *Beichtpfennig*; he wishes it were
abolished and some compensation made to the pastors for their
diminished revenues.[3] The disgrace connected with the subject was

---

[1] P. Müller De Numo Confessionario, vom Beicht-Pfennige Commentatio;
Ed. quarta, Jenæ, 1683, pp. 8–12.

[2] Müller, *op. cit.*, pp. 16–17, 19–20, 24–25, 29.

[3] J. H. Böhmer Jur. Eccles. Protestantium Lib. v. Tit. xxxviii. § 66.

keenly felt by sensitive minds. When, in 1727, Friedrich Adolf Lampe was called to a church in Bremen he abolished the *Beichtgeld*, which he stigmatized as *Sündengeld*, and substituted for it a fund of voluntary contributions to secure the pastor against loss, an example which was imitated by all the other congregations in the territory of Bremen.[1] The effort to do away with it succeeded in Prussia in 1817, and in Nassau in 1818,[2] but it is still maintained in many places in spite of the discontinuance of confession, and forms a notable portion of the stipend of the pastor.[3]

Zwingli was more radical than Luther. As early as 1523 he declared that God alone remits sins, and it is idolatry to ascribe it to a creature ; confession to a priest or neighbor is only for consultation and not for remission, while the works of satisfaction are mere human inventions. Still he seems unable to divest himself entirely of the idea of human intervention, for, he adds, that to deny to a penitent the remission of a single sin is to serve as a delegate of the devil and not of God, while to sell remission is to become the associate of Simon and Balaam and the emissary of Satan.[4] In 1536, shortly before his death, he addressed to Francis I. an exposition of faith in which this latter concession to sacerdotalism disappears. All remission of sin is ascribed to Christ, obtainable through faith in remission by Christ and appeal to God through Christ : no man can know the faith of another, so all absolution by man to man is futile.[5] About the same time appeared the "Institute" of John Calvin, subsequently revised and remoulded in 1559, so that in its existing shape it represents his latest views. Although he holds with Zwingli that no man can grant absolution, as no man can measure the degree of another's faith, he makes concessions to sacerdotalism ; ministers as witnesses and sponsors render more assured the consciences of sinners, and thus are said to remit sins and absolve souls. General confession in church is most salutary ; private confession is prescribed by St. James, and though the apostle leaves the penitent free to

---

[1] Herzog's Real-Encyclop. VIII. 383.   [2] Ibid. II. 227.

[3] Wetzer und Welte, II. 249.

[4] Huld. Zwingli Artic. L.–LVI. (Niemeyer, Collectio Confessionum, Lipsiæ, 1840, p. 12).

[5] H. Zwingli Expos. Christ. Fidei cap. XI. *Remissio Peccatorum* (Niemeyer, p. 55).

choose, the pastor is the fittest confessor, as he is trained to correct our sins and to console us, but the penitent is not to be required to enumerate all his sins.[1] Even Calvin, halting in this nebulous field, cannot be wholly consistent, and had not the spirit of the revolt which made him its leader been against it, his sacerdotal tendencies would have developed into a spiritual domination as complete as that of Latin Christianity.[2] In 1561, he expressed his regret at having allowed himself to be overruled into omitting, after the general confession in the service, some form of absolution to be pronounced by the minister.[3] As it was, in 1566, after his death, the Confession of the Helvetic Churches emphatically pronounced that confession to God suffices, whether in private or publicly in the general confession in the service ; confession to the priest and acceptance of absolution from him are superfluous.[4] The Huguenots, however, while they had no formula for absolution, and seem never to have admitted it, except for excommunication, were disposed to encourage the practice of auricular confession by protecting it with the seal. Pastors and elders, to whom crimes were thus made known, were forbidden to reveal them even to the civil magistrate, except in cases of high treason.[5]

The partial reformation which separated the Anglican Church from Rome naturally led to the retention of a larger ascription of power to the priestly order than was admitted by the more radical

---

[1] Jo Calvini Institutionis Lib. III. cap. iv. §§ 12, 22.

[2] Calvin and the Genevan Church declared the invalidity of lay baptism and required it to be repeated (Quick, Synodicon in Gallia Reformata, I. 51), and this was accepted by the French Huguenots (Discipline chap. XI. can. 1, *ap.* Quick I. xliv.).

[3] Jo. Calvini Epist. Ed. Genevæ, 1617, p. 452—" Confessioni publicæ adjungere insignem aliquam promissionem quæ peccatores ad spem veniæ et reconciliationis erigat nemo nostrum est qui non agnoscat utilissimum esse. Atque ab initio hunc morem inducere volui ; sed cum offensionem quidam ex novitate metuerunt nimium facilis fui ad cedendum : ita res omissa est."

[4] Helvetica Confessio et Expositio Christianæ Fidei, cap. XIV. (Genevæ, 1654, p. 23).

[5] Discipline chap. V. c. 28, 30 (Quick I. xxxv.). Bishop Grégoire, writing in 1824 (Hist. des Confesseurs des Empereurs etc. p. 145), tells of a French Lutheran (Calvinist?) minister of the period who required confession of the members of his congregation.

revolutions on the Continent. In the ritual for the Ordering of Priests the Edwardian Liturgy retained the formula " Receive the Holy Ghost : whose sins thou dost forgive they are forgiven, and whose sins thou dost retain they are retained ;" [1] and this still holds its place, although the Thirty-nine Articles (Art. xxv.) expressly limit the sacraments to baptism and the Eucharist. The power of the keys thus granted was not intended to be merely potential. In the Liturgy of 1552, which is still in use, the Order of Morning and Evening Prayer contains a general confession to be uttered by the congregation, after which the minister pronounces a kind of deprecatory absolution, asserting that "Almighty God . . . hath given power and commandment to his ministers to declare and pronounce to his people, being penitent, the absolution and remission of their sins." [2] In this, the somewhat vague phraseology used would seem to have been carefully selected to accord with the assertions of St. Jerome that the priest only makes manifest the pardon accorded by God. In the Office for the Visitation of the Sick, however, the power of the keys is asserted absolutely. The sick penitent is directed to confess any sins lying heavy on his conscience, after which the priest grants him absolution in an indicative formula in which the *Ego te absolvo* is virtually the same as that of the Latin Church —"Our Lord Jesus Christ, who hath left power to his church to absolve all sinners which truly repent and believe in him, of his great mercy forgive thee thine offences : and by his authority committed to me, I absolve thee from all thy sins in the name of the Father and of the Son and of the Holy Ghost." [3] A rubric of the

---

[1] Cardwell, The Two Books of Common Prayer, p. 416.—In the modern prayer-book there is only the unimportant interpolation, made in the revision of 1662, after " Holy Ghost," "for the office and work of a priest in the Church of God now committed unto thee by the imposition of our hands."

[2] Cardwell, p. 27. All this service is absent from the liturgy of 1549.

[3] Ibid. p. 363. In the preliminary rubric the minister is directed to examine the sick man "whether he be in charity with all the world." In the modern formula there is interpolated "whether he repent him truly of his sins," which was introduced in the revision of 1662.—Campion and Beamont, The Prayer-Book interleaved, London, 1871, p. 209.

There is no injunction to withhold absolution from the impenitent, but the modern rubric inserts "if he humbly and heartily desire it," which is not in the Liturgies of 1549 and 1552.

Liturgy of 1549 directs that "the same form of absolution shall be used in all private confessions" the omission of which in the revision of 1552 shows the change occurring in the interval. Apparently in 1549 it had been deemed inadvisable to abolish entirely the sacrament of penitence, for in the Communion Service of that year there is an exhortation to those having troubled consciences to ease them by auricular confession to the celebrant "or to some other discreet and learned priest," and to receive absolution, which, of course, was of the indicative form prescribed for the sick; but this was a voluntary matter which, it was urged, ought not to be a subject of offence between those who availed themselves of it and those who did not. In the revision of 1552 this is modified to the cautious invitation to "open his grief that he may receive such ghostly counsel, advice and comfort as his conscience may be relieved; and that, by the ministry of God's word, he may receive comfort and the benefit of absolution to the quieting of his conscience and the avoiding of all scruple and doubtfulness."[1] There was evidently no desire on the part of the Edwardian divines to deny the opportunity of confession to those who wished it or to deprive the minister of the power of the keys, and when, at the Savoy conference of 1661, the Puritan clergy begged that the absolution formula should be made "declarative and conditional," in place of indicative, the request was refused.[2] Yet the power to bind and to loose thus retained for the priestly order fell practically into desuetude. In 1793, Henry Digby Beste, a Fellow of Magdalen College, Oxford, preached a sermon in which he urged its revival, the first utterance, he says, of the kind for two hundred years, but as, a few years later, he was converted to Catholicism, though his effort attracted some attention at the time, it was soon forgotten.[3] The so-called Tractarian movement revived the dormant claim, which the Liturgy shows to be incontestable, and, in the higher or Ritualistic section of Anglicanism, confession and abso-

---

[1] Cardwell, *op. cit.* pp. 278, 288, 291. In the existing Liturgy there is a slight modification—"That, by the ministry of God's holy word, he may receive the benefit of absolution together with ghostly counsel and advice."

[2] Boyd, Confession, Absolution and the Real Presence, p. 106 (London, 1867).

[3] Rev. Henry Digby Beste, A Sermon on Priestly Absolution, 3d Edition, London, 1874.—Cf. Rev. Orby Shipley, The Church and the World, 1st Series, pp. 527-8; Blount's Dictionary of Theology s. v. *Confession of Sins,* n. 5.

lution are practised, in very much the same fashion as in the Latin Church, except that the rite is voluntary.[1]

---

[1] Boyd, *op. cit.* pp. 55–60. This applies also to the Episcopal Church of the United States. In a recent discussion on the subject of Ritualism, provoked by an address of Bishop Paret before the Maryland Diocesan Convention, a journal remarks "In many of our Episcopal churches to-day the confessional is as distinct a part of the ordinance of the church as the communion."

END OF VOLUME I.